D0771459

PRINCIPLES

OF

EVIDENCE

Fourth Edition

By

Graham C. Lilly

Armistead M. Dobie Professor of Law
University of Virginia School of Law

CONCISE HORNBOOK SERIES®

THOMSON

WEST

Mat #40302817

Concise Hornbook Series, *Westlaw,* and West Group are trademarks
registered in the U.S. Patent and Trademark Office.

© 2006 Thomson/West
     610 Opperman Drive
     P.O. Box 64526
     St. Paul, MN 55164–0526
     1–800–328–9352

ISBN–13: 978–0–314–15616–7
ISBN–10: 0–314–15616–X

*TEXT IS PRINTED ON 10% POST
CONSUMER RECYCLED PAPER*

Preface and Acknowledgments

Readers familiar with earlier editions of this basic text (An Introduction to the Law of Evidence) will quickly note that this, the fourth edition, is significantly different. Although the coverage is basically the same as prior editions, the present offering is lightly footnoted and amply stocked with illustrations and examples. The textual emphasis throughout is on the Federal Rules of Evidence, now adopted by the vast majority of states—well over forty at the last count. This current edition does, however, share a common feature with its predecessors: the approach is didactic, and the aim is to help my readers see evidence law as an integrated whole. With the exception of the various rules that collectively constitute the hearsay doctrine, most features of the law of evidence can be mastered through self-study, at least with reasonable diligence. Each rule or principle, when examined in isolation, seems well within one's grasp. It is the subtle interplay among the various rules and principles, however, that poses a challenge for student and practitioner. Yet mastery of these relationships is essential, and it is to this end that I offer this volume.

When the first edition of this book was published in 1979, the principal references to which students could turn for further study were the multi-volume work by the late Professor Wigmore and the single-volume text by the late Professor McCormick. Fortunately, these excellent works[1] have been revised and updated by noted scholars, and are still available to students and lawyers. Today, however, there are many smaller, more readily accessible hornbooks by a host of nationally recognized scholars, including a 1999 "student edition" of McCormick on Evidence.[2] Here is just a sample of evidence texts written primarily for students or others interested in mastering the basic principles and rules that typically comprise an introductory three- or four-hour course.

C. MUELLER & L. KIRKPATRICK, EVIDENCE (3d ed. 2003)[3]

P. GIANNELLI, UNDERSTANDING EVIDENCE (2003)

---

[1] The revision of Wigmore is not yet complete, but some volumes are available. *See* THE NEW WIGMORE (R. Friedman, ed.).

[2] MCCORMICK, ON EVIDENCE (J. Strong 5th ed. 1999).

[3] Professors Mueller and Kirkpatrick are also the authors of a widely acclaimed five-volume set that is particularly useful for in-depth research, locating authorities, and developing evidentiary arguments.

McCormick, on Evidence (J. Strong 5th ed. 1999)

R. Park, D. Leonard, S. Goldberg, Evidence Law: A Student's Guide (2d ed. 2004)

J. Weinstein & M. Berger, Weinstein's Evidence Manual (6th Student ed. 2003)

These texts, of course, do not exhaust the list of notable offerings, which include a number of excellent longer volumes, specialized texts (such as those on scientific and mathematical evidence), shorter treatments[4] and student outlines exemplified by those found in Thompson-West's "Black Letter" series. Suffice it to say the bookshelves are full, the choices are many, and it is hard for student (or practitioner) to go wrong.

Again, as with past editions, I received generous and extraordinary help from many student assistants in the preparation of this revised edition. Let me single out at least some of them for efforts that far exceeded my expectations—which were, I should add, unrealistically high: Cory Levi, Jonathan Marx, Kari Munro, Nick Peterson, Andrew Rogers, and Nilla Watkins. Of critical importance to this project and deserving of special praise and gratitude were the efforts of my dedicated and able secretary, Diane Cronk; without her help, this project would still be a work in progress.

GRAHAM C. LILLY

Charlottesville, Virginia
April, 2006

---

[4] An example is the text by Professor Arthur Best, Evidence (5th ed. 2004).

Abbreviated Citations

1.   GINNELLI, at 1.

    P. GIANNELLI, UNDERSTANDING EVIDENCE 1 (2003).

2.   1 MCCORMICK § 185, at 642.

    1 MCCORMICK, MCCORMICK ON EVIDENCE § 185, at 642 (John W. Strong ed., 5th ed., 1999).[**]

3.   MUELLER & KIRKPATRICK, EVIDENCE § 6.69, at 594.

    C. MUELLER & L. KIRKPATRICK, EVIDENCE § 6.69, at 594 (3d ed. 2003).

4.   1 MUELLER & KIRKPATRICK, FEDERAL EVIDENCE § 162, at 52–53.

    1 MUELLER & KIRKPATRICK, FEDERAL EVIDENCE § 162, at 52–53 (2nd ed. 1994; Supp. 2005).

5.   PARK ET AL. § 11.04.

    R. PARK, D. LEONARD, S. GOLDBERG, EVIDENCE LAW: A STUENT'S GUIDE TO THE LAW OF EVIDENCE AS APPLIED IN AMERICAN TRIALS § 11.04 (2d ed. 2004).

6.   WEINSTEIN & BERGER, at 1.

    J. WEINSTEIN & M. BERGER, WEINSTEIN'S EVIDENCE MANUAL 1 (6th ed. 2003).

[**]Most of the citations to McCormick are to the two-volume "Practitioner Treatise Series," but corresponding information may also be found in the same section of the one-volume "Hornbook Series," MCCORMICK ON EVIDENCE (John W. Strong ed., 5th ed., 1999).

*

Summary of Contents

*

Table of Contents

PRINCIPLES
OF
EVIDENCE
Fourth Edition

*

Chapter I

INTRODUCTION

The subject you are about to explore—the law of evidence—is a key component of litigation in American courts. Because evidentiary rules and principles apply in all judicial trials in this country, even lawyers who do not engage in litigation must know at least the fundamentals of this body of law. Competent attorneys understand that some day in the future their clients may become disputants in controversies surrounding even garden-variety transactions. Should one or more of these disputes ripen into litigation, the law of evidence will take center stage. It will influence discovery and have a significant impact on the terms of settlement. It will profoundly affect the course and outcome of trial. Therefore, the ability to recognize, develop, and preserve admissible evidence is essential to becoming a competent lawyer.

It is not too early in your evidentiary studies to raise this fundamental question: Why do we have or even need rules of evidence? There is no single answer to this question, but certainly a major reason for the rules is to control the information that reaches the lay jury. The received wisdom is that juries must be shielded from evidence that would be prejudicial or highly inflammatory in order to decrease the likelihood of a verdict prompted by momentary passions or erroneous inferences. (Although the rules of evidence apply in bench (i.e., judge) trials, they are not strictly enforced and appellate reversals of evidentiary rulings in bench trials are rare.[1]) Some of the rules of evidence are also designed to expedite the trial, for example, by forbidding the introduction of irrelevant evidence.[2] Other rules are designed to improve the quality of the evidence that is introduced at trial, for example, by preferring the original of a document to a copy (or to testimony

---

1. The judge is rarely reversed for considering "inadmissible" evidence since her professional training prepares her to evaluate the evidence accurately, taking full account of possible defects. However, her refusal to consider evidence that was in fact admissible may lead to a reversal. The question on appeal is whether the excluded evidence is likely to have substantially affected the trial outcome. Even when trial is to a jury, an erroneous evidentiary ruling by the trial judge will not result in a reversal unless the ruling is likely to have had a substantial effect on the rights of one of the parties. *Cf.* FED. R. EVID. 103. The Federal Rules of Evidence are cited hereinafter as "FRE".

2. *See* FRE 402.

1

about the contents of the original document).[3] In addition, some evidentiary rules implement various social policies such as the preservation of confidences between protected parties like attorney and client or husband and wife.[4] Perhaps, most importantly, many evidentiary rules work to preserve a fair balance in the adversarial system of trials. An example is the hearsay rule which generally forbids the introduction of statements made out of court and thus out of the presence of the trial participants, such as the lawyers and the jury.[5] The hearsay problem typically arises because the testifying witness wants to state what an out-of-court "declarant" said about the event in question. ("The declarant told me that the water was three feet over the deck of the bridge when P, going at least 60 miles an hour in his SUV, tried to cross it.") Note, however, that the witness on the stand will be unable to answer the cross-examiner's questions about the declarant's opportunity to perceive the event he described, to remember it accurately, and to faithfully portray it. The witness can only repeat what the declarant said to him. In other words, the cross-examiner cannot put questions to the "real witness" (the declarant) that might reveal that he was mistaken or lying. Since the cross-examining lawyer wants the declarant placed on the witness stand, he will probably raise a hearsay objection.

Today, the study of evidence focuses on the Federal Rules of Evidence (FRE) which apply not only in the federal courts, but also in most state courts. Well over forty states have now adopted the Federal Rules, sometimes with modifications that serve to preserve or introduce some local rules to which the adopting state wishes to adhere. Until 1975, the year in which the Federal Rules of Evidence took effect in the federal courts, the vast bulk of evidence law was contained in state and federal judicial decisions. Over the next quarter century, however, as more and more states adopted some version of the Federal Rules, a major change took place: the law of evidence was largely transformed from a common law to a code-based subject. With this transition came increased uniformity throughout all American courts.

A final note in this introductory chapter concerns aids to interpreting the Federal Rules. As originally presented to Congress, the Federal Rules had been drafted and were to have been promulgated as judicial rules of court, prescribed by the United States Supreme Court for the governance of trials in lower federal courts. (The Supreme Court is aided in this rule-making task by an administrative body called the Judicial Conference of the United

---

3.　*See* FRE 1002.

4.　*See* FRE 501 which recognizes evidentiary privileges, but leaves it to federal judges (that is, to decisional or common law) to determine the existence and scope of federal privileges.

5.　*See* FRE 801–802.

States).[6] However, Congress was dissatisfied with some of the proposed Rules. It therefore intervened by passing the initial body of the Federal Rules of Evidence as a statute, containing not only many of the rules proposed by the Supreme Court, but also the modifications and new rules approved by the House and Senate. Thereafter, rule-making authority was returned to the United States Supreme Court.[7] Nonetheless, Congress occasionally bypasses the judicial rule-making process and enacts a statute that imposes upon the lower federal courts a new or modified rule of evidence. Thus, the historical background of the Federal Rules of Evidence consists of both congressional legislative history and the commentary generated by the Judicial Conference.[8] Also important in interpreting the Federal Rules is the common law background against which the Rules were crafted. These various background materials are sometimes useful in construing the Federal Rules.[9] Moreover, most judges are receptive to arguments based on the apparent intention of the Rules' drafters. Thus, this text refers periodically to historical materials which, among other things, indicate the intention of the drafters and trace the changes made in a particular rule from its initial draft to its final passage.

6. *See* 28 U.S.C.A. § 331 (1988). The Chief Justice of the United States presides over the Conference, which discharges most of its work through committees. The Conference itself is made up of federal judges, but non-judges, such as practicing lawyers and professors of law, routinely participate in committee work.

7. The current statute granting power to the United States Supreme Court to promulgate rules of evidence for use in the federal courts is 28 U.S.C.A. § 2072. A companion statute, 28 U.S.C.A. § 2073, sets out the procedures to be followed by the Judicial Conference. Rules that are finally approved by the Supreme Court must be transmitted to Congress for review. *See* 28 U.S.C.A. § 2074. If Congress takes no adverse action during the prescribed review period, the proposed rule or rules become effective.

8. For example, commentary is generated by the committees that receive public comments and prepare final drafts for presentation to the Judicial Conference and, ultimately, to the Supreme Court. Be especially attentive to the Advisory Committee Notes.

9. The Federal Judicial Center has provided a "note" following each Federal Rule of Evidence that pinpoints which rule-making authority (Congress or the Supreme Court) promulgated the rule or portions thereof. Background material generated by the Judicial Conference ("Advisory Committee Notes" or "ACN") usually provides a discussion of the common law.

Chapter II

THE FRAMEWORK

Table of Sections

---

§ 2.1 The Adversary System

Anglo–American evidentiary rules and principles are embedded in the adversarial system of justice. The general theory underlying the adversarial model is that the self-interest of each party to the litigation will produce the evidence and the competing arguments necessary for the trier to make a fair and rational decision. The adversarial system, therefore, is driven by the parties, one or more of whom (the plaintiff or plaintiffs) initiate a lawsuit by filing with the trial court clerk a complaint and a summons. These documents are "served" on (i.e., delivered to) the defendants who must respond within a specified time or suffer an adverse judgment by default. From the outset of a lawsuit, the parties have a great measure of freedom to shape their legal positions. (Of course in most cases, the parties are guided by, and speak through, their attorneys.) The plaintiff, for example, can choose the legal theory or theories (such as breach of warranty or negligence) on which she will rely. Likewise, the defendant can select the defenses (such as denial or contributory negligence) he wishes to assert. Of course, the defendant can simply forfeit the contest and allow the entry of an adverse, or "default," judgment. A default judgment is entered on motion of the plaintiff, made after the defendant's failure to respond.

Default judgments, however, are not the norm. In most cases, the defendant contests the plaintiff's claims by filing an answer containing one or more defenses. Thereafter, the parties make

4

various adversarial moves during the pre-trial phase of the case, which usually include motions designed to narrow the issues or to conclude the case prior to trial. Typically, the parties also conduct discovery, which enables them to gather evidence and to identify the issues on which the trial is likely to turn. In recent years, judges have taken a more active role in supervising and, especially, in scheduling discovery, although this important pre-trial process is still largely in the hands of the parties.

As the trial date nears, many judges will call one or more pre-trial conferences. These conferences—which are attended by the judge and the opposing lawyers—are used to settle pre-trial disputes, to encourage settlement, and, more importantly, to prepare the case for trial.[1] For example, the judge may precisely identify the issues to be tried and become generally acquainted with the evidence upon which each party will rely. He may also impose time limits or other restrictions (such as the number of expert witnesses) that will impart structure to the trial and avoid wasteful or cumulative evidentiary presentations.

None of this judicial oversight, however, changes the basic adversarial model in which each party gathers and presents evidence. Each disputant, and not the judge, largely determines what evidence he will present at trial. That is, the parties are responsible for gathering and proffering evidence; the judge merely decides if a given item of evidence is admissible when a party opponent objects that the proffered evidence violates an evidentiary rule. This observation leads to a related point: in addition to controlling her own evidentiary presentation, a party (or more specifically, a party's attorney) can influence the evidentiary record by objecting to the evidence offered by her opponent. If her objection succeeds, she can block the admission of the objectionable portions of her opponent's evidence, which of course tends to tilt the evidentiary balance in her favor. The success of her objection will depend upon whether the judge determines that an exclusionary rule dictates rejection of the proffered evidence. However, a party is not required to object to adverse evidence, even if an exclusionary rule is available to prevent its admission. If by careless omission or deliberate inaction, a party fails to object to inadmissible evidence, the judge will normally admit it. Once admitted, this evidence stands on the same footing as other admitted evidence. Only in extreme cases, and usually on behalf of a criminal defendant, will the court intervene and exclude inadmissable evidence on its own motion (sua sponte).

1. *See* FED. R. CIV. P. 16 for an illustrative list of topics that may be addressed at a pre-trial conference.

As the foregoing discussion implies, the evidence that reaches the trier of fact is by far the most important determinant in the outcome of a trial. The principles of law that govern a case are often clear and uncontested. Even if there are "legal" disputes, these normally take second place to "factual" disputes. Resolution of these factual disputes turns upon the trier's consideration and evaluation of the available evidence. Thus, a lawyer's skill in presenting and objecting to evidence will often determine the success of his client's case.

§ 2.2 Phases of a Trial

Since the plaintiff has the burden of proving her case ("the burden of persuasion"), she makes the first opening statement. The defendant's opening statement usually follows, although sometimes the defendant "opens" just prior to his case in defense. After the opening statement(s), the plaintiff makes the first evidentiary presentation (plaintiff's "case in chief"). Next, the defendant makes his evidentiary presentation (defendant's "case in defense"). Often there are further evidentiary presentations, usually called the plaintiff's "case in rebuttal" and the defendant's "case in rejoinder." When the evidence-taking phases of the trial are over, the plaintiff makes the first closing argument. Then the defendant delivers his closing argument. After the defendant's closing argument, the plaintiff is allowed a final closing argument in which she tries to rebut the defendant's closing remarks. (Since the plaintiff has the burden of persuasion, she is given the last opportunity to address the factfinder.)

The judge has considerable control over the order of trial and will not be reversed by an appellate court unless he abuses his discretion. That said, the sequence below is typical of most trials and for our purposes will suffice:

(a) Jury Selection (Voir Dire)

(b) Counsels' Opening Statements

(c) The Presentation of Evidence:

　　Plaintiff's Case in Chief

　　Defendant's Case in Defense

　　Plaintiff's Case in Rebuttal[2]

　　Defendant's Case in Rejoinder

(d) Counsels' Closing Arguments

2. Although many trials have four evidentiary phases, some trials consist only of the plaintiff's case in chief or, more likely, the plaintiff's case in chief and the defendant's case in defense. Usually the judge allows each party to decide whether or not to present additional evidence.

(e) Judge's Charge

(f) Jury Deliberation and Verdict

A final important observation about the order of trial events: unless the judge rules otherwise, a party has the exclusive right during his "presentation phase" to proffer witnesses, documents, or other items of evidence. The opponent is limited to cross-examination. In other words, the opponent must wait until her presentation phase begins before presenting her own evidence. This rule prevents the cross-examiner from destroying the continuity of the direct examiner's presentation of evidence by interposing "extrinsic" rebuttal evidence.

§ 2.3   Offers of Proof and Objections

The Offer of Proof

In a broad sense, every document proffered as evidence and every statement elicited from a witness on the stand is an offer of proof. Commonly, however, the term "offer of proof" is used more narrowly to refer to the dual showing a proponent must make when the admissibility of her evidence is challenged by objection. The offer of proof includes, (1) a presentation or description of the evidence that a party seeks to introduce and, (2) a statement of the fact or facts she wishes to prove with the evidence. (You can appreciate why offers of proof must often be made outside the hearing of the jury.) Sometimes, the context in which the evidence is proffered makes its nature and purpose so clear that no elaboration—that is, no formal offer of proof—is necessary.[3] If there is any doubt about the evidence and its intended purpose, however, counsel should supplement ("perfect") the record.

Perfecting the offer of proof has two advantages. First, counsel may ultimately persuade the trial judge that the proposed evidence is admissible. Second, even if the judge sustains the opponent's objection, counsel may challenge the judge's ruling on appeal should she (the proponent of the excluded evidence) lose her case at trial. With the offer of proof in the record, the appellate court can make an informed decision about the evidentiary ruling below. Note, also, that an offer of proof gives the opponent a clearer picture of the nature and purpose of the contested evidence, giving him the opportunity to refine, restate, or even withdraw his objection.

An offer of proof may take many forms. Sometimes counsel's question to a witness alone suffices because, in context, counsel's purpose in offering the evidence and the witness's expected response are clear. As noted above, however, if there is doubt or

---

3. FRE 103(a)(2) recognizes this possibility.

ambiguity about the offer, counsel should specify "for the record" precisely what evidence she seeks to adduce and the proposition to which she directs it. She may accomplish this, for example, by summarizing the expected evidence and its purpose or by interrogating the witness out of the jury's presence—that is, in the presence of the judge, opposing counsel, and the court reporter. If the proponent offers a document or tangible object, she should record its purpose and ensure that the writing or the object (or at least an adequate description of the object) becomes part of the trial record. The point is that the steps necessary to complete an offer of proof vary with the particular setting. To illustrate the routine possibilities, consider the following:

(a) In the context in which evidence is offered, its purpose and nature is sufficiently clear without further elaboration;

(b) Counsel for each side and the court reporter approach the bench and the proponent states his offer out of the jury's hearing (a "side bar" conference);

(c) The proponent states his offer in open court, a procedure that suffices when the evidence described is unlikely to improperly influence the jury;

(d) The jury is excused, and the proponent formally interrogates a witness "for the record."

Objections

The objection, like its counterpart the offer of proof, should reveal to the adversary, the trial judge, and the appellate tribunal the basis for contesting the evidence. Hence, the objector should indicate the ground upon which she challenges the proffered evidence.[4] Sound trial administration and fairness to the proponent dictate that the objection should be made as soon as the objecting attorney is able to perceive the defect in the proffered evidence. Usually, counsel will make the objection as soon as the question calling for improper evidence is asked (or as soon as an objectionable item is offered). Sometimes, however, there is insufficient time to object, as when a witness answers quickly or gives an answer that is not responsive to the question asked. In circumstances where the evidentiary defect is not apparent until after a response has been made, a motion to "strike the evidence" is the proper remedy. A successful "strike" is followed by the judge's instruction to the jury to disregard the stricken evidence. Of course, as a practical matter, the jury may find this instruction difficult or impossible to follow.

4. FRE 103(a)(1).

Because offers and objections serve important informational functions, it is not surprising that the rules governing these devices encourage the offeror and objector to state their respective positions accurately. This demand for precision reflects the assumption that the opposing attorneys are familiar with the forthcoming evidence, presumably having had an opportunity to develop, preview (through discovery), and study the available evidence before trial. The judge, who does not have equal familiarity with the forthcoming evidence, is entitled to expect informed and succinct offers and objections. Thus, as we shall see below, the specific rules governing offers and objections favor the judge and operate against the attorney who fails to take appropriate, timely action.

When counsel objects to the admission of her opponent's evidence, the judge, of course, must rule. It is important to note that the trial judge rules on the *offer of proof that is actually presented* by the proponent; the judge also rules on the *objection that is actually stated* by the opponent. The correctness of the judge's ruling is determined by the articulated postures of counsel; it is not determined by the positions they might have but did not assume. Thus, the judge does not err if she rejects an offer of proof that is faulty or that by its terms indicates that the proffered evidence is inadmissible. The fact that a different or revised offer would have made the evidence admissible is beside the point. Likewise, the judge who overrules an erroneous objection has not made an error. The fact that a different, proper objection would have resulted in exclusion of the evidence is, again, of no consequence.

ILLUSTRATIONS

(1) Peter sues a private golf club for negligent maintenance of its golf cart. Peter offers evidence of two other accidents during the month preceding Peter's accident in which other golfers were injured while using the defendant's carts. Peter (through his attorney) states that the purpose of the evidence is "to show that the defendant has been negligent in maintaining its carts on other occasions, which supports the proposition that the defendant was negligent regarding his (Peter's) accident." The judge excludes the evidence, ruling that negligence on one occasion is not admissible to show negligence on another, separate occasion.

There is no error even if the evidence was admissible for another purpose. The fact that Peter might have cast his offer in different terms (for example, to show that similar accidents at the same location or with similar carts put golf club on notice of a possibly hazardous condition) will be unavailing on appeal.

(2) In the same suit, Peter starts to testify that Cousin, a golfer and mechanical engineer, told Peter that he (Cousin) had used the same cart Peter was using when injured, and that the cart had a defective axle and a loose clamp in the steering column. Cousin had rented the cart only a day before Peter rented it. The defendant objects that the evidence is irrelevant, but the trial judge overrules the objection.

Assume the testimony about Cousin's statements was inadmissible on hearsay grounds (Cousin, who is the declarant, is not on the stand), but the evidence is relevant. The judge ruled correctly even though another objection (hearsay) would have resulted in exclusion.

While the foregoing illustrations suggest that the rules governing offers and objections are arbitrary and harsh, this unfairness is ameliorated because the parties (unlike the judge) usually have ample pre-trial opportunities to become familiar with the available evidence. Thus, the parties can anticipate what offers and objections are likely to be forthcoming at trial. On the other hand, the judge does not have similar opportunities to anticipate and study the forthcoming evidence; she is likely to know comparatively little about the evidence until the trial begins. Moreover, an appellate court will occasionally alleviate the harshness of the customary rules by invoking the "plain error" doctrine.[5] Although used sparingly, especially in civil cases, this doctrine permits an appellate court to reverse a trial judgment tainted by obvious or palpable error, even if there was no objection during the trial. Keep in mind, also, that even a ruling which erroneously sustains or overrules an objection may not result in an appellate reversal. The appellate court will not reverse the judgment below unless it concludes that the erroneous evidentiary ruling probably had a substantial effect on the trial outcome.[6]

§ 2.4 Examining Witnesses: General Rules

The Form of Questions

In this section, we examine briefly a cluster of rules that govern the interrogation of witnesses. One of these rules, no doubt

5. This doctrine is acknowledged in FRE 103(d).

6. FRE 103(a) ("substantial right ... affected"). When an erroneous evidentiary ruling results in a violation of the United States Constitution, a different standard of review applies. Generally speaking, an appellate court will reverse the judgment below unless it determines beyond a reasonable doubt that the constitutional error was harmless. See Chapman v. California, 386 U.S. 18, 22 (1967).

familiar to most readers, generally prohibits attorneys from asking leading questions during direct examination. The rule rests upon two assumptions. The first, a factual assumption, is that a cooperative relationship exists between the direct examiner and his witness. Presumably, the witness is prepared to give testimony favorable to the examiner's client, precluding any need for leading questions. Moreover, it is likely that examining counsel and the friendly witness have discussed or even rehearsed the latter's testimony prior to trial. The second assumption, a psychological one, is that if the direct examiner phrases his questions in language that implies or suggests the desired answer, the witness will respond by providing that answer. The second assumption is linked to the first: the friendly witness is more likely to respond to a suggestive question by giving an answer that favors the examiner's client.

Thus, as a general rule, the direct examiner is prohibited from asking leading questions—that is, he is generally forbidden to ask questions that suggest the desired answer. Determining whether a question is leading involves a contextual judgment that takes account of such factors as phrasing and, occasionally, voice intonation. For example, in a suit for breach of contract for the sale of goods, the question set out below would constitute a leading question. After establishing that the defendant had spoken with the plaintiff, counsel for the plaintiff asks his witness:

> "During your conversation with the defendant Neill Jones, didn't Mr. Jones declare that he would not deliver the merchandise?"

On the other hand, counsel could avoid leading his witness by rephrasing the question:

> "Will you state what, if anything, the defendant, Neill Jones, said, during your conversation, relating to the delivery of the merchandise?"

The rephrased question avoids the suggestiveness that makes the initial question leading. To generalize: the correct approach to the interrogation of a witness who is not hostile is to use non-suggestive questions, especially when asking about matters that are actually disputed by the parties.

The leading questions doctrine promotes the principle of neutrality in the adversarial system: the trier of fact should hear a witness's unadulterated testimony, not testimony that has been influenced by partisan counsel. Although this goal is difficult to achieve, partisan influence is at least reduced by prohibiting leading questions during direct examination.

Qualifications to the "Leading Questions" Prohibition

There are a number of qualifications to the general rule prohibiting leading questions during direct examination. First, a leading question may be allowed because the opponent decides not to object. (The judge will not ordinarily intervene.) For example, the opponent may conclude that the damaging effect of such question(s) is insufficient to justify the interruption and possible jury impatience caused by an objection. Second, as we will see below, there are situations outside the reach of the general prohibition against leading questions.

Leading questions are permitted, for example, to establish *preliminary, uncontested facts,* such as a witness's identity, address, and other incidental matters. This exception to the general rule is simply a concession to trial efficiency. Leading questions are also proper, at least for a brief period, if the *witness is forgetful.* Here the theory is that a leading question or two may spark the witness's recollection. For example, in stating his question, counsel may direct the witness's attention to an event or a conversation in issue and reveal a portion thereof. There is, of course, some risk that if the leading questions do not revive memory, the witness may nonetheless give an answer based upon the implied suggestion in the examiner's question. Whatever the theoretical extent of this risk, however, it is minimized by two practical controls: first, the opponent can object on the ground that recollection has not been refreshed and, second, during cross-examination the opponent can attempt to prove the limited extent of the witness's recollection. For example, the opposing attorney could ask about other closely related features of the incident about which the witness testified. If the witness has little or no recollection of these features, her memory may not be trustworthy. Leading questions are also usually permitted in the *interrogation of a very young witness.* Again, some risk to the neutrality of testimony exists, especially since a youthful witness is presumably quite susceptible to suggestion. As a practical matter, however, leading questions may be the only effective method of eliciting the testimony of a young witness. Finally, as developed below in greater detail, leading questions may be used during direct examination to *interrogate a hostile witness.* When leading questions are allowed on direct, the trial judge has ample power to prevent abuse. On objection, or occasionally on his own initiative, he can restrict or terminate a leading inquiry.

In contrast to the general rule governing direct examination, the prohibition against leading questions is generally inapplicable during cross-examination. Here the assumption is that the cross-examiner and the witness are antagonistic, and that there has been no pre-trial preparation or testimonial rehearsal. Moreover, the risk of suggestive influence, assumed to be present during direct examination, is thought to be absent in the supposedly hostile atmosphere of cross-examination. The use of leading questions also aids the cross-examiner in controlling the damage that an adverse witness might inflict on his client's case. For instance, counsel can frame his inquiries narrowly in order to limit the witness's range of response, or he can consciously frame a question in a manner designed to elicit the desired answer. Thus, the cross-examiner can question a hostile witness on the examiner's own terms, thereby minimizing the negative impact of the witness's testimony.

It should be apparent that the factual assumptions of cooperativeness (during direct examination) and hostility (during cross) that underlie the rule governing leading questions may not always be accurate. Some witnesses, for example, have no allegiance to either of the parties. Furthermore, the direct examiner may need to call a hostile witness, or the cross-examiner may have the opportunity to interrogate a friendly witness. (An attorney's choice of witnesses is, after all, limited to those witnesses who have personal knowledge of the events to which they testify.) In these instances, the interrogating counsel or the opposing counsel may request a change in the mode of examination. The trial judge has the power to grant or deny counsel's request, depending upon her assessment of the actual relationship between examiner and witness. In administering the rules governing leading questions, the trial judge will be guided by the following provisions of Federal Rule of Evidence 611:

> **(a) Control by Court.** The court shall exercise reasonable control over the mode and order of interrogating witnesses and presenting evidence so as to (1) make the interrogation and presentation effective for the ascertainment of the truth, (2) avoid needless consumption of time, and (3) protect witnesses from harassment or undue embarrassment.
>
> . . .
>
> **(c) Leading Questions.** Leading questions should not be used on the direct examination of a witness except as may be necessary to develop the witness' testimony. Ordinarily leading questions should be permitted on cross-examination. When a party calls a hostile witness, an adverse party, or a witness identified with an adverse party, interrogation may be by leading questions.

Note that Rule 611 makes special reference to calling an adverse party (or a close associate). When a party calls his opponent to the stand, a hostile exchange is likely to ensue. Consequently, the general rule is that the sponsoring counsel can, from the outset, treat the adverse party as a hostile witness and conduct her examination by leading questions. As to unfriendly witnesses not readily identified with the opposing party, counsel should ordinarily seek the court's permission before conducting her examination by leading questions.

Scope of Cross–Examination

Another rule governing the interrogation of witnesses prescribes the scope of cross-examination. There are two versions of this rule. Under the so-called English Rule, a cross-examiner can inquire into any relevant matter. Conversely, under the predominant American Rule, the cross-examiner is limited to the subjects or topics that were covered by the direct examiner *and* to matters relating to the witness's credibility. In Rule 611(b), the Federal Rules of Evidence adopt the (majority) American Rule:

> **(b) Scope of Cross–Examination.** Cross-examination should be limited to the subject matter of the direct examination and matters affecting the credibility of the witness. The court may, in the exercise of discretion, permit inquiry into additional matters as if on direct examination.

As you perhaps anticipate, the restriction imposed by the American Rule is intended to achieve an orderly evidentiary presentation. When each witness addresses the same subject matter during both direct examination and cross-examination, the jury presumably can more readily follow and understand the testimony.

Obviously, situations arise in which it is debatable whether the cross-examiner is venturing outside the scope of direct examination. The mosaic of human events does not always permit sharp divisions between the various topics of descriptive testimony. It falls to the trial judge to set the proper limits of cross-examination, although she is likely to await an objection before she acts to limit the cross-examiner's inquiry. Generally speaking, judges administer the American Rule in a practical fashion, allowing cross-examination on topics that are very closely linked to the subject matter of direct examination. This permissive posture defeats the strategy of a direct examiner who attempts to elicit from a witness only a fragment of an event or conversation in the hope of confining the cross-examiner to the same arbitrarily restricted scope of inquiry.

Questions Relating to Credibility

Notwithstanding its otherwise determinate nature, the American Rule permits the cross-examiner to ask questions related to a witness's credibility. Questions directed to the credibility (impeachment) of a witness are allowed, even if those questions introduce new topics. For example, the examiner may ask the witness whether he holds a grudge against one of the parties, whether he has a financial stake in the outcome of the case, or whether he has been convicted of a kind of crime that raises doubts about his credibility—for example, perjury or fraud. Two reasons justify this practice. First, the credibility of a witness is always implicitly at issue during trial. Second, the central purpose of cross-examination is to weaken or negate the testimony given during direct examination. Impeachment helps achieve this purpose. However, even though the cross-examiner is entitled to expand her examination by asking questions pertaining to impeachment, it does not follow that she can interrupt her opponent's evidentiary presentation by calling her own "impeachment" witnesses or introducing documentary evidence designed to impeach. Normally, counsel must present this additional ("extrinsic") evidence during her own evidentiary presentation, such as her case in defense. The rule prohibiting the cross-examiner's introduction of extrinsic evidence during her opponent's presentation phase is designed to facilitate an orderly evidentiary presentation without major digressions and interruptions.

The Lay Opinion Rule

We conclude this section with a brief discussion of the "opinion rule" which forbids a lay witness from giving opinion testimony. (A quite different rule applies to expert witnesses.) The rule confines the lay witness to a statement of "facts." In other words, the lay witness should give testimony that is descriptively neutral and relatively concrete, and avoid testimony that is infused with his own opinions or inferences. It is the jury's responsibility, and not that of the lay witness, to draw inferences from the evidence. Thus, the opinion rule places a limit on how far a lay witness can go in stating his own characterizations and conclusions.

Note that the opinion rule is based on a tacit assumption; namely, that once the jury has heard the "bare facts" from the witness, it is in as good a position as the witness to draw reasonable inferences. Sometimes, however, the witness is in a superior position. We then say that the witness's opinion is "helpful" to the jury's understanding and thus his opinion is admissible. Note also how "fact" and "opinion" shade into one another. For example, when a witness describes a tree as "gnarled and decaying," is he making a factual statement or is he giving his opinion? There is usually no clear division between the two. The difference, rather, is a matter of degree. Indeed, "fact" and "opinion" are simply labels. We use these terms in an effort to differentiate testimonial concreteness and neutrality from testimonial generality and predilection. (Courts would probably characterize the statement describing the tree as factual; even if the description were labeled an opinion, it would be helpful and thus permissible.) It should come as no surprise that trial judges administer the opinion rule in a very practical fashion, admitting so-called "opinion" testimony that is non-prejudicial and helpful.

The more inference-laden and conclusive a witness's statement is, the more likely it is to be his opinion. When a lay witness testifies, "Fog was so heavy that the cyclist ran off the pavement and lost control", he is stating his opinion as to causation. Would his statement nonetheless be allowed because it would be helpful to the jury? Probably not, although the issue is at least debatable. The question for the judge is whether the witness can describe adequately the density of the fog and the movement of the cycle and rider, leaving it to the jury to decide whether lack of visibility caused the cyclist to lose control. Consider the following statements of opinion:

(1) "When the party ended, Puck appeared to be drunk."

(2) "After several hours of searching for the child, Portia looked exhausted and worried."

(3) "I would say that he was old, probably 75 or more."

(4) "When Henry heard that Paulina had gone out with Duncan, he looked really angry."

(5) "The white Porsche then pulled into the left lane and passed all three cars at a high rate of speed–probably eighty or more miles an hour."

(6) "Yes, I do recognize that handwriting. It is my sister, Lillian's."

Assume that in each of these instances the witness has actually observed the event or condition to which he testified. Note that in many of these instances, it would be difficult or impossible for the witness to recite the constituent "facts" that underlie his testimony. For example, how can a witness convey her perception of speed without saying the driver was "going fast" or that the driver was going about "eighty miles an hour"? Even when it may be possible to reduce a statement to its underlying components (as, for example, in Illustration (1)), the witness's opinion is still helpful. Testimony that Puck slurred his words and lost his balance on the dance floor helps the jury. But so, too, does the witness's opinion, formed from his first-hand observation, that he (Puck) was drunk. The reason this opinion is helpful is probably apparent: we often ob-

serve other persons as an integral whole, without a distinct awareness of each particular feature or trait. From this kind of observation, we characterize a trait (such as age) or activity (such as
speeding). General perceptions and characterizations, such as those
noting fear or anger, often aid the jury—as, for example, in resolving the issue of intoxication.

The foregoing testimonial samples are illustrations of allowable
lay opinion because, in the words of Federal Rule 701, each is based
on "the perception of the witness" and each is "helpful to a clear
understanding of the witness's testimony or the determination of a
fact in issue," Rule 701 is judicially administered by asking the
simple question whether the proffered form of testimony is *helpful*.
Appellate reversals based on the misapplication of the opinion rule
are quite rare, at least among modern appellate courts. There is
now general agreement that the administration of the lay opinion
rule rests largely in the discretion of the trial judge. Note again
that Rule 701 governs only the testimony of a lay witness. The Rule
does not apply to a witness whose testimony is "based on scientific,
technical, or other specialized knowledge...."[7] Such a witness
must be presented and "qualified" as an expert witness. Thus,
while a lay witness could testify that a substance on the victim's
clothing appeared to be blood, he could not testify that blood loss
was the cause of death.[8]

§ 2.5   Examining Witnesses: When Memory Fails

We have already noted that examining counsel may ask leading
questions to elicit testimony from a forgetful witness. There is
another courtroom technique that attorneys use to stimulate memory, should leading questions fail to do so. Counsel may attempt to
refresh a witness's memory by showing him some object (usually a
writing) or by having him listen to a recording. Indeed *any* object or
device—such as a photograph, a map, a song, or even a scent—that
will refresh the witness's memory is fair game. The important
restriction is that the object or reminder, whatever its nature,
serves *only* the purpose of stimulating the witness's recall: the
object or device used to refresh recollection is *not* an independent
source of evidence. If a witness regains her memory of the event by
consulting, say, a writing that describes it, she may continue to
testify. For example, a witness who examines the minutes of a past
committee meeting may thereafter recall the committee's discussions and the resulting committee action. However, it is her *testimony* given from restored memory, and not the committee minutes,
which constitutes the evidence received. The fact that she may

---

7. FRE 702 (expert testimony).   **8.** FRE 701 Advisory Committee's
Note (hereinafter ACN).

occasionally have to look again at the minutes (or other reminder) does not necessarily mean that she has no present recollection.

The courtroom procedure for refreshing present recollection though the use of writing or other aid to memory often calls upon the trial judge to make a difficult judgment. The problem is most acute when the reminder—for example a writing or recording—describes the event the witness is asked to recall. The judge must determine whether the witness's recollection has actually been refreshed or, alternatively, whether she is in fact merely reciting the contents of the writing or other memorial that she is consulting.

If the judge rules that the witness's recollection has not been restored, then of course her testimony cannot constitute the evidence received. The actual evidence is the reminder itself. This raises the question of whether the writing or other object is admissible for the purposes of proving what it records. We shall address this question momentarily. For now, let us assume that the witness's present recollection is refreshed. The object used to refresh recollection, which has been marked as an exhibit and shown to opposing counsel, has served its purpose. The examining lawyer is not entitled to admit it into evidence, but she may, of course, continue to elicit testimony based upon the witness's restored memory.

At the end of the direct examination, the questioner relinquishes the writing or other object to her opponent, who may use it in conducting his cross-examination. The opponent may then try to show that the witness's present recollection is faulty, for example by demonstrating that she cannot recall important details contained in the writing. The cross-examiner may also expose discrepancies between the witness's testimony and the writing (or other recordation), raising a question about which is accurate. Finally, the cross-examiner may introduce into evidence the item used to refresh recollection. The limited purpose of this evidence is to allow the jury to compare it with the witness's testimony. Technically, the item may be used only for "impeachment" purposes, that is, to cast doubt on the witness's testimony.

Rule 612 of the Federal Rules of Evidence is pertinent to the present discussion. It provides:

Writing Used to Refresh Memory. Except as otherwise provided in criminal proceedings by [the Jencks Act,[9]]

---

9. The Jencks Act, 18 U.S.C.A. § 3500 (1970), gives the accused the right to inspect written or recorded statements of any prosecution witness if the statement has been adopted by the witness or if the statement is essentially

> . . . if a witness uses a writing to refresh memory for the purpose of testifying, either—
>
> > (1) while testifying, or
> >
> > (2) before testifying, if the court in its discretion determines it is necessary in the interests of justice,
>
> an adverse party is entitled to have the writing produced at the hearing, to inspect it, to cross-examine the witness thereon, and to introduce into evidence those portions which relate to the testimony to the witness. . . .

Under these provisions, there is no absolute right to compel production of a writing used to refresh a witness's memory *prior* to his courtroom appearance, but neither is such a writing invariably protected from disclosure. Access to the writing previously used to refresh recollection lies within the judge's discretion, influenced by such factors as the importance of the "refreshed" testimony and the nature of the document used to refresh. Rule 612 reflects a judgment that in view of other means, notably discovery, available to parties to gain access to pertinent materials in the adversary's hands, it suffices to leave to the judge's discretion the question whether the opponent is entitled to a writing used as a memory aid prior to trial.

Another point deserves comment and it, too, arises when a document or other recorded communication is used to refresh a witness's memory *prior* to his testimony at trial. There is some question whether a judge may order the production of such a recorded statement if the recordation would ordinarily be protected by an evidentiary privilege. Suppose, for example, that the writing used prior to trial to restore a witness's memory is subject to the attorney-client privilege. A similar question surfaces with respect to a writing protected by work product immunity—the immunity that generally protects from disclosure documents prepared in anticipation of litigation by a party, his attorney, or other representative.[10] By refreshing a witness's memory prior to trial, the party entitled to the privilege or immunity has avoided the open disclosure and resultant waiver that inevitably occurs when a privileged document is used in courtroom proceedings. Thus, the opponent's claim that any privilege (or immunity) is waived—a claim that is uniformly upheld when memory is refreshed during a witness's testimony—is not necessarily compelling. The issue is a close one, and the

---

a verbatim recording of the witness's prior oral statement. The Act does not apply unless the statement deals with the subject matter of the prosecution witness's testimony.

10. *See* Fed. R. Civ. P. 26(b)(3).

response of the courts has not been uniform.[11] Certainly, the fact that a writing used to refresh recollection is of such a nature that it ordinarily would be protected is an important factor in the judge's decision whether to exercise his discretion and order production. However, it may not be a conclusive factor. If the judge decides that under Rule 612 "it is necessary in the interests of justice" that the writing be produced, there is some authority holding that neither privilege nor work product immunity will defeat production.

Past Recollection Recorded

Let us now suppose that neither leading questions nor the use of a writing (or other stimulus) results in restoring memory. In other words, counsel's attempts to "refresh present recollection" have failed. Suppose, further, that the examiner has in his possession a writing (or other recordation) prepared at an earlier time by the very witness on the stand. This setting raises the possibility of introducing into evidence the witness's prior statement describing the event the examiner wishes to prove. As you will more fully appreciate when we reach the chapter on hearsay, the difficulty with introducing this writing lies in the disadvantage accruing to the *cross-examiner*. Recall that hearsay evidence is generally excluded (there are many exceptions) because the cross-examiner cannot test the credibility of the out-of-court speaker (the "declarant"). The declarant's statements are revealed to the trier of fact either through the testimony of a witness who heard them or by the introduction of a recordation, often a writing, that contains the declarations. If Davy tells Warwick that "Puck shot Victim," and Warwick so testifies in an effort to prove Puck was the assailant, a hearsay issue arises. Puck's lawyer wants to cross-examine the declarant, Davy, the person who actually observed the shooting. (Davy may be mistaken or lying.) The same hearsay problem arises if Davy's diary contains the accusation "Puck shot the victim" and the diary is introduced by the prosecutor. Only the author of the diary entry (Davy) can provide adequate responses to the cross-examiner's questions.

Now suppose Davy *is on the stand* but he simply cannot recall whether Puck or Peter or someone else fired at the victim. In other words, he has no present recollection of the event. Suppose, however, Davy is able to testify that he keeps a diary and that he made a descriptive entry in his diary soon after the shooting in question, when his memory was fresh. In short, he can give testimony vouching for *the accuracy of the entry* even though he cannot recall the event it describes. The point is that Davy's testimony gives his earlier, out-of-court statement, added credibility. The first key to

---

11. For discussion and citations to conflicting authorities, see CHRISTOPHER V. MUELLER & LAIRD KIRKPATRICK, EVIDENCE § 6.69, at 594 (3d ed. 2003).

admissibility is that the witness's past recollection has been preserved in a writing or some other recorded form (hence the descriptive label "past recollection recorded" or simply "recorded recollection"). The second key to admissibility is that the witness is able to testify that he recognizes the writing or other recording, that he recalls making it (or adopting it) soon after the event in question when his memory was fresh, and that he believes the earlier recorded statements are accurate.

The difference between present recollection refreshed and past recollection recorded should now be apparent. In the first setting, the witness's testimony is the actual evidence; in the second setting, the past recording is the actual evidence. The key features of past recollection recorded are set out as an exception to the hearsay rule in Federal Rule of Evidence 803(5):

> **Recorded Recollection.** A memorandum or record concerning a matter about which the witness once had knowledge but now has insufficient recollection ... to testify fully and accurately [is admissible if] ... made or adopted by the witness when the matter was fresh in the witness' memory and [if shown] to reflect that knowledge correctly ....

The bar of the hearsay rule is overcome by a "recorded recollection" since the witness on the stand can testify that the statements in the prior recording were accurate when made because he made or verified them when his memory was fresh. Of course, the fact that the writing or other recording is admitted into evidence simply means that the trier may consider it along with all of the other evidence in the case. The trier—let us say the jury—might decide that Davy was mistaken when he recorded in his diary that Puck shot the victim. All trials, of course, have conflicting evidence and, ultimately, the trier must decide which portions of the evidence to believe.

§ 2.6   Role of Judge and Jury: An Overview

Lawyers often generalize that the jury decides questions of fact and the judge resolves questions of law. This description of functions loosely accords with prevailing practice. The rationale for such a division is clear: the judge, through training and experience, is particularly qualified to resolve legal questions, while the jurors, who bring to the courtroom the common experience of the community, are better equipped to settle factual disputes. As we shall see, however, it is not as easy to distinguish the responsibilities of judge and jury as this lawyers' colloquialism suggests.

The first qualification to this general statement of functions is that the jury discharges its fact-finding role only in those cases where the state of the evidence reasonably justifies a finding in favor of either party. If from the evidence there is no *reasonable* dispute as to the historical (adjudicative) facts, the judge may use an instruction, judgment as a matter of law, or some other appropriate procedural device to prevent the jury from making any finding contrary to the overwhelming, conclusive evidence. The judge's intervention may take the whole case from the jury or only a portion of it. In any event, the function of adjudicating historical facts, a function that normally belongs to the jury, is assumed by the judge in those instances where the evidence reasonably supports only one factual conclusion.[12]

A second qualification to the general allocation of judge-jury responsibility arises when, in rendering a general verdict, the jury applies the substantive law (as described in the judge's charge) to the particular facts of the case. That is, the jury first determines the facts and then applies the applicable substantive law. In some instances, notably where community values and standards are particularly important, the substantive law is phrased in very general terms. A defendant is negligent, for example, if he fails to "act reasonably" or does not exercise "due care." Similarly, an employer is liable for his employee's conduct only if the employee was acting in the "scope of employment" and "scope" is determined in the context of each case. In cases like these, when the applicable law is expressed as a general legal standard, the jury must not only find the facts, but must also *characterize* or label these facts in light of the indeterminate standard.[13] In a sense, the jurors are giving substantive, particularized content to the legal principle involved by construing it in the context of the specific facts before them.

---

12. *See, e.g.,* FED. R. CIV. P. 50(a) (permitting judgment as a matter of law in civil cases). In criminal cases, by uniform tradition and constitutional compulsion, the jury always applies the law to the facts unless the defendant waives his right to jury trial. *See* FED. R. CRIM. P. 29(a) (abolishing motions for directed verdicts in criminal cases). Of course, the judge can take the case from the jury and render a judgment in the criminal defendant's *favor* by granting a motion for acquittal. *See* FED. R. CRIM. P. 29(a).

13. There are control devices, including summary judgment, jury instructions, and judgment as a matter of law (directed verdict), that can be used to limit the jury's characterization. These devices ensure that the jury is not allowed to reach an irrational characterization of the conduct in question. For example, it would be irrational to characterize as negligent a hazardous, but correctly performed, surgical procedure if it were the only known means of saving the patient's life and the patient was fully informed of the risks involved. Nonetheless, substantial latitude is inherent in such imprecise terms as "reasonable" and "scope," and if the facts as well as the issue of reasonableness or due care are disputed, the jury's verdict normally is decisive.

The judge, too, assumes functions that vary from the more familiar task of deciding questions of law. There are numerous occasions when she makes factual determinations. In the pre-trial process, the judge resolves factual questions pertaining to the jurisdiction of the court over the subject matter or over the parties. For example, in determining whether the court has personal jurisdiction over the defendant, the judge resolves any factual dispute that arises with respect to the defendant's activities or "contacts" with the forum state. The judge also settles factual disputes that may arise in connection with discovery proceedings. She resolves, for example, factual disagreements associated with issues concerning whether a privilege protects materials from discovery. Furthermore, in the course of a (pre-trial) summary judgment proceeding or at a pre-trial conference, she determines which, if any, factual issues are reasonably in dispute. Even after a jury trial commences, the judge monitors the evidence and, as already noted, removes from jury consideration any factual determinations that in light of the evidence before the jury could rationally be resolved in only one way.

Judge's Fact–Finding Role in Applying the Rules of Evidence

The judge also plays an important fact-finding role in administering the rules of evidence. Rules of evidence often refer to factual circumstances that attend their application. The judge determines the existence or nonexistence of factual circumstances that control whether a particular rule of evidence is applicable. For example, the "Best Evidence Rule"[14] states that when proving the terms of a writing, the original document must be produced unless it is destroyed or is otherwise unavailable. Suppose the proponent claims that the original was destroyed or lost, but the opponent contests this assertion, thus raising a factual dispute.[15] In order to avoid prolonging the trial and overburdening or confusing the jury, the judge makes the preliminary factual determination necessary to apply the rule of evidence. Similarly, when a witness is offered for the purpose of giving expert testimony, the judge determines whether she has the training or experience to qualify as an expert. Moreover, the judge often determines preliminary facts when one party seeks to adduce evidence that her opponent claims is "privileged" and thus inadmissible. For example, suppose the plaintiff offers evidence of a statement made by one of the corporate defendant's employees to defense counsel. The defendant objects on the ground of the corporate attorney-client privilege. The judge has to decide whether the defendant preserved the privilege by direct-

---

14. *See* FRE 1002, 1004.

15. This example appears in 1 McCormick, On Evidence § 53, at 234 (John W. Strong ed., 5th ed., 1999).

ing its employee to speak in confidence to defense counsel for the purpose of facilitating legal advice to the corporation. Generally speaking, if these "preliminary facts" exist, the statement is privileged.

In some instances, the judge determines preliminary factual issues that relate to, but are distinct from, the events being litigated. (For example, the judge decides whether the proffered witness is an expert on, say, the subject of ballistics and is thus able to give testimony on this specialized topic.) In other instances, the judge determines preliminary factual issues that are closely associated with the litigated events. A striking example is the factual determinations a judge must make when ruling on the hearsay exception for "dying declarations." In a prosecution for murder, the victim's dying declarations pertaining to the cause or circumstances of her impending death are admissible over a hearsay objection[16] if she spoke while firmly holding the belief that she was about to die.[17] (The theory is that, facing death, she would be unlikely to lie or falsely accuse.) Whether she spoke with the sense of "impending death" and whether her statement addressed "the cause or circumstances" of her death are preliminary facts, determined by the judge.

ILLUSTRATION

Just after a private aircraft touches the runway while landing, it lurches sharply to the left and crashes into an airliner that is awaiting take-off on an adjacent runway. Peter, a passenger on the waiting airliner, observes these events through the window next to his seat. Fifteen minutes later, Peter, who sustained minor injuries in the collision, relates what he saw to Airport Investigator. At a subsequent trial in which both the owner and pilot of the out-of-control aircraft are defendants, Investigator is called to the stand to testify as to what Peter told him. Defense counsel objects to Investigator's testimony about Peter's remarks, arguing that the proffered evidence is hearsay. The plaintiff's lawyer argues that Investigator's testimony falls within an exception to the hearsay rule that allows into evidence "excited utterances."[18] Out of the jury's hearing, plaintiff presents evidence indicating that Peter spoke while in a state of excitement and shock—a state

---

16. The hearsay problem arises because the opponent who seeks to have this evidence excluded cannot cross-examine the deceased victim, whose statements are likely to incriminate the accused.

17. FRE 804(b)(2).

18. FRE 803(2).

that was produced by witnessing the accident and being jolted and injured himself. Defense counsel.produces rebuttal evidence that when Peter made his statements, fifteen minutes after the accident, he had regained his composure.

The rule of evidence governing this hypothetical permits the introduction of hearsay statements that *relate* to the event being litigated, if the person (the "declarant") making the statements spoke while in a state of excitement, shock, or stress. (The theory is that under these circumstances, the declarant would be unlikely to deceive or lie.) The judge decides the disputed factual question whether Peter spoke while in a state of emotional upheaval. Note that this preliminary fact closely relates to the events being litigated—the crash, its cause, and the results.

Why do we allocate to the judge the task of deciding preliminary facts that are integrally linked to the application of a rule of evidence? We do so primarily because it would be impractical and unwise to assign these factual questions to the jury. The typical juror is uninterested in the technicalities of the rules of evidence and their underlying policies; usually she simply wants to find out all she can about the case. Moreover, as we have observed, these preliminary facts are often closely linked to the very evidence in dispute, so that deciding the preliminary facts requires consideration of the disputed evidence. Consider, for example, the two rules of evidence that, respectively, admit dying declarations and excited utterances if certain conditions—that is, certain preliminary facts—exist. To make an informed, intelligent decision about the existence or nonexistence of the preliminary facts, the decision-maker needs to consider the content of the dying declaration or, in the latter instance, of the excited utterance. (Recall that, to be admissible, dying declarations must *pertain to the cause or circumstances* surrounding the impending death; excited utterances must *relate to* the exciting event.) A juror would find it impossible, as a practical matter, to ignore the very statements in question once these statements were revealed as part of a preliminary fact-finding process. Thus, even if the evidence turned out to be inadmissible, the jury would be unlikely to ignore it.

Rule 104 of the Federal Rules of Evidence is captioned "Preliminary Questions." It provides in part:

(a) Questions of Admissibility Generally. Preliminary questions concerning the qualification of a person to be a witness, the existence of a privilege, or the admissibility of evidence shall be determined by the court.... In making its determination it [the court] is not bound by the rules of evidence except those with respect to privileges.

This portion of Rule 104 assigns important fact-finding responsibilities to the judge. Note also the last sentence of subsection (a), which frees the judge from the usual rules of evidence when she is deciding a preliminary fact. (The only exception is for rules of privilege, which are designed to prevent *any* coerced disclosure of the protected information.) We noted in Chapter I that a principal reason for the creation of rules of evidence is the existence of the lay jury; we also noted that the rules are not strictly enforced in trials to the bench.[19] Since the judge presumably understands the possible deficiencies in "inadmissible" evidence, she can take account of these weaknesses when she is determining preliminary facts. Hence, the normal evidentiary rules are suspended by operation of Rule 104(a) when the judge is finding preliminary facts. In short, we trust the judge to make a reliable determination of preliminary facts, even though she considers evidence that is technically "inadmissible."

§ 2.7 Shortcuts to Proof: Judicial Notice and Other Devices

A careful litigator uses the pleadings, motion practice, and discovery to identify and isolate contested factual issues. She then determines which portions of the evidence gathered prior to trial bear upon (are "relevant to") the contested issues. Next, she determines which portions of this evidence are likely to be admissible in court and, within this category, which portions are likely to be admissible without protest or objection. There are at least two possibilities for gaining admission of evidence during the trial without opposition: first, the evidence in question may be so clearly admissible that the opposing attorney is unlikely to contest its admission; second, the evidence may bear on facts that are relatively unimportant, thus making a contest by the opponent unlikely. There are other—usually tactical—reasons why an opponent may decline to object to evidence, but an examination of these reasons falls within the purview of such courses as trial practice. Note, however, this possibility: an opponent may concede certain factual propositions in an effort to render unnecessary the introduction of any evidence to prove the conceded point. Sometimes the concession is less damaging than the evidence.

There are various devices, most of which are available prior to trial, for gaining factual concessions from opposing counsel. These include admissions in the pleadings, admissions during discovery or at a pre-trial conference, and stipulations. For example, counsel might invoke Rule 36 of the Federal Rules of Civil Procedure

---

19. *See* Chapter I, at n.1.

(governing requests for admissions) and request that her opponent admit certain propositions. ("You are requested to admit that at the time of the accident [described] your employee [name and employment capacity] was acting in the scope of his regular duties and of his employment.") Stipulations by counsel offer another means of avoiding formal proof. For example, an attorney may ask his opponent for a written stipulation that the residential area in which the accident in question occurred has "four-way stop signs." The basic idea is simply to narrow the number of disputed factual propositions by taking full advantage of the available procedural devices.

Judicial Notice

In certain limited circumstances, counsel can invoke the doctrine of judicial notice to avoid the need for formal proof. Courts will take judicial notice of facts that are beyond reasonable dispute. The kind of facts most commonly subject to judicial notice are those that directly pertain to the parties and the circumstances surrounding their dispute. Because these facts would normally be decided by a jury, they are often labeled "adjudicative facts" or "historical facts."

The core feature of judicial notice is the uniformly recognized requirement that this evidentiary device applies only to those adjudicative facts that, in the language of Federal Rule 201(a), are "not subject to a reasonable dispute." It is helpful to think of two general categories of facts that are likely to be beyond reasonable dispute. The first category consists of facts either *widely known* throughout the country or widely known to persons living in the area where the court taking judicial notice is located. The results of a closely-contested presidential election, a recent build-up of the armed forces, an economic depression, or a large-scale domestic terrorist attack are examples of facts likely to be widely known throughout the country. On the other hand, facts such as the area of a city where local government is housed, the main subway routes, the streets and highways that are likely to be congested during rush hours, and the general seasonal weather patterns are examples of local facts likely to be widely known in the vicinity where the court sits.

The second category of facts that are likely to be beyond reasonable dispute are those which can be *accurately determined* by consulting reliable sources such as maps, charts, tables, and reference materials in such varied fields as engineering, biology, medicine, history, mathematics, astronomy, physics, and so forth. This second category consists of facts that are unlikely to be widely known but which—in the words of Federal Rule 201(b)—are "capable of accurate ... determination by resorting to sources whose accuracy cannot reasonably be questioned." For example, a court might consult a reliable source to determine the tides or the depth of a body of water. Similarly, a court might consult an appropriate reference to determine the effective date of a treaty and whether one of the signatories was at war when the treaty became effective. Another example: In prosecutions for drug possession, it is sometimes necessary to determine whether an investigating officer had probable cause to arrest the accused. Suppose the officer testifies that he was suspicious of the accused because the accused was wearing a heavy, bulky coat in very warm weather, thus suggesting concealment. The judge, after consulting a reliable reference, could take judicial notice of the local temperature on the date in question.[20]

When Judicial Notice is Conclusive

Recall that a jury's role is to decide pertinent facts that the parties to the suit reasonably dispute. In other words, the jury deals with factual disputes that, on the basis of the admitted evidence, could reasonably be resolved in favor of either party. Since judicial notice is taken only of those facts that are not subject to reasonable dispute, it would seem to follow that once a fact is judicially noticed, the jury is bound by the court's action and cannot make a contrary finding. In civil cases, the jury is so bound and, accordingly, the judge will instruct the jury to accept the judicially noticed fact as conclusive.

The same rule would apply in criminal cases were it not for the well-established principle that the government must prove each element of a charged crime beyond a reasonable doubt. In a criminal trial to a jury, it is incumbent upon the government to prove each element to the *jury's* satisfaction. The judge is without power to direct a verdict of guilty *against* the accused, even if the evidence points strongly toward his guilt. This prohibition in criminal jury trials has led to a modification of the usual approach to judicial notice. Under Federal Rule of Evidence 201(g), a fact that is judicially noticed is conclusive *except* in criminal jury trials. In these proceedings, the judge instructs the jury that it "may, but is not required to, accept as conclusive any fact judicially noticed."

A court *may* take judicial notice of a fact on its own motion. Under Federal Rule 201(d) a court *must* take judicial notice of an appropriate fact "if requested by a party and supplied with the necessary information." Of course, counsel may disagree on the question whether judicial notice is proper. Under Federal Rule

---

20. When the judge takes judicial notice of a fact in a civil trial, the "noticed" fact is conclusively established. However, in criminal trials, the judge instructs the jury that it "may, but is not required to accept as conclusive any fact judicially noticed." FRE 201(g). See the textual discussion above.

201(e), a party is entitled "to be heard as to the propriety of taking judicial notice and the tenor of the matter noticed." For example, the attorney opposing judicial notice may argue that the fact proffered for the court's notice is neither widely known nor verifiable through reliable sources. The judge makes the final decision as to the propriety of judicial notice, using as her guide the "indisputability" standard of Rule 201(b).

Legislative Facts

Federal Rule of Evidence 201 deals only with judicial notice of "adjudicative facts" which are the facts that collectively make up the litigated event—that is, those facts that deal with the contested occurrence. However, courts, and especially appellate courts, sometimes take judicial notice of legislative facts. So-called "legislative facts" are related to the disputed transaction, but only in the sense that they constitute the context or background in which the case at hand arose and will be resolved. A particular labor dispute, for example, may arise in the context of depressed prices, high unemployment, widespread labor unrest, and an economy that is in transition from wartime to peacetime. An injury to a professional football player during a game may arise in the larger context of the combative nature and physical demands of professional football.

Courts necessarily make explicit or, very often, implicit determinations or assumptions about the context or environment in which the case arose and in which the law declared by the court will be applied. These determinations or assumptions often influence the way a court interprets a statute or crafts a judge-made rule of law. A well-known example of judicial notice of legislative facts is the Supreme Court's consultation of sociological studies in Brown v. Board of Education[21] as part of its effort to determine the deleterious effects upon children of segregated public schools. The point is that courts, and particularly appellate courts (which have some latitude to modify legal rules) often need to acquaint themselves with the factual context in which the legal rule controlling the case before them will operate.

The standard that courts use when they "find" or "notice" legislative facts is not the beyond-reasonable-dispute standard that applies to the judicial notice of adjudicative facts. Although we have no definitive answer to the question of what less restrictive standard does apply, it is very likely a standard of probability—that is, based on the available information, it is at least probable (more likely than not) that the setting in which the case arose and in which this legal rule will operate has the characteristics identified by the court. For example, a court might conclude that labor

---

21.   347 U.S. 483, 494 (1954).

dispute before it occurred "in a coal mining labor environment, where unemployment is very high, and strikes have been frequent and often violent."

Lawyers sometime make arguments in their briefs that draw upon legislative facts. This argumentative technique has a distinguished pedigree. In a famous case,[22] decided almost a century ago, attorney (later Supreme Court Justice) Louis Brandeis successfully argued that a state could constitutionally restrict the number of hours women were allowed to work. Almost the entirety of his "Brandeis Brief" was devoted to medical and empirical evidence that showed the harmful effects on women of working long hours. Brandeis' ground-breaking brief introduced a mode of appellate argument that continues today.

22. Muller v. Oregon, 208 U.S. 412, 419 (1908).

Chapter III

RELEVANCE: GENERAL PRINCIPLES AND SPECIAL APPLICATIONS

Table of Sections

---

§ 3.1   Basic Concepts

Relevance is the basic principle underlying all of the evidentiary rules. The threshold test of admissibility is the test of relevance; if evidence is not relevant, it is not admissible.[1] Because the fundamental principle of relevance pervades the law of evidence, it serves as both the dominant and unifying theme.

What is meant by the term "relevant evidence?" In its simplest form, relevant evidence helps prove the existence (or nonexistence) of some fact that is pertinent to a legal dispute between parties. Drawing upon an observation of reformer and philosopher Jeremy

---

1. FRE 402. However, not all relevant evidence is admissible, since the Constitution, statutes, and other Federal Rules of Evidence may exclude relevant evidence.

Bentham, we can say that the effect of relevant evidence "when presented to the mind, is to produce a persuasion concerning the existence of some ... matter of fact—a persuasion either affirmative or disaffirmative of its existence."[2] Of course, all evidence tends to prove or disprove *some* fact, but not all facts are relevant to a legal dispute. In a judicial trial, the substantive law or, perhaps, the state of the pleadings circumscribes those facts that have pertinent (*i.e.*, legal) consequences. Thus, evidence that *V*, the victim of a robbery, consumed four martinis during the hour before he was robbed tends to show he was intoxicated at the time he was victimized. But this fact—*V*'s intoxication during the robbery—is of no legal consequence in a criminal trial in which *D*, the accused, is prosecuted for robbery. Intoxication of the victim is not a defense to the charge of robbery, nor does it ordinarily increase or decrease the severity of the crime. On these assumptions, therefore, the degree of *V*'s intoxication is irrelevant to *D*'s guilt. More precisely: in a prosecution of *D* for robbery, evidence directed toward *V*'s intoxication is irrelevant if its sole use is to prove that *V* was intoxicated when he has robbed.

The law rejects irrelevant evidence for several reasons. First, the exclusion of irrelevant evidence advances the goal of efficiency: it is wasteful to receive evidence that has no proper bearing on the case. Second, the exclusion of irrelevant evidence advances the objective of unbiased factfinding within the requirements of the substantive law: although some evidence does not logically assist the trier of fact in resolving *pertinent* factual issues, it may nonetheless pose a risk that the trier will use that evidence inappropriately. Consider again the case involving an intoxicated robbery victim. If the trier of fact strongly disapproved of excessive drinking, it might express that disapproval by acquitting *D*, the defendant, even if the relevant evidence tended to show that *D* was guilty of robbery. Suppose, for example, the intoxicated victim unintentionally drove his car into an unfamiliar area of the city with a high rate of crime, and he was robbed when he ran out of gas. The trier could believe that the victim "brought it on himself" by drink-induced imprudence, and refuse to convict *D*. The potential for this sort of misuse is precisely why irrelevant evidence is excluded. (Even some evidence that is relevant is sometimes excluded due to its potential for inflaming the jury or otherwise causing undue prejudice.)

2. Jeremy Bentham, Rationale Of Judicial Evidence, Specially Applied To English Practice 16 (1827).

Federal Rule of Evidence 401 defines relevant evidence as follows:

Definition of Relevant Evidence

"Relevant evidence" means evidence having any tendency to make the existence of any fact that is of consequence to the determination of the action more probable or less probable than it would be without the evidence.

Although we may loosely think of relevant evidence as that which "tends to persuade," it is important to note that the principle of relevance embodies two distinct relationships. First, relevance connotes the *probative relationship* between the *evidence proffered* and the *factual proposition* to which that evidence is addressed. In other words, one aspect of relevance is concerned with whether proffered evidence is logically probative of the proposition toward which it is directed. For example, evidence that a particular horse kicked Wolsey two years ago is somewhat probative as to whether it kicked Philo last month. (Note, however, that it might be helpful to know more about the circumstances surrounding each occasion.) However, compare the weak probative force of this evidence—one event, two years ago—with evidence showing that during the same month in which the horse kicked Philo, it kicked three other persons under similar conditions. Clearly, the latter evidence is more persuasive: the probative relationship is increased by proximity of time, by repetition, and by similarity of conditions.

The second aspect of relevance is concerned with whether the factual proposition to which the evidence is directed is *consequential* under the substantive law. A fact is consequential only if it helps to prove (or disprove) an element of a charge, claim, or defense. For example, in a suit against Davy for breach of a contract to build a walkway, evidence that Davy had two illegitimate children is probably irrelevant. The principal elements necessary to recover for breach of contract are: (1) existence of valid contract; (2) plaintiff's performance of all conditions precedent; and (3) defendant's breach or non-performance. The fact Davy had two illegitimate children is unrelated to any of these three elements.

To summarize: evidence is relevant only if it, (1) tends to prove or disprove a proposition of fact that, (2) is of consequence under the substantive law that applies to the case. In due course, we shall explore more fully the degree of probative force necessary to "prove or disprove" a factual proposition. For now, it is sufficient to remember that evidence is relevant only if it supports a factual proposition that is "of consequence" (*i.e.*, "material") to the legal issues at trial. In the text that follows, we shall look more closely at what is meant by this term "of consequence" (or "consequential"). Bear in mind that even if evidence strongly supports a factual proposition, the judge (on objection) will reject the evidence unless the proposition is "of consequence" to the lawsuit in which the evidence is offered.

Determining Consequential Facts

Determining what facts are consequential involves a careful analysis of the statutory or common law that applies to a particular case. These substantive provisions of law, made applicable to the case by the pleadings, dictate what legal effects attach to various factual propositions. The only factual propositions that legitimately govern the outcome of a lawsuit are those that constitute the elements of a criminal or civil charge, claim, or defense. Therefore, evidence is consequential (or, under the older common law terminology, "material")[3] only if it tends to establish the existence or nonexistence of an element of the controlling substantive law. Suppose that in a suit filed by Prospero against Duncan for assault and battery, Duncan offers evidence that he mistakenly thought Prospero was another person, Puck. This evidence should be rejected if the factual proposition to which it is directed—mistaken identity—is of no legal consequence under the substantive law governing the case. In other words, if the law of intentional torts imposes the same liability notwithstanding this kind of mistake, the judge should declare this evidence irrelevant.[4]

Although the requirement of consequentialness involves an independent analysis of the relationship between the substantive law (which prescribes what facts have a bearing) and the factual proposition to which the evidence is directed, it is important to remember the role of pleadings. The plaintiff's complaint (or the prosecutor's indictment or information) determines the theory of recovery (or of prosecution) and thus invokes the substantive law on which the plaintiff (or prosecutor) will rely. For example, a plaintiff's complaint alleging a defendant's breach of warranty invokes the substantive law of warranty and not, for example, the law of negligence. Similarly, the responsive pleading of the defendant (or the accused) indicates the general nature of the defense and thus the substantive law on which the defendant relies. A

3. "Immaterial" historically meant that the proffered evidence bore no relationship to the legal issues raised by the substantive law made applicable by the pleadings, although the term sometimes was used indiscriminately to refer merely to a lack of sufficient probative force between the evidence proffered and a consequential proposition. *See* FRE 401 ACN.

4. Note, however, that if mistaken identity were consequential under the law governing damages, then evidence of mistake could be considered for the purpose of determining the amount of the plaintiff's recovery. Evidence of mistake would be consequential, not to excuse liability, but to the assessment of the appropriate award.

defendant in a civil case, for instance, may not only deny certain of the plaintiff's allegations, he may also offer defenses such as contributory negligence or breach of warranty, thus invoking the substantive law pertaining to these defenses. Likewise, an accused in a criminal trial may simply enter a plea of not guilty; in addition, however, he may offer affirmative defenses such as entrapment, self-defense, and so forth. The point is that both the plaintiff's (or prosecutor's) legal theory and the defendant's (or accused's) legal theory affect the legal rules that are "in play" and hence affect which facts will be consequential.

It is worth noting, however, that while pleadings initially determine the substantive law that applies to a case, they are easily amended—particularly if they are amended early in the litigation. Amendments often result in a shift in the applicable law. Furthermore, modern procedural systems often permit parties to make pleading allegations that are sufficiently broad to invoke all the substantive rules that are likely to apply to the case. In other words, in most modern procedural systems, pleadings may be drafted generally (for example, by simply alleging what occurred) or in the alternative (so as to support multiple theories of recovery or defense). Pleadings that invoke the substantive law supporting several different theories of recovery, *e.g.*, negligence and breach of warranty, or several different theories of defense, *e.g.*, assumption of risk and release, have the general affect of increasing the number of consequential propositions in a particular case.

Even though pleadings are not a very important feature of modern litigation, they can still affect the admissibility of evidence. Suppose, for example, in a plaintiff's suit for breach of contract, the defendant's pleading (*i.e.*, her "answer") alleges as her *only* defense the running of the statute of limitations. When this case goes to trial, she could not (over objection) introduce evidence that there never was a valid contract To clear the way for this evidence, she would have to amend her pleading. Under the traditional common law approach, the judge would rule that without an amendment, evidence tending to prove there was never a valid contract should be excluded as *immaterial* (in modern terminology, inconsequential) because the defendant conceded the validity of the contract in her answer by failing to deny it.

A judge following the modern approach embodied in the Federal Rules of Evidence would resolve the problem caused by this pleading omission somewhat differently, although she would reach the same result. Consistent with the common law approach, the Federal Rules take both the plaintiff's complaint and the defendant's answer into account. In order to state a valid contractual claim, the complaint must allege that there was a valid contract, which the defendant breached. Under the Federal Rules' approach, the fact that the defendant's answer relies solely on the statute of limitations and thus *concedes* that there was a valid contract does not mean that her *evidence* showing there was no valid contract is inconsequential (immaterial). After all, the plaintiff's complaint invoked the law of contractual breach, including the essential precedent allegation that the plaintiff had a *valid* contract with the defendant. More to the point, under the Federal Rules the *relevance* of evidence pointing to a consequential fact *does not depend on whether that fact is disputed*. Since the defendant's proffered evidence is directed to the existence of a valid contract, the evidence is consequential and therefore relevant.

Without an amendment to her answer, however, the defendant's evidence is nonetheless inadmissible under the Federal Rules, just as it is under the common law. The reason her evidence is objectionable is that to receive it under the present state of the pleadings would be a waste of time. In other words, the Federal Rules, unlike the common law, exclude the evidence showing there was no valid contract by relying on the general evidentiary principle, embodied in Federal Rule 403, that even relevant evidence should be excluded when its probative force is "substantially outweighed" by such considerations as wastefulness, jury confusion, or unfair prejudice. Of course, if the trial is in its early stages, the judge is very likely to grant the defendant's request to amend her answer by adding another defense; namely, that no valid contract ever existed. Then, of course, the receipt of evidence bearing on this issue would not be a waste of time because the defendant's former concession in the pleading has been superseded by a denial.

Let us now return to our principal theme. You can readily appreciate the dual inquiry raised by a lack-of-relevance objection. One task, as we have noted, is to examine the probative link between the proffered evidence and the factual proposition to which it is directed. The other task is to examine the relationship of that proposition to the substantive law. These investigations can be performed in either order, but evidence is admissible only if it has probative value to prove or disprove a consequential fact. Under the approach of the Federal Rules, it is the substantive law and not the pleadings that determine what facts are consequential, although evidence that falls outside of the pleading allegations will still be rejected as superfluous or wasteful.

To illustrate the fundamental principles of relevance, consider a hypothetical posed by Professor Arthur Best: plaintiff sues the owner of an office building on the theory that inadequate maintenance of the lobby caused the plaintiff's injuries.[5] Three items of evidence are proffered:

5. ARTHUR BEST, EVIDENCE 3 (5th ed. 2004).

(1) The office building is one story taller than permitted by the applicable zoning regulations;

(2) The lobby, once painted pink, was recently repainted yellow;

(3) The lobby was dimly lit.

Of these, only the third is directed to a consequential fact. In order to state a valid claim, the plaintiff must allege, among other things, that a hazardous condition was the proximate cause of her injuries. The excessive height of the building would be relevant (consequential) in a dispute over a zoning violation, but has nothing to do with the maintenance of the lobby. Similarly, the color of the lobby probably has no bearing on its maintenance with respect to safety. On the other hand, dim lighting does have a tendency to point toward an unsafe or hazardous condition and might show, for example, that lobby users could not see a step or a loose tile. Thus, because the evidence about lighting is offered to show that there was an unsafe condition in the lobby, it is consequential.

Note, however, that although evidence must normally be consequential under the substantive law, certain background evidence, having little or no consequence to the law governing the case, is routinely admitted. In order to convey fully the "story of a case" to the trier of fact—that is, to permit the jury or judge trying the case to comprehend fully and contextually the consequential facts that gave rise to the lawsuit—it is almost always necessary to present background information. The trier needs to know contextual facts about the setting and the occurrences that collectively make up the events on which the lawsuit is based. This background information is conveyed through a variety of evidentiary forms, such as testimony, charts, maps, photographs, and so forth. Some of this evidence would fail to meet the test of relevance if the test were strictly applied. For example, in the suit for failure to properly maintain the interior of an office building lobby, testimony that the lobby "is on the west side of the building and is entered from Chancellor Street by either a revolving door or a handicap ramp" may not have a tendency to affect the probability of any consequential fact. Nonetheless, evidentiary facts of this sort are routinely admitted. The reason is that this kind of background evidence *aids the jury's understanding* of the evidence that is "relevant" in the strictest—Rule 401—sense of the word.

Similarly, incidental (background) evidence about a witness may not be relevant in the strictest sense. Such details as the witness's address or occupation may come into evidence simply as contextual information. On the other hand, evidence about a witness may sometimes bear strongly on a consequential fact and thus easily satisfy the strict definition of relevance. For example, evidence that a witness has poor vision or impaired hearing might affect the jury's assessment of her account of the litigated event. In the language of Rule 401, evidence that the witness has abnormal hearing or vision has a tendency to reduce the trier's belief in the "existence of . . . [those] facts of consequence" to which the witness testifies. Evidence directed to the credibility of a witness bears on the trier's assessment of the truth or accuracy of her account of consequential facts, and thus is relevant because it has a tendency to make such facts more or less probable.

Bearing in mind that the test of relevance involves assessing the probative value of proffered evidence to affect the existence or nonexistence of a consequential fact, consider the following problem. Suppose that in April a prison guard, *V-1*, is murdered and that in May another guard, *V–2*, is murdered. The investigation by authorities intensifies and, in late May, *D,* a prisoner, tries to escape from prison. In a subsequent trial for the murder of *V–1* in which *D* is named the accused, is *D*'s attempted escape relevant?[6]

Persons responding to this question may disagree. Clearly the evidence does not establish the accused's guilt. However, only the total evidence introduced need be sufficient to justify a finding of guilt. A single item of evidence is relevant if it has any tendency to increase (or decrease) the probability of a consequential factual proposition. It is not even necessary to demonstrate that it is *more probable* that escape was motivated by the fear of detection in connection with *V–1's* murder than by other possible motives, such as feared detection in connection with *V–2's* murder or the simple desire to gain freedom. The question is whether the probability that the accused committed the murder for which he is on trial is to some degree increased by evidence that he attempted to escape. So put, it may at least be argued that the evidence is relevant and, hence, it should be considered along with other circumstantial evidence (such as fingerprints, blood stains, and the like) in determining whether the defendant is guilty beyond a reasonable doubt. In a jury case, the judge simply asks herself whether a reasonable jury could rationally conclude that the proffered evidence of attempted escape tended to make a consequential fact (*D* murdered *V–1*) more or less probable.[7]

The foregoing examples suggest that the test of probative value is derived from commonplace experience. That is, the test usually involves no more than a common sense determination whether

6. This problem, with some variation, is posed in 1 McCormick § 185, at 642.

7. As you will see, however, the judge may exclude relevant evidence if other considerations, such as prejudice or jury confusion, substantially outweigh the probative value of the evidence. The risk of prejudice is the particular point of concern in the hypothetical above.

proffered evidence reveals events or conditions that increase or decrease the likelihood of other, associated, events or conditions. In the words of an early evidence scholar, Professor James Bradley Thayer, relevance is an "affair of experience and logic, and not at all of law."[8] Common observation teaches that if one fled the scene of a crime, his guilt is made somewhat more probable than it would be in the absence of flight. Similarly, human experience indicates that if one had a motive for murder, it is more probable that he murdered than it would be if no motive existed. The touchstone of relevance, at least in the first sense—probative value—is therefore the presence of a logical relationship between the evidence and the ultimate proposition to which it is directed. Of course, this logical relation may be established not only by common observation, but by the principles governing probabilities in specialized disciplines, such as statistics, science, medicine, architecture, or engineering. In these latter instances, an expert witness testifies as to the probabilities or other causal relationships within the specialized field. The trier of fact, however, ultimately determines the probative force of even technical or "scientific" evidence.

It remains to examine more closely the probative (logical) relationship between the proffered evidence and the consequential fact to which it is directed. Suppose the question in a case is whether Portia, who leased her pasture to Diana for a period of one year, reserved for herself the right to graze twenty cattle on the leased land. Since the lease was oral, the outcome of the case turns upon whether the jury believes Portia, who testifies she made the reservation, or Diana, who testifies that Portia did not.

Consider the following evidence offered by Portia:

(a) Three years ago, Portia leased the same tract of pasture land to Duncan for a three year period, and she reserved grazing rights for the twenty head of cattle she then owned. At the time Portia leased the land to Diana, Portia had twenty head of cattle.

(b) During each of the past four years, Portia has leased this same tract of pasture land. On each of these occasions, she owned approximately twenty head of cattle, just as she did at the time of the (fifth) lease with Diana. In each of the prior leases, which were with various lessees including Diana, Portia had reserved the right to graze her herd of about twenty cattle.

Clearly, the evidence described in (b) has greater probative force than the evidence described in (a). First, the evidence shows a consistent *pattern* of reserving grazing rights. Second, at the time

8. JAMES THAYER, A PRELIMINARY TREATISE ON EVIDENCE 269 (1898).

each lease was executed Diana owned approximately twenty head of cattle. Third, one of the prior leases was with the defendant, which tends to increase somewhat the likelihood that the current lease with the defendant contains the same reservation of grazing rights that was in the earlier lease.

This example illustrates the simple proposition that the probative force of evidence directed toward a consequential fact (here, the existence of a grazing reservation) can be increased or decreased by changing the evidence offered. To carry the example a step further, suppose there was evidence that the day after Portia and Diana had agreed to the lease in question, Diana had said to her accountant, "I got the lease I wanted, except for a grazing reservation for twenty head of Portia's cattle." Evidence of this deserving statement, called a "party admission," has strong probative force. Again, changes in the evidence offered to prove a consequential proposition are very likely to affect the probative force between the evidence and the proposition.

We will now see how changing the *consequential proposition* (defined by the substantive law) affects the probative value of the *same* proffered evidence. Suppose Portia has a dispute with the Internal Revenue Service (IRS), which claims that her pasture has no market value. (Her taxes are reduced if it has value.) Assume that Portia has available the evidence described in (a) above, which, as we have seen, has only weak probative value in the suit against Diana. In the imagined case now before us, however, this evidence is directed to a different consequential proposition; namely the proposition that Portia's pasture has market value. If the lease to Duncan, described in (a) above, was during or near the taxable year that is the subject of dispute between Portia and the IRS, evidence of the lease has considerable probative force. Assuming Portia and Duncan were dealing at "arm's length" and that Duncan paid significant rent for the pasture land in question, evidence of the Portia–Duncan lease has strong probative force to show that Portia's pasture has market value.

Summary

Here, then, are the simple core principles of relevance, the unifying theme of evidence law. In order to meet the first part of the relevance test, counsel's proffered evidence must tend to increase or decrease (*i.e.*, affect) the likelihood of the fact to which it is directed. In order to meet the second part of the relevance test, the fact to which counsel's proffered evidence is directed must be a *consequential* fact, that is, a fact made consequential by the substantive law governing the case. (Although these basic principles are denominated "first" and "second" the order of their application does not, of course, make any difference.) Finally, counsel can affect the probative force of evidence either by changing the evidence proffered *or* by changing the consequential proposition to which it is directed. Nonetheless, since the range of consequential propositions is limited by the substantive law, there are only a limited number of consequential propositions in any given case.

§ 3.2   Exclusionary Counterweights

Meeting the test of relevance often, but certainly not always, satisfies the test of admissibility. Recall Federal Rule 402: "All relevant evidence is admissible, except as otherwise provided by the Constitution ... Act of Congress, or by [other of] these rules...." It may be helpful to think of relevant evidence as "assumptively admissible," that is, admissible unless excluded by some other applicable evidentiary provision found in the Federal Rules or elsewhere. There are many such exclusionary provisions, including the rule against hearsay evidence, and many of these provisions (particularly those found in the Federal Rules themselves) are quite specific. For example, evidence that one party to a suit offered to settle the case is generally inadmissible.[9] The theory is that a party who offers a compromise should not be penalized (by evidence that he did not stand firmly behind his initial claim or defense) for his attempt to resolve the dispute. The law favors compromise agreements and the law of evidence is crafted to encourage offers of compromise.

Of course, the United States Constitution, and particularly the first eight amendments, might render relevant evidence inadmissible. The study of those constitutional rules of exclusion is covered only partially in this text, but is more fully explored in texts dealing with criminal procedure. Statutory provisions, too, sometimes operate to exclude relevant evidence.

In addition to numerous, specific exclusionary rules, the Federal Rules contain a general exclusionary rule that applies broadly to almost all proffered evidence. This rule, embodied in Federal Rule 403,[10] contains a balancing test. Because of its pervasive importance, the Rule is set out in full below:

Exclusion of Relevant Evidence on Grounds of Prejudice, Confusion, or Waste of Time

Although relevant, evidence may be excluded if its probative value is substantially outweighed by the danger

9. *See* FRE 408. The rule contains limited exceptions to the general prohibition. *See generally* infra, Ch. IV, § 4.3.

10. FRE 403 does not apply to certain convictions offered under FRE 609(a)(1) and (2), nor to 609(b). Nor does the Rule apply to a victim's sexual behavior under FRE 412(b)(2). Both Rule 609 and Rule 412 contain balancing tests that differ from the test contained in Rule 403.

of unfair prejudice, confusion of the issues, or misleading the jury, or by considerations of undue delay, waste of time, or needless presentation of cumulative evidence.

Rule 403 has several noteworthy features. As its title indicates, the rule provides for the exclusion of relevant evidence on, essentially, three grounds: (1) prejudice, (2) confusion (including misleading the jury), and (3) waste of time (including undue delay and the presentation of needless, cumulative evidence). As noted above, Rule 403 provides a balancing test that allows the judge to exclude relevant evidence if "its probative value is *substantially outweighed*" [emphasis supplied] by one or more of the counterweights of prejudice, confusion, or wastefulness. This test tips the scales in favor of admissibility: only if the "probative value is substantially outweighed" by one or more of the countervailing factors is the judge permitted to exclude relevant evidence. Finally, since the balancing test is necessarily an inexact one that takes into account the applicable law, the facts, and the evidence in each case, the trial judge has considerable discretion in applying this test. Her determinations under Rule 403 will not be reversed by an appellate court unless she has clearly abused that discretion.[11]

Old Chief v. United States[12] is perhaps the most notable case construing Rule 403. Old Chief was charged with assault with a dangerous weapon and use of a firearm in a violent crime. Additionally, he was charged as a felon in possession of a firearm. To sustain the last charge, the prosecutor had to prove, first, that Old Chief had been convicted of a felony-grade offense that raised a prohibition against future firearm possession and, second, that Old Chief had thereafter possessed a firearm. To establish the first point, the prosecutor, over a defense objection, introduced the record of the prior criminal judgment. It showed that Old Chief had been convicted of a criminal assault causing serious bodily injury, for which he received a five-year prison term.

Although the introduction of this evidence seems unremarkable, a problem arose because prior to trial defense counsel had offered to stipulate that Old Chief had been convicted of a felony-grade offense, thus removing this issue from dispute. Defense counsel also asked the judge to instruct the jury that the accused had a prior felony conviction, leaving as the sole issue his subsequent possession of a firearm. (Counsel was concerned about the jury's adverse reaction when it learned that the prior offense was a serious criminal assault.) When the prosecutor refused to accept or join in this stipulation, the trial judge permitted him to produce

---

11. 1 McCormick § 185, at 647   **12.** 519 U.S. 172 (1997).
nn.64–66.

evidence showing the name and nature of the prior conviction. The prosecutor did so by introducing the judgment of conviction described above.

The central question before the United States Supreme Court was whether the trial judge abused his discretion by refusing the accused's offer and permitting instead the prosecutor's evidence of the prior offense. Before reaching that issue, however, the Court rejected Old Chief's contention that the proffered stipulation rendered the name of the prior offense irrelevant. Noting that the relevance of an item of evidence does not turn upon whether it bears on a *disputed* issue, the Court found that the type of past crime committed by Old Chief had probative value bearing on a consequential fact. The named prior offense had probative force to place the accused within the class of persons convicted of a type of felony-grade offense that was within the statutory category[13] of offenses raising a prohibition against future firearm possession. (If, for example, Old Chief's prior offense had been a misdemeanor or had been a felony-grade income tax violation, no such prohibition would have arisen.) Nor was the name of the prior offense rendered irrelevant because there was alternative evidence, such as an admission or stipulation, that also placed the accused within the statutory ban on possessing a firearm. When a party concedes a consequential fact that his opponent's proffered evidence tends to prove, this concession does not render the evidence irrelevant. This concession does suggest, however, that the judge should often exclude the evidence under Rule 403 on grounds such as prejudice or wastefulness. In other words, the availability of the stipulation has the effect of discounting the probative value of the prior criminal judgment which may then be substantially outweighed by the risk of prejudice to Old Chief.

Next, in a wide-ranging discussion, the Court approved and elaborated upon the general principle that a prosecutor normally has the right to choose the evidence with which he wishes to prove his case.[14] Ordinarily an accused has no right to block the prosecutor's evidence by offering admissions or stipulations. The prosecutor's right of evidentiary choice, said the Court, has at least three grounds of support. First, an item of evidence very often points in more than one relevant direction. Testimony about a shooting may tend to establish "capacity and causation," while at the same time it may tend to establish "the triggerman's motive and intent."[15] In other words, the prosecutor is entitled to use evidence that is not

---

13. *See* 18 U.S.C.A. § 921, 922 (2002).

14. *See* Parr v. United States, 255 F.2d 86, 88 (5th Cir.), *cert. denied*, 358 U.S. 824 (1958).

15. *Old Chief*, 519 U.S. at 187.

confined to narrow, abstract linear reasoning, but narrates the story of the case with "descriptive richness"[16] that may capture more than one relevant point. Second, an evidentiary narration of the defendant's conduct aids the jury in drawing inferences, in faithfully adhering to the law governing the case, and in appreciating the moral foundations of the law. Third, the prosecutor's right of evidentiary choice helps ensure that the jury receives the evidence it is likely to expect. Through a carefully planned evidentiary presentation, the prosecutor usually can avoid both unexplained gaps and truncated narrative accounts in his evidentiary sequence.

Nonetheless, the Court held, by a five to four majority, that the particular circumstances in *Old Chief* required a limited departure from the general practice of allowing a prosecutor ample latitude to select his evidence. That latitude is restricted when, as here, one or more of the counterweights contained in Rule 403 substantially outweighs the probative value of the proffered evidence. That probative value must be discounted when other evidence, equally probative but less prejudicial, is available. The Court's principal concern was the unfair prejudice likely to result when evidence of the nature of the prior conviction (assault causing serious bodily injury) was offered for the sole purpose of proving the *status* of the accused. The status that had to be proved, of course, was that of a convicted felon who was prohibited from possessing a firearm. In *Old Chief* there was a substantial risk that the jury would not confine its use of evidence disclosing the exact prior offense to the permissible issue of Old Chief's status. Rather, the jury might have used evidence of the prior conviction to reason that he had a propensity to commit violent crimes such as assault with a dangerous weapon. In other words, the prosecutor's evidence, which was presumably offered to show only that Old Chief had "felon" status, might have had the strong, even primary effect of tainting the jury's attitude toward the question of his guilt of the gun-related crimes with which he was also charged.

Note, however, that Rule 403's reference to "unfair prejudice" *does not refer* to evidence that simply damages the opponent's case. Evidence favorable to one side is usually damaging to the opponent. The rule refers to prejudice that is likely to result from the trier's misuse of the evidence—in other words, the rule is concerned only with evidence that is likely to distort the trier's proper evaluation. In *Old Chief*, there was a risk that evidence of the prior convictions, introduced for the sole legitimate purpose of establishing the accused's status, would be used improperly by the jury. To reprise: the jury might conclude that Old Chief had a violent, assaultive

16. Id.

disposition (character) and therefore was guilty of the other crimes with which he was presently charged.

As suggested above, the opinion in *Old Chief* teaches that a Rule 403 determination is contextual in nature. That is, the trial judge must assess the challenged evidence not in isolation, but rather in the "full evidentiary context of the case. . . ."[17] This means that the probative force of the proffered evidence (the criminal judgment) and its potential for unfair prejudice must be evaluated in light of the importance of the evidence, its place in the narrative cohesion of the evidentiary presentation and, notably, in light of the availability of other evidence (the stipulation) directed at the same point. If "alternative evidence" were found to have the same or greater probative value but a lower danger of unfair prejudice, sound judicial discretion would discount the value of the item first offered. This is not to say, the Court cautioned, that the existence of two items of evidence supporting the same consequential fact "necessarily mean[s] that only one of them might come in."[18] Even though the two items may differ in their probative value and potential for prejudice, the existence of other available evidence is simply a factor that the trial judge takes into account in ruling on the admissibility of the challenged evidence. Finally, the Court noted, the contextual approach endorsed in *Old Chief* does not mean that the accused can block relevant evidence by simply conceding the point to which it is directed. Generally, such a move by the accused is ineffectual.

The Supreme Court's opinion in *Old Chief* is a study in contrast. The dictum, which dominates the opinion, is decidedly favorable to the prosecution and, by extension, supportive of the general principle that parties may usually select the evidence they wish to present. The specific holding, however, favors the accused. In a narrowly tailored ruling, the Court held that the trial judge abused his discretion by permitting the prosecutor to reject the accused's offer (to stipulate his prior felony conviction) and to introduce instead evidence revealing the name and nature of the prior offense. The key to the holding is that the only *legitimate* use of evidence pertaining to the prior conviction was to establish the accused's status as a felon prohibited from possessing a firearm. Furthermore, using the accused's stipulation or admission neither impedes the flow of the prosecutor's narrative, nor frustrates the expectations of the jury. Since Old Chief was not on trial for his past crime, the jury would not expect to receive evidence concerning its details; it would only need to know whether the prior conviction raised a bar against firearm possession.

---

17. Id. at 182.   **18.** Id. at 183.

While the *Old Chief* case focuses primarily on prejudice as a counterweight to probative value, there are other counterweights contained in Federal Rule 403. Two of these—"confusion of the issues ... [and] misleading the jury"—bear a kinship to unfair prejudice in that they are designed to safeguard the factfinding process. The remaining counterweights—"undue delay, waste of time, or needless presentation of cumulative evidence"—are simply time-saving devices that promote judicial efficiency. These latter counterweights substantially overlap since each one bears upon the dispatch and efficiency with which the trial moves forward.

Suppose that in a civil trial involving a pedestrian (the plaintiff) who was hit by the defendant's car, counsel for the plaintiff requests that the jury be taken to the scene of the accident so that the members can view the physical surroundings. Assume that the scene of the accident is forty miles from the courthouse. If the physical surroundings can be accurately depicted by testimony, photographs, diagrams, or other means, the trial judge would probably deny this request on the ground that allowing a jury view would be a waste of time or would unduly delay the trial.

Under the terms of Rule 403, a court may also exclude evidence on the ground that it is needlessly cumulative. The emphasis here is on the term "needlessly," as parties may often choose to emphasize a particularly crucial fact by introducing more than one item of evidence to support it. Needlessly cumulative evidence often relates to a minor or undisputed issue. For example, if the parties to the traffic accident (above) do not seriously dispute the facts that the defendant was driving a European sports car capable of high speeds and that the accident occurred at noon on a clear day, the trial court may decline to allow several witnesses to be called to the stand simply to testify as to these facts. On the other hand, if a defendant in a criminal trial denies involvement with a charged robbery, a trial court would likely allow several or more of the prosecution's witnesses to testify that they saw the defendant at the scene of the crime. Note, also, the court is quite likely to allow the *accused* a greater degree of latitude in presenting cumulative evidence, at least if the evidence is directed at a significant point. The accused's constitutional right to present a complete defense will, except in the clearest cases of redundancy, outweigh the court's interest in judicial efficiency.[19]

§ 3.3 Evidentiary Foundations

Rules of evidence require evidentiary foundations or predicates—that is, evidentiary steps that precede the introduction of testimonial, real, or demonstrative proof bearing on a consequential

---

19. *See, e.g.*, Chambers v. Mississippi, 410 U.S. 284, 302 (1973).

fact. Often, these foundations fit so naturally within the customary scheme of adducing evidence that they blend into the trial proceedings without notice or attention. Consider, for example, the foundational requirement of Federal Rule 602, which states in part:

Lack of Personal Knowledge

A witness may not testify to a matter unless evidence is introduced sufficient to support a finding that the witness has personal knowledge of the matter....

Yet a trial attorney does not routinely ask a witness "do you have personal knowledge of the matters to which you will testify?" The witness's personal knowledge is ordinarily revealed by her preliminary testimony establishing her presence at the event to which she will testify. In the course of her preliminary testimony, the witness will quite naturally disclose that she was in a position to perceive the relevant occurrence. Should there be a "foundation" objection, the judge has only to determine whether the trier of fact (here, let us assume, a jury) could reasonably find that the witness had perceived—that is, had first-hand knowledge—of the event or condition she describes in her testimony. Observe that in this instance the judge acts in a supervisory or "screening" capacity: his only role is to ensure that the jury has before it sufficient evidence to reasonably conclude that the witness saw or heard the occurrence in question. The assumption is that if the jury concludes that the witness lacks personal knowledge, it will ignore her testimony.

Many rules of evidence call upon the judge himself to determine the preliminary or foundational facts. In these instances, the judge does not merely screen the evidence, but rather he makes the necessary factual determination. Recall, for example, the hearsay exception for recorded recollection.[20] In administering this rule of evidence the judge determines the preliminary (foundational) facts. These foundational components consist of determinations, (1) whether the witness is unable to testify accurately from present memory, (2) whether the witness once had knowledge of the event in question, and (3) whether the witness made a recordation of the event when his memory of it was fresh. If the judge admits the recordation into evidence, the jury decides what probative weight to give it. The foundational or preliminary facts, however, have already been determined by the judge.

---

20. Supra Ch. II, § 2.5.

ILLUSTRATION

The plaintiff, Paulina, brings suit again Dora, claiming that Dora, a dealer in fine art, is liable to the plaintiff on grounds of fraud, or breach of warranty, or both. Paulina's complaint alleges that Dora sold to the plaintiff an expensive painting which Dora represented was the work of the Swiss painter, Paul Klee. In fact, Paulina claims, the work was by an unknown artist, most likely one who had worked as Klee's understudy. Dora, however, contends that the painting in question is actually one of Klee's early works.

During Dora's case in defense, her attorney calls Ella to the witness stand. Ella gives her name, address, and college major (commercial art); she then testifies that she has worked for more than twenty years for the Phillips Gallery of Art, where she specializes in arranging and conducting private tours of the gallery. Paulina's attorney then asks Ella if she has examined the painting in question. Receiving an affirmative answer, the attorney asks Ella whether she has an opinion as to who painted the disputed piece of art. The plaintiff objects on the ground of inadequate foundation.

Federal Rule of Evidence 702 permits testimony by an expert if her knowledge will "assist the trier of fact" and if she is qualified "by knowledge, skill, experience, training, or education" to address the specialized topic in question. The party calling an expert must provide a proper foundation before she testifies regarding a technical or scientific topic. The judge himself determines whether the foundation is adequate, because under Rule 104(a) it is he who determines the "qualifications of a person to be a witness. . . ." The foundation needed here requires[21] evidence that the topic to be addressed is within the realm of "scientific, technical, or other specialized knowledge" *and* that the proposed witness has the necessary expertise. In this Illustration, the foundation is inadequate. The principal defect is defense counsel's failure to adduce evidence that Ella was qualified by training or experience to determine the authenticity of a painting by an early twentieth-century European painter. Majoring in commercial art and serving as a director and guide of private tours do not, standing alone, yield the expertise necessary for her to render an opinion of the genuineness of the disputed work.

---

21. For a full explanation of the foundational requirements for expert testimony, *see* Ch. XI, §§ 11.3–5.

Notice again that in some instances, foundational requirements are fulfilled if the judge determines that the evidentiary predicate is *sufficient* for a jury to conclude that the foundational facts exist. The judge only screens the evidence to ensure that it is adequate to support the jury's determination. In other instances, the judge determines the existence (or nonexistence) of the foundational facts. In the next section, we will examine more closely the roles of judge and jury in foundational fact-finding. For now, it suffices to recall that subsection (a) of Federal Rule 104 assigns to the judge, and not to the jury, fact-finding responsibilities concerning "the qualification of a person to be a witness, the existence of a privilege, or the admissibility of evidence...."

Authentication

The term "authentication" denotes a particular foundational requirement that emerges in almost every trial. Its most frequent application is to documents and other items (exhibits) of real proof, but the requirement of authentication is not limited to tangible items. Whenever a lawyer offers evidence that she asserts is genuine (e.g., a telephone call from X to Y), she must provide a foundation sufficient for a reasonable trier of fact to conclude that the evidence is authentic. Generally speaking, if an item of evidence is not authentic, it is not relevant. That is, unless a party is attempting to prove that an item is not authentic (*e.g.*, because it is counterfeit), it is generally required that the party offer sufficient evidence that the item is genuine. Items that are forged or otherwise false are, of course, usually without probative value.

The evidentiary foundation ("authentication") required by the law of evidence to help assure authenticity is somewhat more demanding than daily experience might lead us to expect. In everyday affairs, if we receive a letter from a stranger that concludes with a typed or longhand signature ("Sincerely, Alena Leitner"), we normally assume that the signatory wrote the letter. Likewise, when the telephone rings and an unfamiliar voice says, "This is Alena Leitner calling," we normally assume it is she.

The law of evidence is more circumspect, however, for it operates in a milieu of conflict with a lay jury often acting as the factfinder. Under evidentiary principles, for example, the presence of a signature on a proffered document is not, standing alone, sufficient to satisfy the requirement of authentication. The proponent of the document must provide additional evidence that helps confirm its authenticity. Similarly, self-identification by a telephone caller is not, standing alone, sufficient to meet the requirement of authentication. The party wishing to show that the caller who identified herself was in fact that person must provide additional confirming ("foundational") evidence.[22]

Nonetheless, the requirement of authentication (which includes identification) is not stringent. Furthermore, there are no fixed rules of authentication that require a specific evidentiary procedure or routine. This flexible approach allows trial attorneys to think creatively about how to provide the evidentiary clues that meet the authentication requirement. All that is needed is evidence sufficient for the judge to conclude that a reasonable jury *could* find that the evidence in question (*i.e.*, the evidence being authenticated) is genuine. For instance, in the foregoing example involving self-identification by a telephone caller, authentication would be satisfied if the person receiving the call testified that she recognized the caller's voice as that of Alena Leitner. The authentication requirement would also be met by evidence that the caller revealed information likely to be known only by Alena Leitner. Similarly, authentication could be achieved by evidence that Alena Leitner frequently stutters and so did the caller. You should think of authentication as simply the process of providing evidentiary confirmation that a proffered item of evidence is in fact what it appears to be.

In a bench trial, after the judge hears evidence supporting authentication and any contrary evidence introduced by the opponent, she decides if the proffered evidence (to which authenticating evidence is addressed) is genuine. However, in a jury trial, the judge simply *screens the authenticating evidence* in order to determine whether the evidence *supporting* authentication, if believed by the jury, is sufficient to allow it rationally to conclude that the proffered evidence is genuine. Whether the judge personally believes the proffered evidence is authentic is of no consequence. If the process of authentication is satisfactory, the evidence in question is introduced; the jury evaluates it; and the jury ultimately decides if it is genuine. If the jury concludes it is not—for example, if it concludes that Alena Leitner did not make the telephone call in question—it will then ignore the evidence, for it has no probative value. More specifically, assuming the evidence is consequential under the substantive law only if Alena Leitner made the call, and the jury concludes that she did not, it will then ignore the evidence simply as a matter of common logic.

---

22. But if the proponent is trying to prove *that a person called* was in fact the person reached (respondent), it suffices for purposes of identification (authentication) to show that the caller dialed the number in the telephone directory that was assigned to the respondent and that the person reached identified herself as the respondent or provided other clues that confirmed her identity. *See* FRE 901(b)(6).

ILLUSTRATION

In a dispute over the value of an antique clock, counsel for the plaintiff, Howard Carter, wants to introduce a business letter from one Duncan Pearce, a reputable antique dealer, who appraised the clock and offered to buy it. Pearce has since closed his business, retired, and moved to a foreign country. There are, nonetheless, a number of possibilities for satisfying the requirement of authentication. Preliminarily, however, counsel must have Pearce's letter marked as a numbered or lettered exhibit (which in many jurisdictions is called an "exhibit for identification"). The exhibit is then shown to opposing counsel. Thereafter, counsel might use one of the following techniques of authentication:

(a) A lay witness who is familiar with Pearce's signature could testify that the letter was signed by Pearce.[23] (Thereafter, the letter would be introduced into evidence and read or shown to the jury.[24])

(b) An expert witness, having been qualified by the required foundational questions,[25] could compare Pearce's signature on the exhibit with specimens of Pearce's signature (or his handwriting) that have been authenticated.[26]

(c) The jury could compare Pearce's signature on the letter with specimens of Pearce's signature (or his handwriting) that have been authenticated.[27]

(d) If Pearce's letter containing the offer was responsive to an earlier letter from, say, Howard Carter to Pearce, then Carter could take the stand, authenticate his letter (or a copy thereof) and testify that the contents of Pearce's letter were responsive to his (Carter's) earlier letter.[28] This means of authenticating Pearce's letter invokes the *reply doctrine*. The theory of this doctrine is that if *A* writes to *B*, and a reply letter that purports to be from

---

23. FRE 901(b)(2) permits authentication by "Non-expert opinion as to the genuineness of handwriting, based upon familiarity not acquired for purposes of litigation."

24. As you will see in Ch 5, this letter also presents a hearsay question. Perhaps that question can be answered by invoking FRE 803(6) or, possibly, 804(b)(3).

25. See the earlier Illustration, § 3.3, at note 21.

26. FRE 901(b)(3) permits authentication by "Comparison . . . by expert witnesses with specimens which have been authenticated."

27. FRE 901(b)(3) also permits authentication by "Comparison by the trier of fact . . . with specimens which have been authenticated."

28. FRE 901(b)(4) permits authentication by evidence that shows "distinctive characteristics" by revealing such features as "appearance, contents, substance, internal patterns, or other distinctive features, taken in conjunction with circumstances."

B is responsive to *A*'s letter, a reasonable jury could find that *B* actually wrote the reply letter.

The techniques set out above are simply possibilities, and are not intended to foreclose other means of authentication. Counsel's task is to provide confirming evidence. Note that in all of the examples above, authentication is achieved by the introduction of evidence extrinsic to the proffered document.

There are two major patterns of authentication (or identification). The first pattern involves the introduction of evidence extrinsic to the proffered item—evidence which tends to confirm that the item is authentic. The second pattern, which we will consider shortly, involves only the limited step of showing that the item in question contains on its face the necessary indicia of authenticity.

Pattern One Authentication: Extrinsic Evidence

Federal Rule 901(b) sets out illustrations of pattern one authentication. An authenticating process conducted in conformity with one of these illustrations satisfies "authentication ... as a condition precedent to admissibility...."[29] One of these illustrations embodies the "ancient documents" rule which permits the authentication of an old document if certain requirements are met. The rule is sometimes very useful, since finding authenticating evidence for an "ancient" document may prove difficult. Age alone, however, is insufficient to authenticate an old document. Federal Rule 901(b)(8) specifies that in addition to age—set by the rule at twenty or more years—the document (or data compilation) must "be in such condition as to create no suspicion concerning its authenticity" and, furthermore, must be retrieved from or found in "a place where it, if authentic, would likely be ...."

To appreciate the utility of the ancient documents rule, consider its application in a 1997 deportation case.[30] There, lawyers for the United States used documents stored in archives of the former Soviet Union to help prove that the defendant, a Russian native, had engaged with Nazis in the persecution and murder of Lithuanian Jews during the Second World War. The records in question showed no indications of tampering or fraud. Furthermore, the repository from which they were taken was not only a likely storage facility, but also housed many other War documents that the trial testimony showed were authentic.

This case was tried to a judge. Had it been tried to a jury, the judge would have allowed the records into evidence after they had been authenticated as "ancient documents." (The judge would

---

29. FRE 901(a).

30. United States v. Stelmokas, 100 F.3d 302 (3d Cir. 1996), *cert. denied*, 520 U.S. 1242 (1997).

decide if a reasonable jury could find the records were genuine.)[31] The jury would then have to decide if the records were in fact genuine. Obviously, the opposing party is entitled to produce before the jury counter evidence indicating that the documents are not authentic or are otherwise inaccurate. Application of the ancient documents rule makes only a prima facie case that an aged document is genuine. The rule rests on the assumption that if a document that appears genuine has survived twenty or more years without encountering suspicion and is stored in a normal place, the jurors should at least be entitled to determine its authenticity. In other words, satisfaction of the ancient documents rule provides sufficient evidence to support a jury finding of genuineness.

Next, consider the following provision, which is set out in subsection (9) of Federal Rule 901(b). That subsection provides that a document or other piece of evidence may be authenticated thusly:

> **Process or system.** Evidence describing a process or system used to produce a result and showing that the process or system produces an accurate result.

This illustration is within the pattern-one category because the proponent of an item of evidence must produce extrinsic evidence that shows the accuracy of the process or system that produced the proffered evidence. Suppose, for example, a trucking company wanted to introduce evidence in the form of a computer printout that displayed the average monthly cost of service, maintenance, and repairs on its fleet of 200 trucks over the last five years. Evidence showing how the basic data were collected, how this information was arranged for computer processing, and the basic features of the company's software program would provide an adequate foundation to authenticate the resulting product—for example a printout displaying average monthly costs.

ILLUSTRATIONS

(1) Law enforcement officers have been trying to secure evidence that Dromio is a drug dealer. So far, they have been unsuccessful in their attempts to entice Dromio to sell drugs to a police undercover agent. The authorities

---

31. There is also an ancient documents exception to the hearsay rule. *See* FRE 803(16). When the proponent of an ancient document wants to prove that the statements within it are true, he must not only authenticate the docu- ment, but also offer it under Federal Rule 803(16) as an exception to the hearsay rule. The judge would then *decide* whether the proffered document is at least twenty years old. *See* FRE 104(a).

have, however, identified a parking lot adjacent to a storage building that is thought to have been used by Dromio to make two narcotics sales. A surveillance officer equipped with night-vision binoculars is posted on the second story of a nearby building.

Several days later, at 2:00 a.m. on Monday, July 18, 2005, a man wearing a cap and carrying a leather or vinyl pouch emerges from a parked car and greets another man, later identified as Davy, who enters the parking lot from an adjacent sidewalk. After a brief conversation, the men stroll around the side of the storage building, out of the sight of the observing officer. Unbeknownst to the two men, law enforcement officers have installed a small camera behind the gutter of the storage building. The camera is activated by the motion of a subject within the range of its lens. When activated, it runs for twenty minutes and records the date and the time frame during which it was operative. Video film from the hidden camera, when developed by the police, shows two men exchanging cash for packages taken from a pouch. The packages, which are examined by Davy, appear to contain a white powder. On the film, the man delivering the packages and receiving the money appears to be Dromio.

At the trial of Dromio for selling a narcotic, the prosecutor could authenticate the film—and thus identify Dromio as the seller—by calling witnesses who could establish the installation of the video camera and the technical details of how it works. This testimony would then be linked with the testimony of someone familiar with Dromio's appearance. (Of course, the prosecutor could simply allow the jury to compare the features of the man shown in the film with the features of the accused, Dromio.) Since the ultimate goal of the prosecutor is to convince the jury that the seller was Dromio, the prosecutor would probably first obtain the testimony of the surveillance officer who, even if he could not identify Dromio, would provide the context for the jury to believe that Dromio was the person depicted in the film.

(2) Twenty minutes after the transaction described in Illustration (1), law enforcement officers arrest Davy in his car. They seize a bag containing plastic packages—and these contain a white powdery substance.

Critical to the prosecution of both Dromio and Davy is proof that the plastic packages contained a narcotic. Suppose laboratory tests confirm that the substance in question is cocaine. At trial, the prosecutor wants to introduce the packages of white power along with expert testimony that the packages contain cocaine. By what means can she authenticate the powdery substance in the plastic bags?

Items such as a blood sample, a glove, a broken cable, or seized drugs pose special problems of authentication. The difficulty is that these items—and many others—usually bear no distinctive features, such as a peculiar appearance or a serial number, that allow them to be differentiated from similar items of the same variety. Of course, when potential items of evidence come into the possession of law enforcement personnel, these authorities usually assign numbers, names, or other identifying data to the items. Nonetheless, the lawyer proffering these tangible items in court usually has to employ an authentication technique called "chain of custody."[32] This simply means that counsel offers authenticating testimony or, perhaps, official (public) or business records,[33] that account for the whereabouts of the proffered item from its original seizure to its presence in the courtroom. The chain of custody technique is also useful when it is important to show that the evidence in question is in the same condition (at trial) that it was at the time of the litigated event. For example, it may be important to show that the evidence has not been subjected to climatic extremes, tampering, or some other source of alteration or contamination between the time of seizure and the courtroom presentation. (Evidence of a chain of custody may show the item in question was stored in a secure place, thus reducing or eliminating the opportunities for alteration or change.)

A chain of custody need not be flawless. However, links that forge the custodial oversight, coupled with any purposefully added identifying names or marks, must at least be sufficient to allow a jury to find, first, that the item proffered in evidence is the same one that was involved in the events being litigated and, second, that its condition has not changed to a degree that makes it misleading. A minority of jurisdictions is more demanding, and requires that the evidence establishing the chain support authentication by "a reasonable certainty."[34]

---

32. Although the Federal Rules of Evidence do not expressly mention chain of custody, the technique is everywhere recognized. It is simply an example of using circumstantial proof to establish genuineness. *Cf.* FRE 901(b)(9).

33. The Confrontation Clause, contained in the Sixth Amendment to the United States Constitution, places limits on documents and other hearsay evidence that can be introduced against a defendant in a criminal trial. *See* Ch. VIII.

34. Roger C. Park, et al., Evidence Law: A Student's Guide to the Law of Evidence as Applied in American Trials § 11.04 at 565–66 (2d ed. 2004). This more stringent requirement is not, however, called for by the text of FRE 901.

Pattern Two Authentication: Self-authentication

Federal Rule 902 lists twelve categories of documents, including labels and trade inscriptions, that are "self-authenticating." These items have sufficient indicia of genuineness "within their four corners," so to speak, to pass the threshold test of authentication. Of course, compliance with the requirement of authentication means only that the judge admits the authenticated item into evidence; it does not mean that there can no longer be a dispute concerning its genuineness. A generous sample of Rule 902's self-authenticating documents includes:

— Domestic public documents[35]

— Foreign public documents[36]

— Certified copies of public records[37]

— Official publications[38]

— Newspapers and periodicals[39]

— Trade inscriptions and the like[40]

— Acknowledged documents[41]

— Commercial paper[42]

Each of the twelve categories of documents enumerated in Rule 902 has some feature that adds the necessary degree of assurance of authenticity. Unlike Rule 901, which provides a *nonexclusive* list of authentication possibilities, Rule 902 provides a *closed* list of specific categories that meet various criteria for self-authentication. Many of the categories, such as public documents, describe records and instruments that bear a public seal or attestation (including certification) by a public official. Other categories, such as those providing for the authentication of newspapers and trade inscriptions, describe writings that carry little risk of forgery or other alterations; furthermore, in these latter categories it is usually easy for an interested party to confirm genuineness or reveal falsity. Consider, for example, how easy it would be to expose as a forgery an article falsely claimed to be from the January 12, 2005 edition of the New York Times.

In the year 2000, an amendment to Rule 902 added two additional categories—eleven and twelve—of self-authenticating

---

35. FRE 902(1), (2) (sealed or signed by a public officer).

36. FRE 902(3) (attested by a foreign official).

37. FRE 902(4) (documents filed in a public office, certified by custodian).

38. FRE 902(5) (books, pamphlets, etc. issued by public authority).

39. FRE 902(6) (printed materials).

40. FRE 902(7) (labels, signs, etc., affixed in course of business).

41. FRE 902(8) (*e.g.*, a notarized document).

42. FRE 902(9).

documents. These recent additions allow domestic and foreign business records to be authenticated by certification. Generally speaking, authentication is satisfied when a qualified person, such as the custodian of the proffered records, provides a written declaration that the records were properly prepared in the regular course of business.

Demonstrative Evidence: Illustrative and Substantive

Demonstrative evidence, as the name suggests, is typically used to demonstrate, illustrate, or explain. Often, this kind of evidence is used to add clarity or vividness to a witness's testimony. Thus, the diagram of an intersection might be used in a personal injury case; a model of a portion of the human body might be employed in a medical malpractice case; a chart might be displayed to remind the jury of the key evidence in a business conspiracy case; and a map might be presented in boundary-dispute litigation. Photographs might also be used simply to illustrate a witness's testimony, although photographs are sometimes used as substantive evidence, as we saw earlier in Illustration (1).

Note that this brief treatment of demonstrative evidence is concerned with various exhibits that either illustrate a witness's testimony or depict a party's factual contentions. The prevailing practice is to have the demonstrative exhibit marked (numbered or lettered) as an exhibit, although many judges do not even require this. (Judges, you might have surmised, have considerable discretion in handling demonstrative evidence.) Probably, the prevailing practice is for the judge to admit the marked exhibit into evidence with a cautionary instruction that its only purpose is illustrative. The practice regarding whether jurors have access to demonstrative exhibits during their deliberations is mixed, although many modern courts allow at least some of the exhibits to be taken into the jury room.[43]

Common sense will usually suggest the proper foundation for demonstrative evidence. The purpose of demonstrative evidence is to demonstrate fairly and accurately that which it depicts. Consequently, absent a stipulation, there must be testimony that the proffered item (map, model, photograph, etc.) is a fair and accurate representation of whatever it displays. It is usually necessary that the witness providing the evidentiary foundation have personal familiarity with the subject that is displayed by the demonstrative evidence. For example, a witness familiar with a particular airport runway might testify that a photograph or diagram of it is a fair and accurate representation. (The witness need not be the photog-

---

43. For thoughtful elaboration of these and many other points about demonstrative evidence, *see generally* PARK et al., *supra* note 34, § 11.05–11.10 at 568–88.

rapher or draftsman.) When an exhibit is drawn or constructed "to scale" a somewhat more elaborate foundation is required in order to establish the ratio of the scale used (e.g., one inch equals thirty feet) and to demonstrate that the distances reflected in the exhibit are accurate.

Bear in mind that courts usually associate *real* evidence with items that were actually part of the litigated event (e.g., the gun used by the accused); conversely, courts usually associate *demonstrative* evidence with illustrative exhibits (e.g., the diagram of a hillside that was strip mined). But there is an area of overlap between "original" real evidence and demonstrative evidence. This overlap occurs when an item of evidence is a recordation—for example, photograph, disk, X-ray, motion picture, or sound recording—that depicts a relevant part or feature of the litigated event. Although such an item may be used illustratively, its principal use will usually be substantive, that is, to prove a consequential fact— for example, that the bank robber in the surveillance film is the accused. The required foundation, however, is a predictable application of the general requirement of authentication. The proponent must provide evidence sufficient to support two propositions:

(1) The subject or thing pictured or heard is in fact the subject or thing that counsel contends it is;

(2) The recorded image or voice is an accurate reproduction.

Sometimes counsel can meet these requirements by simply presenting a witness who saw the subject that is displayed (such as a film alleged to be obscene) or heard a voice that is reproduced, and who can thus testify that the display or reproduction is accurate. Sometimes, however—as, for example, in the case of X-ray plates—authentication is a blend of testimony detailing that which can be observed (Smith had his lower spine X-rayed on a particular date; the X-ray film was labeled) with testimony "describing a process or system used to produce [an observable] result and showing that the process or system produces an accurate result."[44] Since the use of X-ray machines is an accepted medical technique, the judge will take judicial notice[45] that the scientific *principle* underlying X-rays is sound. Nonetheless, absent a stipulation, counsel will still have to show that the X-ray equipment was an acceptable type, that it was in proper working order, that a qualified operator took the picture, and that an appropriate labeling and tracking procedure was followed, all to the end of providing assurance that the proffered X-ray plate is accurate.

44. FRE 901(b)(9).

45. *See* supra Ch. II, § 2.7.

§ 3.4　Conditional Relevancy

The relevance of one item of evidence (Item A) frequently depends upon another connected item of evidence (Item B). Suppose, for example, Puck sues Dora for breach of an oral contract, claiming that, in response to his classified ad in the "wanted to buy" column, Dora telephoned him and offered to sell a four-piece bedroom suite for $3,500. Puck alleges he accepted the offer. Dora, in her answer, denies making (or authorizing) such a call—or any call whatsoever—to Puck.

At trial, Puck takes the stand and starts to testify about the terms of the offer. Dora objects on the ground that this testimony is irrelevant because she did not telephone Puck. It is true that Puck's evidence of the terms of the contractual offer is relevant only if Dora (or her agent) made the offer. This evidentiary deficiency becomes even more obvious if you imagine that the call was made by a complete stranger—a third person whose name happened to be Dora. Since that person is not the defendant, Puck's testimony about the content of the offer is irrelevant. Simply put, testimony about the offer supports a consequential fact if, and only if, defendant (and not a third party) made the offer.

Puck's problem stems from the fact that trials consist of an evidentiary sequence in which events portrayed by the evidence necessarily unfold one at a time. Puck must produce evidence not only of the terms of the offer, but also of the identity of the offeror—that the offeror was *defendant* Dora. The problem can be quickly resolved if Puck can testify, for example, that he recognized the voice of the defendant and, having provided the necessary authentication, he then proceeds to describe the offer. Suppose, however, his only evidence of identity (authentication) comes from a witness, W, who overheard Dora making the telephone call. Suppose, further, that W's testimony is scheduled for later in the trial. The relevance of Puck's testimony concerning the terms of the telephone offer *is conditioned* on the connected fact (not yet supported by evidence) that the defendant made the offer.

When the relevance of proffered evidence depends upon (*i.e.* is conditioned upon) a related fact that must be supported by other evidence, we say that the proffered evidence is *conditionally relevant*. The probative force (*i.e.*, relevance) of the evidence is conditioned upon a fact that is shown by other evidence. That "other evidence" must be sufficient to permit the trier to conclude by a preponderance of the evidence that the connected fact exists. To return to our example, the judge would admit evidence of the terms of the offer conditioned upon the assurance of Puck's lawyer that he would subsequently produce evidence that the offeror was Dora.

Federal Rule 104 is concerned primarily with the allocation of fact-finding responsibilities between judge and jury. In making this allocation, the rule addresses conditional relevancy in subsection (b). As we have seen, subsection (a) of this rule states that the judge alone shall determine "preliminary [factual] questions concerning the qualification of a person to be a witness, the existence of a privilege, or the admissibility of evidence . . . ." In other situations, such as the reception into evidence of authenticating testimony, the judge does not determine facts from the evidence presented. Rather, under Rule 104(b) she screens or monitors the evidence in order to ensure that it is sufficient to support a jury finding. (It is sufficient if a reasonable jury could find by a more-likely-than-not standard or, put otherwise, by a preponderance of evidence, that the supported fact—for example, that Dora made the offer—exists.) The judge assumes this monitoring role in situations involving conditional relevancy.[46] Subsection (b) of Rule 104 states:

Relevancy conditioned on fact. When the relevancy of evidence depends upon the fulfillment of a condition of fact, the court shall admit it upon, or subject to, the introduction of evidence sufficient to support a finding of the fulfillment of the condition.

The application of Rule 104 to our illustrative contract dispute is simple and straightforward. The judge will allow Puck's testimony about the terms of the telephone offer either, (1) "upon" his testimony that he recognized or otherwise identified defendant Dora's voice, or (2) "subject to" the condition that other (forthcoming) evidence will be sufficient to support a jury finding that the caller was Dora.

ILLUSTRATION

Each of the following examples presents a problem of conditional relevance. The fact supported by the evidence in Column A is conditionally linked to the fact supported by the evidence in Column B. The judge must ensure that, at some point in the trial, the proponent produces sufficient evidence of the factual condition(s) [Column B] on which relevance depends. Note that the order in which the evidence supporting the connected facts is presented does

---

46. Academic commentators have leveled insightful criticism at the conditional relevancy rule. A leading article is Ronald Allen, *The Myth of Conditional* *Relevancy,* 25 LOY. L.A.L.REV. 871 (1992). Nonetheless, courts continue to apply the rule as described in the text and illustrations above.

not matter. For example, in Illustration (1) below, evidence that D was driving a black sedan might be offered first, subject to the later "condition" that the black sedan was speeding.

(1) Proposition: defendant was speeding through the intersection.

A.	B.
Witness testifies that a black sedan sped through the intersection	D was the driver of the black sedan

2. Proposition: accused shot victim with a handgun.

Ballistics expert testifies that the fatal bullet was fired from a particular handgun proffered as Prosecutor's Exhibit 1	The handgun was owned or possessed by the accused

3. Proposition: defendant Duncan sold his stock after illegally receiving "inside information" that Company would sustain huge losses.

Confidential memorandum from Company President to Chairman of Board of Directors expressing fear that outside accountants had apparently discovered questionable transactions and false entries overstating company's profits	Prior to the sale of his stock, defendant saw the memorandum or otherwise learned of its contents

4. Proposition: Antony criminally assaulted Davy, inflicting serious injury to Davy's face and groin.

Davy raped and seriously injured Alice, a college senior	Alice and Antony had close ties, such as those of affection or kinship, that would be sufficient to motivate Antony to avenge the rape when he learned of it

5. Proposition: Alena ran away from boarding school because she was depressed about her poor grades and hated her coursework.

A crumpled, detached diary page, discovered in the drawer of a desk used by Alena and her roommate. The author of	Alena made the diary entries

the diary entries expresses remorse about low grades and antipathy toward her courses and teachers

6.   Proposition: Plaintiff, a delivery man, was contributorily negligent when he was injured by a dynamite blast at a construction site.

The construction supervisor yelled a warning when he saw plaintiff driving a truck toward the blast site	The plaintiff heard or should have heard the warning in time to stop

In Section 3.3 of this Chapter, we examined the requirement of authentication. In essence, this foundational requirement states that when a proponent proffers an item of evidence that she claims is genuine or authentic, she generally must offer additional evidence to confirm its authenticity. Thus, if the prosecutor proffers the accused's glove stained with the victim's blood, she must produce evidence that is sufficient for the jury to find, (1) the blood on the glove came from the victim and, (2) the glove belonged to or was in the possession of the accused.

You can see from this simple example that authentication is a form of conditional relevance. The authenticating evidence supplies the factual predicate that makes the glove relevant. A glove—even the defendant's glove—stained with ketchup has no relevance to show D was the murderer; neither does a blood-stained glove that was never in the possession of the accused.[47] The jury must have before it evidence that, if believed, is sufficient to support its conclusions that the victim's blood stains are on the accused's glove. The usual standard governing factual determinations by the jury applies: the jury ordinarily finds facts using a more-likely-than-not ("preponderance-of-the-evidence") standard.

Before it can apply the *simple* test of relevance, the jury must find the connected facts (*D's* glove; *V's* blood) that increase the probability (the simple test) that D was the killer. That simple test, as we have seen, is met if the evidence has a tendency to make the fact to which it is directed more (or less) likely. A glove belonging to the accused and stained with the victim's blood increases the likelihood that the accused was the murderer. Note that the simple relevance test requiring "some probative value" applies to most evidence. It is only when an item of evidence is conditionally relevant that the more stringent "preponderance test" is invoked

---

47. Of course, this evidence is relevant to the accused's claim that he was not the killer.

by the judge as she screens evidence supporting the conditioning fact.

Even in a criminal trial, a judge will not apply a higher standard of proof (than the preponderance test) to questions of conditional relevance. Do not make the mistake of applying the "reasonable doubt" standard to individual items of evidence in a criminal case. Such items are subjected to the usual, "simple" test of probative value—does the evidence tend to persuade?—or, in the case of conditional relevance, to a "preponderance" test. The reasonable doubt standard applies to the aggregate evidence that is available to the jury. Collectively, the evidence supporting the accused's guilt must be adequate to support a jury determination that the defendant is guilty beyond a reasonable doubt—that is, the state's evidence supporting each element of the offense must be adequate to justify a finding beyond a reasonable doubt that each element exists.[48]

We shall conclude this discussion of conditional relevance with a practical consideration. Suppose the plaintiff wishes to introduce evidence that the defendant, Drake, drove the black car that sped through the intersection in violation of the stop sign and struck Victim, a pedestrian. Wolsey can testify as to the speeding black car; Windsor can testify that Drake (the driver) was the only person in the car when, prior to the accident, it stopped at a gas station three miles from the intersection. Suppose that when Wolsey starts to testify about the speeding black car, Drake's counsel objects that the evidence is irrelevant because Wolsey did not see who was driving. Although that objection may on the surface appear meritorious, we have seen that the plaintiff can meet the objection by assuring the judge that she will "connect up" or link this evidence with forthcoming evidence showing that Drake was driving the black car. Thus, as we have also seen, the evidence of the speeding black car is admitted "subject to the fulfillment of the condition of fact"[49] that forthcoming evidence will be sufficient to support a jury finding that Drake was driving the black car. If the proponent fails to provide the necessary connecting evidence, the objector is entitled to strike the conditionally admitted evidence and to an instruction to the jury to ignore the evidence that was struck.

48. For example, in a prosecution for breaking and entering a home during the evening hours for the purpose of committing a serious crime, the prosecutor would ordinarily have to produce evidence sufficient to justify a "beyond-reasonable-doubt" finding that the accused *broke into* and *entered* a *dwelling place* in the *nighttime* with the *intent of* *committing a felony* therein. The reasonable doubt standard would apply to each element, but any particular piece of evidence proffered as proof of each element need only be probative and satisfy Rule 403's balancing test.

49. FRE 104(b).

The important point is to note carefully the respective roles of judge and jury. Rule 104(b) allocates to the jury the determination of whether the connected or "conditioning facts"—that is, those that form a predicate for the proffered evidence—actually exist. Why is this responsibility given to the jury when Rule 104(a) allocates to the judge the task of determining preliminary facts bearing on the admissibility of evidence? The answer lies in the nature of the question to be allocated to either judge or jury. There is very little chance that the jury will be misled or act irrationally in discharging its task under Rule 104(b)'s provision governing conditional relevance. The only issue for the jury is a common-sense relevance question. To return to an earlier Illustration, if the question is whether Alena was depressed, and the jury finds that the diary entry indicating depression was not written by Alena, it will ignore the entry. Similarly, if the question is whether Drake drove the speeding black car that struck the pedestrian, and the jury determines that Drake was not driving the offending vehicle, it will not hold him responsible. Thus, when the jury's task in dealing with evidence *is confined to a determination solely of relevance*, there is virtually no risk that it will misuse the evidence.

These "relevance-only" determinations, governed by Rule 104(b) and assigned to the jury, are quite different from determinations governed by Rule 104(a) and allocated to the judge. Rule 104(a) is concerned with findings of fact that pertain to the applicability of an exclusionary rule of evidence, including the qualifications of a witness. If the judge did not make these factual findings, the exclusionary rules would be ineffective. For example, if the judge did not herself determine the factual issues related to admissibility, but merely "screened for sufficiency" she would often have to provisionally admit evidence that might ultimately be excludable. She would also have to instruct the jurors to ignore the evidence should they find that it is inadmissible under the exclusionary rule or rules that might apply. This evidentiary task is beyond the jury's capacity. Furthermore, the jury has no interest in technical exclusionary rules, nor are its members likely to ignore "inadmissible" evidence.

Note also how intolerably complex the jury's task would become if the jurors had to apply the technical exclusionary rules, such as the hearsay rule, the rules governing privilege, and so forth. For example, the jurors would have to determine whether evidence which they had already seen or heard was admissible. Then, depending on how they resolved the factual questions governing admissibility, they would be expected to either assess the probative value of the evidence (if admissible) or ignore it (if inadmissible). To give a simple example, the jury would be told that if a communication between client and lawyer *was intended* to be confidential and was for the *purpose* of receiving legal advice or services, and was *not disclosed* to outsiders, the communication was subject to the attorney-client privilege and the jury should ignore it. While only one such instruction might not sound intolerable, in the course of a complete trial there might be dozens of such evidentiary factual issues with different rules of evidence law governing each. Jury confusion and incapacity would be inevitable.

The Application of Relevance Principles
to Evidence of Similar Events

Suppose the plaintiff, attending her favorite play, slips on the theater stairs during intermission. She subsequently brings suit against the theater, alleging its negligence in allowing the carpet of the stairs to buckle. At trial, the attorney for the plaintiff offers evidence that two weeks prior to the plaintiff's fall, another patron slipped and fell on the same stairway.

Whether the evidence is admissible depends upon the circumstances surrounding each event—the principal (litigated) event and the collateral one. More to the point, the admissibility of evidence of "similar events" depends upon the trial judge's careful application of Rule 403. Collateral events, similar to the one that is the subject of a trial, sometimes have probative value to show a dangerous condition, or that the defendant had "fair warning" or notice that a hazardous condition might exist, or that the condition in question was the cause of the plaintiff's harm or injury. On the other hand, the judge must take account of dissimilarities between the events, the possibility of conditions having changed between the collateral and principal event, jury distraction, and the consumption of trial time. In the example above, for instance, there may be significant differences in lighting on the two occasions,[50] the number of persons using the stairs, the youth and agility of the two persons who fell, and the probability of other explanations for the two mishaps, such as a beverage spilled on the carpet in question. Sometimes, changed conditions diminish the probative value of a similar event, as where vegetation that blocked visibility at an intersection in July has been cut back by the highway department or has simply lost its leaves by November, and hence is no longer an obstacle to the observation of oncoming traffic.

Two basic points emerge from this simple example. First, there must be sufficient evidence of the other (collateral) event or condition to permit a finding by the trier of fact that it occurred or existed. Here, the judge simply screens the evidence, exercising his monitoring authority under Rule 104(b)—conditional relevance. Second, the judge must determine whether the probative value of

---

50. Perhaps one was in daylight, the other at night.

evidence of the similar event(s) is substantially outweighed by Rule 403's counterweights to admissibility, such as jury distraction, time consumption, and prejudice.

§ 3.5 Direct and Circumstantial Evidence

Attorneys and judges often speak of evidence as being "direct" or, alternatively, "circumstantial." The difference between these types of evidence is straightforward: direct evidence, if believed, supports a consequential fact without the need for inference drawing: "I saw Dali thrust a knife into Picasso's chest." Circumstantial evidence, if believed, supports a consequential fact through inference drawing: "I saw Dali flee the scene of the stabbing and throw a knife into the river." Note that both direct and circumstantial evidence must meet the test of relevance: each must have probative value and each must point to a consequential fact. But in the case of direct evidence, the trier of fact does not have to reach the consequential proposition (Dali stabbed Picasso) by a process of inference. The trier's only task is to decide whether the direct evidence is accurate (*i.e.* believable). In the imagined case above, the trier would have only to decide whether to believe the witness who testifies that she saw Dali stab Picasso.

The testimony about flight and discarding the knife, however, calls for a different mental process by the trier. As with direct evidence, the first step is to determine whether the proffered testimony is credible. (Should the witness who testifies that Dali fled and threw a knife into the river be believed?) Assuming the trier believes the testimony, (i.e., determines that more likely than not, it is true), it then becomes necessary for the trier to draw inferences that increase the probability that Dali stabbed Picasso. For example, the trier might draw inferences such as these: flight is associated with guilt; disposal of the knife points toward a coverup; a coverup suggests guilt, and so forth. Note that in order to be relevant, the circumstantial evidence, once believed, does not have to establish by a preponderance of evidence (or beyond a reasonable doubt) that Dali stabbed Picasso. The evidence need only increase the probability that he did so. Of course, when all the evidence has been received, the judge must decide whether or not, taken collectively, the evidence justifies a jury finding by a preponderance of the evidence (in a civil case) or by a reasonable doubt standard (in a criminal case). If it does not, the judge herself will rule in favor of the defendant.

Circumstantial evidence is not intrinsically inferior (*i.e.* less probative) than direct evidence. Suppose, for example, that *D* is accused of breaking into *V*'s apartment in the nighttime and stealing a diamond watch and other items of jewelry. He denies the offense and claims that he was in another city on the night of the crime. Nonetheless, *D*'s fingerprints are found on *V*'s windowsill and on her jewelry box, and there is testimony that during the afternoon preceding the crime, *D* was seen near *V*'s residence. This circumstantial evidence may be more convincing than testimony by *V*'s husband that he saw *D* take the jewelry, particularly if the lighting were bad, the time for observation fleeting, or *D*'s physical or facial features were partially obscured. The probative force of both circumstantial and direct evidence is determined by the particular evidence presented and the surrounding circumstances, not by a formal classification.

§ 3.6 Determinate Rules of Relevance Related to Character

Introduction: Protective Rules

In most instances, a trial judge rules on questions of relevance by assessing probative value and then determining whether that value is "substantially outweighed" by the countervailing concerns set out in Rule 403—concerns such as prejudice, jury confusion, and wastefulness. These rulings are contextual and trial judges are given broad discretion to admit or exclude evidence that is challenged on relevance grounds. The judge's discretionary ruling will not be reversed unless an appellate court determines that she abused her discretion.

Over the years, certain relevance questions recurred with such frequency that appellate courts began to forge definite principles and rules to control trial courts' evidentiary decisions. Over time, these judicial principles and rules became fairly uniform across American courts and, in 1975 when the Federal Rules of Evidence were adopted, these appellate determinations were crafted into specific provisions of the Federal Rules. They appear in Article IV of the Rules.

Various policies and practical concerns undergird the "fixed" or "determinate" relevance rules but, broadly speaking, two themes predominate. One cluster of rules—the group discussed here in § 3.6—is concerned primarily with fairness in the trial process. The central issue is whether to admit evidence that a party has a particular character trait or propensity that increases (or decreases) the likelihood that he acted in conformity with that trait on a particular occasion. Suppose, for example, John Claggart, who is prosecuted for assaulting Billy Budd, is a man of violent, aggressive temperament. Should the court receive evidence of other occasions on which Claggart had been aggressive and violent? Alternatively, should the court receive testimony of witnesses who know Claggart, each of whom will give his opinion that Claggart is an aggressive, violent man? Finally, should the court permit witnesses familiar with Claggart's reputation to testify that he is reputed to be aggressive and violent? Whatever the *form* of the testimony (that is, whether it reveals other incidents, the opinion of associates, or Claggart's reputation), evidence depicting Claggart's violent disposition (a character trait) would be at least somewhat probative of his action on the day in question.

However, a basic tenet of American justice is that a trial is focused on the litigated event and not upon other misdeeds or upon the character traits of the parties. After all, the purpose of a trial is to resolve the event in question, and not to rectify other wrongs or redress undesirable features of a party's character. Furthermore, common observation suggests a person may sometimes act inconsistently with a particular character trait. Note also that judicial inquiry into character carries with it the price of distraction from the principal event and the consumption of trial time. Quite aside from these considerations, however, evidence of character or propensity raises a genuine risk that the trier of fact may base its decision upon a party's "good" or "bad" character and not upon the strength of the evidence concerning the litigated event. Thus, the rules and principles that appear in this subsection are designed to strike a desirable balance between probative character evidence, on the one hand, and countervailing concerns, especially trial fairness, on the other.

Chapter IV, which follows this subsection (§ 3.6), deals with additional determinate rules of relevance. Generally speaking, these latter rules control admissibility in circumstances in which probative value (suggesting admissibility) comes into conflict with public or social policy (suggesting inadmissibility). An example would be proffered evidence that the defendant, an alleged tortfeasor, paid the hospital bill of the injured plaintiff. Although defendant's voluntary payment might suggest that he felt that he was legally liable, the law should probably encourage "Good Samaritan" acts. The rule of evidence[51] that rejects disclosures that the defendant paid the plaintiff's medical expenses is designed to protect the benefactor from adverse evidentiary consequences.

Character Evidence: In General

In everyday affairs, we often rely on assessments of character. This is true in many settings. Consider, for example, the likelihood that a character appraisal will affect the decision of an employer who is selecting a new employee; or the decision of a college admissions officer who is selecting matriculates, or the decision of a lender who is deciding whether to make a loan; or the decision of a professional sports executive who is considering whether to bid on

51. FRE 409.

or trade for an athlete. And, note again the sources of information available to one who is attempting to determine the character of another (*X*). First, witnesses could testify that *X* has a reputation for a certain character trait in his residential or employment community; second, witnesses acquainted with *X* could each give his opinion about *X*'s character; and third, witnesses who have observed *X's* conduct on various occasions could describe his actions. Arguably, this third source of information is the most accurate; the second less so, and the first the least accurate. This generalization, however, assumes a sufficient number of occasions or displays of *X*'s pertinent conduct to permit a reliable conclusion about his character based on specific events.

These possibilities of the use of character in ordinary affairs are pertinent to the use of character in the courtroom. As you will see, one set of specific evidentiary rules revolves around the central question in the area of character evidence, namely, whether character evidence is admissible at all. (Here, for example, one of several determinants is whether the issue arises in a criminal, as opposed to a civil, case.) A second set of rules, less important and simpler than the first, revolves around the question of *what kind* of evidence is acceptable for the purpose of proving character in those instances where proof of character is permitted. For example, a rule might allow "reputation evidence" and "opinion evidence," but disallow "conduct evidence" because evidence describing particular instances of conduct, despite its possibly superior reliability, is often unduly distracting and time consuming. Indeed, as you will see, opinion and reputation evidence are the preferred means of proving character, although in one circumstance, evidence of past conduct is also available.

When lawyers and judges speak of proving a subject's "character" they have in mind everything from a rather general character ("law abiding and moral") to specific character traits such as carelessness in driving, jealousy in love affairs, and caution in financial matters. Character involves a propensity to act in a certain way and this predisposition may surface across a broad spectrum of conduct, ranging, for example, from general law abiding, responsible behavior, on the one hand, to quite specific tendencies, such as punctuality or excessive drinking, on the other.

The materials that follow contain a number of subtle distinctions. Perhaps these fine distinctions are a reflection of the law's ambivalence about character. As you make your way through the text immediately ahead, be especially attentive to the purpose for which character evidence is being offered. Purpose is the most important determinant in the admissibility of character evidence, although—as you will see—it is not the only one. As noted above, another important determinant is whether the case in which character evidence is proffered is criminal or civil. The use of character evidence in civil cases is severely restricted.

Character Evidence: When Character is an Essential Element

Sometimes the substantive law makes the nature of one's character a dispositive issue at trial. That is, the existence or nonexistence of a character trait is itself an issue that determines the outcome of the trial.

Consider the following hypothetical case:

Shylock files a character defamation suit against Antonio. In the complaint, the plaintiff alleges that Antonio, in the presence of third persons, referred to Shylock as a "usurious cheat." In his answer, Antonio asserts the defense of truth and at trial he offers a witness who will *testify* that Shylock has a *reputation* as a lender who charges exorbitant interest rates and cheats uninformed borrowers by making misleading and false statements. Antonio also offers two witnesses (former employees of Shylock) who are familiar with Shylock's business practices and each will testify that in his *opinion* Shylock is deceptive and dishonest in his lending practices. Finally, Antonio offers three witnesses who will testify as to specific *past events*; namely that each of them had received loans from Shylock only to discover later that Shylock had provided false information about the true rate of interest.

Notice the role that character plays in this hypothetical. The task of the trier of fact is to decide if Shylock's character is in fact that of a "usurious cheat." They *do not have to go on to decide whether on a particular occasion Shylock cheated one of his borrowers.* Shylock's character, in other words, is an end in and of itself—an ultimate issue.

Federal Rule 405 is entitled "Methods of Proving Character." As we shall observe more fully, in most cases where character evidence is allowed, Rule 405(a) restricts the kind of evidence that may be used to prove character. First, witnesses familiar with the reputation of the subject (the person whose character is in question) may testify as to that reputation. Second, witnesses who know the subject may give an opinion as to his character. Evidence of specific instances of conduct, however, is normally disallowed. The reason for restricting the allowable types of evidence to reputation and opinion is that presentation by those two methods does not require a significant expenditure of time. In contrast, proof of character by evidence of specific instances of conduct is usually time consuming and distracting, and for these reasons is normally rejected. However, subsection (b) of Rule 405, which reads as follows, suspends the usual restriction concerning modes of proof:

(b) Specific Instances of Conduct. In cases where character or a trait of character of a person is an essential element of a charge, claim, or defense, proof may *also* be made by specific instances of that person's conduct. [emphasis added]

Thus, in the imagined case above, *all three methods of proof* are available to Antonio. Obviously, this is because Shylock's character takes center stage as an ultimate issue or, in the words of Rule 405(b), an "essential element" of the claim and defense. His character is not being used to prove conduct on a particular occasion, for example, by drawing the inference that since Shylock has the character of a cheater, he probably cheated the plaintiff to whom he lent money. This illustrative suit is not, of course, brought by a plaintiff who claims he is a victim of Shylock's dishonest lending practices. The key to the hypothetical is that since character is an essential element of Antonio's defense of truth, he is entitled to prove character by reputation evidence, opinion evidence, or specific instances of conduct.

Cases in which character "is an essential element of a charge, claim or defense" and thus important enough to be within the embrace of Federal Rule 405(b) are infrequent. In addition to cases based on defamation of character (where truth is a defense), there is a cluster of cases involving a claim against an employer or principal for hiring an unfit employee or agent. Typically, the defendant's liability hinges on proof that he negligently hired a person of unfit character. In practical terms, the employer will be liable *only if he* hired a person whose character made her unfit for the position she filled and, further, *if the* employer knew or should have known about her unfit character.

ILLUSTRATIONS

(1) Henry, Jr., a ten-year-old, is injured while aboard a carnival ride called Whip–A–Roo. Through a guardian, he brings suit against Carnival Inc., the owner and operator of the carnival. The complaint alleges that Carnival was negligent in hiring and retaining one Hyde, the operator of the Whip–A–Roo, because Hyde was "an intemperate vagabond who was addicted to drugs and the excessive use of intoxicating beverages...."

(2) In a custody battle over Oliver, aged three, Mrs. Sowerberry seeks sole custody on the ground that Mr. Sowerberry is an "unfit parent." She offers evidence that he is a spendthrift with an abusive, violent personality.

Illustration (1) is a straightforward application of the type of case just described in the text: the employer's liability hinges on proof that he hired a person of "intemperate character." That person's character is essential to the plaintiff's claim and thus all three types of character evidence are available to the plaintiff.

Illustration (2) is more subtle and requires a more precise analysis. If the plaintiff's evidence pertaining to character—evidence such as reputation, opinion, or specific events—is offered solely to prove Sowerberry's *traits* of profligacy, violence, and abuse, it is admissible. His character is alleged to be "unfit" and Mrs. Sowerberry's evidence supports this proposition. However, were this same evidence offered for the purpose of showing, by a process of inference-drawing, Sowerberry's conduct on a particular occasion Rule 405(b) would not apply. (For example, suppose Mrs. Sowerberry offered evidence of Mr. Sowerberry's violent character to support her claim that on Christmas day he beat Oliver with a belt.) Furthermore, as you will see, the general rule in *civil* cases is that character evidence, *no matter what its type, is inadmissible to prove conduct on a particular occasion.* Thus, we are reminded that when a party offers character evidence, the opponent must consider whether character evidence is admissible at all and, if it is, what type of character evidence is permissible.

Notice how the principle of relevance applies to proving character. When a proponent is allowed to prove character, there are two separate relevance questions. First, is the proffered character *evidence* probative of the character trait alleged? Second, is the alleged character trait a consequential proposition or probative of some consequential proposition? As to the second inquiry, suppose the plaintiff sues a small loan company for hiring a dishonest employee (whose actions were the immediate cause of the plaintiff's loss) The consequential character trait at issue is dishonesty, rather than carelessness, intemperance, or violence. The trait of dishonesty, an essential component of the plaintiff's claims is clearly a consequential fact. As to the first inquiry, evidence demonstrating that the employee became angry and truculent when under stress should be rejected as irrelevant: such evidence is not probative of the character trait at issue: dishonesty. Likewise if violent temperament is the consequential trait in question, evidence of dishonesty or sexual profligacy would fail the test of relevance because it is not probative of violence.

To summarize: you must determine whether a character trait is itself consequential or whether it makes another consequential proposition more (or less) likely. Next, you must determine whether the proffered character evidence has probative value to establish the trait in question. Of course, it is comparatively rare for a character trait, standing alone, to be an ultimate (consequential) proposition. More frequently, a character trait has probative value to prove conduct on a particular occasion. However, as you will see, the law of evidence allows this use of character only in limited circumstances and, in most jurisdictions, only in *criminal* cases. Character evidence is viewed differently when it is offered to impeach a witness. For this purpose it is allowed in both civil and criminal cases.

§ 3.6–1 Character Evidence: Criminal and Civil Cases Distinguished

We have seen that occasionally "character or a trait of character of a person is an essential element of a charge, claim, or defense."[52] Cases in which character plays such a central role are probably confined to civil cases. Today, it would be rare to find a criminal prosecution in which the character of the accused or of the accused's victim was an essential element of a criminal charge. The Advisory Committee Note to Federal Rule 404 illustrates such a case by citing a prosecution for seduction in which the chastity of the "seduced" victim is an essential element of the offense.[53] Criminal seduction statutes, however, are rare and prosecutions under them are unlikely. Thus, as a practical matter, civil cases constitute the primary if not exclusive domain in which character is an "essential element" of a lawsuit.

The "Circumstantial" Use of Character

We turn now to what is sometimes called the "circumstantial use of character." More precisely, in the language of Federal Rule 404(a), circumstantial use refers to the use of "[e]vidence of a person's character or a trait of character . . . for the purpose of proving action in conformity therewith on a particular occasion. . . ." Use of one's character to prove his conduct at a specific time or on a particular occasion is disfavored. The traditional justification for rejecting character evidence offered to prove conduct is that its probative value is substantially outweighed by the introduction of collateral issues, by the consumption of time, and by the risk of prejudice. The last factor carries particular weight. There is, for example, a risk that the character of one of the parties may unduly sway the jury and deflect its attention from evidence of

52. FRE 405(b). *See* supra Ch. III,   **53.** FRE 404 ACN.
§ 3.6.

the *conduct* that is the subject of the trial. Furthermore, there is a risk that the jury may conclude that even if there are doubts about liability or guilt, the party with bad character "deserves" to lose. The risk of prejudice is especially high in a criminal prosecution in which the government portrays the accused as a person of unsavory disposition.

Use of character evidence to prove particular conduct (usually, conduct during the litigated event) is controlled by Federal Rule 404. It reads in part:

Character Evidence Not Admissible to Prove Conduct; Exceptions; Other Crimes

(a) Character Evidence Generally. Evidence of a person's character or a trait of character is not admissible for the purpose of proving action in conformity therewith on a particular occasion, except:

(1) Character of accused. Evidence of a pertinent trait of character offered by an accused, or by the prosecution to rebut the same, or if evidence of a trait of character of the alleged victim of the crime is offered by the accused and admitted under Rule 404(a)(2), evidence of the same trait of character of the accused offered by the prosecution;

(2) Character of alleged victim. Evidence of a pertinent trait of character of the alleged victim of the crime offered by the accused, or by the prosecution to rebut the same, or evidence of a character trait of peacefulness of the alleged victim offered by the prosecution in a homicide case to rebut evidence that the alleged victim was the first aggressor;

(3) Character of witness. Evidence of the character of a witness, as provided in rules 607, 608, and 609.

(4) Other crimes, wrongs, or acts. Evidence of other crimes, wrongs, or acts is not admissible to prove the character of a person in order to show action in conformity therewith. It may, however, be admissible for *other purposes* such as proof of motive, opportunity, intent . . . or absence of mistake . . . . [emphasis supplied]

Observe that Rule 404 begins with a general prohibition, followed by exceptions. The third exception, Rule 404(a)(3), deals with witnesses and, as you will see in Chapter IX, permits evidence pertaining to a witness's character for truthfulness. This evidentiary process ("impeachment"), involves casting doubt on the truthfulness of a witness's testimony (in other words, her testimonial "conduct" at trial). The rules of impeachment apply, with minor variations, in *both criminal and civil cases*. The fourth "exception" to the general prohibition in Rule 404(a) is contained in rule 404(b). Close examination of this subsection reveals that it does not provide an exception at all, but rather it draws a distinction. After reaffirming the general prohibition against the use of character to prove particular conduct, Rule 404(b) generally permits evidence that is offered to show distinct features of the crime charged, such as motive or identity.

Imagine, for example, that *D* is engaged in extortion and money laundering. The government convinces *D's* henchman, Cairo, to testify for the prosecution. Two weeks before *D's* scheduled trial, Cairo disappears; three months later his body is found and, thereafter, *D* is charged with homicide. At *D's* homicide trial, the judge admits evidence of *D's* illegal commercial activities and Cairo's intention to testify against him in the extortion trial. Although a by-product of this evidence is to negatively affect *D's* character (for it shows he has engaged in other criminal activities), the principal purpose of this evidence is to establish *D's* motive for murdering Cairo. The key to admissibility lies in the purpose for which the evidence is offered. It is not being offered on the ground that since *D* engaged in other crimes he has a "criminal disposition or character" and therefore it is more likely that he murdered Cairo. Rather, the evidence is offered to prove a specific point: motive.

Let us now return to the major exceptions contained in Rule 404(a), namely, subsections (a)(1) and (a)(2). Observe that these exceptions are *confined to criminal trials*. Note also that these subsections do not apply unless the accused, in his evidentiary presentation, makes the first or opening move. We shall take up the details of these provisions in the material that follows. The picture that is emerging, however, is that, aside from character evidence used to impeach a witness, there is general reluctance to admit character evidence. In criminal cases, this reluctance gives way to the accused's right to present character evidence. In civil cases, however, this reluctance is generally firm unless character is an essential element of the claim or defense. Furthermore, the preferred types of character evidence are opinion evidence and reputation evidence. However, in those comparatively rare (civil) cases where character is "an essential element of a charge, claim, or defense"[54] evidence revealing the subject's past conduct may also be used to prove his character.

54. FRE 405(b).

§ 3.6–2 Character Evidence: Circumstantial Use of Character in Criminal Cases

Because most criminal acts involve calculated, deliberate conduct, the character of the accused often has probative value. If, for example, *D* has engaged in false advertising and embezzlement in the past, his deceitful character (as shown by this misconduct) increases the likelihood of his guilt when he is subsequently indicted for insurance fraud. The stronger the relationship between the character trait and the crime charged, the greater the probative value of character evidence. However, as we saw in the last subsection, there are countervailing considerations that push against admitting evidence of *D's* character. For example, the trier of fact might accord undue probative force to evidence of *D*'s character, paying little heed to the evidence directly bearing on his conduct in connection with the charge of insurance fraud. That is, the jury might use his "bad character" as the major determinant of his guilt. Or perhaps the trier will de-emphasize the consequences of a false determination that the accused committed the crime charged (insurance fraud) because evidence of his unfavorable character has provoked the trier's belief that he deserves to be confined or otherwise penalized.

These dangers of prejudicial effect, when combined with other counterweights to admission, such as misleading the jury and time consumption, have led to the general prohibition embodied in Rule 404(a): Character evidence is not usually admissible to prove *D's* (or, for that matter, any other actor's) conduct on a particular occasion. What this prohibition means in the present context is that the prosecutor cannot introduce evidence of *D's* character for the purpose of helping to prove that *D* committed the crime with which he is charged.

The Accused's Right to Introduce Character Evidence

The first major exception to this general exclusionary principle (Rule 404(a)) is set out in Rule 404(a)(1) which allows the *accused* to introduce evidence of "a pertinent trait of character." In practical terms, this means that the defendant is entitled to introduce evidence of his character provided the character trait supported by this evidence is inconsistent with the crime charged. This requirement of inconsistency is, of course, nothing more than an application of the familiar principle of relevance. A character trait consistent with the crime charged has no probative value to demonstrate that the accused did not commit the alleged offense.

Why is it that the criminal defendant is excepted from the general prohibition against the "circumstantial" use of character evidence (*i.e.*, use that entails inferring specific conduct)? This concession is part of the deeply embedded American tradition favoring the accused in a criminal trial. In general, the American Constitution and the judicial systems that operate under it take special precautions to reduce the risk that an innocent defendant will be falsely convicted. Familiar precautionary principles include the right of the accused to be represented by counsel, to confront and cross-examine adverse witnesses, to gain access to exculpatory evidence in the prosecutor's possession, and to be convicted only if proof of guilt is convincing beyond a reasonable doubt. The accused also has a Constitutional right—although its contours are not sharply defined—to make a full defense.[55] His right to produce evidence that his character is inconsistent with the charges against him, even if not guaranteed by the Constitution, aligns nicely with his generally recognized right to fully defend himself. Furthermore, since a major ground for excluding character evidence is apprehension about its prejudicial effect, the accused's use of evidence of good character can be justified because, in this context, there is a reduced risk that the trier will evaluate the evidence irrationally or emotionally. The only "prejudice" that might occur is the weakening of the prosecution's case.

Evidence of the Victim's Character

In addition to the right to portray his own character, Rule 404(a)(2) extends to the accused the right to introduce evidence regarding the victim's character when this evidence is relevant to the accused's defense. Again, however, the principle of relevance applies with full force: it is essential that the victim's character (or character trait) is, in fact, relevant to the accused's defense. Suppose in a criminal assault case the accused defends on the ground of self-defense. It would be relevant to show that the victim was a violent, aggressive person; it would not be relevant to show that the victim was a cheat or a drug addict.

The Prosecution's Rebuttal

A feature common to both Rule 404(a)(1) and Rule 404(a)(2) is that, with one minor exception,[56] it is the exclusive right of the

---

55. *See* Crane v. Kentucky, 476 U.S. 683, 690 (1986) (accused entitled to introduce evidence that his confession was coerced despite judge's contrary finding); Chambers v. Mississippi, 410 U.S. 284, 302 (1973) (accused denied due process when he was barred from introducing confession of third party that latter committed the crime in question and, also, barred from impeaching key witness.)

56. If the accused in a homicide case introduces evidence that the alleged victim was the first aggressor, the prosecution may rebut this evidence by introducing evidence that the victim had a peaceful character. *See* FRE 404(a)(2). Note that in this limited circumstance, the accused's introduction of "noncharacter" evidence pointing toward the victim's initial aggression triggers the prosecutor's right to introduce character

accused to initiate the introduction of character evidence to prove conduct. Of course, once the accused has made the first move during his evidentiary presentation, the door is open for the prosecution to show that the accused (or victim) does not have the character trait portrayed by the defendant's evidence. Two attacks are available to the prosecutor: the first is to rigorously cross-examine D's character witness(es);[57] the second is to offer one or more character witnesses who will portray D's character as consistent with the offense charged. For example, if D's character witnesses have testified to his peaceful, nonviolent nature, the prosecution's character witnesses could testify to D's violent and bellicose disposition.

A difficult question arises when the accused makes an "indirect attack" on the victim's character *in a homicide case*. That is, the accused does not call witnesses to testify about V's character, but through other evidence, the defense portrays V, the deceased, as the first aggressor. Since D has not called to the stand any character witnesses, it can be argued that D has not opened the door to (rebuttal) *character* evidence by the prosecutor. It is, as we have seen, generally true that the prosecution cannot call character witnesses unless the accused has first done so.

A close reading of Rule 404(a)(2), however, reveals that if the accused introduces evidence (not necessarily character evidence) in a homicide prosecution for the purpose of showing that the victim was the first aggressor, the door is partially open. That is, the prosecutor is now entitled to introduce "evidence of a character trait of peacefulness of the alleged victim...."[58] This rule governing rebuttal recognizes that in murder cases where the central question is who was the initial aggressor, a character trait such as peacefulness or aggressiveness can have significant probative force. In order for the trier to assess these traits accurately, it seems fair to allow the prosecution to counter the accused's evidence that the victim was the first aggressor. Since the alleged victim is now dead, the prosecutor's only available means of rebutting D's evidence may be to call witnesses who will testify that V was a peaceful, nonviolent person. The risk of prejudice to the accused is limited, first, because the prosecution's character evidence is confined to V's (not D's) character, and, second, because that allowable evidence is restricted to V's peaceful nature and does not include other admirable traits. Testimony that would establish other desirable character

evidence supporting the victim's peaceful disposition. *See* text at note 57.

57. These would either be opinion witnesses or reputation witnesses. Recall that witnesses proffered to testify to the subject's past conduct as evidence of the subject's character trait(s) are disallowed unless character "is an essential element of a charge, claim, or defense." FRE 405(b).

58. FRE 404(a)(2).

traits of the victim is not within the allowance of Rule 404(a)(2) and should be excluded. In sum, the evidence of *V's* peaceful character is allowed on the grounds of evidentiary balance and the unlikelihood that the trier will use this evidence irrationally. The expectation is that the trier will use evidence of *V's* peaceful character for its intended purpose, namely, to determine who initiated the deadly encounter.

A related but distinct pattern is found when *D does* present character witnesses who testify to some feature of *V's* character that is related to *D's* defense. Clearly this presentation by the defense triggers the prosecutor's right of rebuttal—that is, to challenge *D's* portrayal of *V's* character. Suppose, for example, in a prosecution for criminal assault, *D* pleads self-defense and presents character witnesses who testify that *V* has a violent, aggressive character. It is clear that the prosecutor can present rebuttal character witnesses who portray *V* as nonviolent and peaceable. But suppose the prosecutor goes further and offers character evidence *that D* is a violent, aggressive individual. In terms of Rule 404, the issue is whether the accused's use of character evidence to establish a relevant trait of the alleged victim triggers the prosecutor's right to use character evidence to prove that the defendant has the *same* character trait. The current version of Rule 404 (reflecting an amendment in 2000) yields an affirmative answer.

In short, when *D's* evidence of *V's* character trait is admitted under Rule 404(a)(2), the prosecutor can invoke Rule 404(a)(1) and introduce evidence that *D* has the same trait. The common sense underlying this rule of parity is obvious enough: if the trier is made aware only of the victim's character trait, and shielded from evidence that the accused has the same character trait, there is an increased risk that the trier will draw an erroneous inference about who provoked the violent encounter.

The Presentation and Cross–Examination of Character Witnesses

Recall that Federal Rule 405 restricts the evidentiary means by which a subject's character can be proven. When character is offered for the inference that the subject acted in conformity therewith on a particular occasion, Rule 405(a) provides that "proof [of character] may be made by testimony as to reputation or by testimony in the form of an opinion." The "reputation witness" must be familiar with the subject's reputation in a setting (such as the subject's community or work environment) which is sufficiently communal for her reputation to develop. The "opinion witness" must be sufficiently acquainted with the subject to be able to form a reliable opinion concerning the latter's character. The attorney presenting a character witness must initially elicit "foundation" testimony that establishes the required familiarity. The character witness then testifies as to the pertinent character or character trait.

A reputation witness testifies as to the subject's reputation for the trait in question (for example, honesty); an opinion witness testifies that in her opinion the subject possesses the trait in question (for example, nonviolence). As we have seen, evidence of *specific instances* of the subject's conduct for the purpose of inferring that she has the character trait in question is disallowed.[59] Although such evidence is often the most accurate measure of the subject's character, its introduction is both time consuming and a source of significant jury distraction.[60] Therefore, Rule 405(b) allows evidence of the subject's specific conduct only in cases where character is a principal issue, that is, *only* "[i]n cases in which character ... is an essential element of a charge, claim, or defense...." In these relatively rare civil lawsuits,[61] character may be proven by any of the available means: reputation, opinion, or specific instances of conduct.

All witnesses, including character witnesses, are subject to cross-examination and impeachment. One technique for attacking the credibility of a character witness is to weaken or negate the character witness's assertion that she is familiar with the subject's reputation or (in the case of an opinion witness) that she is well acquainted with him. The cross-examiner can, of course, ask straightforward questions that probe, for example, how long the reputation witness and the subject have lived or worked in the same community. Such a question would test the validity of the propositions underlying the witness's direct testimony, namely, that the subject has been a member of the community long enough to have developed a reputation and that the witness is familiar with it. A parallel question, appropriate for the opinion witness, probes the length and closeness of the witness's acquaintance with the subject.

Beyond these obvious inquiries, however, the cross-examiner can ask the reputation witness questions about events involving the subject that would be likely to affect the subject's reputation for the trait(s) in question. Correspondingly, the cross-examiner can ask the opinion witness about events that would be likely to affect her opinion about the subject's character for the trait(s) in question. The questions take either the form of "Have you heard that ... ?" (appropriate for the reputation witness) or "Did you know that ... ?" (appropriate for the opinion witness). Suppose, for example, an opinion (character) witness testifies that in her estimation the

---

59. FRE 405(a), (b).

60. There is often disagreement about the specific events.

61. It is highly unlikely such cases will be criminal in nature. *See* supra Ch. III, § 3.6–1.

accused, Churchill, is very brave and would never have deserted the Army. The cross-examiner might ask the witness if she knew that during a training exercise in which live ammunition was used, Churchill left his squad and hid in a storage building. If the witness answers "no," the cross-examiner has weakened her assertion (made during direct) that she is knowledgeable about Churchill's character for bravery. If the witness answers "yes," the cross-examiner has raised doubts about the standard she used on direct when she characterized Churchill as "very brave."[62]

ILLUSTRATION

Benedict Arnold is charged with spying for a foreign country and planting false evidence that was designed to incriminate a CIA agent, Iago, for Arnold's deceitful acts. Arnold defends on the ground that in fact *he* was framed by Iago, the alleged victim, who was scheming to advance his own career. In addition to his own testimony, Arnold calls a reputation witness, Lord Venice, and an opinion witness, Cassio, who will each provide character evidence that Arnold is law-abiding and honest. The accused also calls Roderigo, an ex-CIA agent who served as a subordinate to Iago for over ten years. Roderigo testifies that Iago is "deceitful, treacherous, and obsessively ambitious."

What evidentiary opportunities are available to the prosecutor as a result of the testimony presented by the defense?

First, *any* witness (e.g., Arnold, Venice, Cassie, and Roderigo) is subject to the traditional impeachment techniques described in Chapter IX. For example, by testifying on his own behalf, Arnold runs the risk that the prosecutor will present evidence that Arnold has been convicted of crimes that involve deceit and thus reflect adversely on his character for truthfulness. The prosecutor could also present evidence that Arnold has made prior statements that are inconsistent with his courtroom testimony. Furthermore, during his cross-examination of Arnold, the prosecutor can inquire about prior "bad acts" (not resulting in a conviction), such as falsifying an application for a business license or filing a false insurance claim, that cast doubt upon Arnold's credibility.

Second, the prosecutor can try to weaken the testimony of Lord Venice (Arnold's reputation witness) and Cassio (Arnold's opinion witness) by exposing their lack of familiarity with Arnold's reputation or with Arnold himself. One means of achieving this end is to

---

62. The cross-examiner would also cast doubt on the character witness's truthfulness, at least in the context of this imagined case.

ask "have you heard" or "did you know" questions. Note that these questions test not only the character witnesses' familiarity with the subject's reputation or the subject himself, but also the standard these witnesses are using when they assert that Arnold is law-abiding and honest. For example, the prosecutor might ask Cassio, the opinion witness, whether he was aware that Arnold had been fired from his job because he falsified his travel expenses when seeking reimbursement from his corporate employer. Observe that by using witnesses to portray his character as "law-abiding," Arnold presents the prosecutor with a considerable range of possible did-you-know (or have-you-heard) questions, since a number of activities might be inconsistent with Arnold's reputed "law-abiding" character. (Suppose, for example, the prosecutor were to ask Cassio, "Did you know that Arnold was convicted of reckless and drunken driving on August, 15, 2005?")

Third, by introducing character evidence that the victim, Iago is "deceitful, treacherous, and obsessively ambitious," Arnold triggers the prosecutor's right not only to present character witnesses who will testify that Iago is, say, truthful, fair, and honest, but also to present character witnesses who will testify that Arnold is deceitful, treacherous, and obsessively ambitious. (These are the same character traits that Arnold has attributed to Iago.) If the trier of fact believes this evidence bearing on Arnold's bad character, it might draw the inference that Arnold was guilty of the charged spying and planting false evidence.[63]

Evaluation of Rules Governing the Cross–Examination of Character Witnesses

The allowance of "have-you-heard" and "did-you-know" questions during the cross-examination of the accused's character witnesses presents an overzealous prosecutor with opportunities for abuse. Although such questions are designed to test the knowledge of the character witness and the standard he is using in his assessment of the subject's character, these inquiries necessarily describe the subject's unfavorable conduct. ("Have you heard that the accused, Arnold, was twice taken into police custody and twice jailed during the summer of 2005 for inflicting physical injury on his wife?") One judicial safeguard against abuse is the requirement that the prosecutor's questions to the character witness must be in good faith. In practical terms, this good-faith requirement means that the prosecutor, after a reasonable investigation, must be satisfied that the event that is the basis for the cross-question actually occurred. In the case of a reputation character witness, the

---

63. The traits of deceit and treachery also bear on impeachment, that is, these traits cast doubt on the credibility of Arnold and also Iago—assuming he testifies.

prosecutor must also be satisfied that the actual event would have been widely enough known to have affected the subject's reputation. Nonetheless, there is a risk that the trier, especially a jury, will be unduly influenced or even inflamed by the accused's past conduct. Of course, the defense is entitled to an instruction that the sole purpose of asking a character witness about alleged conduct of the accused is to test the witness's familiarity with the accused (or his reputation) and to reveal the witness's standard of evaluation. The instruction will go on to direct the jury not to consider these past events as evidence of guilt in the present trial. Such an instruction, however, may at best be only modestly effective.

Consider the evidentiary options available to the prosecutor if the rules of evidence disallowed cross-questions in the form of have-you-heard or did-you-know inquiries. The prosecutor would still be entitled to impeach the accused's character witnesses by any of the standard techniques of impeachment, such as revealing a prior criminal conviction that bears on credibility, producing evidence of bias, or disclosing prior statements inconsistent with the witness's present testimony. The prosecutor could also ask straightforward questions that probe how familiar the witness really is with the accused (or his reputation). For example, the prosecutor could ask the opinion witness how long he has known the accused and how often (and under what circumstances) they have associated with each other. Finally, the prosecutor could call her own character witnesses to testify that the accused has character traits consistent with the crime charged.

These available counterattacks may appear quite adequate; sufficient, indeed, to justify the elimination of the prosecutor's right to ask such questions as, "Did you know that in September, 2003, the accused was tried for assault with a deadly weapon?" There are, however, arguments in favor of the present rules governing the prosecutor's cross-examination of the accused's character witnesses. Recall that it is the accused who has the right to control the introduction of character evidence. When he elects to introduce evidence of his own "good" character, he is likely to select character witnesses whose personal histories are not tainted by the kind of misconduct that will allow them to be impeached by the traditional methods.[64] Furthermore, the accused is likely to choose character witnesses whose *familiarity* with her or her reputation cannot be effectively challenged. Thus, the prosecutor's cross-examination may be ineffectual unless he can ask questions about the character witness's knowledge of prior instances involving the accused.

64. The only standard technique of impeachment that is likely to be available is bias. The prosecutor may be able to show, for example, that the character witness's close ties to the accused motivated her favorable testimony.

It is true, of course, that the prosecutor always has the right to rebut the accused's character evidence by calling witnesses who will attest to the accused's pertinent "bad character." The prosecutor's difficulty lies in implementing this right: it is unlikely that such witnesses will come forward and, even if they can be located, they are often reticent or fearful to give character testimony that will estrange and anger the accused. Thus, the question whether the present rules governing the cross-examination of character witnesses are justified should be addressed in the larger context of trial strategies and practical realities. The issue is close, and the legitimacy of the current rules (allowing cross-questions pertaining to knowledge of particular events) depends heavily on the careful oversight and control of the trial judge. Under Rule 403, she can reject unduly prejudicial evidence.[65]

"Circumstantial" Use of Character Evidence in Civil Cases

Federal Rule 404 generally disallows character evidence when offered to prove specific conduct. As we have observed, the rule then sets out exceptions to this broad prohibition. Except for allowing character evidence that bears on a witness's credibility, Rule 404's exceptions to its general prohibition are confined to criminal cases, which means that evidence of character to prove conduct on a particular occasion is normally inadmissible in civil cases. The rationale is that character evidence offered circumstantially in civil cases is not worth its cost in time consumed, distraction of the trier, and potential prejudice. The justification underlying the admission of circumstantial character evidence in criminal cases—special precautions against an erroneous conviction and the accused's right to make a full defense—are absent in civil trials. In addition, many civil trials are based on a party's unintentional behavior, such as negligent conduct. In lawsuits involving careless behavior, character evidence has weak probative value.

The strongest case for admitting character evidence in civil cases is made where a party defending a civil claim is alleged to have engaged in conduct that is also criminal in nature. Suppose, for example, a civil party is defending a claim (or counterclaim) that he has committed securities fraud or, perhaps, assault and battery. The alleged conduct is not only deliberate, but stigmatic. Thus, even though the reasons supporting a criminal defendant's right to introduce character evidence are not fully applicable, a few courts have broken ranks and permitted character-to-conduct evidence in a civil case when the alleged conduct is also criminal in

65. *See* Ch. III, § 3.2. *See also* FRE 611(a) which states that the "court shall exercise control over the mode and order of interrogating witnesses and present-ing evidence so as to (1) make the interrogation and presentation effective for the ascertainment of the truth...."

nature.[66] Perhaps there is little harm in this occasional departure from the text of Federal Rule 404,[67] but the practice does cast a shadow over the bright-line drawn by Rule 404(a). When considered with the exceptions contained in subsections (b) and (c), Rule 404 prohibits character evidence offered *to prove conduct* in civil cases unless that evidence bears on credibility.[68]

§ 3.6–3 Evidence of Habit Distinguished from Evidence of Character

Habit is related to, but different from, character. The term "habit" refers not to a character trait such as careful driving, but rather to a specific, repeated response to a particular situation, such as always fastening one's seatbelt. If evidence of the regular use by X of her seatbelt were offered to show she was a careful person, it would be excluded. However, if her regular use was shown for the inference that on the day in question she fastened her seatbelt, it would be admissible "habit evidence." Similarly, X may have a *character trait* for punctuality and a *habit* of returning to her office from lunch between 12:50 and 1:00 p.m. Evidence of the former would be rejected, while evidence of the latter would normally be received. Evidence of a regularly repeated response to a particular situation (habit) has probative value that generally exceeds the probative force of evidence of a character trait. Furthermore, unlike evidence of character, evidence of habit is "unlikely to provoke such sympathy or antipathy as would distort the process of evaluating the evidence."[69]

Federal Rule 406 states:

Habit; Routine Practice.

Evidence of the habit of a person or of the routine practice of an organization, whether corroborated or not and regardless of the presence of eyewitnesses, is relevant to prove that the conduct of the person or organization on a

66. Perrin v. Anderson, 784 F.2d 1040, 1044–45 (10th Cir. 1986). *Contra*, Securities and Exchange Comm. v. Towers Financial Corp., 966 F.Supp. 203, 205–06 (S.D.N.Y. 1997).

67. The Advisory Committee Notes make it clear that the drafters of Rule 404 rejected the use of character evidence to prove conduct in civil cases. *See* Rule 404(a) ACN.

68. As we have seen, however, character evidence is admissible in civil cases when character "is an essential element of a charge, claim or defense...." FRE 405(b). Furthermore, as suggested earlier, in instances involving a witness's credibility, the Federal Rules allow various kinds of evidence designed to reveal bad character for truthfulness. *See e.g.*, FRE 608(1) (opinion and reputation evidence admissible). Observe that when character evidence is used to attack credibility, the specific conduct to which the evidence is directed is the witness's false or misleading testimony. *See generally* Ch. IX.

69. 1 McCormick, § 195, at 687.

particular occasion was in conformity with the habit or routine practice.

Note that the Rule makes specific reference not only to evidence of the habit of a person, but also to the "habit" (sometimes called custom or routine practice) of an organization such as, for example, a business entity, fire department, hospital, library, or government office. Because organizations generally adhere to prescribed routines and procedures, it is comparatively easy to discover established organizational habits or practices. For example, a hospital may have a routine practice of isolating patients with certain highly contagious diseases; a polling organization may have a routine procedure for its selection of respondents or interviewees, and so forth.

Proving a Habit or Practice

Rule 406 does not specify how a habit or an organizational practice (custom) is to be proved. The rule does, however, specify that admissibility does not depend upon the presence of eyewitnesses to the event in question or other corroborative evidence. Such evidence should not be required, for if the habit or custom evidence has probative force, it should be admitted if it is not excluded by some other rule. The proponent of habit or "routine practice" evidence needs to convince the trial judge that a person or organization repeatedly reacted to a specific setting or stimuli with sufficient uniformity to establish a habitual response. The usual means of establishing this foundation is by the presentation of witnesses who have observed the actor's consistent behavior over a significant time period. (In the case of a business or other organization, written rules, standards, or procedures are also probative.) The greater the number of observations or samples, the more likely it is that a uniform pattern can be shown. This is not to suggest that there can never be a deviation from habitual conduct; it is to say, however, that foundational evidence is weakened by variable conduct, as well as by eyewitness observations that span only a short period of time, or include only a small number of instances. Obviously, the trial judge must be allowed considerable discretion both in determining whether conduct is narrow and specific enough to constitute a habit (as opposed to a character trait) and whether the foundational evidence of repetitious activity suffices to establish a habit or practice.

ILLUSTRATION

Two days after Alice visited her Uncle Herbert and Aunt Louise, Herbert died of a sudden, unexpected heart attack. The present suit, Aunt Louise v. Alice, concerns ownership of a valuable oriental vase (worth $25,000 or more) that had originally belonged to Herbert's great grandmother.

Louise claims that Alice stole the vase in question at the conclusion of the latter's week-long visit with Herbert and Louise. Alice, however, says that the vase was a gift. She claims that Herbert gave it to her when she went into his study to thank him for the visit and to say goodbye.

A week before trial, the presiding judge calls a pretrial conference. At the conference, Alice's attorney indicates he expects to offer opinion (character) witnesses who will testify that Alice is honest and law-abiding. He also expects to put on the witness stand friends and family members who knew Herbert prior to his death. They will testify that he was exceedingly generous, and was especially so with his nieces and nephews since he and Louise had no children. Each witness has observed one or more instances over the years during which, especially at Christmas, Herbert made generous gifts to his nephews and nieces, such as weekend vacations, gold wristwatches, gift certificates for expensive clothing, and season tickets to sporting and cultural events. Alice is prepared to testify that she has visited Herbert and Louise twice each year for ten years. At the conclusion of each visit, Herbert gave her a valuable item of china or jewelry that was a family heirloom.

Louise's attorney argues to the judge that none of this evidence is admissible. Is he correct?

Since this is a civil case, Rule 404 renders inadmissible evidence of character offered to prove particular conduct. Evidence of character is, of course, freely admissible in a civil case when character is an essential element or a claim or defense, but character is not such an element here. It would appear, therefore, that Rule 404(a) rules out the character evidence that Alice is honest and law-abiding. Alice can argue, of course, that since she is being "charged" with conduct (theft) that is criminal in nature, she should be permitted to introduce character evidence inconsistent with this alleged conduct. There is some (minority) judicial support for this position.

Alice's best argument rests not upon character evidence, but upon evidence of habit. The testimony of family members and friends that Herbert is generous and has made various gifts to his relatives, especially his nieces and nephews, probably falls short of the specificity and regularity that is the essential foundation for habit evidence. The judge will probably characterize this evidence as tending to establish a character trait (generosity), rather than a habit. On the other hand, Alice's own testimony of her uncle's practice of giving her a valuable heirloom at the conclusion of each of her semi-annual visits does establish his specific, repeated response to a particular situation (the conclusion of Alice's visit).

The fact that Alice is a self-interested witness might affect her credibility with the jury, but does not affect admissibility. Alice can also argue that even though testimony by friends and family concerning generous gifts to other nieces and nephews may not constitute evidence of habit, it provides the background and context for her habit evidence and ought to be admitted. The argument is especially compelling, she might urge, because she is being charged with illegal, dishonest conduct. In other words, Alice's argument is that in order to allow her to "tell the full story of her defense" the judge should exercise his discretion and allow at least some of the evidence about generous gifts to other family members. Were the judge to do so, he probably would not be reversed on appeal because it is doubtful that he abused his discretion in allowing this contextual evidence. Even if he disallows it, he might permit Alice to include in her testimony a brief description of her uncle's generous conduct toward his nieces and nephews. (This evidence, not involving other witnesses, would not be time consuming.)

Special Rules in Cases Involving Sexual Misconduct

As you will see in Section 3.6–7, special rules of evidence prevail in both criminal and civil cases involving specified kinds of sexual misconduct (essentially, sexual assaults and child molestation). Generally speaking, in these cases (governed by Federal Rules 412–15), evidence of other instances of sexual misconduct by the party alleged to have committed the charged sexual offense is admissible. Evidence of these "collateral" sexual acts is usually allowed even if the only basis for receiving the evidence is to show the defendant's predisposition toward certain (defined) sexual conduct. Another general feature of these special rules, and in particular Rule 412, is to restrict the admissibility of evidence that discloses collateral sexual activity of the alleged victim of the charged sexual misconduct. The point to keep in mind is that Rule 404 is superseded by Rules 412–15 and these special rules shift dramatically the protections afforded the accused under Rule 404(a). Indeed, it is fair to say that the pendulum swings sharply away from protecting the accused and toward protecting the alleged victim of a sexual crime. Several of these special rules also carve out exceptions to the prevailing rule that evidence of character used to prove particular conduct is inadmissible in civil cases.

§ 3.6–4 Other (Collateral) Crimes and Wrongful Acts

The focus of this section is on Rule 404(b). It states:

> **(b) Other crimes, wrongs, or acts.** Evidence of other crimes, wrongs, or acts is not admissible to prove the character of a person in order to show action in conformity therewith. It may, however, be admissible for other purposes, such as proof of motive, opportunity, intent, preparation, plan, knowledge, identity, or absence of mistake or accident, provided that upon request by the accused, the prosecution in a criminal case shall provide reasonable notice in advance of trial, or during trial if the court excuses pretrial notice on good cause shown, of the general nature of any such evidence it intends to introduce at trial.

The use of a collateral crime or wrong to prove some feature of the crime charged does not violate the general rule that forbids the prosecution from introducing evidence of the accused's character to prove his conduct in connection with the present (charged) crime. What Rule 404 prohibits is prosecution evidence to establish that the accused has a character trait or predisposition (*e.g.* an aggressive character) pertinent to the crime charged, thus allowing the trier to infer that because the accused has this trait or propensity, he is more likely to have committed the charged crime. The forbidden sequence is character evidence, to propensity (predisposition), to conduct in connection with the charged crime. What Rule 404(b) allows is evidence of a collateral wrong, committed before or after the offense charged, that has probative value to prove some element of the crime charged. Of course, evidence disclosing a collateral (uncharged) offense or wrongful act reflects negatively on the accused's character, but the trier can use this evidence properly without traveling the forbidden inferential route from character evidence, to propensity, to conduct. Evidence of the collateral misconduct can be permissibly used to draw inferences about some particular feature of the present crime. Ultimately that feature points either *to the accused's conduct (including identity)* during the charged crime or his *state of mind* during the charged crime.

A simple example will set the stage for the discussion that follows. Suppose the accused, *D*, an accountant, is charged with embezzling money from the charity that employed him. The indictment alleges that *D* attempted to hide his theft by making false financial entries in his employer's accounts. *D* defends on the ground that he did not misappropriate the funds in question and that any false entries were an innocent mistake. The prosecution offers evidence that five years earlier, *D's* Canadian employer had fired him for misappropriating company funds and covering up his theft by making false accounting entries. Subsequently, Canadian authorities successfully prosecuted D, who was fined and given a suspended sentence.

This evidence would be admitted, in the words of Rule 404(b), to show "knowledge ... or the absence of mistake or accident." The point to emphasize is that the prohibition *barring the introduction of collateral crimes evidence is limited to situations where the only use of that evidence is to establish D's unfavorable character trait* which would then be used by the trier to draw inferences about D's criminal propensity and, hence, to his conduct during the charged crime. Think of the prohibition as a rule that rejects character evidence if its only probative value is to show propensity or predisposition.

ILLUSTRATION

Assume that in the embezzlement trial described above, D's defense is that any misappropriations or false financial entries were made not by D, but rather by X, a part-time accountant who periodically worked for D's employer. The prosecutor offers evidence that five years ago, D was fired by his Canadian employer for misappropriating funds and making false entries and that D was subsequently convicted of embezzlement. D objects.

Should this evidence be admitted?

It should not. The defense is not mistake, but mistaken identity. Even though the Rule 404(b)'s list of "purposes," for which evidence of other crimes or wrongs may be admissible is illustrative only, the list does include the most frequently encountered purposes for which this evidence is received. One of these permissible purposes is to show identity. However, identity cannot be established simply by showing that the accused has committed collateral offenses similar to, or the same as, the charged offense. Thus, if D is charged with bank robbery and denies that he was the robber, the prosecution cannot introduce evidence that before (or after) the charged crime, D robbed a bank. The reason this evidence is rejected is because in order to use it, the trier will necessarily draw the following inference: since D has committed a similar collateral crime, he has a propensity to commit bank robbery, and thus he is more likely to have committed the robbery in question.

This forbidden line of reasoning is even more apt to occur if D has committed *multiple crimes similar to or the same as* the charged crime. If evidence of similar collateral (uncharged) crimes were freely admissible, prosecutors could obtain convictions more easily, even in the face of weak evidence that *D* committed the offense charged. Furthermore, a person with a criminal record, especially one reflecting offenses similar to the offense being investigated, is likely to be the focus of a police investigation and is more likely than is a person with a "clean" record (or even a record involving *dissimilar* crimes) to be arrested and charged. Thus, having a criminal record can haunt the accused throughout the process of enforcing the criminal law, that is, from the police investigation through final judgment.

Suppose, however, in the Illustration above, the accounting "cover-up" scheme used in the collateral Canadian theft was the same as the one used in the crime charged. And suppose further that the pattern of false entries was unusual—that is, the accounting scheme used to conceal the missing funds was uncommon enough to strongly suggest that the same accountant conceived and executed both cover-ups. When the collateral crime and the charged crime bear the same unusual characteristics or earmarks, evidence of the collateral offense *can* be used to prove identity. The evidence has specific probative value to prove identity and the trier can draw legitimate inferences that move directly from the evidence of the collateral misconduct (patterned false entries) to identity without the necessity of moving from "other crimes" evidence, to propensity, to conduct (identity). While, as we have noted, evidence of collateral misconduct does taint the accused's character, this ancillary effect is tolerated if the evidence has significant probative force, independent of character, to establish an element of the crime charged.

Certainty with which a Collateral Crime must be Shown

A preliminary issue sometimes arising in connection with an offer of collateral crimes evidence is the degree of certainty with which the commission of the other crime must be shown.[70] It may be useful to recall the basic principle that individual items of evidence need not meet the standard of proof that applies to the totality of the evidence. Although the sum of all the evidence in a criminal case must support belief of the accused's guilt beyond a reasonable doubt, this standard of proof is not applied to individual items of evidence. Indeed, if it were, the prosecution would find it virtually impossible to obtain a conviction.

70. The term "other crime" is used broadly here to embrace any misconduct that tends to establish a feature of the charged crime, such as identity, motive, or absence of mistake. The term includes crimes for which there has been a conviction, as well as misconduct that has gone unpunished. Note that there is nothing in the language of FRE 404(b) that limits its application to criminal cases. While it is certainly true that collateral crimes are also admissible in civil cases, such as a suit for a fraudulent act, the vast majority of cases involving FRE 404(b) are criminal.

Observe that the use of other (collateral) crime evidence is yet another illustration of the principle of conditional relevance. Suppose *D* is prosecuted for lying to customs officials and concealing behind the lining of her suitcase an undeclared, expensive diamond bracelet. Her defense is that she placed the bracelet in a secure place to prevent its theft, and then forgot to declare it. The prosecutor now offers evidence that a year prior to the present offense, *D* was detained by customs officials because she failed to declare on her customs declaration a valuable diamond ring that was hidden inside the toe of one of her shoes. In order to use this evidence to infer knowledge or the absence of mistake, the trier of fact first must find that *D* concealed and failed to declare the diamond ring. To make the point more emphatically: if the collateral event (crime) or the pertinent features of the collateral event did not occur, the trier cannot draw inferences about knowledge, the absence of mistake, or other particular features of the crime charged. These inferences about specific features of the charged crime are *conditioned upon* the existence of the defendant's collateral misconduct.

Under Rule 104(b), which governs conditional relevance, the proponent of other crimes evidence must produce evidence of the collateral event that is sufficient "to support a finding"[71] of its existence. The judge screens the evidence to ensure its sufficiency; the jury, using a more-likely-than-not standard, determines if the collateral event did in fact occur. This, at least, is the practice in the federal courts and most state courts. The leading case, which determined that the Federal Rules require only sufficient evidence to support the other (uncharged) crime, is Huddleston v. United States.[72] Since this case is simply a construction of the Federal Rules of Evidence as applied in the federal courts (and is not a constitutionally based decision), it is not binding on state courts. These courts are not only free to interpret their own version of the "federal rules" differently, but also (if authorized by statute) to amend them. Some states have not followed the *Huddleston* construction, and have demanded a larger role for the judge or higher standard of proof for collateral crimes.[73] The argument for these additional protections rests upon the probable adverse impact of other crimes evidence upon the accused. Whatever the standard of proof, however, evidence of a collateral crime is probative if, and only if, the trier finds that the other crime was committed and that it was committed by the accused.

---

71.   FRE 104(b).

72.   485 U.S. 681 (1988).

73.   *See, e.g.*, People v. Garner, 806 P.2d 366, 372 (Colo. 1991) (judge, not jury, must find by a preponderance of the evidence that accused committed the other crime); State v. Cofield, 127 N.J. 328, 605 A.2d 230, 234–36 (1992) (evidence showing other crime must be clear and convincing).

Acquittal of the Collateral Crime

A special difficulty arises if the accused has been tried and acquitted of the commission of the collateral crime. In a technical sense, an acquittal means only that the jury (or the judge, in a bench trial) decided that the evidence admitted was insufficient to convince it beyond a reasonable doubt of the existence of each essential element of the collateral offense. This negative determination does not preclude a subsequent finding of the criminal conduct by a lesser standard, such as one requiring only a preponderance of the evidence (or even clear and convincing evidence); nor does an acquittal preclude reconsideration of only one particular aspect or element of the collateral incident. It may be, for example, that the evidence pertaining to one feature of the collateral offense (*e.g.*, conduct) was very strong, whereas evidence pertaining to another feature (*e.g.*, intent) was comparatively weak. Perhaps the aspect of the other crime that has significance in the trial of the charged offense is the accused's conduct in the collateral event.

In the hypothetical above, for example, assume the accused had been tried and acquitted of an *initial* charge of concealing a diamond ring from customs agents and knowingly falsifying her declaration. Imagine, further, that the jury rendered a verdict of innocence even though there was strong evidence that the undeclared ring was concealed in *D's* shoe. A year later, *D* is apprehended and tried for the separate and recent offense of concealing a diamond bracelet from customs agents and falsifying her declaration. Her defense is "innocent mistake." Should the acquittal in the first trial preclude the prosecutor from introducing evidence pertaining to the earlier misconduct? It is true that the use of this evidence has the practical effect of forcing the defendant to defend against the same evidence a second time, in that she will normally attempt to challenge, explain, or rebut the evidence of the first charge. Nonetheless, the federal courts and most state courts reject the position that an acquittal of the collateral offense bars relevant evidence pertaining to it in the trial of another (charged) offense.[74] If acquittal were to erect an absolute bar, consider the evidentiary outcome in the following case.[75]

ILLUSTRATION

In the early morning hours of January 1, 2001, *D* called the police station. He reported that when he awoke at 12:30 a.m. and went to the kitchen for a glass of milk,

74. The decisive case for the federal courts is Dowling v. United States, 493 U.S. 342, 347–354 (1990).

75. The Illustration that follows in the text is an adaptation of Tucker v. State, 82 Nev. 127, 412 P.2d 970 (1966).

he discovered a dead man on his living room floor. The police arrived to discover that *V–1*, a deceased male who had been fatally shot with a large caliber pistol, was in fact lying on *D's* living room rug. *D* appeared disoriented and under the influence of liquor or some other intoxicating substance. *D* claimed that he had no idea how *V–1*, whom he hardly knew, was shot or how *V–1* got inside *D's* unlocked house. D was not indicted.

At 2:10 a.m. on February 3, 2002, *D* summoned the police. He led them to *V–2*, who lay dead on *D's* kitchen floor. *D*, who appeared intoxicated, said that when he heard a noise, he arose from his bed and discovered *V–2*. The latter, lying in a pool of blood on *D's* kitchen floor, had been fatally shot with a large caliber pistol. Subsequently, *D* was indicted and charged for the murder of *V–2*, a woman he had once dated. The trial judge rejected evidence pertaining to the earlier murder because in his jurisdiction the earlier crime had to be shown by clear and convincing evidence and the prosecutor's evidence connecting *D* with *V–1's* murder fell short of that standard of proof. At the conclusion of the trial, the jury acquitted *D* of *V–2's* murder.

At 1:30 a.m. on January 3, 2003, *D* called 911. He reported that he had discovered *V–3* in his recreation room. *D*, who seemed disoriented and perhaps intoxicated, stated that he could not sleep, so he went for a walk. When he returned and went into his recreation room to watch television, he discovered *V–3*, apparently shot to death, lying on the floor. *V–3* had been a member of *D's* National Guard unit.

At *D's* trial for the murder of *V–3*, the prosecutor offers evidence of the earlier murders. Evidence pertaining to *V–1's* murder was rejected on the ground that *D's* connection with that alleged offense could not be established by clear and convincing evidence. Evidence pertaining to *V–2's* murder was also rejected on the ground that *D* had been acquitted of that murder and evidence of a collateral crime is not admissible if an earlier trial for that offense had resulted in an acquittal.

Was the judge correct?

This Illustration may seem far-fetched, but cases do in fact arise in which a series of related events or acts, when considered cumulatively, have strong probative value with respect to some feature of the charged crime. In one such case,[76] the accused was

76. United States v. Woods, 484 F.2d 127 (4th Cir. 1973), *cert. denied*, 415 U.S. 979 (1974).

charged with infanticide when a child in her care died of cyanosis. She claimed that the child's death was accidental. The prosecutor offered evidence that over an extended period, children in the accused's care had suffered twenty cyanotic episodes. The extraordinary frequency of these unlikely incidences, argued the prosecutor, had the cumulative effect of increasing the likelihood that they were accompanied by purposeful conduct. On this theory, the judge admitted evidence of these collateral events. What is at work here is the doctrine of chances.

Professor Edward J. Imwinkelried observes that,

> Under both the doctrine [of chances] and the character theory ..., the trier of fact begins at the same starting point, the evidence of the accused's uncharged [collateral] crimes. However, when the trier engages in character reasoning, the initial decision facing the trier is whether to infer from the evidence that the accused has a personal bad character. In contrast, under the doctrine of chances, the trier need not focus on the accused's subjective character. Under the doctrine of chances, the initial decision facing the trier is whether the uncharged incidents are so numerous that it is objectively improbable that so many accidents would befall the accused....[77]

In the text ahead, which deals with the trial court's obligation to protect the accused from undue prejudice, you will see that one of the several factors that weighs against the introduction of evidence of collateral crimes is an earlier acquittal. Indeed, one of the central points of the forthcoming discussion of other crimes evidence is the critical role played by judges, and particularly by the trial judge, in protecting the accused from unwarranted disclosures of his alleged participation in collateral misconduct. Nonetheless, neither an acquittal nor a prosecutor's decision not to bring charges in connection with the collateral offense(s) should be an absolute bar to the introduction of other crimes evidence.

Other Crimes Evidence: Illustrations

Rules 404(b) sets out a number of propositions for which collateral crimes evidence is often received. Although the purposes

---

77. Edward J. Imwinkelried, *The Use of An Accused's Uncharged Misconduct to Prove Mens Rea: The Doctrines which Threaten to Engulf the Character Evidence Prohibition*, 51 Ohio St. L.J. 575, 586–87 (1990). For a thoughtful argument that the doctrine of chances is not an escape from the rule forbidding propensity evidence, but in fact violates the rule, see Paul F. Rothstein, *Intellectual Coherence in An Evidence Code*, 28 Loy. L. A. L. Rev. 1259, 1261–65 (1995) (actor's propensity accounts for the unusual frequency of his involvement in the series of events).

listed in this subsection are illustrative only, many of the decided cases focus on one or more of the propositions listed. Nonetheless, it is clear from the language of the rule, as well as its legislative history, that the drafters of subsection (b) created an open-ended system in which the trial judge neither mechanically excludes, nor routinely accepts, other crimes evidence. Rather, she determines admissibility on the basis of such factors as probative value, potential prejudice, and the availability of alternative forms of evidence.[78]

The elaborative material below sets out a sampling of circumstances in which consequential propositions normally *can* be established by the introduction of other crimes evidence. The chain of inferences based upon this evidence ultimately leads to an inference about either the *actor's conduct, or his state of mind, or both.* For example, suppose evidence of the collateral crime, such as the illegal acquisition of explosives, indicates *D's* plan or preparation for the crime charged, such as detonating a bomb in a crowded public square. The collateral crime evidence allows the trier to infer plan or preparation, which in turn allows it to infer conduct or identity. Other illustrations appear below:

(1) In the prosecution of *D* for the murder of *V*, evidence that *V* had threatened to expose *D's* participation in a land fraud scheme is relevant to show *motive*; in other words, to reveal the inducement or reason why *D* might have committed the criminal offense charged. Existence of a motive usually supports an inference about conduct, but motive might also have probative value in establishing a mental state such as intent or purpose.

(2) In the trial of *D* for car theft, the defendant asserts that he was in a distant city on the day in question. Evidence that on the same day as the car theft, *D* purchased illegal drugs from a supplier in the city where the car was stolen is relevant to show that *D* had the *opportunity* to commit the theft. Similarly, if the car thief had used specialized tools to deactivate the stolen car's alarm system and to rig the electrical system so the engine would start, evidence that *D* possessed such tools during the period in question would be relevant to show he had the *capacity* to commit the theft.[79]

(3) In the prosecution of *D* for the theft of a rented automobile, he asserts that he intended to return the car. Evidence of the theft of other rented cars is relevant to establish *D's* intent. The term "intent" is, generally speaking, synonymous with "purpose"; it denotes the desire to achieve a particular end and an awareness that the action undertaken is likely to produce it. Thus, since the

78. FRE 404(b) ACN.

79. In this example, possession of the tools may not constitute a criminal offense; nonetheless, absent some expla-

nation from the defendant, the jury would probably draw unfavorable inferences from *D's* possession of these specialized tools.

crime of theft is usually defined so as to require a taking of goods with the purpose of depriving the owner (either permanently or for a substantial period of time), evidence of other thefts bears upon the mental element of intent.

(4) In the prosecution of *D*, a nurse, for murdering *V* by lethal dose of morphine, evidence that prior to the murder *D* stole from the hospital dispensary enough morphine to cause death is relevant to show *preparation* (or capacity). Preparatory steps increase the likelihood that the act charged was performed. Preparation may also reveal the accused's state of mind, *e.g.*, by showing deliberateness or purposefulness.

(5) In the prosecution of *D* for arson of building *A*, evidence that *D* had wrongfully burned building *B* covered by similar fire insurance is relevant, if coupled with other evidence, to show that *D* had a *plan* (scheme or design) to destroy these buildings in order to collect insurance proceeds. If the crime charged is shown to be part of a plan, inferences can be drawn concerning conduct or, often, state of mind. In its pristine form, this exception entails the evidentiary use of acts separate from, but nonetheless related to, the crime charged in order to infer the existence of a plan or scheme. An inference is then drawn that the act charged is part of the larger scheme. From this conclusion, further inferences can be made about the actor's conduct or mental state in connection with the offense charged. In other words, when there is no direct evidence of a plan, the prosecution can prove circumstantially the existence of a plan by the separate but related prior bad acts, and then try to connect the charged incident to the plan.

(6) In the trial of *D* for receiving stolen property from *A*, evidence that on other occasions and under similar circumstances *A* had supplied *D* with goods (probably known by *D* to have been stolen) is relevant to show that *D* had *knowledge* that the goods in question were stolen. It is necessary that the prosecutor provide sufficient evidence for the trier of fact to conclude that *D* knew or should have known that the other goods were stolen. Perhaps, for example, the sale of the other goods was attended by suspicious circumstances such as a price far below market value, "after-hours" delivery, or the absence of proper documentation. The element of knowledge is closely related to and frequently overlaps that of intent (or purpose) since both require awareness.[80] The element of knowledge appears to require only an awareness of wrongfulness or criminality, whereas the element of intent seems also to call for a purpose or desire to achieve a particular end.

---

80. *See* Model Penal Code § 2.02(5) (1962) (proof of purpose sufficient for conviction when crime requires knowledge, but knowledge insufficient when crime requires purpose).

(7) In the prosecution of *D* for passing a forged "paycheck" for $150, purportedly made payable to *D* by *A* Company, evidence that *D* passed similar false checks from *A* Company under like circumstances (*e.g.*, buying a small item, describing *A* Company's products, using the same false documents of identification, and receiving a substantial sum in change) is relevant to *identify D* as the actor in the offense charged. However, there must be more to link *D* to both the charged and uncharged crime then simply passing forged checks. Evidence of other crimes is admissible to prove identity when identity is in question (that is, when the accused denies that he participated in the charged crime) and when the modus operandi of the two crimes is sufficiently distinctive and similar to be substantially probative of identity. It is often said that the conduct associated with the collateral and principal crime must be sufficiently *similar* and sufficiently *distinctive* that the resulting pattern is the "perpetrator's signature." This may overstate the requirement, but it is quite clear that a mere showing that D has committed other crimes in the same class as the offense charged is insufficiently probative of identity to justify admission. However, even when the principal and collateral crimes are largely dissimilar, it may be possible to introduce evidence that a distinctive feature linking the defendant to the collateral crime(s) is also involved in the crime charged. For example, it may be possible to show that a certain unusual weapon was used in committing both crimes or that some object acquired during the collateral crime (*e.g.*, a check-writing machine) was used in the commission of the crime charged (passing forged checks). Note the possibility that a collateral crime may bear upon both preparation and identity, or for that matter, other propositions.

(8) In the trial of *D* for the murder of his wife, *V–2*, he claims that the shooting was accidental and occurred when he was preparing to clean his pistol and pulled the trigger to ensure that the gun was "decocked" so he could disassemble it. Evidence that *D* had shot and killed his first wife, *V–1*, while claiming to have dropped his pistol as he was preparing to clean it, thus causing its accidental discharge, is relevant to show lack of accident or mistake.

(9) In the trial of *D*, a firearms dealer, for selling assault weapons that were banned from importation and sale, evidence that *D* destroyed invoices and sales receipts and altered his financial statements is relevant to show consciousness of guilt. Other conduct, such as bribing or threatening witnesses, would be relevant for the same purpose.

Sometimes two criminal acts are so closely related by causation, geographic closeness, or (especially) time, that it is necessary to reveal the uncharged crime in order that the trier of fact can fully understand the event charged. For example, suppose *D* is charged with reckless driving that resulted in the death of an elderly pedestrian who was crossing the street. Assume that just before the accident, *D* was leaving a nearby department store when the alarm buzzer sounded, indicating that he was carrying "unpaid-for" goods. As the security guard approached, *D* ran. The incident at the department store is clearly relevant to show the motive or reason why *D* was driving at a high rate of speed. Furthermore, the incident suggesting *D's* shoplifting could be viewed as so intertwined with the reckless driving charge that it does not constitute a "collateral" offense.

In all of the examples and illustrations discussed in this subsection, other crimes evidence has been offered by the prosecution against the accused. This is the typical setting, although Rule 404(b) is not confined to this pattern: it speaks simply of the admissibility of evidence not offered for the purpose of proving character or propensity, but offered instead for purposes such as motive, intent, or identity. The rule is broad enough to include civil cases,[81] as well as the comparatively rare cases in which an *accused* invokes Rule 404(b). (The so-called "reverse 404(b) case.") Suppose, for example, two crimes, C–1 and C–2, bear so many similarities that it is likely they were committed by the same person. *D*, who is prosecuted for C–2, has evidence that the victim of C–1 identified another person, *X*, as the perpetrator of that crime. This evidence is relevant to show mistaken identity—that is, to show that *D* is innocent of C–2, the crime with which he is now charged. *D* is not attempting to prove the "criminal" character of the perpetrator of C–1, but is introducing the evidence on the specific point of identity. Furthermore, the risk of prejudice, with which we are very concerned when other crimes evidence is offered against the accused, shrinks from importance in the reverse Rule 404(b) case. Any anger or passion aroused in the jury is directed not at *D*, but toward a third person, *X*.

§ 3.6–5 Protective Exclusion of Other Crimes Evidence

Evidence of collateral offense(s) to prove a particular point, such as intent, motive, or identity, carries a considerable risk of prejudice. In the typical case, this evidence is offered against the accused. As we have noted before, when evidence of the accused's collateral misconduct comes before the trier of fact, it may produce an impassioned or angry response. This possible reaction raises the risk the trier will use the evidence for the forbidden "propensity purpose," or that it will conclude that the defendant's past justifies his incarceration (or other penalty) even if he did not commit the crime with which he is now charged. Thus, the judge should be

---

81. *See* supra, note 70.

especially cautious when ruling on the prosecution's offer of other crimes evidence.

All courts agree that, with the exception of certain incidents of sexual misconduct,[82] evidence of collateral crimes must have probative value directed to a specific point if it is to clear the hurdle of exclusion; it does not suffice for admissibility that the evidence reveals a propensity to commit crime or even a *proclivity to commit the particular kind of offense* that is charged in the present trial. The general requirement that evidence of collateral offenses must have probative force above the propensity level begins our inquiry, but does not end it.

It will be readily seen that collateral crimes often may have *some* probative force bearing upon one or more legitimate propositions such as intent, motive, absence of mistake, and so forth. Nonetheless, there may be ample other evidence bearing on this (or these) particular feature(s) of the present crime, so that resort to other crimes evidence is unnecessary. Furthermore, the inflammatory nature of the past crime may be such that evidence pertaining to it is likely to unduly influence the jury. Special caution is also warranted when the collateral crime bears a close resemblance to the crime charged (e.g., another bank robbery). This similarity increases the likelihood that the trier of fact will resort to a propensity inference. All of these factors must be taken into account when a judge rules on the admissibility of other crimes evidence.

It is also important to consider whether the accused has assumed a defensive posture that heightens the probative importance of the other crimes evidence. Suppose, for example, the accused, a retailer, is charged with knowingly receiving stolen property. He offers the defense that he had no knowledge that the goods were stolen. Evidence that he has received other goods from the same supplier under suspicious circumstances (*e.g.*, unaccompanied by a bill of sale, priced far below market, large volume purchase, delivered after hours, etc.) would be admissible to rebut this defense. Likewise, a defense of entrapment by the accused in the case imagined would point toward admissibility of the collateral evidence. By invoking this latter defense, the accused is claiming that law enforcement authorities lured him into committing the crime charged. The fact that the defendant has committed similar collateral crimes tends to rebut the proposition that he would not have committed the charged crime absent police encouragement.

On the other hand, suppose the accused claims that although he did receive a large quantity of goods at a discounted price (in connection with the crime charged), the goods were not stolen, but

---

82. Sexual misconduct is treated *infra* § 3.6–7.

were legally imported from a foreign country with "cheap" labor. Since the goods were not the subject of a theft, he could not possibly have "known" they were stolen. He offers documentation from the country of origin and the shipper. The probative value of the collateral incident (receiving stolen goods on prior occasions) falls considerably, for now the collateral evidence is limited to supporting the inference that since the accused on a prior occasion received goods that were probably stolen, the goods in question in the present trial are more likely to have been stolen. The defense attorney should argue that none of the particular purposes of the sort illustrated in Rule 404(b) applies; the most obvious inference is that since the accused received stolen goods on another occasion, and it is known that he received goods at a discounted price in the charged crime, these articles were more likely to have been stolen. The evidence of the collateral event strongly points toward *propensity* to deal in *stolen* goods and thus should be excluded. The prosecutor can at least argue that evidence of the collateral offense is offered to show the absence of mistake—the accused *did know* the goods were stolen. The fallacy in this argument is that the accused is not claiming he did not know the goods were stolen; he is claiming the goods were not stolen.

The general point is this: in each case posing the issue of other crimes evidence, the judge must take full account of the circumstances before him. Major factors that counsel against the admission of other crimes evidence (although one or even several may not be decisive) include the following:

(1) An acquittal of the collateral crime;

(2) The inflammatory nature of the collateral crime;

(3) The similarity of the collateral crime to the charged crime;

(4) The availability of other evidence to prove the particular point toward which evidence of the collateral crime would, if admitted, be directed;

(5) The defensive claims of the accused, including whether or not the point to be proved by the collateral evidence is disputed.

These and other contextual factors often complicate the trial judge's decision when he is faced with an offer of collateral-crimes evidence. In resolving the question of admissibility, the judge is applying Rule 403 in an effort to determine whether the probative value of the other crimes evidence is substantially outweighed by considerations such as jury confusion, time consumption, and, especially, prejudice. Because of the potential impact of evidence involving collateral crimes, as well as the need for full consideration of the evidentiary issues, Rule 404(b) entitles the accused to demand notice from the prosecution that it intends to offer evidence of a collateral crime.

§ 3.6–6 Reputation, Threats, and Collateral Incidents Affecting the Defendant's State of Mind

A criminal defendant who pleads self-defense raises the issue whether, in light of all the circumstances, he acted reasonably in defending himself against the alleged victim (V). A similar issue is posed in a civil suit for battery in which the defendant pleads self-defense. The trier of fact considers not only the conduct of V and the defendant (D), but also the related but distinct question of D's apprehension of harm. Of course, V's conduct toward D at the time of the offense is a major factor in determining whether the latter took reasonable steps to defend himself. But this conduct may not be the only factor. For example, suppose V had threatened D on an earlier occasion; or perhaps V is reputed to be a violent, dangerous person. In the present context, the key to admitting evidence of V's reputation, his prior threats to harm D, or V's violent conduct directed toward others, is D's *knowledge* of V's reputation, threats, or violent activities. The purpose of the evidence disclosing V's violent or threatening nature is to demonstrate that D had a reasonable basis for fearing V, and thus was justified in taking protective steps.

As we noted, the evidentiary use described above requires that prior to the litigated incident, D had knowledge of V's threats, aggressive conduct toward others, or reputation for violence. To this general requirement of D's awareness, there is a notable exception: evidence of a threat by V to harm D is generally admissible even if it was disclosed to a third person and not to D. Since, as we will now assume, D was unaware of V's statement, evidence that V threatened D cannot derive its probative force from the probable effect that V's statement had on D's mental state. Yet, when there is a violent exchange between two people, the fact that one (V) had threatened to harm the other (D) has probative value in resolving the question of who was the aggressor. Even though one person's threat to harm another is unknown to the latter, the threat increases the probabilities that the party making the threat carried it out.

Confirm your understanding of this evidentiary principle with the following hypothetical. V confides in W that he (V) is going to kill D, who is living with V's former girlfriend. Subsequently, V is killed or seriously injured and D is prosecuted; he pleads self-defense. Counsel for the accused (D) calls W, who will testify that V threatened to kill D. As we have seen, the relevance of this testimony is apparent. Recall that Rule 401 says that evidence is relevant if it has "any tendency to make the existence of any fact that is of consequence ... more probable or less probable...." *V's* threat meets this test. Of course, relevant evidence is excludable if its admission would contravene another rule of evidence. The evidence of *V's* threat would be rejected, for example, if it constituted inadmissible hearsay. As you will see in Chapter VII,[83] however, an assertion by an out-of-court speaker (the "declarant") that he will take certain action in the future is admissible under an exception to the hearsay rule.[84] It suffices at this juncture to conclude that unless some other exclusionary rule is applicable, *V's* threat against *D* is admissible even though *D* was unaware of it. Equally admissible would be *W's* statement to *D*: "Be careful *D, V* told me he was going to kill you."

§ 3.6–7 Special Rules: Cases Involving Sexual Misconduct

Introduction

Certain kinds of sexual offences, namely sexual assault and child molestation, are specifically addressed in Federal Rules 412–415. These rules apply generally to both criminal and civil cases, although different provisions may be applicable depending on whether the case being tried is criminal or civil. A word of caution: although state jurisdictions usually have special evidentiary rules that apply in cases involving sexual misconduct, you should expect considerable variation from state to state, including significant departures from the federal evidentiary scheme.

Rules 412 through 415 contain a number of technical provisions, but the overarching scheme is fairly straightforward. It is helpful to think of Rule 412 as a "rape shield provision" designed to protect the alleged victim of a sexual assault from unwarranted disclosures of her reputation or sexual history, particularly as that history pertains to sexual behavior with persons other than the accused. It is useful to think of Rules 413 through 415 as "sexual predisposition" provisions, since the premise underlying these rules is that an alleged offender's collateral sexual behavior of the same type that is claimed or charged in the case being tried has strong probative value.

Rules 413–15 reject the general principle of Rule 404 that excludes evidence of collateral conduct (such as a crime) when its only probative value is to demonstrate a character trait or predisposition. As we have already observed, the premise of Rule 404 is that evidence of character offered to prove particular conduct is general-

---

83. See Ch. VII, § 7.2(c) in particular.

84. The applicable exception allows into evidence statements that reflect the declarant's "existing state of mind," provided it is not just a statement of the declarant's belief about, or recollection of, past events. *See* FRE 803(3).

ly excluded since its probative value is insufficient to overcome countervailing considerations such as prejudice, confusion, and time consumption. Congress overrode Rule 404's exclusionary principle when it enacted Federal Rules 413–15.[85]

Background

Suppose *V* has consensual sexual relations with *A*. On another occasion, *V* has sexual intercourse with *D*. *V* claims *D* raped her; *D* claims *V* consented. At *D*'s trial for sexual assault, defense counsel offers evidence supporting the fact that *V* consented to sexual intercourse with *A*. How should the judge rule when the prosecutor objects?

During the first half of the Twentieth Century, judges would have usually admitted this evidence. Furthermore, they would usually have allowed reputation evidence that *V* had an "unchaste" or promiscuous character. The leading American evidence scholar during this period, John Henry Wigmore, confidently asserted:

> Modern psychiatrists have amply studied the behavior of errant young girls and women coming before the court in all sorts of cases. Their psychic complexes are multifarious, distorted partly by inherent defects, partly by diseased derangements or abnormal instincts, partly by bad social environments, partly by temporary physiological or emotional conditions. One form taken by these complexes is that of contriving false charges of sexual offenses by men. The unchaste (let us call it) mentality finds incidental but direct expression in the narration of imaginary sex-incidents of which the narrator is the heroine or the victim. . . . The real victim, however, too often in such cases is the innocent man; for the respect and sympathy naturally felt by any tribunal for a wronged female helps to give easy credit to such a plausible tale. . . .[86]

The last half of the Twentieth Century ushered in new attitudes, a critical reappraisal of the judicial practice of allowing evidence of the victim's collateral sexual behavior, and legislative reform efforts ("rape shield statutes") that eventually prevailed in all jurisdictions. There was a growing acknowledgment that in sexual assault prosecutions, evidence of the victim's reputation or consensual sexual behavior with third persons had marginal or (usually) no probative value. *V*'s consensual sexual behavior with *A*

---

85. Congress decided to enact these rules, even though they were rejected by the Judicial Conference of the United States (the body that proposes to the United States Supreme Court additions and modifications to the Federal Rules of Evidence).

86. 3A J. WIGMORE, EVIDENCE IN TRIALS AT COMMON LAW § 942(a), at 736 (Chadbourn rev. 1970). More recent versions of WIGMORE would, of course, present a different view.

(as in the example above) usually tells us little or nothing about whether her sexual behavior with D was consensual. After all, the victim did not accuse her other partner or partners of rape, but she *has* accused the defendant.[87] Beyond this, there is the pragmatic concern that publicly subjecting V to embarrassing disclosures and innuendoes has a chilling effect on her willingness to come forward and report a sexual assault to law enforcement authorities.

Federal Rule 412

Federal Rule 412 begins, in subsection (a), by generally prohibiting specified kinds of evidence "in any civil or criminal proceeding involving alleged sexual misconduct...." The term "sexual misconduct" encompasses a broad range of cases and it is immaterial whether or not the victim or the person accused is a party to the litigation.[88] The evidence generally forbidden is, first, that which shows that the "victim engaged in other sexual behavior" and, second, that which portrays the "victim's sexual predisposition."

The Rule is indifferent to the particular form of proffered evidence, for its prohibition is equally applicable to reputation evidence, opinion evidence, and evidence of specific sexual acts. As we shall see below, there are limited exceptions to Rule 412's general exclusionary provision, but these exceptions are specified in the body of the rule itself. Thus Rule 412 is a "gatekeeping" provision and *if evidence of a victim's sexual predisposition or collateral sexual behavior is to gain admissibility, it must pass through (or around) the portals of Rule 412.* This means that the evidence must either fall outside the broad exclusionary ban of Rule 412[89] or it must fall within one of the enumerated exceptions. Before we turn to these exceptions, we should take up a procedural point.

Rule 412 has a procedural component, set out in subsection (c). The prescribed procedural process must be followed in both criminal and civil cases. The party who seeks to escape the general exclusionary rule of subsection (a) must file a written motion describing the evidence to be offered and its purpose. Thereafter, the court conducts an in camera hearing at which the proponent, the victim, and all parties may appear and advance their respective

---

87. "[W]e would not expect a person—regardless of whether she is sexually active—to claim falsely that a consensual sexual act in which she participated was actually a rape." Sherry F. Colb, *"Whodunit" Versus "What Was Done": When to Admit Character Evidence in Criminal Cases,* 79 N.C.L. Rev. 939, 974 (2001).

88. FRE 412 ACN.

89. The prohibition, as noted above, embraces V's "sexual behavior" as well as V's "sexual predisposition." FRE 412(a)(1), (2). It is clear that sexual behavior includes physical contact. However, there is authority holding that V's false accusations of sexual assault made against third persons does not involve sexual behavior and is thus outside the reach of the rape shield provision. *See* State v. Smith, 743 So.2d 199, 202–03 (La. 1999).

arguments. On the basis of the materials and arguments presented at this proceeding, the judge rules on the admissibility of the proffered evidence. "The motion, related papers, and the record of the hearing"[90] are thereafter sealed and, absent a court order of release, remain so. The general purposes of these required procedures are to facilitate an informed decision by the judge and to protect the victim from unwarranted public disclosures and innuendoes.

We turn now to the exceptions to the broad prohibition contained in Rule 412(a). These exceptions, set out in subsection (b) of Rule 412, are divided into two broad categories: criminal cases and civil cases. Note that the provisions of subsection (b) specify not only the *purposes* for which evidence of an alleged victim's sexual behavior or predispositions is admissible, but also the *particular type of evidence* that is allowed—that is, evidence of specific instances, but not reputation or opinion evidence. Subsection (b) also makes it clear that evidence is admissible only if it is permitted by that subsection *and* is also "otherwise admissible under these rules." For example, if evidence is not blocked by Rule 412, but nonetheless runs afoul of some other exclusionary rule, such as the hearsay rule or one of the rules governing privilege, it will be rejected. Furthermore, in a criminal case, Rule 403 will block evidence if its prejudicial effect, resulting jury confusion, or time consumption substantially outweigh its probative value. Rule 412(b)(2) prescribes a special balancing test in civil cases involving sexual misconduct; that test is described later.

In *criminal cases* there are three exceptions to the general exclusionary rule of Rule 412(a):

First, Rule 412(b)(1)(A) allows evidence of "specific instances of sexual behavior by the alleged victim" when the accused offers this evidence in an effort "to prove that a person other than the accused was the source of semen, injury or other physical evidence." For example, the accused might offer evidence of *V*'s sexual relations with a third person as the explanation for her pregnancy, venereal disease, or physical injuries such as bruises or fractures.

Second, Rule 412(b)(1)(B) allows "evidence of specific instances of sexual behavior by the alleged victim with respect to the person accused . . . offered by the accused to prove consent or by the prosecution." Collateral (uncharged) sexual encounters between the accused and the victim have more probative force than do sexual encounters between the victim and third persons. Note that "consent" is the only allowable purpose for which the accused may offer evidence of other sexual activity with the victim. In contrast, the prosecution can offer such evidence for any relevant purpose.

90. FRE 412(c)(2).

Suppose, for example, D is charged with sexually assaulting his stepdaughter, V. He denies the prosecution's allegation. The prosecution may be able to enter evidence of specific instances in which D sexually abused or assaulted V, even though these events are not charged in the state's indictment. For example, the prosecutor could argue that these collateral events show a plan or pattern of conduct, thus increasing the likelihood that D assaulted V on the day in question.[91] The task for the trial judge is to assess the probative value of the proffered evidence and to apply the counterweights to relevance (prejudice, jury confusion, and time consumption) set out in Federal Rule 403.

Third, Rule 412(b)(1)(C) allows any evidence, "the exclusion of which would violate the constitutional rights of the defendant." Since the Constitution would override any contrary statute or evidentiary rule, this provision is superfluous. Nonetheless, it may serve to remind trial judges that occasionally a rejection of the defendant's proffered evidence would violate the due process clause, the accused's right of confrontation, or some other constitutional provision.

The occasions when the exclusion of evidence would comport with the Federal Rules of Evidence, yet violate the constitutional rights of the accused, are infrequent. This comparative rarity is explained by the fact that the drafters of the Federal Rules were alert to the possible impact of constitutional principles on evidentiary rules, particularly in criminal cases. As a result, they crafted the Rules so as to minimize constitutional concerns.[92] Nonetheless, there are circumstances in which application of Rule 412 or other (state) versions of rape shield statutes may have such a restrictive effect on the accused's ability to defend himself that constitutional principles override the statutory prohibition that usually disallows evidence revealing the victim's sexual behavior.

ILLUSTRATIONS

(1) V testifies that D used false statements to lure her from a barroom and that he thereafter sexually assaulted her. Following this alleged sexual assault, D drove V to X's (her boyfriend's) home where she was permitted to leave the car. X testified that he observed V as she left D's car

---

91. FRE 413 and 414, as you will see, facilitate the introduction of the accused's collateral (uncharged) sexual behavior by making evidence of such behavior admissible for any relevant purpose—including propensity.

92. *See, e.g.,* FRE 201(g) (fact judicially noticed is not conclusive in criminal cases).

and that she immediately complained to *him* that *D* had raped her.

D's defense to charges of rape and forcible sodomy is consent. He also offers evidence that *V* and *X* were lovers and that *V* had fabricated the rape story in order to preserve her relationship with *X*, who grew suspicious when he observed *V* leaving *D*'s car. Additionally, *D* offers evidence that by the time his trial began, *V* and *X* were living together. *D*'s proffered evidence is excludable under Rule 412 and many state rape shield statutes *unless* the Constitution requires that *D*'s evidence be received.[93] How should the trial judge rule?

(2) Prosecution for attempted rape. *V* testifies that *D* knocked on her door and, after she invited him into her home, he became sexually aggressive. As *D* was forcibly removing *V*'s clothing, she was able to free herself and run (screaming) into a nearby room where relatives were sleeping.

D testifies that after a period of talking and sexual foreplay, he and *V* had consensual sex. He then offers to testify that while engaged in sexual intercourse, *D* had asked *V* whether she liked a particular sexual position, remarking that a mutual male acquaintance, *X*, had told *D* that she did. *D* then made a remark about *V* "switching partners." *V* thereupon angrily ordered *D* to get dressed and leave at once.[94]

At *D*'s trial, he offers the defense of consensual intercourse. How should the trial judge rule on the prosecutor's objection to *D*'s testimony concerning what he said to *V*?

In Illustration (1), the accused can successfully argue that rejection of his proffered evidence would violate his constitutional right to "confront" an adverse witness.[95] This right can be violated by a court's denial of *any* opportunity for the accused to cross-examine a witness against him; it can also be violated by a court's *undue restriction* of the accused's cross-examination of an adverse witness.[96] The prevailing argument in Illustration (1) is that *D* has

---

93. The facts in this Illustration are drawn from Olden v. Kentucky, 488 U.S. 227 (1988).

94. The facts in this Illustration are drawn from Stephens v. Miller, 13 F.3d 998 (7th Cir.) *(en banc), cert. denied*, 513 U.S. 808 (1994).

95. The Confrontation Clause is contained in U.S. Const. Amend. VI. There

is also an argument that the judge's restriction violated the Constitution's "due process" clause, contained in the Fourteenth Amendment. See *infra*, text at notes 96–100.

96. There are other features of the Confrontation Clause. *See* Ch. VIII.

a right to ask questions designed to reveal V's bias and motive to lie, both of which grow out of her past and current relationship with X.

It would be a mistake, however, to conclude that the Confrontation Clause (or any other constitutional provision) disallows all restrictions that inhibit an accused's ability to impeach the alleged victim's credibility. It appears that constitutional protection surrounds only evidence of those events or statements that bear a *close relationship* to the case being tried, such as evidence revealing V's bias or ulterior motive.[97] *General* attacks on V's credibility, assuming they reveal V's sexual behavior or sexual predisposition, fall within the *general* prohibition of Rule 412(a) and cannot escape by reason of constitutional interdiction.

Illustration (2) is a close case and the answer is uncertain. Certainly, the Constitution would accord to the accused the right to introduce evidence that he made remarks to V that angered her. Several Supreme Court decisions, taken together, support the general proposition that the Constitution guarantees to accused persons "a meaningful opportunity to present a complete defense."[98] This "meaningful opportunity" includes, of course, the accused's right to present witnesses and to testify himself. Suppose, however, the judge applies evidentiary rules that severely circumscribe the accused's testimony. In the case[99] on which Illustration (2) is based, the trial judge restricted D to testimony that "he had said something to ... [V] that angered her and caused her to fabricate the attempted rape charge."[100] Testimony about V's preferred sexual position as reported by X and about switching partners was excluded.

A closely divided federal appellate court, sitting en banc, found no constitutional violation. The majority opinion reveals a part of the trial transcript that perhaps influenced the appellate court: a defense witness admitted during cross-examination that, at the direction of D, he had given false testimony during direct examination. The witness had falsely testified that, on the night of the alleged offense, he did not drive D to V's home, as the prosecution alleged, but rather he drove D to a store in the vicinity of V's home. This fabrication, prompted by D, points strongly toward his guilt.

97. *See* Boggs v. Collins, 226 F.3d 728, 736–39 (6th Cir.), *cert. denied*, 532 U.S. 913 (2001) which contains a helpful discussion of the leading Supreme Court decisions.

98. Crane v. Kentucky, 476 U.S. 683, 690 (1986). The right to make a complete defense is usually traced to Chambers v. Mississippi, 410 U.S. 284 (1973), where the Court relied on the due process clause of the Fourteenth Amendment, and Washington v. Texas, 388 U.S. 14 (1967), where the Court relied on the compulsory process clause of the Sixth Amendment.

99. *See Stephens* 13 F.3d 998, *supra* note 94.

100. Id. at 1002.

(He suborned perjury to bolster his defense.) In any event, a bare majority of the Court of Appeals for the Seventh Circuit held that the trial judge's ruling was not arbitrary and that he had struck a fair balance between the defendant's constitutional right to tell his story and victim's statutory right to be shielded from invasions of privacy and public denigration. Still, there is likely to be a substantial difference (in jury impact) between vague and general testimony (allowed by the trial judge) that *D* said something to offend *V* and precise and detailed testimony (disallowed) revealing what *D* claims he said. As one dissenter put it, "[t]he judge required . . . [*D*] to convince the jury of the truth of his story without allowing him to reveal the fragments on which its plausibility turned."[101]

Rule 412: Civil Cases

Subsection (b)(2) of Federal Rule 412 applies to civil cases and governs the introduction of evidence bearing upon the "sexual behavior or sexual predisposition" of the alleged victim. Usually, but not always, *V* is the plaintiff. Protection against evidence revealing her sexual past is considerable, but not as stringent as that which she is afforded in criminal cases. Recall that one of the public policies underlying rape shield statutes in criminal cases is that of encouraging *V* to report a sexual assault to proper authorities. That policy is inapplicable in civil cases.

Although the principal feature of Rule 412(b)(2) is a balancing test, the proponent of evidence that discloses *V*'s sexual behavior or sexual predisposition faces imposing obstacles. First, as is generally true when evidence is admitted under Rule 412, that evidence must be admissible under any other evidentiary rule that might apply. Second, that evidence must surmount a special balancing test that is contained in, and specific to, Rule 412(b)(2). Under this special test governing civil cases, the *proponent* of the evidence must convince the judge that the probative value of the evidence of sexual behavior or predisposition *substantially outweighs* "the danger of harm to any victim and of unfair prejudice to any party." This is a different balancing test than the one of general application which favors admissibility and is contained in Federal Rule 403. Under Rule 403, evidence is admissible unless the *opponent* convinces the judge that its probative value is *substantially outweighed* by the counterweights of undue prejudice, jury distraction or confusion, or waste of time. Furthermore, as the Advisory Committee notes, the special balancing test of Rule 412(b)(2) puts "harm to the victim" on the scale in addition to prejudice to the parties.[102]

Another feature of Rule 412(b)(2) addresses the admissibility of reputation evidence that portrays the victim's sexual predisposi-

---

101. Id. at 1010.

102. FRE 412 ACN (1994 Amend.)

tion. Such evidence is inadmissible unless *V* opens the door by introducing her reputation—presumably one for a virtuous or chaste character. She might, for example, offer evidence of her "good" reputation as bearing on the issue of damages.[103]

New Principles of Admissibility: Special Rules in Cases of Sexual Assault or Child Molestation

Congress enacted Federal Rules 413 through 415 in 1995, bypassing the usual rulemaking process.[104] Building upon a line of cases that had shown increasing receptivity to the admission of evidence of collateral sexual misconduct similar to the charged sexual offense, Congress took bold—and many would say unprincipled—steps to facilitate the introduction of similar sexual offenses. The legislative history of Rules 413–15 reflects a congressional concern that "too often, crucial evidentiary information is thrown out at trial because of technical evidentiary rulings."[105] The "corrective" measures taken by Congress and embodied in Federal Rules 413–15, are far-reaching. Although we will examine these rules in detail, do not expect to find that they have been widely adopted by the states, for these rules remain highly controversial.

Under these Federal Rules, evidence of similar sexual offenses is admissible in both civil and criminal cases when specified sexual misconduct is alleged.

Rule 413(a) provides:

Evidence of Similar Crimes in Sexual Assault Cases

(a) In a criminal case in which the defendant is accused of an offense of sexual assault, evidence of the defendant's commission of another offense or offenses of sexual assault is admissible, and may be considered for its bearing on any matter to which it is relevant.

The rule goes on to require that the government must give timely notice to the accused of its intention to offer evidence of similar sexual offenses, including a disclosure of what evidence will be offered.[106] Note that Federal Rule 413, like its companion rules, 414 and 415, limits "other offense" evidence to sexual offenses of

---

103. Such evidence would not violate the general rule that evidence of character is inadmissible in civil cases. That rule of inadmissibility applies only if evidence of character is being used to prove conduct on a particular occasion. *See* supra Ch. III, § 3.6–1.

104. Pub. L. No. 103–322, 108 Stat. 2135–2137 (effective July 9, 1995).

105. 113 Cong. Rec. S15072–3 (1993) (statement of Senator Dole).

106. FRE 413(b).

the same type as the charged offense. Since Rule 413 addresses only *sexual assault* prosecutions, it lets in only evidence of other *sexual assault* crimes. The rule would not, for example, allow evidence of a prior sexual assault committed by one who was being prosecuted for homicide or armed robbery. Similarly, the rule would not allow evidence of dissimilar offenses (such as a criminal battery) in a prosecution for sexual assault. The issue of admissibility in these settings continues to be governed by Rule 404(b) or, in the case of impeachment, by Rules 608 and 609. Sexual assault is, however, broadly defined in Rule 413(d) and includes any nonconsensual sexual contact between the defendant and the victim, any violent act toward the victim from which the defendant derived sexual pleasure or gratification, and any attempt or conspiracy to engage in this prohibited sexual behavior.

What is most striking about Rule 413 (and the companion Rule 414 dealing with child molestation) is its nullification of the established evidentiary principle that an accused should be shielded from the prosecution's use of character or propensity evidence. In the words of Rule 404(b), which embodies that longstanding principle, "[e]vidence of other crimes, wrongs, or acts is not admissible to prove the character of a person in order to show action in conformity therewith." Rule 413(a), in contrast, allows evidence of a collateral sexual assault "for its bearing on any matter to which it is relevant," including propensity. Recall, also, that the alleged victim of the sexual assault being prosecuted is given substantial protection under Rule 412 against evidence disclosing her sexual behavior or predisposition.

Rule 413 is subject to other evidentiary rules that would deny or qualify admissibility, of which the most notable is the now familiar Rule 403.[107] Thus, the trial judge has some discretion in deciding whether the probative value of the other sexual assault(s) is substantially outweighed by undue prejudice or other counterweights, such as jury confusion or time consumption. Many factors, such as the similarity of the collateral sexual assault(s) to the charged offense, the recency and the other offense(s), the number of collateral offenses, the strength of the evidence supporting the collateral offense(s), and whether there was an acquittal of the other offense(s), should bear on the trial judge's Rule 403 determination.

It appears that the jury and not the judge will decide whether or not an alleged collateral assault actually took place. That is, the judge will treat evidence of the other sexual assault under the usual approach to issues of conditional relevance;[108] he will thus limit his

107. *See* supra Ch. III, § 3.2.
108. *See* supra Ch. III, § 3.4.

role to screening evidence of the collateral sexual assault in order to ensure that there is sufficient evidence of its existence to allow a reasonable jury to conclude (by a preponderance of the evidence) that it did occur.[109] This is the approach that is taken with regard to "other-crimes" evidence under Rule 404(b).[110] The dispositive case under Rule 404(b) is Huddleston v. United States.[111]

Professors Christopher Mueller and Laird Kirkpatrick point out, however, that although *Huddleston* may be controlling because it

> deals with a closely analogous situation ... the present [Rule 413] situation is different in one important respect: Here the jury is actually *allowed* to draw the otherwise-forbidden character inference, so the risk of unfair prejudice is even higher, and there is even more reason to insist on certainty in admitting the proof. Greater judicial involvement in passing on preliminary questions is amply warranted, and this fact alone would justify the court in treating such issues as affecting admissibility under FRE 104(a).[112]

Recall that Federal Rule 104(a) addresses "preliminary questions [of fact] concerning the qualification of a person to be a witness, the existence of a privilege, or the admissibility of evidence," and places fact-finding responsibility in the trial judge.

Federal Rule 414, which applies to cases of child molestation, parallels Rule 413 in its general content and structure. It provides in subsection (a):

Evidence of Similar Crimes in Child Molestation Cases

> (a) In a criminal case in which the defendant is accused of an offense of child molestation, evidence of the defendant's commission of another offense or offenses of child molestation is admissible, and may be considered for its bearing on any matter to which it is relevant.

Note the "similarity" requirement: in prosecutions for child molestation, the ostensibly admissible other crimes or collateral offense evidence is limited to incidents of child molestation. The other subdivisions of Rule 414 generally track their Rule 413

---

109. Johnson v. Elk Lake School District, 283 F.3d 138 (3d Cir. 2002) (holding that under Rule 415, dealing with civil cases of sexual misconduct, judge's role is to screen evidence for sufficiency).

110. *See* supra Ch. III, § 3.6–4.

111. 485 U.S. 681 (1988).

112. 2 MUELLER & KIRKPATRICK, FEDERAL EVIDENCE § 162, at 55 (2d ed., Supp. 2005).

counterparts. For example, Rule 414(b) provides for the government's notice and disclosure of evidence of other offenses of child molestation that it intends to proffer. It will thus be seen that in most respects Rule 414 is the mirror image of Rule 413; the major difference is that Rule 413 applies to a charge of sexual assault, whereas Rule 414 applies to a charge of child molestation. Even the definition of child molestation, set out in Rule 414(d), generally tracks its counterpart in Rule 413(d), but is restricted to sexual assaults directed toward persons "below the age of fourteen."

Civil Cases Involving a Sexual Assault or Child Molestation

Rule 413 and 414 coalesce in Rule 415 which addresses the admissibility of evidence of other offenses of sexual assault and child molestation in civil cases. Rule 415(a) provides:

Evidence of Similar Acts in Civil Cases Concerning Sexual Assault or Child Molestation

(a) In a civil case in which a claim for damages or other relief is predicated on a party's alleged commission of conduct constituting an offense of sexual assault or child molestation, evidence of that party's commission of another offense or offenses of sexual assault or child molestation is admissible and may be considered as provided in Rule 413 and Rule 414 of these rules.

Rule 415(b) contains the "notice and disclosure" provisions found in subsection (b) of Rules 413 and 414. As you will now anticipate, other rules of evidence may deny or qualify the admissibility of evidence within the ambit of Rule 415. As we have elsewhere observed,[113] character evidence is almost always disallowed in civil cases, except where it is an "essential element of a charge, claim, or defense."[114] Under Rule 415, however, evidence of other acts of sexual assault or child molestation of the same type alleged in the civil case come into evidence as bearing on the conduct in question. In essence, this is using evidence of other acts to prove a character trait or predisposition and ultimately to prove the sexual misconduct in question. This line of proof appears to be a one way street: unless the party charged with sexual misconduct in the civil suit (usually the defendant) can counterclaim and allege the opposing party's sexual misconduct (so as to bring the counterclaimant's claim within Rule 415), he would not be allowed to prove that party's character. Furthermore, since that party, let us say the

---

113. *See* supra Ch. III, § 3.6.

114. FRE 405(b).

plaintiff, is alleging she is a victim, Rule 412's application to civil suits calls upon the judge to apply Rule 412(b)(2)'s special balancing test that favors inadmissibility.[115] These and other difficulties with Rule 415 may take some years to resolve fully.

115. *See* supra Ch. III, § 3.6–7.

Chapter IV

RELEVANCE: SPECIAL APPLICATIONS DRIVEN BY SOCIAL POLICY

Table of Sections

§ 4.1　In General

In this chapter, we continue our examination of special relevance rules, that is, determinate rules of relevance that yield solutions to recurring patterns of evidentiary issues. In the preceding chapter, such fixed rules responded primarily to considerations of whether or not the probative value of the evidence in question was overcome by factors such as prejudice, jury confusion or distraction, or misuse (waste) of trial time. Some of these same factors surface in connection with the evidentiary rules under consideration in this chapter.

The unifying theme in this chapter, however, is that social or public policy play an important, often dominant, role in resolving the issue of admissibility. In other words, a significant and often principal goal of the evidentiary rules examined here is to avoid discouraging socially beneficial behavior. This goal is presumably accomplished by excluding evidence that is offered for the *forbidden purposes specified* in the various rules we will encounter.[1] Generally speaking, however, the same evidence offered for another purpose— one that is not forbidden—usually falls outside the exclusionary ban and is admissible unless barred by some other evidentiary rule

---

1. As you will see, there are questions regarding whether or not some of these exclusionary rules actually affect the behavior of the individuals who are their beneficiaries.

or principle. Often, a critical issue in deciding whether evidence is admissible for some permissible purpose is whether or not the parties have a genuine dispute about the permissible proposition for which the evidence is ostensibly offered.

Suppose, for example, a rule states[2] that evidence that a party took precautionary steps following an accident or injury is inadmissible to prove *that the party was negligent* in not taking such steps prior to the harmful event. Aware of this exclusionary rule, the plaintiff's lawyer offers evidence that following an accident in the defendant's machine shop, the defendant added safety devices designed to reduce or eliminate the occurrence of similar accidents. In making his offer of proof, the plaintiff's lawyer states that evidence of the newly installed safety devices is not offered for the purpose of proving the defendant's negligence, but rather for the limited purpose of showing that safer machines were feasible. If the defendant has never contested the proposition that it was feasible to make his machines safer, the judge will reject the plaintiff's evidence. The protective rule of exclusion would be emasculated or negated if a party could successfully avoid it by offering the forbidden evidence for a "different" purpose that was not even contested.

§ 4.2   Subsequent Remedial Measures

Federal Rule 407 addresses evidence of remedial measures taken after an event that has caused harm or injury. Such measures take a variety of forms such as repairs, design changes, new or amended safety regulations, warnings to users, product recalls, new or amended instructions, disciplinary action against the employee causing the harm, closing the particular geographic area which was the site of injury, and so forth. The policy-based assumption underlying Rule 407 is that admitting evidence of subsequent remedial measures would discourage potential defendants from taking precautions that are in the public interest.

It is no doubt true that some persons taking remedial steps after an injurious event are unaware of the principle embodied in Rule 407 or its state counterpart. Ignorance of this evidentiary principle by some actors, however, is not necessarily a fatal objection; other actors (especially business enterprises) are aware of the principle embodied in Rule 407. Furthermore public policy might be served by protecting responsible actors from adverse evidence even if they acted without an awareness of this evidentiary protection.

Rule 407 also draws support from the weak probative force of evidence of post-accident remedial measures. The proponent of remedial-measure evidence is attempting to raise the inference that

2. *See* FRE 407, discussed in § 4.2.

subsequent remedial steps were taken because the actor thought the prior condition was hazardous or harmful; therefore (the further inference goes), it is more likely that it was. Note, however, that the potential defendant who takes precautionary measures after an injury-causing event is usually acting on the basis of new information. Put otherwise, "the rule [barring evidence of remedial steps] rejects the notion that 'because the world gets wiser as it gets older, therefore it was stupid before.' "[3] There also exists the possibility that the person taking remedial steps was exercising extraordinary caution to avoid any possibility of future injuries and did not believe that the prior condition was a dangerous one.

Observe carefully the text of Federal Rule 407. It reads:

Subsequent Remedial Measures

When after an injury or harm allegedly caused by an event, measures are taken that, if taken previously, would have made the injury or harm less likely to occur, evidence of the subsequent measures is not admissible to prove negligence, culpable conduct, a defect in a product, a defect in a product's design, or a need for a warning or instruction. This rule does not require the exclusion of evidence of subsequent measures when offered for another purpose, such as proving ownership, control, or feasibility of precautionary measures, if controverted, or impeachment.

The rule states the purposes, such as proving negligence or a defect in a product or its design,[4] for which evidence of subsequent remedial measure is not admissible. But it goes on to say that such evidence may be admissible if offered for other purposes. This structure is typical of most of the various "public policy" rules that are the subject of this chapter. The intention of the drafters of Rule 407 and kindred rules is to foreclose specified evidence (such as

---

3. Rule 407 ACN quoting Baron Bramwell's statement in Hart v. Lancashire & Yorkshire Ry. Co. 21 L.T.R.N.S. 261, 263 (1869).

4. As currently written, Rule 407 (amended in 1997) expressly prohibits evidence of subsequent remedial measures in order to prove the defendant's product was defective. Some state jurisdictions allow remedial measures in product liability cases. The theory is that the manufacturer has such strong incentives to correct defects and contain or prevent injuries by product modifications, warnings, recalls, and the like, that a rule that blocks evidence of post-accident remedial measures is not needed. This justification is questionable. It is not always clear to the manufacturer that its product was at fault and that it needs to guard against future incidents by taking remedial steps. It is clear (in states that do not apply Rule 407 to product liability cases) that such steps could and probably will be used as adverse evidence in litigation. Thus, in close cases, the admissibility of evidence of subsequent remedial measures might be an important consideration.

remedial measures) if offered for particular, forbidden purposes (such as proving negligence), while leaving open the possibility that the specified evidence might be admissible if offered to prove other propositions in the case. Of course, evidence offered for permissible purposes may encounter other evidentiary rules that foreclose admissibility; nonetheless, the first concern of the proponent is *purpose*.

Construing Rule 407

Rule 407 speaks of taking remedial measures after the "event" causing harm or injury. Remedial or precautionary measures taken prior to the injury causing event are outside the protection of the rule.

ILLUSTRATION

Suppose that in year *one* the defendant company (*D*) manufactures and sells a new model in its line of electric circular hand-saws. In year *two* company officials learn that under certain unusual conditions, the axle bolt that secures the circular saw blade can break, causing the blade to dislodge and, sometimes, to be propelled through the air. To eliminate this hazard, the defendant begins using axle bolts made of more durable metal, coupled with a specifically designed washer that reduces the tension on the axle bolt. In year *three* the plaintiff (*P*) is injured when the circular blade on his saw (manufactured by *D* and purchased by *P* in year *one*) dislodges, takes a downward course, and inflicts serious injuries to *P*'s knee and lower leg.

At trial *D* claims that his product is safe and that *P*'s injury was occasioned by his misuse of the saw. *P* responds by offering evidence that *D*'s product was defective and that *D* made design and material modifications to eliminate the defect. Should the trial judge exclude the evidence under Rule 407? Would the judge rule differently if *P*'s injury from the saw occurred in year *one*?

The key phrase in Rule 407 speaks of remedial measures taken "after an injury or harm allegedly caused by an event." The "event" is the occasion, occurrence, or mishap that is the immediate cause of the harm or injury.[5] Here the defendant made remedial changes in year *two*, but the event immediately causing the harm occurred later in year *three*. Thus, Rule 407 does not bar the proffered evidence. The practical effect of this limiting feature of

---

5. FRE 407 ACN to the 1997 amendment.

Rule 407 is to increase the pressure on persons and enterprises taking remedial measures to embrace within those measures the protection of persons, such as prior purchasers, who have exposure to a potential harm or injury that has not yet materialized. Of course, with respect to the judge's second ruling, had the plaintiff sustained his injuries in year *one*, the defendant's remedial measures, taken in year *two*, would have been within Rule 407's protective ambit and evidence of *D*'s remedial measures would have been excluded.

Guided by the policy underpinning of Rule 407, courts have held that remedial measures taken not by the defendant but by a third party are not protected from evidentiary exposure. When a third party takes remedial action, evidentiary disclosure does not harm him (he—the actor—is not the defendant). Put otherwise, disclosure of the remedial measures does not exact a penalty from the one who took the socially responsible action that the defendant failed to take. Of course, cases of third-party remedial interventions are infrequent. But suppose, for example, there is a bicycle accident on a riding trail owned by *X* city. Subsequently, members of a private bicycle club post a warning sign, "Steep Rough Grade. Walking Advised." In a suit against *X* city filed by the injured bicyclist, evidence of the warning sign would not be banned by Rule 407,[6] although other exclusionary rules might apply.

The Principal Escapes From Rule 407: Ownership, Control, Feasibility, and Impeachment

Rule 407 states explicitly that its exclusionary ban applies only when evidence of post-accident remedial measures is offered, essentially, to prove fault in the defendant's conduct or product. Other purposes for which evidence of such measures might be offered, "such as proving ownership, control, or feasibility of precautionary measures, *if controverted*, or impeachment"[7] are not within Rule 407's proscription. Although the enumeration in Rule 407 of the purposes that fall outside its exclusionary ban is illustrative only, the bulk of case law addressing excepted purposes has focused on the ones enumerated in Rule 407,[8] especially the troublesome "feasibility" purpose.

6. *See* Pau v. Yosemite Park & Curry Co., 928 F.2d 880, 887–88 (9th Cir. 1991).

7. FRE 407 (emphasis supplied).

8. One unenumerated purpose (supporting the introduction of "remedial" evidence) that has found approval in the cases is rebutting the defendant's claim that the plaintiff was contributorily negligent. Suppose, for example, the defen-dant asserts that the plaintiff contribut-ed to her injury for the reason that the danger about which the plaintiff com-plains would have been apparent to a reasonable person. The defendant's im-plementation of a subsequent remedial measure (taken after the plaintiff's inju-ry) weakens this assertion. *See* Mueller & Kirkpatrick, Evidence § 4.24, at 240 (3rd ed. 2003).

The first thing to note is that three out of the four illustrative purposes do not escape the exclusionary ban of Rule 407 unless "controverted" by the parties. If the existence of a dispute or controversy were not required, it would be relatively easy for the proponent of the remedial evidence to offer it as bearing on some permissible purpose such as the feasibility of improving the product in question or making the premises in question safer. Of course, it is often a close question whether defendant's pleadings and evidence actually controvert "ownership, control, or feasibility of precautionary measures...."[9]

Ownership and Control

Sometimes an issue arises over whether or not the defendant owns or controls the premises, product, instrumentality, or process alleged to have injured the plaintiff. Suppose, for example, in a suit against a highway contractor for failing to erect warning signs at a road construction site, a dispute arises as to whether the contractor or the highway department controlled the portion of the road where an accident occurred. The plaintiff could introduce evidence that after the accident, the contractor erected warning signs.[10] The purpose of the evidence would, of course, be limited to proving that the contractor had control over the locus. Similarly, a remedial measure such as a post-accident repair to the structure where an accident occurred has probative value in resolving a dispute about ownership of the structure.

Feasibility of Precautionary Measures

The purpose most frequently invoked by litigators to elude the prohibition of Rule 407 is "feasibility of precautionary measures."[11] The issue most often faced by the trial judge is whether "feasibility" is "controverted" as required by Rule 407. The difficulty begins with the meaning of "feasibility," or in its adjectival form, "feasible."

To say that something, such as a particular design or an added safety device, is not feasible often means that the actor (decision maker) simply took due account of constraints such as the current state of technology, the cost, the availability of materials or labor, anticipated delays, and so forth. The change or modification under consideration might be possible, but taking all factors into account, it is not practical. On the other hand, to say something is not feasible may mean, as one court put it, that it is not "physically, technologically, or economically possible."[12] It sometimes happens,

---

9. FRE 407.

10. *See* Powers v. J. B. Michael & Co., 329 F.2d 674, 677 (6th Cir. 1964).

11. FRE 407.

12. Tuer v. McDonald, 347 Md. 507, 701 A.2d 1101, 1109–11 (1997) (discussing divergent approaches to what is meant by "feasible.")

of course, that a remedial measure that was taken subsequent to the litigated event was not possible (in the latter sense just noted) at an earlier time—for example, when the product or medical procedure causing the injury was first manufactured or instituted. If a defendant asserts, for example, that a safer design was not possible at this earlier time, the issue is joined. The plaintiff will try to show that the post-accident remedial measure or at least an equivalent measure was possible at the earlier date.

Often, however, a given design, production process, security measure, medical protocol, or other feature under consideration involves a trade-off in which the ideal product or procedure is compromised because of constraints such as costs, availability of labor, or other practicalities. In other words, a person—for example, the defendant—weighs all the factors, including hazards, risks, and costs, and settles on the course of action he believes is preferable.

ILLUSTRATION

The defendants, Carl and his wife, Janet, own and operate a motel in a small town. Prior to opening their business, they consult the village police chief about security measures.[13] The police chief recommends additional lighting (which the owners install), but declines to suggest the installation of peep holes and chain locks on the entry door to each room. Since each room has a six-foot picture window adjacent to a solid entry door and standard (Triple A) door locks, the police chief advises the owners that additional security devices are unnecessary.

Subsequently, plaintiff's, Husband and Wife, check into the defendant's motel. During Husband's brief absence, Stranger knocks on the plaintiffs' door; Wife responds by opening it, whereupon Stranger enters the room and rapes her. Eventually Husband and Wife sue Carl and Janet, claiming that the defendants breached their warranty to provide safe lodging and were negligent in failing to provide the plaintiffs with a room that was reasonably safe.

At trial, Carl testifies during cross-examination that since the picture window in each motel room afforded a view of the area outside the entry door, the installation of safety chains and peep holes was "unnecessary" and would

---

13. The facts in this case are based on those in Anderson v. Malloy, 700   F.2d 1208 (8th Cir. 1983).

have "provided false security." The trial judge thereafter rules that the plaintiffs' proffered evidence that following the rape of Wife, the defendants installed safety chains and peep holes was inadmissible under FRE 407. At the conclusion of the trial, the defense lawyer, in his closing argument, asserts that in following the advice of the police chief, the defendants had done all they "could or should have done." He then asks rhetorically, "What more can they do?"[14]

Did the trial judge err in rejecting the plaintiff's evidence of the defendants' subsequent remedial measures?

A defendant can always protect himself from evidence of subsequent precautionary measures bearing on feasibility by stipulating that other arrangements, designs, or protocols were feasible.[15] Most courts, however, hold that even without such a stipulation, a defendant can present evidence that his product, procedure, or process comported with reasonable safety measures without thereby "controverting" feasibility. In the Illustration above, had the defendants simply asserted that they had consulted the police chief, followed his advice, and concluded at that time that room security was reasonably safe, they would not have "controverted" feasibility. However, Carl testified, in essence, that the addition of peep holes and safety chains would have been redundant, of no utility, and would have amounted to "false security."

In the case on which this Illustration is based, a divided panel of the Eighth Circuit Court of Appeals held that the trial judge abused his discretion when he rejected evidence of the defendants' subsequent precautionary measures. The court declared that " 'feasible' means not only 'possible,' but also means 'capable of being ... utilized, or dealt with successfully.' "[16] The Court's majority held that the defendants' evidence controverted feasibility because the defendants contended, in essence, that peep holes and safety chains could not have been successfully employed. The subsequent installation of these devices indicated not only the utility (feasibility) of these additional precautionary measures, but also served to impeach Carl's testimony which stated, in essence, that he and Janet had "done everything necessary for a secure

---

14. Id. at 1214.

15. A few courts have taken the dubious position that a stipulation is essential in order to render evidence of subsequent precautions inadmissible. See, e.g., Herndon v. Seven Bar Flying Service,

Inc., 716 F.2d 1322, 1329 (10th Cir. 1983), cert. denied, 466 U.S. 958.

16. Anderson, 700 F.2d at 1213 (quoting from Webster's Third New International Dictionary).

motel, and that chain locks and peep holes would not be success-ful. . . ."[17]

Impeachment

Rule 407 lists impeachment as one of the illustrative purposes for which evidence of subsequent measures is admissible. The key to admissibility is a showing that the testimony of a witness (typically the defendant) is contradicted by a subsequent remedial measure that he, himself, ordered or implemented. Note that the "if controverted" requirement of Rule 407 applies to evidence of subsequent precautionary measures introduced to show ownership, control, or feasibility; the requirement does not, however, apply to evidence of such measures introduced to impeach a witness. The application of the "if controverted" requirement to impeachment would be superfluous: a witness's credibility is always implicitly an issue. Observe that impeachment sometimes overlaps with feasibili-ty, as the last Illustration demonstrates. To give a further example, if the defendant testified that his product design was the "safest possible," evidence of a subsequent safety modification that was available when the initial product design was chosen bears on both feasibility and credibility.

Professors Mueller and Kirkpatrick summarize the case law bearing on evidence of subsequent remedial measures to impeach a witness, by observing:

> Impeachment may be allowed if the witness denies the existence of a particular hazard, testifies that the product was as safe as it could be, or characterizes an alternative design or protective measure subsequently adopted as unnecessary, inef-fectual, or otherwise inadmissible.[18]

§ 4.3   Compromise and Offers to Compromise

The importance of the evidentiary rule encouraging compro-mises lies in the fact that the vast majority of lawsuits filed are settled prior to trial. Were it not for the frequency of settlements, our judicial systems would have to be revamped in order to accom-modate the large increase in trial activity. Quite aside from the effect of settlements on caseloads and public expenditures, the private resolution of disputes is generally more desirable than one forced upon the parties through the imposition of state authority.

Suppose that Plato sues Descartes for $100,000, claiming pla-giarism. Descartes offers to settle the suit for $75,000, but Plato

---

17.   Id. at 1214.

18.   MUELLER & KIRKPATRICK, EVIDENCE § 4–24, at 239–40. Of course, other ex-clusionary rules might apply. Note espe-cially FRE 403 which calls for balancing probative value against such factors as prejudice and jury confusion. Id. at 240. *See also* Ch. III, § 3.2.

declines the offer. At trial Plato offers testimony and documents that detail Descartes' rebuffed offer. Because of the substantial amount of the offer, it has probative value to indicate that Descartes thought his defense to Plato's claim was weak. In other words, the evidence of the offer is relevant. Contrast the foregoing offer with an offer by Descartes of $500 to settle the case. Here, probative value pointing toward Descartes' liability is weak to nonexistent. The sum offered is such a small percentage of the damage claimed that the most plausible inference is that Descartes simply wanted to avoid the time and expense necessary to defend against Plato's claim. Now suppose Descartes offered a settlement of $25,000. Here a reasonable jury might draw the inference that Descartes thought he might incur significant liability—in other words, that Descartes had concluded that there was some risk in going to trial. On the other hand, Descartes might have had other reasons for making a settlement offer. Perhaps negative publicity was affecting the sales or general acceptance of his book that, you will recall, Plato claims contains plagiaristic materials.

You can see that, generally speaking, probative value increases or decreases in proportion to the amount of the settlement offer. However, other factors, such a negative publicity, may influence a party's "settlement behavior." The most efficient and easily administered means of using an evidentiary rule to encourage offers of compromise is to fashion a rule that disregards the amount of the offer and simply declares that evidence of an offer of compromise is inadmissible:

(a) If made by the plaintiff, to show that his claim is weak;

(b) If made by the defendant, to show that his defense is weak.

With this brief introduction in mind, examine carefully the text of Rule 408:

Compromise and Offers to Compromise

Evidence of (1) furnishing or offering or promising to furnish, or (2) accepting or offering or promising to accept, a valuable consideration in compromising or attempting to compromise a claim which was disputed as to either validity or amount, is not admissible to prove liability for or invalidity of the claim or its amount. Evidence of conduct or statements made in compromise negotiations is likewise not admissible. This rule does not require the exclusion of any evidence otherwise discoverable merely because it is presented in the course of compromise negotiations. This rule also does not require exclusion when the evidence is offered for another purpose, such as proving bias or prejudice of a witness, negativing a contention of undue delay, or proving an effort to obstruct a criminal investigation or prosecution.

Rule 408 has a number of noteworthy features. First, the rule protects not only offers of compromise, but also compromises that were agreed to but not implemented. The rule also includes settlement activity between a party and a third person.[19] Second, the rule protects evidence of "conduct or statements made in compromise negotiations," thereby making it unnecessary for a negotiating party to constantly resort to such protective statements as "assuming arguendo my client was speeding ...," or alternatively, employing such prefatory remarks as "without prejudice" or "hypothetically speaking." Prior to the widespread adoption of the Federal Rules of Evidence, lawyers routinely used these cautionary phrases during negotiations in order to avoid making an inadvertent statement of "fact" that could be used against their clients should there be a trial. Federal Rule 408 renders unnecessary these awkward precautionary remarks by protecting statements made during "compromise negotiations" whether or not they are couched in hypothetical terms.

A third noteworthy point about the text of Rule 408 is that it protects only statements or conduct made in an effort to compromise a claim that is "disputed as to either validity or amount." For example, suppose the plaintiff sues the defendant for $5,000, alleging that the latter negligently failed to put a railing on a stairwell. During compromise negotiations the defendant's lawyer admits that his client's failure to erect a railing violated the applicable safety code. Even if such a violation were negligence per se, the lawyer's statement is nonetheless protected if he disputed the amount of damages to which the plaintiff was entitled. However, should the plaintiff's lawyer acknowledge that his client was negligent and also admit that the plaintiff has suffered at least $5,000 in damages as a result of the stairwell accident, this statement, as well as an offer to settle for, say, $3,000, would be outside the evidentiary protection of Rule 408. The policy underlying Rule 408—to encourage the resolution of disputes—is not served by protecting a party who simply refuses to satisfy a claim that he acknowledges is valid. Of course, if there were other grounds, such as contributory negligence, on which the defendant disputed plaintiff's claim, Rule 408's protection would apply.

19. Suppose, for example, A, B, and C are involved in a three car automobile accident. In the A v. B suit, A offers evidence that B paid C $30,000 to settle C's claim. Rule 408 applies to protect the compromise.

Purposes for Which Evidence of Compromise
is Not Forbidden by Rule 408

First, observe that Rule 408 expressly thwarts a tactic designed to bring material *within the exclusionary protection of the rule.* Suppose a party or a party's attorney holds evidence that she knows is discoverable by her opponent. In order to protect this evidence from disclosure, she presents it during compromise negotiations. This stratagem will fail under the provision of Rule 408 that deprives the rule's evidentiary protection to "any evidence otherwise discoverable merely because it is presented in the course of compromise negotiations."

Next, note the final sentence of Rule 408 contains a familiar theme: the protective provisions of the rule do not apply when evidence concerning a compromise is offered for purposes other than to show that a claim or defense is weak. The rule gives some illustrations, "such as proving bias or prejudice of a witness, negativing a contention of undue delay, or proving an effort to obstruct a criminal investigation or prosecution." Suppose, for example, *P* sues *A*, a truck driver, and *B*, the truck company. Prior to trial, *P* and *A* settle *P*'s claim against *A*, and *A* agrees to testify for *P* in his trial against *B*. After *A* testifies, *B* could disclose *A*'s possible bias by introducing evidence of his (*A*'s) compromise with *P*.

ILLUSTRATION

Following American Creditcard's termination of its contract with Universal Creditcard, Universal sues American for breach of contract.[20] American's defense against Universal's claim of contract breach is that the plaintiff, Universal, had failed to comply with the contract in question and should be denied a recovery. In particular, American asserts that Universal breached their agreement by steering its (Universal's) customers to American's competitors through a process called "rolling over accounts." Universal's position was that the rollovers occurred only after Universal thought it had reached a settlement agreement with American under which the rollovers to other banks were permitted. (The settlement under which Universal claimed it was acting was never finalized.) After the settlement was abandoned and litigation was resumed,

---

20. The facts in this Illustration are based on those in Bankcard America, Inc. v. Universal Bancard Systems, Inc., 203 F.3d 477 (7th Cir.), *cert. denied*, 531 U.S. 877 (2000).

Universal stopped rolling over accounts to American's competitors.

When, at trial, Universal's president starts to testify about the tentative agreement under which his bank engaged for a period of time in rollovers, American objects, citing Rule 408. How should the trial judge rule?

Universal offered evidence of the failed compromise for the purpose of explaining why it rolled over accounts in an apparent violation of the contract between Universal and American which American, the defendant, terminated. It was this termination, of course, which led to Universal's claim that American had breached their contract, which in turn led to American's claim that Universal should be denied a recovery because it had violated their contractual provisions through its rollover practices. When this lawsuit appeared to have been settled, Universal began to shift accounts to other banks as it thought it was entitled to do under the terms of the compromise. It would be unfair to allow American to cite Universal's rollover practice as the reason for denying Universal's breach of contract claim, while at the same time allowing American to foreclose "compromise" evidence that explained and perhaps justified the practice. From a policy standpoint, settlements are not encouraged when one party uses settlement discussions to lead his opponent into a contractual breach, and then uses the breach to escape liability.[21]

§ 4.4 Payment of Medical Expenses

Suppose that at the annual Spartan Township Memorial Day Picnic, there is always a "fathers against sons" softball game. When Phil attempts to steal second base, he collides with the second baseman, Drew, and sustains serious head injuries. Drew, who is clearly upset, declares "I'm so sorry. It was all my fault and I want to pay your medical bills."

Subsequently, Phil sues Drew, alleging negligence. Drew, who has had several months to think further about how the accident happened, denies negligence and asserts Phil's contributory negligence.

As you would anticipate, Phil wants to offer testimony that reveals what Drew said after the two collided. Drew's statement is clearly relevant and it would normally be considered a "party admission" and thus admissible against him. Note that Rule 409 states that "evidence of furnishing or offering or promising to pay medical ... expenses occasioned by an injury is not admissible to prove liability...." This provision renders inadmissible at least

21. Id. at 484.

that portion of Drew's statement relating to his desire to pay Phil's medical bills. The exclusion of this evidence serves the policy objective of not penalizing one who engages in humane acts. However, Rule 409 does not protect collateral statements made in conjunction with offers to pay medical bills. Thus, that portion of Phil's statement relating to fault gains no protection from Rule 409; neither does it gain any protection from Rule 408 because, at the time of Drew's statement, Phil and Drew were not compromising a "claim ... disputed as to either validity or amount."[22]

Of course, had Phil and Drew actually been in settlement negotiations, Rule 408 would have protected all "statements made in compromise negotiations...."[23] This broader protection is necessary in the extended give and take of settlement negotiations. But such protection is unnecessary under Rule 409. Professor George Fisher makes the following observation:[24]

> Consider the position of the average driver involved in an accident. She is probably not a lawyer and may not be thinking ahead to how her words could be used against her at trial. She is in any event probably unaware of Rule 409.... So a more protective rule—one that excluded her ... [collateral remarks]—would have little impact on whether she ... [made these remarks]. Any excess protection offered by the rule therefore comes as a windfall to her....

§ 4.5 Pleas and Related Statements

Federal Rule 410, which applies to pleas and the plea-bargaining process in criminal cases, bears a relationship to Federal Rule 408, which applies to the compromise process in civil cases. Both rules facilitate the voluntary resolution of disputes by the adverse parties. Rule 410 addresses withdrawn guilty pleas and pleas of nolo contendere; the rule also addresses statements made at plea hearings or proceedings and statements during the course of plea discussions between defendant (often speaking through his counsel) and the attorney for the prosecution. In the absence of these protections, the process of plea discussions and negotiations would be hampered by a lack of candor. Furthermore, unfair practices would probably develop as, for example, when the prosecutor produced evidence at a criminal trial that the defendant offered to plead guilty to a lesser offense. The jury might view evidence that the defendant was prepared to enter a guilty plea to a lesser offense as a convincing indication that he was guilty of the crime charged. However, as Professors Lempert, Gross, and Liebman point out:

---

22. FRE 408.
23. Id.

24. George Fisher, Evidence 105 (2002).

[M]any factors ... might lead an innocent defendant to offer a plea to a lesser charge: she might be unable to make bail while waiting for trial, and the likely sentence on the lesser charge might be less than the expected period of pretrial detention; the likely penalty if convicted on the greater charge might be so severe that she does not wish to take the risk; or she might have been advised that the trial will come down to her word against a police officer's, and that in such circumstances juries usually convict.[25]

When you examine Rule 410, which is reproduced below, note carefully its structure, which contrasts with that of the other policy-based rules we have studied. Heretofore, these "policy" rules have singled out a purpose or two for which specified evidence is not admissible. However, the specified evidence may be admissible if offered for some other purpose. For example, evidence of remedial measures taken after an injury-causing event cannot be introduced to prove negligence, but it can be used for other purposes, such as impeachment. However, Rule 410 provides:

Inadmissibility of Pleas, Pleas Discussions, and Related Statements

Except as otherwise provided in this rule, evidence of the following is not, in any civil or criminal proceeding, admissible against the defendant who made the plea or was a participant in the plea discussions:

    (1) a plea of guilty which was later withdrawn;

    (2) a plea of nolo contendere;

    (3) any statement made in the course of any proceedings under Rule 11 of the Federal Rules of Criminal Procedure or comparable state procedure regarding either of the foregoing pleas; or

    (4) any statement made in the course of plea discussions with an attorney for the prosecuting authority which do not result in a plea of guilty or which result in a plea of guilty later withdrawn.

However, such a statement is admissible (i) in any proceeding wherein another statement made in the course of the same plea or plea discussions has been introduced and the statement ought in fairness be considered contemporaneously with it, or (ii) in a criminal proceeding for

---

25. Richard Lempert, et al., A Modern Approach To Evidence 273 (3rd ed. 2000).

perjury or false statement if the statement was made by the defendant under oath, on the record and in the presence of counsel.

Unlike the other policy-based relevance rules, Rule 410 has a "closed" structure. The rule prescribes what evidence is inadmissible and then carves out two exceptions. Observe that the provisions of the rule that declare certain evidence inadmissible do so by addressing:

    (1) pleas and statements

    (2) civil and criminal proceedings

    (3) the party (namely, the defendant) entitled to the rule's protection.

Put otherwise, the Rule 410 protects defendants from evidence of certain pleas and statements entered or made during various stages of the plea proceedings. That protection extends to both criminal and civil cases, and it embraces any stage of these cases that is subsequent to the protected statement or plea. That the civil or criminal case was filed before the protected statement or plea is immaterial.

What Pleas and Statements are Protected and Why

Subsection (1) of Rule 410 renders inadmissible evidence of "a plea of guilty which was later withdrawn." Once a defendant enters a guilty plea, he cannot withdraw it without the court's permission.[26] The trial judge who grants this permission has found a sufficient reason. Perhaps the plea was coerced, or the defendant was inadequately represented, or he did not fully understand the consequences of entering a guilty plea, or the factual basis underlying the plea was weak. The point is that if a guilty plea was improperly entered, evidence that it was entered and withdrawn should not be used against the defendant in subsequent criminal or civil proceedings.

Rule 410 also renders inadmissible evidence disclosing that the defendant entered a plea of nolo contendere. A "nolo plea", which is essentially a "no contest" plea, says, in essence, "I admit nothing, but I will not contest the charges against me." The court must approve the entry of this plea. A defendant wishing to enter a nolo plea is usually concerned about the effect that an adverse (criminal) judgment will have on a civil suit (or suits) based on the same conduct that is the subject of the criminal charge. If there

---

26. This is the long-standing rule in the federal system, but it does not prevail in all states. Those states that allow a unilateral withdrawal may decline to exclude evidence of the withdrawn guilty plea in future proceedings.

were no opportunity for entering a plea of nolo contendere, the defendant might decide to contest the criminal charge simply to protect against civil liability. Nolo pleas are often entered by corporate defendants faced with multiple civil suits based on the alleged criminal conduct or faced with a civil suit (such as an anti-trust action) that carries a treble-damage penalty. The nolo plea avoids what a guilty plea would not: the introduction of evidence in the civil trial that the defendant had pled guilty to a criminal charge based on the conduct that now forms the basis of the plaintiff's civil claim.

Before a defendant is permitted to enter a guilty plea, the court holds a hearing to determine whether the tendered plea is voluntary, whether the defendant understands the charges against him and the consequences of pleading guilty, and whether there is a factual basis for his plea. A similar hearing attends the entry of a nolo contendere plea. In the federal system, these hearings are conducted pursuant to Rule 11 of the Federal Rules of Criminal Procedure. It is important that the defendant and his counsel speak openly and candidly when responding to the court's inquiries. Thus, Rule 410 prohibits the introduction of evidence (in any subsequent criminal or civil proceeding) that reveals "any statement made in the course of any proceedings under Rule 11 ... or comparable state procedure regarding" either a *withdrawn* guilty plea or a nolo contendere plea. Note that Rule 410's protection surrounds withdrawn guilty pleas, nolo pleas, and, as we will see, plea discussions between the defendant and the government's attorney that do not eventuate in a guilty plea. The *entry of a guilty plea that is not withdrawn* is outside the protective ambit of Rule 410. A defendant who elects to plead guilty usually enjoys the benefits of pleading to a lesser charge or a reduced sentence (or both). However, he is not entitled to the additional benefit of using Rule 410 to block the subsequent evidentiary use of the guilty plea or statements he may have made during "plea-bargaining" discussions with the prosecutor.

As we have just observed, Rule 410's protection extends to defendant's statements made during his exchanges with the prosecutor and directed to the possibility of a plea bargain. Specifically, Rule 410 renders inadmissible evidence of "any statement made in the course of plea discussions with an attorney for the prosecuting authority which do not result in [an unwithdrawn] plea of guilty...." Were it not for this protection, statements by the defendant or his agent (the defense attorney) could be used against him in any subsequent criminal or civil proceeding in which they were relevant. They might be used, for example, to prove his guilt or to impeach his testimony by showing the inconsistencies between his testimony and earlier statements made during the plea-bargaining stage.

The protection afforded by Rule 410 is intended to promote candor and thus increase the productiveness of plea discussions. The rule does not apply to discussions between the defendant and persons, such as police, who are not acting as "an attorney for the prosecuting authority. . . ."[27] However, a few cases have found that a law enforcement officer who held discussions with the defendant was acting as the prosecuting attorney's agent.[28]

Admissible Statements

Rule 410 contains two exceptions to its general exclusionary sweep. The first is designed to avoid misleading the trier of fact. Suppose the defendant introduces evidence of a statement that Rule 410 would exclude if offered against the defendant. This opens the door for his opponent to introduce evidence of any related statement, "made in the course of the same plea or plea discussions . . . [that] ought in fairness [to] be considered contemporaneously with" the statement the defendant introduced.[29] Think of this exception as an application of the "completeness" principle that underlies Federal Rule 106. That rule provides that when a party introduces a writing, in whole or in part, "an adverse party may require the introduction . . . of any other part or any other writing . . . which ought in fairness to be considered contemporaneously. . . ."[30]

The second exception contained in Rule 410 is designed to thwart a defendant's attempt to shield himself from a perjury prosecution. If during the plea process the defendant makes a statement "under oath, on the record and in the presence of counsel"[31] and is later prosecuted for "perjury or false statement,"[32] evidence of the statement is admissible in the trial for the allegedly false testimony. The formal requirements that attend this exception, namely the oath, a transcript, and the presence of counsel, largely confine it to prosecutions for false or perjurous statements made during a plea hearing conducted under Rule 11 of the Federal Rules of Criminal Procedure.

Special Situations Not Expressly Covered by Rule 410

We have seen that in the adversarial system of litigation, the parties largely control the evidence that comes before the court. The parties decide, for example, what evidence to present, when to

---

27. FRE 410.

28. *See, e.g.,* United States v. Millard, 139 F.3d 1200, 1205–06 (8th Cir.), *cert. denied,* 525 U.S. 949 (1998).

29. FRE 410 (4).

30. FRE 106.

31. FRE 414.

32. Id.

object to an opponent's evidence, whether to waive a privilege, whether to stipulate that certain evidence is (or is not) admissible, and whether to settle a case and thus remove it from the judicial system. This tradition of party control permeates the evidentiary rules. With this background in mind, consider whether a prosecutor could refuse to "plea bargain" with a defendant unless the latter waived some of the evidentiary protections afforded to him by Rule 410.

This issue came before the Supreme Court in United States v. Mezzanatto.[33] There, the defendant arranged to meet with the prosecutor to discuss cooperating with the government. At the outset of the meeting, the prosecutor set forth his conditions: the defendant had to be completely truthful and he had to agree that any statements made during the plea discussions would be admissible if a trial ensued and if the defendant gave testimony that contradicted his statements during the plea discussions. Further, the prosecutor stated that if the defendant declined these conditions, the plea discussions would not go forward. After conferring with his counsel, the defendant agreed to the prosecutor's demands.

During the ensuing discussions, the defendant made statements that the prosecutor knew were untrue. As a result, the prosecutor terminated the plea discussions and brought the defendant to trial. During his trial testimony, the defendant made statements that were inconsistent with some of the statements he had made to the prosecutor during their plea discussions. The prosecutor then introduced evidence of the earlier statements despite the defendant's objections that the protections afforded by Rule 410 could not be waived. To allow a waiver at the behest of the prosecutor, he argued, creates an unfair procedure, frustrates the goal of party settlement, and "invite[s] prosecutorial overreaching ... [because of the] 'gross disparity' in the relative bargaining power of the parties to a plea agreement...."[34]

Ultimately, however, a majority of the Supreme Court rejected these contentions. Speaking generally, the Court endorsed the view that evidentiary rules are "presumptively waivable." In this case, the waiver resulted in an appropriate outcome: the trier was apprised that the defendant had made conflicting statements under oath. The Court also noted that Rule 410 favored the defendant, not the prosecution. Although some defendants may eschew plea discussions rather than waive a right protected by Rule 410, the prosecutor may, nonetheless, decline plea discussions unless the defendant agrees to such a waiver. As to the defendant's claim that allowing waivers will lead to prosecutional abuse, the Court was

33. 513 U.S. 196 (1995).
34. Id. at 209.

unwilling to endorse the belief that there would be widespread misconduct. It suffices, said the Court, "to permit case-by-case inquiries into whether waiver agreements are the product of fraud or coercion."[35]

Recall that Rule 410 is a one way street: it confers evidentiary protections upon the defendant, but not upon the prosecution. There are occasions, however, when statements by the prosecutor during plea discussions would be useful to the defendant at a subsequent trial. Suppose for example the prosecutor admits that there are gaps in his evidence, or that his witnesses may not be credible, or that in light of the entire evidentiary record he is willing to reduce the charge to a lesser offense if the defendant will then plead guilty. If the defendant offers evidence of statements like these at his subsequent trial, Rule 410 appears inapplicable. However, routinely allowing this kind of evidence appears to discourage prosecutorial candor.

ILLUSTRATION

Prosecutor (P) convenes a grand jury which returns an indictment charging Defendant (D) with armed robbery. Subsequently, P and D enter into plea bargaining discussions. At the conclusion of these talks, P offers to reduce the charge to grand theft if D agrees to plead guilty to this lesser charge. D refuses.

At D's trial for armed robbery, defense counsel offers evidence that P offered to reduce the charge against D from armed robbery to grand theft. P objects. How should the trial judge rule?

Rule 410 states that specified evidence that is adduced during various plea proceedings "is not, in any civil or criminal proceeding, admissible against the defendant. . . ." The rule does not protect the prosecution from adverse evidence. However, there is some judicial authority excluding evidence derived during plea proceedings and offered by the defendant against the government. The

---

35. United States v. Mezzanatto, 513 U.S. 196, 210 (1995). There is still some question about the sweep of *Mezzanatto*, since its particular facts make the approval of the defendant's waiver at least a defensible outcome. After all, the defendant apparently made a number of false statements both to the prosecutor and during his trial testimony. In any event, some of his testimonial statements contradicted statements made to the prosecutor so that both could not be true. That said, a defendant's waiver of Rule 410 protections is likely to be upheld absent a finding by the trial judge of ineffective (defense) counsel or prosecutional misconduct or coercion. *Compare* United States v. Ruiz, 536 U.S. 622, 629–33 (2002). (No constitutional violation if prosecutor fails to disclose impeaching evidence "that might aid defendant and proceeds to negotiate a plea.")

concern of at least some courts is that allowing "plea-bargaining" evidence against the prosecution will have an adverse effect on plea discussions and plea offers by the prosecutor.[36]

Perhaps Rule 403 is the proper rule under which to accept or reject the defendant's proffered evidence. That rule gives the trial judge considerable discretion in ruling on the defendant's offer of proof. There are a number of reasons why a prosecutor might wish to conclude a plea arrangement. For example, she may be willing to reduce the charge against the defendant and reach a plea agreement because she has other cases of greater significance that she wishes to bring to trial. Or perhaps she offers to reduce the charge against the defendant because she wants to gain his cooperation with respect to gathering evidence against other persons who may have been involved in the offense charged. Other reasons could be suggested, but the point is that the jury might conclude that the prosecutor had a weak case against D when, in fact, she offered to reduce the charge for an entirely different reason.

Rule 403, you may recall, empowers the judge to reject relevant evidence when its probative value is "substantially outweighed by the danger of unfair prejudice, confusion of the issues, or *misleading the jury*, or by considerations of undue delay, [or] waste of time...."[37] An additional difficulty stems from the long tradition, often implemented by a specific rule, that it is generally inappropriate for a lawyer who represents a party to litigation to act as a trial witness. Thus, if the accused introduces evidence that the prosecutor offered to reduce the charge, the jury may never learn what actually motivated the offer. The judge, however, in exercising her authority under Rule 403, may hear arguments from both the prosecution and the defense outside the jury's presence, and then make her ruling.

§ 4.6   Liability Insurance

Federal Rule 411 prohibits evidence that "a person was or was not insured against liability" when this evidence is offered as bearing on whether the person "acted negligently or otherwise wrongfully." The rule is broad enough to preclude evidence that a person had no insurance, but its main application is to forbid evidence of insurance coverage. Furthermore, even though the rule

---

36. *See, e.g.,* United States v. Verdoorn, 528 F.2d 103, 107 (8th Cir. 1976) (evidence of prosecutor's plea-bargaining stance as proof of government's weak case is inadmissible); United States v. Delgado, 903 F.2d 1495, 1499 (11th Cir. 1990) (Rule 403 supports rejection of defense evidence of statements of prosecutor and plea offer because reasons other than weakness in government's case may be explanatory). *But see,* United States v. Biaggi, 909 F.2d 662, 690–93 (2d Cir. 1990), *cert. denied,* 499 U.S. 904 (1991) (defendant allowed to show he rejected immunity offer).

37. Emphasis added.

forbids evidence that "a person" was (or was not) insured, its primary effect is to prohibit evidence that one who is allegedly liable for some action or activity has liability insurance. Rule 411 draws support from at least two sources. The first—and most important—is the apprehension that if jurors were made aware that a party charged with liability was insured, they might impose liability when they otherwise would not or, perhaps, increase the damage award.[38] The second justification for the rule is its marginal effect on the purchase of insurance. If evidence of liability insurance were routinely admitted for whatever probative force[39] it might have on the conduct of the insured, the incentive to purchase insurance might be weakened. The insured would have to consider the possible impact of this evidence on the jury; the insurer would have to consider the impact of this evidence on premiums it charges.

The prohibition of Rule 411 is not absolute. Exclusion is not required when evidence of liability insurance is "offered for another purpose, such as proof of agency, ownership, or control, or bias or prejudice of a witness." Suppose, for example, a witness for the defendant is an employee or agent of the defendant's liability insurer. Evidence of this relationship is admissible to impeach the witness, even though it incidentally reveals the fact that the defendant has liability insurance.

ILLUSTRATION

Plaintiff, a truck driver, sues both the owner and the lessee of a truck stop for injuries incurred when the plaintiff fell into a grease pit on the premises.[40] At trial, there is conflicting evidence as to whether the owner, the lessee, or both were responsible for maintaining the premises. The owner testifies that the lessee had sole responsibility for maintenance. Plaintiff thereupon starts to cross-examine the owner concerning whether the latter had liability insurance that protected against damages for injuries sustained on the truck stop premises. The defense

38. Of course, in some contexts insurance coverage is either quite common or mandatory, so it is reasonable to suppose that the jury probably assumes that there is some insurance coverage. This is probably true, for example, in automobile accident cases.

39. In cases involving negligent conduct, probative value would appear to be either very weak or nonexistent. Thus, rejection of evidence of liability insurance could rest on the justification of minimal probative value. But Rule 411 does not leave the issue of admissibility of evidence of liability insurance to a mere relevance determination and its attendant fluctuations from case to case.

40. *See* Pinckard v. Dunnavant, 281 Ala. 533, 206 So.2d 340 (1968).

objects, citing Federal Rule 411. How should the trial judge rule?

The evidence probably falls within one of the enumerated exceptions to Rule 411's prohibition against the disclosure of liability insurance. Arguably, the evidence in question is offered on the issue of "control." However, since the list of exceptions (allowable purposes) in Rule 411 is illustrative, not exhaustive, it is unnecessary to fit the evidence within one of the enumerated purposes. The evidence in the Illustration was not offered on the issue of owner's negligence or wrongful conduct, but was addressed to the disputed issue of which defendant had responsibility (an adequate surrogate for "control") for maintaining the truck stop. Thus the judge should overrule the defendant's objection.

Chapter V

HEARSAY: WHAT IS IT?

Table of Sections

---

§ 5.1 Overview

The general understanding among lay persons that hearsay evidence is characterized by a courtroom witness's testimony about what someone else said is partially accurate. Hearsay, in fact, does involve a serial repetition: generally speaking, one person, the witness, repeats what was previously said by another person, whom we shall call the *declarant*. But not all statements made by an out-of-court declarant are hearsay. To constitute hearsay, the repeated statement must be offered for the purpose of proving that what the declarant said is true.

Suppose, for example, Owner lends a painting by Alfred Sisley to Museum so that it can be included in an exhibit of Impressionist painters. During the exhibition, the painting is stolen and, subsequently, Owner sues Museum. A member of the maintenance crew testifies that as he walked past the entrance to the exhibit he caught a brief glimpse of a man in uniform. The man said to a person the witness could not see, "I made sure all the visitors had left the gallery area and then locked both doors." If this statement were offered to prove that the visitors were cleared from the gallery and the doors were then locked, it would be hearsay. Put otherwise, the witness's testimony describing what the declarant said would be hearsay because it would be offered for its truth. However, if the witness's testimony were offered only to prove that the guard was at his station near the exhibit, the statement would not be hearsay.[1] The declarant's statement makes it more likely that he was a security guard, even if he was mistaken or lying about his actions. Note, however, that the principle of relevance confines the purposes

---

1. *See* Arthur Best, Evidence 66 (5th ed. 2003).

for which an out-of-court statement can be offered. If the presence of the security guards near the exhibit did not bear on a consequential proposition, the statement of the speaker (declarant) could not be admitted for the "nonhearsay" purpose of proving he was on duty.

Why do we confine the rule against hearsay evidence to out-of-court statements that are offered "to prove the truth of the matter asserted?"[2] The principal basis for the rule against hearsay is that a cross-examiner who is confronted with adverse hearsay evidence is denied the opportunity to cross-examine the "real" witness (the declarant) and to expose weaknesses in his statement. In other words, the cross-examiner is unable to put questions to the declarant that are designed to show that the declarant is mistaken, evasive, or lying. Cross-examining the witness on the stand is of little value for he can only relate what the declarant said to him. However, an adverse interrogation of the declarant is unnecessary when his statement is not offered for the truth of its contents. If his statement is not offered for its truth, the *only* question for the trier of fact is whether the declarant in fact made the statement to which the witness on the stand testifies. As to this question, the cross-examiner can conduct an effective cross-examination because he can ask questions of the witness that are designed to show that the witness is mistaken or lying about *the declarant's statement—* that is, exactly what, if anything, the declarant said.

ILLUSTRATION

Andy's Bar and Grill is located near an Air Force base from which soldiers often fly to their new duty station, sometimes located in a combat zone. On a particular Saturday night a group of soldiers who were about to be "shipped out" went to Andy's for drinks. As the evening hours passed, arguments ensued between the soldiers and anti-war protesters who were also having drinks at Andy's Bar and Grill. A fight broke out; then another; and a melee ensued.

Your client, Hemmingway, suffered serious injuries to his head, which he thinks were inflicted, without provocation, by Corporals Buck or Spitz or both. Hemmingway says he unsuccessfully tried to fend off his attackers with an empty gin bottle and a wooden stick. Two eyewitnesses substantiate Hemmingway's account.

---

2.   FRE 801(c) (defining hearsay).

Unfortunately however, by the time Hemmingway consults you, most of the soldiers involved in the fray have been sent abroad and many of the protesters cannot be located. However, you do locate a reporter, Woodward, who wrote an article about the brawl for the local newspaper. Woodward interviewed Buck and Spitz before they left for the war zone; he also interviewed Bartender and Waitress, who observed the events in question. On the basis of the statements of these four "declarants," Woodward concluded that Hemmingway, who had drunk an entire bottle of gin, attacked Buck and Spitz from behind with an empty gin bottle and the leg of a broken chair. Subsequently, Buck and Spitz return to the base and you, on Hemmingway's behalf, file suit against them for assault and battery.

Suppose that during the third day the defense calls Bartender and Waitress. You cross-examine each of them. During the fourth day of trial, you learn that Buck and Spitz have suddenly been ordered to participate in a field maneuver in a remote section of the base. However, Woodward will testify in their place and, after refreshing his recollection by consulting his interview notes, will give their account of the relevant events of the brawl.

What kinds of questions, designed toward what ends, were useful to you when you cross-examined Bartender and Waitress, but are of little value to you in your cross-examination of Woodward? In other words, which practical limitations, not applicable in your cross-examination of Bartender and Waitress, seriously hamper your cross-examination of Woodward?

This Illustration is designed to encourage you to think about what ends are likely to be pursued by a cross-examiner. Often, she focuses on ways in which she can discredit the witness or at least raise doubts about the accuracy of his testimony. For example, she may ask questions designed to reveal that the witness was not in a good position to observe the event in question; that he has poor eyesight; that his memory is faulty, that he is being evasive or deceptive, and so forth. As we have seen, such questions are of limited value when the witness on the stand has recited what someone else—the declarant—has said about the event. The witness, who was not, himself, a first-hand observer can say no more than what he was told by the declarant. This is why hearsay testimony carries with it certain infirmities, often called hearsay "dangers" or "risks". These potential dangers to testimonial accuracy are:

(a) *Defects in Perception*: the declarant's statements may be unreliable because he did not observe or hear accurately.

(b) *Defects in Memory*: the declarant's statements may be unreliable because his memory (of the event about which he spoke) may have been weak, inaccurate, or incomplete.

(c) *Defects in Sincerity*: the declarant's statements may be unreliable because he purposefully gave a biased, incomplete, or false account.

(d) *Defects in Narration or Transmission*: The declarant's statements may be unreliable because his language was ambiguous, or because he inadvertently left out an important word or phrase, or because he used a word or phrase that is peculiar to his culture or social group—although to the trier it may have seemed quite plain.

The assumption underlying the hearsay rule is that cross-examination can test for and reveal these infirmities. Accordingly, the lack of opportunity to cross-examine the declarant is the fundamental reason for excluding hearsay evidence. This rationale is, of course, consistent with a major tenet of the adversary system: cross-examination is the essential means for testing the accuracy of testimony and discovering the truth. Despite the usefulness of cross-examination, however, an unremitting exclusion of all hearsay statements would actually impede accurate fact-finding. Hence, as the next two chapters demonstrate, there are numerous exemptions and exceptions[3] to the hearsay rule. Bear in mind, then, that *classification of a particular statement as hearsay does not necessarily mean that the statement will be excluded.* Quite often, a declarant's hearsay statement is admissible because it falls within one of the various exemptions or exceptions.

§ 5.2 A Definition of Hearsay

We begin a detailed analysis of the hearsay rule by examining the "definitional" portions of Federal Rule 801. This rule first defines "statement" and then goes on to incorporate "statement" (as thus defined) into the definition of hearsay. Rule 801(a) says that "[a] 'statement' is (1) an oral or written assertion or (2) nonverbal conduct of a person, if it is intended by the person as an assertion." The crux of this definition is this: a person makes a statement when she asserts something either through the use of words or through conduct (such as nodding her head or using hand signals) that is intended as a substitute for words. Rule 801(c) uses the word "statement" (as defined in subsection (a)) in its definition of hearsay:

3. A statement falling within an exemption or exception may be used to prove the truth of the matter asserted in the statement.

"Hearsay" is a statement other than one made by the declarant while testifying at the trial or hearing, offered in evidence to prove the truth of the matter asserted.

This definition captures the principle we have just discussed: the hearsay rule is concerned with an out-of-court statement (that is, a statement not made from the witness stand)[4] offered for the purpose of convincing the trier of fact that the statement is true. Of course, as we know, a declarant's statement must be probative of one (or more) consequential propositions or it would fail the basic test of relevance. However, a hearsay statement, even if relevant, is inadmissible unless it falls within an exemption or exception. This basic proposition is affirmed by Federal Rule 802 which declares that "[h]earsay is not admissible except as provided by these [Federal] rules or by other rules prescribed by the Supreme Court . . . or by Act of Congress."

In its several subsections that define hearsay, Rule 801 consistently speaks of hearsay declarations *of a person*—the declarant. Machines or devices such as radar units, heart monitors, surveillance cameras, or clocks do not make hearsay statements; neither does an animal such as a tracking dog that follows the scent of the accused from the scene of the crime to his hiding place, or a parrot who calls out the name of the accused as someone (whose identity is in issue) enters the victim's house. Judges may sometimes exclude evidence derived from these various sources, but not because of the hearsay rule. The cross-examiner would be no better off if we placed the radar unit, parrot, or the bloodhound in the witness chair. Evidence derived from devices or animals is tested for reliability by the cross-examination of persons who are acquainted with the operating principles and particular features of the device or the training and history of the animal.

§ 5.3 Statements that Are Not Hearsay: A Sampling

We have seen that the hearsay stigma attaches when, and only when, the proponent offers evidence of the declarant's statement for the purpose of convincing the trier of fact that the statement is true. Of course, some statements have no "truth content," so to speak. Thus questions and commands do not usually constitute hearsay. However, the hearsay rule should apply to a question such as "Did you bring my gun" (offered to show the speaker had a gun)

---

4. We often speak of hearsay statements as "out-of-court" assertions offered for their truth. This is a convenience; technically, however, any statement made anywhere other than from the stand in the *present* trial is hearsay if offered for its truth. For example, statements made during testimony rendered in another trial (and thus given "in court") would be hearsay; so too—at least ordinarily—would a statement made prior to trial by a

or a command such as "Move the red Honda motorcycle out of a 'No–Parking' zone near the fire hydrant" (offered to show where the motorcycle was parked). But even if a statement makes an assertion, it is often possible to skirt the hearsay rule.

As we have seen, if the proponent's probative purpose can be realized without the factfinder's reliance upon the truth of the declarant's statement, the hearsay rule is inapplicable. Thus, it is important to focus closely on the *purpose* for which the declarant's statement is offered. Sometimes it is readily apparent that a proffered statement is not being offered for its truth. Yet, at other times, the proffered statement appears to have its greatest probative force if its assertion is used for its "truth content," rather than for the other relevant (and permissible) nonhearsay purpose for which the proponent proffers it. In these situations, the trial judge must consider whether to exclude the evidence on one (or more) of the grounds set out in Rule 403,[5] especially the ground of "unfair prejudice." If the trial judge decides to admit the evidence for a nonhearsay purpose, the opponent of the evidence is entitled to have the judge instruct the jury members that they can consider the evidence only for its proper (nonhearsay) use and not for its forbidden hearsay use. (If the judge does not give such an instruction sua sponte, the opponent can assert his right to it.) Sometimes, however, the opponent declines to request the instruction, since he does not want to emphasize the evidence by calling it to the jury's attention.

The material that follows contains examples of statements that are not hearsay. These nonhearsay "patterns" are based on the text of Federal Rule 801, as well as cases that involve the various nonhearsay exemplars that will be described. Of course, other patterns arise, but the central issue remains constant: Is the declarant's statement offered for its truth? As you examine the examples and illustrations below, note whether the witness on the stand has first-hand (personal) knowledge of what the declarant said. Occasionally, the declarant X speaks to (or in the presence of) Y, who subsequently tells W (the witness) what the declarant X said. At trial, the proponent of the declarant's statement offers W to testify that "Y said that the declarant X said...."

This "double hearsay" (there are two declarants, Y and X) presents a special difficulty because the cross-examiner cannot effectively cross-examine W concerning what the first declarant X said. W only knows what Y, the second declarant, said the first declarant, X, said. Put otherwise, W's testimony describing X's

---

testifying witness and offered for its truth.

5. Rule 403 states that the judge may exclude evidence "if its probative value is substantially outweighed by the danger of unfair prejudice, confusion of the issues, or misleading the jury, or by considerations of undue delay [or] waste of time...."

statement (as related by *Y*) is offered for its truth, that is, with the expectation that the factfinder will believe that the *initial declarant (X) made the statement in question*. Yet, the cross-examiner has no means of effectively interrogating *W* concerning what *X* said.

Suppose, for example, the first declarant's (*X*'s) statement is, "I'm hungry." If offered for its truth, it is hearsay. Imagine, however, that it falls within an exemption or exception to the hearsay rule. In the double-hearsay context, applying the exception to the statement of the first declarant (*X*) solves only half of our hearsay problem. The cross-examiner still cannot test *Y*'s perception, memory, sincerity, or narration because *Y* is not on the witness stand. In other words, there is no way to cross-examine *W*, the witness on the stand, as to what *X* actually said. Obviously, cross-examining *W* is not helpful, because he can only testify that declarant *Y* told him that declarant *X* said he was hungry. Yet the trier is asked to believe *Y*'s statement that *X* expressed hunger. Perhaps *X* said nothing of the kind. Perhaps he said, "I'm not hungry," or "I have a hangover," or "I will be hungry by noon."

In the lexicon of evidence teachers and trial lawyers, the person who has personal knowledge of what the (first) declarant said is called the *auditor*. Usually, but not always, the auditor is the testifying witness. We will address the problem of multiple hearsay later in this text. For now, simply consider the *possibility* that *X*'s statement ("I'm hungry") is within an exemption or exception to the hearsay rule *and Y*'s statement to *W* ("*X* told me he was hungry") *also fits* within an exemption or exception. By linking two exceptions or exemptions, or by linking an exception and an exemption, the hearsay barrier can be surmounted.

Verbal Acts
(Words that have Independent Legal Significance)

A statement that is instrumental in creating or shifting a legal relationship is not hearsay. Such a statement is often called a "verbal act,"—suggesting the analogy between conduct that has legal significance (for example negligent conduct or criminal conduct) and words that have legal significance, quite independent of the declarant's perception, memory, sincerity, or narration.

Suppose the declarant runs into an opera house and excitedly yells, "fire, fire—there's a fire in the basement!" Later, he is prosecuted for giving a false alarm. A witness (auditor) who was in the opera house testifies as to the defendant's actions and words. These words were a "verbal act"—they had *independent legal significance* because they constituted an offense, namely, giving a false alarm in a public place. The declarant's words are not being used for the hearsay purpose of proving there was a fire in the basement. To illustrate further, suppose the issue at hand is whether *B* accepted *A*'s offer for certain painting services. A witness testifies that she heard *B* said to *A*: "I accept your offer to paint my porch for $500." Under the objective theory of contract formation, *B*'s statement resulted in a binding contract. Imagine that prior to *B*'s acceptance he had confided in his wife that he intended to tell *A* that he (*B*) accepted *A*'s offer, but that he would really be lying because he wanted to use the $500 to buy a kitchen appliance. *B*'s insincerity is of no consequence; there is still a contract; the words of acceptance completed the bargain. Similarly, a *contractual offer* is a verbal act because it shifts the legal relations between the parties by empowering the offeree to accept the offer.

An early case,[6] still cited in many evidence texts, concerned a suit against a bank for the conversion of plaintiff's corn. It was critical that the plaintiff prove that the corn in question belonged to him and not to his tenant. It was clear that one portion of the corn crop belonged to the tenant and that the other portion belonged to the plaintiff; the issue at trial was what corn belonged to whom. The plaintiff testified that after the corn was harvested, he went to his farm to inspect the yield. Upon seeing several or more cribs filled with corn, the plaintiff asked, "Which corn is mine?" The tenant responded by pointing to certain cribs and telling the plaintiff that these cribs contained the corn that belonged to the plaintiff. Subsequently, the corn in one of these designated cribs was attached and sold by the bank to satisfy a debt that the *tenant* owed the bank. The plaintiff's suit against the bank for conversion followed.

It first appears that the tenant's statement which said, in essence, "That's your corn in cribs A and B" was hearsay. However, under the controlling substantive law, the tenant's statement had the effect of making the plaintiff the sole owner of the corn designated by the tenant. Until the tenant's statement, ownership in the corn, a fungible crop, was undivided; his statement had the legal effect of vesting in the plaintiff title to that portion of the corn that was stored in the designated cribs. In other words, the utterance of the words that marked off the plaintiff's share had the independent legal effect of vesting sole ownership in him. It was unnecessary for the trier of fact to rely on the credibility of the tenant-declarant since, whatever might have been his motives, ownership was conferred when he spoke the words of division.

Note, however, that the tenant's statement would have been hearsay if it had identified corn that had already been divided. Imagine, for example, that on day *one* the tenant made a statement that resulted in vesting ownership in the plaintiff (landlord) to the

6. Hanson v. Johnson, 161 Minn. 229, 201 N.W. 322 (1924).

corn in cribs A and B. On day *two*, the tenant told an insurance agent that the plaintiff owned the corn in cribs A and B. Suppose that corn in these cribs was destroyed by a fire and the plaintiff sued his insurance company to recover the value of the lost corn. At trial, the insurance company contends that the corn that was destroyed belonged to the tenant. To meet this contention, the plaintiff presents a witness (auditor) who heard the tenant tell the insurance agent (on day two) that the corn in cribs A and B belonged to the plaintiff. Since the corn was divided on day one, the tenant's statement on day two had no independent legal significance. Stripped of any legal effect, the proffered statement would be hearsay, offered to prove that the plaintiff owned the corn in cribs A and B.

Verbal acts are fairly common in both civil and criminal cases, as the following illustrations suggest.

ILLUSTRATIONS

(1) An issue at trial is whether Smith illegally impersonated a United States ambassador named Bruce. *W* testifies that when Smith met a representative of the Immigration and Naturalization Service, Smith said, "I am Ambassador Bruce."[7]

(2) An issue at trial is whether Father put a deposit in trust for Daughter or for Son. Bank Teller testifies that when Father handed him a check for $50,000, Father said, "I want the entire amount of this check put in trust for Daughter."[8]

(3) An issue at trial is whether *A*, an Army Officer, gave to *B* a Rolex watch or whether *A* simply put the watch in *B*'s care during the time *A* was engaged in a dangerous combat mission. *W* testifies that when *A* handed the watch to *B* he (*A*) said, "We have been friends through thick and thin; whatever happens, I want to give you this Rolex."[9]

---

7. The words of impersonation constitute the offense.

8. In most jurisdictions, the father's statement would result in the deposit being held in trust for Daughter. Even in a minority jurisdiction, Father's declaration is *part* of a shift in legal relations, and as such, is not hearsay.

9. In most jurisdictions, a transfer of property accompanied by words of donation results in a gift, even if the donor did not intend to make a gift.

(4) An issue at trial is whether *D* spoke words that defamed a corporate vice-president, *P*. *W*, a witness for *P*, testifies that at a meeting of the Board of Directors, *D* appeared before the Board and said, "You should all know I have completed my investigation of *P*'s activities; he has been defrauding the company."

(5) An issue in an adverse possession case is whether *D*, who claims adverse possession of Greenacre, held the property adversely and notoriously. *W* testifies that on several occasions *D* appeared before the local zoning board. On each occasion *D* identified himself as the owner of Greenacre.

(6) An issue at trial is whether *B*, a defendant bank, guaranteed to pay Hospital's bills for certain medical supplies should Hospital fail to pay the plaintiff, Supplier. *W* testifies that *B*'s Vice–President said to Supplier, "Go ahead and ship the supplies to Hospital; we guarantee payment."

In the foregoing Illustrations, the declarant's words either shift the legal relationship between the declarant and some other person or else the words are an operative part of a shift in relationship. In Illustration (4), for example, the declarant's words gave rise to *P*'s cause of action for slander (obviously *P* is not trying to prove the truth of *D*'s statement); in Illustration (5), the statements of ownership play an operative role in the legal rule governing adverse possession. Generally speaking, that rule requires that the adverse possessor hold the property in question for a specified number of years, and that he do so openly (notoriously) and adversely. Thus, *D*'s assertions may be received as evidence that he openly claimed ownership. However, these same assertions would be hearsay if offered to show, for example, that *D* owned Greenacre. In Illustration (6), the Vice–President's words created Bank's obligation to cover Hospital's bill, (assuming the substantive law acknowledged a verbal, as opposed to written, commitment). The point to bear in mind is that whenever declarant's words, or conduct accompanied by words, affect the legal relationship between the declarant and another person (or entity), there is a non-hearsay rationale for admitting the declarant's statement.

Statements Affecting Another's State of Mind

Another pattern in which a declarant's statement is not offered for its truth emerges when the purpose of the proffered statement is to show the probable effect of the statement on the state of mind of another person who heard (or read) it. Suppose, for example, a grocery store customer sues the store for injuries she sustained when she slipped on a broken bottle of olive oil that someone had dropped in the aisle.[10] The defendant store calls to the witness stand a checkout clerk (the auditor) who will testify that he heard the store manager cry out, "Lady don't step on the spilled olive oil in the aisle." This evidence is, of course, relevant because the patron's conduct, which may constitute contributory negligence, should be evaluated in light of the warning. The evidence is also relevant because it bears on whether the grocery store took reasonable steps to prevent an injury. These "consequential" purposes are satisfied if the trier of fact concludes that the manager issued a warning. The trier is not being asked to use the manager's statement to prove there was olive oil in the grocery aisle. Without relying on the truth of the manager's statement, the factfinder can evaluate the reasonableness of each party's conduct.

Another example of a "statement offered for its probable effect" appears in a British case involving a prosecution for the forbidden possession of ammunition in a battle zone.[11] The accused tendered the defense of duress. He claimed that he had been captured by enemy terrorists and forced to take up arms against the British. To establish his defense, he offered evidence of his captors' orders and threats. These statements were not hearsay because they were not offered to prove that their contents were true. They were not offered, for example, to prove that the terrorists would have carried out their threats to torture the accused or bury him alive should he refuse to join them. Instead, the statements were offered because their mere utterance was significant in establishing duress. Evidence that the threats were made enables the trier to assess the probable effect of the terrorists' words on the accused's state of mind and to judge his conduct accordingly.

Further examples of statements that could be offered to show their probable effect on the listener:

(1) On the issue of whether D was negligent when he drove a car that had defective tires, a statement made to D by X, a service station attendant, who looked at the front tires and said, "Both of these front tires are bad and the one on the left front already has a tear."

(2) On the issue whether D was anxious and worried about his health, a statement to D by his physician (declarant) that "You have had a series of small heart attacks and strokes; one heart artery is closed and the others are badly congested."

---

10. A case involving similar facts is Safeway Stores, Inc. v. Combs, 273 F.2d 295 (5th Cir. 1960).

11. Subramaniam v. Public Prosecutor, 100 Solicitor's Journal 566 (Judicial Comm., Privy Council 1956).

(3) On the issue of whether D had purposely and fraudulently failed to file an estate tax return, a letter to D from his accountant stating that "Your available deductions will eliminate any concern about estate tax liability."

(4) On the issue whether Police Officer had probable cause to arrest X, a statement to the officer by an excited and angry woman, "that man (X) broke into my car and took the money out of my purse."

In each of these illustrations, there is a nonhearsay use for the declarant's statement. In the first example, the station attendant's statement warned D (i.e., put him on notice) that he had a defective tire. This statement would be hearsay if offered to prove that the tire was defective. It could not be used for this purpose unless it came within a hearsay exemption or exception,[12] but it could be used for the nonhearsay purpose of showing that D was aware of the possibly dangerous condition of his tires. Other evidence, such as expert testimony (or the station attendant's testimony from the stand), could be used to prove the defective condition of the front tires. In the second illustration, the physician's statement has probative force to prove that D was anxious and worried about his health. Note that we are assuming that D's state of mind is consequential under the substantive law governing the case. Perhaps, for example, D's mental state is relevant to whether he attempted suicide or whether he was justified in revoking a trust that he had established (for his former wife) because he anticipated needing the trust proceeds to cover his medical expenses. In the third illustration, the accountant's assurance that no estate taxes would be due make it less likely that D would have willfully and fraudulently failed to file an estate tax return. Finally, in the fourth illustration, the evidence helps to prove that the officer acted reasonably when he arrested X.

Declarant's Own Statement to Show Knowledge, Awareness

Sometimes a declarant's statement reveals her knowledge of a fact or condition. If her knowledge is consequential in a subsequent lawsuit, her statement is admissible for a nonhearsay purpose. For example, a driver might have stated that her car had defective brakes; an estranged father, against whom a contempt order is sought for visiting his child, might have remarked that he, the father, was forbidden by court order from visiting his child,[13] or a corporate vice-president might have stated that run-off from the company's newly installed disposal system was poisoning nearby

12. As you will see in Chapter VII, the statement probably comes within a hearsay exception called "present sense impression."

13. Assuming the father's statement was made prior to his visit, the remark shows that he knew he was violating a court order when he visited his child.

aquatic life. Each of these statements reveals the declarant's knowledge or awareness of a fact or condition. In cases in which the declarant's knowledge or awareness a consequential fact, these statements have a nonhearsay use. Of course, should statements such as those above fit within a hearsay exemption or exception, they are admissible not only to show awareness, but also to prove that the statements are true.

Declarant's Own Statement Used Circumstantially

We often encounter statements that assert something ("New York City is intellectually and culturally exciting"), but carry an unstated message or implication ("I like New York City.") Someone who dominates the dinner conversation with animated accounts of the accomplishments of various baseball players is impliedly asserting that he likes baseball.

Suppose the issue before a college Academic Review Board was whether Beth, who did not sit for Professor Sophocles' Greek Tragedies examination, was enrolled in his course. Beth claims that she did not enroll in Sophocles' class and that the appearance of her name on his roll resulted from a computer error in the Registrar's office. Wilma (the auditor) takes the stand on Beth's behalf and testifies that prior to the beginning of the college term, she and Beth were discussing various courses and teachers. Wilma was about to enroll in Greek Philosophy, a course taught by Professor Sophocles. Beth remarked that the year before she had taken a course from Sophocles and that he was "arrogant, uninterested in his students, and gave mostly low grades." This testimony was not offered to prove the truth of these unfavorable remarks; rather it was offered for the implied or circumstantial proposition that Beth disliked or at least did not admire Professor Sophocles. So viewed, it is plausible to argue (and most judges would agree), that Beth's statement is not hearsay because it is not offered for its truth. If the trier concludes that Beth's statement shows (circumstantially) that she held Sophocles in low regard, it is then less likely that she registered for his course. Her feelings about the professor were implied by her statement detailing his specific traits or conduct. However, as we have seen, her statement is not being offered to prove Sophocles' arrogance, indifference, or grading patterns.

There is, however, a rather indistinct line separating a declarant's statements that the trier can use circumstantially for their implication (thus avoiding the hearsay rule) and statements in which the implied proposition is so close to the surface of the expressed statement that the declarant was probably aware that she was making two assertions: one explicitly and the other implicitly. If the declarant refers to X as a "dirty, lying cheat" and the issue is whether she disliked X, you can certainly argue that her statement is equivalent to "I hate *X*" and thus this statement is offered for its truth.[14] On the other hand, you can argue that the evidence of declarants' statement is not offered to prove that *X* has these traits. The question is close, but most judges would admit these declarations for the limited purpose of showing declarants' dislike of *X*. Rather clearly *within* the definition of hearsay, however, are statements constituting an aphorism or metaphor, or statements clothed in irony or sarcasm. In the following examples, the declarant is clearly aware of the assertion he is making:

"the clouds burst," (heavy rain)

"he was burning with desire," (passionate)

"the barber scalped him," (very close haircut)

"of course, *you* would never have eaten the rest of the cake," (you ate the cake)

"fools rush in where angels fear to tread," (you were foolish to do that)

"forget the trial—put him in the jug and throw away the key." (he is guilty of the offense charged)

Before allowing a declarant's statement into evidence on a *nonhearsay*—circumstantial use—basis, the judge should be satisfied that the declarant did not intend to be asserting the proposition that is supposedly "implied." This requirement accords with the basis for classifying statements used circumstantially as nonhearsay: when a statement is implied by the declarant (or, put otherwise, inferred by the listener) the hearsay danger of insincerity is reduced because the declarant was not focused on the proposition for which his statement is offered at trial.

ILLUSTRATION

Suppose the issue is whether Testator (*T*) intended to omit from his will Nephew (*N*). A witness testifies that several months before his death, *T* remarked to his sister (*N*'s mother), "*N* has turned out to be an incorrigible spendthrift, too lazy even to hold a job. You shouldn't let him spend your family into bankruptcy."

This declaration is offered not to prove *N*'s traits, but rather as circumstantial evidence that *T* disapproved of *N*'s conduct and thus probably intended to omit *N* from his will. For this latter purpose,

---

14. Here, however, is a nonhearsay rationale: The fact that a declarant speaks derogatory or hateful words about *X* is circumstantial evidence of the declarant's dislike of *X*. Even if the statement is "I hate *X*" and the issue is whether the declarant hates X, the use of vituperative words, standing alone, is circumstantial (nonhearsay) evidence of the declarant's feelings.

most courts would treat T's declaration as nonhearsay. A similar analysis would admit as nonhearsay the declarations of a wife accusing her husband of neglect, cruelty, and infidelity, when offered for the limited purpose of showing the wife's disaffection— which we will assume is consequential. Note, however, that if there were issues in the case concerning the husband's neglect, cruelty, or unfaithfulness, the judge might invoke Rule 403 and exclude the wife's declaration on the ground that despite a limiting instruction the jury would probably not confine its consideration of the wife's remarks to its determination of her feelings. There is considerable risk that the jury would also use the wife's declarations as proof of the husband's conduct—a line of proof that involves hearsay.

A famous English case[15] considers in detail the issue of implied assertions. There, the proponents of a will proffered letters to the testator from X, Y, and Z because the tone and content of the letters impliedly manifested the writers' belief that the recipient was sane and competent. (His sanity was the central issue in the case.) So far as the letters disclosed on their surface, the writers (declarants) intended only to communicate various business and social matters. However, the letters were not offered to prove anything expressly said within them. Rather, they were offered for the implied assertion that the writers believed the testator was competent. In other words, the writers' use of normal, unguarded language, coupled with the fact that the writers entrusted to the testator the discharge of certain business and social affairs, implied that they thought he was sane.

Although the English court ruled that the letters were hearsay, American Courts applying the Federal Rules of Evidence would classify the letters as nonhearsay. Of course, the proponent would still need to show that the writers had the opportunity to observe and interact with the testator within a relatively recent period. Otherwise, the trial judge should reject the evidence as lacking sufficient probative value. If the declarants' source of information was outdated, their letters would have only marginal probative value to suggest the testator was sane.

ILLUSTRATION

The police receive a reliable tip that X's house is being used for illegal bookmaking. During the police raid several telephones in X's library ring and a policeman answers. Each caller identifies himself and then places a bet. At

15. Wright v. Doe d. Tatham, 7 Ad. & E. 313, 112 Eng. Rep. 488 (Exch. Ch. 1837).

trial, the officer answering the phones testifies, over a hearsay objection, as to what the callers said. On appeal X's counsel argues that the trial judge made an error in allowing this "hearsay" evidence. Was the trial judge mistaken in her ruling?

Under the Federal Rules, the trial judge's decision was correct. The callers were simply placing their bets; they were not making a direct assertion that "X's house is used for gambling transactions." This latter assertion was implied, but implied assertions are not hearsay under Federal Rule 801. That rule defines a hearsay statements as an "oral or written assertion"[16] (or conduct that substitutes for words) that is intended by the declarant to assert the proposition for which the statement is offered. Suppose, for example, one of the callers had said, "You owe me seventy-five dollars because Black Beauty won the fifth race." Evidence of this assertion is not offered for the purpose of proving either the amount owed or that Black Beauty won. The hearsay rule applies only to words or conduct offered to prove the assertion the declarant intended.

Ledgers, Inscriptions, and the Like

Suppose that in connection with the raid on X's house the police had seized a bookkeeper's ledger containing the details and amounts of various gambling transactions. At X's trial, the prosecutor offers the ledger as proof that X engaged in gambling activities. If the prosecutor's offer is limited to showing the general nature of the entries as circumstantial evidence that gambling transactions took place in X's house, the ledger would not be hearsay.[17] In the same nonhearsay category as the ledger would be items such as X's address book listing Y's address and telephone number or a receipt showing that X had paid ten-thousand dollars to Y, if these items were offered for the limited purpose of showing that X and Y were acquainted.[18] The key to avoiding a hearsay characterization of these entries is to offer them not for their truth, but as circumstantial evidence that X was acquainted with Y. Again, however, it is essential that X's acquaintance with Y be consequential (relevant) under the applicable substantive law. Suppose, for example, X were charged with illegal drug sales. If Y were involved in assisting persons such as X in "laundering" illegal drug proceeds, it would probably be relevant that X knew Y. Obviously, entries offered to

---

16. FRE 801 (a).

17. *See, e.g.,* United States v. Alosa 14 F.3d 693, 696–97 (1st Cir. 1994).

18. As you will see in Ch. VI, statements made by a party constitute party admissions. Such admissions are exempted form the hearsay rule and thus may be admitted for their truth.

prove what they assert (e.g., the receipt and sale of heroin) would be hearsay.[19]

Keep in mind that the sole purpose of this chapter is to flesh out the definition of hearsay. In many of the foregoing illustrations and examples, the evidence, even if hearsay, might be admitted as an exemption or exception[20] to the hearsay rule. The number of exemptions and exceptions allowing hearsay statements into evidence curtail the number of occasions in which a judge must make subtle distinctions between hearsay and nonhearsay. There is no practical necessity for drawing a fine line between hearsay and nonhearsay if the proffered evidence, even if classified as hearsay, would nonetheless be admitted.

ILLUSTRATION

An issue in a hit-and-run case is whether a certain truck belonged to X or Y. A witness will testify that a sign painted on the side of the truck in question said:

X's QUALITY MULCH

We Deliver

X's lawyer objects to evidence reciting the content of the sign on the ground that the statement is essentially that of some declarant, such as the person painting the sign, or the person who engaged him, who is asserting that the truck belong to X. How should the trial judge rule?

Although X's argument favoring a hearsay characterization is plausible, most courts would reject it. One rationale for a nonhearsay characterization is to view the sign as just another external feature of the truck, in the same category as size, color, make, and other identifying features. Professors Mueller and Kirkpatrick[21] suggest another possibility: a label or name on an object has probative value to show that it is owned by a person of that name—in this case, X. The sign is circumstantial evidence that the truck belongs to a person named X, as opposed to a person named Y or Z. Put otherwise: a person named X is much more likely to be responsible for the sign or label than someone not named X. Because the truck is labeled as belonging to one named X and the party we are interested in is also named X, there is an increased

19. *See* note 18. Authenticated entries made by the *defendant* would be admitted as nonhearsay party exemptions.

20. As you will see, hearsay exemptions are essentially like hearsay exceptions. Both exemptions and exceptions allow assertions to be used for their truth.

21. For an extended and insightful discussion, see MUELLER and KIRKPATRICK, EVIDENCE § 8.19, at 735.

likelihood that "our X" and the X whose name appears on the truck are the same person. In addition to these nonhearsay bases for admissibility, there is a strong likelihood of invoking a hearsay exemption called "party admissions." We will consider party admissions in the next chapter.

Statements Revealing Knowledge Derived from a Particular Source

In comparatively rare cases, a declarant's statement reveals knowledge that he must have acquired from a particular source. Even if the declarant is known to be a cunning dissembler, acquisition of the *knowledge revealed by his statement* allows us to infer that he has had access to the source of the information he discloses. Suppose, for example, there were a secret society of ten members. Rosenkreutz, the founder of the society, knows the names of the entire membership. As each member is inducted, he or she is given the means by which to signify membership in the society: a special handshake; three particular questions about international politics; and a handkerchief or tie that contain four specified colors.

At a dinner party, A, a society member, meets B who displays and performs all of the rituals signifying membership. If A can correctly assume that B had little or no chance of acquiring knowledge of the society's rituals unless B was a member, A can be confident of B's membership, regardless of what B says. Perhaps B is a liar or has a poor memory or is not a careful observer; still, A's assurance of B's membership would not be shaken. Without relying on B's credibility, A can confidently draw an inference that B, like himself, is one of the group of ten.

This thought experiment should facilitate your understanding of the well-known case of *Bridges v. State*.[22] There, a child was abducted by the defendant and taken to his house where she was sexually molested. Subsequently, the child described to her mother not only what the exterior of the house looked like, but also what the interior looked like, including the furnishings and various articles in the room in which she was molested. At defendant's trial, the prosecutor introduced detailed evidence depicting the exterior and interior of the defendant's home. He also supplied evidence showing that it was extremely unlikely that the victim could have gained knowledge of these surroundings except through her transport there by the defendant. Next, the prosecutor called the victim's mother who testified to the detailed statements of her daughter's description of the premises to which she had been taken

---

22. 247 Wis. 350, 19 N.W.2d 529 (1945), *rehearing denied*, 247 Wis. 350, 19 N.W.2d 862 (1945).

by the accused. The child's description, given to her mother, matched the actual appearance of the defendant's home.

The mother's testimony did not violate the hearsay rule. Her courtroom narrative of what her daughter had told her was not offered "for the truth" of what the defendant's home looked like. Rather, the child's description, repeated in her mother's testimony, was offered to show the congruence between the actual appearance of the defendant's house and the child's account of that appearance. In other words, the declarant's description showed her knowledge of the physical appearance of defendant's house—a knowledge that was derived from being there. A similar analysis would support a nonhearsay characterization of the child's statement to her mother giving a detailed description of her abductor. If it could be shown that the abductor fit the detailed description and that the only source of the child's knowledge was her observation of him during the abduction, a hearsay objection should be overruled.

Non-Assertive Conduct

We have seen that statements that expressly assert something can sometimes be used for their implied assertions. So used, they are not hearsay under the Federal Rules. Conduct can also give rise to implied assertions. A witness (auditor), for example, sees a trucker stop for a stoplight. At the stoplight, the truck is flanked by a car driven by P. A minute or two later the truck driver accelerates and the truck slowly moves forward toward the intersection. P's car, which can move more swiftly, also starts, enters the intersection, and is struck from the side by D's car. At trial, the issue is who had a green light. The trucker cannot be found. From the angle at which the auditor, a pedestrian, was standing, he could not see the green, yellow, and red lens on the stoplight. But he will testify as to the actions of the truck, followed by the actions of P's car on its flank.

The desired influence is that the light had turned green, prompting the trucker to start forward. Counsel for D objects, citing the rule against hearsay. He argues that the truck driver's actions are the equivalent of rolling down his window and saying to the witness and the driver of the plaintiff's car: "The light is green!" The decisive issue, however, is whether the truck driver *intended* to assert that the light had turned green. Since he was merely moving his truck forward and into the intersection, he probably did not intend to make an assertion about the color of the stoplight.

Sometimes, of course, conduct is intended as an assertion. Suppose, in the foregoing example, there had been construction at the intersection requiring traffic to merge into one lane. To facilitate the flow of traffic, the construction company assigns a worker to assist drivers. The employee uses arm gestures to move traffic forward when the light turns green and to point traffic toward the open lane. He is quite obviously, making assertions. Other instances of using conduct to make an assertion include nodding or shaking the head, pointing a finger at a person to designate or identify him, and using sign language. When conduct is used as a substitute for words, all of the usual hearsay dangers attach. But where the "declarant" (that is, the person whose conduct is observed by the auditor) does not intend to make an assertion, the danger of insincerity as to the unintended (implied) assertion is eliminated.

ILLUSTRATIONS

ISSUE	EVIDENCE
Had it started to rain?	*Dc* opened her umbrella.
Does the bus stop at the corner of Sixth and Main?	A number of people, some holding tickets or tokens, stood at the corner of Sixth and Main.
Is the ship seaworthy?	Dc, an experienced captain, examined the ship during the morning hours and set sail with his family after lunch.
Did *X*, while traveling abroad in a tropical climate, contract malaria?	*Dc*, a physician, prescribed a course of treatment that is the usual therapy for malaria.
Did *A* finish ahead of *B*, the favorite, in the local marathon?	Uncle, (*Dc*) who bet on *B*, paid his nephew (who bet on *A*) $25 as soon as the results of the race were known.

In all of the foregoing illustrations, the conduct in question apparently proceeds from the actors' belief that a certain condition exists. He does not, however, directly state this belief. Rather, his belief is implied by his action or, put otherwise, may be inferred by an observer. Although the key to treating implied assertions as nonhearsay is the reduction or elimination of the hearsay danger of insincerity,[23] it is often the case that one or more of the other

---

23. If a "declarant" is unaware of her implied assertion, then the hearsay danger of insincerity (deliberate lying or misleading) disappears. However, if she

hearsay dangers are minimized. Frequently, the risk of faulty perception is minimized as, for example, in the case of the sea captain inspecting the ship or the person opening her umbrella. Similarly, the risk of faulty memory is often minimized, as it would be in both examples just cited.

Silence
(including nondisclosure and failure to complain)

Silence is usually within the nonhearsay category of nonassertive conduct. Sometimes one's inaction or silence—his failure to speak out or complain—has probative value to show that an alleged event did not occur or an alleged condition did not exist. Suppose, for example, a plaintiff sues the railroad on which she had taken a trip six months before. In her complaint, she alleges that during a lengthy stopover at a railroad station in Cleveland, Ohio, the temperature in her passenger car dropped far below normal. As a result, a preexisting physical ailment from which she suffered was exacerbated. In its defense, the railroad offers the testimony of the conductor and the porter. Each is prepared to testify that no one else complained about the temperature in the passenger car. The hearsay rule should not prevent this testimony because the passive passengers were not making an assertion.[24]

ILLUSTRATIONS

ISSUE	EVIDENCE
(1) Was the restaurant's fish chowder spoiled or otherwise deleterious?	Other customers ate the same chowder and no one complained.
(2) Did *A*, representing the *ABC* partnership, agree to license one of the partnership's patents to the *X* Company?	When *A* returned from a business trip and reported his activities (which included a meeting with *X*'s president) to his partners, *B* and *C*, he made no mention of licensing patent rights to *X*.

is aware of her implied assertion, she could deliberately manipulate her conduct to deceive others. Suppose, for example, the ship captain wanted to give the false impression that a ship was seaworthy. He could inspect the ship in the morning; set sail with his family in the afternoon; but go into port soon

after he was out of the observer's (auditor's) sight. The judge decides if the declarant intended to make the relevant assertion. *See* FRE 104(a).

24. *See* Silver v. New York Cent. R. Co., 329 Mass. 14, 105 N.E.2d 923 (1952).

Although passive conduct, including silence, is not usually hearsay because no assertion is intended,[25] problems of relevance may arise. In order for inaction, failure to complain, or silence to be probative, persons who did not react or speak out must have been exposed to the event or condition that allegedly occurred or existed. In Illustration (1), for example, noncomplaining customers must have eaten chowder from the same pot or batch from which the plaintiff was served. Furthermore, silence has little probative value unless a complaint or protest can be made without undue difficulty. If lodging a complaint were onerous or impractical, the fact that other persons did not complain has little or no probative value because there is a likely alternative explanation for their passive behavior.

Polls or Opinion Surveys

Persons conducting surveys often ask their respondents questions that are designed to elicit a truthful response. Questions such as "Did you vote in the last presidential election?" or "Do you think the Country is moving in the right direction or the wrong direction?" are obvious examples.[26] Nonetheless, courts increasingly admit the results of a properly conducted poll. Often, one or more hearsay exceptions apply so that hearsay obstacles are avoided. For example, the hearsay exception that allows into evidence statements of a declarant's presently existing state of mind[27] would apply to a response such as "I think we should initiate diplomatic relations with Cuba." There is also the possibility that an expert witness could testify and give an opinion that was based in whole or in part on survey results. (Experts may rely on evidence that might be technically inadmissible in court if that evidence is "of a type reasonably relied upon by experts in [the testifying expert's] ... particular field....")[28] There is yet another possibility: a "catch-all" or residual exception to the hearsay rule provides for the admission of hearsay evidence that does not fit within one of the regular, specific exceptions, and yet is as reliable as hearsay evidence that does fall within these customary exceptions.

Of course, when polling results come before the trier of fact, it is important to afford the cross-examiner an adequate opportunity to test the design and execution of the poll. Such features as the selection of a sampling area, the determination of a random selec-

---

25. Consider, however, the following: "Keep talking into the cell phone until you see her enter; then remain perfectly silent for thirty seconds and hang up."

26. Of course, if a poll sought only to establish the number or percentage of respondents willing to express an opin-

ion on a particular topic, the response of the person polled would not be hearsay. She would either give her opinion (any opinion) or decline to do so.

27. FRE 803(3).

28. FRE 703.

tion within it, the design of the questions, and the execution of the interviews can be important factors in the survey's accuracy.

Incidentally, there is usually a double or multiple hearsay problem with surveys: the declarant (respondent) speaks to the pollster (auditor) who typically records the response and communicates it to a third person, often the witness. The cross-examiner may object that not only is the respondent's statement offered for its truth, but it is also impossible to examine the witness on the stand as to *what* the respondent actually said. In other words, the pollster's *recorded declaration of what* the respondent-declarant said is offered as evidence of the words the declarant spoke to the pollster. However, these "double hearsay" objections will usually fail because hearsay exceptions can often be linked so as to surmount the hearsay barrier. For example, the content of the respondent's statement often qualifies under an exception such as the one that applies to expressions of a declarant's present state of mind; the pollster's recordation (statement) of what the declarant said will usually qualify as business entry and, as such, also falls within a well-established exception to the hearsay rule.[29]

Prior, Out-of-Court Statements by the Witness on the Stand

An imaginary case will reveal a central feature of the problem addressed in this subsection. Suppose Henry Ford sues Walter Chrysler and the main issue in the case is whether a particular automotive prototype was black or some other color. If Ford can prove the car was black he will win the suit, but if Chrysler can show that the car was another color, such as green, he will prevail.[30] The plaintiff, Ford, calls his key witness, Edsel, a freelance automotive journalist. To Ford's surprise, Edsel testifies that the car in question was green. Subsequently, Ford adduces evidence (either during the cross-examination of Edsel or from another witness) that two months prior to the trial, Edsel told a Ford engineer that the car in question was black.

It seems reasonable to assume that each party has now produced conflicting evidence on which a jury could make a finding one way (black) or the other (green). However, if Ford has the burden of persuasion and if the only evidence he has that the car was black consists of Edsel's prior inconsistent statement, the judge will direct a judgment as a matter of law for the defendant Chrysler.

---

29. FRE 803(6).

30. Of course, if the jury cannot decide one way or the other because it believes the evidence points equally in both directions, the party with the burden of persuasion will lose. Usually, that party is the plaintiff; however, the defendant normally bears the burden of persuasion on affirmative defenses and, of course, on counterclaims.

The explanation for this odd result may be found in the definition of hearsay. Federal Rule of Evidence 801 defines "hearsay" as "a statement, other than one made by the declarant while testifying at the [present] trial or hearing, offered in evidence to prove the truth of the matter asserted." Edsel's prior statement that the car in question was black meets the definition of hearsay—it was not made from the stand at the present trial. Therefore, unless it fits within an exemption or exception, it is inadmissible if offered for its truth. Yet, it seems plain enough that the trier of fact should be made aware of evidence indicating that Edsel had made an earlier inconsistent statement, for the earlier statement casts doubt on his credibility.

Common law judges did not hesitate to admit evidence of the witness's prior inconsistent statement, but, true to the hearsay rule, disallowed use of the prior statement to prove the truth of its content. This convoluted result was accomplished by instructing the jury (when requested by a party to do so) that the witness's prior statement could be used to cast doubt on—that is, impeach—his trial testimony. The prior statement could not, however, be used for its truth. In other words, since the witness has given inconsistent accounts of the same event, the jury may consider his prior statement as bearing on whether the witness's trial testimony is unreliable.

Thus, in our imaginary case, if the jury members believe that prior to trial Edsel had said the car was black, they may consider this inconsistency in evaluating the credibility of his testimony that the car was green. But unless the prior statement comes within a hearsay exemption or exception, it cannot be used as the basis for a jury finding that the car was black. That is why Ford could not prevail *if* he had the burden of proving the car was black and *if the only evidence supporting that fact* was Edsel's prior statement.[31] Of course, if Ford had other admissible evidence *sufficient to support a finding* by the trier that the car was black, the judge would not grant a judgment as a matter of law (i.e., a directed verdict). Although in theory the jury would still be confined to using the prior inconsistent statement only for the nonhearsay purpose of evaluating Edsel's credibility, a general verdict in Ford's favor would be sustainable. The other admissible evidence that *could* be used to support a finding that the car was black would adequately support the jury's verdict. Furthermore, there would be no practical means of discovering whether the jury had also (improperly) consid-

---

31. We are assuming, of course, that the prior statement does not qualify as an exemption or exception.

ered Edsel's prior out-of-court statement as proof that the car in question was black.[32]

ILLUSTRATION

Federal Authorities bring charges against Humbert Humbert for illegally transporting his girlfriend, Lolita, in interstate commerce for the purpose of having the latter engage in prostitution. Prior to trial, Lolita, who had broken up with Humbert, gave several statements to the police in which she disclosed her activities as a prostitute. However, the day before trial Lolita and Humbert reconcile. When Lolita takes the witness stand for the government, she surprises the prosecutor by testifying that she has never engaged in prostitution. He thus proceeds to impeach her with evidence of her prior written and oral statements to the contrary. At the close of the prosecution's case, defense counsel moves for a directed acquittal and calls the court's attention to the fact that the only evidence that Lolita had ever engaged in prostitution consists of her own prior inconsistent statements. How should the trial judge rule?

With comparatively minor modifications, the Federal Rules of Evidence endorse the common law view that prior statements of a witness offered for their truth are hearsay. When the prior statements are inconsistent with the witness's trial testimony, they may, as we have seen, be introduced for purposes of attacking the witness's credibility. However, unless the earlier statements qualify as an exemption or exception to the hearsay rule, they cannot be used to prove the truth of the assertion they contain. This rule applies to both bench trials and jury trials. In jury trials, a party[33] may request that the judge instruct the jury regarding the restricted purpose for which evidence of the inconsistency is admitted.

The hearsay characterization of a witness's own prior statements has been justly criticized.[34] Since earlier statements are often made before the pressures of litigation are brought to bear on the witness, they may be more reliable than trial testimony. Furthermore, the earlier statements are made closer to the event in

---

32. Even if the jury did use the prior statement for its truth, the error would probably be harmless in light of the other evidence that the car was black.

33. The party requesting the instruction will almost always be the one trying to convince the jury to believe the truth of the witness's statements from the stand, and to disbelieve the prior inconsistent statement.

34. Early criticism, which has not lost its trenchancy, was offered by the late Professor Edmund M. Morgan in a classic article, Hearsay Dangers and the Application of the Hearsay Concept, 62 HARV. L. REV. 177, 192–96 (1948).

question thus reducing the risk of memory loss. The cross-examiner can question the witness not only about the latter's present testimony from the stand, but also about what he said prior to the trial. With both the witness's testimony and his earlier statements before them, the jury members should be able to decide which version is more reliable. In performing this task of evaluating the witness's present (testimonial) and past (inconsistent) statements, the jury is able to observe the witness's demeanor as he responds to questions about both his trial testimony and his previous account. Of course, if the witness's prior statements *are consistent* with his testimony, there is usually no need for the earlier statements and the trial judge can prohibit their introduction. Rule 403 permits the judge to reject relevant evidence that results in "undue delay, waste of time, or the needless presentation of cumulative evidence." The prior consistent statements of a witness, like his prior inconsistent statements, are hearsay. Thus, if the sole purpose of a witness's prior consistent statement is to bolster her testimony, evidence of the consistent statement should be excluded.[35]

Over the years, the debate has continued over the hearsay classification of a witness's prior inconsistent statements. Many trial lawyers support the rule that such statements are hearsay and, absent an applicable exemption or exception, cannot be used "substantively"—that is, to prove the truth of the facts they assert. Apparently, some trial lawyers believe that a cross-examination directed to testimony a witness has just given is more effective than a cross-examination directed at the witness's earlier inconsistent statement. Note that each of the opposing lawyers wants the jury to accept the witness's statement favorable to her client, but reject the witness's statement unfavorable to her client.

Defining Hearsay: A Minority View

A small minority of states define hearsay somewhat more broadly than do the Federal Rules. As we have seen, the focus of the Federal Rules is on the declarant's *assertion*: the central question is whether the declarant makes a conscious (intended) assertion that is subsequently "offered in evidence to prove the truth of the matter asserted."[36] A few common law jurisdictions shift the focus from the declarant's *statement* to the *declarant*. If the declarant's credibility is implicated when her statement is proffered, her statement is classified as hearsay. Of course, it may still be admissible because, for example, it comes within an exception. Nonetheless, a declarant-based definition of hearsay shifts some statements from nonhearsay (under the assertion-based approach of the Federal Rules) to hearsay, thus affecting admissibility

35. See, however, Ch. VI, § 6.2.
36. FRE 801(c).

in some cases. A simple but not infallible guide to recognizing hearsay in a declarant-based minority jurisdiction is to ask whether the probative value of the declarant's utterance hinges on what the declarant really believed.

ILLUSTRATIONS

(1) During a raid on a residence that was a suspected headquarters for illegal betting, the police answer the telephone in the parlor. After identifying themselves, the callers place bets on horse races and other sporting events. The police want to testify as to what the callers said.

(2) *X* is suspected of making a large drug sale in Boston. When the police visit *X*'s Boston residence the day after the sale, *X*'s wife says, "*X* isn't here. He flew to Los Angeles day before yesterday to attend his aunt's funeral and will be back tomorrow." Several hours later the police discover that *X* has spent the last twenty-four hours in a Boston motel and that his aunt in Los Angeles is alive and in good health. A policeman wants to testify as to the wife's false statement.

The declarations in these illustrations would not be hearsay under the Federal Rule. In Illustration (1), the callers are making implied (unintended) assertions that the house in question is used for gambling. In Illustration (2), the prosecutor is offering the wife's statement to show she was lying—that is, covering up for her husband, *X*. (Obviously, the prosecutor is not trying to prove that *X* was in Los Angeles.) However, in a minority, declarant-based jurisdiction the probative value of the evidence in the illustrations hinges on what the declarants actually believed and thus would be hearsay.

[There is a short Hearsay Quiz in Appendix I.]

Chapter VI

HEARSAY EXEMPTIONS

(Definitional or Statutory Nonhearsay)

---

§ 6.1 Introduction

In the last chapter we defined and illustrated hearsay evidence. In this chapter we refine the definition of hearsay by examining two classes of evidence that meet the basic definition of hearsay (that is, an intended assertion offered for its truth), yet because of subsection (d) of Federal Rule 801 are treated as nonhearsay. Generally speaking, these *exemptions* from the hearsay rule were applied by common-law judges as *exceptions* to the hearsay rule. But the drafters of the Federal Rules thought that these particular common-law exceptions had characteristics that distinguished them from the other common-law exceptions. They decided, therefore, not only to address these two classes of evidence separately, but also to transform them from hearsay (under Rule 801(c)) to non-hearsay (under Rule 801(d)).

Most courts and commentators refer to these two classes of evidence, formally considered hearsay exceptions (at least for the most part), as hearsay *exemptions* or *exclusions*. In this text we will denote these special classes with the term "exemptions" or, occasionally, with the phrases "statutory nonhearsay" or "definitional nonhearsay." The idea is Rule 801(d) *exempts* two classes of evidence (that are hearsay under Rule 801(c)) from the hearsay category or, put otherwise, *statutorily redefines* them so as to remove them from the basic definition of hearsay. An important point to bear in mind is that hearsay exemptions and hearsay exceptions have a common central feature: an out-of-court state-

166

ment within either category surmounts a hearsay objection and thus the proponent may use the statement to prove the truth of the matter it asserts. At the *practical level*, therefore, *exemptions and exceptions operate identically.*

Two Categories of Exemptions

There are two broad categories of statements transformed into nonhearsay by Rule 801(d):

(1) Certain prior statements by a testifying witness; and

(2) Statements made by a party or a party's representative ("Party Admissions") offered in evidence by that party's opponent.

The first category (Rule 801(d)(1)) includes certain prior *inconsistent* statements made by a testifying witness, as well as certain prior *consistent* statements made by her. Also within the first category are out-of-court *identifications* made by a testifying witness. Within the second category (Rule 801(d)(2)) are statements *made by a party* as well as statements made by other declarants (such as a party's agent) *associated with a party*. These nonhearsay "party admissions" are confined to statements that are offered *against a party by her opponent*. A party cannot introduce her own (presumably favorable) party admission as nonhearsay under Rule 801(d). The party admissions portion of Rule 801(d)[1] is, so to speak, "a one way street."

§ 6.2   Category I: Prior Statements of a Testifying Witness

We have already observed[2] that the hearsay rule applies to any statement "other than one made by the declarant while testifying at the trial or hearing, offered in evidence to prove the truth of the matter asserted."[3] Yet Rule 801(d)(1) removes from the hearsay category certain prior statements of a testifying witness. As we noted above, these exemptions from the basic definition of hearsay fall into three classes:

1. Specified Prior Inconsistent Statements

2. Specified Prior Consistent Statements

3. Prior Identification of a Person

1. FRE 801(d)(2) addresses party admissions.

2. Ch. V. § 5.2.

3. FRE 801(c).

Prior statements that fit within one (or more) of these classes become nonhearsay because they are specifically exempted (or excluded) from the basic definition of hearsay set out in Rule 801(c). We shall take up each class in the order in which it is set out in Rule 801(d)(1). Note, however, that each of the three exempted classes of prior statements by a testifying witness has a basic requirement in common: the prior statement is not converted from hearsay to nonhearsay unless the "declarant testifies at the trial or hearing and is subject to cross-examination concerning the prior statement. . . ."[4] This requirement that the hearsay declarant (who has made a pretrial statement) take the stand and testify applies to all of the exemptions contained in Rule 801(d)(1), but not to the exemptions set out in 801(d)(2) which covers party admissions. Furthermore, hearsay *exceptions*, as you will see in Chapter VII, usually do not require that the hearsay declarant testify.[5]

Prior Inconsistent Statements

A prior inconsistent statement of a testifying witness can be used to impeach his credibility.[6] So used, the proponent of the statement offers it to show that on another occasion the witness gave an account that differed from, and is inconsistent with, his testimonial account. Therefore, the proponent will argue, the witness is not reliable. A prior inconsistent statement used *only to impeach* does not violate the hearsay rule because it is not offered for the truth of the assertion it contains. Rather, the earlier inconsistency is offered to show that at another time the witness has given a conflicting version of the same event and therefore his account from the witness stand is not reliable.

If the proponent of the prior inconsistent statement wants to use it to prove the truth of the assertion it contains (that is, to establish facts), he must fit it within either an exemption or an exception to the hearsay rule. Rule 801(d)(1)(A) exempts from the hearsay rule a testifying witness's prior inconsistent statement if it "was given under oath subject to the penalty of perjury at a trial, hearing, or other proceeding, or in a deposition. . . ."

ILLUSTRATION

Rafael is prosecuted for transporting illegal immigrants into the United States. The grand jury's indictment alleges that he owned the van that carried eleven illegal

---

4. FRE 801(d)(1).

5. One exception, however, does require that the hearsay declarant testify. See FRE 803(5) which sets out the exception for a "Recorded Recollection."

6. Certain requirements, imposed by FRE 613, must be met.

aliens across the Mexican border, and that the driver, Miguel, was acting as Rafael's agent and coconspirator. After the Border Patrol stopped the van and apprehended its occupants, Miguel was taken to a nearby border patrol station. There, he gave sworn, tape-recorded statements to Pearce, an investigator for the Border Patrol. Subsequently, Miguel testified before the grand jury that indicted Rafael.

At Rafael's criminal trial, the prosecution calls Miguel, who unexpectedly testifies that he had borrowed Rafael's van on the pretense of hauling produce. Miguel also testifies that Rafael had no knowledge that Miguel was using the van to transport aliens across the border.

The prosecutor then impeaches Miguel with evidence of his prior inconsistent statements to the border patrol agent and to the grand jury. At the close of the evidence, defense counsel moves for a directed acquittal. She argues that Miguel's prior inconsistent statements may only be used to impeach him, and hence do not constitute substantive evidence that Rafael was involved in the illegal transportation of immigrants. Since these prior statements cannot be used substantively, she argues, there is insufficient evidence for the jury to find beyond a reasonable doubt that Rafael was involved in the crime charged. How shall the trial judge rule?

Rule 801(d)(1)(A) allows a prior inconsistent statement to be used substantively if it was made "under oath subject to the penalty of perjury at a trial, hearing, or other proceeding, or in a deposition. . . ." Of course, a prior inconsistent statement not made under oath can be used substantively (i.e., to prove its truth) if it comes within another hearsay exception or fits within another hearsay exemption. Grand jury "hearings" or "proceedings" fall squarely within Rule 801(d)(1)(A): the witness who appears before a grand jury testifies under oath and is subject to a prosecution for perjury if he lies. Therefore, Miguel's statements before the grand jury are nonhearsay ("statutory nonhearsay"). Whether a "hearing" or "proceeding" conducted by a member of the United States Border Patrol also fits within Rule 801(d)(1)(A) is a closer question.

One way to approach the question is to examine the reasons that support Rule 801(d)(1)(A)'s requirement of an oath and exposure to a perjury charge. First, these two requirements add to the likelihood that the declarant will tell the truth. Second, statements given under oath and subject to a perjury penalty are almost invariably recorded by a court reporter or some other official acting on the government's behalf. The existence of a transcript, tape recording, or some other recordation is generally a reliable means of proving that the declarant (who is a testifying witness at trial) made a prior inconsistent statement. Furthermore, the recordation is normally a reliable method of proving exactly what the declarant said on the prior occasion. The existence of a recordation thus minimizes trial disputes that center on whether the witness even made a prior inconsistent statement at all or, if he did, what exactly he said on the earlier occasion.

Since Miguel made a sworn, recorded statement before the Border Patrol investigating officer, and was subject to a perjury charge if he lied, there is at least a plausible argument that his prior statement can be used to establish Rafael's guilt.[7] On the other hand, police interrogations do not qualify as "proceedings" under Rule 801(d)(1)(A). The language of the rule, which embraces prior inconsistent statements made "at a trial, hearing, or other proceeding, or in a deposition," implies a formal inquiry, officially sanctioned by statute, regulation, or court rule, and conducted by a person or body that routinely receives witnesses' testimony "under oath subject to the penalty of perjury...."[8] The border patrol proceeding is in a twilight area between, say, a grand jury hearing and a police investigation or proceeding.

Prior Consistent Statements

Prior consistent statements, like their counterpart, prior inconsistent statements, fall within the general definition of hearsay.[9] Even if such statements were not hearsay, there would be good reason not to accept them as evidence since they add very little to the trial testimony. Suppose, for example, on the issue of the color of a car, the witness testifies that it was black. Prior statements to the same effect add very little, and their admission into evidence consumes trial time especially if evidence of the prior consistent statements is provided by other witnesses. Furthermore, if prior consistent statements were freely admissible, parties would be motivated to enhance favorable testimony by having their witnesses make prior out-of-court statements that would coincide with their subsequent trial testimony.

There is, however, one circumstance in which a witness's prior consistent statement has enhanced probative value. When a cross-examiner directly or by fair implication charges that a witness's testimony is a "recent fabrication," or is the product of an "im-

---

7. In circumstances similar to those in the Illustration, one court held that statements given before a Border Patrol agent could be used substantively. United States v. Castro–Ayon, 537 F.2d 1055, 1057–58 (9th Cir.), *cert. denied*, 429 U.S. 983 (1976) (immigration hearing very similar to grand jury proceeding).

8. FRE 801(d)(1)(A).

9. FRE 801(c).

proper influence or motive,"[10] a prior consistent statement may have considerable probative force to rebut this charge. It is imperative, however, that the prior consistent statement(s) predate the alleged corrupting influence or purported fabrication.[11]

ILLUSTRATION

In *D*'s prosecution for distributing drugs, two of his former associates testify for the prosecution. On cross, *D*'s attorney establishes that prior to trial, the two witnesses were incarcerated in the same jail cell; he then asks questions designed to show that during that incarceration they decided to frame *D* in order to minimize their own punishments. In rebuttal, the prosecutor presents a police detective who will testify that the two prosecution witnesses made statements consistent with their testimony after they were arrested and during a period (preceding their incarceration in the same cell) in which they were held in separate cells and could not communicate with each other. The defense attorney objects to the officer's testimony.[12]

It is not always easy to identify the point in time at which a corrupting influence might have caused a witness to give false or misleading testimony. Pursuant to Federal Rule 104(a), the judge must determine whether a prior consistent statement predated the time at which a fabrication was allegedly conceived or some motive or improper influence attached. In the Illustration, the defense attorney charged that the witnesses' frame-up was conceived and planned while they were cell mates. The police detective's testimony, however, rebuts this charge since he asserts that the two witnesses made statements consistent with their testimony prior to the time they were placed in the same cell where they could communicate with each other.

Other cases present more difficult factual questions for the judge. For example, suppose an arresting officer says to an arrestee, *X*, "If you cooperate with us and the prosecutor, you will get a lot lighter sentence." Subsequently, *X* agrees with the prosecutor to testify adversely to *D* in return for a reduced sentence. At trial,

10. FRE 801(d)(1)(B).

11. The leading case interpreting FRE 801(d)(1)(B) is Tome v. United States, 513 U.S. 150, 156–60 (1995).

12. This Illustration is a variation of the facts addressed by the Third Circuit in United States v. Anderson, 303 F.3d 847 (7th Cir. 2002), *cert. denied*, 538 U.S. 938 (2003) (consistent statements admissible since they predated alleged frame-up). *Compare* United States v. Prieto, 232 F.3d 816, 819–20 (11th Cir. 2000) (admissible prior consistent statements predated any discussion of cooperation with authorities).

after X has given testimony damaging to D, the cross-examiner asks leading questions suggesting that X's testimony is unreliable because, in return for a lighter sentence, X gave a skewed and partially false account of D's activities. Later, the prosecutor proffers a police detective willing to testify that after X's arrest, but before X spoke with the prosecutor, he gave an account of D's activities consistent with his (X's) testimony.

The issue for the judge is whether it is more likely than not that X's incentive to give false or misleading testimony preceded his pre-trial consistent statement; if this motive existed prior to his consistent statement, Rule 801(d)(1)(B) would not be satisfied and the pre-trial consistent statement would be hearsay.[13] In a case with strong factual similarities to this example, a federal Court of Appeals held that statements consistent with the witness's trial testimony did not precede his motive to give misleading or false testimony.[14] Initial conversations with the police had included police assurances about the benefits that would accrue from aiding the prosecution; therefore any subsequent statements to prosecutors necessarily came after the motive for supporting the state's case had attached.

Two reminders bring to a close our discussion of prior consistent statements which are rendered nonhearsay by Rule 801(d)(1)(B). First, there is no requirement that the prior consistent statement be made "under oath subject to the penalty of perjury ...," which, you will recall, is a requirement for a prior inconsistent statement proffered under Rule 801(d)(1)(A). Second, factual determinations of the trial judge are important under all three subsections of Rule 801(d)(1), but they are especially so under Rule 801(d)(1)(B)—prior consistent statements. That is because it is often unclear exactly when the influence, motive, or incentive to falsify arose. The ruling of the trial judge on the issue of whether the prior consistent statement preceded the corrupting motive or event is not easily overturned on appeal. The appellate standard for overturning factual determinations by a trial judge is generous: normally, her findings of fact will not be reversed on appeal unless they were "clearly erroneous."[15]

---

13. An adverse determination, however, does not necessarily mean that X's statement is inadmissible. Perhaps it comes within an exception (or another exemption) to the hearsay rule, although in the context of this example, that is not likely.

14. United States v. Awon, 135 F.3d 96, 99–100 (1st Cir. 1998).

15. Fed. R. Civ. P. 52(a). A roughly similar standard governs an appellate

court's review of a trial judge's ruling in situations where she has discretion. *See, e.g.,* FRE 403. A trial judges' discretionary determination will not be reversed unless the appellate court determines that she abused her discretion. *See, e.g.,* United States v. McRae, 593 F.2d 700, 706–07 (5th Cir. 1979), *cert. denied,* 444 U.S. 862 (1979). *Compare* Bhaya v. Westinghouse Elec. Corp., 922 F.2d 184, 187 (3rd Cir. 1990) *cert. denied,* 501 U.S. 1217 (1991) (reversal warranted only if

Prior Identifications

Federal Rule 801(d)(1)(C) exempts from the general definition of hearsay (contained in 801(c)) a statement "of identification of a person made after perceiving the person." As with all three of the exemptions contained in Rule 801(d)(1), it is essential that the declarant take the stand, subject to cross-examination. Generally speaking, an earlier out-of-court identification is more reliable than one made in the courtroom. The earlier identification is, of course, closer in time to the event that is the subject of the litigation than is a similar identification made at the trial. Two other factors may affect the accuracy and reliability of courtroom identifications. First, the person who is the subject of the identification may have changed his appearance by the time of trial. Second, when that person is a party, his location within the courtroom (as, for example, at counsel's table) may suggest who he is.

Some technical points emerge from a close reading of Rule 801(d)(1)(C). Subsection (C) operates independently of subsections (A) and (B), so that it is immaterial whether the prior identification is consistent or inconsistent with an identification made in the courtroom. There is also no requirement that the identification be sworn to or recorded. Subsection (C) does not require that a *courtroom* identification precede evidence of a prior identification. Indeed, Subsection (C) does *not require* that there be a courtroom identification at all. The subsection simply requires that the prior "statement" (which could, of course, consist of pointing to the subject in question) be an "identification of a person made after perceiving the person."[16] This language is broad enough to include not only an identification made at a "lineup" or "showup"[17] but also an identification made in any other setting, such as one made at the scene of an accident or crime, during or after an arrest, and so forth. Of course, in criminal cases, law enforcement officials must be obedient to constitutional requirements such as the presence of counsel at a lineup and to the constitutional proscription against unduly suggestive identifications.[18]

ILLUSTRATION

After a brutal attack on John Foster, a federal correctional counselor, an FBI agent visits him in the hospital. Although Foster's head injuries have impaired his memory,

---

trial judge's discretionary determination was "arbitrary and irrational").

16. FRE 801(d)(1)(C).

17. In a showup the identification is made without the display of other persons who generally fit the description of the person sought.

18. *See* 4 Mueller & Kirkpatrick, Federal Evidence § 410, at 206 (2d ed.).

he is able to identify his assailant, Owens, from an array of photographs that display eight prison inmates who were in the general proximity of the assault and thus a position to attack Foster. At Owens' trial for assault with intent to kill, Foster takes the stand. Foster's recollection of the attack is hazy and on cross-examination he admits that he cannot now remember seeing Owens during the attack. However, Foster does recall the visit of the FBI agent and he also recalls identifying his attacker's picture from a group of photographs. However, when Foster is shown the same array of photographs, he cannot be certain whether he had pointed out Owens or Ramsey, another pictured inmate.

Subsequently, the prosecution calls the FBI agent who had visited Owens in the hospital. Over objection, the agent is allowed to testify that when Foster was shown photographs of the eight inmates, he identified Owens as his attacker. On appeal, Owens' counsel argues that (1) a photographic identification is not within Rule 801(d)(1)(C) and, (2) since Foster's memory was still badly impaired at the time trial was held, he was not effectively "subject to cross-examination concerning the prior statement" of identification, as required by Rule 801(d)(1). How should the appellate court rule?

The photographic identification of Owens meets Rule 801(d)(1)(C)'s requirement that the prior statement be one that identifies a person that was perceived by the identifier. Owens was identified after an earlier perception, even though a photograph was the means by which Foster made the identification. The fact that at trial Foster cannot recall seeing Owens might affect Foster's credibility, but does not establish Foster's lack of perception. The earlier identification was based on his recollection of the assault and its perpetrator. Nor does it matter that it was the FBI agent's testimony that established that Foster pointed out Owens' picture. The same principle would apply if the identifier picked *D* out of a lineup and stated that he (*D*) was the bank robber. At trial, someone who saw and heard the identifier pick *D* could so testify, even if the identifier could not point to or otherwise identify *D* during his (the identifier's) testimony.

In United States v. Owens,[19] the Supreme Court addressed Rule 801(d)(1)'s requirement that a witness's prior statement is exempted from the hearsay rule only if the witness "testifies ... and is subject to cross-examination concerning the [prior] statement...." *Owens* bears a close factual resemblance to the Illustra-

19.   484 U.S. 554, 561–64 (1988).

tion above. There, the witness, who had suffered severe memory impairments after a brutal attack by a prison inmate, testified on direct that he only partially recalled the assault. Even though he could not now (at trial) remember seeing his assailant during the attack, he did recall making a photographic identification while in the hospital and in the presence of a particular FBI agent. However, he had little or no recollection of other relevant particulars of his hospitalization, such as the names of other visitors or whether any of them had suggested Owens was his assailant.

Nonetheless, the Supreme Court held that Foster was "subject to cross-examination" as that term is used in Rule 801(d)(1). It was sufficient, the Court said, that Foster was on the stand responding to cross-questions, even though his answers did not contain many of the "facts" the cross-examiner wanted to elicit. The Court did suggest that "limitations of the scope of examination by the trial court or assertions of privilege by the witness may undermine the process [of cross-examination] to such a degree that meaningful cross-examination within the intent of the Rule no longer exists."[20] However, the *Owens* opinion yields the general impression that in most cases the presence of the witness on the stand coupled with his responses to cross-questions will satisfy Rule 801(d)(1). Even an obdurate witness should not nullify cross-examination, so long as he at least responds to cross-questions.

The key to the *Owens* case is its recognition that a poor performance on the stand by the witness who has made a prior identification usually has the effect of undermining the reliability of that identification. Had *Owens* held that Rule 801(d)(1) required that the cross-examiner must be afforded at least the opportunity for a thorough and effective cross-examination, trial judges would constantly have to measure the adequacy of a particular cross-examination under that subsection. *Owens* removes this difficult determination from most trials, with the possible exception of a witness's refusal to respond to some cross-questions because of a claim of privilege or because a ruling by the trial judge severely narrows the allowable field of inquiry.

§ 6.3   Category II: Party Admissions: In General

As the name suggests, party admissions are statements or equivalent actions by a party that can be construed as admitting some relevant, damaging fact. The idea is that the party's *opponent* is entitled to introduce evidence of the "admitting" party's statements (or other communicative actions), although these admissions are in no way conclusive.[21] The party against whom evidence of an

---

20. Id. at 562.

21. Compare, for example, an admission made in a pleading such as the

admission is introduced may produce rebuttal evidence that shows, for example, that in fact there was no party admission or that there is a benign explanation for what was said or done. Think of party admissions as simply manifestations of the adversary system: a party's past statements, which appear to weaken his contentions at trial, may be introduced against him by his adversary.

The hearsay rule is not a barrier to the admissibility of party admissions since Rule 801(d)(2) *exempts* these admissions from the Rule 801(c)'s general definition of hearsay. Even the pervasive principle of Rule 602, generally requiring that a witness or hearsay declarant[22] have personal knowledge of the event or condition about which he speaks, has no application to party admissions. The assumption is that a party who makes an out-of-court statement about an event or condition must have had some basis for his assertions.[23] The gist of the rule that exempts party admissions from the hearsay ban is that a party bears the responsibility of having to confront in the courtroom evidence that he has allegedly made statements or taken other assertive actions that are inconsistent with his position at trial. Note, also, that if a party, herself, (as opposed to a party's representative or agent) makes a party admission and then raises a hearsay objection to its subsequent admission, she is saying, in essence, that she needs to cross-examine herself in order to expose a mistake or falsehood. This position, on its face, is untenable.

Despite the liberality with which party admissions are received in evidence, it is a mistake to assume that these admissions are always received into evidence. Suppose, for example, the defendant in a personal injury case is sued for having lost control of his car as he sped through a turn. Assume further that the plaintiff calls a witness who is prepared to testify that bystander (the auditor) told witness that after the accident the defendant lamented, "I should have seen the 'Loose Gravel' sign and slowed down." The proffered testimony by the witness would be hearsay: there is no way for the defendant's lawyer effectively to cross-examine the witness in an effort to prove that the defendant did not make this "party admission." The witness can only report what bystander said the defendant said. (There are too many links in the hearsay chain; in other words, multiple hearsay.)

defendant's answer. This admission is conclusive (unless the pleading is subsequently amended) and removes the matter admitted from the parties' dispute.

22. This principle expressed in Rule 602 also generally applies to hearsay declarants.

23. Of course, the party making the admission can take the stand and explain, for example, that he was mistaken as to the true facts, was simply guessing, or had been misled.

Furthermore, some party admissions are excluded by rules of evidence that reject relevant evidence in order to avoid undue prejudice or to advance a social policy. For example, if an accused in a bank robbery prosecution (the crime charged) had admitted to an undercover agent that on another occasion he had robbed a different bank (a collateral offense), his party admission would probably be excluded in the trial for the principal crime.[24] Likewise, statements made by a party in the course of compromise negotiations or plea bargaining are not usually admissible against him.[25] The point is that although party admissions usually escape the hearsay rule and are thus generally admissible against the party who made them, these admissions are sometimes rendered inadmissible by the application of an exclusionary rule or principle contained elsewhere in the Federal Rules.

There is yet another point to keep in mind: a party admission is admissible *only against the party* who, through his own action or the action of his agent or representative, made the admission. His party admission is inadmissible against other parties who are merely aligned as co-plaintiffs or co-defendants with the "admitting" party. However, if these other parties are so closely associated with the admitting party that they can be deemed his principals or accomplices, then his party admission is also admissible against them. For example, if one coconspirator makes a party admission in connection with advancing the aim of the conspiracy, his statement is admissible not only against himself, but also against the other coconspirators.[26] Similarly, statements by an agent are usually treated as party admissions of both the agent and his principal and, under this assumption, the agent's declarations would also be admissible against his principal—assuming the principal is a party.

The rule that party admissions are admissible only against the parties who are responsible for them flows from the fact that party admissions, unlike most admissible hearsay statements,[27] are not admitted into evidence because they are deemed trustworthy. As we have seen, the nature of the adversary system, with its emphasis on the thrusts and parries of the adverse parties, explains why party admissions are allowed into evidence. Of course, some—perhaps

24. See FRE 404(b) and the discussion in Ch. III, § 3.6–4, 3.6–5.

25. See FRE 408, 410 and the discussion in Ch. IV, §§ 4.3, 4.5. *See also* FRE 407 (evidence of subsequent remedial measures inadmissible), 409 (evidence of payment of medical expenses inadmissible).

26. This is true even if the coconspirator who made the damaging statement is not joined as a party. This statement is attributed to his fellow conspirators and is admissible against those coconspirators who are made a party. But the declarant's statement would not be admissible against other parties to the suit who were not part of the conspiracy.

27. At common law, and in some states even today, party admissions are treated as an *exception* to the hearsay rule, not as a (nonhearsay) exemption.

even most—party admissions are reliable, but this fact does not account for either their early common law recognition or their continued acceptance in evidence codes. Generally speaking, judges do not attempt to screen out "unreliable" party admissions; rather the judges leave it to the admitting party to negate the probative force of his party admissions.

Since party admissions are admissible only against the party or parties responsible for them, other ("nonresponsible") parties are entitled to a limiting instruction that directs the jury to confine its consideration of these admissions to the admitting party. An instruction to the jury usually suffices in a civil case, but in a criminal prosecution with multiple defendants, it may be necessary to hold separate trials in cases in which a party admission of *D–1* also implicates *D–2*, yet *D–2* is not an "admitting" party such as a coconspirator. If *D-1* and *D–2* were jointly tried, the jury might improperly consider *D-1's* statement as evidence not only of his guilt, but of *D-2's* as well. In civil or criminal trials where a party admission is admissible against one party, (*A*), for example, but not against her co-party, (*B*), evidence of *A*'s admission may not be used against *B*, nor is such evidence considered in determining the sufficiency of the evidence for (or against) *B*.

§ 6.4 Individual and Adopted Party Admissions

An individual party often makes an out-of-court statement that is at odds with his contentions at trial. For example, the owner of a machine shop may have told an insurance adjuster that one of the owner's employees was badly injured because the machine on which the latter was working was not equipped with a safety shield. Suppose the owner is subsequently sued by the injured employee and the owner contends that the machine was safe and that the accident was due to the employee's own carelessness. The employee can introduce the owner's statement against him—for example, by calling the adjuster to the stand and having him relate what the owner said. Federal Rule 801(d)(2) exempts from the hearsay rule a statement that "is offered against a party and is (A) the party's own statement in either his individual or representative capacity...."

Objections by the owner that he did not see the event (no personal or first-hand knowledge) or that he was merely offering an opinion would not preclude evidence of the owner's admission. Of course, the owner can take the stand and explain that he was mistaken or misinformed when he made the statement in question. Note, also, that the quoted portion of the rule makes it clear that it is of no consequence whether a party made the admission in a personal (individual) capacity or in his capacity as a representative. Thus, if a trustee is a party to a suit, his party admission may be used against him even though he made it in an individual capacity.[28] Of course, the statement in question must be relevant to his representative duties or conduct.[29]

ILLUSTRATION

Deuce is prosecuted for the possession of controlled drugs. He pleads not guilty and contends that the drugs in question belonged to his erstwhile apartment mate, a Columbian national who has returned to his native land. Anita, Deuce's estranged girlfriend, is willing to testify that Deuce once told her that "he made a hell of a good living moving drugs right under the nose of the cops." Deuce's lawyer objects to Anita's proffered testimony on the ground of irrelevance and on the further ground that Deuce has not testified, and probably will not take the stand. How should the trial judge rule?

Deuce's statement increases the likelihood that the drugs in question were his. Recall that evidence is relevant if it has "any tendency to make the existence of any [consequential] fact . . . more probable or less probable than it would be without the evidence."[30] Whether or not a party testifies has no bearing on the admissibility of his party admission. For tactical reasons, however, it may be advantageous to withhold evidence of an opponent's party admission until he has testified on direct. If his direct testimony is inconsistent with his earlier party admission, the statement constituting the admission may be used both to impeach him and as substantive evidence—that is, to prove the truth of the prior statement. If an opponent's party admission is introduced before he testifies, he may decline to testify or structure his testimony so as to minimize any conflicts between his earlier statement (party admission) and his statements from the stand.

Party Admissions by Conduct

Assume that the issue in a case is whether the plaintiff, a truck driver, attempted to drive his truck over a small bridge covered by flood water, despite a warning not to. The defendant, a highway department employee, asserts that the plaintiff stubbornly drove onto the flooded bridge despite the defendant's warning shouts. Conversely, the plaintiff contends that the defendant, who had just measured the depth of the water, used arm gestures to signal that the truck should go forward and onto the bridge. Evidence that the defendant used gestures to indicate the bridge was passable is

28. Rule 801(d)(2) ACN.   **30.** FRE 401.
29. Ibid.

exempt from the hearsay rule even though the defendant's conduct was intended as an assertion and thus falls within the general definition of hearsay. His party admission could be introduced against him by the truck driver, but of course the jury will ultimately determine who is telling the truth.

Consider which, if any, of the following actions fall within the general definition of hearsay (Rule 801(c)):

(1) During a police raid on a warehouse that contained stolen property, *D* was found hiding in a large cardboard container.

(2) Soon after a hit-and-run accident in which a motorcyclist was severely injured, *D* had the dents removed from the front of his car and the car painted a different color.

(3) Dr. *D*, charged with writing bogus prescriptions for drugs that he and a pharmacist sold on the black market, destroyed many of his medical and financial records just prior to his arrest.

(4) *D*, sought for questioning in connection with an attempted murder, shaved his head, began wearing dark glasses and a false mustache, and dressed in military attire.

(5) Immediately after a serious accident at a construction site, apparently the result of a construction worker's negligence, *D*, a construction worker, fled from the scene of the accident.

In each of these instances, many common law judges would consider *D*'s action a party admission evincing *D*'s awareness of his guilt, his probable liability, or in more general terms, the weakness of his legal position. As we have seen, under the common law, a party admission is an *exception* to the hearsay rule. Under the Federal Rules of Evidence, however, *D*'s conduct in the various instances described above would not be hearsay *even* under Rule 801(c)'s general definition of hearsay. In each instance, *D*'s nonverbal conduct was apparently not intended by him as an assertion of his guilt or liability. In all probability, *D* was hoping that his conduct would escape detection. For example, when *D* took his car to a body shop to be repainted, he did not intend to communicate to the manager of the shop, "I hit a motorcyclist and I want to change the color of my car." Nor did *D*, who hid in a cardboard container, intend to assert that he was involved in storing stolen property. On the contrary, he wanted to avoid being discovered in the building that housed the stolen goods. In short, if conduct is not hearsay under the Federal Rules' general definition of hearsay (801(c)), it is not necessary to invoke the hearsay exemption of Rule 801(d)(2) (definitional nonhearsay) to escape the hearsay rule.

Adoptive Admissions

Sometimes a party will, in the words of Rule 801(d)(2)(B), manifest "an adoption or belief in ... [the] truth" of someone else's statement, thereby putting the statement on the same footing as a party's own statement. Suppose, for example, a land developer uses the results of a pollster's opinion survey to try to persuade a zoning board to rezone residential property for commercial use; or a patient uses the written opinion of a physical therapist to make an insurance claim; or a businessman distributes to current and potential customers or investors a newspaper article that describes his company as financially sound and increasingly profitable; or an evangelist "pro-life" minister distributes to his congregation a pamphlet in which the author, a doctor, claims that use of the "morning-after" birth control pill is the equivalent of murder.

These are straightforward examples of the adoption by one person of the statement of another. The law of evidence treats a statement adopted by a party as that party's admission and exempts the adopted statement from the hearsay rule. More troublesome, and often more problematic, are statements that a party "adopts" through his tacit acquiescence in another person's statement. Sometimes, the other person's statement has an accusatory tone:[31] "Your insect control device wouldn't work and you knew it." Silence in the face of this kind of statement often constitutes a party admission. The judge must decide if the statement in question (whether or not accusatory) was heard and understood and whether, in the circumstances in which the statement was made, a reasonable person would have expressed his disagreement with it. The preferred, though not universal practice, is for the judge initially to make these determinations, treating the issues before her as involving "preliminary questions concerning ... the admissibility of evidence" and, as such, allocated to the judge (and not the jury) by Federal Rule 104(a).[32] The jury may then be instructed that the probative value, if any, that the jury attaches to the evidence depends on whether, upon hearing the statement, a reasonable person in the party's circumstances would have denied or protested its accuracy if he believed it was untrue. Unless the judge makes the initial determination about whether a reasonable person would have responded, there is a risk that the jury will accept the truth of the speaker's statement even though it does not conclude that the party adopted it. If the party did not adopt the statement, and the

31.   However, this is not always true. For example, in United States v. Beckham, 968 F.2d 47 (D.C. Cir. 1992), *X*, a cocaine seller, said that he only had one bag left, but that the buyer (an undercover agent) could purchase another bag from supplier, *Y*. Upon hearing this, *Y* walked over to a container containing crack cocaine and opened it. Held: *Y* adopted *X*'s statement.

32.   For a good discussion of the judge and jury problem, see MUELLER & KIRKPATRICK, EVIDENCE § 829, at 779–80.

statement is a hearsay declaration that does not qualify as an exemption or exception, the statement should not be accepted by the jury for its truth. The risk that the jury will use an "unadopted" hearsay declaration for its truth is reduced if the judge makes an initial determination of the question of whether or not a statement was adopted by the party.

Admissions by silence are particularly troublesome when the accused fails to deny inculpatory statements by (or in the presence of) law enforcement officials. In some settings, we do not yet have a definitive answer concerning admissibility. If the defendant is in custody, and has been given *Miranda* warnings, his right to remain silent is constitutionally protected[33] and failure to speak cannot be used against him. The same result should obtain if the defendant is in custody and should have been given *Miranda* warnings, but has not. Of course, a defendant may waive his right to remain silent. If he does so knowingly and intentionally, and thereafter freely converses with the police, he runs the risk that he may tacitly acknowledge the truth of some of the statements made by the police or others in attendance. For example, he may firmly deny certain statements by the police, but remain mute as to others.

A separate problem arises when the accused's pre-arrest silence—prior to a *Miranda* warning—has probative value to *impeach* testimony that he gives at trial. Suppose, for example, the accused testifies that he killed the victim in self-defense. He may be impeached by evidence that he did not report the incident for several weeks.[34]

A related but distinct evidentiary problem arises when the prosecution seeks to offer silence as substantive evidence (as opposed to impeachment) when the defendant's silence occurs before receiving a statement of his *Miranda* rights, as, for example, before he is actually arrested or immediately thereafter. In this setting, law enforcement officers are usually involved. A trial judge should be extremely cautious about allowing "adoptions by silence" in an accusatory environment, since the defendant is usually under considerable pressure and his interrogators probably have incentives to "trip him up." It is probably common knowledge among Americans that the United States Constitution provides a right not to incriminate oneself and there is probably also a general belief that one is entitled not to give self-incriminating information to police. If these

---

33. Miranda v. Arizona, 384 U.S. 436 (1966). See also Doyle v. Ohio, 426 U.S. 610 (1976).

34. Jenkins v. Anderson, 447 U.S. 231, 235–38 (1980). Of course, the nonconstitutional evidentiary rule governing adopted admissions must be satisfied: generally speaking, a reasonable person in the defendant's position would have spoken out and denied or corrected the accuracy of the statement made in his presence. Or, in the context of *Jenkins*, a reasonable person would have reported being attacked and having to defend himself.

assumptions are accurate, it seems unfair to permit evidence that the defendant's failure to deny or respond to an interrogator's accusations gives rise to a party admission. However, Circuit Courts are divided over whether to allow a defendant's silence prior to receiving a *Miranda* warning to be admitted against him.[35]

§ 6.5   Statements by Authorized Spokespersons and Other Agents

Rule 801(d)(2)(C) exempts from the hearsay rule "a statement by a person authorized by the party to make a statement concerning the subject" about which the person speaks. This subsection simply says that when a party has delegated "speaking authority" to an agent, statements made in the course of exercising that authority are admissible against the party. There are many instances in which *P* (the principal) gives speaking authority to *A* (the agent). Familiar examples are a client's authorization to a lawyer to speak for her in connection with a case or other legal matters and her authorization to her accountant to speak for her with respect to financial matters.[36]

The business world is replete with instances in which designated agents are permitted to speak for their company, as, for example, where a construction company's manager is permitted to negotiate with suppliers of materials or a corporate CEO is given authority to initiate product recalls. Federal Rule 801(d)(2)(C) makes no distinction with regard to the persons with whom a "speaking agent" is communicating, so long as the agent is within the range of his delegated speaking authority.[37] Thus, if the construction foreman of a general building contractor is given authority to render oral and written reports evaluating the work of subcontractors, the foreman's oral or written statements to anyone about this subject will constitute the general contractor's party admissions. It is immaterial, for example, whether the foremen's statements were made to a fellow employee, corporate management, a sub-contractor, or someone outside of the construction

35. *Compare* United States v. Frazier, 394 F.3d 612, 619–20 (8th Cir. 2005) (defendant was under no "compulsion to speak" during this time thus his *Miranda* rights were, including the right to remain silent, not triggered), *with* United States v. Velarde–Gomez, 269 F.3d 1023, 1029–30 (9th Cir. 2001) (en banc) (an individual's *Miranda* rights are triggered as soon as the government places him in custody).

36. The courts are split on whether an expert witness's out-of-court statements may be used as a party admission of the party retaining the expert. It is clear that when a party engages an expert to testify at trial, the agent has speaking authority. One the other hand, an expert is supposed to render an independent opinion. Compare Collins v. Wayne Corp. 621 F.2d 777, 782 (5th Cir. 1980) (admissible as party admission) with Kirk v. Raymark Indust. Inc., 61 F.3d 147, 163–64 (3rd Cir. 1995) (not admissible). Perhaps the correct answer lies in the circumstances of each case— the judgment should be contextual.

37. Rule 801(d)(2) ACN.

business. The pivotal issue under Rule 801(d)(2)(C) is apt to be whether the putative principal had in fact delegated to the agent the authority to speak. If not, the agent's statement is not admissible against the "principal" *under this subsection*, but would, of course, be admissible against the agent if she were a party and if the statement were relevant to her claim or defense.

The decision as to whether the purported agent had speaking authority is governed by Rule 104(a) which allocates to the judge "questions concerning . . . the admissibility of evidence. . . ." Sometimes the very statement in question contains an assertion that supports the conclusion that the agent was authorized by the principal to speak for the latter. ("My company, *D*, has asked that I speak with you about selling your property before the EPA launches an investigation as to whether the underground water is contaminated by mercury.") Can such a statement be used by the judge as evidentiary support for her conclusion that the agent had speaking authority? Under Rule 801(d)(2), it can. However, the "contents of the statement . . . are not alone sufficient to establish the declarant's [agent's] authority" to speak for the party-principal. Thus, the judge cannot conclude there was speaking authority unless there is at least some evidence of its existence that is extrinsic to the statement of the purported agent.

The "Scope Rule"

Common law judges had a very restrictive view with respect to when a principal had delegated speaking authority to an agent. For example, agents hired to deliver goods (truck drivers) or services (ushers), or to engage in construction or repairs (electricians or masons) were usually regarded as lacking the authority to speak for the principal. The theory was that the principal hired the agent to perform various physical tasks, not to speak for him and, particularly, not to speak adversely to his interests. Rule 801(d)(2)(D) rejects the traditional common law position by declaring that "a statement by . . . [a] party's agent or servant concerning a matter within the scope of the agency or employment" constitutes a party admission of the principal.

The judge decides whether the statement concerns "a matter within the scope of the agency or employment," since that question controls the admissibility of the statement and thus implicates Federal Rule 104(a). In resolving this issue, the judge may consider any portion of the statement itself that is helpful, although the agent's statement, standing alone, is not sufficient to establish the scope of his duties.[38] Rule 801(d)(2)(D) makes it clear that in order to qualify as a party admission under the scope rule, the agent's

---

38.   FRE 801(d)(2).

statement must have been made before the termination of the agency or employment relationship.[39] This limiting feature protects the principal from damaging statements by terminated employees or agents who may bear ill will against their former employer.

ILLUSTRATION

Alex was hired to perform maintenance services for the Draper Chemical Corporation. One of Alex's duties was to inspect daily certain pipelines that carried toxic chemicals, in order to ensure that there were no leaks. One Friday Alex decided to leave work before lunch in order to depart early for a weekend of fishing. That night a sensor alarm sounded, indicating the presence of toxic substances. Several night-shift employees were rushed to the hospital after inhaling fumes from the chemicals that had seeped from a leak in one of the pipes Alex was responsible for inspecting.

On Monday, when Health and Safety Authorities spoke with Alex, he admitted that he had not inspected the pipe in question on the preceding Friday. On Wednesday, Alex submitted his resignation (effective immediately) to Draper Chemical in order to be eligible for three weeks of "transition pay" which was not available to employees who were fired. On Friday, Alex visited one of the injured employees, Perrozzi, at the hospital. During their conversation, Alex remarked that the pipe in question was old and corroded and that he had twice told his supervisor it should be replaced.

During Perrozzi's suit against Draper Chemical for personal injuries, Perrozzi offers to testify as to what Alex had told him about the defective pipe. Perrozzi also offers a co-worker who will testify that on the Monday before Alex quit he heard Alex admit to a Health and Safety Inspector that he, Alex, had not conducted the required pipe inspection on the Friday of the accident. How should the judge rule on these offers of proof?

There are two approaches to the admissibility of Alex's statement to the Health and Safety Inspector. The most obvious is to apply Rule 801(d)(2)(D) and point out that Alex was speaking about "a matter within the scope of his ... employment" and that he made the statement in question while still employed. Thus, Alex's statement is admissible against Draper Chemical as the latter's party admission. Of course, if Alex were joined as a party defen-

---

39. FRE 801(d)(2)(D).

dant, his statement would also be admissible against him as an individual party admission.

It is also plausible to conclude that Alex had speaking authority and thus his statement also falls within Rule 801(d)(2)(C) because it was authorized by Draper Chemical. Even though, traditionally, common law courts were reluctant to find speaking authority when agents or employees were engaged primarily to perform "nonspeaking" tasks, a minority of common law courts were breaking with tradition as early as 1975,[40] when the Federal Rules of Evidence were first adopted. A modern court is likely to find that Draper Chemical had delegated speaking authority to Alex, at least with respect to matters relating to the chemical leak. If the court so concludes,[41] Alex's statement is admissible as Draper Chemical's party admission. However, the more certain avenue to admissibility is Rule 801(d)(2)(D), the "scope rule".

Alex's statement to Perrozzi during their hospital conversation stands on a different footing. Since Alex's employment terminated prior to this conversation, neither Rule 801(d)(2)(C) (speaking authority), nor Rule 801(d)(2)(D) (scope rule) applies. Even if Alex were joined as a party defendant, Perrozzi probably could not introduce Alex's earlier statement against Alex as an individual party admission: the most obvious thrust of the statement is to *exonerate* Alex and place the blame on Draper Chemical. However, the statement is not admissible against Draper—it is not Draper's party admission. The statement, of course, would be relevant to Draper Chemical's liability, but the statement is hearsay[42] and is not removed from the hearsay rule by the party admissions exemption. Furthermore, Alex's statement cannot be shown through the testimony of Perrozzi for the limited nonhearsay purpose of proving Draper Chemical had notice of a dangerous condition. There are too many links in the hearsay chain.[43]

Coconspirators' Statements

A conspiracy is roughly analogous to a business partnership[44] in the sense that in each enterprise the members act in concert to

---

40. FRE 801(d)(2)(C)(D) ACN.

41. The court would be making a determination pursuant to FRE 104(a).

42. Presumably, the statement would be offered to prove that the leaky pipe was old and corroded and that Alex had made Draper Chemical's management aware of this defect. The trier is asked to believe that the pipe was in this defective condition and that Alex had warned his supervisor. As to these factual propositions, Perrozzi cannot be effectively cross-examined. He only knows

what Alex said about the condition of the pipes and the warning.

43. Perrozzi can only testify that *Alex said* he warned Draper's management. Of course, Alex—or someone who heard Alex warn his supervisor—could provide admissible testimony that Draper was "on notice" about a dangerous condition.

44. The statements of one partner relating to the activities of the partnership are generally admissible against the partnership.

further and achieve desired objectives. As coconspirators implement their plans, one or more of them may make statements that will be offered in subsequent litigation as a party admission. For example, suppose A, B, and C conspire to embezzle funds from their corporate employer. Unbeknown to A, a conversation he has with X, an accountant, is secretly recorded. During this conversation, in which A tries to persuade X to join the company's accounting section, A enticingly describes certain activities of himself, and of B and C, which have resulted in huge financial gains. A's recorded statements, subsequently produced at A's criminal trial, are not only his party admissions; they also constitute party admissions of B and C.

Moreover, if X were to join the conspiracy, statements of his coconspirators made in furtherance of the conspiracy would be admissible against X as his party admissions. Even coconspirators' statements made by A, B, and C *before* X joined the conspiracy would be admissible against him. The rationale is that when X elected to join the conspiracy he took it as he found it; that is, he subscribed to both its potential for gain and its preexisting risks. Finally, it is not necessary to charge the coconspirators with a conspiracy in order to invoke the coconspirator party admissions rule. The rule is available in both criminal and civil trials regardless of whether or not a conspiracy is charged in the indictment or alleged in a civil complaint. Of course, the proponent who wishes to invoke the coconspirator exemption to the hearsay rule must provide foundation evidence of a conspiracy.

These broad, even breathtaking rules of admissibility are tempered by several important restrictions, one of which is the "in-furtherance" requirement. Not only must a coconspirator's statement be made *during the course of the conspiracy*, but it must also be a statement *in furtherance* of the conspiracy.[45] Although courts usually take a generous view of what statements advance the conspiracy, the in-furtherance requirement precludes use of the coconspirator exemption to admit simple narratives about past events, idle chatter, bragging, and the like. Even more obviously, statements which may be incriminating but are designed to defeat the conspiracy are not made in furtherance of it. On the other hand, statements in furtherance of the conspiracy should include those designed to launch the conspiratorial transaction, to recruit new members (as in the example above), to recount past conduct or events *in order* to plan future strategy, to keep members aware of progress, and to reassure members or elicit their cooperation. The same can be said for transactional records, inventories, status reports, and other entries that are designed to track the financial condition or progress of the conspiracy.

---

45. FRE 801(d)(2)(E).

As we have noted, the party admissions rule for coconspirators' statements applies only to statements made during the course of the conspiracy. When the conspiracy is over, Rule 801(d)(2)(E) is no longer applicable. Determining when a conspiracy begins and ends can be difficult, for often there are no clear lines of demarcation. Obviously a conspiracy takes root when two or more persons agree to jointly seek a common end. The fact that additional persons later join the conspiracy does not affect the point in time at which the conspiracy originated. The conspiracy terminates when the conspirators achieve their objective or when they abandon their quest. Invoking Federal Rule 104(a), the judge must decide when a conspiracy begins and ends.

ILLUSTRATIONS

In which (if either) of the following hypothetical problems has the conspiracy (comprised of A, B, and C) terminated?

(1) A, B, and C conspire to set fire to a building owned by A and B, and thereafter to collect the fire insurance proceeds. C, the coconspirator who actually sets the fire, is arrested one month after the building burns. Faced with the possibility of a long prison term, C (two weeks after his arrest) reveals to the prosecutor details about the conspiratorial plot of A, B, and C. Meanwhile, A and B have filed a claim for the insurance proceeds and threatened suit against the fire insurance company should it fail to honor their claim.

(2) A, B, and C conspire to rob a bank. Several days after the successful heist, they decide to break the getaway car into component parts and destroy it. Furthermore, since some of the stolen currency may be marked, the conspirators also agree that each of them will hide his separate share in a safety deposit box and leave it there for at least three years.

In Illustration (1), the first issue is when C effectively withdrew from the conspiracy. Once he terminates his membership in the conspiracy, his statements are no longer admissible as the party admissions of A and B, nor are *their* statements party admissions of C. Generally speaking, a participant in the conspiracy remains a member until he takes affirmative steps to withdraw. Of course, an arrest might be viewed as an involuntary withdrawal by the arrestee. More clearly, C's decision to reveal the conspiratorial plot to the police signals a voluntary withdrawal. (Furthermore, these statements do not advance the conspiracy). Of course, it is possible that an arrested coconspirator could promote the conspiracy even after his imprisonment by, for example, giving false information to the authorities or even communicating with the other coconspirators. The decision as to whether an arrest or other event (such as "confessing") terminates the arrestee's membership in the conspiracy ought to be a contextual one, turning on the facts of each case. The judge, of course, resolves this issue.

For example, an arrestee who remains silent after his arrest and has no opportunity to communicate with fellow conspirators until their subsequent apprehension ought to be viewed as having withdrawn, perhaps involuntarily, from the conspiracy at the time of his arrest. In Illustration (1), the trial judge would have to decide, based on facts peculiar to the case before her, when *C*'s withdrawal became effective. The conspiracy itself survived *C*'s arrest because the ultimate aim of the conspiracy was to collect the insurance proceeds and *A* and *B* were pursuing that end, even though *C* had been apprehended as a suspect. If, during the continuance of the conspiracy, *A* or *B* made statements that incriminated *C*, those statements would be admissible against *C only if they predated* his withdrawal. At least, it seems clear that *C* had withdrawn from the conspiracy when he began to cooperate with the police and reveal the coconspirators' plot.

Illustration (2) also raises a question as to when the conspiracy terminated. In the federal courts (but not those of all the states), the coconspirator party admissions rule usually ceases to operate during the concealment phase—that is, when the members are trying to avoid detection. However, the concealment phase does not begin until the principal goal of the conspiracy has been either achieved or abandoned. In crimes involving the illicit acquisition of money, the principal objective of the conspiracy is not realized until the money has been received *and* divided among the members. In the present Illustration, two separate acts, destruction of the car and secreting the money, arguably fall within the concealment phase and, so viewed, are not part of the initial conspiracy in most jurisdictions.

The question of when concealment constitutes a separate phase is often a close one and the cases are not consistent.[46] If acts of concealment are part of the original conspiratorial plan, as opposed to separately conceived (later) plans to hide the crime, it seems arbitrary to divide the conspiracy into two phases. In Illustration

---

46. Compare United States v. Medina, 761 F.2d 12, 16–18 (1st Cir. 1985) (conspiracy extended through conspirators decision to bury vehicle used in kidnaping) with United States v. Floyd, 555 F.2d 45, 48 (2nd Cir. 1977) (arrangement to have bank robbery getaway car burned not within principal conspiracy).

(2), however, the concealment schemes appear to have originated after the principal aim of the conspiracy had been achieved, and thus would fall outside of the coconspirator admissions doctrine.

The Essential Requirements of the Exemption

The coconspirator hearsay exemption has three requirements:

(1) the declarant and the party against whom the declarant's statement is introduced were members of the same conspiracy; and

(2) the declarant made the statement during the course of the conspiracy; and

(3) the declarant's statement was made in furtherance of the conspiracy.

Although the coconspirator exemption is most often encountered in criminal cases, it is applicable to civil cases as well. The proponent must convince the judge that his evidence meets the requirements listed above. It is not necessary that a conspiracy be charged in the indictment or, in a civil suit, alleged in the pleadings. It is immaterial whether a coconspirator's party admission is made to another coconspirator or to an outsider. Furthermore, it does not matter whether or not the declarant-coconspirator is joined as a party to the civil or criminal trial.

The breadth of the coconspirator exemption sometimes causes parties and judges to rely on it unnecessarily. The exemption is needed only when a coconspirator's statement is offered for its truth. When the statement has a nonhearsay use, its admission need not rest on Rule 801(d)(2)(E). Suppose, for example, A, B, and C agree to extort money from local store owners by threatening injury to the owner or his family. A threatening statement by A to a shop owner ("If you don't pay weekly protection money your son will have an unfortunate accident") is a verbal act—it has independent legal significance because making the statement constitutes an offense. The statement comes in as nonhearsay; the *substantive* law of conspiracy determines whether B and C share A's criminal responsibility.

Coconspirator Admissions: The Judge's Role

In the leading case of *Bourjaily v. United States*,[47] the United States Supreme Court rendered an important interpretation of the relationship between Federal Rule 801(d)(2)(E) (coconspirator party admissions) and Federal Rule 104 (allocation of fact-finding responsibilities between judge and jury). First, the Court held that the judge must determine, under the provisions of Rule 104(a), whether

---

47.   483 U.S. 171 (1987).

the requirements of the coconspirator exemption have been satisfied. For example, the judge, not the jury, determines whether there was a conspiracy, whether the declarant and the party to the suit (usually, the defendant) were members of it, and whether the declarant's statement was in furtherance of the conspiracy. (Sometimes, in order to prevent prejudicing the jury, these determinations have to be made outside the jury's presence.) Second, the judge should use a preponderance-of-the-evidence standard in making her determination. Third, the burden of convincing the judge of the foundational facts lies with the proponent of the evidence. Fourth, it is appropriate for the judge to consider the declarant-coconspirator's statement itself in resolving the issue of whether all of the requirements of the coconspirator exemption have been met. Finally, the Court declined to decide whether that statement, standing alone, would be sufficient evidence upon which to base a finding that all of the requirements of the exemption were satisfied. This question, reserved by the Court in its *Bourjaily* opinion, was subsequently answered by an amendment to Rule 801(d)(2)[48] stating that the "contents of the statement shall be considered but are not alone sufficient to establish . . . the existence of the conspiracy and the participation therein of the declarant and the party against whom the statement is offered."

In essence, the *Bourjaily* Court interpreted Federal Rule 104(a) as applying to the requirements to the coconspirator exemption because, in determining whether these requirements are satisfied, the judge is dealing with "[p]reliminary questions concerning . . . the admissibility of evidence"[49] and therefore is not bound by the usual exclusionary rules.[50] Of course, as with other Supreme Court decisions that simply construe the Federal Rules of Evidence, states are free to interpret their version of the Federal Rules differently. For example, a state might interpret or amend its Rule 801(d)(2)(D) so that state judges cannot even consider the statement proffered (as falling within the coconspirator exemption) in determining whether the requirements of the coconspirator party admissions exemption have been met.

The Coconspirator Exemption: A Reprise

The traditional justification for the coconspirator exemption is founded on the analogy between a business partnership and a conspiracy. The analogy is imperfect, however, because there usually is actual authority for a partner to speak for the partnership,

---

48. The amendment became effective December 1, 1997.

49. FRE 104(a).

50. In deciding preliminary questions of fact that govern the admissibility of evidence the court "is not bound by the rules of evidence except those with respect to privileges." FRE 104(a).

which has a separate legal identity from the individual partners. However, another possible justification for the coconspirator exemption is the difficulty of proving the existence of a conspiracy which, by its nature, is clandestine and covert. Furthermore, neither the courtroom testimony of a coconspirator nor the observable activities of the conspirators adequately reveals the true nature of the conspiracy. The Supreme Court has remarked:

> Because [coconspirators' statements] . . . are made while the conspiracy is in progress, such statements provide evidence of the conspiracy's context that cannot be replicated, even if the declarant testifies to the same matters in court. . . .

Conspirators are likely to speak differently when talking to each other in furtherance of their illegal aims than when testifying on the witness stand. Even when the declarant takes the stand, his in-court testimony will seldom have the evidentiary value of his statements made during the course of the conspiracy.[51]

Of course, a pragmatic justification for the coconspirator exemption does not speak directly to the question whether or not the statements of one coconspirator are sufficiently reliable to be used against his compatriots. That question can be answered only in the context of a particular case. In the final analysis, the justification for this exemption may rest upon how it is administered, that is, the care with which judges determine the preliminary facts and the wisdom with which they exercise their exclusionary power under Rule 403.

51. United States v. Inadi, 475 U.S. 387, 395 (1986).

Chapter VII

HEARSAY EXCEPTIONS

Table of Sections

§ 7.1   Overview

The Federal Rules of Evidence contain twenty-nine exceptions to the hearsay rule. Most of these are quite specific and state with particularity the requirements that must be satisfied in order to escape the rule. For example, Rule 803(2) contains an exception for a "statement relating to a startling event or condition made while the declarant was under the stress of excitement caused by the event or condition." Two of the twenty-nine exceptions are more general in content. These exceptions are designed to address situations that can be generally described, but cannot be foreseen in detail. Rule 804(b)(6) allows into evidence statements of a declarant offered against a party who has wrongfully prevented that declarant from testifying. Rule 807, the so-called "catch-all" or "residual" exception, also addresses statements made in circumstances that can be generally foreseen, but not precisely described. The residual exception allows into evidence statements that the judge finds are as trustworthy as the various hearsay statements that are admitted into evidence under the specific exceptions. For example, a declarant might make a statement in circumstances that would assure that the statement has trustworthiness equivalent to a statement that was prompted by a startling event, yet the declarant's statement does not fit within Rule 803(2) or any of the other specific exceptions.

The Rationale Underlying the Exceptions

The exceptions to the hearsay rule have been developed incrementally over many years. Most of the exceptions contained in the Federal Rules were first articulated by common law judges; many of these were judicially modified and refined with the passage of time. The ancestor of the rules of evidence is judicial experience rather than social science methodology and investigation. Nonetheless, each of the exceptions has at least one feature that serves to eliminate or reduce one or several of the hearsay dangers, namely, insincerity, faulty perception, deficiencies in memory, and errors in narration. For example, Rule 803(2), noted above, allows into evidence statements relating to an exciting event, but only if the declarant speaks while still under the influence of the stress or excitement caused by perceiving the event. Since the time between the event and the declarant's statement is usually short, there is a reduced concern that she has a faulty memory. More importantly, since she spoke excitedly, and presumably, unreflectively, there is a reduced concern that she is dissembling.

The Layout of the Exceptions

The drafters of the Federal Rules divided the exceptions into two major groups or categories. Rule 803 contains the first group; Rule 804 contains the second. The feature that differentiates these groups is this: the twenty-three exceptions listed and defined by Rule 803 may be used whether or not the declarant is available to testify; conversely, the six exceptions listed and defined by Rule 804 may not be used unless the proponent proves to the judge that the declarant is unavailable as a witness.

All of the exceptions except one are conveniently placed in Rules 803 and 804. The only exception that appears elsewhere is the residual or catch-all exception. In 1997, that rule, which had appeared redundantly in both Rule 803 and 804, was transferred to a new location where it now appears as Rule 807.

§ 7.2 Federal Rule 803 Exceptions: In General

We have seen that the courtroom availability of a Rule 803 declarant is immaterial—with one minor qualification, the exceptions contained in this rule are available whether or not the declarant testifies. No single rationale explains or justifies the twenty-three exceptions set out in Rule 803. However, factors that often account for the legislative and judicial recognition of these exceptions include:

(1) A motive for the declarant to speak truthfully;

(2) The lapse of only a brief period of time between the declarant's perception of an event or condition and her statement(s) about the event or condition;

(3) A state of mind, attributable to the declarant, that makes it unlikely that she could (or would) contrive a falsehood;

(4) Scrutiny of the declarant's statement(s) by third persons (including the general public) who are in a position to detect falsehoods or inaccuracies;

(5) A duty, imposed by law, to speak or report accurately.

(6) Reliance by others on the accuracy of the declarant's statement.

Sometimes more than one exception will apply to the same statement; likewise, an exemption (such as a party admission) may apply to a statement that also falls within a Rule 803 exception. It does not usually matter which exception or exemption a proponent invokes—the objective is to have the evidence in question admitted. Recall, however, that a party admission is admissible only against the party who made it (or whose representative made it). Thus, if a given statement were both a party admission (Rule 801(d)(2)) and, say, an excited utterance, which is a Rule 803(2) exception, the proponent may wish to proffer the evidence under Rule 803(2) or under both rules. The advantage of having the judge rule that the evidence satisfies the excited utterance exception is that the evidence may then be freely used against any party.

§ 7.3 Spontaneous Declarations: Excited Utterances and Present Sense Impressions

The term "spontaneous declarations" as used here includes two related but distinct hearsay exceptions for statements made under circumstances that minimize the hearsay dangers of insincerity and inaccurate memory. There is also a kinship between these two Rule 803 exceptions and the Rule 804 exception for statements made when the declarant believes she is facing impending death. All three of these exceptions are supported by reduced risks of insincerity and faulty memory, and all three require that the excepted statement address events or conditions that the declarant recently perceived.

Present Sense Impression

This exception is of comparatively recent origin; it did not have widespread approval until it was included in the Federal Rules in

1975.[1] The exception is contained in Rule 803(1) which removes from the hearsay ban:

> **Present Sense Impression**. A statement describing or explaining an event or condition made while the declarant was perceiving the event or condition, or immediately thereafter.

Reasonable people can—and do—disagree on the question of how much time may elapse between the event or condition and the declarant's descriptive or explanatory statement. That judgment is contextual and it falls to the trial judge to make it. The judge has two guidelines: one is textual, the other is derived from the rationale supporting this exception. First, the text of the rule states that the declarant must make the statement as she is perceiving the event or condition in question or "immediately thereafter." Thus, there must be a close temporal nexus between the event (or condition) and the declarant's descriptive or explanatory statement. Second, a principal rationale for admitting a declarant's statement of her present sense impression is that the brief period between the declarant's perception and her statement allows very little time for devising a fabrication.[2] Taken together, the text of the rule and its supporting rationale suggest that the intervention of more than just a few moments between the declarant's perception and her descriptive statement would normally render the present-sense exception inapplicable.

Note that the text of Rule 803(1) *confines the content* of the declarant's statement: it must describe or explain the event or condition that the declarant has just perceived. Suppose, for example, a declarant, caught in a late afternoon rush-hour traffic jam, observes a fire engine speeding down the highway in the opposite direction. She then remarks to her passenger, "Look how fast he is going—over ninety, I'll bet." This would be a descriptive statement that would qualify as a present sense impression. On the other hand, suppose the declarant said, "As I was driving to the airport to pick you up, I saw two brush fires down in Pleasant Valley, and no one attending them." This statement does not describe or explain the declarant's observation of the fire engine. Perhaps the presence of the fire engine reminded her of the brush fires or perhaps she is simply speculating about its destination. Note, also, that the lapse of time between the declarant's statement and the

---

1. The leading pre-Rules case supporting this exception is Houston Oxygen Co. v. Davis, 139 Tex. 1, 161 S.W.2d 474, 476–77 (Tex.Com.App. 1942).

2. Of course, the hearsay risk that the declarant's memory was faulty is also reduced or eliminated.

observation of the brush fires appears to preclude the application of Rule 803(1).

The simple example above suggests two additional observations about the present exception. This exception, like most hearsay exceptions, requires that the declarant have first-hand (personal) knowledge of the event or condition about which he speaks. (This pervasive requirement not only applies to most in-court testimony, but to most out-of-court hearsay declarations as well.[3]) Note that in the foregoing hypothetical, the driver was speaking to her passenger who, presumably, was able to make her own observations of the fire engine. When a declarant is speaking to someone who can also observe the event or condition she describes, she is less likely to speak falsely or inaccurately. Nonetheless, the exception for present sense impressions does *not* require that the person to whom the declarant speaks can also observe the event or condition the declarant describes.

ILLUSTRATION

Lena has disappeared and at Frank's trial for her murder, the prosecutor wants to establish that Frank and Lena were together the night of her disappearance. Janet will testify that on the night in question Lena called her at about 7:15 p.m. During their conversation Lena said that she was waiting for Frank at the Skylight Lounge, but that he was so late they would probably have to skip dinner and go directly to the theater. Lena then said to someone, "Well finally! Where have you been?" Janet then heard an indistinct male voice, and Lena said to her, "Frank just came in and our cab is waiting outside. Got to run. I'll call you tomorrow."

Should the judge sustain or overrule defense counsel's hearsay objection to Janet's testimony?

Let us assume that Janet is familiar with Lena's voice and is thus able to authenticate her caller's identity. The remaining issue is whether the prosecutor can surmount the defendant's hearsay objection. Preliminarily, note that the generally applicable requirement of first-hand (personal) knowledge is expressly incorporated into Rule 803(1): the rule admits statements "made while the declarant was perceiving the event or condition or immediately thereafter." The personal-knowledge requirement is easily satisfied

---

3. Kornicki v. Calmar Steamship Corp., 460 F.2d 1134, 1138 (3rd Cir. 1972). As we have seen, however, this requirement does not attach to party admissions. See Ch. VI, § 6–3. *See also* FRE 803(13) (allowing into evidence hearsay statements contained in family records; first-hand knowledge is not required). *See also* FRE 703 (expert testimony).

as to Janet because she has first-hand knowledge of what Lena said to her. A separate issue is whether Lena also had first-hand knowledge of Frank's arrival at the Skylight Lounge.

Whether a witness or hearsay declarant speaks from personal knowledge is normally a question for the jury. The judge's responsibility under Rule 104(b) is to ensure that there is sufficient evidence for the jury to conclude that the witness or, in the case of out-of-court statements, the declarant had first-hand knowledge.[4] Sometimes, however, a hearsay exception makes the perception of an event or condition part of the rule that defines or sets forth the exception. Rule 803(1) does so by its requirement that the declarant perceive an event or condition and contemporaneously or immediately describe or explain it. In making her determination of the facts that pertain to this evidentiary rule, the *judge* is necessarily finding that (1) there was an event or condition, and (2) the declarant perceived it—or, put otherwise, had personal knowledge of it.

The usual standard of proof, preponderance of the evidence, applies to these determinations by the judge and the burden is on the proponent to convince her of these preliminary facts, as well as the fact of the immediacy of declarant's statement.[5] However, the proponent is aided by a provision in Rule 104(a) stating that when finding facts pertaining to an evidentiary rule of admissibility, the judge "is not bound by the rules of evidence except those with respect to privileges." Thus, the judge is free to consider the declarant's statement itself for whatever probative force it may have on (1) the existence of an event (or condition), (2) the declarant's perception of it, and (3) the immediacy with which the declarant spoke. Indeed, the statement alone is usually a sufficient evidentiary basis for the judge to conclude there was an event (or condition), and will often suffice to demonstrate immediacy and perception.[6] Assuming these requirements are met and the evidence in the Illustration is admitted, the jury is now free to use the statement for the same inferences.

The key to the judge-jury relationship in this Illustration is that the judge, by admitting the evidence, has now ruled that the evidence escapes the hearsay rule, and, hence, it may be considered for its truth, as well as for any reasonable inferences the jury wishes to draw. Of course, the jury may give the evidence little or no weight, and the opponent of the evidence is free to argue, for

4. MUELLER & KIRKPATRICK, EVIDENCE § 6.5, at 428–29. The assumption is that if the jury ultimately finds the witness or declarant lacked personal knowledge, it will ignore the testimony or statement.

5. Miller v. Keating, 754 F.2d 507, 510–11 (3rd Cir. 1985).

6. 2 McCORMICK, EVIDENCE § 272, at 206. In the Illustration above, the declarant spoke immediately after Janet heard a male voice.

example, that the declarant's perception was inaccurate or that her statement was motivated by bias. The opponent should not, however, be entitled to an instruction to the jury that if they find the declarant did not perceive the event, his statement should be ignored just as if it had been declared inadmissible. Such an instruction is improper because the judge was required, as part of her preliminary fact finding under Rule 104(a), to determine an issue (first-hand knowledge) that is usually for the jury. In most circumstances, however, the judge considering the question of a witness's or declarant's first-hand knowledge is proceeding under Rule 104(b) and her task is only to screen the proponent's evidence to ensure that the jury could reasonably find that the declarant perceived the event about which he spoke.

Observe that in the Illustration above, the exception for a present sense impression is applicable even though the person to whom the declarant spoke (the auditor, Janet) was not able to confirm the declarant's statement that Frank had arrived. As noted earlier, Rule 803(1) does not require that the person to whom the declarant spoke must be positioned so as to confirm the accuracy of the declarant's statement. Nonetheless, in a close case this additional assurance of the reliability of the declarant's statement may be influential in the judge's ruling on admissibility.

Excited Utterance

Rule 803(2) provides a hearsay exception for a declarant's

> **Excited utterance.** A statement relating to a startling event or condition made while the declarant was under the stress of excitement caused by the event or condition.

A close reading of the text of this rule suggests several contrasts between the exception for an excited utterance and the exception for a present sense impression. The latter, as we have seen, limits the subject-matter range of declarant's statement: the declaration must *describe or explain* the event or condition in question. The subject-matter ambit of an excited utterance is broader: the declarant's statement need only *"relate to"* the exciting event.[7] In addition, the exception for excited utterances requires that the declarant speak while under the influence of stress or excitement; no such requirement attends a present sense impression.

---

7. Suppose, for example, the excited declarant who witnessed a car bombing makes a statement about the late arrival of medical personnel. Her statement would "relate" to the explosion—the cause of the excitement.

The fact that an excited utterance, as the name suggests, is grounded on the declarant's mental state (excited, startled, stressed) suggests that the time lapse between the event and the declarant's statement relating to it is usually not the central issue. The question is whether the declarant was in a state of emotional upheaval when she spoke. It is this feature—"excitement," broadly defined—that reduces the risk that the declarant is lying or consciously misleading the listener. The risk of inaccurate memory is also reduced because, as a practical matter, the declarant's emotional state will subside before her memory significantly declines.

Note, however, that the hearsay danger of inaccurate perception is probably increased: emotion and stress are associated with faulty perception.[8] The question, however, is not whether this or any other hearsay exception is flawless. The issue is whether allowing the trier of fact to evaluate the evidence in question is preferable to excluding the evidence and thus depriving the factfinder of relevant material. The party who unsuccessfully opposes the admission of hearsay evidence remains free to try to discredit its probative force.

Under the provisions of Rule 104(a), the judge, not the jury, decides if the declarant's statement satisfies the requirements of Rule 803(2). The essential elements are (1) an exciting event, (2) followed by the declarant's statement which relates to it, and (3) which was made under stress, before there was time for reflection and (hence) fabrication. The familiar requirement of personal knowledge also applies. The statement itself usually has considerable probative force in establishing these elements. As we have seen, the judge (freed from the usual rules of evidence under Rule 104(a)) may consider the declaration itself in ruling on the admissibility of the proffered statement. Suppose, for example, the driver of a car calls 911 and says,

> There has been a terrible accident on Route 340 at Jacob's Creek Bridge! Get help right away. A cement truck crossed into the wrong lane and hit a motorcycle. He's in the water—I mean the motorcyclist—may be dead. The truck just kept going. Hurry!

The judge could find that the statement alone establishes all of the elements of an excited utterance. The statement strongly points toward an exciting event; the recitation of the details of that event suggest that the caller observed it; and his manner of speech and the phrasing of his report to the operator have considerable probative force to show that the accident caused the requisite emotional state in the observer-declarant.

8. *See* Hutchins and Slesinger, *Some Observations on the Law of Evidence:* *Spontaneous Exclamations*, 28 Colum. L. Rev. 432 (1928).

Of course, there are only rare occasions when the proponent must rely solely on the declarant's statement to establish the essential elements of an excited utterance. In this example, there would be abundant evidence of the accident. Furthermore, there would be evidence, perhaps supplied by the declarant, of the approximate period of time between the accident and the declarant's telephone call. And finally, the 911 operator could testify that the declarant seemed distressed and excited, or a recording of his call, if available, could be offered in evidence.

Now suppose the motorcyclist was unconscious when rescue workers pulled him from the water. Ten hours later, in the presence of his physician and his wife, he regains consciousness in the hospital. His wife says, "You are going to be all right; the doctors all say so. You are going to be all right. Do you know what happened?" He replies, "I...." "I was on the bridge, and a truck—a big cement truck—came right at me, right in my lane." The fact that the motorcyclist's statement came ten hours after the exciting event does not necessarily preclude the application of the excited utterance exception. Neither does the fact that the declarant spoke in response to a question. The now-familiar issue is whether the declarant spoke while still under the stressful influence of the startling event. The required immediacy, indispensable to the application of the exception for a present sense impressions, is not always an operative feature of an excited utterance. Of course, had the declarant not been unconscious during the intervening ten-hour period, his statement would presumably not be within the present exception. At some point, fairly soon after the accident, he would have regained sufficient composure so as to be capable of contriving a false or misleading statement. In the present example, however, the declarant appears to have been in the requisite mental state of stress and shock when he spoke.

Observe, also, that the declarant in the example just above—the motorcyclist—was also a participant in the exciting event. Generally speaking, participant-observers are likely to maintain the required emotional state for a longer period than mere observers. Other factors bearing on the duration of the state of excitement include the declarant's age, her physical and mental state, and the probable emotional impact of the event itself. An additional feature bearing on admissibility is whether or not the declarant can be identified.

Suppose someone who is walking past a liquor store sees a robbery in progress. He dashes down the street to a shoe repair shop and says to the owner, "Quick! Call the cops. Two teenage kids with an assault rifle are robbing the liquor store." The call is made, but the declarant is never identified. Subsequently, A and B, two teenagers, are arrested and placed on trial for robbery. Should the fact that the declarant cannot be identified preclude testimony by the shoe repairman as to what the declarant said? The prevailing view is that an inability to identify the declarant is not, standing alone, fatal to the applicability of Rule 803(2).[9] Nonetheless, courts proceed with more caution when the declarant is anonymous, since it is impossible for the objector to demonstrate that the declarant lacked first-hand knowledge or to introduce impeaching evidence (such as bias) designed to weaken the probative force of the declarant's statement.

Sometimes, days or months after an emotional event such as a sexual assault or a car jacking, the declarant encounters something (e.g., the crime scene), or some person (e.g., the perpetrator), that vividly renews the memory of the exciting event and reignites the emotion and nervous stress that accompanied it. ("There he is— that's the man who tried to lock me in the car trunk and kidnap me!") Although the risk that declarant's memory may be inaccurate is somewhat increased, the exception for excited utterances is ordinarily applicable in situations such as this because its essential requirements are usually satisfied.[10]

§ 7.4 Physical or Mental Condition

The hearsay exceptions for a declarant's statements concerning her physical or mental condition are well established. Their recognition is based in part on primacy: a principal means of learning about a person's bodily or mental condition is through her own statements. The declarant is usually in a favorable position to perceive and report her own physical or mental condition ("There is sharp pain is in my lower back" or "I am depressed"). Even if the declarant is not always a reliable source of information, her declarations are nonetheless likely to facilitate evaluations by health care professionals and even family members. The emphasis in this section, of course, is upon using the declarant's statements for their truth. The danger of mistaken perception is minimal. So, too, is the danger of inaccurate memory, at least when the exception is applied to statements disclosing a presently existing state of mind or bodily condition. Thus, Rule 803(3) provides that the hearsay rule will not exclude:

---

9. *See Miller,* 754 F.2d at 510, supra note 5. An argument can be advanced, however, that the evidentiary use of the unidentified declarant's statement violated the defendants' constitutional right to confront the witness against them. This contention however, would probably fail. See Ch.VIII, at note 32 and following.

10. State v. Brown, 112 Ohio App.3d 583, 679 N.E.2d 361, 373 (1996) (child experienced nervous excitement when he returned to the crime scene where, three days earlier, he had witnessed his brother's murder).

Then existing mental, emotional, or physical condition. A statement of the declarant's then existing state of mind, emotion, sensation, or physical condition (such as intent, plan, motive, design, mental feeling, pain, and bodily health), but not including a statement of memory or belief to prove the fact remembered or believed unless it relates to the execution, revocation, identification, or terms of declarant's will.

Note that the rule adopts the general requirement limiting the excepted declaration to a "then existing" condition, but suspends that requirement for statements regarding the declarant's will.

The drafters of the Federal Rules concluded that a declarant's statement concerning "the execution, revocation, identification, or terms of . . . [his] will" falls into a special category. The unavailable declarant is the person who presumably knows the most about his will: typically his declaration concerns his own conduct, and normally a testator considers the execution or revocation of his will a serious matter. These considerations, coupled with the need to at least consider evidence concerning the testator's relevant statements, have carved out a special qualification to Federal Rule 803(3)'s general requirement that admissible declarations must refer to an existing mental state.

ILLUSTRATIONS

Suppose Florence Nightingale is willing to testify concerning the following statements made by her late friend and patient, Thomas:

(1) "Today, the pain in my lower back is very acute."

(2) "I am so discouraged and depressed. For me, life is no longer worth living."

(3) "I am not in this business just to be competitive—as soon as I recover, I'm going to drive Cartwright, my last competitor, out of business."

(4) "Don't try to convince me of Fred's redeeming features! I can't stand the guy. When I revised my will last month I left every nephew $50,000—except Fred. For him, zero."

(5) "I vividly recall the year 2000; I was miserable for most of it—migraine headaches every day or two."

(6) "Didn't I tell you? Don Purcell has quit his job with Benchmark and will start working for me in January."

(7) "When I saw firsthand the way Edgar abuses Alice—even batters her—that's when I decided not to leave him a cent."

The first four illustrations appear to fit within the language of Rule 803(a); the next two (5 and 6) do not; and the last (7) is problematic. As always, of course, the initial question is the now familiar one of relevance: does the proffered evidence tend to prove or disprove a consequential fact? If we assume, for example, that the proponent of the evidence in Illustration (1) needs to prove that the declarant suffered back pain, evidence of the declarant's statement is relevant and, under Rule 803(3), admissible. Likewise, if we assume the declarant's depressed state of mind is relevant in Illustration (2)—as it would be, for example, if the issue were suicide—the declarant's statement also fits within the terms of Rule 803(3).

Let us assume, then, that each statement in the Illustration is relevant. Illustration (3) has probative value to show the declarant's presently held intention to drive his competitor out of the market. Illustration (4) falls within the special provision of Rule 803(3) dealing with wills. Illustration (5) is "backward looking," so to speak, and is simply a statement of the declarant's memory or belief. Thus, it is not within Rule 803(3). If statements of a past fact remembered or believed were to qualify generally for admission under Rule 803(3), there would be nothing left of the rule against hearsay. In Illustration (6), the declarant expresses his belief or state of mind regarding a past event (Don has quit) and a predicted future event. But the predicted future event (Don will work for me) primarily concerns not the declarant's conduct, but the conduct of another. Therefore, assuming this evidence is offered to prove that Don quit his job at Benchmark and went to work (or intended to go to work) for the declarant, it is hearsay as to both propositions and is not admissible under Rule 803(3).

The last Illustration is problematic because it is unclear what relevant fact the proponent is trying to prove. If the hearsay declaration is offered to prove that Edgar abused Alice, it is hearsay and not admissible under Rule 803(3). However, if it is offered to prove that the declarant intentionally omitted Edgar from his will, at least the last portion of the statement would fit the special provision of 803(3) dealing with wills. The judge would have to decide whether to admit the entire statement or, perhaps, exclude the first portion as prejudicial to Edgar, assuming he is a party.[11]

Rationale and Applications of the State of Mind Exception

When a declarant is speaking about her current state of mind, the hearsay dangers of mistaken perception and faulty memory are inapplicable. Furthermore, the frequency with which state of mind is an issue in litigation adds a practical need for this evidence. Often, the most convincing evidence of a declarant's state of mind is her own declaration. Thus, at an early date, common-law judges began admitting into evidence a declarant's statement concerning her own mental (or physical) condition.

Note the various contexts in which one's mental state becomes a relevant issue in litigation, both criminal and civil. For example, a crime is normally defined so as to require a particular mens rea or state of mind; the measure of civil damages sometimes depends on the mental suffering of the victim or the malicious intent of the defendant (e.g., intentional infliction of emotional harm). The cases are replete with other instances in which mental state is an issue: the question of where one is domiciled is answered in part by ascertaining her intention; the issue of whether a will was validly executed (or revoked) may turn upon intent; the question of whether one fraudulently conveyed assets turns primarily on his intention; and a business tort is usually defined so as to include the intention of the alleged wrongdoer. In these and similar instances, the substantive law itself specifies a particular state of mind and thus an actor's mental state often becomes a pivotal element at trial. In other words, mental state is often an ultimate proposition to which the parties address their conflicting evidence.

State of mind, once established, can also serve as circumstantial evidence of behavior. In this context, the declarant's state of mind is not itself an element of the case or an ultimate proposition; rather, state of mind, when determined by the trier of fact, provides an intermediate basis from which the trier may draw one or more additional inferences that lead toward the declarant's probable conduct. Suppose, for example, there is an issue at trial concerning whether an individual has left the United States and returned to his native country. Evidence that he often expressed deep affection for his homeland and that he also declared that he intended to return there permanently provide a basis for the inference that in fact he did. Observe that even though the state of mind exception is, aside from wills, limited to the expression of a presently existing state of mind, the trier can make reasonable inferences that the

11. The best argument for admitting the entire statement is that the first portion explains and strengthens the latter proposition that Edgar was intentionally omitted from the will.

same state of mind existed at an earlier or later date. Thus, if a declarant stated in August that he missed his native country and was anxious to return to it, the trier could ordinarily infer that this same state of mind existed, for example, in July or September.

The Hillmon Doctrine

In Illustration (3) above, the declarant expresses his intention to take certain action in the future—that is, to drive his competitor, Cartwright, out of business. We noted that the declarant's statement was within Rule 803(3)'s exception. This application of the state-of-mind exception to the hearsay rule was first articulated by the United States Supreme Court in a famous case, Mutual Life Ins. Co. v. Hillmon.[12]

The central issue in *Hillmon* was whether a body discovered at Crooked Creek, Colorado, was that of Hillmon, the insured, or that of Walters, a companion. In an effort to prove that Walters was present at Crooked Creek (and thus the body could have been his), the defendant insurance company offered as evidence several letters written by Walters to his family and fiancée. In these letters, Walters declared his intention to leave Wichita, Kansas, and travel with a new acquaintance, a sheepherder named Hillmon, to the vicinity of Crooked Creek. The Supreme Court held that Walter's written statements were admissible under the state of mind exception since they showed his presently held intention to travel with Hillmon to Crooked Creek. This intention was, of course, relevant because it increased somewhat the probability that Walter's embarked upon his intended journey, reached his destination, and that the body was his. Notably, there was no issue in the *Hillmon* case concerning whether or not Hillmon was present at Crooked Creek; the parties agreed that he was there.

Assume, however, that the issue in the case was whether Hillmon was at Crooked Creek at the time of the death in question. Obviously, a declaration by Hillmon that he intended to go there would be admissible[13] under Rule 803(3). Suppose, however, the plaintiff, who claims the body found at Crooked Creek was that of Hillmon (the insured), offers Walter's statement that he intended to leave Wichita with a sheepherder named Hillmon and travel to the vicinity of Crooked Creek. As we have seen, this was, essentially, the statement that was admitted in the *Hillmon* case, for it had probative value on the contested issue of whether Walters was

---

12.　145 U.S. 285 (1892).

13.　Of course, there would have to be admissible evidence that Hillmon made the declaration. If Walters, in a letter to his family, wrote that Hillmon stated he was going to Crooked Creek, the letter would be inadmissible. The opponent would be unable to conduct a cross-examination testing whether Hillmon really made the statement (double hearsay or too many "links in the chain").

there. The fact that Walters intended to travel *with* Hillmon introduced the contingency that Hillmon might or might not go, but that contingency did not negate altogether the probative force of the evidence insofar as it pointed to Walters' whereabouts. The statement is roughly the equivalent of a declaration by Walters that "if the cold weather doesn't set in before the end of the month, I'm leaving Wichita for Crooked Creek." (There is also the possibility that even if Hillmon decided not to make the journey, Walters would have gone alone.) The problem we confront is whether Walter's declaration is admissible under the state of mind exception on the issue of *whether* Hillmon was at Crooked Creek.

In the course of the *Hillmon* opinion, Justice Gray, its author, stated:

> The letters in question were competent . . . as evidence that, shortly before the time when other evidence tended to show that he went away, he had the intention of going, and of going with Hillmon, which made it more probable *both that he did go and that he went with Hillmon* than if there had been no proof of such intention.[14]

Thus, at least in forceful dictum, the Court approved of the evidentiary use of Walter's declaration for proof not only of Walter's future conduct, but Hillmon's as well. This apparent extension of the *Hillmon* doctrine, exceeding the facts actually before the Court, applies only if the declarant's statement not only addresses his own future conduct, but also embraces the cooperative conduct of another. Even a broad reading of *Hillmon* does not support the admission into evidence of a statement by, say *X*, that another person, *Y*, intends to pursue a certain course of conduct. To apply the state-of-mind exception for the sole purchase of proving *Y*'s conduct would result in using *X*'s state of mind for the singular purpose of proving *Y*'s future conduct.

ILLUSTRATION

(1) Larry, a high school student was apparently kidnapped—at least his father received demands for a ransom. Even though Larry was never found, Angelo is brought to trial on a kidnapping charge. The prosecution calls several of Larry's friends who testify that, on the day Larry disappeared, he told them he was going to meet Angelo at 9:30 p.m. in the parking lot of Sambo's Restaurant to pick up a package of marijuana. One friend, for example, testified over objection that while he and Larry were sitting at a table in Sambo's, Larry said that it was

14. *Hillmon*, 145 U.S. at 295–96 [emphasis supplied].

"time to pick up the pot from Angelo in the parking lot" and that he "would be right back."[15]

Assuming there was no evidence of Angelo's whereabouts, is this testimony admissible?

(2) Assume the same facts as in (1), except there is other evidence from which the trier of fact could reasonably conclude that Angelo was in Sambo's parking lot at the appointed hour.

Should this be the decisive factor in the trial judge's ruling?

The difficulty in Illustration (1) is apparent: Larry's statement really has two assertions: "I am going to meet Angelo" and "Angelo is going to meet me." Implicit in these assertions is some prior arrangement between Larry and Angelo by which Angelo agreed to meet Larry in Sambo's parking lot to deliver a package of marijuana. A statement such as "Angelo and I agreed that we would meet at nine o'clock in Sambo's parking lot" does not fit within the state-of-mind exception. It is a statement of memory or belief about a past fact. Furthermore, Larry's statement in Illustration (1) is, at least in part, a declaration *about what someone else—Angelo—will do in the future.* So too, however, was Walter's statement in the *Hillmon* case, asserting that he and Hillmon would soon leave Wichita, bound for the Crooked Creek area. Of course, in *Hillmon*, there was not an issue as to Hillmon's presence at Crooked Creek, for it was conceded that he was there.

There is a decided tendency among courts to admit statements by X that he intends to do something jointly (or in cooperation) with Y.[16] In other words, Justice Gray's dictum in the *Hillmon* case has usually proved decisive. Some of these courts attempt to confine the state-of-mind exception by instructing the jury, for example, that the declarant's statement may be used only as evidence of his intention and conduct[17] or by holding that the declarant's statement is admissible only if there is evidence corroborating the conduct of the other person.[18]

15. This Illustration, with only minor departures, tracks the facts in United States v. Pheaster, 544 F.2d 353 (9th Cir. 1976), *cert. denied*, 429 U.S. 1099 (1977).

16. Id. at 376–80; State v. Terrovona, 105 Wash.2d 632, 716 P.2d 295, 298–301 (1986) (victim tells girlfriend that he is going to help accused who ran out of gas at 116th St.; subsequently victim's body found at 116th St.); People v. Alcalde, 24 Cal.2d 177, 148 P.2d 627, 631–32 (1944) (victim states she is "going out with [the accused] Frank tonight;" victim is murdered that night).

17. *Alcalde*, 148 P.2d at 632.

18. United States v. Delvecchio, 816 F.2d 859, 863 (2nd Cir. 1987).

The first restriction noted above—curtailing the permissible use of the declarant (*X*'s) statement so that it does not apply to the conduct of the other actor (*Y*)—is too technical for the jury to adhere to or even understand. If *X* says "I'm going out with *Y* tonight" and the jury is allowed to hear the entire statement, it is difficult, to say the least, for the jury to ignore the portion of the statement referring to *Y*'s participation. On firmer ground is the requirement enforced by some courts that there be other (corroborative) evidence of *Y*'s conduct. Independent evidence of *Y*'s conduct makes it unnecessary for the jury to rely solely on *X*'s assertion about *Y* in order to determine what *Y* did. If there is enough corroborative evidence to sustain independently a jury finding of *Y*'s conduct, the difficulties of interpreting *Hillmon* broadly (or narrowly) largely disappear. As in Illustration (2), the jury now has before it evidence of the declarant's (*L*'s) future conduct (his declaration) and independent evidence that is sufficient to uphold a jury finding of *A*'s conduct.

Although the requirement of corroborative evidence is a safeguard against the hearsay dangers implicit in allowing the use of *X*'s statement for *Y*'s (cooperative) conduct, not all courts require an independent evidentiary confirmation. The reason is, in part, that such independent evidence is often unavailable. The issue then comes down to whether to admit or exclude *X*'s statement. The pull of relevance is particularly strong when *X* firmly declares her intention to undertake certain activity in conjunction with *Y*, and the time span between her declaration and the intended activity is short. ("We will meet tomorrow at noon to discuss whether to lease or buy.") As a New York court remarked:

> Everyday experience confirms that people frequently express an intent to see another under circumstances that make it extremely likely that such a meeting will occur. Indeed, it is not uncommon for such expressions of intent to be more trustworthy evidence that the meeting took place than many statements of intent with regard to the performance of acts not involving any inference with regard to another person.[19]

Bear in mind that the principal dispute over the boundaries of the *Hillmon* doctrine center on statements in which *X* declares her intention to meet *Y* or to undertake some joint activity with *Y*, and *X*'s declaration is offered not only as proof of her conduct, but of *Y*'s as well. Even the expansive version of *Hillmon* does not permit the use of a declaration by *X* that does not embrace her own conduct, but simply predicts *Y*'s future conduct.

19. People v. Malizia, 92 A.D.2d 154, 460 N.Y.S.2d 23, 27 (App. Div. 1983), *aff'd*, 62 N.Y.2d 755, 476 N.Y.S.2d 825, 465 N.E.2d 364 (1984).

ILLUSTRATIONS

Examine the following hearsay statements and determine whether either (or both) of them should be admitted under Rule 803(3)'s exception for state of mind (or bodily condition):

(1) In the prosecution of husband (*Y*) for the murder of wife (*X*), the latter's statement, "I'm so afraid of what *Y* will do. He has threatened to kill me and I know he will as soon as he thinks he can get by with it."

(2) In the prosecution of *Y* (an illegal drug dealer) for the murder of *X* (a drug distributor), *X*'s statement to his girlfriend, "I'll be back in about an hour and we can go out; first, I need to see *Y* and I'm going over to his condo now."

In Illustration (1), assume that *Y*'s defense is that he did not kill his wife, *X*, but someone else did. In this event, as in many cases of murder, the *victim's* state of mind is irrelevant under the substantive law; that is, her state of mind is not an element of the crime. Therefore, the only relevant purpose of the evidence is to show what *Y did* and for this purpose the wife's statement is inadmissible hearsay.

Of course, the victim's mental state sometimes bears on her *relevant conduct*. Suppose the victim says, "Tonight I'm going to tell him it's over—that I'm leaving and I'm taking the kids." Such a forward-looking statement is within the *Hillmon* doctrine. The declarant is stating what *she* intends to do (confront the other person and announce her departure) and the fact that she must locate the other person in order to carry out her intention is just a contingency.

However, as we noted above, the victim's statement in Illustration (1) is relevant only for its bearing on what the husband allegedly said and did. Therefore it is inadmissible hearsay. *X*'s statement that *Y* threatened to kill her is simply a statement of her recollection. Furthermore it carries another hearsay difficulty: there is no way to cross-examine the deceased, *X*, as to whether or not *Y* actually made these threats. (If there were admissible evidence of his threatening statements, *Hillmon* would permit evidence of *Y*'s threats to kill *X* because these threats increase the probabilities that, in the future, he carried out his intention.) *X*'s statement that she held the belief that in the near future *Y* would kill her is forward looking. However, it is not a declaration of *her* intended conduct, but rather that of her husband. Thus, the statement in Illustration (1) should be inadmissible, and most courts would so hold.[20]

Illustration (2) falls comfortably with the *Hillmon* doctrine. The declarant, *X*, states his presently-held intention to go to *Y*'s condominium and return. There is no statement about *Y*'s activities or even his presence in the condominium. If it is relevant that *X* was there—for example, because it provided *Y* or *Y*'s henchman with the opportunity to kill *X*—the statement is admissible. *X*'s assertion avoids the hearsay rule because it is excepted from it by Federal Rule 803(3). There is no doubt that Rule 803(3) includes the declarant's statement of what he intends to do; difficulties arise only when the declarant's assertion includes what he intends to do in association with another.[21]

The Supreme Court had occasion to revisit the famous *Hillmon* doctrine in *Shepard v. United States*,[22] decided four decades after *Hillmon*. In this case, Dr. Shepard was prosecuted for the murder of his wife by poisoning her. There was evidence that shortly before dying, Mrs. Shepard summoned her nurse and asked to examine the contents of a whiskey bottle. Stating that this was the liquor she drank just before collapsing, she asked whether there was enough remaining in the bottle to permit a test for the presence of poison. After remarking that the taste and smell were strange, she concluded, "Dr. Shepard has poisoned me."

At trial, Mrs. Shepard's statements were admitted under the hearsay exception for dying declarations.[23] On appeal, however, it was held that the prosecution had failed to provide adequate evidence of an essential feature of that exception, namely, that the declarant spoke while believing that her death was imminent. There remained, however, two possibilities for upholding the trial court's decision to admit Mrs. Shepard's statements. First, admission of this evidence might be sustained on the ground that her statements had probative value to rebut defense evidence that Mrs. Shepard was depressed and had suicidal intentions. (The government pressed this contention.) Under this theory, the evidence would not be used to prove any fact stated or suggested by Mrs. Shepard's statements, but only for the limited purpose of showing that her state of mind was consistent with a will to live. (This theory of admissibility involved characterizing Mrs. Shepard's

---

20. *See, e.g.*, United States v. Joe, 8 F.3d 1488, 1492–93 (10th Cir. 1993); United States v. Brown, 490 F.2d 758, 763–64 (D.C. Cir. 1973). *Contra* State v. Alston, 341 N.C. 198, 461 S.E.2d 687, 704 (1995).

21. Even the legislative history of Rule 803(3) contains conflicting indications of whether that subsection admits a declarant's statement as proof that he intended to participate in certain activity with a designated person and he did. *Compare* FRE 803(3) ACN with H.R. REP. No. 93–650, at 13–14 (1974).

22. 290 U.S. 96 (1933).

23. *See* FRE 804(b)(2).

statements as nonhearsay, since they would be admitted only for the inference that she wanted to continue living.) Second, even if Mrs. Shepard's statements were hearsay, it could be argued they were within the state-of-mind exception to the hearsay rule.

Justice Cardozo's opinion for the Supreme Court rejected both of these possibilities. As a preliminary matter, Cardozo condemned the tactic of offering evidence at trial on one theory and then, on appeal, attempting to sustain the trial judge's admission of the evidence on another. Such a tactic is usually unfair to the opponent of the evidence. In this case, for example, the prosecutor offered the evidence as Mrs. Shepard's dying declaration and the trial judge, over objection, admitted it as such. To sustain the judge's ruling on appeal by invoking a theory of admission not presented at trial denies to the opponent the opportunity to rebut the new theory at trial—for example, by presenting counter evidence and arguments to contest admissibility, or by seeking a limiting instruction, if appropriate.

Cardozo nonetheless addressed the possibilities that the trial judge's ruling, though not sustainable under the exception for dying declarations, might nonetheless rest on a different footing. He found unconvincing the argument that Mrs. Shepard's statements could have been properly received for the limited, non-hearsay purpose of showing her will to live. The overriding feature of her statements was their accusatory thrust, directed toward the defendant's conduct and guilt. Even a carefully crafted limiting instruction to the jury, restricting its members to a consideration of Mrs. Shepard's statement solely to determine her state of mind, could not overcome "[t]he reverberating clang of those accusatory words, [which] would drown out all weaker sounds."[24]

The final question was whether Mrs. Shepard's statements might qualify for admission under the exception for a declarant's expressions of her state of mind. Here, of course, the theory is that although the statements are hearsay, they may nonetheless be admitted for their truth because the applicable exception renders cross-examination of the declarant unnecessary. Observing that the principal probative force of the statements in question was directed toward *past* acts of *another* person, Cardozo emphasized the limits of the *Hillmon* doctrine:

> Declarations of intention, casting light upon the future, have been sharply distinguished from declarations of memory, pointing backwards to the past. There would be an end, or nearly that, to the rule against hearsay if the distinction were ignored.

24. *Shepard*, 290 U.S. at 104.

The testimony now questioned faced backward and not forward. This it did, in at least its most obvious implications. What is even more important, it spoke to a past act, and more than that, to the act of someone not the speaker.[25]

The *Shepard* opinion reaffirms the principal limitations on the *Hillmon* doctrine. Generally speaking, that doctrine, now embodied in Federal Rule 803(3), is restricted to forward-looking declarations in which the declarant states his intention to undertake a course of conduct in the future. As we have seen, however, statements by the declarant about his will fall into a special category: such statements not only may look to the future ("I intend to execute a codicil tomorrow."), but may refer to the past as well ("After Emma died, I tore up my will."). Statements of joint or cooperative activity ("Ned and I will take the train to Chicago on Saturday.") are usually admitted as evidence of the future conduct of both participants. Of course, many statements fitting comfortably within Rule 803(3) are not about conduct, but rather describe a physical or mental condition that is relevant to an issue in the case being tried. An example is a statement by a patient to her physician describing the presently existing stiffness and pain in her knees. Finally, as we observed in Chapter V, a declarant's statement sometimes permits the trier to infer the existence of the relevant mental state without the necessity of accepting her statement as true. ("I always buy advance season tickets to the symphony, but then have to stand in line for the ballet and opera," leads to the inference that the speaker enjoys music.)

The next section considers Rule 803(4)'s exception for statements made for the purpose of obtaining a medical diagnosis or treatment. As with the special provision in Rule 803(3) that applies to wills, the exception in Rule 803(4) is broad enough to include statements that embrace past events or conditions. As you will see, the central focus of Rule 803(4) is on statements made to medical personnel that facilitate the diagnoses or treatment of the person who is the subject of the statements—usually, but not always, the speaker.

§ 7.5 Statements for Purposes of Medical Diagnosis or Treatment

The traditional basis for this exception rests on the assumption that persons seeking medical treatment have an incentive to be truthful: proper treatment may depend on the patient's accurate description of his condition and symptoms. In addition, a lay person is likely to assume that a physician, trained in medicine, might easily detect a patient's exaggerations and falsehoods. Taken to-

25. Id. at 105–06.

gether, however, these traditional rationales do not fully justify the breadth of Rule 803(4), for it includes not only declarations made in pursuit of treatment, but also those made in the sole pursuit of a diagnosis. While we often think of a diagnosis as the first step in the process of treatment, a diagnosis may have other objectives, such as prevailing in a lawsuit or increasing a damage or medical insurance award. If the diagnosis is for one or more of these latter purposes, incentives for the declarant's candor are either missing or considerably diminished. As we shall see, however, there is a pragmatic justification for admitting statements relating to a medical diagnosis, even when no treatment is contemplated.

Rule 803(4) excepts from the hearsay rule:

> **Statements made for purposes of medical diagnosis or treatment.** Statements made for purposes of medical diagnosis or treatment and describing medical history, or past or present symptoms, pain, or sensations, or the inception or general character of the cause or external source thereof insofar as reasonably pertinent to diagnosis or treatment.

Frequently, statements falling within Rule 803(4) will be made by the patient to her physician. The rule, however, is not limited to this typical setting. The central requirement of this hearsay exception is that the statement in question be made "for purposes of medical diagnosis or treatment" including medical history, past as well as present symptoms, and the external cause of the patient's condition if relevant to the diagnosis or treatment.

ILLUSTRATION

A mother takes her tearful and injured six-year-old daughter to the hospital emergency room. When she arrives at the desk of the intake nurse, the mother says, "Please have her examined right away. She lost control of her bicycle and went over the curb and into the street. An old man who wasn't looking where he was driving sideswiped the bike, and she hit the pavement really hard. She was unconscious—then in a few minutes she came to and started crying."

A close reading of Rule 803(4) leads to the conclusion that, with the exception of one portion, the mother's statements qualify for admission. Her account makes it reasonably clear that she had firsthand knowledge. Her statements are made to the nurse for purposes of diagnosis and treatment, clearly satisfying the rule. Such statements could be made to anyone in the medical care field or even to family member or colleague. (For example: "Quick, get me to the hospital—I have severe pains in my chest and my arms feel numb.")

The language of the Rule 803(4) includes within the exception statements pertaining to "the inception or general character of the cause or external source thereof insofar as reasonably pertinent to diagnosis or treatment." The facts that the child was thrown from her bicycle and onto a hard surface after being obliquely struck by a car are pertinent to diagnosis or treatment. (For example, the attending physician would be more alert to serious internal injuries.) The only portion of the mother's account that falls outside the boundaries of Rule 803(4) is her remark that her daughter was hit by "an old man who wasn't looking where he was driving." As the Advisory Committee states, Rule 803(4) is broad enough to include "a patient's statement that he was struck by an automobile ... but not his statement that the car was driven though a red light."[26] Consider, however, the possibility that the portion of the mother's account not within Rule 803(4) might qualify as an excited utterance. It is certainly plausible to argue that the mother was still stressed and excited when she spoke to the nurse and that her statement about the old man's inattention "relates to" the exciting event.[27]

Very often, statements that are within Rule 804(4)'s purview are contained in a medical record. The proponent offers the record to prove what the declarant's words were, and she then invokes Rule 804(4) in order to permit the trier to use the declarant's statement for its truth. This process involves linking two hearsay exceptions. Normally, we require that the auditor take the stand and testify as to what the declarant (e.g., the patient) said. The presence of the auditor on the witness stand permits the opponent to cross-examine the auditor regarding whether or not the declarant did in fact make the statement that the proponent claims. When the proponent uses a medical record in lieu of the live witness (the auditor), it is necessary for her to invoke a hearsay exception that permits the trier of fact to find that the statement was made. In other words, since the opponent cannot cross-examine the medical record in an effort to disprove any statement allegedly made by the declarant (or to show that the statement actually made was different from the one recorded), the record itself must comply with the terms of a hearsay exception.[28] The exception that usually

---

26. FRE 803(4) ACN.

27. See FRE 803(2). We are assuming, of course, that the mother had personal knowledge.

28. Rule 805 states that "[h]earsay within hearsay is not excluded under the hearsay rule if each part of the combined statements conforms with an ex-

facilitates this line of proof is contained in Rule 803(6); that exception removes from the hearsay rule statements contained in regularly prepared and maintained business records.

ILLUSTRATION

> In a civil proceeding in which a state agency sues to terminate the custody rights of a stepfather, Morris, the agency's lawyer proffers a medical record. The record was prepared by Dr. Wolf, who had examined Morris' step-daughter, Hilda, age 12. After the examination, Dr. Wolf made medical-record entries indicating that his examination disclosed "vaginal ruptures, the presence of semen in the vagina, and psychological trauma." Another entry made by Wolf states that "Patient, Hilda, says that her stepfather, Morris, came into her bedroom last night around midnight and raped her."

How should the trial judge rule on Morris' hearsay objection?

The physician's medical findings were made in regular course of business and, as we shall later see, should qualify for admissibility under Rule 803(6). Dr. Wolf's entry recording Hilda's account of the events of the preceding night was also made in the regular course of the doctor's (or hospital's) business, thus permitting the use of the medical record to prove what Hilda told Wolf. Rule 803 (4)—statements for purposes of medical diagnosis and treatment—permits the trier to use Hilda's statement for the truth of its contents—that she was sexually assaulted by Morris.[29] In many situations, the identity of perpetrator or tortfeasor would not be pertinent to diagnosis or treatment. In the Illustration, however, Morris' identity would be pertinent. Proper psychological counseling (or proper referral by the examining physical) would be influenced by the nature of the relationship (stepfather and stepdaughter) between Morris and Hilda. Furthermore, proper treatment hinges in part on not returning Hilda to Morris' care.

We have noted that Rule 803(4) removes from the hearsay ban statements made solely for the purpose of a medical *diagnosis* (as opposed to treatment). When the diagnostician is not engaged to treat the patient, but only to render a diagnosis (usually for purposes of subsequent expert testimony), the patient's statements

ception to the hearsay rule provided in these rules."

29. If this were a criminal case, and if Hilda were not available as a witness (and thus could not be cross-examined

by Morris), there would be an issue as to whether the Sixth Amendment's Confrontation Clause should bar Hilda's declarations about Morris. See generally Ch. VIII at notes 14–15.

of present and past conditions carry greater hearsay risks then would be present if the patient were also seeking treatment. The stimulus to truth telling that presumably exists when the patient is aware that proper treatment depends in part on his candid disclosures to the physician is not operative where the patient seeks a diagnosis for partisan purposes.

The risk that the patient's statements to medical personnel might be false or misleading in these circumstances caused most common law judges to hold that these statements could not be admitted for their truth. In short, these judges limited the scope of the hearsay exception for statements to physicians and other medical personnel. Nonetheless, under the common-law approach, the patient's statements of medical history as well as past and present conditions were admissible not for their truth, but rather to apprise the trier of the basis (or at least part of it) upon which the expert grounded his opinion.[30] Thus, the jury was made aware of the patient's remarks to, say, the examining physician, following which the jurors were instructed to consider the patient's statements solely for their bearing on the physician's expert opinion, and not for their truth.

Most jurors were probably bewildered by such an instruction and, in any event, found it difficult to follow. Moreover, jurors can usually appreciate the potential for the patient's (typically, plaintiff's) partisanship and thus, when appropriate, can discount the probative value of his statement to the examining physician. Thus, the federal drafters took the pragmatic view that there was little or no practical gain in attempting to carry forward the common-law approach by perpetrating the highly technical approach of treating a patient's statements to a nontreating physician as outside Rule 803(4)'s exception. As we have seen, Rule 803(4) includes descriptions of medical history, as well as past and present symptoms, when "made for purposes of medical diagnosis or treatment. . . ."

§ 7.6 Recorded Recollection (Past Recollection Recorded)

We have made the observation that the hearsay exceptions are based more upon the commonplace observations of judges and lawyers than upon academic disciplines such as the social sciences. Most of us, for example, have had the experience of not being able to recall a particular fact or event, only to have it reenter conscious memory when someone—or something, like a writing—reminds us of the relevant historical context or points out some salient feature of the forgotten incident. This common experience of recovering

---

30. Typically, the expert's opinion will be based on medical tests and the patient's account of his medical history, including past and present symptoms.

memory in response to some stimulus or catalyst underlies the evidentiary rule that allows counsel to use leading questions, a writing, a sound recording, or some other means to refresh a witness's recollection. If one or more of these techniques is effective, then the witness's testimony (based on her refreshed recollection) constitutes the evidence for the jury's consideration. The technique or device used to prompt the now-revived recollection has served a useful function; it is not, however, evidence.

The hearsay exception for past recollection recorded (or simply, "recorded recollection") draws upon another widely-shared experience. Most persons have had the experience of observing something, promptly making a record of the observed event, and, at a later date, having confidence that the recordation is accurate, even though the event itself has faded from memory.

Rule 803(5) removes from the hearsay ban:

> **Recorded recollection.** A memorandum or record concerning a matter about which a witness once had knowledge but now has insufficient recollection to enable the witness to testify fully and accurately, shown to have been made or adopted by the witness when the matter was fresh in the witness' memory and to reflect that knowledge correctly. If admitted, the memorandum or record may be read into evidence but may not itself be received as an exhibit unless offered by an adverse party.

The contrast between refreshing a witness's memory and having a witness affirm the accuracy of a prior recordation becomes even clearer when Rule 803(5) is carefully examined. The "Rule 803(5) witness" either has no recollection of the event or condition in question or her partial recollection is insufficient to enable her to testify "fully and accurately." Thus, it is the recordation itself that serves as proof of the matter it describes. The witness's role is to provide foundational testimony that is akin to the testimony of an authenticating witness. When the proper foundation is complete, the memorandum or record is read (or played) in the jury's presence. The recordation itself is not received into evidence as an exhibit, unless "offered by an adverse party." The intent of this latter provision is to reduce the chance that the jury will exaggerate the probative force of the recordation, since exhibits are not only examined by the jury when received in evidence, but also often carried to the jury room when the jury retires to deliberate. The opponent, of course, has the option of offering the recordation into evidence, which he would ordinarily decline to do unless he thought the writing or recordation was inaccurate and that this inaccuracy would be highlighted by the jury's further examination.

The central features of Rule 803(5) are these:

1. The witness once had personal knowledge of the event or condition in question, but by the time she takes the stand her memory has faded to the point that she is unable "to testify fully and accurately."

2. The witness made or adopted a recordation of the event or condition in question *when her memory was fresh*; there is no requirement that the record be made or verified "immediately" or "promptly" after the witness's observations.

3. There must be evidence—and the testifying witness usually supplies it—sufficient for the trier of fact to conclude that the record correctly reflects the witness's knowledge at the time the record was made or verified.

In the typical setting, the witness who prepared the writing or other recordation will take the stand and supply all of the necessary foundational conditions, including her present inability to recall sufficiently the event or condition in question. The evidentiary routine is essentially the same when a recordation is prepared by one person—for example, the secretary to a commission or committee—and verified as accurate by another, such as the Committee Chairman, when the latter's memory of the recorded event or condition was fresh. A slightly different evidentiary routine is followed when a declarant-observer reports her observations to another, who then records them but does not show the resulting recordation to the declarant for her verification.

ILLUSTRATION

Bystander, who is searching for a coffee shop in City, sees a hooded man dash out of a bank and run quickly to a parked car in a nearby alley. As he speeds away, Bystander is able to read his license plate. When Bystander reaches the bank he is met by Security Guard who tells Bystander the bank has just been robbed and is closed until further notice. Bystander then reports what he saw and gives the license number and state of registration of the getaway car as "VA–YT468." The Security Guard records the information, as well as Bystander's name, address, and telephone number.

At trial, the prosecutor wants to show that the defendant's car (VA–YT468) was at the scene of the crime and was driven away by the robber. Both Bystander and Security Guard are available to testify. Bystander, who cannot now recall the license plate number, wishes to testify that he gave the plate number to Guard when his (Bystander's) memory was fresh and that the number he then gave was accurate. Guard will, if allowed, testify that he accurately recorded the license plate number that Bystander stated was on the getaway car.[31]

Should the trial judge allow the proffered testimony and admit into evidence Security Guard's memorandum as past recollection recorded?

Suppose that after observing the license plate number, Bystander promptly recorded it on his pocket-sized appointments calendar. At trial he takes the stand and testifies that his memory was fresh when he made the entry, that the entry accurately records what he saw, and that he cannot now remember the license number. Bystander's recordation should be admitted as past recollection recorded.

If this result is correct, then why should not the collaborative efforts of two persons with firsthand knowledge—one who saw and spoke, the other who heard and recorded—also satisfy the requirements of Rule 803(5)? Although a recordation is normally "made" by the observer, there is no reason why the two separate functions (observing and recording) cannot be carried out by two persons. As you might anticipate, however, it is necessary that both participants take the stand and testify. From an analytical perspective, there is one witness who once had reliable knowledge about the event observed (but who cannot now remember) and another witness who once had reliable knowledge about what he recorded (but who cannot now remember). Each, respectively, can testify that what was said or recorded was accurate. This is the essence of Rule 803(5).

Here are two final, but important points. First, suppose that in the Illustration above, Bystander was not available to testify. Security Guard is then able only to provide the foundation that he is confident that he recorded accurately what Bystander said. The problem is that the exception for recorded recollection embraces *only* the proposition that Guard accurately *recorded* what Bystander said—for that is all that Guard was able to perceive. But the exception does not include the very important proposition that what Bystander said is true. Yet it seems clear that Bystander's statement is being offered for its truth. This will be seen even more

31. For similar facts, *see* United States v. Booz, 451 F.2d 719 (3rd Cir. 1971), *see also* United States v. Lewis, 954 F.2d 1386 (7th Cir. 1992).

strikingly if Bystander said (and Guard had recorded), "The man who ran out of the bank was a very tall white man; he carried a black satchel, and he had a slight limp as he ran to a blue Lincoln, license 'VA–YT468' and sped away." All of the hearsay dangers are, presumably, present. Thus, in order to have the recordation admitted, it is necessary to link the exception for recorded recollection (to show that Bystander made the statement) with another hearsay exception (or exemption) to allow Bystander's statement in for its truth. For example, Bystander's statement may have embodied a "present sense impression"[32] or perhaps it constituted an "excited utterance."[33]

The second, and closing, comment about the "recorded recollection" exception concerns the occasional difficulty of providing evidence sufficient to allow the trier to conclude that the witness's earlier recordation reflected his "knowledge correctly."[34] Sometimes the foundational evidence is necessarily circumstantial, for the witness cannot recall making the particular entry in question. Suppose, for example, the witness, a security guard, is able to recall only that when he checks the security system, he "always records the working condition of each alarm and, when he fills out his report, specifically notes any problems he detected." Although the guard may not recall the night in question, his systematic routine of checking and recording (habit or custom) should provide sufficient evidence for the trier to conclude that his entries were correct.

§ 7.7　Business and Public Records

Introduction

This section covers two frequently used hearsay exceptions: business records and public records. Since these exceptions share some characteristics, it is useful to consider them in tandem. Each of these exceptions requires that the declarant's hearsay statements be contained in a writing or other recordation that can be accessed by persons in addition to those who created the recordation. Furthermore, declarations within the purview of these exceptions are relied upon by others, who are often in a position to detect mistakes or false entries. Finally, the declarant is usually disinterested insofar as the *content* of his recordation is concerned and he typically is motivated to be careful and accurate because unreliable entries may adversely affect his job performance.

Note that, a business document or public record is often a composite of several business or public entries made by different

---

32. *See* FRE 803(1).　　　　**34.** *See* FRE 803(5).
33. *See* FRE 803(2).

persons. Let us begin with an example from the business world. A "Statement of Current Inventory" reflecting items in a clothing store might be based upon entries from the receiving department, from accounting, from persons who stock the display areas, and from the sales and return departments. Generally speaking, if each person supplying the information for an entry did so in the regular course of business and had personal knowledge of the facts she supplied, the composite record is admissible. In other words, it suffices for admissibility that the business employee *supplying the information* had personal knowledge, even if the recorder did not. For example, if someone in the receiving department e-mails a clerk in the accounting department that a particular shipment of men's shoes is defective and is being returned to the distributor, subsequent entries by the accounting clerk are admissible. The person who was the source of the information had personal knowledge and (we will assume) was making his report in the regular course of business; the clerk also (let us assume) had a regular business duty to record returned shipments as reported by the receiving department.

This transaction and many others are likely to be reflected in the composite inventory tally that appears on the "Statement of Current Inventory." It is not necessary to call each person who contributed entries that appear in, or affect, the totals in the inventory report. Neither, of course, is it required that the person who provides the evidentiary foundation for the current inventory statement have personal knowledge of each underlying transaction. It is, however, necessary that the person authenticating the inventory statement be familiar with the record-keeping procedures of the clothing store, for he must confirm that each statement or entry that contributed to the composite record was made in the regular course of business.

In due course, we shall examine more closely the foundation required for the admission of business records, as well as the foundation required for public records. These requirements usually differ. Generally speaking, the proponent of a business record must provide testimonial or written evidence that the record was compiled in the regular course of business. The proponent of a public record must have an appropriate public official enter a certification on the record that attests to its genuineness.

Business Records

The term "business records" embraces a wide variety of regularly conducted activities, including the activities of such disparate enterprises as hospitals, charities, fire departments, public utilities, and in the language of Rule 803(6), "calling[s] of every kind, whether or not conducted for profit." The key is regularity and, in particular, regularity in record keeping. A business (or other enterprise) relies on its own records and, typically, so do third parties that interact with it. This reliance, as we noted earlier, is one of the factors that justifies the business-entry exception to the hearsay rule. Those who place reliance on recorded facts and figures have an incentive to monitor the accuracy of their informational base.

Rule 803(6) provides an exception to the hearsay rule for:

> **Records of Regularly Conducted Activity.** A memorandum, report, record, or data compilation, in any form, of acts, events, conditions, opinions, or diagnoses, made at or near the time by, or from information transmitted by, a person with knowledge, if kept in the course of a regularly conducted business activity, and if it was the regular practice of that business activity to make the ... [record], all as shown by the testimony of the custodian or other qualified person, or by certification that complies with Rule 902(11), Rule 902(12), or a statute permitting certification, unless the source of information or the method of circumstances of preparation indicate lack of trustworthiness. The term "business" as used in this paragraph includes business, institution, association, profession, occupation, and calling of every kind, whether or not conducted for profit.

You should be attentive to several features of the quoted text. First, the rule requires that the record be made "in the course" of regular business activity and that it was the "regular practice" of the business to make the entry. This latter requirement is designed to ensure that the entry is routine and not one that is made for some special, nonrecurring purpose—perhaps motivated by a desire to create evidence. Second, the rule demands that the entry be "made at or near the time" of the event, act, or observed condition that it records. This feature of the rule minimizes the hearsay danger of lapsed or faulty memory. Third, a proviso near the end of the rule permits the judge to exclude an entry that appears suspicious or untrustworthy. This provision vests the judge with discretionary oversight that takes account of the "source of information or the method or circumstances of preparation" of the proffered entry. Sometimes conditions or events surrounding the preparation of a record (or an entry within it) suggest that it is "untrustworthy"; if so, the judge should exclude it, and she is specifically empowered to do so by the proviso in Rule 803(b). For example, she is likely to reject entries made in anticipation of litigation or by an employee with a motive to shift blameworthy conduct from himself to another.

ILLUSTRATION

Assume that, at noon on a given day, there is a collision at a railway crossing between a train and a delivery truck. The driver of the truck, the engineer of the locomotive, and a bystander all witness the event. Within ten minutes of the accident, police officers Blue and Shield arrive at the scene. They conduct interviews and examine the physical evidence. Only Truck Driver is injured, and he is taken to the hospital.

Subsequently, Truck Driver and his employer, Trucking Company, file suit against Railroad Company, alleging that Engineer was speeding and, also, failed to blow the train whistle, which may have been in disrepair. (Engineer is not named as a defendant, since he has left Railroad's employ and his current address is unknown). Railroad denies negligence, claims the whistle blew several times, and asserts that Truck Driver was contributorily negligent because he was speeding and, also, failed to stop, look, and listen for an oncoming train.

At trial the following evidence is offered by the party indicated below. There is a hearsay objection to each of the proffered items of evidence. Nonetheless, the judge uniformly rules for the proponent and admits each item of evidence in question.

(1) Railroad offers an accident report of a type that, in accordance with its by-laws, it routinely prepares after any accident involving personal injury, death, or property damage. A sentence in the report declares that Railroad's Chief Investigator (a railroad employee) inspected the locomotive whistle three hours after the accident and found it in good working order. The report also states that Investigator interviewed Engineer the day after the accident. Engineer declared that he blew the whistle twice before the train reached the intersection where the collision occurred. This statement was dutifully recorded by Investigator.

(2) The defendant, Railroad, offers a portion of a police report prepared by Officer Blue. The report states that when Blue arrived at the scene, he interviewed Bystander. According to Blue's report:

Bystander had just finished a jogging workout. He says that he heard the train whistle twice, than saw the truck in question. The Truck Driver was going about sixty-five or seventy miles an hour. When the driver saw the railroad crossing, or maybe the train, he jammed on his brakes and the truck began to skid. Since the driver apparently couldn't stop before reaching the railroad crossing, he accelerated, but the train hit the back of the truck before the driver could clear the railroad.

(3) The defendant, Railroad, offers another portion of the police report. In this portion, Officer Blue reports, "Officer Shield states that he just measured the tire (skid) marks that were made by the truck's wheels. The skid marks were 45 feet long, and formed an undulant pattern, indicating the rear of the truck was swinging back and forth during Driver's stopping maneuver."

(4) During Truck Driver's cross-examination of the Railroad's Chief Investigator, the latter admits that, following his investigation, Engineer was fired. Investigator also admits that before Engineer was dismissed, he told Investigator that he thought the train was "going about seventy-five or eighty miles an hour" when it hit the back of the truck. When asked why this statement was not in his accident report, Investigator states that interviews with other members of the train crew convinced him that Engineer's estimate of speed was "entirely too high— twenty-five or thirty miles an hour above the actual speed."

Assume that the written statements above were accompanied by foundational evidence showing that they were routinely made in the regular course of business. Was the trial judge correct in ruling that all of the written entries described above were admissible?

In Illustration (1), the first question is whether Railroad's accident report is a business record. An early, pre-Rules Supreme Court opinion took the view that such a report was not a business record because it was prepared for the purpose of litigation, not for the purpose of operating a business.[35] It is highly doubtful that this view would prevail today. It is now generally accepted that business enterprises have a "business" reason to carefully investigate accidents because accidents, even in the absence of litigation, are costly

35. Palmer v. Hoffman, 318 U.S. 109, 113–14 (1943).

events that businesses try to prevent. The Advisory Committee Note to Rule 803(6) indicates the Committee's belief that routine accident reports are business records. That conclusion, however, does not mean that an accident report (or selected entries within) is admissible. Even if an entry within the report was made in the regular course of business and contains information supplied by an employee (e.g., Engineer) with personal knowledge, it might be rejected by the judge because attending circumstances make the entry untrustworthy. As we have seen, Rule 803(6) expressly provides for this contingency. Engineer certainly had motives to deny any fault: he might be fired if he were negligent or irresponsible in operating the train; furthermore, he knows that he is a potential defendant and thus may be reluctant to admit fault. In any event, the judge would have to determine if Engineer's self-serving statements were sufficiently trustworthy to be admitted under Rule 803(6). Perhaps less suspicion attaches to the Chief Investigator's statement that the whistle was in working order, but, again, the judge must determine admissibility. (At least, Investigator was not a potential defendant.) Note that if Investigator is available to testify, the Railroad may prefer to offer his testimony about the condition of the whistle.

In Illustration (2), Officer Blue records the statements of Bystander. The officer had a business duty to record, but the declarant (Bystander) did not have a business duty to speak. Courts have consistently held that a business entry that contains a statement by an "outsider" with no business duty to speak cannot be used to prove the truth of the declarant's statement unless the statement is within some other exception or exemption to the hearsay rule.[36] It is clear that Bystander's statement is being offered for its truth; therefore it needs to be supported by a hearsay exemption or exception. There is at least a ten-minute gap between the accident and Bystander's statement to the police—too much time for the statement to be characterized as a present sense impression.[37] It might be possible for the proponent of this evidence to lay the foundation necessary to characterize Bystander's statement as an excited utterance. His statement does relate to the startling event, as required by Federal Rule 803(2). To successfully invoke this exception, Railroad would have to convince the judge that Bystander spoke while still under the influence of the stress and excitement caused by the collusion. The fact that Bystander was not, himself, involved in the accident tends to strengthen his

---

36. The Advisory Committee was aware of these court decisions, and approved of them. *See* FRE 803(6) ACN. A leading case is Johnson v. Lutz, 253 N.Y. 124, 170 N.E. 517 (1930).

37. Federal Rule 803(1) states that the declarant's statement "describing or explaining an event or condition" must be made "while the declarant was perceiving the event or condition, or immediately thereafter."

credibility (sincerity), but, on the other hand, his status as a nonparticipant suggests that he would regain his composure more rapidly than would the individuals who were actually involved in the collision. Success in admitting the evidence in Illustration (2) depends upon linking Officer Blue's duty to record with Bystander's excited utterance.

In Illustration (3) both the speaker (Officer Shield) and the recorder (Officer Blue) had a business duty. The entry was made "at or near the time"[38] of Officer Shield's observation and measurement of the skid marks. After a proper foundation is laid,[39] this entry is admissible as a business record.

Illustration (4) does not really involve the business records exception, although Chief Investigator's concessions during cross-examination cast doubt on the accuracy of his report. Note that Engineer's declaration about the speed of the train, made before he was fired, is admissible against Railroad as a party admission. The applicable Federal Rule is 801(d)(2)(D). It is critical that Engineer's statement preceded the termination of his employment because, had it been made after his discharge, it would not have been exempted from the hearsay rule under that subsection. Under the facts of this Illustration, however, the Engineer's pre-termination declaration is exempted for the hearsay rule ("definitional nonhearsay") because his statement concerned "a matter within the scope of . . . [his] agency" and he made the statement "during the existence of the [employment] relationship."[40]

Medical Diagnoses in Business Records

Prior to the widespread adoption of the Federal Rules of Evidence, some courts were very skeptical of a hospital (business) record that contained a medical diagnosis. A recorded diagnosis of a routine medical condition, such as a broken limb or a kidney stone, caused no problem; neither did a diagnosis that was supported by "objective" findings such as an X-ray plate or the electronic images produced by magnetic resonance imagining (MRI). But some diagnoses, especially those which were not routine or which rested heavily on "subjective" professional judgments,[41] were labeled "conjectural" or simply "opinions" and rejected.

The text of Federal Rule 803(6) states that the business records exception includes entries that record "acts, events, conditions,

---

38. FRE 803(6).

39. There must be testimony or other admissible evidence that the information in the entry was supplied by an individual with first-hand knowledge who had a business duty to speak and that the written record (the police report) was prepared in the ordinary course of business.

40. FRE 801 (d)(2)(D). The engineer might also have had delegated "speaking authority" under FRE 801(d)(2)(C).

41. For example, psychiatric diagnosis.

opinions, or diagnoses...." The textual language means that medical records containing opinions or diagnoses are prima facia admissible. Recall, however, that Rule 803(6) permits the judge to exclude a business record when the "source of information [in the record] on the method or circumstances of preparation indicate a lack of trustworthiness." Suppose, for example, a plaintiff claims that job-related stress and mistreatment by his employer had caused him to suffer "transient global amnesia."[42] Prior to trial, plaintiff had spent three days in the hospital where, according to his hospital record, he was diagnosed as suffering from the amnesia noted above. The hospital record did not elaborate on the nature of this infirmity, nor—more importantly—did the record indicate a causal connection between the plaintiff's work experiences and his transient global amnesia. This hospital entry would be untrustworthy because of its cryptic nature, which left to sheer speculation both the particulars of the disease and its causation.

Laying a Foundation

The proponent of a business record must provide a proper foundation. That foundation includes evidence that the record (or entry) in question was "kept in the course of regularly conducted business activity, and ... [that] it was the regular practice of that business to make"[43] the record (or entry) in question. The proponent must also show that the information contained in the record was "transmitted by a person with knowledge"[44] and that the record was prepared in timely fashion—"at or near the time" of the recorded event.[45] In practice, the various foundational requirements are often treated as a composite and satisfied by evidence that shows the record-keeping procedures of the business enterprise. For example, a custodian of the records or some other person familiar with the record-keeping routine can take the stand and give the required testimony. (The emphasis usually falls on whether the document in question is a regularly-kept business record.) A useful amendment to Rule 803(6), effective in 2000, permits the custodian or other qualified person to provide a written certification that attests to the propriety of the proffered records.[46]

Today, of course, most businesses use computers to establish and maintain their business records. Although the general rule is that no special foundation is required for computer-generated busi-

---

42. *See* Fowler v. Carrollton Public Library, 799 F.2d 976 (5th Cir. 1986).

43. FRE 803(6).

44. Id.

45. Id.

46. Certifications of domestic records must comply with 902(11). *See* FRE 803(6). Foreign business records that are offered in federal court trials must comply with FRE 902(12). *See* FRE 803(6).

ness records,[47] it is usually necessary to lay a foundation that shows how data are gathered, stored, and retrieved. Sometimes, more detail is required, such as evidence about the software program used to manage the business data. Of course, if the opposing parties stipulate or otherwise agree to the introduction of specified business records, no further foundation is required.

Absence of an Entry in Business Record

If a regularly-kept business entry is admissible to show a fact or event, the absence of an entry that would normally record such a fact (or event) has probative force to show the unrecorded fact never existed. For example, if X company routinely records shipments of goods that are prepaid by the customer, the absence of such an entry pertaining to customer Z's order makes it less likely that he prepaid. Federal rule 803(7) makes it clear that "[e]vidence that a matter is not included" in a business record that would normally record it, is admissible "to prove the nonoccurrence or nonexistence of the matter. . . ." Again, however, as in the case of Rule 803(6), the judge is empowered to exclude this evidence if she finds it untrustworthy.

Observe that the hearsay exception contained in Rule 803(7) is actually superfluous. When there is no entry pertaining to a particular matter or event, no assertion is being made by the declarant. The Advisory Committee to the Federal Rules recognized this, but, noting some contrary authority, proposed Rule 803(7) in order to ensure a uniform practice.[48]

Public Records: In General

The hearsay exception for public or governmental records rests upon a number of grounds. The first is an assumption that public (governmental) officials will generally discharge their duties faithfully and honestly. The second is a recognition that the volume of public records makes it unlikely that a public official will have any recollection of the contents of most of the public documents within her responsibility. The third is that public documents are relied on by others, such as members of the general public, persons within the governmental agency that created the records, or members of another governmental business or department.

Generally speaking, but subject to an important qualifications to be noted shortly, the information contained in a public record originates from a person with a public duty and first-hand knowledge. In this respect, the exception for public records is analogous to the exception for business records. It is also true that those who

---

47. *See, e.g.,* United States v. Linn, 880 F.2d 209, 216 (9th Cir. 1989).

48. FRE 803(6) ACN.

create public records are usually engaged in routine, systematic practices and that they typically record events shortly after their occurrence. However, *there is no* requirement under Rule 803(8), which is the principal (but not the only) Federal Rule governing public records, that a record be created *soon after* the event that it records. Nor does Rule 803(8) require that a public record (or an entry within a public record) be made as part of a *regular, systematic routine*. Thus, a non-routine entry by a government geologist about the composition, texture, or color of certain volcanic ash would be a public-record entry, even if the recordation were not made soon after the official's observations. Of course, the exceptional and untimely nature of the record or entry could affect its weight and credibility. Furthermore, the last provision in Rule 803(8) authorizes the judge to exclude a public record or entry if the "sources of information or other circumstances indicate lack of trustworthiness." This provision parallels a similar one in Rule 803(6) that deals with business records.

Public Records: Rule 803(8)

The Federal Rules of Evidence contain a number of provisions governing the admissibility of public documents.[49] Principal among these is Rule 803(8), which provides a hearsay exception for:

> **Public Records and Reports.** Records, reports, statements, or data compilations, in any form, of public offices or agencies, setting forth (A) the activities of the office or agency, or (B) matters observed pursuant to duty imposed by law as to which matters there was a duty to report, excluding, however, in criminal cases matters observed by police officers and other law enforcement personnel, or (C) in civil actions and proceedings and against the Government in criminal cases, factual findings resulting from an investigation made pursuant to authority granted by law, unless the sources of information or other circumstances indicate lack of trustworthiness.

There are three kinds of public records set out in subsections (A), (B), and (C) of Rule 803(8), although there is some overlap, particularly between the first two subsections ((A) and (B)). The public records within subsection (A) bear a close resemblance to business records. Subsection (A) includes entries such as those pertaining to payroll, personnel, inventories, disbursements, and, generally speaking, the internal or "office" operations of a governmental department, agency, or commission. Public records falling within subsection (A) are admissible in both civil and criminal cases

---

49. See FRE 803(8), (9), (10), (12), (14), (22), and (23).

and may be introduced by or against any party. As you will see momentarily, criminal defendants are given special protection in subsections (B) and (C), and, generally speaking, public records within these two subsections cannot be introduced *against* such defendants.

Subsection (B) embraces recordations of "matters observed" pursuant to a public duty to observe and report. Typically, these observations are made outside an office environment—"in the field," so to speak. Recorded observations within subsection (B) would include, for example, a policeman's arrest of a suspect, the Weather Bureau's observations of weather conditions, an induction officer's observation that an inductee refused to take the required oath, a safety inspector's citation to an employer detailing safety violations, and an INS officer's report that he had deported a particular individual.

It is not always clear, however, whether a particular record should be characterized as within subsection (A) because it describes an "activity of . . . [a public] office or agency" or whether the record more comfortably fits with subsection (B) because it records "matters observed pursuant to . . . [a legal] duty . . . as to which matters there was a duty to report. . . ." Classification of the record is sometimes important because Rule 803(8)(B) states that it does not apply to criminal cases if the proffered public report contains "matters observed by police officers and other law enforcement personnel." Suppose, for example, a Customs Service Agent finds a powdery substance hidden in the lining of a traveler's suitcase. Suspecting the substance is heroin, the agent sends the powder to a Customs Service forensic chemist, who tests it. The chemist then files a routine report that identifies the substance in question as heroin. An argument can be made that this report, filed by a chemist who routinely tests and identifies various substances, is simply a recordation of an office activity within Rule 803(8)(A). However, in a case involving these essential facts,[50] a federal Court of Appeals found that the chemist's report was prepared pursuant to either Rule 803(8)(B) or, even more likely, pursuant to Rule 803(8)(C), to which we shall turn shortly. The court also found that the chemist could properly be included in the "law enforcement personnel" category to which subsection (B) makes specific reference.

Note that subsection (B) of Rule 803(8) appears to state categorically that any "law-enforcement" report is inadmissible in

---

50. United States v. Oates, 560 F.2d 45 (2d Cir. 1977). The *Oates* case has been criticized and, generally, other courts have founds ways to distinguish it or to depart from its construction of Rule 803(8)(B). *See, e.g.,* United States v. Baker, 855 F.2d 1353, 1359–60 (8th Cir. 1988), *cert. denied,* 490 U.S. 1069 (1989). (Chemist's drug analysis report is admissible). See infra at note 54.

criminal cases. Yet the intent of the drafters of this subsection was to protect the criminal defendant. Therefore, as most courts have wisely held,[51] subsection (B) excepts from the hearsay rule (and thus makes admissible) reports by police and other law enforcement agents that the *accused offers against the government*. In other words, the prohibition in this subsection applies only to reports offered *against the accused*. Of course, some other rule of exclusion may apply, but the point is that subsection (B) is a one-way street. This interpretation of Rule 803(8)(B) is consistent with the text of subsection (C), which shields the criminal defendant, but permits public records within that subsection to be introduced "against the government in criminal cases. . . ."

Subsection (C) of Rule 803(8) generally confers admissibility upon investigative findings by a public official who is pursuing an official investigation, but again, not when offered against the accused in a criminal case. The protective provision is probably required by the accused's constitutional right to confront witnesses against him.[52] The text of subsection (C) provides a generally applicable hearsay exception for public records or reports that present "factual findings resulting from an investigation made pursuant to authority granted by law. . . ." Public reports within subsection (C) should include, for example, an investigative report by the Army setting out the extent and causes of lost military supplies or a report of the Bureau of Mines detailing the probable cause of an explosion.

In conducting an investigation "pursuant to authority granted by law", the investigating officer frequently obtains information from persons who have no public duty to speak. They may, for example, be merely witnesses and not governmental officers or employees. When we examined the hearsay exception for business records, we saw that under that exception it was necessary that both the "speaker" (the source of the information) and the recorder have a business duty to act. However, under the public records exception contained in Rule 803(8)(C) (investigative reports), it is not necessary that the person who is the source of information contained in the report be speaking pursuant to a public (or business) duty. The theory is that the investigating officer(s) has expertise in the area in which she conducts her investigation, and thus can reliability evaluate the probable accuracy of declarations by witnesses or other persons with knowledge. Of course, subsection (C) is not a license to admit recordations of hearsay statements by members of the general public. The officer's findings are admissible.

51. *See, e.g.*, United States v. Smith, 521 F.2d 957, 963–68 (D.C. Cir. 1975).

52. U.S. Const. Amend. VI. See Ch. VIII at note 13 et. seq.

There is yet another salient feature of Rule 803(8)(C): its language confines the admissible content of public investigative reports to "factual findings." The judicial construction of this phrase is important because a narrow reading of "factual findings" would exclude significant portions of the investigator's report on the ground that they contain evaluations, opinions, or conclusions—not bare facts.

ILLUSTRATION

During a Navy training exercise, one of the participating aircraft departs from the prescribed flight pattern. In an effort to avoid a collision with an adjacent aircraft, the pilot of the errant plane banks sharply. Thereafter, the plane plunges downward, crashes, and burns. The pilot and her student are both killed. Subsequently, survivors of the decedents file suit against the manufacturer of the doomed aircraft. The plaintiffs contend that the crash was caused by a defect in the plane's fuel system; the defendant contends that the accident resulted from errors made by the pilot as she tried to maneuver the plane back on course.

At trial, the defendant offers an investigative report prepared by a JAG officer who conducted an exhaustive post-accident investigation of the crash. The report contains numerous "factual findings", as well as a section labeled "Opinion." In the latter section, the investigator reconstructs the evidence bearing on pertinent events and concludes that the "most probable cause of the accident was the pilot's failure to maintain proper interval."[53]

The plaintiffs object to the admission into evidence of the "Opinion" section of the JAG report. How should the trial judge rule?

This Illustration is based on Beech Aircraft Corp. v. Rainey,[54] decided by the Supreme Court in 1988. Speaking for the Court, Justice Brennan held that Rule 803(8)(C) does not exclude an investigative report containing opinions or conclusions. To begin with, said Justice Brennan, the term "factual findings" is usually construed so as to include reasonable inferences drawn from observable evidence. More importantly, the language of Rule 803(8)(C) is plainly addressed to the admissibility of *reports*, and in the context of subsection (C), the requirement is that the *report in question* must be based on factual findings. So construed, Rule

53. Beech Aircraft Corp. v. Rainey,   **54.** Id.
488 U.S. 153, 158 (1988).

803(8)(C) does not distinguish between facts and opinions by approving the former, but rejecting the latter. Finally, Rule 803(8) itself provides protection against the admission of speculative or unsubstantiated hearsay assertions. If the "sources of information or other circumstances" cast doubt on the reliability of statements in a report, the judge may exclude them. Similar, but even broader protection against misleading or unwarranted evidence is provided by Rule 403. The existence of these several protective provisions permits the trial judge to take full account of such factors as the expertise of the investigator, her possible bias or motive to distort, the thoroughness of her inquiry, and the strengths and weaknesses of the factual bases that underlies her report.

The Relationship Between Rule 803(8) and Rule 803(6)

We have seen that there is a rather close kinship between Rule 803(6), governing the admission of business records, and Rule 803(8), controlling the admission of public records. The term "business" is so broadly defined in Rule 803(6) that it surely embraces most public entities such as governmental departments, agencies, commissions, and the like. Therefore, many recorded hearsay declarations will meet the conditions of both Rule 803(6) and Rule 803(8). As to many of the hearsay statements contained in these documents, it is a matter of indifference whether the proponent offers his recordation as a public record or as a business record. The record will be admitted under the rule he cites, assuming the conditions of the rule are satisfied.

However, as we have just observed, Rule 803(8) contains special protections for the accused in a criminal prosecution. For example, a recorded observation by a law enforcement official falls within the exclusionary provision of 803(8)(B). In this context, the overlap of Rule 803(8) and Rule 803(6) raises an important issue: may the proponent of a hearsay declaration that is barred from admission by one of the protective provisions of Rule 803(8), nonetheless gain admission of the declaration by offering it as a business record presumptively admissible under the terms of Rule 803(6)? After all, a general governing principle of evidence holds that if evidence is admissible under the theory or rule cited by the proponent, it will not be rejected simply because it would be inadmissible if offered under another theory or pursuant to another evidentiary rule. If, however, this general principle were to apply in the setting under consideration, the protective provisions of Rule 803(8) would be seriously emasculated. Consider whether the following records should be admitted as public records, or business records, or under some other exception to the hearsay rule.

ILLUSTRATIONS

(1) In a prosecution for the possession and use of a dangerous weapon during the commission of a felony, the prosecutor proffers a police report that states, "When Abel [the accused] was arrested, approximately 20 minutes after the robbery, he had in his possession, encased in a shoulder holster under his jacket, a Beretta 92FS, 9mm, semiautomatic pistol, serial number BER400817."

(2) In a prosecution for a conspiracy to violate federal firearms laws, the government needs to prove that certain weapons were transported to Northern Ireland. The prosecutor proffers a routine inventory report prepared by the Northern Ireland police. Among the inventoried items are weapons seized by the police, some of which bear serial numbers that match weapons formally owned or possessed by the defendants.

(3) The police report in Illustration (1) is proffered as the past recollection recorded of the officer who prepared it. The officer cannot now recall what, if any, weapon was carried by the arrestee, Abel. However, the officer can verify that he prepared the report soon after the arrest, when his memory was fresh, and he is sure the entry is accurate.

(4) In a perjury prosecution, the District Attorney offers a transcript of the testimony of the accused in an earlier case. The purpose of this evidence is to establish the exact content of the accused's testimony and also, to establish that the accused had been sworn.

(5) In a "hit-and run" prosecution, in which the defendant is charged with colliding with an ambassador's car and leaving the scene, the government offers a police report. The report was prepared by an investigating police officer who, using skid marks and other physical evidence, estimated the speeds of the two vehicles involved, the point at which the cars collided, and the trajectories of the two cars before and after the collision. This kind of report is routinely prepared, and the officer who prepared it is on the witness stand. The prosecutor offers the report as both a public record and a business record.

The evidence in Illustration (1) is inadmissible under Rule 803(8)(B) since it is a record of "matters observed pursuant to duty imposed by law," prepared by a police officer and offered against the defendant in a criminal case. The report is also a business record, but to allow the proponent to defeat the protection afforded the accused under Rule 803(8)(B) by the simple device of offering the police report under Rule 803(6) as a business record would defeat the purpose of 803(8)(B). One case, United States v. Oates,[55] goes so far, at least in dictum, as to say that if a public report is inadmissible against a criminal defendant because it is within the protective provisions of Rule 803(8), subsections (B) or (C), the report cannot be admitted under *any other* rule of evidence. The *Oates* court refused to admit a lab report by a Customs Service chemist in which he concluded that the substance he tested was heroin. Concluding that the chemist had conducted an "investigation" within Rule 803(8)(C) and was probably also a law enforcement officer recording matters he "observed" pursuant to 803(8)(B), the *Oates* court disallowed the use of Rule 803(6) to skirt the protective provisions of Rule 803(8).

It is not at all clear that a laboratory analysis is an "investigation" within the ambit of Rule 803(8)(C). At least this kind of routine analysis bears only a remote kinship to the typical 803(8)(C) investigation in which the investigating officer gathers and assesses evidence from a variety of sources and tries to reconstruct an event. A prototypical subsection (C) "investigation" would be one undertaken by a fire marshal in an attempt to determine the cause or origin of a fire. Nor is it clear that a Customs Service chemist is within the "law enforcement personnel" category to which Rule 803(8)(B) refers.[56] Even more problematic is the broad assertion of the *Oates* court that a report that is caught in the exclusionary grip of 803(8)(B) or (C) is barred from admissibility under *any* other rule of evidence.

While it is sound to say, of a general matter, that the business entries exception contained in Rule 803(6) cannot be used to nullify the protective provisions of Rule 803(8), the ironclad "*Oates* doctrine" is neither necessary nor sound.

Other courts have departed from *Oates* in significant ways, and Illustrations (2) through (5) are designed to elucidate these disparities. Most courts draw a distinction between non-adversarial (routine or ministerial) law enforcement reports and law enforcement reports that are prepared in an adversarial context in which the attention of law enforcement officials is fastened upon one or more suspects. A routine property inventory is ministerial, and thus the

---

55. *Oates*, 560 F.2d at 69.

56. *Cf.*, United States v. Hansen, 583 F.2d 325, 333 (7th Cir.), *cert. denied*, 439 U.S. 912 (1978) (building inspector not considered a law enforcement officer even though building code violations can constitute criminal offense).

police report in Illustration (2) would be admissible in most courts.[57]

The police report described in Illustration (3) is offered under Rule 803(5) as the officer's past recollection recorded. The author of the report is on the stand; his demeanor can be observed by the trier of fact; he can be cross-examined about what he can (and cannot) recall and about the circumstances surrounding his recordation. In short, Rule 803(5), by its terms, requires that the author of the "recorded recollection" testify and, thus, be subject to cross-examination. This context is significantly different from one in which a public record is offered against the accused and the person or persons preparing the report do not appear and testify. This difference has persuaded most courts that the protective provisions of Rule 803(8) do not prohibit the introduction into evidence of a police report that meets the requirements of past recollection recorded.[58]

Illustration (4) raises the issue of whether a court reporter is included in the term "law enforcement personnel" which is used in Rule 803(8)(B) to generally identify those persons who enforce the criminal laws. This term should not be so broadly construed that it embraces purely administrative personnel. A court reporter has a clerical or ministerial role and should not be considered an officer or employee charged with enforcing the criminal laws.[59] Finally, Illustration (5) rests on the proposition that when the author (with personal knowledge) of a public report testifies, the concern that underlies the protective provisions of Rule 803(8)—the inability of the accused to confront adverse hearsay declarants—disappears and the report is admissible,[60] unless of course, the judge finds that it is untrustworthy. Note also the possibility of using the police report to refresh the officer's recollection

The Absence of a Public Record

Rule 803(10) bears a close resemblance to Rule 803(7), for both rules address the absence of an entry or recordation. Rule 803(10)

---

57. *See, e.g.,* United States v. Grady, 544 F.2d 598, 604 (2d Cir. 1976). Once it is determined that the protective provisions of Rule 803(8) are inapplicable, the proffered record may be received as either a public record or a business record.

58. *See, e.g.,* United States v. Picciandra, 788 F.2d 39, 44 (1st Cir. 1986); United States v. Sawyer, 607 F.2d 1190, 1193 (7th Cir. 1979).

59. *See* United States v. Arias, 575 F.2d 253, 254–55 (9th Cir.), *cert. denied,* 439 U.S. 868 (1978).

60. *See* United States v. Sokolow, 91 F.3d 396, 404–05 (3d Cir. 1996). The concern underlying Rule 803(8) does disappear insofar as the author has first-hand knowledge of the matters recited in the public report. The concern is ameliorated if the other contributors to the report were operating under a public or business duty to speak. However, the fact that the author of the request is on the stand does not justify admitting the declarations of members of the general public, such as witnesses, for the truth of their declarations, unless, of course, some other hearsay exception (or exemption) applies.

may be invoked to prove, first, the absence of a public report or, second, the "nonoccurrence or nonexistence of a matter" that would routinely be filed and preserved in a public office. The appropriate public official must certify that she has made a diligent search. Technically, the fact that there is no public record of an event is not a hearsay declaration, but merely circumstantial proof. Thus, if the custodian or other appropriate person were to testify that her diligent research failed to locate the putative record in question, no hearsay problem arises. Note, however, that the written certification of the appropriate public officer that she conducted a diligent, but unsuccessful, search is a declaration by a person not on the witness stand which is offered for its truth. Her certification is a public entry and, as such, is admissible for its truth.

§ 7.8 Miscellaneous Rule 803 Exceptions; Rule 804 Exceptions

Ancient Documents

We have seen that a document that is twenty or more years old, regular (unsuspicious) on its face, and located in a "place where it, if authentic, would likely be" needs no additional foundational evidence in order to be admitted as authentic.[61] Of course, the opponent may continue to dispute its authenticity. The foundational facts of age, regularity, and location suffice, however, under the "ancient documents" authentication rule to permit a reasonable trier to determine that the document is genuine.[62] There is a second aspect to the ancient documents rule: it creates a hearsay exception for the declaratory content of old documents. Rule 803(16) excepts from the hearsay rule:

> **Statements in Ancient Documents.** Statements in a document in existence twenty years or more the authenticity of which is established.

There is technical issue raised by this rule, but it should be of little consequence. It will be recalled that jury has the last word on whether a recordation, such as a writing, is authentic. The judge simply screens the foundational evidence to ensure that a reasonable jury *could* find that the proffered evidence is sufficiently convincing to support a conclusion that the item in question is genuine. On the other hand, as to facts surrounding the admissibili-

---

61. FRE 901(8). See Ch. III, § 3.3.

62. This is not the only means by which an ancient document can be authenticated. For example, a witness with knowledge may testify that the docu-ment in question is genuine. Authentication requires only that there be foundational evidence sufficient to permit a reasonable trier to conclude that the proffered document is genuine.

ty of evidence (such as facts necessary to the application of a hearsay exception), the judge ordinarily makes the final determination.[63]

However, the most sensible and practical way to administer Rule 803(16) is for the judge to defer to the jury.[64] This deference can be extended by a simple instruction to the jurors that if they find that the document in question is genuine, they *may* also accept the statements in it as true. This solution avoids the awkward procedure of allocating to the judge (as part of his hearsay-exception fact-finding responsibility) the determination of whether the document in question is at least twenty years old, while giving the jury the responsibility of determining authenticity—a determination that often involves a jury decision as to the document's age.

It remains to ask whether a hearsay exception for ancient documents is justified. Certainly, necessity played a part in the creation of this exception, for finding available witnesses to an event so long past would be unusual, if not rare. Further, even if one or more such witnesses exist, their memories of the occurrence would be impaired by the passage of time. The probable reliability of an old document is enhanced by the fact that it was nearly always created long before the dispute that led to the present trial, and that the evidence is in recorded form (thus, *what* the declarant said is known). As a practical matter, if the authenticity of the proffered document had been seriously disputed on other, earlier occasions, the trial judge could caution the jury, or could even exclude the document by invoking Rule 403.

Learned Treaties

Generally speaking, at common law an expert witness could be impeached by showing that an author, also an expert in the witness's field, held professional views that contradicted those of the witness. The Federal Rules of Evidence go a step further in Rule 803(18) by creating a hearsay exception for statements in a learned treatise or other professional or scholarly publication,

> [t]o the extent [the work is] called to the attention of an expert witness upon cross-examination or relied upon by the expert witness in direct examination ... [provided the work is] established as a reliable authority by the testimony or admission of the witness or by other expert testimony or by judicial notice.

---

63. FRE 104(a).

64. Alternatively, the judge, pursuant to the hearsay exception contained in Rule 803(16), could determine the

single fact *expressly* mentioned in this rule: that the document in question is at least twenty years old.

Statements in a learned treatise, journal, pamphlet, or similar publication that qualify under the present exception to the hearsay rule are read into evidence, but are not received as exhibits. To treat them as exhibits would normally entitle the jury to use the learned volume, pamphlet, or periodical during its deliberations, thereby affording these works more prolonged jury attention then the expert testimony presented at trial. Even more importantly, if the jury had access to a treatise or similar work during its deliberations, jury members might attempt to interpret and apply the work without the benefit of expert guidance.[65]

Before passages in a treatise (or similar publication) qualify as an exception to the hearsay rule under Federal Rule 803(18), the proponent of this evidence must establish that the work in question is "a reliable authority." Perhaps the expert being challenged by a cross-examiner will admit that the work is authoritative. If not, another expert can provide this foundational testimony. In some instances, a court may take judicial notice that the work is reliable. Suppose, for example, the work is widely adopted by medical schools as a required text or the author is a renowned authority. In any event, the judge must be persuaded by whatever foundational evidence is presented that the proffered work is "a reliable authority" before a proponent will be allowed to invoke Rule 803(18).

Another signal feature of the present rule is that an expert on the stand must have the opportunity to interpret or comment upon the passages in the learned work that are read to the jury. This end is achieved by that provision in Rule 803(18) that directs that the work in question is admissible only "[t]o the extent called to the attention of an expert witness upon cross-examination or relied upon by the expert witness in direct examination . . . ." Thus, as a practical matter, the rule ensures that the trier of fact will have the benefit of a knowledgeable expert's view as to the validity of the textual passage in question and, just as importantly, how those passages bear upon the issue(s) in the case before the court.

The exception for learned treatises is probably used with the greatest frequency to secure textual evidence that contradicts or at least is at variance with the testimony of an opposing expert. In other words, the cross-examiner invokes the exception to impeach the opposing side's expert. But the rule is not limited to his setting. A "friendly" expert could provide the foundation for the introduction of the text, treatise, or other authoritative publication, presumably to give greater currency to his own opinion.

Judgment of a Criminal Conviction: Background

Rule 803(22), to which we will more fully turn in a moment, is concerned with using a prior criminal conviction in a subsequent

---

65. FRE 803(18) ACN.

criminal or civil trial as *evidence*. The heart of the rule is simply the proposition that a criminal conviction based on essential fact *A* (e.g., breaking and entering), fact *B* (e.g., a residence), and fact *C* (e.g., with intent to commit a felony), has considerable probative force in a subsequent case to prove any of these same facts that are in issue. For example, a prior conviction might help the government prove an element in a crime being prosecuted because a crime for which the accused has already been convicted has probative value to prove an element of the presently charged crime, such as intent, motive, knowledge, lack of accidental causation, and so forth. Criminal convictions, of course, have various other evidentiary uses, such as impeaching the credibility of a witness who has been convicted of an offense (e.g., perjury or fraud) that bears strongly on truth telling.

A criminal conviction can also have res judicata effects in subsequent litigation; in particular, an issue resolved in one trial (Suit 1) may foreclose the relitigation of that issue in a subsequent trial (Suit 2) based on a different claim or defense. The key is that the two suits have a common issue that is essentially, factual, and that issue was resolved in the earlier suit.

ILLUSTRATIONS

(1) Clem is convicted of willfully setting fire to a large warehouse that he owns. Subsequently, Clem sues the fire insurance company that insured the destroyed warehouse, claiming that he is entitled to the insurance proceeds. The defendant offers in evidence the judgment of criminal conviction from Clem's arson trial, as well as pertinent parts of the trial transcript. Is the fire insurance company entitled to a summary judgment or directed verdict—that is, a judgment as a matter of law?

(2) Oscar and Seth, each driving his own car, are involved in an automobile collision. Oscar is prosecuted and convicted of driving while intoxicated. Subsequently, Oscar sues Seth, alleging that Seth's negligence caused the collision and Oscar's resulting injuries. The state in which the accident occurred and in which Oscar's civil suit is filed has a statute declaring that one who is intoxicated when he is involved in an automobile accident shall be deemed contributorily negligent and cannot recover against the other driver. Is Seth entitled to use the earlier criminal judgment to receive a favorable judgment as a matter of law in the present civil suit?

(3) Suppose that in Illustration (2) Oscar had not contested the drunken driving charge, but had entered a guilty plea. Would Seth be entitled to a judgment as a matter of law (directed verdict) in the present civil suit?

It is likely that all, and certainly most modern courts would conclude that the insurance company in Illustration (1) was entitled to summary judgment or judgment as a matter of law (often called a directed verdict). The first trial was for a serious felony offense—arson. In the second suit Clem is seeking to profit from what a criminal court concluded was his own wrongdoing. Furthermore, the standard of proof in the first trial was high—beyond a reasonable doubt. An old common law principle, called the doctrine of mutuality, limited the application of issue preclusion (collateral estoppel) to instances in which suits 1 and 2 involved the same parties,[66] and, of course, the fire insurance company was not a party to the first suit. The early reasoning was that issue preclusion had to be a "two-way street:" It was thought unfair to let a party to the second suit (who was not a party to the first suit and thus could not be bound by doctrines of res judicata) invoke issue preclusion against one who was a party to the first suit. Modern courts recognize that the focus should be on the person *who was a party to the first suit*. If that person had a full and fair opportunity to contest an issue, and the issue was resolved against him in Suit 1, why should he be entitled to relitigate the issue in Suit 2?

Probably a majority of modern courts would resolve Illustration 2 consistently with the resolution of Illustration 1. (If so, there would be no trial.) However, driving under the influence of alcohol is usually not as serious an offense as arson. The drunken driving offense might be only a misdemeanor and some of the constitutional and statutory protections designed to ensure a full and fair trial may not be applicable.[67] Thus, some courts would refuse to apply issue preclusion and would allow Oscar to relitigate the issue of his intoxication. These courts might, for example, apply the old doctrine of mutuality or they might say that even though that doctrine is no longer followed, the application of issue preclusion depends on the context of suits 1 and 2 and, in particular, the incentives and opportunities to fully litigate the common issue in the first suit.

Illustration (3) raises the question of whether a guilty plea in a criminal prosecution has issue preclusive effects. The traditional rule is that issue preclusion (collateral estoppel) applies only to

---

66. It sufficed if a party to the second suit had her interests represented in the first suit even though she was not formally a party to that suit. For example, if a trustee in the first suit represented the interests of a beneficiary, the beneficiary could be issue-precluded in Suit 2.

67. Perhaps, for example, there would be no right to have counsel appointed or to demand a trial by jury.

those facts *actually and necessarily litigated* in the first suit—that is, only to those facts that were actually disputed by the parties and resolved by the trier of fact. Therefore, under the traditional approach, Oscar's conviction based on his guilty plea would not preclude the relitigation of the issue of his intoxication. Note, however, that his plea to the charged offense of driving while intoxicated can probably be introduced against him as a party admission, to which the jury may give such weight as they deemed appropriate. Although courts are sometimes hesitant to allow a guilty plea to a traffic offense to be used as a party admission in a subsequent trial, driving under the influence is a serious enough charge that the judge in Suit 2 would probably allow the plea to be introduced against Oscar as his party admission. A guilty plea to drunken driving is distinguishable from a guilty plea to an alleged minor violation (e.g., 40 m.p.h. in a 25 m.p.h. zone), which may be entered simply to avoid the inconvenience and expense of a judicial contest.

Some modern courts depart from the traditional rule that issue preclusion applies only to factual determinations that were actually and necessarily litigated in the first trial. Where the first trial is a prosecution for a criminal offense that has substantial consequences—for example, a felony or a serious misdemeanor—these modern courts apply issue preclusion to the resulting conviction, thus foreclosing relitigation of the facts that constitute the criminal offense.[68]

Judgment of a Criminal Conviction: Rule 803(22)

Rule 803(22) provides a hearsay exception for

> **Judgment of Previous Conviction.** Evidence of final judgment, entered after a trial or upon a plea of guilty (but not upon a plea of nolo contendere), adjudging a person guilty of a crime punishable by death or imprisonment in excess of one year, to prove any fact essential to sustain the judgment, but not including, when offered by the Government in a criminal prosecution for purposes other than impeachment, judgments against persons other than the accused. The pendency of an appeal may be shown but does not affect admissibility.

---

68. *See, e.g.,* United States v. Killough, 848 F.2d 1523, 1528 (11th Cir. 1988) (defendants' guilty pleas to charge of conspiracy to defraud the United States sufficient to give rise to issue preclusion in subsequent civil suit by U.S. to recover misappropriated funds).

This exception does not address issue preclusion, which is not properly included within the law of evidence, but rather is part of the body of law generally known as the "law of judgments." Rule 803(22) is concerned with using a prior criminal conviction as an *evidentiary* tool employed in an effort to prove a "fact essential to sustain the [prior criminal] judgment." Obviously, that fact has to be relevant to a consequential fact in the subsequent civil or criminal trial. The proponent of the prior criminal judgment would, of course, prefer that the law of judgments, and in particular issue preclusion, foreclose altogether the relitigation of the fact(s) claimed to underlie the prior conviction. But sometimes issue preclusion is not available,[69] so the proponent turns to the evidentiary use of the prior conviction, and the possible application of Rule 803(22).

Note that under 803(22), it is immaterial whether the prior judgment rests on a guilty plea or upon a conviction after trial. It is essential, however, that the judgment represents a conviction of a felony grade offense—one that is "punishable by death or imprisonment in excess of one year...." A conviction based on a plea of nolo contendere is not within the exception; "nolo pleas" are not an admission of guilt by the pleader. He agrees not to contest the government's case, in return for which he does not have to bear the adverse collateral consequences of the plea and resulting conviction. A judgment of acquittal is also outside the scope of Rule 803(22), since it implies only that some factual element necessary to a conviction was not found to exist beyond a reasonable doubt.

Recall that the essence of Rule 803(22) is that it permits the introduction into evidence of a prior felony-grade conviction "to prove any fact essential to sustain the judgment."[70] The prior judgment is usually against a party to the present suit, but in a civil case this congruence of party identity is unnecessary—and the same is true in a criminal case in which where the accused offers a prior conviction of another person *against the government* in an effort to prove some exculpatory fact. Thus, imagine a civil suit in which *A*'s executor (the plaintiff) claims that the defendant *B* (and not *C*) negligently shot and killed *A* while the three of them were hunting. *B* could introduce a criminal judgment showing that *C* was convicted of the involuntary manslaughter of *A*.

A final example illustrates a restriction appearing near the end of Rule 803(22). Suppose that the present trial (Trial 2) is a criminal prosecution in which *D* is charged with the receipt of rare

69. Generally speaking, the judge in the second suit or prosecution must apply the law of judgments of the state in which the first judgment was rendered, giving the earlier judgment the same preclusive effect it would have in the jurisdiction that rendered the first judgment. *See* 28 U.S.C.A. 1738.

70. FRE 803(22).

and valuable (stolen) stamps. To prove that the stamps were in fact stolen, the government introduces a judgment, obtained in an earlier criminal trial (Trial 1), showing that X had been convicted of stealing the stamps in question. The prior judgment is offered for the hearsay assertion by the trier of fact in the first trial that the stamps were stolen. Rule 803(22) would disallow this evidence.[71] The previous criminal judgment was against a person "other than the accused" in the present trial; the evidence is not offered for the purpose of impeaching the credibility of a witness; and, more importantly, the present accused is unable to confront and cross-examine the witness against him. The Confrontation Clause of the United States Constitution accounts largely for the restriction in Rule 803(22).[72]

ILLUSTRATION

Carla is charged with selling a firearm to a convicted felon. In order to show that the buyer was a convicted felon, the government offers a judgment from a 2002 criminal trial in which Carla's buyer was convicted of bank robbery. Carla's attorney objects to this evidence, citing the restriction that appears near the end of Rule 803(22). How shall the judge rule?

The government is not offering the prior conviction in an effort to prove that the buyer robbed a bank. The buyers' criminal conviction is offered as a public record[73] only to show that he has the status of a convicted felon, whether or not he actually robbed a bank. The restrictive provision of Rule 803(22) has no application. Indeed, Rule 803(22) is not applicable because the prosecutor is not using the prior criminal judgment in an attempt "to prove any fact [about the bank robbery] essential to sustain the judgment ...."

Other Miscellaneous Rule 803 Exceptions: A Sample

We have addressed the Rule 803 exceptions most often studied in evidence courses and most often discussed in the reported cases. Recall, however, that Rule 803 has twenty-three exceptions, of which we have examined twelve. The remaining rules, some with a long common law history, are fairly narrow in scope and comparatively easy to grasp. A sample follows:

    1. Rule 803(9) excepts from the hearsay rule "records or data compilations" that contain statistics pertaining to "births, fetal deaths, deaths, or marriages." The strong analogy here is

---

71. *Cf.* Kirby v. United States, 174 U.S. 47, 54–62 (1899).

72. FRE 803(22) ACN.

73. FRE 803(8).

to public records, the subject of Rule 803(8). This helpful comparison will be readily seen by examining the provisions of Rule 803(9): the vital statistics controlled by this rule must be reported to a public office "pursuant to requirements of law" by such persons as physicians, ministers, coroners, undertakers, and the like. Many of the persons required by law to file the report are not public officers, but they are performing a publicly imposed duty when they file the reports named in Rule 803(9).

2. Rule 803(17) excepts from the hearsay rule published compilations "used and relied upon by the public or by persons in particular occupations."[74] Stock quotations, telephone directories, weather conditions, census statistics, commodity market reports, price and inflation indexes, and a host of other tabulations and quotations are admissible under this rule. The source of the published information may be either public[75] or private. Note that the person or entity that is the source of these published materials usually has an incentive to be accurate or, at the very least, no incentive to falsify information. Furthermore, falsity is likely to be detected by those who rely on the data. Thus, the combination of a disinterested source and public reliance justify this exception to the hearsay rule. The accuracy of the compilation, list, or directory may be challenged by the opponent. If the judge believes the proffered material is outdated or otherwise misleading, she can invoke Rule 403 and exclude it. The admission of a Rule 803(17) report is not conclusive as to the accuracy of the reported data. The reliability (probative force) of this evidence is finally determined by the trier of fact.

3. Rule 803(19) is one of several hearsay exceptions contained in Rule 803 that allow evidence of reputation as an exception to the hearsay rule.[76] Under this subsection, reputation evidence is admissible to prove "a person's birth, adoption, marriage, divorce, death, legitimacy, relationship by blood, adoption, or marriage, ancestry, or other similar factual personal or family history".[77] There are three sources from which relevant reputation evidence may be obtained: within the family, within the community, or among associates familiar with the reputation concerning persons whose relationship is in

---

74. FRE 803(17).

75. There will be instances in which a public record, admissible under Rule 803(8), will be published and thus fall within Rule 803(17).

76. *See also* FRE 803(20) (proof of boundaries), (21) (proof of character).

Rule 804(b)(4) also contains a hearsay exception that pertains to family history. In the case of 804(b)(4), hearsay *declarations* by family members about family relationships are admissible.

77. FRE 803(19).

question. A witness who testifies concerning this person's reputation must have personal knowledge of the reputation, but need not have personal knowledge of the relationship in question. ("The reputation throughout the village is that she was Bert Grant's illegitimate daughter.")

A Transitional Note

We have seen that Rule 803 exceptions apply whether or not the declarant is available to testify. This is not true of Rule 804 exceptions: The four exceptions set out in Rule 804(b) are inapplicable *unless the declarant is unavailable*. To determine whether or not the declarant is unavailable, recourse is had to 804(a), where the technical phrase "unavailability as a witness" is elaborated. The categories of unavailability set forth in Rule 804(a) are not exclusive, and circumstances not enumerated in subsection (a) could justify a judge's determination that a declarant was unavailable as a witness.

Rule 804 is a rule of preference at two levels. First, the rule prefers a declarant's live testimony to her hearsay declaration. Second, with one exception to be noted subsequently, the rule prefers the declarant's deposition to other evidence of her hearsay statement. As a general matter, the drafters of the Federal Rules thought that the Rule 804 exceptions, taken collectively, were not generally as reliable as live testimony, but superior to no evidence at all. Thus, they built in a preference for the declarant's live testimony. And, as just noted, if that cannot be reasonably secured, there is a general preference for receiving the declarant's deposition. This second-level preference does not, however, attach to the exception for former testimony. Testimony from an earlier trial or proceeding is normally proved through the introduction of the court reporter's transcript, although there are other possibilities. Nonetheless, there is no point in preferring a deposition to courtroom testimony.

Rule 804(a): Unavailability Defined

Since Rule 804's first preference is for the witness-declarant to appear and testify, it becomes necessary to determine when she is unavailable. The death or incapacity of the declarant are obvious examples of unavailability. Suppose, for instance, the declarant has suffered a disease or injury that renders him incapable of testifying.

In an effort to give some consistency to judicial rulings on "unavailability," the drafters of Rule 804 provided, in subsection (a), a non-exclusive list of circumstances in which a witness would be considered unavailable. In addition to death or incapacity, Rule 804(a) also states that a witness is unavailable if

(a) she successfully invokes a claim of privilege;

(b) she refuses to testify in defiance of the judge's order to do so;

(c) she testifies that she cannot remember the event in question; or

(d) the proponent of her hearsay declaration "has been unable to procure the declarant's attendance by process or other reasonable means."

Rule 804(a) goes on to provide that if the proponent is able to show that the declarant is unavailable, he must surmount yet another hurdle. Before he is able to invoke the hearsay exceptions for dying declarations, statements against interest, or family history (all contained in 804(b)), he must show that the declarant's deposition cannot be procured "by process or other reasonable means."[78] The preference for the declarant's deposition rests largely on the opportunity afforded the opponent to conduct a cross-examination. As we have already observed, this second-level preference for taking the declarant's deposition does not apply to Rule 804(b) exception for former testimony. First of all, the opportunity for cross-examination has already been afforded under the "former testimony" exception to the hearsay rule. Second, it is highly likely that the former testimony was recorded as part of the court reporter's transcript of trial or proceeding, so that the reason to insist a deposition disappears entirely.

Former Testimony

The central feature of this exception is the principle that if a party has had the opportunity to develop (by direct or cross-examination) a witness's testimony in the first trial (or proceeding), the witness's (trial-one) testimony should be admissible against that party in trial two. The hearsay dangers are minimized by the prior opportunity to develop the testimony. It can be argued that the witness's former testimony should not be hearsay at all since it was given in some formal proceeding (usually, but not always, judicial), under oath, and subject to examination by the opposing parties. Alternatively, it can be argued that prior testimony should be a Rule 803 exception, so that the declarant's availability is immaterial.

As a technical matter, however, the prior testimony is hearsay, since Federal Rule 801 defines hearsay as "a statement, other than

---

78. FRE 804(a).

one made by the declarant while testifying at the [present] trial or hearing, offered in evidence to prove the truth of the matter asserted." Even if former testimony were *exempted* from the hearsay rule by Rule 801 ("definitional nonhearsay"), some restrictions concerning the quality of the prior examination (or, at least, the adequacy of the opportunity) should apply, unless one were to take the position that the oath alone is sufficient to remove a witness's statements from the hearsay rule. As to the argument that former testimony should be a Rule 803 exception, the best response is that a witness's demeanor is an important factor in the trier's assessment of the witness's credibility. Note, also, that prior testimony usually consists of a series of declaratory responses, unlike, say, an excited utterance, present sense impression, and many other hearsay declarations that typically consist of one—or just a few—sentences. Thus, live testimony should be preferred to past testimony, since the former affords the trier of fact in the second suit an important opportunity to observe the witness's demeanor.[79]

Rule 804(b)(1) creates an exception from the hearsay rule for:

> **Former Testimony.** Testimony given as a witness at another hearing of the same or different proceeding, or in a deposition taken in compliance with law in the course of the same or another proceeding, if the party against whom the testimony is now offered, or, in a civil action or proceeding, a predecessor in interest, had an opportunity and similar motive to develop the testimony by direct, cross, or redirect examination.

Observe that the rule requires only an *opportunity* to develop the witness's testimony in the first proceeding. Furthermore, it is immaterial whether that opportunity is afforded at the juncture of direct examination or at the point of cross-examination. Thus, if, say, the plaintiff calls *W*, asks only several questions and, following his opponent's cross, declines redirect, the rule is satisfied. The rule would also be satisfied if a co-plaintiff conducted a direct examination, but the other co-plaintiff (against whom *W's* testimony is later offered) declined to conduct a direct examination. Even more clearly, the rule is satisfied if a cross-examiner (against whom *W's* testimony is subsequently offered) waived cross-examination. Recall that modern rules governing the interrogation of witnesses provide flexibility:[80] a direct examiner, faced with a hostile witness, may

---

79. Of course, if witnesses' testimony were routinely videotaped, "demeanor evidence" would be available to the trier of fact in the second proceeding.

80. *See* FRE 611.

secure the court's permission to ask leading questions; a cross-examiner, who interrogates a friendly witness may, after a successful objection, be confined by the court to nonleading questions. These flexible approaches to witness interrogations are reflected in Rule 804 (b)(1), which draws no distinction between direct and cross-examination.

Rule 804(b)(1) makes an important distinction between criminal and civil cases. Before we note that distinction, observe that in both criminal and civil cases, the focus is on *the party against whom the former testimony is now offered.* The central question is whether the prior testimony of a witness should be admissible against that party on the ground that he was adequately protected by an earlier examination of the witness or by an earlier *opportunity* to "develop the testimony"[81] of that witness. In criminal cases, there is a *"same-party"* requirement: the party against whom the former testimony is offered in the second proceeding must have also been a party to the first proceeding. This coincidence of parties is not required when the second proceeding is civil in nature. In some civil settings, a different party (from the one against whom the prior testimony is now offered) may have adequately protected the interests of the present party.

ILLUSTRATIONS

(1) Pate and his passenger (and girlfriend) Pam, are both injured when Pate's car is struck by a train at a railroad crossing. Pate and Pam join as co-plaintiffs and sue the railroad company for installing a mechanically defective signal. Bystander testifies for the plaintiffs that the signal in question was not working and he is cross-examined by the railroad. Although the plaintiffs win, the appellate court reverses and orders a new trial on the ground that the judge gave the jury an erroneous instruction. At the time of the second trial, Bystander is in the armed forces, stationed in a war zone and his presence as a witness cannot be secured. Pat and Pam offer a transcript of Bystander's former testimony against the railroad. Is it admissible?

(2) Assume the same car-train collision described in Illustration (1). Assume further, however, that Pate and Pam do not join as co-plaintiffs, but Pam alone brings the first suit alleging the railroad's negligence. Now imagine

---

81. FRE 804(b)(1).

that in this first suit, Bystander is called as a witness by the *railroad* and he testifies that the signal was functioning properly. There is a verdict for the defendant.

Months later, Pate sues the railroad, alleging that the signal was defective and inoperative.[82] Bystander is in the armed services and unavailable. The railroad offers a transcript of Bystander's prior testimony (given in Pam's trial) against Pate. Should the trial judge admit it?

(3) Dellinger, an alleged drug dealer, is prosecuted in state court for the murder of two rival dealers. He claims someone else committed the homicides. Wiley, a witness for the state, testifies as to the bitter rivalry between Dellinger and the two victims, and of Dellinger's threat to "blow them away with my AK–47 assault rifle." However, the jury acquits Dellinger.

Subsequently, the federal government prosecutes Dellinger for federal firearms violations in connection with the alleged murders.[83] Wiley is unavailable, so the prosecutor offers that portion of Wiley's testimony concerning Dellinger's threat to use his AK–47 assault rifle. Admissible over objection?

(4) Assume the facts as presented in Illustration (3), except Wiley's testimony in the first trial is not about Dellinger's threat, but rather that "just after [the victims] completed the drug sale, at about midnight, Dellinger waited for them to walk outside the warehouse, gunned them down with an assault rifle, and jumped in the back seat of a waiting escape car."

Illustration (1) meets the requirements of Rule 804(b)(1). The railroad had the opportunity to "develop" Bystander's adverse testimony and, indeed, attempted to weaken that testimony by cross-examination. Its motive in the earlier proceeding is "similar" to its motive at the new trial, namely, to show that the signal was operating properly at the time of the accident. Note that the issue to which Bystander testified is the same in both trials. Although rule 804(b)(1) does not require similar or identical issues in the first and second proceedings, similarity of issues is still a relevant concern in applying the rule. Similarity of issues sheds light on

---

82. Pate was not a party to the first suit, and thus could not be bound (issue precluded) by a finding that the signal was operating properly.

83. This Illustration is partially based upon United States v. Lombard, 72 F.3d 170 (1st Cir. 1995).

similarity of motive and the rule does require the latter. The greater the divergence of the issues in the first and second trials, the greater the likelihood that the similarity of motive required by the rule is lacking. Of course, the fact that, say, trial 1 and trial 2 have a number of different issues is of no consequence: the *only* issue (or issues) of importance in the application of Rule 804(b)(1) is the issue *toward which the former testimony is directed.*

Illustration (2) tests the limits of the phrase "predecessor in interest" that appears in Rule 804(b)(1). In this Illustration, Pam had the opportunity to develop Bystander's adverse testimony, but the transcript of his former testimony is offered against Pate in subsequent litigation. It is probable that Pam, through her attorney, had the motive of weakening or discrediting Bystander's testimony that the signal was operating properly. Pate would have a similar motive if Bystander were available and the railroad called him to the witness stand. Nonetheless, the language of Rule 804(b)(1) disallows the use of Bystander's former testimony against Pate unless Pam is Pate's "predecessor in interest" as that term is used in 804(b)(1). This phrase liberalizes Rule 804(b)(1)'s "same-party" requirement that applies in criminal cases.

The phrase "predecessor in interest," which some courts use interchangeably with the phrase "parties in privity," has an exasperating imprecision about it. At common law, the expression generally refers to a predecessor from whom the present party received the right, interest, or obligation that is at issue in the current litigation. For example, a decedent is a predecessor in interest to (or "in privity with") both her personal representative and those, such as heirs and legatees, who inherit from her. So, too, is the grantor of property a predecessor to the grantee. The terms "predecessor" or "privity" have also been used to characterize instances in which two parties are linked by representation, as where, for example, a trustee is a party to the first suit and a beneficiary is a party to the second suit. The common law concept of privity is of limited value in the solution of evidentiary problems such as the application of the hearsay rule.

It is not surprising, then, that modern courts interpreting Rule 804(b)(1) have shown a marked tendency to interpret functionally its predecessor-in-interest language.[84] For example, in Lloyd v. American Export Lines,[85] two seamen, A and B, got into a violent fight. In the first proceeding, in which both combatants were represented by counsel, the Coast Guard held a hearing. Acting on

84. *See, e.g.,* Supermarket of Marlinton, Inc. v. Meadow Gold Dairies, Inc. 71 F.3d 119 (4th Cir. 1995) (core of Rule 804(b)(1) is not privity, but rather similarity of motives between predecessor party and present party).

85. 580 F.2d 1179 (3d Cir.) *cert. denied,* 439 U.S. 969 (1978).

the report of a Coast Guard investigator, the hearing examiner sought to establish that *A* had constantly harassed *B*, and that *A*, while intoxicated, started the fight. Subsequently, *B* sued the corporate owner of the freighter on which the fight occurred, claiming that company officials had failed to take reasonable steps to protect him from *A*'s harassment and violence. *A* was unavailable as a witness, so the defendant company offered a transcript of *A*'s testimony at the Coast Guard hearing. The trial judge excluded the transcript, but the Third Circuit Court of Appeals reversed his ruling. It held that the Coast Guard was a predecessor in interest to *B*, the current civil plaintiff. The Coast Guard and *B*'s motives were similar, in that each wanted to establish that *A* had harassed *B* and, while drunk, instigated the violent encounter with *B*. Thus, *B*'s interests were protected by the Coast Guard's similar motives and its opportunity to develop *A*'s prior testimony; Rule 804(b)(1) was satisfied and *A's* account of the relevant activities should be revealed to the trier of fact in the civil trial through his prior testimony given at the Coast Guard Hearing.

In Illustration (2), Pam and Pate do not stand in a relationship of privity as that term has been historically used; no property interest has passed between them, nor was Pam, the plaintiff in the first suit, Pate's legal representation or fiduciary. Thus, if the trial judge equates "predecessor in interest" with privity, Bystander's former testimony is inadmissible against Pate, who is not a successor in interest.

A functional approach, on the other hand, favors admissibility. Pam's motive to weaken or discredit Bystander's testimony is similar to Pate's, and Pam had the opportunity to do so. Thus, a modern court is likely to rule that since both Pam and Pate had the common objective of showing that the signal malfunctioned, and since this is a common issue in both trials, Bystander's prior testimony is admissible against Pate.

Illustration (3) is a reminder that multiple or "double hearsay" problems that can exist in many hearsay settings, including the present context. Often, the content of a witness's prior testimony consists of a description or account of events that are relevant to the disputed issue. For example, a witness, *W*, might testify that he saw the accused provide crack cocaine to *B*, a teenager. We have seen that if the witness is unavailable at a subsequent trial, his former testimony may be admissible against the accused, who has had an opportunity to examine *W* and "develop ... [his] testimony."[86] The trial transcript, a public record is admissible to show what *W* said and the opposing party's opportunity to develop *W's* testimony permits *W's* statements to be accepted for their truth.

86. FRE 804(b)(1).

Suppose, however, *W* testifies as to something the *declarant said* ("Sam said he locked all three entry gates at 5:30 that afternoon.") The direct or cross-examiner can "develop" *W's* testimony with respect to what, if anything, the declarant (Sam) said. However, the examiner has no means of examining *W* as to the truth or falsity of the declarant's statement.[87] Sam may be lying, or he may have had a different day in mind, or perhaps his memory has faded. It thus becomes necessary to link the exception for public records (to prove *W's* words) with the exception for former testimony and then to forge a third link to allow Sam's statement to come in for its truth. Put otherwise, the former testimony exception provides *only the means* of allowing the trier of fact in the second trial to accept *as true W's testimony* that Sam *made the statement* above; the prior testimony exception does not allow the trier to accept as true the hearsay *contents* of Sam's statement. ("I locked the gates at 5:30.")

This observation is relevant to the problem described in Illustration (3). First, the transcript from the initial trial is proof of Wiley's words. Second, Wiley's testimony is within Rule 804(b)(1) which permits the trier to find that Dellinger made the threat. (Dellinger's defense counsel had an opportunity to "develop" Wiley's testimony regarding what Dellinger said.) But the prosecutor wants the trier to believe Dellinger, so she must link the exception for former testimony with an exemption or another exception. Dellinger's statement is a party admission and, as definitional nonhearsay, is exempted from the hearsay rule by Rule 801(d)(2)(A). Incidentally, Dellinger's statement is also within Rule 803(3)'s exception for declarations of one's present state of mind.

Do not cabin prior testimony within only Rule 804(b)(1). Statements made in a testimonial context have many possibilities, including the impeachment (by prior inconsistent statements)[88] of a witness or hearsay declarant. If the witness who gave the former testimony is on the stand in the present proceeding, the prior testimony might be used to refresh recollection under Rule 612. Furthermore, inconsistent prior statements made under oath by a present witness are exempted from the hearsay rule by Rule 801(d)(1)(A), since she can be cross-examined as to those statements. There is also the possibility that prior testimony of a now-unavailable witness might fall within the hearsay exception for declarations against interest.[89]

Illustration (4) requires only limited application of the linking principle because Wiley's testimony describes an *event* rather than

---

87. Put otherwise, there are two hearsay declarants: the witness in the first trial and Sam.

88. *See* Ch. IX § 9.3 at note 42.

89. FRE 804(b)(3).

someone else's statement. The transcript, a public record, can be used to show what Wiley said. The question is whether the former testimony exception applies so as to permit the trier to conclude that Wiley's statement about the assault rifle is true. The second proceeding is a criminal trial and thus Rule 804(b)(1)'s requirement of party identity applies: the party against whom the former testimony is now offered must himself have had an adequate opportunity to develop the testimony of the now-unavailable witness. This condition is satisfied in the present Illustration.

The difficulty arises with respect to Dellinger's motive. The first trial was for a double homicide, and Dellinger's defense was that some other person committed the murders. In "developing" Wiley's testimony by cross-examination in the first trial, it is highly unlikely that Dellinger's counsel focused her attention on the particular weapon allegedly used in the commission of the murders. It is, of course, the judge's responsibility to determine if Dellenger "had ... a similar motive to develop" Wiley's testimony in the first trial, and this is a contextual judgment. The transcript of the earlier proceedings, as well as the indictment, would inform the judge's determination.

The Supreme Court has emphasized that similarity of motive in the first and second proceedings is an indispensable feature of Rule 804(b)(1). In United States v. Salerno[90] the Court addressed the issue of whether defendants in a criminal trial could introduce against the government the prior grand jury testimony of two (now-unavailable) witnesses. The admissibility of this testimony, the Court said, turns upon whether the prosecutor in the grand jury proceedings had a motive to develop the witnesses' testimony that was similar to that of the prosecutor at trial. The fact that the grand jury testimony (to the prosecutor's surprise) was favorable to the defendants does not estop the government from objecting to the admissibility of the prior testimony on the ground of dissimilarity of motive.

On remand, the Second Circuit found that under the facts of this particular case, the government's motives were dissimilar:[91] in the grand jury proceeding, the prosecutor's motive was to secure evidence to indict *other* defendants. The defendants in *Salerno* were already under indictment at the time the prior testimony was given. Contextual determination of the kind illustrated in *Salerno* must also be made in a related criminal context, namely, where the

90. 505 U.S. 317, 321–24 (1992).

91. United States v. DiNapoli, 8 F.3d 909, 915 (2d Cir. 1993). *Compare* United

States. v. Miller, 904 F.2d 65, 67–68 (D.C. Cir. 1990) (similar motive).

first proceeding is a preliminary hearing and the second proceeding is a criminal trial.[92]

In the foregoing Illustrations and discussion, it has been assumed that the statements contained in a witness's former testimony were shown by the introduction of a transcript, or at least the portion thereof containing his prior sworn statements. As we have seen, the transcript is a public record, and thus is admissible to show what the witness said. And we have noted that the former testimony exception—assuming its conditions are satisfied—allows the witness's statements to be received for their truth. Use of the transcript from the former proceeding is an efficient means of proving what the witness said and it has the added advantage of probable accuracy. The proponent may, however, use other methods to prove the witness's prior statements. For example, one who heard the former testimony can take the stand in the present trial and state what the testimony was, i.e., recite what the present witness heard the declarant say. If the witness made notes, these might be used to refresh her recollection or, if she is unable adequately to recall the testimony, come into evidence as her past recollection recorded.

Unavailability: A Reprise

We have observed that although Rule 804 requires a declarant's unavailability as a witness, the rule might be more accurately characterized as requiring the unavailability of the declarant's testimony. While it is true that Rule 804(a) mandates "witness unavailability" as a condition that attends the application of the exceptions set out in 804(b), all of those exceptions but one—former testimony—are attended by a second requirement: the *testimony* of the declarant must also be unavailable. In practical terms, then, the proponent must show that he cannot produce the declarant's deposition. Stated otherwise, the Rule 804(b) exceptions for dying declarations, statement against interest, and statement of personal or family history are attended by levels of preference in the following order: (1) live testimony (witness on stand); (2) testimony secured in quasi-judicial context (deposition), and finally; (3) extra-judicial statements (ordinary hearsay). Rule 804(a) obligates the proponent to show that he is unable to secure the declarant's "attendance or testimony by process or other reasonable means."

Dying Declarations

The hearsay exception for statements made in contemplation of death (dying declarations or "deathbed statements") has the impri-

---

92. *See, e.g.*, Glenn v. Dallman, 635 F.2d 1183, 1186–87 (6th Cir. 1980), *cert. denied*, 454 U.S. 843 (1981) (preliminary hearing testimony admissible against accused).

matur of age, but remains, even in its modern form, rigid and arbitrary. During the Nineteenth Century, courts increasingly admitted *in criminal homicide prosecutions* the victim's dying statements identifying his slayer or otherwise revealing the cause of his impending death. Over the years, courts and commentators have advanced several justifications for this hearsay exception. The principal justification rests on the proposition that a declarant faced with what he believes is his certain death is unlikely to lie. The motivation to speak truthfully might be rooted, as the early cases said, in the religious belief that one "about to face his Maker" will not conclude his earthly activities with the deceitful act of lying. Aside from this religiously-based notion, there is a current of psychological opinion that one facing death has nothing to gain by promoting a fabrication. Finally, in functional or pragmatic terms, the lapse of time between the relevant events and the declarant's declaration is likely to be short, thereby reducing the hearsay danger of a faulty memory. This observation is buttressed by the restriction for "dying declarations" that limits their content to "the cause or circumstances of what the declarant believed to be [her] impending death."[93]

If a declarant's statements, made at the brink of impending death, are sufficiently reliable to be admitted as a hearsay exception, they should be admitted in any kind of case. As we will see, however, they are not. Furthermore, if the admissibility of statements in contemplation of death is explained on the grounds of need, then they should be rejected if there are other witnesses to the circumstances leading to death. But they are not so rejected. There may be multiple witnesses to the relevant "death causing" events or circumstances, but the declarant's dying declarations would still be admissible.

The exception to the hearsay rule pertinent to the present discussion appears in Rule 804(b)(2):

> **Statement under belief of impending death.** In a prosecution for homicide or in a civil action or proceeding, a statement made by a declarant while believing that the declarant's death was imminent, concerning the cause or circumstances of what the declarant believed to be impending death.

The exception applies in one and only one kind of *criminal* prosecution: homicide. However, the exception is available in all civil cases. The crux of the exception is declarant's settled expectation that death is inevitable. ("I might be dying" does not qualify.) Observe, also, the restricted scope of the permissible subject of the dying statement: "cause or circumstances" of the "impending death." As with all Rule 804 exceptions, the declarant must be unavailable. Obviously, this requirement is always satisfied in homicide prosecutions. In civil cases, however, unavailability could be an issue. Suppose, for example, the declarant, certain he is about to die, makes a statement within the scope of Rule 804(b)(2). Contrary to his expectation, he survives, but cannot be found at his last known address. The proponent of his "dying" declaration must show that the declarant is unavailable under the criteria of Rule 804(a), and that his deposition cannot reasonably be produced. Once these facts are established, the declarant's dying declaration is admissible.

ILLUSTRATIONS

(1) Mrs. Shepard, who suddenly feels desperately ill, calls for her caretaker-nurse. "Call Dr. Knight immediately," she says, "because I am probably dying." And, she continues, "bring me the bottle of sherry my husband, Dr. Shepard, bought for me; he gave me a glass before dinner and I'm sure he poisoned me!"[94] The next day, Mrs. Shepard dies and, subsequently, her husband, Dr. Shepard, is prosecuted for murder by poisoning. The prosecution offers the decedent's dying declaration. Admissible?

(2) Mae is viciously assaulted and raped. In a statement to a member of the medical team that answered her 911 call, she says, "I'm dying" and then in a barely audible voice, she identifies her assailant as Troy. After two weeks in intensive care, Mae begins to recover. A month later, however, she dies from a brain aneurysm. Troy, who denies he was the assailant, is prosecuted for rape with intent to kill. The prosecutor offers the 911 medical assistant who will testify as to Mae's dying declaration. Admissible?

(3) Suppose Mae's husband sues Troy for civil damages. He offers Mae's dying declaration. Admissible?

94. For a case that is similar on its facts, see Shepard v. United States, 290 U.S. 96 (1933).

In Illustration (1), the declarant does not have a firmly held conviction that she is about to die. That fact alone defeats the application of the exception for dying declarations. Furthermore, the declarant appears to be speculating about her condition (poisoned) and about the culprit (Dr. Shepard). Generally, a hearsay declarant's statement is inadmissible for lack of personal knowledge unless, from all the surrounding circumstances, a reasonable trier could conclude that the declarant had personal knowledge.[95]

The declarant in Illustration (2) does have a settled expectation of death. But the dying declaration exception applies to only one kind of criminal prosecution: homicide. In the Illustration, the prosecution is for rape with intent to kill, so the present exception does not apply.[96] As you will see below, however, there are other possibilities for escaping the hearsay rule.

In the civil suit brought by Mae's husband in Illustration (3), the declarant's statement should be admissible. Mae thought she was about to die, although she did not die until later. The cause of her death may have been related to the sexual assault, but apparently the causal connection was not definite, or else the prosecutor would have probably prosecuted Troy for homicide in Illustration (2). Had Troy been convicted in Illustration (2), he should be precluded (issue preclusion) from contesting, in the subsequent civil trial, his commission of the rape with intent to kill. Note, also, that if the jurisdiction in Illustration (2) did not apply issue preclusion,[97] Rule 803(22) would permit admission into evidence of the criminal judgment. The judgment would not be conclusive, but would be evidence—probably quite persuasive evidence—that Troy committed the acts charged in the civil suit.

The Federal rule governing "statement[s] under belief of impending death"[98] should be amended to permit these statements in any suit in which they are relevant. Dying declarations are at least reliable enough to be considered by the trier of fact. Furthermore, a victim's family members should be outraged by an evidentiary rule that forecloses any consideration of her final statements explaining the cause of her impending death.

95. The personal knowledge requirement does not apply to party admissions (a Rule 801(d)(2) exemption), nor to statements of personal or family history (a Rule 804(b)(4) exception).

96. See Hansel v. Commonwealth, 260 Ky. 148, 84 S.W.2d 68 (1935) (rape victim dies during childbirth).

97. The res judicata law of the jurisdiction rendering the initial judgment determines the claim or issue preclusion effect of the judgment not only in its own courts, but in the courts of other jurisdictions as well. See 28 U.S.C.A. § 1738, which demands that a judgment of the rendering state shall have the same force and effect in other courts located in the United States as the judgment has in the rendering state.

98. FRE 804(b)(2).

Until and unless Rule 804(b)(2) is revised, however, other evidentiary possibilities must be explored. One who speaks while under a sense of impending death is usually under the influence of stress or excitement. Thus, statements made in contemplation of death may often be received under Rule 803(2), the exception for excited utterances. The use of this hearsay exception has an added advantage. Whereas dying declarations under Rule 804(b)(2) are limited to statements concerning "the cause or circumstances . . . of [the declarant's] . . . impending death," excited utterances under Rule 803(2) extend to statements "relating to . . . [the] startling event or condition" that produced the emotional state. The expanded subject matter (permissible content) of Rule 803(2) declarations offers the proponent a greater potential for securing a favorable evidentiary ruling.

Another possibility for circumventing the shortcomings of Rule 804(b)(2) is found in Rule 807, the "residual exception."[99] This exception may be invoked when a proffered hearsay declaration does not fit within any of the specific hearsay exceptions contained in Rules 803 and 804, and yet has "equivalent circumstantial guarantees of trustworthiness."[100] For example, factors such as the disinterestedness of the speaker, the short duration between the event and her declaration, the likelihood that a false statement would be discovered, and reliance on the statement by persons the declarant would not want to deceive are some of the relevant considerations in determining the trustworthiness of a statement proffered under Rule 807.

Statements Against Interest

The rule that admits statements against a declarant's interest is based on the psychological assumption, which is probably generally accurate, that a person does not make personally disserving statements unless they are true. For the assumption to be applicable, the statement in question must have been against the declarant's interest at the time it was spoken and, additionally, the declarant must have realized that the statement was detrimental to her interest.

The impracticality of assessing the psychological profile of a declarant who makes an against-interest statement has caused courts to resort to a "reasonable-person" test in applying this exception. The Federal rules adopt this approach. However, if a particular declarant characteristically indulges in making false disserving statements, the judge could exclude her proffered statement under Rule 403. Alternatively, the judge could permit evidence of

---

99. The rule is discussed infra, Ch. VIII, at note 1.

100. FRE 807.

her psychological tendency toward self-denigration, allowing the trier of fact to take this trait into account in assessing the reliability of her against-interest hearsay declaration.

It is important at the outset to distinguish declarations against interest from party admissions. Although most party admissions are against the party-declarant's interest when made, this disserving element is not an essential feature of the party admission exemption. All that is required for a party admission is that the party is against whom the statement is offered is responsible for the statement. In practical terms, of course, the opponent will have made a determination that the admission is adverse to the admitting party's litigating posture (claim or defense).

Recall that "unavailability" is essential to the admissibility of a declaration against interest. This requirement does not, of course, apply to a party admission. Typically, the party against whom the admission is offered is present at the trial and prepared to try to rebut or explain the admission. Another important difference between a party admission and a declaration against interest is this: a party admission is admissible only against the party responsible for it; a declaration against interest, however, is freely admissible against any or all parties to the suit. Of course, the against-interest declaration would have to be relevant to the claims and defenses of a particular party (in a multi-party suit) in order for it to be admissible against him.

Because admissibility of a declaration against interest is conditioned upon a showing of unavailability, the exception has its most frequent application when the declarant is not a party. As we just observed, when the declarant is a party, she is usually available to testify and thus the party admissions exemption is the proper means for her opponent to surmount the hearsay rule. Although a party cannot introduce her own statement as a party admission, she could in theory (but rarely in practice) put into evidence her own declaration against interest. Note, however, the difficulties: (1) the declaration would have to be against interest when made, but helpful to the declarant-party's case at the time of trial; and (2) the party would have to meet at least one of the conditions of unavailability (such as loss of memory or physical or mental infirmity) set out in Rule 804(a). Hence, we may generalize that declarations against interest are usually disserving statements made by unavailable *nonparty declarants*.

We have spoken about a declaration against a declarant's interest as if it were apparent when his interest is undermined or threatened by a "disserving" statement. Of course, the nature of a declaration is not always evident. First, it must be determined what kind of interests are embraced within the present exception. There are various possibilities, ranging from a statement inimical to one's social interest ("When I'm drunk, I'm cruel to my wife, when sober, I'm cruel to her dogs")[101] to a statement against penal interest that could lead to criminal punishment "(I shot my wife"). Most of the common-law cases, especially the early ones, limited the present exception to statements that were directly adverse to the declarant's pecuniary or proprietary interest. Thus, assertions coming within the exception tended to have a business or financial flavor, and thus often were spoken in a context where rational behavior is the expected norm.

Statements against penal interest were usually rejected, primarily because of the context in which they most frequently were proffered. Assume that Alex is prosecuted for the murder of *V*. He offers the testimony of *W* (his cousin) who will testify that Cassius said that he murdered *V*. Cassius cannot be located and is possibly now in another country. The trial judge is apprehensive that *W* may be lying or that even if Cassius made the statement in question, he was lying. In other words, the judge is concerned that false evidence will raise a reasonable doubt in the jury's mind and that Alex will be erroneously acquitted. Common law judges—or at least most of them—responded to this concern by refusing to recognize declarations against penal interests as within the present exception. As you will see, penal interests are included in the Federal Rule's definition of declarations against interest.

Suppose we take as a working hypothesis the proposition that modern courts, operating under the Federal Rules or their state counterparts, recognize three kinds of interests that a Rule 804(b)(3) declarant can impair: pecuniary, proprietary, and penal. There remains the problem of deciding whether a particular statement is adverse to one of these interests. *This determination is made in the context in which the statement is made.* Of course, when paramount consideration is given to the context of the statement, it sometimes occurs that the nature of the statement will vary from its most obvious purport. Take, for example, the statement, "I owe Alex $5,000." This remark appears to be against the speaker's interest, and usually is. But suppose Alex is claiming that the speaker owes him $10,000, not the $5,000 claimed by the declarant. In this broader context, the speaker's statement is actually self-serving. So, too, would be a declarant's statement to investigators that he committed a crime at noon on day 1 in City X, when he is suspected of committing a more serious crime in City Y at that approximate time. What of a written entry or verbal declaration by a creditor that he just received $10,000 from his

---

101. Although the Federal Rules do not recognize statements against social interest as within the present exception, a few states do. See, e.g., Cal. Evid. Code § 1230 (1966).

debtor? This statement is disserving because it acknowledges a debt in this amount is no longer outstanding—in other words, the creditor no longer has a claim.

The point is that statements that appear self-serving sometimes may be disserving; statements that appear disserving sometimes may be self-serving, and "neutral" statements may not in fact be neutral. Consider, for example, a statement by X that she is still a member of a certain business partnership. Her statement might be disserving if the partnership were in financial difficulty, but self-serving if the firm were improving its financial posture and she wanted a share of its potential profits.

Federal Rule of Evidence 804(b)(3) provides an exception from the hearsay rule for a statement that qualifies as a—

> **Statement against interest.** A statement which was at the time of its making so far contrary to the declarant's pecuniary or proprietary interest, or so far tended to subject the declarant to civil or criminal liability, or to render invalid a claim by the declarant against another, that a reasonable person in the declarant's position would not have made the statement unless believing it to be true. A statement tending to expose the declarant to criminal liability and offered to exculpate the accused is not admissible unless corroborating circumstances clearly indicate the trustworthiness of the statement.

The major innovation of Rule 804(b)(3) is its recognition of penal interests. Although some common law courts refused to recognize statements affecting the probable validity of a civil claim or defense (interests some courts thought too "contingent"), a growing number of these courts had recognized these statements against "civil suit" interests prior to 1975, when the Federal Rules were adopted. Such declarations are, after all, a species of statements affecting the declarant's pecuniary interest. On the other hand, statements against penal interests had only limited judicial recognition prior to the adoption of the Federal Rules. As noted previously, it is perhaps useful to group the interests reorganized by Rule 804(b)(3) into three categories: pecuniary, proprietary, and penal.

Note the proviso at the end of Rule 804(b)(3) that attaches a condition to the admissibility of statements against a hearsay declarant's penal interest ("I shot Ben") and offered as exculpatory evidence by the accused. (Assume Ben was shot by one person; if the declarant shot Ben, the accused did not and is innocent.) The trial judge should not admit the statement "unless corroborating circumstances clearly indicate ... [its] trustworthiness...."[102]

A variety of circumstances could supply the needed confirmation, such as the relationship (e.g., animosity) between the declarant and the victim, the motive of the declarant to be truthful, physical evidence (e.g. presence of the declarant's fingerprints or DNA at the scene of the crime), and the testimony of other witnesses. The rule does not require corroboration when a declarant's declaration against penal interest is offered by the prosecution against the accused ("I got $5,000 and a year's supply of crack just for driving the accused's getaway car"). Nonetheless, concerned that the accused's inability to confront and cross-examine the "real" witness against him (the unavailable declarant) might threaten the accused's constitutional rights,[103] some courts have required corroborating circumstances.[104] Under this protective approach, the accused and the prosecutor are put on equal footing insofar as demonstrating the probable trustworthiness of the proffered "third party" declaration against penal interest.

ILLUSTRATIONS

(1) Harvey and his wife, Ellen, are employed by a successful small business that specializes in selling and laying kitchen and bathroom tile. Harvey, who majored in accounting in college, manages and maintains the company's financial records; Ellen works mostly in the sales department, but sometimes is assigned to help with records and accounting. For more than a year, Harvey has been embezzling small amounts of money from his employer. Recently, he revealed his scheme to Ellen, and enlisted her aid in advancing and covering up his theft. For several months thereafter, the embezzlement scheme worked smoothly, but then a routine outside audit revealed discrepancies in the company's financial records. Both Harvey and Ellen, whose relationship is increasingly acrimonious, fall under suspicion.

As the pressure mounts, Ellen calls the detective from the Fraud Division who has been investigating the case. She reveals her own illegal activities and then explains in detail (and from personal knowledge) exactly how Harvey conceived the scheme, enlisted her aid, and made the false

---

102. FRE 804(b)(3).

103. The accused's rights under the Sixth Amendment's Confrontation Clause is called into question. See infra, Ch. VIII.

104. See, e.g. United States v. Costa, 31 F.3d 1073, 1077 (11th Cir. 1994). A proposed amendment to Rule 804(b)(3) would follow this line of cases.

entries that allowed him to embezzle funds. Although Ellen agrees to testify against Harvey, she is killed in an automobile accident prior to trial. The prosecutor offers her statements to the fraud investigator, who is present and willing to testify. Admissible?

(2) Assume that Harvey and Ellen participate in the embezzlement as described in Illustration (1). However, assume further that Harvey and Ellen are not married, but only close business associates. When the outside auditor discovers the accounting discrepancies, Ellen confides in her husband, Ben, that she has been involved in an embezzlement scheme. She also tells him exactly how Harvey conceived and executed the theft, and how she and Harvey tried to cover up their illegal activities. Since Ellen is unavailable at Harvey's criminal trial, the prosecutor calls Ben. Is Ben's testimony about Ellen's "declaration against interest" admissible?

Illustration (1) raises both constitutional issues and an issue pertaining to the construction of Rule 804(b)(3). As to the latter, the difficulty arises because the portions of Ellen's statements that are relevant to Harvey's prosecution pertain to his illegal activities and are thus not against her penal interests. The problem of "mixed" statements has been variously resolved by courts over the years. One approach, for example, is to examine the components of a single statement or a cluster of related statements and determine if on the whole their character is disserving. If so, the entire statement (or several integrated statements) is admitted. Another approach is to sever and exclude portions of a statement (or several statements) that are self-serving, but allow into evidence "neutral" parts of a single statement (or neutral statements in an integrated cluster). A third approach is to allow into evidence only those statements (or parts of a single statement that can be severed) that are against the declarant's interest. The third approach is the dominant one, and the Supreme Court has adopted it for the federal courts through its construction of the language of Rule 804(b)(3).

In Williamson v. United States,[105] the government sought to use certain statements of one Harris, an alleged accomplice, to implicate the defendant, Williamson. Harris, after his arrest and the seizure of two suitcases of cocaine from the trunk of his rented car, told a DEA officer (in several interviews) that he was transporting the cocaine for Williamson. His statements implicated both himself and Williamson. At Williamson's trial, Harris refused to

---

105. 512 U.S. 594 (1994).

testify and thus was "unavailable" under Rule 804(a). Concluding that Harris's statements were against his penal interest under Rule 804(b)(3), the trial judge allowed the DEA agent to testify concerning what Harris had said about both himself and Williamson.

On appeal, the United States Supreme Court first addressed the meaning of "statement" in the against-interest exception, and concluded that the principle underlying the exception dictates a restricted construction: a single declaration or remark, rather than a report or narrative. The Court went on to say that collateral statements, including ones that are neutral as to the declarant's interest, are outside the ambit of Rule 804(b)(3). As applied to Harris's confession, a majority of the Court held that the against-interest exception of subsection (b)(3) did not apply to the entire narrative, at least in the absence of individual determinations as to whether each statement in his confession was self-inculpatory. The Court cautioned that Harris may have thought that his statements implicating Williamson would ultimately decrease his own punishment. This possibility arises not only because Harris was cooperating with authorities, but also because his account might shift more of the blame to Williamson.

A majority of the Court advocates a cautious approach to statements against penal interest. Narratives, reports, and extended declarations are not to be treated in the aggregate as self-serving or disserving. Each component of a composite narrative requires a discrete analysis.[106] Presumably, this approach would also apply to a single statement with both self-serving and disserving parts. Of course, the components of a simple statement may be so closely intertwined and interdependent that severance is impractical. Thus, the whole statement must be admitted or excluded.

The *Williamson* construction of Rule 804(b)(3) probably applies to civil cases, but with less rigor, since there is no concern about the accused's inability to confront and cross-examine the hearsay declarant. Furthermore, errors by the trial judge are more likely to be harmless. Observe that *Williamson* simply construes Rule 804(b)(3) for application in the federal courts. States may construe their version of the rule differently, provided their construction remains within constitutional boundaries.

In any event, when *Williamson* is applied to the facts of Illustration (1), Ellen's declarations would have to be individually

---

106. Consider the following hypothetical. Late at night Declarant knocks on the door of a friend's apartment. When admitted, he says, "I've got to hide. Sam and I robbed the convenience store at Seventh and Vine. Someone called the cops, so we ditched the car, split the money, and ran in separate directions." Admissible against Sam? Note that the declarant was not currying favor, was not speaking to the authorities, had no apparent motive to lie, and his statement displays an "insider's" knowledge of the illegal activities.

examined. The fact that she made her statements to a law enforcement official and had agreed to testify against Harvey casts considerable doubt on the admissibility of her declarations. Her motives might have been to gain leniency and shift most of the blame to Harvey. Should a court decide (despite the current language or Rule 804(b)(3)) that the corroboration requirement of subsection (b)(3) should apply when an against-interest statement is offered *against* an accused, admissibility is rendered even less likely.

Constitutional issues also strongly suggest the inadmissibility of Ellen's proffered statements. The Confrontation Clause contained in the Sixth Amendment of the United States Constitution guarantees to an accused the right "to be confronted with the witnesses against him." This command is not absolute, however, and the Supreme Court has in the past allowed hearsay declarations that are within a well-established ("firmly rooted") exception to be introduced against the accused. Relatively new hearsay exceptions, such as the one for declarations against *penal* interest, may be invoked against the accused only if the prosecutor is able to convince the judge that the proffered statement is accompanied by "particularized guarantees of trustworthiness."[107] By this is meant that the circumstances in which the declarant spoke provide assurances that her statement is reliable—circumstances that do not appear to be present in Illustration (1).

A 2004 Supreme Court decision, Crawford v. Washington,[108] casts even greater doubt on the constitutionality of admitting Ellen's statements against Harvey. In *Crawford* the Court embarked on a fresh approach to resolving confrontation clause issues. The issue under this clause, said the Court, is whether the hearsay statement is "testimonial" in nature. If so, the statement is inadmissible unless the declarant is available for cross-examination by the accused or, if unavailable, the accused has had a prior opportunity to cross-examine the declarant. The general test of whether a statement is testimonial is whether it is made in circumstances associated with an anticipated criminal prosecution, such as statements made at a grand jury proceeding or at a preliminary hearing.[109] Statements given to police during "the course of interrogations [concerning criminal activity] are . . . testimonial" under this standard.[110]

The circumstances in Illustration (2) are less likely to provoke constitutional concerns. Ellen's declarations, made to her husband, Ben, are not testimonial. Nonetheless, the older line of confrontation clause cases had held that since a declaration against penal

---

107. See, e.g., Ohio v. Roberts, 448 U.S. 56 (1980).

108. 541 U.S. 36 (2004).

109. Id. at 68.

110. Id. at 52.

interest is not a firmly rooted hearsay exception, the declaration must be accompanied by other indicia of reliability. It is doubtful that this older line of cases has continuing vitality. Even if these cases were to be followed in instances where the declarant's against-interest is nontestimonial, there may be sufficient "particularized" guarantees of trustworthiness surrounding Ellen's statement to her husband. She had no apparent motive to lie and she was not shifting the blame to Harvey. Those same features are relevant to Rule 804(b)(3)'s corroboration requirement, should a court read that requirement into the rule, despite the fact that the declaration in Illustration (2) is not "offered to exculpate the accused...."[111]

It might be argued that a statement that on its face is disserving ("I have been embezzling funds from my employer") is not against interest when the declarant is confiding in family members, close friends, or other confidants. The argument is that even though the *content* of the statement is disserving, *making* the statement was not disserving because the declarant reasonably believed that her interests were not impaired: her confidant would not reveal the statement to a third person. The courts have rejected this argument.[112] This judicial response can be defended on several grounds. First, it is unlikely that the declarant thought her statements were self-serving, or even neutral. Second, the context of trust and confidentiality suggests that the declarant is likely to be candid.

Personal and Family History (Pedigree Exception)

Modern public records concerning births, deaths, adoptions, divorces, and the like limit the need for this exception. The Federal Rule in point is 804(b)(4). It has two major parts. In subsection (A), the exception removes from the hearsay ban statements by an unavailable declarant about *his* birth, adoption, ancestry or other aspects of his "personal or family history."[113] In subsection (B), the exception generally addresses the same subject matters,[114] but focuses on declarations by *family members* (related by adoption, marriage, or blood) and by *family associates* (such as minister or doctor) "likely to have accurate information concerning the matter declared."[115] Rule 804(b)(3) does not require that the declarant have first-hand knowledge. Thus, an entry in (now unavailable) Uncle's diary that "Niece and Husband called from London to report the birth of their daughter, Alana, 6 pounds, 9 ounces, b. Aug. 2, 1993" would fall within the exception.

---

111. FRE 804(b)(3).

112. See, e.g., United States v. Mock, 640 F.2d 629 (5th Cir. 1981).

113. FRE 804(b)(4)(A).

114. Subsection (B) adds "death" to the list of admissible personal and family events and relationships.

115. FRE 804(b)(4)(B).

Chapter VIII

THE FUTURE OF HEARSAY

(Herein: The Residual Exception and the Confrontation Clause)

In this chapter, we will briefly examine the residual ("catch-all") exception to the hearsay rule and the impact of the Sixth Amendment's Confrontation Clause on the hearsay rule. The residual exception has the potential of liberalizing the hearsay exceptions, bringing them in closer alignment with everyday experience where reliance on hearsay statements is commonplace. Conversely, the Confrontation Clause places a restraining hand on the use of hearsay in criminal convictions. American courts and legislatures seem committed to a relatively rigid hearsay system: hearsay is defined and declared inadmissible; then dozens of exemptions and exceptions create irregular patterns of admissibility. This scheme is not inevitable, and perhaps not even desirable. Hearsay evidence might be admissible, except where fairness or suspicious circumstances justify its rejection. However, this alternative approach is unlikely to be adopted in the foreseeable future.

The Residual Exception

Federal Rule 807, which formally (and redundantly) appeared twice[1] in the Federal Rules, creates an exception for

A statement not specifically covered by Rule 803 or 804, but having equivalent guarantees of trustworthiness, is not excluded by the hearsay rule, if the court determines that (A) the statement is offered as evidence of a material fact, (B) the statement is more probative on the point for which it is offered than any other evidence which the proponent can procure through reasonable efforts; and (C) the general purpose of these rules and the interests of justice will best be served by admission of the statement into evidence. However, a statement may not be admitted under this exception unless the proponent of it makes known to the adverse party sufficiently in advance of trial

---

1. Rules 803(24) and 804(b)(5) were combined in Rule 807. No substantive change was intended. FRE 807 ACN.

or hearing to provide the adverse party with a fair opportunity to prepare to meet it, the proponent's intention to
offer the statement and the particulars of it, including the
name and address of the declarant.

Although Rule 807 lists a number of conditions, the important
ones are these: (1) notice to the adverse party, (2) circumstantial
guarantees of trustworthiness equivalent to the specific exceptions,
and (3) probative force exceeding that of other evidence on the
same point that the proponent could secure through reasonable
efforts. Only conditions (2) and (3) warrant any further discussion.
As to the latter, the judge must decide on the basis of the represen-
tations of parties, whether other evidence can be procured by
reasonable efforts. The other evidence may consist of the declarant's deposition, her appearance as a witness, or testimonial or
documentary evidence from other sources. Presumably, the "other
evidence" to which Rule 807 makes reference would either be
nonhearsay or hearsay that fit within one of the specific exceptions.
The judge should take into account the probable reliability of the
proffered Rule 807 evidence, the predicted reliability of the "other
evidence," and the inconvenience, time, and expense associated
with securing evidence from an alternative source. Central to the
judge's determination is the centrality or importance of the hearsay
evidence to the main issues in the case.

As we just observed, Rule 807 commands that hearsay admitted under the "residual" exception must have "circumstantial
guarantees of trustworthiness" that are equivalent to the specific
hearsay exceptions enumerated in Rules 803 and 804. The framework for determining the trustworthiness of a proffered Rule 807
declaration is the organizational structure that supports the entire
hearsay system. Cross-examination is preferred because the cross-
examiner can test a witness's perception, memory, sincerity, and
use of language. However, cross-examination often is impossible or
impractical to achieve. Therefore, hearsay statements are admissible if one or more of the hearsay dangers are significantly reduced.

The next step is to recall the factors or circumstances that
contribute to the reduction of the so-called hearsay dangers. These
include (but are not limited to) such considerations as the time
lapse between the event and the declaration (e.g., present sense
impression), the declarant's mental state (e.g., excited utterance;
dying declaration), the declarant's probable motive to be truthful or
deceitful (e.g., declaration against interest), reliance by others on
the declarant's statement (e.g., business record); the likelihood of a
false statement being detected (e.g., public record), superior knowl-

edge (a declarant's mental or bodily condition), and whether the declaration is recorded (e.g., recorded recollection).

There is little or no gain in describing and analyzing the large (and growing) number of cases decided under Rule 807 and the identical Rules 803(24) and 804(b)(5) that were consolidated in Rule 807. Understanding the framework is the most important task. That said, consider the following examples.

ILLUSTRATIONS

(1) Staywich is a town of 30,000 residents. Recently, the heavy clock tower atop the city courthouse came toppling down, crashed through the roof, and virtually destroyed the courtroom below.

Damage to the building was in excess of $100,000. Subsequently, Staywich brings suit against the company that insured the courthouse against loss by *fire or lightning*. Debris from the clock tower contained charred timbers. Several residents testify that the week before the tower collapsed, it had been struck by lightning. The insurance company contends, however, that the tower collapsed due to a faulty design, improper construction, and progressive deterioration. According to the defendant's experts the *charred wood* and the debris came from a fire in the courthouse tower that occurred sixty years previously, when the courthouse was under construction.

Counsel for the defendant produces an article from the Staywich "Morning Times," the town's only newspaper. The article, which bears the date June 9, 1945, reports that a fire destroyed the unfinished dome of the courthouse, but firemen were able to save the main structure. After counsel authenticates the article as coming from the newspaper's archives, and confirms that she has given the required notice under Rule 807, she offers the newspaper article in evidence. Counsel for the town of Staywich objects on the grounds of hearsay. How should the trial judge rule?

(2) Since his graduation from high school a year ago, David has been working as a day laborer for a construction company. Because his wages are low, he has continued to live in the house owned and occupied by his mother. Lately, she has been increasingly concerned about both his

excessive drinking and his association with two brothers, known for their violent behavior and substance abuse.

Peter has filed a suit against David, alleging that the latter became intoxicated at a local bar and, egged on by the two brothers, covertly followed Peter (under cover of darkness) from the bar to his (Peter's) car. There he viciously attacked Peter causing serious bodily injury.

Although Peter was hospitalized for two weeks due to the gravity of his injuries, David also sustained a sprained wrist, a bloody nose, and minor cuts and bruises. Nonetheless, David managed to drive his motorcycle home, where he dismounted, let the cycle fall on its side, pressed a handkerchief to his nose, and walked unsteadily to the door.

Unbeknownst to David, his mother observed his arrival from her bedroom window. Ten minutes later she quietly went outside, where she saw drops of fresh blood on David's motorcycle tank.

The next morning, after she heard her son "call in sick" and go back to bed, David's mother sought out her pastor. She shared her concerns about David and also disclosed his intoxicated condition the night before, his apparent bloody nose, and the discovery of fresh drops of blood on his motorcycle. A month later, David's mother suffers a massive stroke and died en route to the hospital.

Subsequently, in the civil suit, Peter v. David, for assault and battery, David denies he was Peter's attacker and claims mistaken identity as his defense. During Peter's case-in-chief, he testifies that even though there was no moon on the night in question, he recognized David as his attacker. However, during the case in defense, David and the two brothers testify that the three of them finished their drinks, left the bar together, and immediately drove away—the brothers in their car and David on his motorcycle. During the Plaintiff's case in rebuttal Peter's lawyer, having given the notice required by Federal Rule 807 (or its state counterpart), calls Pastor who is prepared to testify about David's mother's observations on the night of the attack. David's lawyer immediately enters a hearsay objection. Should the trial judge sustain it?

(3) Suppose, prior to the civil suit described in Illustration (2), the prosecutor decides to prosecute David for criminal assault causing serious bodily injury. A grand jury

is convened, and among the witnesses called before the grand jury are Peter, and David's mother. The latter testifies as to David's intoxicated condition, his handkerchief pressed against his nose, and the drops of fresh blood on his motorcycle. The grand jury indicts David. Since David's mother is unavailable at his criminal trial, the prosecutor (after giving proper notice) offers a transcript of her grand jury testimony. Admissible under Rule 807?

Illustration (1) is based on a pre-rules case decided by the Fifth Circuit Court of Appeals.[2] Although there was no residual exception at common law, the court admitted a newspaper article similar to the one described in the Illustration. It found that hearsay dangers were minimized. The reporter presumably wrote the story soon after the fire when his memory was fresh. Faulty perception was not a significant problem because the fire and its aftermath could easily be observed. The reporter had a motive to be truthful because in a small town the accuracy of his story could be verified by local residents. Moreover, there was a need for this evidence, since the passage of time would make it difficult to find witnesses to the fire and, even if one or more could be located, their memories would have dimmed. All of these factors are, of course, present in Illustration (1) and, in combination, they strongly suggest that the Illustration meets the criteria of Rule 807. Although that rule does not require unavailability, it does require that the proffered hearsay evidence be "more probative on the point for which it is offered than any other evidence which the proponent can procure through reasonable efforts." Thus, the availability (or unavailability) of live testimony is a relevant consideration in the application of Rule 807.

Recall that Rule 807 is available only if a proffered hearsay statement is "not specifically covered by Rule 803 or 804...."[3] There is authority holding that at least some periodical or newspaper articles, if twenty or more years old, may be admitted into evidence under the ancient documents exception to the hearsay rule.[4] One difficulty with newspaper and magazine articles is that the writer may not have first-hand knowledge—the entire article may be based on conversations with others. If it is clear that the writer was not in a position to have first-hand knowledge, admission into evidence under the ancient documents rule is more problematic, since that rule requires first-hand knowledge. Recourse to Rule 807 would be appropriate, although lack of personal

2. Dallas County v. Commercial Union Assur. Co. 286 F.2d 388 (5th Cir. 1961).

3. FRE 807.

4. FRE 803(16). *See, e.g.,* Bell v. Combined Registry Co., 536 F.2d 164,

167 (7th Cir. 1976) (magazine articles), *cert. denied* 429 U.S. 1001; Ammons v. Dade City, 594 F.Supp. 1274, 1280 n.8 (M.D. Fla. 1984) (newspaper articles), *aff'd,* 783 F.2d 982 (11th Cir. 1986).

knowledge would be one factor favoring rejection of a proffered article. Other factors, however, such as the absence of more probative evidence, the probable motives of the author, the ability of readers to confirm the accuracy of the story, and the reputation of the newspaper or journal may point toward admissibility. In any event, the decision of the trial judge is unlikely to be overturned on appeal. The standard of appellate oversight used in reviewing rulings under 807 is (appropriately) a generous one: the issue is whether the trial judge's determination was a reasonable one, and the appellate court will not overturn it absent "a firm conviction that the court made a clear error...."[5]

There is some federal authority that would so strictly construe Rule 807 that it would lose almost all of its utility. Under the so-called "near miss" construction of Rule 807, the rule is inapplicable if the proffered evidence is addressed by one (or more) of the specific exceptions, but fails to satisfy all of the conditions of admissibility.[6] Thus a statement by a neutral observer to a utility repairman that from his window, five minutes before, he (the declarant) saw "lightning strike very close to an electrical generator" on a nearby mountainside could not be admitted under Rule 807. The statement would be specifically addressed by Rule 803(1) and (2). The five-minute lapse of time would probably disqualify the statement from admission into evidence as a Rule 803(1), which governs present sense impressions. That rule, you may recall, requires that the declarant speak as he perceives the event or condition he describes or "immediately thereafter." Suppose, further, that the declarant was not "under the stress of excitement"[7] when he spoke, thus ruling out the application of Rule 803(2)—the exception for excited utterances. These "near misses" would make Rule 807 inapplicable.

The problem with the near-miss advocates, led by Judge Easterbrook of the Seventh Circuit,[8] is that almost every hearsay declaration is addressed, at least peripherally, by one or more of the specific exceptions. One of the reasons for Rule 807 is to provide the courts with some flexibility in applying the hearsay rule; another reason is to afford opportunity for patterns of judicial response that could lead to the formation of another specific exception to the hearsay rule. Both of these aims are frustrated by the

5. United States v. North, 910 F.2d 843, 909 (D.C. Cir. 1990).

6. Advocates for the near-miss construction contend that the language in Rule 807 which makes the rule potentially available if a proffered statement is "not specifically covered" by a specific exception should be construed to mean "not addressed." But isn't it more sensible to construe the phrase as meaning "not admissible" under a specific exception?

7. FRE 803(2).

8. *See* United States v. Dent, 984 F.2d 1453, 1465–67 (7th Cir. 1993) (Easterbrook, J., concurring).

near-miss theory which provides little or no room for experimentation. Furthermore, if the near-miss theory is uniformly applied, the price of recognizing the desirability of a new hearsay exception is that a significant number of hearsay statements that should have been received under Rule 807 would have been consistently rejected because they were "near misses." Most courts have rejected the near miss rule and for good reason.[9]

Illustration (2) appears to meet the criteria of Rule 807. The only evidence possibly more probative on David's likely involvement in the assault is his mother's testimony and it is unavailable. There are circumstantial guarantees of trustworthiness: the short period of time between the mother's observations and her perception, her opportunity to observe, and her probable motive to tell the truth to her pastor, from whom she was seeking guidance. Corroborative evidence supplied by Peter's testimony is an additional guarantee of trustworthiness. And, finally, in this setting, the "interests of justice" criterion of Rule 807 might be served, since Peter is faced with the collaborative (opposing) testimony of David and his two confederates. The mother's statements do not fall within any specific exception—she was not, for example, making statements to a member of the medical profession for purposes of "diagnosis and treatment" under Rule 803(4). And, of course, too much time has elapsed for the application of Rule 803(1) [present sense impression] or 803(2) [excited utterance].

Illustration (3), regarding the admissibility of grand jury testimony under Rule 807, raises constitutional concerns. Recall that grand jury testimony is often admissible against the government under the former testimony exception of Rule 804(b)(1). This central issue is usually whether the prosecutor had a motive to develop the testimony of the (now unavailable) grand jury witness that corresponds with the prosecutor's motive at trial. But the former testimony exception cannot be used to introduce grand jury testimony against the accused[10] because he is not represented at the grand jury hearing and, except for the possibility of being called as a witness, is absent from these proceedings. Nonetheless, the prosecutor could proffer the testimony of an unavailable grand jury witness against the accused, citing Rule 807.

Until the Supreme Court's 2004 decision in Crawford v. Washington,[11] the courts would initially respond to Illustration (3) by

9. *See, e.g.*, United States v. Clarke, 2 F.3d 81, 83–85 (4th Cir. 1993) (near miss approach would nullify residual exception).

10. Assume that the accused did not, through wrongdoing, cause the unavailability of the declarant. If so, Rule 804(b)(6) would apply. It states that if a party has "engaged or acquiesced in wrongdoing that was intended to, and did, procure the unavailability of the declarant," the hearsay ban is lifted.

11. 541 U.S. 36 (2004).

applying the criteria set forth in Rule 807. The first issue was whether the proffered testimony complied with the requirements of Rule 807. As we have seen, this is a contextual judgment involving such factors as the probable bias of the declarant, the circumstances under which he spoke, his opportunity to clearly observe, and so forth. The court's search for the "guarantees of trustworthiness" required by Rule 807 could also include corroborative evidence that is consistent with the statement in question and thus adds to the probability that the statement is reliable. Frequently, courts would find that grand jury testimony satisfied the requirements of Rule 807 (or its predecessors, Rule 803(24) and Rule 804(b)(5)).[12]

The second issue in this line of "grand jury" cases was the constitutional question whether the introduction of grand jury testimony against the accused violated his rights under the Sixth Amendment's Confrontation Clause. Generally speaking, until 2004 and the Supreme Court's decision in the *Crawford* case, the Court used a two-pronged test to determine if the Confrontation Clause was satisfied. If hearsay evidence was admitted against the accused under a firmly established exception, there was no constitutional violation. The theory was that years of judicial experience with a firmly rooted hearsay exception validated its trustworthiness. On the other hand, if an exception was not firmly rooted, the prosecutor had to convince the court that the proffered hearsay statement was reliable or, as the Court often put it, was accompanied by adequate "indicia of reliability."[13]

Observe that the factors that are relevant to Rule 807's demand for "circumstantial guarantees of trustworthiness" are also relevant to the constitutional requirement of "indicia of reliability." However, the Supreme Court has refused to allow corroborative evidence to be considered in assessing the reliability of the proffered statement for *constitutional* purposes.[14] In the context of Illustration (3), this means that the corroborative evidence supplied by Peter's testimony may be considered under Rule 807 in assessing the trustworthiness of the declarant's grand jury testimony, but may not be considered in resolving the constitutional issue of reliability. Nonetheless, under the approach followed by the Supreme Court prior to the *Crawford* decision, there is good reason to predict that the mother's grand jury testimony would be admissi-

---

12. *See, e.g.,* United States v. Earles, 113 F.3d 796, 799–801 (8th Cir.1997).

13. Ohio v. Roberts, 448 U.S. 56, 66 (1980).

14. Idaho v. Wright, 497 U.S. 805, 822 (1990). This position is difficult to justify. One would suppose that an important goal of evidence law is to admit reliable evidence and that all factors casting light on reliability should be considered. Perhaps the court was apprehensive that law enforcement agents would use improper techniques to create corroborative evidence.

ble. As you will see, however, Crawford v. Washington, discussed below, forbids this result, and in doing so, takes a new approach in defining the role of the Confrontation Clause.

The Confrontation Clause: A Primer

The story of the Confrontation Clause is a tale of constitutional uncertainty. The seemingly intractable problem in criminal trials is to reconcile the accused's Sixth Amendment right "to be confronted with the witnesses against him" with the government's invocation of the various exceptions to the hearsay rule. These escapes from the hearsay ban allow a declarant's statement to be introduced against the accused for the truth of the declarant's assertion. Yet, in most instances, the accused cannot cross-examine the declarant concerning the reliability of her statement. Perhaps she was lying or mistaken; these possibilities cannot be explored through cross-examination.

In the typical hearsay setting A (the declarant) makes a statement to B (the auditor) who appears as a witness and discloses A's statement to the trier of fact. It is true, of course, that the accused can confront and cross-examine B, but the "real" witness against the accused is A. If the Confrontation Clause were construed so as to forbid the introduction of A's statement unless she testified, the trier of fact would often be denied probative and reliable evidence. One possible escape from this dilemma is to place the accused's constitutional protection on the assumed reliability of the hearsay exceptions. The argument would run: exceptions to the hearsay rule are based on determinations by judges and legislators that some classes of hearsay are reliable. These classes of hearsay may be introduced into evidence even though the opponent has no opportunity to cross-examine the declarant. Thus, the accused is given adequate constitutional protection because of the way the hearsay rule is administered—unreliable hearsay is rejected. The problem with this argument, of course, is that the tail—the evidence rules—is wagging the dog—the accused's constitutional right. It is not surprising that the Supreme Court has rejected this approach and has sought some middle ground between denying the use of hearsay exceptions in criminal trials and placing the constitutional protection of the Confrontation Clause entirely in the hands of the rule-makers and judges who oversee and administer the hearsay rule.

Major Features of Pre–Crawford Confrontation Doctrine

There are two obvious ways in which the accused's constitutional right "to be confronted with the witnesses against him" can override the various hearsay exceptions. The first is to use the Confrontation Clause to require a diligent effort by the prosecutor to try to produce the hearsay declarant for cross-examination by the accused. In other words, a hearsay exception could not be invoked by the government against the accused until the prosecutor has made a good-faith, diligent effort to secure the live testimony of the hearsay declarant. The degree of effort required would be dictated by the Confrontation Clause. The Court might apply this constitutional "unavailability" requirement to Rule 803 exceptions which, generally speaking, make no reference to whether or not the declarant is available to testify. The Court might also supersede some of the unavailability standards set forth in Rule 804(a),[15] that govern the exceptions set out in Rule 805(b), by substituting a more stringent constitutional standard. Although the Court has occasionally used the Confrontation Clause to require the prosecutor to make a diligent effort to produce the accused,[16] this use of the clause has been sporadic and, so far at least, inconsequential. It is probably safe to assume that the Court will usually defer to the terms of the hearsay exception on the issue of unavailability.[17] Thus, for example, if a hearsay exception does not require as a condition of its application that the declarant be unavailable, the Court is unlikely to impose a constitutional requirement that the prosecutor make a diligent effort to produce the declarant.

Two reasons explain and justify the Court's reluctance to require production of an available witness whose hearsay declaration meets the requirements of an exception. First, it frequently happens that the hearsay statement, made closer to the event and usually before the pressures of litigation have developed, possesses reliability that is equal to or better than the declarant's live testimony. Second, if the accused insists upon the testimony of the declarant, he can often secure it by having the court issue a subpoena.

Another obvious way to protect the accused's confrontational right is to develop constitutional standards of trustworthiness (reliability) that exceed those of the hearsay exceptions. These more stringent standards might completely disallow the use of certain hearsay exceptions (e.g. dying declarations) against the accused.

---

15. In the case of the declarant's death, of course, live testimony is impossible. However, the Court could hold that even a deceased declarant's hearsay statement is inadmissible if the prosecutor had an opportunity to take her deposition, but failed to do so.

16. *See, e.g.,* Barber v. Page, 390 U.S. 719, 723–25 (1968) (state government has obligation to try to produce the declarant who was in federal prison before resorting to testimony declarant

gave at a preliminary hearing). *See also Roberts*, 448 U.S. at 65.

17. *See, e.g.,* White v. Illinois, 502 U.S. 346, 355–57 (1992) (government may invoke exceptions for excited utterance and statements made to medical personnel without showing unavailability). United States v. Inadi, 475 U.S. 387, 394–96 (1986) (prosecutor not required to show co-conspirator unavailable before invoking exemption for coconspirator's statements).

Alternatively, the Confrontation Clause could be interpreted to impose more rigorous conditions on the use of some hearsay exceptions. For example, a declarant's statement of intention to participate with another person in a joint undertaking ("I'm going to buy some crack from Spinoza") could not be introduced to show the speaker's conduct unless there was clear and convincing evidence of the other person's conduct or the judge deleted the reference to the other person (the accused).

From 1980[18] until 2004,[19] the Supreme Court's principal approach to reconciling the textual demand of the Confrontation Clause and the hearsay exceptions was to focus primary attention on newly established hearsay exceptions. If an exception had the imprimatur of many years of judicial experience (that is, was "firmly rooted"), the Court would defer to the collective judgments that had determined the hearsay was reliable and, accordingly, hold that the Confrontation Clause was satisfied.[20] However, the Court subjected recent exceptions (or older ones not widely adopted), such as the residual exception (Rule 807) and the exception for statements against *penal* interest, to a more stringent constitutional test. A hearsay declaration introduced against the accused under an exception that was not firmly rooted would violate the Confrontation Clause unless the prosecutor could show that the hearsay statement was attended by indicia of reliability or "particularized guarantees of trustworthiness."[21] As we have seen, most of the same factors indicating that a statement offered under Rule 807 (the residual exception) is reliable also reinforce the "constitutional" trustworthiness of a declaration offered under any "new" exception. However, the Court has refused to consider *corroborative* evidence in its *constitutional* search for indicia of reliability.[22] As you can now anticipate, the *Crawford* decision, discussed below, may relegate many of the pre-*Crawford* decisions to the annals consulted only by legal historians.

There are, however, several areas of pre-*Crawford* confrontation jurisprudence that remain largely unaffected by the *Crawford* decision. First, the Confrontation Clause is not offended by the introduction of a witness's prior statements assuming the accused has a fair opportunity to cross-examine the witness.[23] After all, the

18. Ohio v. Roberts, 448 U.S. 56 (1980).

19. Crawford v. Washington, 541 U.S. 36 (2004).

20. *See, e.g., White* 502 U.S. at 355 n.8 (excited utterances and statements made for medical treatment); Bourjaily v. United States, 483 U.S. 171, 183–84 (coconspirator statements).

21. *See, e.g., Roberts,* 448 U.S. at 66.

22. See supra note 14 and accompanying text. Most courts are willing to consider corroborative evidence in determining the trustworthiness of hearsay in nonconstitutional contexts.

23. California v. Green, 399 U.S. 149, 158 (1970). Thus, a statement admitted under the exemption for certain prior statements of a testifying witness would not ordinarily be constitutionally suspect. See FRE 801(d)(1).

witness can be cross-examined about both her present testimony and her previous declarations. Second, the Confrontation Clause requires that the accused and the adverse witness face each other— that is, be in a position to have eye contact during the witness's testimony.[24] (The assumption is that a face-to-face confrontation reduces the likelihood that the witness will lie.) This requirement affects the ability of the government to use electronic transmission, or a "one-way" screen in order to block the witness's view of the accused.[25] If this arrangement were constitutionally permissible, it would be frequently used when a young child, allegedly victimized by the accused, was called to testify. However, blocking the child's view of the accused is constitutionally forbidden *unless* the trial judge makes a determination, *specific to the case before him*, that requiring the child to testify in the presence of the accused is likely to produce trauma (or, presumably, other serious emotional harm).[26] Third, the Confrontation Clause precludes the use of a confession by one of the accused's confederates against the accused. Suppose, for example, A and B are indicted for kidnapping. Following A's arrest, he signs a written statement that admits his guilt and also implicates B. Later, A repudiates his confession as false on the ground that the police threatened his family. Nonetheless, in the joint trial of A and B, the trial judge allows the prosecutor to use A's prior statements under the party admissions exemption to the hearsay rule. A constitutional violation occurs because A's earlier confession implicates B in the charged criminal activity and B cannot effectively cross-examine A.[27]

The Confrontation Clause generally requires that A and B be given separate trials and that A's prior statements about B be withheld from evidence in B's trial. In some cases, it may be possible to delete B's name from A's admissions, but this technique ("redaction") is constitutionally defective if a jury is likely to infer that the omitted name is that of co-defendant B.[28]

Of course, if A elects to take the stand and testify fully, the Confrontation Clause is satisfied.[29] It does not matter whether A admits the prior statements, denies them, or qualifies them, B (A's co-defendant) can confront and cross-examine A with respect to both A's prior statements and his present testimony. A's prior

24. Coy v. Iowa, 487 U.S. 1012, 1019–20 (1988).

25. The accused, and other trial participants, can, of course, see and hear the witness.

26. Maryland v. Craig, 497 U.S. 836, 857–58 (1990).

27. The cornerstone case is Bruton v. United States, 391 U.S. 123, 136–37 (1968).

28. *See* Gray v. Maryland, 523 U.S. 185, 192–95 (1998).

29. *See* Nelson v. O'Neil, 402 U.S. 622, 629–30 (1971) (prior statement denied; favorable testimony given); La-France v. Bohlinger, 499 F.2d 29, 35 (1st Cir. 1974) (statement admitted; truth of it denied; police threats alleged), *cert. denied*, 419 U.S. 1080.

hearsay declarations might be technically inadmissible against B (and would be unless an exemption or exception provided otherwise), but B could seek an instruction that confines the jury's use of B's prior statements to his criminal liability. The point is that the Confrontation Clause was satisfied when A took the stand and submitted to direct and cross-examination. Whether or not his prior statement or statements are admissible against B is now simply a question of evidence law.

Crawford v. Washington: A Crossroads

In 2004 the Supreme Court adopted a new approach to the Confrontation Clause and *appears*—although it is not certain—to have discarded the constitutional doctrine it had been developing and refining since 1980. The core of that doctrine, set out in the Court's opinion in Ohio v. Roberts,[30] was to distinguish firmly rooted hearsay exceptions from more recent ones (or from ones not enjoying wide acceptance). The government could invoke a well-established hearsay exception against an accused without violating the Confrontation Clause. However, when the government sought to invoke an exception that was not "firmly rooted," the prosecutor had to offer satisfactory proof that the proffered declaration was attended by "particularized guarantees of trustworthiness."[31] The circumstances surrounding the hearsay statement supplied the context in which the government pointed to facts suggesting reliability, such as spontaneity or the absence of any motive to be untruthful. The Court refused to allow the trial judge to consider corroborating evidence as a factor confirming the trustworthiness of the proffered hearsay declaration; the theory was that the statement in question should stand or fall on its own footing.

Two uncertainties infuse the *Roberts* approach described above. First, there is uncertainty as to when a hearsay exception, recent in origin but now widely adopted, becomes "firmly rooted" so that the government need not demonstrate "particularized" trustworthiness. This issue may arise not only with a relatively "new" hearsay exception, but also with amendments or modifications to a traditional one. For example, declarations against interest is a well-established exception to the hearsay rule. But declarations against penal interest, an expansion of the traditional exception, is of more recent origin. Second, as we have observed, hearsay exceptions that are not firmly rooted may nonetheless be invoked against the accused if attended by "particularized guarantees of trustworthiness." In many cases, courts disagree as to when circumstances

30. 448 U.S. 56 (1980).

31. Idaho v. Wright, 497 U.S. 805, 818 (1990) (extending and refining the approach set out in Ohio v. Roberts).

surrounding the application of a "new" hearsay exception suffice to make it "constitutionally" reliable. Hence, appellate reversals and disparities among courts in different jurisdictions became too commonplace for a desirable level of predictability and stability.

It is unclear whether Crawford v. Washington[32] has abandoned entirely the older approach, first articulated in Ohio v. Roberts. What is clear is that the Court carved out a special category of hearsay statements described as "testimonial."

Crawford involved a prosecution for assault and attempted murder. The accused, Michael Crawford, claimed self-defense. An important factual question was whether the victim had drawn a weapon just before the accused stabbed him. Crawford's wife, Sylvia, was present at the assault and indeed participated in the alleged crime by leading Michael to the victim's apartment. However, at Crawford's trial she claimed her privilege not to testify against her spouse, and thus became unavailable. The prosecutor responded by proffering a tape-recorded statement that Sylvia had given to the police. Her statement described the assault in terms that cast doubt on Michael's claim of self-defense. The trial judge admitted the taped statement on the ground that it was a declaration against Sylvia's penal interest that was accompanied by "indicia of reliability" sufficient to overcome Michael's confrontation clause objection. In particular, the trial judge noted that the police questioning of Sylvia was "neutral," that she did not attempt to shift blame to her husband, and that she had first-hand knowledge of the recent event she described.

Eventually, the case reached the United States Supreme Court where the question posed was whether the ruling of the trial judge violated Crawford's rights under the Confrontation Clause. Justice Scalia, speaking for seven members of the Court, concluded that it did. But the Court refused to employ the framework that was established in *Roberts* and its progeny. Instead, the Court adopted, at least in large part, an analysis suggested by Justice Thomas (joined by Scalia) in a concurring opinion filed in a 1992 case, White v. Illinois.[33]

This analysis begins with the premise that the core concern of the Confrontation Clause is to assure that unexamined ex parte declarations that are "testimonial" in character are not introduced against an accused. The *Crawford* Court did not precisely define what constitutes a testimonial statement, but Justice Scalia provides considerable guidance at scattered places in his opinion. Testimonial declarations are directed to proving a fact;[34] they are

32.   541 U.S. 36 (2004).   **34.**   *Crawford*, 541 U.S. at 61–62.
33.   502 U.S. 346, 365 (1992).

characterized by structure and a certain degree of formality,[35] as opposed, for example, to a casual remark or a spontaneous or excited utterance; and such statements are directed at government officials or bodies such as prosecutors, police, judicial officers, grand juries, or other investigative units.[36] In an important passage, the Court said that although it declined to adopt a definitive definition of "testimonial statements," the term

> applies at a minimum to prior testimony at a preliminary hearing, before a grand jury, or at a former trial, and to police interrogations.[37]

These "modern practices," said the Court, have "the closest kinship to the kinds of testimonial abuses at which the Confrontation Clause was historically directed."[38]

The *Crawford* rule as to testimonial statements is absolute. These hearsay statements cannot be introduced into evidence against the accused unless, first, the declarant is unavailable at the accused's trial and, second, the accused had a prior opportunity to cross-examine the declarant. These requirements apply when, and only when, a declarant's statements are offered for their truth, thus implicating the hearsay rule. It is immaterial whether or not a testimonial statement fits within a firmly rooted hearsay exception or whether the exception has only recently gained recognition.

The only possible deviation from these constitutional requirements is when the proffered statement is a dying declaration. Most such declarations would not be testimonial in nature. However, when a public official, such as a police officer, conducts a formal or structured interrogation of a dying declarant, the resulting responses would probably be testimonial. If these statements were nonetheless allowed in evidence, the rationale would be a long historical practice—and dying declarations would be sui generis. Since the statement before the Court in *Crawford* was not a dying declaration, the question of the admissibility of a testimonial dying declaration was left open.

Another—and much more important question—unanswered in *Crawford* is whether the *Robert's* framework remains partially intact and will be applied to nontestimonial hearsay statements. Although the *Crawford* opinion repeatedly and harshly criticizes *Roberts* as both theoretically unsound and practically defective, the

---

35. Id. at 51–52.

36. Justice Scalia mentions other ways of defining testimonial declarations. For example, a statement might be characterized as testimonial if the declarant "would reasonably expect [it] to be used prosecutorially" or, in a variation, if "an objective witness reason-

ably ... [would] believe that the statement would be available for use at a later trial." These formulations, however, are likely to be rejected because of their indefinite, subjective character.

37. *Crawford*, 541 U.S. at 68.

38. Id.

opinion is ambiguous about the complete demise of *Roberts*. The Court is unlikely to abandon all constitutional oversight of the use of nontestimonial hearsay against the accused, yet it need not continue to adhere to the framework and methodology of *Roberts*. For example, where the use of uncross-examined hearsay has rendered a criminal trial fundamentally unfair, the Court could invoke the due process clause to set aside the accused's conviction. So far, however, lower courts have continued to administer the *Roberts* doctrines,[39] even though Chief Justice Rehnquist, dissenting in *Crawford*, expresses disagreement with the Court's decision to "overrule" Ohio v. Roberts....[40]

39. United States v. Saget, 377 F.3d 223, 227 (2nd Cir. 2004). United States v. Dumeisi, 424 F.3d 566, 576 (7th Cir. 2005).

40. *Crawford*, 541 U.S. at 69.

Chapter IX

IMPEACHMENT

Table of Sections

---

§ 9.1 Competency to Testify

The early common law had a number of restrictive rules that declared various persons incompetent to testify. Included among these were infants, insane persons, atheists, spouses of parties, and even parties themselves. The assumption was that these persons were either unduly biased or incapable of giving reliable testimony. With the passage of time, and especially during the Twentieth Century, statutory reform abolished or modified these incapacities.

The opening sentence of Federal Rule of Evidence 601 illustrates the modern rule:

> **General Rule of Competency.** Every person is competent to be a witness except as otherwise provided in these rules. However, in civil actions and proceedings, with respect to an element of a claim or defense as to which State law supplies the rule of decision, the competency of a witness shall be determined in accordance with State law.

Rule 601 has two features. First, it states a general rule that every person is a competent witness unless prohibited from testifying by another Federal Rule. Only a scattering of prohibitory rules are found in Article VI of the Federal Rules, the most notable of which disallows testimony by the residing judge[1] or a member of the jury.[2] But generally speaking, a witness is disqualified only when he is shown to be incapable of perceiving, remembering, or describing the event in question. Second, Rule 601 defers to the

---

1. FRE 605.
2. FRE 606.

policy of Erie R.R. Co. v. Tompkins[3] which dictates that when a federal court is applying state substantive law (e.g., in "diversity" cases), it should also apply those state procedural rules that potentially could have a significant impact on the outcome of the trial.[4] Thus, suppose State X has passed a statute that renders felons convicted of specified crimes incompetent to testify in designated civil trials. If a federal court were entertaining one of these civil suits and applying the substantive law of State X, the court would apply the "witness competency" rule of State X. Of course, since most states have modernized their rules governing the competency of witnesses, there are comparatively few instances in which a witness, competent under the general approach of the Federal Rules, is disabled from testifying because of a specific contrary state rule.

Some states have statutes that may create special rules of competency in suits in which one of the parties (usually the defendant) is deceased and thus represented by a fiduciary, such as an executor. The live party has the potential advantage of taking the stand and testifying, whereas his opponent, now deceased, is denied this opportunity. So-called "Dead Man's Statutes" are a misguided legislative attempt to correct this adversarial imbalance.

There are several means of doing this, the crudest (and most unfair) of which is simply to prohibit the surviving party from testifying. The injustice that results from this approach is apparent in cases where the survivor has a valid claim stemming from an oral agreement with the deceased or, perhaps, from a personal injury caused by the decedent. The living party is prohibited from substantiating his claim by his own testimony. Thus, even in states which retain some version of the Dead Man's statute, there has been widespread reform. For example, the living party may testify, but his testimony triggers the opponent's right to introduce the decedent's hearsay statements pertaining to the event in question. Another technique is to allow the survivor's testimony, but require him to produce corroborative evidence before he can gain a favorable judgment. Finally, the scope of the Dead Man's statute may be restricted. For example, it is likely to apply only when the *defendant* is the deceased party and the statutory prohibition may apply only to *oral communications* between the plaintiff and the decedent. (Older Dead Man's statute typically applied to any "transaction" between live party and the deceased party.)

---

3. 304 U.S. 64, 78–80 (1938).

4. Generally speaking, Congress or the Supreme Court acting pursuant to an enabling statute is free to displace the state "procedural" rule with a uniform federal rule. *See* Hanna v. Plumer, 380 U.S. 460 (1965).

§ 9.2   Impeachment: In General

We turn now to the subject of impeachment. The rules of impeachment govern the means by which a party tries to weaken or discredit the testimony of adverse witnesses (including hearsay declarants).[5] Some of the techniques of impeachment trace their ancestry to rules governing the competency of witnesses. For example, conviction of a serious crime, once a basis for a potential witness's incompetence, is now a basis for impeaching a witness's testimony.

The term "impeachment" generally refers to all evidence *intended* to negate or raise doubts about the reliability of a witness's testimony, including evidence that calls into question the accuracy of his observation, his recollection, or the fidelity of his account. The examiner may, for example, try to extract the witness's concession that he was unable to observe clearly the event in question, that his memory has dimmed, or that he was under the influence of an intoxicating substance when he observed the event to which he testified. Note that this attack on credibility does not *necessarily* imply that the witness is consciously lying. Rather, the principal thrust of this means of impeachment is to show that, sincere or not, the witness is wrong or mistaken.

Error, whether deliberate or innocent, is also suggested by evidence showing the witness has made a prior statement that is inconsistent with her present testimony. Another line of attack is directed at the witness's bias. Perhaps the witness is related to one of the parties or has a financial interest in the outcome of the case. Again, the examiner is suggesting testimonial distortions or inaccuracies that hint at, but do not necessarily rest upon, a conscious fabrication. A third approach is to call other witnesses to contradict the first witness's testimony. Contradictory accounts cast doubt on the accuracy of the first witness's testimony. Of course, all of the foregoing methods of impeachment may carry an innuendo of deliberate fabrication; much depends on how the cross-examiner frames his questions and the subtleties of his body language and voice intonations.

Other methods of impeachment more directly impugn a witness's honesty by revealing his disposition to consciously distort or falsify. In other words, the cross-examiner tries to show the witness himself (and not just his testimony), has a defect. Although impeachment by psychiatric evidence usually points to "a flaw in the witness," there are only limited opportunities to invoke this tech-

---

5. FRE 806 provides that when a declarant's hearsay statement has been admitted under an exception or as statutory nonhearsay (under Rule 801(d)(2)(C), (D), or (E)), the "credibility of the declarant may be impeached ... by any evidence which would be admissible ... if declarant had testified as a witness."

nique. More often, a witness's character for truthfulness is attacked by testimony revealing his misdeeds ("bad acts" that suggest falsity or deceit) or by testimony of lay witnesses who know the witness under attack and can speak to his (bad) character for veracity. Although the law of evidence generally disfavors character or "propensity" evidence, there are exceptions,[6] and impeachment is one of them. Since the outcome of most trials depends upon which witnesses are believed by the trier of fact, the law of evidence is crafted to provide the trier with ample information pertaining to the credibility of the witnesses whose testimony is admitted.

A recurring issue in impeachment is whether the "impeaching party" is entitled to present "extrinsic" impeaching evidence. Extrinsic evidence is evidence that is adduced other than by questions during cross-examination—in other words, evidence presented by calling witnesses or introducing documents. The issue usually arises when the cross-examiner is unable to gain the desired concessions from the principal witness during cross-examination. For example, the principal witness, a mechanic, denies, during cross, that he was fired by his employer for falsifying the number of overtime hours he worked. Counsel now proposes to call the employer who will testify that the principal witness was fired because he made false entries.

You will discover that some methods of impeachment allow the introduction of extrinsic evidence, while others do not. In the example above, the cross-examiner must, as the cases sometimes put it, "settle for the answers on cross." The notion underlying this restriction is that some methods of impeachment do not carry sufficient probative force to justify the introduction of extrinsic evidence. In other words, the price in terms of time consumption and jury distraction from the main issues is too high. Another factor that influences the rules about extrinsic evidence is the nature of that evidence. If the extrinsic evidence is highly reliable and can be presented quickly, the rules are more likely to allow it. For instance, if the mechanic in the example above had been convicted of falsifying employment records, his judgment of conviction (which is extrinsic evidence) would be admissible. It is reliable evidence that a court has determined beyond a reasonable doubt that the principal witness lied to his employer in order to gain unearned compensation. Furthermore, the introduction of the certificate of judgment consumes very little time.

At common law, there was a general rule that prohibited a party from impeaching her own witness. The idea was that by

---

6. *See, e.g.,* FRE 413, 414 and 415, allowing propensity (disposition) evidence in connection with certain sexual offenses. *See also* FRE 404(a) (character of the accused and the victim).

calling a witness to testify, a party "vouched for" her character and credibility. A related notion was based on the perceived unfairness of calling a witness and then attacking her veracity. The rule against impeaching one's own witness might be defensible if a party had a wide choice of witnesses to the same event. In reality, however, a party has very limited choices—or perhaps no choice at all. A party often subpoenas a particular witness because she has knowledge of relevant facts, not because she has an alliance with the party or because her credibility is beyond reproach. Faced with this reality, common law judges and legislatures began to devise means of avoiding the rule against impeaching "your own witness." Here are some of the common law and statutory escapes from the rule:

1. The court would call the witness, so the rule did not forbid impeachment by either party.

2. The rule had no application if the law required a party to call a certain witness—for example, an attesting witness to a deed or will.

3. The rule had no application when a party called her adversary.

4. The rule was suspended if the party calling the witness was genuinely surprised by her unexpected testimony.

5. The rule was not violated when counsel asked a witness about prior statements, inconsistent with her direct testimony, if counsel was simply trying to "refresh" the witness's memory in an effort to secure changes or corrections in her testimony.

In most jurisdictions today, resort to these escape devices is unnecessary. The modern approach to impeaching witnesses is contained in Federal Rule 607. It states:

> **Who May Impeach.** The credibility of a witness may be attacked by any party, including the party calling the witness.

In the commentary accompanying this provision, the Advisory Committee notes the unreality of the assumption that a party has unfettered choices in selecting witnesses.[7] Generally speaking, Rule 607 clears the way for a party to impeach her own witness by any of the techniques discussed in the next section.

___

7. FRE 607 ACN.

§ 9.3 Techniques of Impeachment

It may be helpful to arrange the various techniques of impeachment on a continuum that begins with those methods clearly directed at the witness's character and proceeds to those methods that speak more to the witness's mistaken testimony than to his mendacity. For example, impeaching a witness by evidence of his criminal conviction impugns his character; impeaching him by evidence of his poor eyesight casts doubt on his perception; impeaching him by evidence of his probable bias falls somewhere between.

Conviction of a Crime

One method of impeaching a witness is to show that he has been convicted of a crime. There are, to be sure, limitations having to do with the nature of the crime and its recency, but this impeachment technique, uniformily recognized, is fairly common, especially in criminal trials where witnesses are more likely to have a criminal record. The desired inference is straightforward: a person who has committed a criminal offense is likely—or at least more likely than one who has not—to give false testimony.

Nonetheless, a number of distinctions can be made. Some offenses are more closely linked to credibility than others. For example, convictions for perjury, embezzlement, fraud, or tax evasion yield strong inferences relating to truth-telling, while convictions for manslaughter or reckless driving do not. A distinction might also be drawn between a felony-grade offense and a misdemeanor. Finally, a distinction could be made between ordinary witnesses and an accused who elects to testify. If the accused can be freely impeached by prior convictions, he probably will decline to take the stand. Even if he does testify, the impeaching evidence—supposedly directed only at his *untruthful* character—might be used by the jury to infer that he has a criminal character (disposition) and thus must be guilty of the crime with which he is charged.

The Federal Rule governing impeachment by evidence of a prior conviction is Rule 609. It provides:

> **(a) General Rule.** For the purpose of attacking the credibility of a witness,
>
> (1) evidence that a witness other than the accused has been convicted of a crime shall be admitted, subject to Rule 403, if the crime was punishable by death or imprisonment in excess of one year under the law under which the witness was convicted, and evidence that the accused has been convicted of such a crime shall be admitted if the

court determines that the probative value of admitting this evidence outweighs it prejudicial effect to the accused; and

(2) evidence that any witness has been convicted of a crime shall be admitted if it involved dishonesty or false statement, regardless of the punishment.

(b) Time Limit. Evidence of a conviction under this rule is not admissible if a period of more than ten years has elapsed since the date of the conviction or of the release of the witness from the confinement imposed for that conviction, whichever is the later date, unless the court determines, in the interests of justice, that the probative value of the conviction supported by specific facts and circumstances substantially outweighs its prejudicial effect. However, evidence of a conviction more than ten years old ... is not admissible unless the proponent gives to the adverse party sufficient advance written notice ....

(c) Effect of Pardon, Annulment, or Certificate of Rehabilitation. Evidence of a conviction is not admissible under this rule if (1) the conviction has been the subject of a pardon, annulment, certificate of rehabilitation, or other equivalent procedure based on a finding of the rehabilitation of the person convicted, and that person has not been convicted of a subsequent crime which was punishable by death or imprisonment in excess of one year, or (2) the conviction has been the subject of a pardon, annulment, or other equivalent procedure based on a finding of innocence.

(d) Juvenile Adjudications. Evidence of juvenile adjudications is generally not admissible under this rule. The court may, however, in a criminal case allow evidence of a juvenile adjudication of a witness other than the accused if conviction of the offense would be admissible to attack the credibility of an adult and the court is satisfied that admission in evidence is necessary for a fair determination of the issue of guilt or innocence.

(e) Pendency of Appeal. The pendency of an appeal therefrom does not render evidence of a conviction inadmissible. Evidence of the pendency of an appeal is admissible.

Rule 609 speaks only to the use of a prior conviction to cast doubt on the truthfulness of a witness. Other uses of a criminal conviction are possible, but implicate other rules. For example, Rule

803(22) addresses the use of a prior conviction as proof of "any fact essential to sustain the judgment."[8] Under Rule 404(b), "other crimes, wrongs, or acts" may sometimes be used to prove an element of the crime charged, such as motive, identity, or "absence of mistake or accident."[9]

The rule presently under consideration—609—has the following general structure. Although *any* witness's credibility may be attacked by the introduction of his prior conviction, Rule 609 draws a distinction between an "ordinary" witness and the accused as witness. The accused is given somewhat greater protection from impeachment by conviction, primarily because of a special balancing test, contained in 609(a), that applies only to the criminal defendant. Rule 609 also distinguishes between a conviction of a prior crime involving "dishonesty or false statement,"[10] and conviction of other crimes such as criminal assault or manslaughter, which do not. Prior crimes involving lying or deceit point strongly toward a witness's lack of probity, and Rule 609 favors admissibility of this class of convictions. Finally, Rule 609 discourages the use of "stale" convictions (more than ten years old) and of juvenile adjudications.

Rule 609(a)(1) addresses serious crimes—those "punishable by death or imprisonment in excess of one year"—and opens the possibility of using the conviction of one of these felony-grade offenses[11] as an impeachment tool. In the case of an ordinary witness in a criminal or civil trials, the judge must balance the probative value of the prior conviction against the counterweights contained in Rule 403. Thus, unless the probative force of the prior conviction on the issue of the witness's truthfulness is "substantially outweighed by the danger of unfair prejudice, confusion of the issues, or misleading the jury, or by considerations of . . . waste of time . . . ,"[12] the prior conviction is admissible. In contrast, when the accused is the witness in a criminal trial, the judge may admit the prior conviction only if its "probative value . . . outweighs its prejudicial effect on the accused."[13] Thus, the special balancing test of Rule 609 provides an additional measure of protection for the criminal defendant. In applying this special balancing test, the judge may take into account such factors as the probative value of the prior conviction on the issue of the accused's truthfulness, the nature of the prior offense (in particular, its similarity to the crime charged or the likelihood that it would inflame the jury), the

---

8. FRE 803(22).

9. FRE 404(b).

10. FRE 609(a)(2).

11. The controlling language in Rule 609(a) is "punishable by death or imprisonment in excess of one year." This is usually, but not always, the dividing line between a felony and a misdemeanor. Thus, for convenience, we will use the term "felony" or "felony-grade" to denote this class of serious crimes.

12. FRE 403.

13. FRE 609(a)(1).

centrality of accused's credibility to the main issues in the case, the accused's record as a whole, the age of the conviction, and the importance of hearing the accused's account of the charged event.

Suppose, for example, the accused was on trial for armed bank robbery. He testifies that he was not one of the robbers (mistaken identity). The prosecutor now offers a certified copy of a prior criminal judgment showing that nine years ago the accused was convicted of the armed robbery of a convenience store. In the exercise of her discretion to admit or exclude this evidence, the trial judge should be particularly attentive to the probative force of this evidence, to the span of time between the prior conviction and the accused's testimony, and to the similarity of the past offense to the present one. Although it may be true that one who would rob would also readily lie, the framework of Rule 609 places the greatest probative value on past crimes of falsity or deceit. Furthermore, there is a strong resemblance between the prior offense and the one now charged, which increases the risk that the jurors may use the past crime to infer the accused's guilt in the case before them.

Under the special balancing test of Rule 609(a), the focus is on prejudice *to the accused*. Under Rule 403, which applies to ordinary witnesses, the balancing test is inclined more favorably toward admissibility,[14] and is focused not only on the witness, but on all parties and on judicial concerns such as trial expedition. In any event, the decision of the trial judge, whether under Rule 403 or Rule 609, is not likely to be overturned on appeal. The appellate test is whether the trial court abused its discretion in weighing the appropriate factors for and against admission.

Rule 609 (a)(2) states that a prior conviction of a crime involving "dishonesty or [a] false statement" shall be admitted against any witness in *any civil or criminal case*. No distinction is drawn between the accused and other witnesses in a criminal prosecution. Furthermore, the judge has no discretion to exclude a conviction that falls within this special category. This scheme makes it imperative to determine what crimes are characterized by dishonesty or false statement. The use of "dishonesty" causes the most difficult problems, because that word is sometimes broadly associated with illegal or corrupt acts that do not necessarily involve deceit. But the legislative history of Rule 609(a)(2) strongly suggests that as used in the rule, "dishonesty" is an elaboration of "false statement," and that the reference ("dishonesty or false statement") in 609(a)(2) is to crimes involving deceit, falsification, or untruthfulness.[15] Thus, crimes falling within this special catego-

---

14. Exclusion is justified only if probative value is substantially outweighed by Rule 403's enumerated counterweights.

15. *See* H. R. Conf. Rep. No. 93–1597, at 9 (1974). See also the extensive opinion in United States v. Smith, 551 F.2d 348, 362 (D.C. Cir. 1976).

ry are those such as perjury, mail fraud, embezzlement, forgery, false pretense, counterfeiting, knowingly passing a worthless check, income tax evasion, and larceny by trick. Most trial judges will receive evidence demonstrating that even though the prior crime on its face did not involve deceit or lying, the particular way in which it was executed did involve these traits. Thus, larceny (not on its face within the special category) that was implemented by making a misrepresentation is a crime of dishonesty or false statement.[16]

Proving the Prior Conviction

Under the Federal Rules (and thus in most states) there are two ways of proving a prior conviction: counsel may adduce this evidence, usually during cross-examination, by asking the witness to admit his prior conviction; or counsel may introduce a certified copy of the prior criminal judgment. Neither of these means of proof consumes much time, and thus the introduction of a prior conviction usually poses only the problem of whether the conviction is admissible at all. When a conviction is admissible, judges usually disallow detailed descriptions of the previous offense, confining counsel to such essentials as the name of the crime, the time and place of the conviction, and the punishment imposed. Many judges also allow the impeached witness to give a brief ameliorative explanation of the prior offense.

An accused, of course, need not testify; she has a constitutional right not to take the stand. Of particular concern to an accused who is considering taking the stand is whether he can be impeached by a prior conviction. In order to make an informed decision about whether to testify, he will often seek (by a motion "in-limine")[17] an early ruling on the admissibility of prior conviction(s), tendered by the prosecutor for the purpose of undermining the accused's credibility. An in-limine ruling, which the judge may provide in the exercise of her authority to manage the trial,[18] is subject to revision until the accused actually testifies at trial.

ILLUSTRATION

Clyde is on trial for the armed robbery of a bank. Eight years ago, he was convicted of breaking into a residence and committing an armed robbery. (At the time

16. *See* United States v. Payton, 159 F.3d 49, 56–57 (2nd Cir. 1998).

17. This is a written motion made prior to trial or during its early stages in which a party seeks an early ruling, usually to resolve an evidentiary issue.

18. *See* FRE 611(a). *See also* Luce v. United States, 469 U.S. 38, 41 n. 4 (1984).

of the presently charged offense, he was on parole.) In the current prosecution, Clyde's defense is alibi. He admits that he was in the vicinity of the bank robbery on the day of the crime and that he was arrested while fleeing. He insists, however, that the two witnesses who identified him as one of the robbers were mistaken. As to his presence near the bank, Clyde claims that he was waiting there to meet a friend. He explains his flight on the ground that he was afraid he might be arrested on suspicion, and that his parole might be reversed because he had two unpaid traffic violations.

Prior to trial, Clyde files a motion in-limine, urging the court to rule that the prosecutor cannot introduce his prior conviction to impeach him. The trial judge denies the motion and rules that should Clyde decide to testify, his conviction for residential robbery may be used to impeach his credibility.

1.   Did the trial judge correctly apply Federal Rule 609?

2.   Does Clyde have the option of declining to take the stand, but (assuming he is convicted) nonetheless appealing the ruling of the trial judge?

There is an intentional ambiguity in this Illustration. The trial judge incorrectly applied Rule 609 if he admitted the prior conviction for residential robbery under subsection (a)(2). The prior offense is not one of "dishonesty or false statement" as that phrase is used in this subsection. However, if the trial judge admitted the prior conviction under the special balancing test of Rule 609(a)(1) and entered in the trial record her considered application of the various factors relevant to a determination under that subsection, she would probably not be reversed on appeal.[19] For example, the trial judge might have concluded that the probative value of the prior conviction (a serious offense) was relatively high and that the conviction also had a special informative value in the context of this case. Without knowledge of the prior conviction, the jury might be left with the impression that Clyde, whose good behavior earned his parole from some (unknown) past offense, was the victim of a double misfortune: two traffic tickets and the coincidence of being in the neighborhood where a bank robbery was occurring. On the other hand, had the judge excluded the prior conviction, she might have emphasized the importance of Clyde's testimony, the age of the prior conviction, and the likelihood that (should his prior

19. For a case with many features in common with the present illustration, see United States v. Alexander, 48 F.3d 1477 (9th Cir. 1995) (convictions for residential robbery and possessing cocaine for sale admissible to impeach accused).

conviction be admitted) the jury would infer that his commission of one armed robbery (in a residence) made it likely that he committed another armed robbery (in a bank). Furthermore, had Clyde been on parole for several years without committing any significant offenses, the judge might have been influenced by his interim good behavior.

In Luce v. United States,[20] the United States Supreme Court addressed the appealability of in limine rulings. These early rulings by the trial judge are not final—that is, they are subject to revision during trial. Suppose, then, that an accused files a motion in limine seeking an early ruling by the trial judge that his prior conviction cannot be used to impeach him. The judge determines, however, that the prior conviction may be used to impeach the defendant if he decides to testify. Suppose, further, the judge does not reverse his earlier ruling, the accused testifies, and the prosecutor introduces the prior conviction for impeachment purposes. The defendant, if convicted, can appeal the judge's ruling. On the other hand if the accused declines to testify because of the judge's earlier determination (that the accused's prior conviction is admissible), he waives his right to appeal the judge's in-limine ruling.

Faced with an in-limine ruling that an accused's prior conviction will be admissible if he testifies, defense counsel will sometimes call the accused to the stand and, during direct examination, have him admit that he has a specified past conviction(s). The idea is that by frankly admitting the prior conviction, the jurors will not judge the defendant as harshly as they would if this evidence were revealed by the prosecutor during impeachment. While this may be a useful trial tactic, the defendant nonetheless waives the right to appeal the judge's earlier ruling that the prior conviction is admissible, because the defendant himself introduced this evidence.[21]

Stale Convictions; Pardons; Juvenile Adjudications

Generally speaking, a conviction is "not admissible [under Rule 609] if a period of more than ten years has elapsed since the date of the conviction or the release of the witness from confinement, ... whichever is the later date...."[22] Thus, if a witness was not imprisoned for the prior offense, the ten-year period began to run on the date of the conviction. The ten-year cutoff, however, is not absolute. If more than ten years has elapsed since the conviction or release from prison, the judge may nevertheless admit the conviction "in the interests of justice" if the probative value of the

---

20. 469 U.S. 38, 42–43 (1984).

21. Ohler v. United States, 529 U.S. 753, 756–58 (2000).

22. FRE 609(b).

conviction "substantially outweighs its prejudicial effect."[23] A party who proffers a conviction outside the usual ten-year time limit must give her opponent written notice so that the latter can muster his arguments against admissibility.[24]

Rule 609(c) and (d) address other circumstances in which admissibility of a prior conviction is either absolutely barred or is disfavored. A pardon, annulment, or certificate of rehabilitation will render the prior conviction inadmissible if the forgiving act was based on either a finding of innocence or rehabilitation.[25] Generally speaking, juvenile adjudications are inadmissible. There is, however, an exception to this general rule. In criminal trials, the judge can admit a juvenile judgment (adjudication) if "necessary for a fair determination of ... guilt or innocence," *and if a* "conviction of the offense would be admissible to attack the credibility of an adult" *and if* the witness being impeached is *not the accused*.[26]

Prior Bad Acts

Suppose a witness has committed an act in the past that reflects unfavorably upon her truthfulness. We have seen that if her prior conduct led to a criminal conviction, Rule 609 often permits the introduction into evidence of that conviction to impeach her credibility. But if there were no conviction, can the "bad" act (the conduct itself) be proved? Generally, the modern answer is yes[27] and the Federal Rule in point is 608(b).

Two difficulties attend this method of impeachment. First, there may be an issue of relevance because not all bad acts cast doubt on one's credibility. This, of course, is a familiar problem— one that we also encountered in connection with Rule 609. The solution turns upon the careful application of the general principle of relevance. Filing false statements on an application for a retail license clearly involves deceit and has considerable probative force upon the issue of a witness's credibility. On the other hand, engaging in drunken or disorderly conduct has little or no bearing on one's willingness to testify truthfully. Theft, if unaccompanied by falsehood or stealth, falls somewhere between the crimes suggested above. Thus, it is not surprising that courts have divided when ruling on the admissibility of various prior bad acts.[28] A

---

23. Id. Note that this balancing test differs from the one in Rule 609(a) and also differs from the balancing test in Rule 403. It is doubtful that these nuances in wording have much practical impact.

24. Id.

25. FRE 609(c).

26. FRE 609(d).

27. In the past, and possibly in a few jurisdictions today, courts rejected impeachment by prior bad acts on the grounds of limited probative force and (more importantly) distraction from the main issues.

28. Even in a single jurisdiction, the supreme court may alter its view. *Compare* Gustafson v. State, 267 Ark. 278, 590 S.W.2d 853, 858 (1979) (inquiry

second problem—growing out of the practical aspects of trial administration—arises from the generally shared concern that trials stay focused on the principal issues and not be unduly prolonged. In short, courts resist conducting a mini-trial within a trial by adjudicating the circumstances of some alleged act that has relevance *only because it brings into question a witness's credibility*. In an effort to limit the distraction and expenditure of time associated with impeachment by prior bad acts, common law courts usually ruled that the examiner must settle for the admissions and concessions he is able to adduce during cross-examination. He cannot resort to additional or "extrinsic" evidence to prove the existence of (or circumstances surrounding) the prior bad act. This is the position taken in Federal Rule 608(b) which provides in part:

> **Specific Instances of Conduct**. Specific instances of the conduct of a witness, for the purpose of attacking or supporting the witness' character for truthfulness, other than conviction of a crime as provided in Rule 609, may not be proved by extrinsic evidence. They may, however, in the discretion of the court, if probative of truthfulness or untruthfulness, be inquired into on cross-examination of the witness (1) concerning the witness' character for truthfulness or untruthfulness, or concerning the character for truthfulness or untruthfulness of another witness as to which the witness being cross-examined has testified.
>
> . . .

Rule 608 emphasizes discretionary control by the trial judge. In exercising her discretion, the judge may take into account a number factors such as the centrality of the witness's testimony (and hence the importance of fully assessing credibility), whether the accused is the witness, whether the nature of the prior bad act is likely to inflame the jury, and, of course, the probative value of the past act on the issue of truthfulness. Other considerations include the remoteness in time of the prior bad act, as well whether revealing this past misdeed is likely to cause unwarranted prejudice to a party.

Although the text of Rule 608(b) makes no mention of the cross-examiner's good faith, there is a judicially-imposed requirement that the cross-examiner have a good-faith belief that the event he inquires about actually occurred. The application of this good-faith standard means that the attorney who intends to inquire

about theft proper) *with* Rhodes v. State, 276 Ark. 203, 634 S.W.2d 107, 110–11 (1982) (improper).

about a prior bad act must take reasonable steps to confirm its past existence.

As we noted above, the range of "bad" acts that may be the subject of the cross-examiner's questions is limited by Rule 608(b)'s requirement that the past conduct be "probative of truthfulness or untruthfulness." Obvious candidates for inclusion within this category are acts such as forgery, bribery, threatening witnesses, using false documents, or making false entries in an application or an official document, such as a tax return. There is at least a rough congruence between the bad acts that can be used to impeach under Rule 608(b) and the convictions that are "automatically" admissible under Rule 609(a)(2) because the underlying offense "involved dishonesty or false statement." However, under Rule 608(b) the trial judge does have considerable discretion to admit or exclude evidence of a prior bad act that bears on credibility. She should not be reversed unless she has clearly abused that discretion. In contrast, under Rule 609(a)(2) if an appellate court has ruled that a particular crime is (or is not) one of dishonesty or false statement, the trial judge is without discretion; he must abide by the characterization.[29]

Recall that Rule 608(b) forbids *extrinsic* evidence of prior conduct that relates to the witness's "character for truthfulness or untruthfulness...." There is usually no issue concerning what constitutes extrinsic evidence: it is evidence other than the witness's testimony on cross-examination—that is, extrinsic evidence is characterized by the testimony of other witnesses or the introduction of documentary evidence. As to the latter, merely having a document marked as an exhibit and then asking the witness about it does not constitute the introduction of extrinsic evidence. Introducing the document through another witness would, however, violate Rule 608(b)'s prohibition against extrinsic evidence.[30] Suppose, however, the witness being impeached concedes that the document about which he is being questioned is authentic and that the cross-examiner's accusations about the witness's connection to the document are true. For example, suppose the witness denies that he misrepresented his "straight A" educational accomplishments on a past civil service application, and the cross-examiner confronts him with his (the witness's) college transcript. The witness acknowledges that the transcript is his, and the judge admits the transcript so that the jury can assess the disparities between

---

29. The trial judge could, however, determine that a crime that, on its face, was not one characterized by dishonesty or false statement was accomplished by means of falsity or deceit.

30. Of course, the document may be admissible under some other rule of evidence. The prohibition against extrinsic evidence applies when the purpose of showing the witness's previous conduct is to cast doubt on her truthfulness.

the witness's testimony, affirming his "A" average, and his actual academic record. Since the cross-examiner did not have to call another witness to authenticate the transcript, the judge's ruling may not be a violation of the no-extrinsic-evidence rule[31] and even if it is, it should be a harmless error.

ILLUSTRATION

Rob, who sells "new and second-hand discount goods," is on trial for receiving stolen property consisting of twenty-five large screen, high definition television sets. He admits that he received the electronic equipment in question, but claims that he had no idea the sets were stolen. Rob's business records show that he paid $25,000 for the twenty-five, unused TV's. The prosecutor has a witness (a former Rob employee) who will testify that Rob actually paid only $10,000 for the twenty-five units, but entered a price of $25,000 in his account records.

Confronted with this alleged disparity on cross-examination, Rob vehemently denies that he paid only $10,000 for the equipment in question. Later in the trial, the prosecutor proffers the former employee who is willing to testify, on the basis of first-hand knowledge, that Rob paid only $10,000 for the television sets, but made false entries reflecting a price of $25,000. Rob's defense attorney points to Rule 608(b) and contends this extrinsic evidence is inadmissible. How should the judge rule?

If the only relevance of the former employee's testimony were to show that Rob's past conduct increased the likelihood that his testimony was untrue, Rule 608(b)'s prohibition against extrinsic evidence would apply. However, this evidence (false entries to cover up the crime) has another probative role: it undermines Rob's claim that he had no suspicion that the television sets were stolen. This prior act is an integral part of the crime charged. Thus, Rule 608(b)'s rule against extrinsic evidence is inapplicable.

Examine again Rule 608(b)(2). It allows specific instances of conduct to show "the character for truthfulness or untruthfulness of another witness as to which character the witness being cross-examined has testified." Sometimes a "character" witness is allowed to testify to the character for truthfulness of another witness—the "principal" witness. Like all witnesses, the character witness is subject to the test of cross-examination. Is A, the character witness, being honest and forthright when he testifies that B, the principal witness, has good character with respect to truth and

---

31. The courts disagree on this relatively unimportant technical point. *See*   Mueller & Kirkpatrick, Evidence § 6.27, at 488–89.

veracity? One means by which the cross-examiner can weaken A's testimony is to ask A if he is aware of certain instances of B's misconduct that reflect badly on B's character for truthfulness. Rule 608(b)(2) clears the way for the cross-examiner to ask[32] such questions as, "Are you aware that in January 2003, B was fired from his job as a mechanic because he stole tools from his employer?" We will revisit this setting in connection with reputation or opinion testimony that is directed at a witness's character for truthfulness.

Occasionally, a cross-question concerning a witness's prior bad acts calls for an answer that would violate his privilege against self-incrimination. This may occur with an ordinary witness or when the accused takes the stand. It is clear that in either instance the constitutional privilege is available and may be claimed. Indeed, the last paragraph in Rule 608(b) provides that:

> The giving of testimony, whether by the accused or any other witness, does not operate as a waiver of the accused's or the witness' privilege against self-incrimination when examined with respect to matters that relate only to character for truthfulness.

Of course, should the witness neglect to claim the privilege, her answer disclosing the prior bad act may be freely used to assess her credibility.

Bad Character Regarding Truth and Veracity

We have already observed that prior convictions and prior bad acts (not resulting in a conviction) are often admitted into evidence for the ultimate inference that a witness's testimony should not be believed. The trier is invited to draw the following inferences: the witness's prior conduct indicates that his character for truthfulness is defective; therefore his testimony in the present trial is likely to be false or misleading. Basically, the evidence of past conduct is used to show that the witness has a character trait that predisposes him to falsify.

Another means by which counsel can establish this same character trait is to offer one or more witnesses who testify that they are familiar with the principal witness and that his character for truthfulness is bad. There are two means by which the character witness may establish his familiarity with the principal witness:

---

32. The examiner must act in good faith—that is, he must have grounds to believe the specific instances that form the basis of his question actually occurred.

one means is to be *personally acquainted* with the principal witness; the other is to be acquainted with the principal witness's *reputation* for truthfulness ("truth and veracity"). Of course, in a mobile, largely urban society, the principal witness may not have a reputation bearing upon his truthfulness. The traditional approach of the common law was to require that the principal witness have a reputation concerning truthfulness *in the community* in which he resided. Today, it suffices that he has a reputation concerning truthfulness in some associational setting (such as a work environment) in which more or less the same group of persons frequently interact. Often, however, counsel presents "character evidence" through witnesses who know the principal witness and are thus able to give a personal opinion concerning his character for truthfulness.

The direct examination of a reputation or opinion witness has a ritualistic character. Counsel first establishes the necessary foundation. In the case of a reputation witness, this consists of eliciting testimony that demonstrates that the witness is or has been in a position to learn of the principal witness's reputation for truthfulness, and that he is in fact familiar with this reputation. In the case of an opinion witness, the foundation consists of the character witness's testimony that he is personally acquainted with the principal witness, and that this acquaintance has been sufficiently close to permit the character witness to have an informed opinion of the principal witness's character for truthfulness. Next, with little or no elaboration, the character witness states the principal witness's *reputation* for truthfulness (or "truth and veracity") is good; or that, in the character witness's *opinion*, the principal witness has good character with regard to truthfulness.

The governing Federal Rule of Evidence is Rule 608(a) which states,

> **Opinion and Reputation Evidence of Character.**
> The credibility of a witness may be attacked or supported by evidence in the form of opinion or reputation, but subject to these limitations: (1) the evidence may refer only to character for truthfulness or untruthfulness, and (2) evidence of truthful character of a witness is admissible only after the character of the witness for truthfulness has been attacked by opinion or reputation evidence or otherwise.

Subdivision (2) of Rule 608(a) ensures that the opposing parties cannot engage in a "bolstering" contest by having one or more character witnesses support the credibility of the principal witness.

Such a practice, if allowed, would be distracting and time consuming. Thus, every witness who takes the stand is assumed to have a good (or at least acceptable) character for truthfulness—at least, until the witness's character has been attacked "by opinion or reputation evidence or otherwise."[33] For example, cross-examiner might attack a witness's character for veracity by introducing evidence showing that he has been convicted of a crime that bears on credibility. This attack opens the door for the opposing party's introduction of evidence directed at "rehabilitating" the witness. For instance, the opponent might present an opinion witness who testifies that the principal (attacked) witness has a good character for truthfulness.

All witnesses, including those who appear for the limited purpose of testifying about someone else's character, are vulnerable to the various forms of impeachment, including an attack based on character for truthfulness. A character witness, however, is also subject to a special form of impeachment, conducted during cross-examination. This special technique of impeachment does not necessarily imply that the character witness is giving false or distorted testimony. It does imply, at the very least, that the witness's testimony is inaccurate. The technique is available during the cross-examination of any witness who has testified to a relevant character trait of another person (the subject). For example, the witness might give testimony that subject's character is, say, peaceful, and thus inconsistent with the commission of the violent crime with which she (the subject) is charged;[34] or the witness might testify that the subject (for example, the principal witness) has a good (or bad) character for truthfulness.

During the cross-examination of a character witness, the examiner is entitled to test *how well-informed the* character witness is and, also, to reveal the *standard she is using* when she portrays the subject's character. A simple example will make the point. Suppose witness *A*'s character for truthfulness has been attacked on cross-examination by the introduction into evidence of an eight-year-old conviction for selling counterfeit watches (*i.e.*, they look like and are sold as brand-name watches but are not). In an effort to repair the damage to his witness's credibility, counsel (*A*'s direct examiner) subsequently calls *B*, who testifies that he has known *A* for seven years and that, in his opinion, her character for truthfulness is excellent. On cross, *B* can be asked "do-you-know" questions that pertain to specific incidents during the last seven years that cast doubt on *A*'s credibility and, more to the point, cast doubt on *B*'s opinion. For example, the cross-examiner may ask *B*, "Are you aware that *A* was arrested and placed on trial in June, 2004, for

33.   FRE 608(a)(2).

34.   *See* FRE 404(a)(1).

making false entries in her application for unemployment benefits?" If *B* answers that he is unaware of this event, his assertion on direct that he is familiar with *A*'s character is undercut. If *B* answers that he is aware of this event, his assertion on direct that *A*'s character for truthfulness is excellent is undercut.[35] (Of course, the cross-examiner must have conducted an investigation and concluded, in good faith, that the arrest and trial actually occurred.) A reputation witness may be subjected to the same kind of cross-examination with the minor difference that the cross-examiner frames his question in a "have-you-heard" format.[36]

Impeachment by Evidence and Bias

The term "bias" denotes a variety of mental attitudes—either conscious or unconscious—that may incline a witness to give misleading or false testimony. In general, bias signifies a witness's interest in the outcome of a trial, including a friendly or hostile association with one of the parties that could induce him to shade, distort, or falsify his testimony. The cross-examiner can expose a witness's probable bias by probing to discover links between the witness and the case. For instance, the examiner's questions might reveal that the witness is related to a party, employed by a party, bears a grudge against a party, has an economic stake in the outcome of the trial, received compensation for testifying, was promised immunity from prosecution, received favored treatment from the prosecutor in return for his testimony, or has a strong identification with the subject of the litigation (such as environmental protection). These are simply illustrations; the sources of a witness's bias are almost infinite.

Although there is no Federal Rule of Evidence addressing impeachment by bias, this technique of impeachment is uniformly acknowledged in both federal and state courts. Furthermore, across the federal (and most state) courts, there is general agreement about the evidentiary rules governing this method of impeachment. The cross-examiner probing the possible bias of a witness does not have to "settle for" or "take" the witness's answer on cross, but can produce extrinsic evidence through other witnesses or documents. It is usually unnecessary to lay a foundation for extrinsic evidence by first asking the witness about the sources of his possible bias. Some federal courts,[37] however, do require such a foundation where the evidence showing bias consists of the wit-

---

35. Put otherwise, this answer raises questions as to the standard *B* was using when she testified as to *A*'s "excellent" character for veracity.

36. For example: "Have you heard that in June, 2004, *A* was arrested and placed on trial for making false entries in her application for employment benefits?"

37. FRE 611(a) gives the judge "reasonable" control over the mode and order of interrogating witnesses and presenting evidence.

ness's prior statement ("I hate that SOB [the defendant] and hope the plaintiff reduces him to poverty"[38]). Those judges requiring that the witness be asked about her prior statement before it is proved by extrinsic evidence do so on the grounds of fairness and expedition: the witness should be afforded an opportunity to explain or deny her prior statement; furthermore, if she frankly admits having made it, extrinsic evidence becomes unnecessary.

The admissibility of evidence of bias for impeachment purposes in the federal courts was strongly affirmed by the Supreme Court in United States v. Abel,[39] decided in 1984. In that case, a bank robbery prosecution, the government called witness A, who had earlier entered a guilty plea to the same robbery with which defendant Abel was now charged as a co-participant. A's testimony fortified Abel's guilt. Later in the trial, Abel called witness B in an effort to refute A's damaging testimony: B testified that A had once admitted to him that A intended to falsely implicate Abel so that A would receive lenient treatment from the government. The prosecution was now faced with the task of rebutting B's testimony. First, the prosecutor asked cross-questions in an unsuccessful attempt to elicit an admission from B that he and Abel shared membership in a secret organization. Subsequently, the prosecutor recalled A, who testified that Abel, A, and B had previously belonged to a secret prison gang. According to A, membership in that gang required that each member deny the existence of the secret group and "lie, cheat, steal [and] kill to protect each other."[40] Thus, A testified, it would have been "suicide" for him to have told B that he (A) intended to falsely implicate Abel. (Note that the probative force of A's testimony supports both the unlikelihood that he would have disclosed a plan to frame Abel and, more importantly, the likelihood that B's testimony in Abel's favor was biased.)

Ultimately, the United States Supreme Court approved the trial judge's admission of A's rebuttal testimony. The Court found that the probative force of this testimony on the issue of B's possible bias (favoring Abel) justified its reception. Reverting to first principles, Justice Rehnquist noted that relevant evidence is admissible unless blocked by an exclusionary rule, and that evidence supporting bias clearly meets the test of relevance. Such evidence diminishes the likelihood that the facts to which the biased witness testified are accurate. Here, the membership of B and Abel in an organization embracing secrecy and falsehood "supported the inference that [B's] testimony was slanted or perhaps

---

38. This out-of-court statement would be offered for its truth, thus implicating the hearsay rule. However, the exception for the declarant's presently existing state of mind (FRE 803(3)) would overcome a hearsay objection.

39. 469 U.S. 45, 50–51 (1984).

40. Id. at 48.

fabricated in ... Abel's favor."[41] Furthermore, the Court said, the jury was entitled to hear evidence concerning the type of organization in question—closely knit, secret, and sworn to perjury and mutual protection. Knowledge about the prison gang and its tenets allowed the jury to identify the source of *B*'s possible bias and to assess its strength.

Note that *B*'s membership in the secret prison gang is also a prior bad act bearing on truthfulness. So viewed, however, the restriction against the introduction of extrinsic evidence would apply. But evidence of *B*'s membership also discloses his possible bias. On the issue of bias, the cross-examiner need not settle for testimony she adduces during cross-examination; extrinsic evidence (i.e., *A*'s rebuttal testimony) is admissible. Thus, we see again the familiar principle that evidence admissible for the purpose for which it is offered is usually not rendered inadmissible simply because it would be excluded if offered for some other purpose.

Impeachment by Prior Inconsistent Statements

A frequently used impeachment technique is to introduce evidence that a testifying witness has made prior statement(s) inconsistent with her testimony. The prior statement might be contained in a writing or it might have been an oral remark. In any event, its impeaching value is obvious: unless the witness has a convincing explanation as to why she gave an earlier contradictory account, the force of her trial testimony is considerably weakened. Of course, she may deny ever having made a prior inconsistent statement. In this event, the trier of fact has to resolve the issue of whether she even made the alleged contradictory remark.

This all seems simple enough; nonetheless, impeachment by prior inconsistent statements is attended by a subtle point or two, and hedged by several restrictions. Recall that a statement "other than one made by the declarant while testifying at the trial" is hearsay if it is offered to prove the truth of the earlier declaration.[42] Thus, generally speaking, the prior statement of a witness on the stand is hearsay if it is offered for its truth. (Prior inconsistent statements "under oath and subject to the penalty of perjury" are exempted from the hearsay rule.[43]) Of course, sometimes a witness's prior statement fits within an exemption or an exception to the hearsay rule. However, if it does not, it can still be used by the trier of fact, but only for the limited purpose of discrediting the witness's trial testimony. The prior inconsistent statement cannot be used as proof of the truth of the assertion contained within it. Thus,

---

41. Id. at 52.

42. FRE 801(c).

43. FRE 801(d)(1)(A). There are other prior statements by a witness that are

exempted from the hearsay rule. *See* FRE 801(d)(1).

suppose a witness testifies that the car in question was black; previously she has said that the car was white. She is impeached with evidence of her prior inconsistent statement. Unless her earlier statement is exempted or excepted from the hearsay rule, her prior statement cannot be used to prove the car was white. The sole purpose of the evidence is to show that the witness's testimony ("The car was black") may not be credible because she gave a different account on an earlier occasion.

Counsel who impeaches a witness by her prior inconsistent statement may have to confront the rule that bars extrinsic evidence. There is general agreement that counsel may *cross-examine* a witness about a prior inconsistent statement that, when viewed in light of the central issues in the trial, appears incidental or "collateral." The theory in allowing this inquiry is that if the witness has made an inconsistent statement about comparatively unimportant topics to which she testified, she may have been inaccurate in her account of the central topics. Thus, if she testifies that the bank teller wore an orange dress (a minor point, we will assume), the cross-examiner can ask, "Didn't you tell Detective Larkin, when you spoke with him the day after the robbery, that the teller's dress was green?" If the witness was mistaken about the color of the teller's dress, perhaps her description of the getaway car (a central point) is inaccurate.

Difficulties arise when the cross-examiner proffers extrinsic evidence (another witness or a document or recording) to prove that the witness made the alleged inconsistent statement. If the prior statement concerns a "collateral" or incidental matter, extrinsic evidence is forbidden. Allowing proof by methods other than cross-examination is disallowed because of the associated costs of time consumption and distraction from the principal issues. The difficulty is this: how do we identify statements that are collateral and thus within the no-extrinsic-evidence rule? In the varied factual patterns that judges face, it is not always easy to determine if a topic is collateral. Ultimately, the judge must apply Rule 403 and determine whether the probative value of the proffered extrinsic evidence is "substantially outweighed by the danger of unfair prejudice, confusion of the issues, or misleading the jury, or by considerations of undue delay, waste of time, or needless presentation or cumulative evidence."[44] As a rough guide, the common law's approach to determining when the subject matter of a prior statement is collateral may be helpful. Common law judges would ask whether the subject of the prior inconsistency could be shown in evidence for some purpose other than to simply impeach the witness.

44. FRE 403.

ILLUSTRATION

Phillip is suing the Ajax Corporation for breach of contract. For some years, Ajax has been mining gravel under a lease with Phillip. That lease was recently renegotiated. Under the new lease, Ajax claims that Phillip's royalties are based only on "first quality" gravel, which is mined on a tract of Phillip's land adjacent to a river. Phillip contends that he is also entitled to royalties on the second quality gravel that is mined on hillsides some thousand yards from the river's edge.

During the course of renegotiating the contract, Phillip dealt with several Ajax representatives, including Wilford, who first approached Phillip about the possibility of increased mining near the river and the extension of mining activities to the nearby foothills.

Ajax, the defendant, calls Wilford to the stand. Describing himself as a "corporate officer," Wilford goes on to testify that he clearly explained the terms of the proposed contract to Phillip—the same terms that Ajax claims were inserted in the new contract by Ajax's lawyers, who completed the contractual arrangement with Phillip. On cross, Phillip's lawyer reminds Wilford that he described himself as a corporate officer. He then asked, "Isn't it true that you are not a corporate officer, but only the foreman of mining operations?" Wilford insists that he is considered a corporate officer. Subsequently, counsel proffers a letter from Wilford to Phillips, thanking the latter for his courtesy during their initial consultation and saying that Ajax's lawyers would "follow up and complete our arrangements." The signature block of the letter contained Wilford's title, "Foreman, Mining Operations." Furthermore, on the letterhead there was a list of corporate officers; Wilford's name did not appear. Should the trial judge admit the letter?

If we assume that the sole purpose for which this letter can be used is to impeach Wilford, the strict application of the common-law test would exclude it. This does not necessarily mean that the trial judge applying Rule 403 would reach the same conclusion. Since Wilford first explained Ajax's proposal to Phillip, the judge might conclude that his credibility is sufficiently important to permit the proffered extrinsic evidence. The question of admissibility is easily answered if Wilford's letter has probative value for some other appropriate purpose. For example, if it contained the preliminary terms of the proposed new lease, it might be independently admissible for that purpose and would also serve the secondary purpose of impeaching Wilford. Further, if there were an issue as to whether Wilford had authority to speak for Ajax, his corporate position might be relevant. If Wilford's letter was either "authorized" by Ajax or concerned "a matter within the scope of" Wilford's employment,[45] it could be introduced against Ajax as a party admission. What is worthy of note is, first, the common law approach to extrinsic evidence is simply a useful guidepost, not an invariable rule. Second, under the Federal Rules, the prohibition against extrinsic evidence should be applied flexibly through the application of Rule 403.[46]

There are two other notable features of impeachment by prior inconsistent statements. The first is obvious: the prior statement must, in fact, be inconsistent with the witness's testimony. However, a blatant, irreconcilable contradiction is *not* required. It suffices that the previous statement is sufficiently at variance with the witness's trial testimony to weaken or undermine it. It also suffices that a significant point that was included in the witness's testimony was omitted from his prior statement.[47] Second, under Federal 613, a witness who is impeached by extrinsic evidence of her prior inconsistent statement must ordinarily be afforded "an opportunity to explain or deny it...." Specifically, Rule 613(b)[48] provides:

> **Extrinsic Evidence of Prior Inconsistent Statement of Witness.** Extrinsic evidence of a prior inconsistent statement by a witness is not admissible unless the witness is afforded an opportunity to explain or deny the same and the opposite party is afforded an opportunity to interrogate the witness thereon, or the interests of justice otherwise require. The provision does not apply to the admissions of a party opponent ....

Common law judges required that a witness be asked about a prior inconsistent statement *prior* to the introduction of extrinsic evidence offered to prove the content of the statement. Thus, the

---

45. FRE 801(d)(2).

46. The extrinsic-evidence prohibition applies not only to prior inconsistent statements, but to impeachment by prior bad acts and by contradiction. We shall take up the latter method shortly.

47. United States v. Strother, 49 F.3d 869, 874–75 (2d Cir. 1995). (Witness's testimony included assertion that defendant specifically requested that she

make payment on a particular check; earlier written statement omitted any reference to this request).

48. Rule 613(a) abolishes an ancient common law rule ("Rule in Queen's Case") that required a cross-examiner to show a written inconsistent statement to the witness *before* she could be questioned about it.

cross-examiner had to lay a foundation by identifying the prior statement with sufficient detail (e.g., time, place, person spoken to) to allow the witness to explain, deny, or qualify her prior remark. Under Rule 613, it suffices that the witness be afforded an opportunity at some point in the trial to address her prior inconsistency and to respond to questions about it by the attorney supporting her credibility.[49] Even this requirement (an opportunity *at some point*) can be waived by the judge "in the interests of justice ...."[50] Furthermore, the requirement of a chance to response has no application when the out-of-court statement in question is a party admission. Statements that constitute a party admission are admissible *whether or not* the party testifies, and even if a party *does* testify, Rule 613 does not apply to prior statements that fall within the party admission exemption.

Impeachment by Contradiction

Suppose counsel for the plaintiff has two witnesses to a single-car automobile accident. The principal issue in the case is whether the accident was caused by a defect in the road, or by the plaintiff's negligent driving. Witness *A* gives an account of the relevant event that, at best, mildly favors the plaintiff's version of the facts; witness *B*'s description of the accident is more favorable to the plaintiff.

This imagined case presents a commonplace sequence of events: the testimony of two or more witnesses vary on one or several points. The fact that *B*'s testimony is not entirely congruent with *A*'s testimony does not mean that *A* has been impeached. On the other hand, suppose that while *A* is on the stand, the lawyer who called him seeks and receives the court's permission to examine witness *A* "as if under cross-examination." He then conducts a hostile examination as to the condition of the road at the time of the accident. Assume that he fails in his attempt to have *A* retract or alter her account of the condition of the road. Counsel now calls *B*, and directs his attention to the condition of the road or, perhaps, even to *A*'s testimony. *B*'s testimony conflicts with *A*'s account. *A* has been impeached by a technique of impeachment called "contradiction."

Typically, "contradiction" is employed by the cross-examiner who, unable to get the witness to modify her testimony, attempts to impeach her by the introduction of extrinsic evidence that contra-

---

49. Some federal appellate courts have construed Rule 611 (judges' control over testimony) broadly enough to allow a trial judge, in her discretion, to require that a witness be asked about his prior inconsistency before he is impeached by extrinsic evidence. *See, e.g.,* United States v. Schnapp, 322 F.3d 564, 571–72 (8th Cir. 2003).

50. For example, suppose the witness completes his testimony, leaves the court's subpoena jurisdiction, and thereafter counsel discovers that the witness has made a prior inconsistent statement.

dicts that testimony. There is no difficulty if the extrinsic evidence is independently admissible for some relevant purpose—such as the condition of the road.[51] However, extrinsic evidence is not permitted if it is not independently admissible and it contradicts the witness on a tangential or "collateral" point. The cross-examiner will often argue that if the witness is mistaken as to a collateral fact, she may also be mistaken as to the important facts. But the courts have generally held that to receive evidence of contradiction on tangential portions of a witness's testimony exacts too great a price in distraction and time consumption.

ILLUSTRATION

Herbert is on trial for burglary of guns and related items. In his defense, his lawyer calls Herbert's mother as a material witness and as a character witness.[52] Mother first testifies that she was at home with her son for the entire evening of the burglary. She then testifies that Herbert was a good husband who "worshiped" his former wife and their child, and that she (the mother) had seen him stay at home and nurse his sick child and "spend his last dime to give his family whatever they needed—clothes, toys, and food." On cross, the mother adheres to her testimony and denies the prosecutor's accusations that Herbert had abused his former wife or neglected his child. Later, over defense objection, the prosecutor calls the former wife who testifies that Herbert threatened her with a gun, tried to run over her with his truck, beat her, and frequently abused their son. Should the trial judge have allowed this "rebuttal" testimony?

Note, first, that a portion of the mother's direct testimony is objectionable. To establish Herbert's character, she is limited to opinion or reputation testimony, but her testimony drifted off into specific instances of conduct which is forbidden.[53] More importantly, the "character-evidence" part of her testimony raises a relevance issue. Although the accused has the right to introduce evidence that his character is inconsistent with the crime charged,[54] it is doubtful that devotion to and support of his wife and child has probative value to show that he is unlikely to have committed burglary. Thus,

---

51. If the extrinsic evidence also constitutes impeachment by some method (such as showing bias) that permits such evidence, there is no difficulty; extrinsic evidence is allowed.

52. FRE 404(a)(1) allows the accused to call character witnesses who (pursu-

ant to FRE 405) can give opinion or reputation evidence showing that the accused's character is inconsistent with his commission of the charged crime(s).

53. FRE 405.

54. FRE 404(a)(1).

the prosecutor had two grounds for objecting to the mother's direct testimony—which, let us assume, he failed to assert.

The prosecutor also has two possibilities for neutralizing the mother's testimony: cross-examination and the introduction of extrinsic evidence. Unable to get the defendant's mother to recant her testimony during cross-examination, the prosecutor subsequently called Herbert's former wife for the purpose of contradicting the mother's direct testimony. The difficulty, again, is that Herbert's devotion and support—or lack of it—to his former wife and child has no bearing on the case other than to establish a character trait that is, at best, only marginally inconsistent with the crime charged. A character trait that has more probative force is that of being a "law-abiding" person.

Recall that the cross-examiner who puts did-you-know questions to an opinion witness (or have-you-heard questions to a reputation witness) must settle for such evidence as he can adduce on cross. He cannot introduce extrinsic evidence to establish that the event he asks about actually occurred.[55] Thus, a strict application of the traditional evidentiary rules arguably forbids the extrinsic evidence provided by Herbert's ex-wife.

On the other hand, there are two possibilities for gaining admission of the ex-wife's testimony, or at least those portions of it that the judge is willing to admit. The Federal Rule that controls this Illustration is the now-familiar Rule 403. If the judge determined that leaving the mother's testimony unanswered might mislead the jury, he might permit at least some parts of the wife's contradictory testimony.[56] In essence, the judge would rule that the probative value of her testimony was not "substantially outweighed" by the various reasons for exclusion set out in Rule 403. Of course, the judge might conclude that the jury can easily detect the mother's possible bias, and that no extrinsic evidence will be allowed on a point that appears collateral—Herbert's devotion to his family.

Curative Admissibility

Another possibility is found in the common-law doctrine variously called "opening the door" or "curative admissibility." The doctrine is really a waiver rule, and the idea underlying it is simple enough. When one party introduces evidence that, if left unan-

---

55. However, the cross-examiner must have grounds to believe the event he asks about did occur. Otherwise, he cannot ask the question. Note that if the witness, in this case Herbert's mother, is unaware of the event, her direct testimony is weakened.

56. *See* United States v. Benedetto, 571 F.2d 1246, 1250 (2d Cir. 1978) ("trial judge has broad discretion to admit extrinsic evidence ... even if ... [the testimony contradicted] concerned a collateral matter").

swered, would mislead the jury, the opposing party is entitled to meet the evidence with rebuttal "inadmissible" evidence. The party who first introduces a line of proof waives his right to keep out her opponent's counter evidence.

In its traditional and most common form, curative admissibility is allowed where one party, without objection, introduces inadmissible evidence and his opponent is subsequently allowed to counter it with inadmissible evidence. The party who first introduces an improper line of proof is said to have waived any objection to her opponents "inadmissible" rebuttal evidence. (Of course, the rebutting party bears some responsibility, for he failed to object).

A variation of the curative admissibility doctrine occurs when *over objection* the first line of evidence is allowed. Later, the objector presents "inadmissible" rebuttal evidence to counter his opponent's earlier evidence. If the judge concludes that the rebuttal evidence is admissible, she will overrule an objection. But what if the judge concludes that the rebuttal evidence is inadmissible? Some judges will exercise discretion and allow at least some counter evidence on the ground that permitting at least some rebuttal evidence achieves the fairest adversarial balance. In other words, allowing at least some rebuttal evidence is a better means of protecting the rebutting party than simply ruling that he must stand solely on his earlier (overruled) objection. Of course, when the "curative" evidence is admitted, the usual result is to render harmless any error the judge may have made when she permitted the initial line of proof. The objector has now had a chance to rebut that proof with counter evidence, so he usually cannot successfully complain on appeal.

In the Illustration, let us again assume that the prosecutor did not object to the mother's direct testimony. The judge might determine that the defense "opened the door" to at least some rebuttal (extrinsic) evidence. Much would depend on how effective the prosecutor's cross-examination was. For example, the judge might determine that without at least some extrinsic counter-evidence, the jury would be left with the erroneous expression that Herbert was a devoted husband and father. The curative evidence doctrine imparts a measure of discretionary leeway in the adversary system and, along with Rule 403 and Rule 611,[57] leavens the structural rigidity of a detailed evidence code.

The main point about impeachment by contradiction is this: on cross-examination, counsel can seek to have a witness express doubt or retract his testimony on a minor point. But the introduction of extrinsic evidence to contradict a witness on a collateral

---

57. FRE 611 gives the judge "reasonable control over the mode and order of interrogating witnesses and presenting evidence...."

point is usually disallowed.[58] Thus, if a witness testifies that she was returning from church when she saw the accident in question, the cross-examiner can ask in good faith, "Isn't it true that you were actually returning from a nude Sunday-morning swim with your boyfriend?" However, if the witness denies the tryst, the cross-examiner will have to "take the answer" on cross. This does not mean that the examiner cannot press the witness; it only means that extrinsic evidence is ordinarily inadmissible if its only value is to impeach this witness on a minor (collateral) point. And, again, a rough guide for determining whether a point or topic is collateral is to ask whether it is relevant to the proof of some consequential fact in the case or whether its *only* relevance is to contradict the witness. Ultimately, however, a trial judge should decide the admissibility of extrinsic evidence on a so-called "collateral" point by applying Rule 403.

Sensory Impairments

Here we speak of various impairments that hinder a witness's ability to accurately observe, remember, and relate. The sensory defect may range from a mild impairment (the witness wasn't wearing her glasses) to total incapacity (psychosis). Common impairments are poor eyesight, defective hearing, intoxication, drug use, or memory loss. Although the focus is usually on the witness's condition at the time of the event in question, issues about a witness's capacities can also arise when she is called to testify. (The communication of an earlier sensory perception may be impaired.) For example, some event, such as memory loss, or a debilitating psychological condition may have intervened between the witness's observation and her proffered testimony, or the witness may be under the influence of drugs at the time of her testimony.[59] The

---

58. Assume the accused is prosecuted for a robbery that took place in Seattle on June 14. His defense is alibi and in support of it, R, a restaurant owner, testifies that on the night of the robbery the accused—a regular patron—had dinner in R's restaurant in Portland. On cross, the prosecutor presses R on the frequency of the accused's visits to R's restaurant, which employed the accused's girlfriend. R testifies that he thought the accused had been in the restaurant every night for two months. Later in the trial, the prosecutor proffers X to testify that he saw the accused in Seattle a month before the robbery; and that he also spoke with the accused, who said he had been in Seattle for a couple of days.

Assume the accused does not deny that he sometimes travels to Seattle, but

does deny that he was in Seattle on the night of the crime. Should the trial judge disallow X's testimony as an attempt by the prosecutor to introduce extrinsic evidence on a minor or collateral point? The Supreme Court of Washington thought so, noting that X's testimony, even if believed, does not place the accused in Seattle on or even near the date of the robbery. See State v. Oswalt, 62 Wash.2d 118, 381 P.2d 617 (1963). Today, in the federal system and most state jurisdictions the issue would be decided under Rule 403. No matter which way the trial judge ruled, it is doubtful that she would be reversed on appeal.

59. An issue that sometimes arises is whether a witness may be impeached by

availability of extrinsic evidence to prove a sensory defect is controlled by Federal Rule 403. The general practice is to permit extrinsic evidence unless the witness's admission during cross-examination renders unnecessary any further proof.

Psychiatric Condition

Some mental illnesses, often not apparent to the trier of fact, affect a witness's credibility. For example, a mental condition might impair a witness's capacity to perceive accurately or to testify truthfully. In rare cases, the judge may order a potential witness to submit to an examination by an impartial physician. Usually, however, the question before the court is whether a witness may be impeached by existing evidence of a mental illness that could affect his credibility. An expert witness, knowledgeable about the disease in question and its probable impact on credibility, is ordinarily essential to the introduction of psychiatric evidence. Since this form of impeachment is usually time consuming (and embarrassing to the witness), courts use it sparingly. Three considerations are particularly influential: (1) the nexus, according to medical authorities, between the alleged mental condition and testimonial accuracy; (2) the importance of the witness's testimony; (3) the time involved in receiving the psychiatric evidence.

Impeaching a Hearsay Declarant

We have seen that the hearsay rule applies only to statements that are proffered to prove the truth of the assertions contained within them. Since the trier is asked to believe the hearsay declarant, the credibility of the declarant is important. Federal Rule of Evidence 806 allows the credibility of a hearsay declarant to be attacked by the same impeachment techniques that are available to discredit a testifying witness. In practice, there are minor differences. For example, if the hearsay defendant is unavailable as a witness, she cannot be asked about her prior bad acts (bearing on credibility) during cross-examination. Thus, this method of impeachment presumably would not be available since extrinsic evidence of a prior bad act (not resulting in a conviction) is ordinarily inadmissible.

---

showing she is addicted to alcohol or drugs. That is, although counsel has no evidence that the witness was under the influence of an intoxicating substance at the time of the event (or at trial), she does have evidence of the witness's general addiction. Rule 403 is the governing evidentiary provision. The general practice is to exclude evidence of addiction. *See* United States v. Ramirez, 871 F.2d 582, 584 (6th Cir. 1989). *But see* United States v. Lochmondy, 890 F.2d 817, 824 (6th Cir. 1989) (limited inquiry into heroin addition permissible).

Abusing Impeachment

Suppose counsel knows that a particular witness, *W*, will give unfavorable testimony. However, counsel has identified an inconsistent statement, made by *W* on a prior occasion, that is favorable to counsel's client. Assume the prior inconsistent statement would be inadmissible hearsay if offered for its truth. However, as we have seen, a prior inconsistent statement is normally admissible not for its truth, but the limited purpose of impeaching the witness who made it. In the present setting, however, there is a risk of abuse. Counsel should not be allowed to call a witness for the sole purpose of impeaching him by a prior inconsistent statement. Herein lies the vice: if the lawyer knows the witness will give unfavorable testimony, then his reason for calling the witness must be to reveal the latter's prior inconsistent statement. Although we are assuming the prior statement can only be introduced for the purpose of impeachment, there is a risk the jury may use it for the truth of its assertion—which is exactly what the lawyer must intend. In short, counsel should not be permitted to call a witness for the purpose of eliciting testimony he does not want the jury to believe and then to introduce the witness's prior statement (ostensibly only to impeach) which he does want the jury to believe. This practice is condemned in both criminal and civil cases; the remedy is to disallow the impeachment by prior statements.

Accrediting the Witness (Rehabilitation)

The starting point for this discussion is the basic principle that the credibility of a witness may not be supported in the absence of an impeaching attack on his character. Federal Rule 608(a) makes this general principle clear. The assumption is that most witnesses are conscientious and honest, so there is no reason to prolong the trial by receiving evidence pertaining to credibility when truthfulness has not been questioned. Not all of the impeachment methods we have discussed provide a justification for additional evidence designed to accredit or rehabilitate the witness. The question is whether the impeaching evidence strikes at the witness's character for truthfulness or merely suggests that she is mistaken. The dividing line is not sharp, and much depends on context.

Generally speaking, when the attacking party impeaches by prior conviction, prior bad acts, or reputation (or opinion) evidence showing an untruthful character, the party supporting the witness is entitled to respond with evidence designed to bolster the witness's credibility. At the other extreme, when the attacking party questions the witness's perception—for example, by evidence of a sensory defect—or memory, he is not assailing the witness's character. Occupying the middle ground are impeachment techniques such as bias, prior inconsistent statements, and contradiction. Here the trial judge must decide if the tenor of the impeaching evidence strikes at the witness's character for truthfulness. In most, but not all instances, these methods of impeachment are not accusations that the witness is consciously lying. It is important to note, however, that the supporting party is always entitled to use redirect examination to try to rebuild the witness's credibility. The witness may, for example, refute the impeaching evidence, recharacterize it, or offer a benign explanation.

ILLUSTRATION

Zeke, an African–American, is prosecuted for the robbery of a jewelry store. Just as the robber, who was wearing a mask and gloves, was dropping rings, watches, and other items of merchandise into his satchel, a police siren sounded. As the robber ran out of the door to the sidewalk, muscular, athletic Passerby pulled off the robber's ski mask. As Passerby was about to wrench the satchel away from the robber, the latter shot him in the leg and escaped down an alley.

At trial, Passerby is one of the prosecution witnesses. He testifies that he cannot be certain that Zeke was the person running out of the jewelry store. He does state, however, that the robber was a young black male, about six feet. (Zeke fits this description.) On Cross, Zeke's defense attorney asks, "Isn't it true that after the robbery you told Officer Clack that the robber was Hispanic?" Passerby's response is a denial: "No, I said the robber's skin color was light enough for him to be Hispanic, but that he was African–American."

Later in the trial, the defense calls Officer Clack, who reluctantly admits that when he interviewed Passerby, an hour after the robbery, the latter had told him that the robber was "Hispanic—rather young and about six feet tall." Still later in the trial, the prosecutor presents, Curtis, one of Passerby's friends who belongs to the same health and fitness club as Passerby. Curtis is prepared to testify that he returned from vacation about ten days after the robbery. The day after his return, he and Passerby worked out together, and Passerby described the robber as "fairly young, around six feet, and a black guy." Should the judge sustain a defense objection to Curtis's testimony?

Passerby has, of course, been impeached by the introduction of his prior inconsistent statement. The impeaching evidence, furnished by Officer Clack, was proper, although at some point Passerby should be afforded an opportunity to respond to Clack's testimony.[60] Note, also, that the judge was correct in receiving extrinsic evidence (Clack's testimony). On cross, Passerby refused to admit that he had previously said that the robber was Hispanic, which means that Officer Clack's testimony was not redundant or superfluous. Furthermore, since Passerby's testimony addresses a central point—the identity of the robber—the rule that forbids extrinsic evidence on a collateral topic has no application.

The prosecutor's attempt to rehabilitate Passerby by introducing the latter's prior consistent statement will probably fail. Had the defense attorney charged or insinuated that Passerby had recently fabricated his trial testimony or was responding to some improper influence or motive, the prior consistent statement would be admitted *if an important condition were met.*[61] It would be essential that the prosecutor convince the judge that the prior consistent statement predated the alleged influence, motive, or recent fabrication.[62] If this foundation is provided, the prior consistent statement has heightened relevance in that it has probative value to show that Passerby was not responding to a corrupt or improper stimulus. (He made an earlier statement (to Curtis) that is consistent with his testimony and the prior statement *predated* the alleged influence or fabrication.) In the Illustration, however, the defense attorney simply impeaches Passerby with a prior inconsistency. The trier of fact now has before it Passerby's testimony and evidence of a prior statement inconsistent with that testimony. Producing evidence that Passerby also made a statement consistent with his testimony adds very little: the trier already has before it two conflicting accounts of the robber's race.

In the foregoing Illustration, Passerby denied that he had ever said that the jewelry store robber was Hispanic. Note that one way to rebut impeaching evidence is to produce evidence that the impeaching evidence is false and should not be believed. Counsel may attempt to negate the impeaching evidence during redirect examination or—unless the impeaching evidence is forbidden because it pertains to a minor point—by producing extrinsic evidence. For example, if a witness is impeached by evidence that he was intoxicated at the time he observed the event in question, supporting counsel can offer evidence that the witness was sober. If the witness is impeached by opinion evidence that his character for truthfulness is bad, supporting counsel can offer an opinion witness to testify to the principal witness's good character for truthfulness.

---

60. FRE 613(b).

61. The Federal Rule in point is 801(d)(1)(B). If this rule applies, the prior statement is also admitted for its truth. See the discussion in Ch. XI, § 6.2.

62. *See* Tome v. United States, 513 U.S. 150, 156–60 (1995).

A second means of attacking impeachment evidence is to produce evidence that rebuts *the inference of untruthfulness* from the impeaching facts. Suppose, for example, the witness is impeached by evidence that eight years ago he was convicted of a crime that casts doubt on his credibility. Supporting counsel might respond by producing evidence that the witness currently has a good reputation for truthfulness. Obviously, this rebuttal strikes not at the impeaching fact (the conviction), but rather at the inference of untruthfulness that can be derived from the impeaching fact.

This second means of rebutting impeachment evidence—countering the inference of untruthfulness—often raises issues of relevance. If, for example, impeachment is by evidence of bad reputation for truthfulness, rebuttal evidence that shows the witness has made prior statements consistent with her testimony usually has little or no probative force. The courts would reject it for the obvious reason that the witness's prior assertions may also have been false. A similar result can be expected when the witness is impeached with evidence of bias, and supporting counsel seeks to accredit the witness with evidence of prior consistent statements. Unless these previous accounts predate the alleged inception of the bias, they fail to negate the inference to be drawn from the impeaching evidence. On the other hand, if the evidence of bias involved corruption or dishonesty, the witness's character has been assailed and opinion or reputation evidence that suggests the witness's good character for veracity should be admitted.

Chapter X

PRIVILEGE

Table of Sections

§ 10.1 Rationale and Characteristics

As we have seen, the law of evidence generally seeks accuracy in factfinding by receiving relevant evidence thought to be reliable, while rejecting evidence deemed untrustworthy. Recall, however, that some of the specific evidentiary rules of relevance, such as those that prohibit evidence of post-accident remedial measures or offers of settlement,[1] are based on social or policy concerns. In other words, relevant evidence is rejected on the ground that an extrinsic policy is more important than the factfinder's consideration of the excluded evidence. Evidence that reveals a privileged communication bears a kinship to these specific relevance rules, in that extrinsic policies—rather than the law's search for truth—dictate the rejection of probative evidence.

Privileged communications are excluded because their disclosure would be inimical to a governmental interest or to a private relationship that courts and legislatures deem worthy of preserving or fostering. For example, the President of the United States has a privilege not to reveal communications that would compromise national security;[2] a client has a privilege not to reveal confidential communications made to her attorney.

---

1. See generally Ch. IV.

2. The President also has a qualified privilege that protects confidential com- munications with his subordinates. *See* United States v. Nixon, 418 U.S. 683, 708–09 (1974).

The cost of evidentiary privileges is apparent in the courtroom: probative evidence is suppressed, and the trier makes factual determinations without it. This means, of course, that the application of an evidentiary privilege increases the probability of an erroneous trial outcome. On the other hand, the benefits of conferring a privilege are difficult to measure. For example, confidential communications between husband and wife are privileged. It is fair to ask whether this privilege encourages spousal communications—which is said to be its immediate purpose. The answer here, as with many privileges, is uncertain. The most that can be said is that privileges rest largely on unproven assumptions; some of these assumptions are highly probable, others are highly problematic.

There are two justifications for the recognition of privileges. The principal rationale is utilitarian or instrumental: privileges are justified because their existence encourages behavior that is socially desirable. For example, the attorney-client privilege encourages full and candid revelations by the client, thus enabling the attorney to provide the appropriate legal advice. Furthermore, the existence of the privilege encourages persons who need legal advice to seek it. The second rationale for privileges rests upon notions of personal autonomy and privacy. Certain intimate relationships, such as those of husband and wife, priest and penitent, and lawyer and client, should be protected from governmental intrusion and prying.

A unique feature of evidentiary privilege is that the right to claim it belongs exclusively to the person or persons for whom the privilege was created—that is, the holder(s). The holder may be a party to litigation and thus conveniently situated to claim his privilege if he wishes. Sometimes, however, the holder is not a party litigant; in this event, none of the parties to the suit has standing, in his own right, to object to the introduction of privileged evidence. The claimant's right is reserved for the holder, who may or may not wish to exercise it. Nonetheless, a party or some other person is sometimes permitted to assert the privilege on behalf of the holder—as the holder's agent or representative. This is the case, for example, where the holder gives express authorization to someone else to claim the privilege on the holder's behalf; the same is true where authorization may be fairly implied, as it is when a lawyer invokes the attorney-client privilege on behalf of the client, who is the holder. In still other circumstances, the law may authorize a presiding judge to invoke a privilege on the absent holder's behalf.

Since a privilege is created to benefit the holder and only the holder can claim or waive it, there are occasional problems of standing to appeal rulings by the trial judge pertaining to privilege. There is no difficulty if the holder is a party: if he claims the privilege, but the judge erroneously denies the claim, the party-holder has standing to appeal this ruling. He has been harmed both as a party and as a holder. Suppose, however, the party is not the holder, but the holder (or someone on his behalf) asserts the privilege; nonetheless, the trial judge erroneously denies it. For example, suppose a witness who is not a party claims the privilege not to reveal a statement to her husband because it was a confidential marital communication. The judge, however, mistakenly denies her claim and orders that she disclose the statement. The communication disfavors the defendant who, after losing at trial, appeals the judge's ruling. The person whose rights were violated by the erroneous ruling is the holder of the privilege, not the complaining party. The result of the judge's error was to provide additional relevant evidence for the trier's consideration. Furthermore, reversing the judgment below does nothing to help the holder. (The communication in question has now been revealed.) A reversal only nullifies a judgment that, itself, is presumably sound, even though based on a fuller evidentiary record than it should have been. Thus, since the losing party has no standing to complain on appeal, the judgment below will be upheld.

Be careful, however, to distinguish a case in which the trial judge erroneously upholds a claim of privilege and *excludes* evidence pursuant to the privilege claim of a nonparty holder. In this instance, the trier of fact has been precluded from considering relevant, admissible evidence. The party who is disadvantaged by the judge's improper ruling *does* have standing to appeal. (He stands in the same position, for example, as a party who complains on appeal that the trial judge excluded evidence as hearsay, when it was not.) The appellate court can correct the lower court's error by holding that the claimed privilege was not applicable and a new trial should be held.

The various privileges share some other common features. For example, they may be waived either expressly or by implication as, for example, when the holder shares privileged information with an "outsider." If a client shows to her friend a copy of a "confidential" letter she has written to her attorney, she has probably waived the attorney-client privilege. In the context of discovery, a trial, or some other proceeding, failure to assert a privilege by a timely claim or objection constitutes a waiver. Most importantly, privileges protect communications from disclosure, *but they do not insulate* from discovery or disclosure at trial events or facts that *are the subject* of these communications.

ILLUSTRATION

Clyde, whose expensive luxury car is only two years old, has just been told by his mechanic that the car will soon need costly repairs. Doubtful that the mechanic is correct, Clyde (who is mechanically inclined) verifies for himself the imminent repairs. Since the manufacturer's warranty on the car has expired, Clyde decides to sell it without disclosing its defects.

Subsequently, the buyer sues Clyde and Clyde retains a defense lawyer. He tells his attorney about the mechanic's report and about his own confirmation of the impending mechanical failures. During discovery, the plaintiff's lawyer takes Clyde's deposition. He asks Clyde the following series of questions.

(1) Q: "Did you know this car had these [named] serious mechanical defects?"

(2) Q: "Did your mechanic, at Bosch Bros. Luxury Cars, inform you on June 3, 2005, that the car had these [named] defects?"

(3) Q: "Do you have mechanical skills?"

(4) Q.: "Isn't it true that on or about June 5, 2005, you personally verified that the car you sold to the plaintiff had precisely the defects and problems identified by the Bosch Bros. mechanic?"

Clyde's attorney objects to these questions on the ground that they call for responses that are protected by the attorney-client privilege. How should the judge rule?

None of these questions is improper, and Clyde must provide answers to each. The attorney-client privilege does not apply to facts or events that are the subject of, or described in, a confidential communication. If it did, there would be little or no evidence for the jury to consider. A client could simply relate all the relevant facts to his attorney and thereby insulate the client's knowledge of the underlying events from discovery. Of course, the attorney-client privilege does protect Clyde's *communications* to his lawyer. If it did not, these statements would be admissible as party admissions. The attorney-client privilege, and privileges generally, facilitate confidential communications by permitting socially desirable disclosures without penalizing the speaker. In the absence of a privilege, the speaker's communication would result in the creation of evidence that an opponent could use against her.

Finally, do not confuse privileges with various professional codes that obligate persons such as lawyers and doctors to preserve their clients and patient's confidences and secrets. Violating these ethical codes can lead to disciplinary action by the appropriate authorities. However, disclosures that violate a professional code are not barred from evidentiary use unless they also fall within a privilege.

§ 10.2 Privileges Under the Federal Rules of Evidence

In the 1970's when the proposed Federal Rules of Evidence were considered and amended in Congress, there was widespread disagreement about what privileges should be recognized and what should be their proper scope. Since Congress could not agree on the detailed privilege provisions that were contained in the proposed Federal Rules, a compromise was reached. Congress deleted the detailed privilege rules, which recognized nine privileges, and in their place passed a single rule, Federal Rule 501. It reads:

> **General Rule.** Except as otherwise required by the Constitution of the United States or provided by Act of Congress or in rules prescribed by the Supreme Court pursuant to statutory authority, the privilege of a witness, person, government, State, or political subdivision thereof shall be governed by the principles of the common law as they may be interpreted by the courts of the United States in the light of reason and experience. However, in civil actions and proceedings, with respect to an element of a claim or defense as to which State law supplies the rule of decision, the privilege of a witness, person, government, State, or political subdivision thereof shall be determined in accordance with state law.

The key phrase directs that "principles of the common law as . . . interpreted . . . in the light of reason and experience" shall determine the law of privilege in the federal courts. Of course, pursuant to the Supreme Court's decision in Erie Railroad Co. v. Tompkins,[3] federal courts often apply state common and statutory law. They do so, for example, in "diversity cases," that is, civil cases in which the federal courts have jurisdiction to entertain the litigation only because the parties are citizens of different states. Federal courts also apply state law in civil cases where the plaintiff's principal claim is based on federal law, but he "tacks on" a state law claim that arises from the same cluster of facts or related events that underlie his federal claim. Federal Rule 501 directs that in civil cases the state law of privileges shall apply to the trial of claims and defenses based on state law. Thus, if a plaintiff from Virginia sues a defendant from Delaware in a federal court in

---

3.   304 U.S. 64 (1938).

connection with an automobile collision that occurred in Virginia, the substantive law of Virginia would apply. The federal judge presiding over the case would also apply Virginia's law of privilege, including any Virginia laws that might defer to the privilege law of another state (*i.e.* Delaware). This diversity case is straightforward because it involves only *state* substantive law.

Suppose, however, a plaintiff sues a defendant in federal court and the plaintiff's claim is based on a federal anti-trust statute. Suppose further, the plaintiff appends a second claim based on state "unfair competition" law. The federal court can entertain the state claim by invoking its supplemental subject matter jurisdiction,[4] if the events giving rise to the state claim are the same as or closely related to the events that underlie the federal claim. The intertwining of facts supporting jurisdiction over both the federal and state claims make it likely that some witnesses will give testimony that is relevant to both claims. Suppose a witness whose testimony is relevant to both claims asserts a privilege. What happens when the state law of privilege is different from the federal law? For example, suppose state law confers a privilege on part or all of a witness's testimony, but federal law does not. Where the facts to which a witness will testify are relevant to both the federal and state claims, federal courts generally apply federal privilege law.[5]

§ 10.3   The Attorney–Client Privilege

We have seen that privileges rest uneasily in an adversarial system because they promote values that are unrelated to the general principle that disputes should be resolved on the basis of all reliable evidence. This tension suggests that jurisdictions are likely to vary somewhat in the number and scope of privileges they recognize; it also suggests that even within a single jurisdiction some privileges are more durable than others. And, in fact, these variations do exist. For example, in a particular jurisdiction a privilege may or may not be recognized; it may or may not survive the holder's death, or it may or may not be subject to a judicial override for good cause.

The privilege protecting communications between attorney and client is recognized in every American jurisdiction. It is firmly rooted and unqualified—that is, once it attaches, it is not subject to

4. 28 U.S.C. § 1367 is the "supplemental jurisdiction" statute.

5. *See* Pearson v. Miller, 211 F.3d 57, 66 (3rd Cir. 2000). The question is one of congressional intent, which in this instance is unclear. There is no doubt that if Congress intended federal privilege law to prevail, it could so provide. Congress has authority to provide rules of practice and procedure for the federal courts, and valid federal laws override conflicting state laws under the Supremacy Clause, Art. VI of the United States Constitution.

a judicial override. Furthermore, it can be claimed, even after the client's death, by her personal representative. The privilege rests both on privacy concerns and, more importantly, on a utilitarian rationale. As to the latter, the existence of the privilege encourages frank and full disclosure by the client, thus improving the quality of legal representation. Furthermore, since the existence of the privilege is widely known, it may encourage persons in need of legal advice to seek it. That said, it is still not easy to craft the proper bounds of the attorney-client privilege.

Here are some of the difficulties. The client may wish to conceal evidence, or hide his identity, or prevent disclosure of his whereabouts. Note that the protection of information like this is only tenuously connected to the purpose of the privilege—full and frank disclosure. Thus the privilege is generally inapplicable in situations like these. Another difficulty arises because, in the course of legal representation, lawyers and clients necessarily interact with a wide range of third parties, such as investigators, paralegals, accountants, physicians, and consulting attorneys. Thorny problems emerge in determining whether communications with and among these secondary actors fall within the boundaries of the attorney-client privilege. And numbers alone magnify the difficulty of marking the appropriate bounds of this privilege, especially when the holder is a business enterprise, such as a corporation, partnership, or other business association. Wide disclosure of "privileged" communications may suggest that the communications were not intended to be confidential or that even if the privilege initially attached, it has been waived. Special problems also exist when shareholders in a corporation sue management on behalf of the corporation—an increasingly common practice in American business life. In theory, the overriding purpose of management is to advance the interests of the stockholders. Yet management's interests can diverge, especially as between the managers and dissident minority shareholders. Should these "minority" litigants be able to defeat the corporate attorney-client privilege when management claims it? Other problems arise when a lawyer represents several clients on a common matter and they subsequently become adversaries, or when separately represented clients cooperate and pool their resources.

In resolving these and other problems, it is important to keep in mind the core objective of the attorney-client privilege: to promote full and candid confidential communications between client and attorney so as to facilitate the rendition of legal services. Obviously, judicial opinions and statutory enactments often elucidate the application of this core principle in various contexts. Additional guidance is provided by proposed Federal Rule 503. Even though neither this rule nor the other proposed privilege rules were adopted when Congress enacted the Federal Rules of Evidence in 1975, Congress made it clear that its decision to allow the law of privilege to evolve by judicial decision was not a disapproval of any of the proposed enumerated privileges.[6] Proposed Rule 503 is a carefully crafted, detailed provision, covering many aspects of the attorney-client privilege. It has been an influential "standard" in both federal and state courts and its influence has prompted greater uniformity across jurisdictional lines. You should be aware, however, that some differences in the scope of the attorney-client privilege do exist among the jurisdictions and this is particularly true among the various states. Thus, the following textual materials should be viewed as representing the position of most courts and, in particular, of most federal courts.

The Privilege Defined

Proposed Rule 503 broadly defines the attorney-client privilege. Subsection (b) states:

> **General rule of privilege.** A client has a privilege to refuse to disclose and to prevent any other person from disclosing confidential communications made for the purpose of facilitating the rendition of professional legal services to the client, (1) between himself or his representatives and his lawyer or his lawyer's representative, or (2) between his lawyer and the lawyer's representative, or (3) by him or his lawyer to a lawyer representing another in a matter of common interest, or (4) between representatives of the client or between the client and a representative of the client, or (5) between lawyers representing the client.

Proposed Rule 503 contemplates the protection of not only the direct communications between attorney and client, but also of communications between and among various representatives of each. The rendition of legal services often involves non-lawyer specialists such as investigators, physicians, economists, investment bankers, accountants, scientists, and mathematicians. It is important to note, however, that to be protected by the attorney-client privilege, these representatives must either be communicating to the lawyer (or his representative) or the client (or his representative) for the purpose of assisting the lawyer in delivering legal services. Proposed Rule 503(a)(3) affirms this observation by defining an attorney's "representative" as one who is engaged "to assist the lawyer in the rendition of professional legal services."

6. S. Rep. No. 93–1277, at 4 (1974).

ILLUSTRATIONS

Cusp. Associates is a dental partnership consisting of partners White and Phil and three employees: two hygienists and an administrative assistant. Recently, a successful elderly dentist ("Seller", age 68) has mentioned to friends that he has decided to retire at age 70 and to sell his dental business. Seller owns the modern building in which his office is located and he leases approximately half the square footage in this building to an accounting firm. He has told several of his friends and associates that he intends to sell the building, the one-acre tract on which it is located, all of his office furnishings and dental equipment, and his "goodwill." The asking price will be about four and a half million dollars.

Since Seller's dental office is just two blocks from Cusp. Associates, White and Phil are considering making an early bid. To that end, they decide to consult lawyers Todd and Sheila, who specialize in legal work for small businesses. At the initial consultation, the two potential clients discuss with the lawyers the possibility of buying the Seller's practice and moving their own practice into his larger and newer building; they also discuss the possibility of hiring a third dentist and maintaining two offices. One difficulty is that there is considerable animosity between the retiring dentist and partners, White and Phil. Therefore, the partners suggest that their identity as potential buyers remain secret. Near the conclusion of this initial consultation, the four participants discuss fee arrangements, the advantages and disadvantages of changing from a dental partnership to a professional or limited liability corporation, various ways in which the contemplated acquisition might be financed, and the general terms of a contract for sale. Overwhelmed by the complexities of the purchase, White and Phil say they need a "few days to think everything over" before they decide to go forward.

(1) Assume the two dentists abandon their tentative plan to acquire Seller's business. Assume further that Todd and Sheila provide an initial consultation to potential clients without charge. Only if they (the lawyers) are retained do they enter into a formal fee agreement with new clients. Are the initial conversations among White, Phil, Todd, and Sheila within the attorney-client privilege?

(2) Assume White and Phil decide to make an early bid on the Seller's dental business. Thus, they return to Todd and Sheila and engage them "to handle the whole transaction." Here are some of the events that follow:

(a) White and Phil send Cusp., Associates' [hereafter "CA"] latest financial statements to Todd and Sheila. In order to expedite delivery, CA's administrative assistant puts the relevant statements in a file, marks the file "confidential," and hand-delivers it to the dental firm's new lawyers.

(b) Sheila personally contacts the managing partner of the accounting firm that currently leases half of the building owned by Seller. In the privacy of the partner's office, they discuss the general terms of the accounting firm's current lease, whether the accountants may need additional space, the probability that the accountants will want to renew their lease, and their willingness to accept a clause that ties the rent to the rate of inflation.

(c) Todd and Sheila engage Real Estate Associates to conduct "a highly confidential appraisal" of Seller's lot and office building. The firm is to consult tax records, compare the selling price of comparable property, evaluate the soundness of the building, calculate its total and usable square footage, gain access to the interior by using some pretext such as seeking accounting or dental services, and, finally, the firm is to prepare a confidential report, summarizing findings, to be delivered to Todd and Sheila.

(d) Todd and Sheila dispatch a young associate from their law firm to the offices of White and Phil. There, over lunch with the two dentists, their hygienists and their administrative assistant, the associate describes and explains a bill pending in the state legislature that, if passed, would change the tax liability of business partnerships.

(e) Subsequently, the bill is amended and passed. The young associate prepares a memorandum in which he discusses and analyzes the potential tax liability of CA if, (a) it remains a partnership and if, (b) it becomes a professional corporation. This memorandum is delivered to Todd, who reviews it and forwards a copy (marked "confidential") to White and Phil.

(f) Later, with the assistance of Todd and Sheila and the Seller's attorney, CA ("Buyer") and the retiring dentist ("Seller") close the deal. However, the real identity of White and Phil is not revealed. Instead, the contract of sale is signed by Seller and "Dental Associates, P.C." a corporation controlled by White and Phil. The contract calls for a certified check at closing. It also contains a number of conditions, one of which is that the Seller agrees to allow an accountant or other financial expert retained by the Buyer (Dental Associates) to conduct an in-depth financial analysis of the Seller's dental business. A copy of this report is to be delivered to Seller's attorney. Since this report could affect the final selling price, the Seller is given 75 days to have his own report prepared. If the parties thereafter fail to agree, an arbitrator will be appointed.

(g) The bank that is financing the Buyer's purchase insists that White and Phil have adequate life and health insurance. Thus, both men undergo a thorough physical conducted by a Dr. Brooke. The doctor sends a copy of his confidential report to the bank, with copies to White, Phil, Todd and Sheila.

Suppose, prior to closing, Seller learns the true identity of the buyers. Thereafter, the deal sours as animosity develops and the contracting parties accuse each other of misrepresentation and bad faith. Subsequently, Seller brings suit for breach of contract, naming as defendants CA, Dental Associates, PC, and White and Phil as individuals.

Which, if any, of the conversations and documents described in Illustration (2)(a)–(g) are protected by the attorney-client privilege?

The attorney-client privilege is available not only to individual clients, but also to partnerships, various business entities (such as associations and corporations), and to governmental officers and agencies. Proposed Rule 503(a)(1) defines "client" as a person or entity "who is rendered professional legal services by a lawyer, or who consults a lawyer with a view to obtaining professional legal services from him." The availability of the privilege is not dependant on the payment of legal fees or on a formal contract between client and attorney. The language of Proposed Rule 503(a) ("[consulting] a lawyer with a view to obtaining profession legal services") confirms the well-established principle that the privilege applies to an initial attorney-client consultation, even if the client[7]

---

7. If the privilege did not apply, the client seeking the benefit of the privilege would be in the awkward position of having to retain the lawyer before re-

(or the attorney) declines representation. Although the initial conversations between the dental partners and their attorneys addressed some topics that, viewed in isolation, related primarily to business (as opposed to legal) matters, these subjects were intimately associated with the rendition of legal services such as the structure of the combined dental offices and the general terms of a contract for sale. When rendering legal services to a business, lawyers often require information about the business enterprise itself. The context for providing legal advice or legal services must be fully developed in order for the consulting attorney to give the appropriate legal advice. If these "business disclosures" are intended to be confidential (often they are not) and if the disclosures are made for the purpose of seeking legal advice or to aid the lawyer in rendering legal services, the attorney-client privilege applies.[8] Thus, the privilege probably attaches generally to the communications in Illustration (1), and it certainly attaches to some of them, such as the terms of the contract of sale and the possible legal restructuring of CA's business. Generally speaking, if a client consults a lawyer for the purpose of receiving legal services, the confidential communications between them are privileged, even though some of the communications, viewed in isolation, appear to be unrelated to legal advice or services. The key factor is the purpose of the consultation.

Although the attorney-client privilege was initially formulated to protect only the client's confidential communications, modern courts recognize that the privilege also applies to the attorney's confidential communications. The client's statements and the attorney's statements often interlock. If the privilege did not attach to the attorney's statements, her disclosures could often be used to infer at least the general content of the client's confidential communications to the attorney. This is especially true when the attorney renders legal advice based on what the client has told her. Thus, considerations of both practicality and preserving confidentially have prompted courts to apply the privilege to the confidential communications of both client and attorney.

In Illustration (2)(a), the partners provide their lawyer with financial documents pertaining to the partnership. First, the fact that these documents were delivered by the client's agent should not affect the existence of the attorney-client privilege. A client may use agents or representatives, such as secretaries or designated

---

vealing his legal problem. Also, the lawyer would be in the equally awkward position of having to agree to represent the client before knowing the facts giving rise to the client's legal difficulties.

8. Most courts apply a "dominant-purpose" test which requires that the lawyer's work for or advice to the client be primarily legal (as opposed to business). *See, e.g.*, Sedco Intl., S.A. v. Cory, 683 F.2d 1201, 1205–06 (8th Cir. 1982), *cert. denied*, 459 U.S. 1017.

spokespersons, to communicate confidentially with the attorney (or with the attorney's representative) on behalf of the client. A client might even designate an examining physician as his appointed representative to convey the client's physical or mental condition to an attorney, provided of course, this information was for the purpose of securing legal advice or services. If the client has a practical need for a representative or spokesperson and if caution is exercised so as to ensure confidentiality, the attorney-client privilege is applicable.

However, the attorney-client privilege *does not apply* to letters, documents (such as CA's financial statements), or other inscribed items that were not prepared for the purpose of facilitating legal services. If the rule were otherwise, a client could place "preexisting" documents beyond the reach of discovery by the simple expedient of turning them over to her attorney. Furthermore, the fact that such documents are useful to the lawyer is beside the point. Of course, if the client prepares a confidential letter to the attorney telling him, for example, how to interpret the documents or suggesting trends reflected in the data contained in them, this letter would be protected by the privilege.[9] Furthermore, if an attorney gives confidential legal advice to a client that is based on the attorney's review or analysis of unprotected documents, the *communication from the attorney* to the client is protected by the privilege.

In Illustration (2)(b), the privilege should not apply. The accountant is neither a representative of the client, nor of the attorney. Furthermore, content of the communications appears to be addressed predominantly, and perhaps solely, to business concerns—whether, and under what conditions the accounting firm would renew its lease.

Students of civil procedure may recall the so-called "work-product" doctrine, traceable to the Supreme Court's decision in Hickman v. Taylor.[10] Although that decision concerned the recognition of the doctrine in federal courts, it is generally recognized among the states. In recent years, the central features of the doctrine have often been codified in a rule of court or statute. Federal Rule of Civil Procedure 26(b)(3) sets forth the basic rules of work-product; subsection (b)(4) extends the work-product doctrine (or at least its rationale) to experts engaged by a party to assist in trial preparation. Generally speaking, the work-product doctrine extends *conditional immunity* from discovery by an opponent to written materials prepared in "anticipation of litigation." Typically,

---

9. We are assuming, of course, that the documents and cover letter are transmitted primarily for a legal, not a business purpose.

10. 329 U.S. 495, 510–11 (1947).

the protected materials are prepared by the lawyer, but materials prepared by others—such as an investigator, agent, consultant, or the party himself—are also conditionally immune. Familiar examples of a lawyer's work-product would be his notes about a witness's statement (or his recording of a witness's statement) or his investigator's recorded measurements of skid marks at the scene of an automobile accident. Like the attorney-client privilege, the work-product doctrine protects the *materials or communications* generated by the lawyer, or by a client who is a party to a suit, or by a representation of either. However, the work-product doctrine *does not protect the client's knowledge*, which includes facts known to his attorney who is his agent. In other words, the client would have to answer an interrogatory: "How long were the defendant's skid marks?" Furthermore, the court may order discovery of work-product materials if the party seeking them shows a substantial need or, in the case of a *consulting* expert (who does not testify), exceptional need. The requisite showing of need varies with the particular context and is affected by the discovering party's ability to secure unprotected evidence that is the substantial equivalent of the materials sought.

Suppose in Illustration (2)(b), Sheila had made notes of her conversation with the managing partner of the accounting firm. Of course, it is uncertain whether the notes would have any bearing on a subsequent suit between Seller and Buyer. Even if the notes were material to subsequent litigation, they probably would *not be conditionally protected* by the work-product doctrine. That doctrine would apply *only* if Sheila could convince the judge that she prepared the notes "in anticipation of litigation."[11] This seems highly unlikely since, when the notes were made, there was no indication of forthcoming litigation.

Illustration (2)(c) presents a close question and the answer is uncertain. The issue is whether Real Estate Associates is a "representative of the lawyer" as that phrase is used in Proposed Rule 503 (a)(3). One qualifies as a lawyer's representative only if engaged "to assist the lawyer in the rendition of professional legal services."[12] This is a contextual judgment requiring more information than is included in the Illustration. Sheila and Todd would have to convince the judge that the legal advice or legal services rendered to the client depend upon the condition and market value of the target property. There are some plausible possibilities. For example, perhaps the terms of the contract of sale, or advice as to tax considerations, or the business form[13] of CA are closely linked to value of Seller's real property. That said, a judge might nonetheless

11. Fed. R. Civ. Proc. 26(b)(3).
12. Proposed FRE 503(a)(3).

13. For example, whether to remain a partnership or to incorporate.

rule that the dominant purpose of the realtor's report was to inform the lawyers and their clients about market values—a business concern. Observe, again, that the work-product doctrine would apply to the realtor's report (which was commissioned by the clients through their attorney) *only* if it were prepared in anticipation of litigation—not the case here.

In Illustration (2)(d), the associate is clearly a representative of the lawyers, since his communications bear on legal matters. The problem is with confidentiality. The informal occasion, attended by all of the dental firm's employees strongly suggests that either there was no intention to keep the luncheon communications confidential or, even if there were such an intention, the presence of third parties—the hygienists and assistant—nullified the intended privilege.

Illustration (2)(e) involves, first, a communication from an attorney's representative (the associate) to the attorney, and, second, a direct communication from attorney to client. The communication is clearly legal in nature, and the requisite confidentiality is maintained. This context should be distinguished from one in which a lawyer simply prepares a client's income tax return and the client supplies the necessary financial information. This information would not be privileged. The mere preparation of an income tax return is not legal in nature; indeed most income tax preparers are not attorneys.[14] On the other hand, tax lawyers routinely render legal services, creating many occasions on which communications from their clients (and their communications to their clients) are within the attorney-client privilege.

While in some circumstances, an accountant or financial expert could be a representative of an attorney (or of a client), in Illustration (2)(f) the parties agree that the report of the financial auditor will be shared by the Buyer and Seller. Thus, the attorney-client privilege is inapplicable. There is a second point to be made: note that Todd and Sheila create a corporation controlled by their clients in order to shield White and Phil's identity. The lawyers would have an attorney-client relationship with both CA and the new entity, Dental Associates, P.C.

Incidentally, a question sometimes arises as to whether the name of a client is protected by the attorney-client privilege.[15] For

14. Section 7525 of the Internal Revenue Code extends the attorney-client privilege to confidential communications between a taxpayer and a tax preparer who is authorized to practice before the IRS, but the protection applies only to a "communication . . . [that would be privileged] if it were between a taxpayer and an attorney."

15. Similar questions arise with respect to whether a client has consulted an attorney and what fee arrangements have been made. These incidental subjects, usually unconnected to the facts on which legal advice is based, are nor-

example, a grand jury or the IRS invokes a process such as a summons or subpoena addressed to a lawyer, demanding the identity of the lawyer's client. In most cases, the client has no intention to conceal her identity. Furthermore, concealing a client's identity seldom advances the purpose of the attorney-client privilege—full disclosure. Even if a client desired anonymity, sound public policy usually militates against granting it. Occasionally, however, protection of a client's identity is justified, as when a whistleblower seeks legal advice in connection with revealing wrongdoing or when revealing the client's name would disclose the general content of a confidential communication.[16]

Illustration (2)(g) appears to be far afield from the concerns underlying the attorney-client privilege. The communications in question essentially concern business arrangements between White and Phil, on one hand, and the bank on the other. The bank is not a "representative" of either the client or the attorney, as that term is used in Proposed Rule 503(a). The copies to Todd and Sheila serve to keep them informed, but insofar as the Illustration reveals, are not the basis for giving legal advice or rendering legal services.

The Corporate Client and the Attorney–Client Privilege

Suppose that the client is a corporation (or other business entity) and that the communication in question is made by a corporate officer or employee to the corporation's attorney. Because the corporation can speak only through individuals, the question often arises as to whether the corporation—the client and holder of the privilege—is the communicant. Depending on the context and a particular court's view of the proper scope of the attorney-client privilege, the statements of the official or other employee could be either, (1) communications from the corporate client and within the corporation's privilege or, (2) statements of an officer or employee who is speaking as an individual witness and whose communications are not within the corporation's privilege. Note that if the privilege extends far down into the corporate personnel structure—to middle management or even below—the reach of the privilege may unjustifiably hinder the efforts of an opponent to support his claim or defense. The evidentiary loss occasioned by increasing the number of *corporate* spokespersons (and hence enlarging the scope of the privilege) seems at once obvious, though quite difficult to

mally outside the attorney-client privilege for essentially the same reasons that the identity of the client is unprotected.

16. For example, in United States v. Liebman, 742 F.2d 807, 809–10 (3rd Cir. 1984), the IRS was pursuing taxpayers who had used certain tax shelters thought by the IRS to be illegal. The Service issued a summons that directed a law firm to name all clients who had paid fees for legal services in connection with establishing or using such shelters. Held: the identity of the clients is privileged because their identity reveals the substance of their communications.

measure. (Recall that even if the privilege applies, the officer or employee must reveal what he knows about the event in question, but *not* what, on behalf of the corporation, he told the attorney or the attorney's representative about it.)

The potential informational loss to the adversary may be generally surveyed by comparing the corporate client to the individual client. In the individual setting, the party opponent may depose her adversary-client or call him as a witness and thereby secure valuable information. The individual client is usually very knowledgeable. But in the corporate setting, pertinent information may be widely diffused or fragmented—impossible to trace to just one or two employees or middle managers within the corporate structure. Yet knowledge of the *composite* facts may reside with only a few persons, such as high-level corporate officials who, themselves, may have little or no first-hand knowledge of the events in question. Often, the composite facts are embodied in a document, or a series of related documents. If these materials are protected by the attorney-client privilege (for example, because they were prepared for an attorney's use in connection with a legal matter) they are beyond the opponent's reach. Furthermore, individual communications directly to the attorney from middle and lower-level employees might also be protected by the corporate attorney-client privilege. It is true, of course, that discovery procedures require that the corporate party to a lawsuit disclose (for example, by interrogatories)[17] what it "knows" of the facts, including the names of any employees with knowledge about the events in question. Nonetheless, gathering facts from a large corporate adversary can be a formidable task.

An expansive application of the attorney-client privilege— which is absolute and not subject to judicial nullification—complicates the opponent's evidence-gathering task. It also makes it difficult to discover discrepancies between what a corporate employee says (in a deposition, for example) to his opponent and what he told the corporate attorney or, perhaps, what he told a representative of the corporate client or a representative of the corporate attorney. If the employee is "speaking for the corporation" and his confidential statement is made directly to the attorney (or the attorney's representative) or is clearly destined to reach the attorney, (without unnecessary disclosures), the corporate privilege probably applies. Observe, also, that the corporate attorney is rarely the individual speaker's lawyer, so the informant *cannot usually claim for himself* an individual attorney-client privilege.

The application of attorney-client protection in the corporate setting often strains some of the basic doctrines of privilege law,

---

17. *See* Fed. R. Civ. Proc. 33(a).

rooted as they are in the context of the individual client. The requirement of confidentiality, for example, meshes poorly with the layered structure of the large corporation, where statements may be passed through many hands before reaching counsel or counsel's advice may be widely shared within the corporation. In addition, the often indistinct boundary between legal and business advice is likely to be perplexingly blurred in the corporate context, and this is especially true as to communications between a corporate spokesman and in-house counsel. On the other hand, the modern corporation could not realize the full potential of legal advice without some application of the privilege. It, like the individual client, needs to communicate freely and fully with its attorneys, preferably through the corporate agents with the most knowledge. The problem, therefore, is one of drawing a line that sensibly balances the corporation's need for an attorney-client privilege and the opponent's need for fair access to evidence generated within the corporate structure. The extremes are easily recognized and managed. Clearly protected is a confidential communication from the CEO to the attorney, made for the purpose of receiving legal advice for the corporation. Clearly unprotected is a routinely prepared statement by a lower-level employee, made in the normal course of business, but subsequently sent to the corporate attorney. The difficulties lie in the shadowy area between these polarities. For communications within this area, two general tests have been devised.

Some states still adhere to the "control-group test." Under this test, the privilege attaches only if the corporate officer speaking with the attorney is vested with authority both to seek legal advice for the corporation and to participate significantly in the corporation's response to the attorney's recommendations. The analogy is to the individual client, who can obtain legal advice and then, if he wishes, tailor his conduct consistently with that advice. The problem with this approach in the corporate context is its heavy reliance on the formal delegation of corporate authority. If the person who speaks with the attorney is an officer within the upper tiers of management, he probably "speaks for the corporation." (Of course, it is also necessary that he be empowered to participate significantly in the corporate response to the attorney's legal advice.) Often, however, the high-level corporate spokesperson is not the individual who is fully informed about the matter in question. The attorney will nearly always want to speak with corporate officers and employees who are the most knowledgeable, yet these persons may be outside the circle of upper level empowered to "speak for" the corporation. Although their statements to the attorney may gain qualified protection through the application of the work-product rule (if litigation is anticipated), the unqualified protection of the attorney-client privilege is not available. Thus, from a functional standpoint, the rigidity of the control-group test can have a distorting effect on the choice of corporate spokespersons.

The second approach to the corporate attorney-client privilege is often referred to as the "subject-matter test." It was adopted for the federal courts in Upjohn Co. v. United States,[18] and is the prevailing approach in many states. The facts before the *Upjohn* Court were these: the Upjohn Corporation, through its general counsel, undertook an investigation to discover whether the company made "illegal" payments to certain foreign governments. Subsequently, the IRS issued a summons demanding production of files pertaining to the investigation, including questionnaires prepared by counsel and answered by various corporate managers. The IRS also demanded records of interviews between counsel and some Upjohn managers. The Court noted that in the letter accompanying the questionnaires, Upjohn's Chairman of the Board stated that the investigation was under the direction of counsel, that responses were highly confidential, and that the completed questionnaires should be returned to counsel.

The Court then turned to the question of what approach should guide federal judges in determining the scope of the corporate attorney-client privilege. It rejected as too restrictive the control-group test, in part because of its focus on formal corporate authority. Although the Court declined to announce "a broad rule" to supplant the test it rejected, it did significantly clarify privilege law in the corporate context. In brief, the *Upjohn* approach would allow the privilege when the facts showed that: (1) the communication in question was pursuant to a corporate purpose to obtain legal advice, (2) the communication "concerned matters within the scope of the employee's corporate duties," (3) the employee knew that he was making a confidential statement and was doing so as part of his employer's efforts to secure legal advice or services, and (4) the statements were kept confidential or disclosed on a limited basis consistent with maintaining the privilege.[19]

The last requirement—limited disclosure—can apply in two contexts: disclosure *within* or *outside* the corporate firm. Since corporations depend heavily upon information, there is a practical need that corporate records be accessible to those individuals or groups who need access. Yet, there is always a risk that information collected under the umbrella of the attorney-client privilege may be so widely shared that the privilege is lost. Generally, privileged communications should be disclosed only to person who need access, and care should be taken to ensure that these persons under-

18.   449 U.S. 383 (1981).

19.   Id. at 394–95.

stand the need to maintain confidentiality. If privileged documents are kept in a general filing system, access should be restricted.

Voluntary disclosures outside the company pose an even greater risk of waiver. Here, it is important to ensure the person or firm to whom disclosure is made be a "representative" of the client or of the lawyer.[20] Common sense dictates the importance of signaling the confidential nature of the disclosure through the use of labels, cover letters, or other precautionary measures.

Since litigation often deals with events that occurred several or more years before suit was filed, some of the employees or officers who gave privileged communications on the corporation's behalf may have died or left the company. Their departure from the corporate staff does not affect the availability of the privilege. A closer question attends *post-employment* statements by a former employee to corporate counsel (or her representative). In his concurring opinion in *Upjohn*, Chief Justice Burger suggested that the privilege did embrace these statements[21] and the Fourth Circuit has so held.[22] Obviously, the subject matter of the former employee's statements to counsel should be restricted to events or conditions within the scope of the ex-employee's former duties. Additionally, the other requirements of *Upjohn* must be satisfied.

Several other issues surrounding the corporate attorney-client privilege warrant brief mention. As we have seen, the holder of the privilege is the corporation. The privilege can be waived only by management; sometimes the board of directors will reserve for itself the right to claim or waive the privilege. The power to waive resides with the current board, regardless of when the privileged communications were made. Finally, as we shall see below, on a proper factual showing, the board can lose control of the privilege to the shareholders themselves.

Shareholder suits ("derivative suits") are a common feature of corporate America. In these suits, a group of disaffected shareholders sues corporate management on behalf of the corporation, typically on grounds of self-dealing or some other breach of fiduciary duty. Who should control the privilege in this setting? If the board maintains control, many of their communications will remain impervious to shareholder discovery. On the other hand, well-intentioned managers may communicate with counsel less freely if they believe the corporate privilege can be easily stripped by minority stockholders in a derivative action. Clearly, if the trial judge finds that the communications in question furthered a crime or fraud, the privilege should give way. Beyond this, the best reasoned cases

---

20. Proposed Federal Rule 503(a)(3), (4).

21. *Upjohn*, 449 U.S. at 403.

22. In re Allen, 106 F.3d 582, 605–06 (4th Cir. 1997).

discourage frivolous suits, but allow shareholders to defeat the privilege for good cause. The trial judge considers such factors as the plaintiff's need, the seriousness of the alleged misconduct, the plausibility of claims that wrongdoing occurred, the number of shareholders joining as plaintiffs, and the availability from other sources of the evidence sought.[23] Note that this flexible approach creates an exception to the general rule that once the attorney-client privilege attaches, it is absolute and cannot by overcome by judicial "balancing" of factors peculiar to the case before the court.

Duration of the Attorney–Client Privilege

Traditionally, courts have held that the attorney-client privilege survives the death of the client. It can be claimed by the executor or some other proper successor in interest. In 1998, the Supreme Court endorsed this principle for the federal courts.[24] The Court was persuaded that if the privilege was not durable, at least some clients would be inhibited in their communications with counsel. For example, "[c]lients may be concerned about reputation, civil liability, or possible harm to friends or family."[25] This support for the traditional rule forecloses for the federal judiciary two possible alternatives for which quite plausible arguments have been made: (1) the privilege does not survive death or, (2) courts should undertake a case-by-case determination of whether the privilege should survive death.

There is, however, one situation in which courts agree that the privilege will be terminated. In disputes between persons claiming property or an entitlement through the decedent—"disputes among insiders," so to speak—claims of privilege by the executor or other successor (such as next of kin) are rejected. Suppose, for example, one group of disputants claims under the decedent's will, the other group, by intestacy. Various combinations of claimants can be imagined, but the point is that relevant communications otherwise within the privilege are subject to disclosure. The privilege is inapplicable "regardless of whether the claims are by testate or intestate succession or by inter vivos transaction."[26] The deceased would probably approve of the privilege's termination, since the resulting evidence will shed additional light on the property distribution he favored.

Special Situations: No Privilege or Privilege Waived

Judicial systems in free societies adhere to the principle that every person, guilty or not, is entitled to a fair hearing and

23. *See* Garner v. Wolfinbarger, 430 F.2d 1093, 1100–04 (5th Cir. 1970), a leading case.

24. Swidler & Berlin v. United States, 524 U.S. 399, 410–11 (1998).

25. Id. at 407.

26. Proposed FRE 503(c)(2).

adequate representation by counsel. As a consequence, communications about *past* crimes are shielded to allow lawyers and clients to communicate freely and plan legitimate defenses. Yet the system is subverted, and the privilege properly lost, when lawyer-client communications advance criminal or fraudulent activity. The *client's* objective is the determinant and the privilege does not attach if he "sought or obtained [the attorney's services] to enable or aid anyone to commit or plan to commit what the client knew or should have known to be a crime or fraud."[27]

It is not always easy to determine if the crime-fraud exception applies. For example, the client's communications may disclose past misdeeds, but also allude to concealment or contemplate some future illegality. The party who seeks to negate the privilege must provide the judge with evidence of a prima facie case—that is, evidence which, if believed, would suffice to defeat the privilege. Thereafter, pursuant to the Supreme Court's decision in United States v. Zolin,[28] the judge can conduct an in camera review to determine if the privilege is applicable. There is some authority expanding the crime-fraud exception to embrace other forms of future illegal behavior, such as willful torts.[29]

Certain relational problems between the lawyer and the client can defeat a privilege that initially attached. When a client sues her lawyer for malpractice, for example, the lawyer can use relevant confidential statements to defend herself. Similarly, if a client refuses to pay his attorney, she can support her claim for fees with confidential information. In other words, the privilege is suspended as to any "communication relevant to an issue of breech of duty by the lawyer to ... [her] client or by the client to his lawyer."[30]

In a related context, a client waives his privilege if he asserts an affirmative defense of "reliance on advice of counsel"[31] or calls his attorney as a witness. And, of course, a client may also forfeit the privilege by voluntarily authorizing disclosure of confidential materials. You should, however, distinguish the cases where an intruder seizes confidential lawyer-client materials or an eavesdropper overhears confidential conversations. If the client has taken *reasonable precautions* to protect the communication in question, modern authority holds that the privilege is not lost.[32]

---

27. Proposed FRE 503(d)(1).

28. 491 U.S. 554, 568–75 (1989).

29. *See* Commodity Futures Trading Comm. v. Weintraub, 471 U.S. 343, 354 (1985) (collecting authorities).

30. Proposed FRE 503(d)(3).

31. *See, e.g.,* Chevron Corp. v. Pennzoil Co., 974 F.2d 1156, 1162–63 (9th Cir. 1992).

32. *See* United States v. Noriega, 917 F.2d 1543, 1550–51 (11th Cir. 1990). Older cases would deny the privilege if unauthorized disclosure took place, thus placing the entire responsibility on the client to prevent access by eavesdroppers or other intruders. Modern technology has increased the means of eavesdropping, making it unfair to hold the

It sometimes happens that several clients with a common problem retain a single lawyer or firm to represent them. For example, one lawyer may represent both A and B in a matter of joint or common interest, such as their purchase of real estate or their common dispute with an insurance company. The rule in such situations protects the statements of both clients and those of the lawyer. It seems plain enough that, as against outsiders, *each client* is entitled to claim the privilege as to statements *she has made*, as well as to the attorney's responsive statements. But can client A invoke the privilege (as against outsiders) so as to prevent disclosure of B's statements to the attorney as well as the attorney's responsive statements to B? The courts split on this question. The issue usually does not arise because A and B have a common objective and thus each is likely to claim the privilege or agree to waive it. However, should they disagree, most, but not all courts, allow each client to control the waiver of her communications, at least in situations in which her disclosure does not also reveal the content of confidential communications from the non-waiving client.

In subsequent litigation in which A and B, having fallen out, become adversaries in litigation, the rule is that privilege is lost as to all of their statements. (Here, no "outsider" is involved.) First, when they were joint clients, neither client intended that his communications be shielded from the other. Second, even if, say, A "secretly" communicated with the attorney, the communication would not be privileged as to B because the attorney would have an ethical duty to share it with her other joint client.[33] Proposed Rule 503(d)(5) states that in an action between persons who were formally joint clients, there is no privilege as to communications "made by any [of the joint clients] . . . to a lawyer retained or consulted in common. . . ."

You should, however, carefully distinguish joint-client arrangements from "pooling" or "common-interest" arrangements. In the latter, two or more clients, *each with his own attorney,* agree to pool or share information in order to conserve resources and mount a more effective case—either a defensive or an offensive one. These allied clients have both a mutual and an individual interest: they are sharing information (and perhaps resources) with respect to their common interests, yet each participating client is represented by his own lawyer or firm. These sharing arrangements would seldom materialize if outsiders could successfully argue that confidential disclosures within the composite group lost the protection of the attorney-client privilege because dissemination went beyond the

client or his attorney strictly responsible for any improper disclosures.

33. *See* Henke v. Iowa Home Mut. Casualty Co., 249 Iowa 614, 87 N.W.2d 920, 924 (1958).

several or more individual attorney-client units that comprise the pool. Thus, it is not surprising that courts protect the confidential communications of separately represented parties who pursue a common legal objective. Protection under the common-interest doctrine applies only if the parties claiming the attorney-client privilege can show that they have agreed (orally or in writing) to assume an allied position. It is thus advisable for the parties to a pooling arrangement who wish to protect the attorney-client privilege—and most parties do—to enter into a formal, preferably written, agreement.

Suppose some members of a common interest or pooling arrangement subsequently become adversaries in litigation. Most courts sensibly hold that in pooling arrangements, the attorney-client privilege is available to each of the adversaries. That is, each litigant may claim the privilege as to his own disclosures made during the pooling arrangement. If this were not the rule, candid disclosures would sometimes be discouraged. Furthermore, the fact that each client in the pool has provided for his own separate representation is evidence that his interests are not entirely congruent with those of the other participating clients.[34] Thus, in the context of a common, cooperative undertaking, he has done all he can to protect his own communications.

§ 10.4 Spousal Privilege for Confidential Communications

This "spousal" or "confidential communications" privilege protects private communications between *married*[35] partners. The most frequently invoked justification for the privilege is that it encourages marital partners to share their innermost thoughts and secrets, thus adding to the intimacy and mutual support that strengthens marriage. This rationale is not convincing. It is probably safe to assume that most married couples are unaware of the privilege. Unlike most privileges, this one does not involve a professional such as a doctor, lawyer, or clergyman who is schooled in a particular privilege and can give advice about its existence. Furthermore, even on the improbable assumption that the existence of the privilege is widely known among marriage partners, it is doubtful that it has a significant impact on the flow of information between them.

Justification of the privilege may, however, rest upon a different footing. There is much to be said for the notion that certain

---

34. The Advisory Committee Notes to Proposed Rule 503 acknowledge that some disjunction of interests is likely to exist among those in a pool of clients who nonetheless continue to insist on separate representation.

35. A valid common law marriage will suffice.

aspects of one's private life should be free from public disclosure. This is especially desirable in light of today's diminished privacy in general and the wide availability of sophisticated electronics that can collect, store, and transmit private information. The invasion of marital communications is an indelicate and distasteful undertaking that should be carefully circumscribed.

The privilege for marital communications can be simply stated: it extends to any *confidential* statement made *between spouses* during the existence of a legal marriage. The general rule is that courts will not inquire into the "quality" of the marriage, although some recent decisions hold that communications made after a formal or permanent separation or after one spouse has filed for divorce are not privileged.[36] In other words, some courts are now willing to look for objective evidence that the marriage is not viable. All courts agree that communications made after the marriage is terminated by divorce are outside the protection of the privilege. Nonetheless, those confidential communications made during marriage retain their privileged status.

The scope of the privilege is restricted: it protects only "confidential communications." Unless a third person is present when a marital communication is made, a rebuttable presumption arises that it was intended to be confidential. However, if a third person (including the couple's child) capable of understanding the communication is present, the privilege does not attach, even if the spouses did not want their communication revealed. "Communications" are written or verbal statements, as well as gestures (such as a nod of the head or a hand signal) that are intended to substitute for words.[37] Some state courts go further and broaden the privilege to include noncommunicative actions–such as unpacking firearms–of one spouse in the presence of the other, at least where it reasonably can be inferred that the actor-spouse did not want his activity revealed. This extension of the privilege is ill conceived; if this kind of observation deserves protection at all, that protection should be afforded by the other spousal privilege, discussed in the next section.

The courts have carved out exceptions to the confidential communications privilege. First, the privilege does not attach to a marital communication that addresses an ongoing or future crime. Here, the interests of the public and third persons (the victims) are paramount. Most courts limit this exception to instances in which both spouses are implicated in the criminal activity.[38] Second, the

---

36. *See* United States v. Porter, 986 F.2d 1014, 1019 (6th Cir. 1993), *cert. denied*, 510 U.S. 933 (1993); United States v. Treff, 924 F.2d 975, 982 n.11 (10th Cir. 1991), *cert. denied*, 500 U.S. 958 (1991).

37. *See, e.g.*, United States v. Estes, 793 F.2d 465, 467–68 (2d Cir. 1986).

38. United States v. Hill, 967 F.2d 902, 911–12 (3rd Cir. 1992). *Compare* United States v. Short, 4 F.3d 475, 479

privilege is nullified with respect to communications that pertain to a past or planned crime against immediate family members, such as a spouse or child. Third, the privilege will not attach if the spouses *fail to exercise reasonable care* to ensure confidentiality and their communications are overheard or intercepted by an eavesdropper.

The question often arises whether only the communicating spouse is the holder of the privilege. After all, it is he or she who made the statements in question. If the holder is willing to waive, perhaps she should be free to do so unless the disclosure of her communication would indirectly reveal the probable content of the other spouse's communication. In theory, the purpose of the privilege is to encourage her communication; now she wants to waive it. Some cases flatly declare that the speaker is the sole holder of the confidential communications privilege. However, in the federal system[39] and in many states, substantial authority vests the privilege in both spouses. Thus, if both are holders as to every confidential communication between them, both must waive before the protection of the privilege is lifted.[40]

§ 10.5 The Spousal Testimonial or Incapacity Privilege

This privilege, variously called the "testimonial privilege," the "incapacity privilege" or the "privilege against adverse testimony" is recognized in the federal system and in most states. It is usually confined exclusively to criminal proceedings such as trials and grand jury investigations. The privilege is based on society's aversion to using judicial compulsion in a criminal proceeding to place spouses in an opposing posture that may weaken or destroy their marriage.

The focus of the testimonial privilege is on one spouse (the "witness-spouse") giving *adverse testimony* against the other in a *criminal proceeding* when the couple *are married at the time* the prosecutor *seeks to call* the witness-spouse. Generally speaking, in these circumstances the holder (or holders) can claim the privilege, thus preventing the witness-spouse from taking the stand.[41] Under the majority view, the availability of the privilege is not dependent on the source or timing[42] of the witness-spouse's knowledge. Rath-

(7th Cir. 1993) (since wife unaware of illegality, privilege applies).

39. *See, e.g.,* United States v. Montgomery, 384 F.3d 1050, 1058–59 (9th Cir. 2004).

40. Recall, however, that the privilege is not available as to communications relevant to a spouse's commission

of a crime against his (her) spouse or immediate family.

41. The privilege should be claimed before the witness-spouse is sworn in; if not, the court may rule that the privilege has been waived. It is clearly waived if the spouse begins her testimony.

42. A minority view refuses the privilege as to matters pre-dating the mar-

er, the privilege is concerned with the *negative effect* on the marriage of her (or his) adverse testimony during the marriage. Thus, the privilege has no application if a spouse is called to the stand to give favorable testimony. Furthermore, when she testifies on direct, she is subject to cross-examination like any other witness. She may, however, be able to resist some cross-questions on the ground that answering them would reveal a confidential marital communication or exceed the scope of direct examination. Notice particularly that whereas the privilege for marital confidential communications is selectively claimed during testimony, the testimonial privilege, when applicable, keeps the witness-spouse off the witness stand.

In the federal system, the leading case setting the contours of the privilege against adverse testimony is Trammel v. United States,[43] decided by the Supreme Court in 1980. In *Trammel*, the Court overturned a sizeable body of federal precedent[44] and adopted the rule that the witness-spouse is the sole holder of the privilege. (Some state courts adhere to different views and hold that the accused is the holder or, alternatively, that both spouses are holders). The Supreme Court reasoned that in cases in which one spouse is willing to testify against the other, the marriage is probably beyond repair. It followed from this assumption that the witness-spouse should be the sole holder.

Doubts have been raised about whether the *Trammel* rule affords adequate protection of the marriage when both spouses are implicated in a crime. The prosecutor can then offer lenient treatment to one spouse, but only on the condition that she give adverse testimony against the defendant-spouse. This hard choice ("testify or go to prison") undermines *Trammel*'s point that if one spouse is "willing" to testify the marriage is, for practical purposes, already over. Under some federal decisions, this question about the possible viability of the marriage becomes moot: in some, but not all, federal circuits, the testimonial privilege is not available if the trial judge finds (out of the jury's presence and by a preponderance of the evidence) that both spouses were involved in the charged crime.[45]

There is an occasional problem when, just before trial or just prior to the expected testimony, the accused marries the potential witness. The holder then claims the testimonial privilege. If the trial judge is convinced that the marriage is a ruse or sham, she can declare the privilege inapplicable. However, the artificial nature of

---

riage. *See* United States v. Clark, 712 F.2d 299, 302 (7th Cir. 1983).

43. 445 U.S. 40 (1980).

44. In earlier cases, the Supreme Court had adopted the minority rule that *both spouses* were holders and either could claim the privilege. *See, e.g.,*

Hawkins v. United States, 358 U.S. 74, 77–79 (1958).

45. *Clark*, 712 F.2d at 300–02 (privilege not available if both spouses participated). *Contra,* In re Koecher, 755 F.2d 1022, 1024–28 (2d Cir. 1985).

the marriage is not always easy to discern, as in one case where the newly-weds had lived together for two years before judicial proceedings began and they were married.[46] A scattering of federal case law endorses a minority position that refuses recognition of the adverse-testimony privilege if the acts or conduct under interrogation predated the marriage.[47] While this approach avoids the "sham-marriage" problem, it erodes the purpose of the testimonial incapacity privilege because it pits against each other spouses who are lawfully married (perhaps for many years) at the time of trial.

We have already noted that some courts refuse the testimonial privilege if both spouses participated in the charged offense. The privilege is uniformly denied if the accused spouse is charged with a crime against the witness-spouse or their children. Thus, in domestic violence cases the adverse testimony privilege is usually unavailable, and the prosecutor can call even a reluctant spouse to testify.

ILLUSTRATION

Henry and Anne's relationship was stormy at times, although they have lived together, relatively happily, for almost three years. Two subjects have occupied center stage in most of their arguments: Anne's attraction to Thomas (which infuriated the jealous Henry) and Henry's dismal failure to help provide adequate income to sustain the couple. Eventually, in the face of Anne's threat to leave him, Henry promised to provide for the two of them, and in the next several months he earned a surprising amount of money as a "salesman." Unbeknownst to Anne, Henry was making and selling methamphetamine ("Ice"), a profitable activity until Henry was arrested and indicted. Two weeks prior to his arrest, however, Henry confided in Anne and revealed the details of how he and a friend were making and selling "Ice."

After Henry's arrest, he pleaded with Anne to marry him. She agreed and the two were married in a civil ceremony held near the cell in which Henry was incarcerated, awaiting trial. In the two months that intervened between Henry's marriage and his trial, Anne fell in love with Thomas, although their relationship was hidden from everyone, including Henry, who received frequent visits from Anne. On the eve of trial, however, Anne told the

---

46. *See* In re Grand Jury Proceedings No. 84–5, 777 F.2d 508, 509 (9th Cir. 1985) (adverse testimony privilege upheld).

47. The leading minority case is *Clark*, 712 F.2d at 302. The better and majority view is adopted in United States v. Lofton, 957 F.2d 476, 477 (7th Cir. 1992).

prosecutor she would testify against Henry. When Anne was called to the stand, Henry's attorney objected, citing both the spousal testimonial (incapacity) privilege and the spousal privilege protecting confidential communications. How should the judge rule?

The privilege that protects marital confidential communications applies only to communications made during a legal marriage, so it has no application to premarital communications. The availability of privilege against adverse testimony in a criminal prosecution poses a closer question. In the federal system and some states, the witness-spouse is the sole holder and can claim or waive the privilege as she wishes. Thus, in these jurisdictions, Anne may testify against Henry over his objection. In states that hold that the accused spouse is the sole holder or that both spouses are holders, the adverse-testimony privilege might apply. Since Anne was not a participant in Henry's illegal activity, the "joint-participant" exception (recognized by some state and federal courts) to the testimonial privilege is inapplicable. The prosecutor could argue that Henry and Anne's marriage was a sham, but this argument is weakened by the fact that they had lived together for three years. The prosecutor could also argue that as a practical matter their marriage is over, but this argument is weakened by the fact that the couple has not formally separated and neither spouse has filed for a divorce. The prosecutor's strongest argument is that Anne's love of Thomas and her willingness to testify against Henry provide ample evidence that her current marriage is over. In the *Trammel* case, the Supreme Court found the willingness of one spouse to testify against the other was ample reason to make the witness-spouse the sole holder of the testimonial privilege. Whether a jurisdiction that makes the accused a sole or joint holder would be swayed by Anne's willingness to testify, coupled with her affection for Thomas, is problematic. Probably, Henry's claim would be sustained.

§ 10.6 Psychotherapist–Patient Privilege

Effective psychotherapy depends upon a relationship of candor and trust between the patient and the therapist. Full disclosure by the patient is essential, and to encourage that disclosure the federal courts, as well as those of all the states, recognize a psychotherapist–patient privilege. This privilege was included in Proposed Federal Rule 504 which can serve as a "standard" for the development of federal common law. (As we have seen, federal common law usually controls the law of privilege in the federal courts.)[48] Pro-

---

48. FRE 501. Federal statutes or rules of court passed pursuant to statutory authority will supercede the common law, thus modifying the law of privilege.

posed Rule 504(b) describes the "general rule" governing the psychotherapist–patient privilege:

> A patient has a privilege to refuse to disclose and to prevent any other person from disclosing confidential communications, made for the purposes of diagnosis or treatment of his mental or emotional condition, including drug addition, among himself, his psychotherapist, or persons who are participating in the diagnosis or treatment under the direction of the psychotherapist, including members of the patient's family.

A number of persons, in addition to the patient, himself, can claim the privilege. Under Proposed Rule 504(c), these include his "guardian or conservator," and, in the event of the patient's death, his "personal representative." The psychotherapist who treated the patient may also "claim the privilege, but only on behalf of the patient."[49]

In Jaffee v. Redmond[50] the United States Supreme Court confirmed the existence of the psychotherapist-patient privilege in the federal courts and extended it beyond psychiatrists and psychologists to also include licensed social workers.[51] Moreover, the Court held that the privilege was unqualified, in the sense that it was not subject to judicial nullification through a case-by-case balancing test. The Court hypothesized that the cost of the privilege was minimal because, without it, patients would often refuse to make disclosures against their interests—thus, there would be no statement for possible evidential use. Moreover, even if some evidence were lost by recognition of the privilege, the existence of the privilege was thought to outweigh that loss because of the important private and public interests served by the privilege. The patient is usually helped, thus serving her private interest, and the public is also benefitted because "[t]he mental health of [the] citizenry, no less than its physical health, is a public good of transcendent importance."[52]

The precise dimensions of the federal psychotherapist privilege have yet to be fully developed. The privilege probably does not extend to social workers generally—they have many duties—but only to duly licensed social workers who are providing psychological

---

49. Proposed FRE 504(c). The psychotherapists' authority to do so is presumed. Id.

50. 518 U.S. 1, 15 (1996).

51. The specific issue was whether the plaintiff could discover communications between a police officer and a clinical social worker. The officer had sought therapy after she fatally shot the plaintiff's decedent.

52. Jaffee, 518 U.S. at 11.

therapy and counseling in roughly the same fashion as it would be offered by a psychologist or psychiatrist. And despite its unqualified nature, the psychotherapist privilege has exceptions. The Supreme Court recognized this in its *Jaffee* opinion, commenting it had no "doubt that there are situations in which the privilege must give way, for example, if a serious threat of harm to the patient or others can be averted only by means of disclosure by the therapist."[53] Proposed Rule 504 (d) lists three exceptions: hospitalization or commitment proceedings, a court-ordered mental examination, and litigation in which the patient asserts his mental condition as "an element of his claim or defense...." Courts are also likely to follow the lead of the First Circuit Court of Appeals and craft a future crime-or-fraud exception to the psychotherapist-patient privilege.[54]

§ 10.7 Physician–Patient Privilege

The privilege, almost invariably a creature of statute, is recognized in most states, but not by the federal courts. Of course, as we have seen, federal courts apply state privilege law to claims or defenses based on state law.[55] Variations among the states make generalizations about the physician-patient privilege rather hazardous. The privilege is usually justified on the now familiar ground that it is needed to ensure that a patient will speak candidly to his physician. Such candor, it is said, is essential to the physician's diagnosis and the patient's effective treatment. Whether a patient seeking treatment from his doctor would withhold information without the assurance of a judicial privilege is highly doubtful. A privacy rationale for the privilege provides a better fit: the intimate nature of communications about one's bodily condition justifies the law's assurance of confidentiality.

The essence of the physician-patient privilege is this: it applies when the patient is seeking *treatment* and it clearly covers communications between the patient and the doctor that are pertinent to diagnosis and treatment. Many jurisdictions expand the privilege to include information secured by the doctor through examination and tests. Note, however, that a patient's consultation with a physician for the purpose of securing a medical evaluation unrelated to treatment is usually outside the privilege. Thus, an examination to

---

53. Id. at 18 n.19. In the wake of Jaffee, several courts have recognized a "dangerous patient" exception. The temporal focus for applying this exception is the time when a demand by a court or other official body is made. For example, if a demand is made in connection with a proceeding to involuntarily commit the patient on ground of danger- ousness, the exception would apply. *See* United States v. Glass, 133 F.3d 1356, 1359 (10th Cir. 1998).

54. *See* In re Grand Jury Proceedings (Violette), 183 F.3d 71, 74–78 (1st Cir. 1999).

55. *See* FRE 501.

secure life insurance, a court-ordered examination, and an examination solely for the purpose of litigation are typically outside the boundaries of the privilege. And since the privilege rests upon either a policy of encouraging full disclosure or the protection of privacy, courts require that the information subject to the privilege be confidential—or at least so intended by the patient. However, courts are reasonable in their allowance of what persons may share the presumably privileged information without destroying its confidential status. For example, nurses and other medical personnel associated with the physician may share the confidential information. Even the presence of a close family member, attending the consultation in a supportive role, will probably not break the "circle of confidence." But the casual sharing of information with third parties before, during, or after the consultation will probably prevent the privilege from attaching or, if it has attached, result in its waiver.

Most jurisdictions allow the physician-patient privilege to survive the death of the patient. The privilege can then be claimed by a fiduciary (or, perhaps by the next of kin) acting on behalf of the patient who, during her life, was the *sole holder of the privilege*. This postmortem extension is not justified, for surely the right to claim the privilege after death is not essential to the realization of its principal objective—free disclosure. However, the harmful consequences of generally permitting the survival of the privilege are leavened by statutory provisions (or, sometimes, judicial constructions) that certain circumstances permit postmortem disclosure. For example, in actions by the estate or next of kin to recover money or property from third persons, as in the case of a wrongful death action, the privilege is lifted as to relevant doctor-patient communications. Furthermore, in suits where both litigants are claiming an entitlement or inheritance through the decedent (as for example, in a will contest) the privilege is lifted.

Even more telling are the numerous exceptions that apply during the lifetime of the patient-holder. Often, the privilege is withdrawn from criminal proceedings and even from certain civil proceedings such as workman's compensation, sanity, or child abuse hearings. Inroads into the privilege are also made by statutory provisions that compel physicians and hospitals to report to the proper authorities certain physical conditions such as gunshot wounds, venereal diseases, or the ingestion of controlled substances.

Sometimes, of course, the fragility of the doctor-patient privilege can be overcome by demonstrating that the physician-patient exchange is an integral part of the attorney-client privilege. That is, the physician is a representative of the client or the lawyer, and communications between the doctor and the patient are part of a larger network of communications "made for the purpose of facili-tating the rendition of professional legal services to the client...."[56] Here, it is essential to show that the medical consulta-tion between patient and physician was arranged by the client or the lawyer for the purpose of obtaining legal advice or services. If the attorney-client privilege applies, only very limited exceptions will defeat it.

§ 10.8 The Privilege Against Self–Incrimination: A Primer

Most readers are probably aware that the privilege against self-incrimination is a constitutional privilege contained in the Fifth Amendment of the United States Constitution. The privilege is founded on the principle that our system of government rests upon an accusatorial, not an inquisitorial foundation. Furthermore, as a practical matter, it is unseemly for the government to force one to incriminate himself, or lie, or remain silent and be subjected to contempt proceedings.[57] The privilege is enforceable against both the federal and state governments.[58] The applicable constitutional language reads, "No person . . . shall be compelled in any criminal case to be a witness against himself."[59] This provision (and the privilege it secures) is usually given extensive coverage in criminal procedure courses. However, the basic features of the privilege are often addressed in evidence classes, which accounts for this brief introduction.

The succinct constitutional language conferring the privilege suggests its outlines. It is concerned with "compulsion" in the context of a "criminal case" that induces a "person" to become "a witness against himself." Although "person" in some constitutional provisions means both individuals and business entities such as corporations, here it means just what the noun suggests—individu-als. And even though the context for the application of the privilege is criminal, the privilege is not limited to criminal trials. Any proceeding, civil or criminal, is within its embrace if official compul-sion is used in an attempt to coerce an individual to respond to inquiries that could eventually lead to her criminal liability.

56. Proposed FRE 503(b). A leading state case, pre-dating the Federal Rules of Evidence, is San Francisco v. Superior Court of San Francisco, 37 Cal.2d 227, 231 P.2d 26, 29–31 (1951).

57. *See* Murphy v. Waterfront Comm'n of New York Harbor, 378 U.S. 52, 55–57 (1964).

58. Although the Fifth Amendment originally applied only to the federal government, it (and most other liberties contained in the first eight amend-ments) was made applicable to the states through the "due process" clause of the Fourteenth Amendment which expressly applies to the states. The Supreme Court decision that "incorporated" the privilege against self-incrimination into the due process clause of the Fourteenth Amendment is Malloy v. Hogan, 378 U.S. 1, 6 (1964).

59. U.S. Const. amend. V.

If an individual is shielded from criminal liability, the privilege is not available. Thus, if one has been acquitted (or already convicted)[60] of the crime that is the subject of the official inquiry, the privilege does not attach. Similarly, if the statute of limitations for a particular offense has expired or the person claiming the privilege has been granted immunity from prosecution,[61] the privilege does not apply.

The privilege offers protection only from compelled *communicative* activity. It is not available where official compulsion is used to secure non-testimonial evidence, such as blood samples, other bodily fluids, or fingerprints. Nor does it apply to other non-communicative activity such as participation in a lineup or wearing certain items of apparel.[62] A suspect can also be compelled to speak for purposes of voice identification, or to provide a handwriting sample, so long as what is compelled is not a statement that is an incriminating assertion.

We noted above that only individuals, not separate business entities, are entitled to claim the privilege. Thus, a corporate officer or employee who is subpoenaed to turn over corporate records cannot decline to do so on the ground that the records would incriminate him. The subpoena is directed to the corporation and the individual producing the records is acting as a corporate agent. Since the corporation has no privilege, its records must be turned over to the proper authorities. Even preexisting records of an *individual* must normally be produced, for no compulsion attended their creation and their mere production is usually not a communicative act. The privilege also gives way when the government seeks records which it requires to be kept for *regulatory* purposes, at least when the records are regularly maintained and have a "public aspect" in that they serve a public interest and thus bear a resemblance to public documents.[63]

---

60. The double jeopardy provision of the Constitution, contained in Amendment V would prevent a second prosecution.

61. There are two kinds of immunity: "use" and "transactional." A potential criminal defendant prefers the latter, for it ensures that he will not be prosecuted for any part of the *transaction* to which his testimony relates. The more narrow "use" immunity shields the potential accused from the use of his protected ("immunized") statements in any future prosecution against him. Thus, when only use immunity is granted, the government might be able to

successfully prosecute the witness by using independent (non-shielded) evidence. Either kind of immunity suffices to compel testimony. *See* Kastigar v. United States, 406 U.S. 441, 457–58 (1972).

62. The principal case concerning non-communicative evidence is Schmerber v. California, 384 U.S. 757, 760–65 (1966) (blood sample). *See also,* United States v. Wade 388 U.S. 218, 222–23 (1967) (lineup) *and* Gilbert v. California, 388 U.S. 263, 266–67 (1967) (handwriting sample).

63. *See* Grosso v. United States, 390 U.S. 62, 68 (1968).

ILLUSTRATION

James Bradley is the sole proprietor of a small convenience store which, in addition to selling a variety of foods and beverages, sells lottery tickets. Law enforcement officials suspect that James is also engaged in an illegal bookmaking trade in which his customers phone in bets on various sporting events. On the basis of sworn statements from two disgruntled customers, the authorities obtain a subpoena to James for the production of all records prepared between January 1, 2003 and January 1, 2005 "containing statements, dates, figures, names, addresses, or other information pertaining to bets placed on any collegiate or professional sporting event." James's lawyer advises his client that unless the government grants James immunity, he can successfully resist production. Is the lawyer correct?

Since James is the sole owner of the convenience store, his business is distinguishable from other businesses such as corporations, partnerships, and labor unions which, as separate entities representing common interests, are not "persons" within the meaning of Fifth Amendment's privilege against self-incrimination. However, James's standing as a "person" to claim the privilege does not mean that he is entitled to it. While it is true that the records sought could subject James to criminal liability, the records in question were not subjected to official compulsion when they were prepared. Thus, unless the act of turning them over to the authorities—which is compelled—constitutes a communicative act, the privilege against self-incrimination is inapplicable.

If there were no dispute as to the existence of the records sought—which is usually the case—then producing the records is not incriminating, and is not protected by the privilege. Furthermore, if the government produced independent evidence of the existence of the documents sought, their location, and the identity of the party possessing them, and if the trial judge determined that this evidence was accurate, then production by the possessor probably would not be within the privilege. The argument against the application of the privilege is that delivering the documents sought would not constitute a communication of heretofore unknown incriminating evidence. The trial judge has made a factual determination, based upon independent evidence, that the government already possessed particularized knowledge of the existence, possession, and general content of the reports sought.[64] Even more

---

64. In United States v. Doe, 465 U.S. 605, 614 n.11 (1984), the trial judge found that the government had failed to "satisfy this court" that it had adequate independent proof of the "existence, possession and authenticity" of the

clearly, if the documents in question were discovered and lawfully seized during a proper search of the possessor's premises, the privilege has no application.

In the Illustration, there is no indication that the existence of the records sought was conceded by James or that the government had convincing proof of their existence. The government's knowledge, so far as the Illustration discloses, is based on the statements of several disgruntled customers who would be unlikely to have any knowledge about James's records. James's production of the records described in the subpoena would thus be communicative because it would affirm ("authenticate") the existence of the records, his possession of them, and their genuineness—in the sense that the records conform to the description contained in the subpoena. Therefore, the privilege against self-incrimination would attach.[65]

Several other features of the Fifth Amendment's self-incrimination clause should be noted. *First*, there is a difference in the way the privilege is applied to an accused, on the one hand, and a witness (not the accused), on the other. The privilege of the accused not to be a witness against herself has been construed to confer a right to remain off the witness stand—that is, the prosecutor cannot call the accused to testify. Nor can the prosecutor emasculate the privilege by forcing the accused to claim it in the jury's presence or by commenting to the jury that the defendant has refused to testify.[66] Of course, the defendant can waive the privilege and elect to testify. If she does, the privilege is lifted as to her testimony on direct and cross. However, the constitutional protection afforded by the privilege is probably determined by the non-constitutional evidentiary rule that prescribes the allowable scope of cross-examination. In the federal system and in a majority of states, "[c]ross-examination should be limited to the subject matter

"documents it sought". The Supreme Court took note of this determination and refused to disturb it. Therefore, one can draw the inference that had the government's proof satisfied the trial judge, the compelled production may not have offended the Fifth Amendment's self-incrimination privilege.

65. *See* Id. (privilege applies to government's attempt to compel production of various telephone, banking, and business records since government did not offer immunity and failed to show by independent evidence the necessary foundational facts). The other leading cases are Fisher v. United States, 425 U.S. 391, 397–98 (1976) (accountant's work papers producible) and United

States v. Hubbell, 530 U.S. 27, 34–38 (2000) (accused's disclosure of documents was communicative and prosecutor improperly used evidence to which the disclosure led him).

66. *See* Griffin v. California, 380 U.S. 609, 613–15 (1965) (privilege may be freely exercised and adverse comment by prosecution or judge's instruction that adverse inferences may be drawn from accused's failure to testify will not be permitted). However, in civil cases, when a party refuses to answer a question on Fifth Amendment grounds, there is no constitutional prohibition against adverse comment.

of the direct examination and matters affecting the credibility of the witness.''[67]

The prevailing practice is to determine the extent of the accused's waiver of her self-incrimination privilege by consulting the rule governing the scope of cross-examination. The reasoning is that the testifying-accused waives the privilege against self-incrimination to a degree co-extensive with the permissible scope of cross-examination. This is a bad rule for several reasons. First, it allows the accused to take the stand and restrict her testimony to just one or two features of the activity that constitutes the crime charged. Under the majority rule, the cross-examiner is limited to these same subjects. Presumably, the judge is powerless to exercise his ordinary authority over testimonial evidence and expand the scope of cross-examination beyond the boundaries set by direct examination.[68] Nor can the prosecutor later call the accused to the stand. Furthermore, and more fundamentally, a single constitutional standard should govern the extent to which an accused waives the privilege against self-incrimination when she elects to testify. A sensible constitutional waiver rule would hold that the accused waives the privilege as to the offense or offenses to which she testifies.[69]

A *second* notable feature of the self-incrimination privilege is that only the accused is entitled to avoid testifying altogether. In civil proceedings, and in criminal trials in which the witness is not the accused, the privilege must be selectively claimed. It is available to an ordinary witness (or a person served with an official process such as a subpoena) only if the witness's response would tend to incriminate him. The presiding judge must decide, on the basis of the interrogator's inquiry and all of the surrounding circumstances, whether the response sought would tend to incriminate the claimant. It is sufficient to sustain the privilege that the expected response, though not incriminating on its face, appears to form a part of the circumstantial evidence potentially available to convict the claimant or that the claimant's response may lead to incriminating evidence.

A *third* aspect of the privilege against self-incrimination concerns the obligation of one sovereign to respect a grant of immunity conferred on a witness by another sovereign. The starting point for the discussion is that an individual is entitled to claim the privilege

---

67. FRE 611(b).

68. FRE 611(b) states that the "court may, in the exercise of discretion, permit inquiry into additional matters as if on direct examination."

69. This rule also fits nicely with one of the current rules regarding waiver: it

is settled that when the prosecutor attacks the accused's credibility through impeachment by prior bad acts, the privilege against self-incrimination is available. See FRE 608(b).

if the answer or response sought by the government would tend to subject him to criminal liability under the laws of another sovereign within the United States. Suppose a federal prosecutor grants immunity to a witness who claims that (without immunity) his answer would be incriminating under the law of a state. A similar pattern emerges when a state prosecutor grants immunity to a witness on the ground that his response would be incriminating under federal law. These grants of immunity would be ineffectual unless the "other" (non-granting) sovereign had to respect the immunity granted. And, as indicated above, grants of immunity within the Unites States must be respected by other governments within the United States. This means, for example, that a grant of immunity by State *A* must be acknowledged by State *B* as well as by the federal government.[70] The non-granting sovereign is prohibited from using the immunized incriminating statements, and this prohibition includes using evidence ("fruits") *derived* from the incriminating testimony.

Of course, in the absence of a treaty or an executive agreement, a foreign country is free to prosecute an individual who has been given immunity from prosecution within the United States. This raises the question whether one can successfully claim the privilege in a proceeding within the United States on the ground that his response poses a danger of prosecution under the laws of a foreign country. After some years of uncertainty, during which lower federal courts were split, the Supreme Court resolved the issue in 1998.[71] The basis of recognizing an intergovernmental threat of prosecution in the United States is that all governmental units within this country are bound by the Constitution and, in particular, the Fifth Amendment. This is obviously not true of a foreign government, which suggested to the Court that the traditional (common-law) self-incrimination rule should apply: the privilege against self-incrimination is available only when there is a threat that criminal liability will be imposed by a sovereign within the United States.[72] The Court was also unpersuaded that expanding the privilege (thus often depriving prosecutors within the United States of relevant evidence)[73] would result in international arrangements that would compensate for this loss.

70. The leading Supreme Court case is Murphy v. Waterfront Comm'n of New York Harbor, 378 U.S. 52, 77–79 (1964).

71. *See* United States v. Balsys, 524 U.S. 666, 695–98 (1998).

72. Perhaps there would be a different result if legislation, a treaty, or an executive agreement make it clear that the United States and the other country involved were in close alliance and that the evidence sought would be turned over to the foreign country to facilitate a prosecution in which the United States was interested.

73. To assure immunity, the prosecutor would have to obtain the foreign government's agreement not to prosecute.

§ 10.9 Analyzing Privilege Law: A Suggested Approach

There are many other privileges, both public, such as the privilege ("state secrets") protecting sensitive military and diplomatic information, and private, such as the privilege (priest-penitent) protecting confidences between clergyman and parishioner.[74] Generally speaking, privileges share a common framework. Putting aside the privilege protecting against self-incrimination, privileges are usually designed to encourage the free flow of information between or among those persons within the protected circle. Of course, there are significant variations, but despite these differences, shared characteristics provide a common theme and suggest a common approach to the analysis of privilege law.

The initial step in this suggested approach is to discover the *purpose, rationale, or justification* for the recognition of the particular privilege. The accepted rationale usually provides arguments for or against its application in a particular case. Of course, sometimes there are several justifications for a single privilege, and these several purposes usually support multiple arguments for, or occasionally against, the attachment of a privilege in a specific set of circumstances.

Observe how the identification of the justification for a particular privilege leads naturally to an identification of the *persons within the protection of the privilege.* For example, the privilege may extend beyond the lawyer and her client to the representatives of each. Somewhere within the circle of protected persons is the holder (or holders) of the privilege and her identification is critical for only the holder(s) or someone authorized to act on her or their behalf can claim or waive the privilege. Finally, if the privilege in question does attach, it is necessary to determine *its duration.* Here, the inquiry focuses on such issues as whether the privilege survives death, whether it can be overridden by court order, and most importantly, whether it has been waived. The most common basis for waiver is disclosure of the privileged statements by the holder to persons ("outsiders") not within the protected circle.

---

74. Other notable privileges include a presidential (executive) privilege protecting confidential presidential communications, *see* United States v. Nixon, 418 U.S. 683, 708–09 (1974), and in an increasing number of states, a journalist's privilege protecting confidential sources, *see, e.g.,* N.J. Stat. Ann. § 2A:84A–21.1.

Chapter XI

EXPERT TESTIMONY AND SCIENTIFIC EVIDENCE

Table of Sections

§ 11.1   Introduction and General Principles

We have seen elsewhere, that a lay witness's opinion is allowed only if it is "(a) rationally based on the perception of the witness, (b) helpful to a clear understanding of the witness' testimony or the determination of a fact in issue, and (c) not based on scientific, technical, or other specialized knowledge within the scope of Rule 702 [governing expert testimony]."[1] In an effort to confine inference-drawing to the jury, common law judges unsuccessfully sought to distinguish "opinion" from "fact" and to enforce a rule that, with some exceptions, confined lay witnesses to "facts." The problem is that fact is distinguished from opinion only by specificity (concreteness) or degree. Thus, we might compare a statement that "he walked slowly and unsteadily, stooping so low that his long white hair almost touched the top of his cane," with a less specific one that "he was stooped and grey, and walked with a cane," and, finally, with an even less specific account that "he looked quite old and leaned heavily on a cane or walking stick." Other statements simply do not lend themselves to a "factual" breakdown: "He was speeding—probably seventy-five or eighty miles an hour." And still other statements may or may not be broken down into specific; "factual" or concrete components: "The teller, who at first looked

_____
1.   FRE 701.

359

calm, suddenly became terrified." Note that even if the witness could give a more concrete account of the teller's emotional state, her more vivid statement, somewhat tinged by personal inference, is probably quite helpful to the jury.

Even though in many common law courts today, all of the illustrative statements above might be admitted, the straightforward approach of Federal Rule 701 is much preferable to the common law's rigid categories of fact and opinion. The federal rule requires *rationality* and *helpfulness* to the end that the witness's account assists in promoting the clarity and understanding of her testimony or otherwise aids the trier in resolving a factual issue. Sometimes a short descriptive sentence or phrase is worth dozens of words: "He was dead drunk and when we reached the intersection; he didn't know which road led to the apartment." The trial judge administers the "lay opinion rule" by applying the criteria of Federal Rule 701. Her ruling is unlikely to be disturbed on appeal, for the standard of review is "abuse of discretion." Furthermore, an improper opinion by a lay witness is unlikely to have a significant enough effect on the jury's verdict to constitute reversible error.

§ 11.2   Role and Qualification of the Expert Witness

By definition, an expert witness possesses knowledge and skills that distinguish her from an ordinary witness. The expert is in a position superior to other trial participants, and in particular the jury, to draw inferences and reach conclusions within her field of expertise. She may gain that expertise though either education or experience or both. The point is that she has abilities that are not shared—or at least not fully shared—by lay persons. Thus, if a witness qualifies as an expert, she may render an opinion concerning subjects within her specialty. Even if she does not express her *opinion*, her testimony can still provide assistance to the trier of fact, for she can help *facilitate the understanding* of scientific or technical evidence.

When one of the parties presents a witness who will testify as an expert, the judge must determine whether she has the necessary qualifications. Before resolving that question, however, the judge must decide whether the subject matter to which the witness will address her testimony is sufficiently removed from common experience to qualify as specialized or technical. The trier of fact does not need an expert to testify that persons wearing gloves do not leave fingerprints,[2] or that compulsive gamblers characteristically mis-

---

2. *See* United States v. Booth, 669 F.2d 1231, 1240 (9th Cir. 1981) (expert's not permitted to testify that the reason no fingerprints were on the getaway car was because the occupants "had either

manage their finances.[3] In older cases, the courts often required that the subject matter in question be outside the reach ("beyond the ken") of the trier of fact, thus emphasizing the highly specialized nature of the subject. Modern courts are less demanding and require only that the expert's testimony *be helpful* to the trier of fact. When the subject concerns an aspect of such specialized fields as medicine, economics, statistics, science, engineering, or investment banking, there is usually no question about the legitimacy of expert opinion. But other, less technical subjects, such as burglars' tools, the effect on livestock of drinking salt water, bricklaying, strategies and code words used by drug dealers, trucking practices, and techniques for controlling motorcycles are also appropriate subjects for expert testimony.

Rule 702 of the Federal Rules of Evidence simply states:

> **Testimony by Experts.** If scientific, technical, or other specialized knowledge will assist the trier of fact to understand the evidence or to determine a fact in issue, a witness qualified as an expert by knowledge, skill, experience, training, or education, may testify thereto in the form of an opinion or otherwise, if (1) the testimony is based upon sufficient facts or data, (2) the testimony is the product of reliable principles and methods, and (3) the witness has applied the principles and methods reliably to the facts of the case.

§ 11.3 Background of Current Rule 702

Some background is necessary for a fuller understanding of Rule 702 which, along with Rules 701 and 703,[4] was amended in 2000. A persistent question under the original version of Rule 702 was how to determine whether proffered "scientific" evidence was sufficiently reliable to be admitted. The main battleground was the validity of the scientific principles on which the proffered expert based his opinion, although admissibility also hinged on the sufficiency of his facts, as well as his methodology in applying the scientific principles to the disputed issued in the case.

---

used gloves or wiped [off] the fingerprints").

3. United States v. Shorter, 809 F.2d 54, 61 (D.C. Cir. 1987), *cert. denied*, 484 U.S. 817 (1987) (trial judge properly excluded "expert" testimony that financial mismanagement is characteristic of a compulsive gambler).

4. Rule 701 was amended to ensure that the requirements for expert testimony in Rule 702 could not be evaded by having an expert testify as a lay witness. Rule 703 was amended to address the admissibility of evidence reasonably relied upon by the expert, but not independently admissible.

As to the validity of the underlying principles, an early federal case, Frye v. United States,[5] was widely recognized as setting the correct standard: a scientific principle or process will not be recognized in the federal courts unless it has "gained general acceptance in the particular field in which it belongs."[6] Most state courts accepted the *"Frye* Test" and some states continue to use it today. But the language of the original[7] (and current) Rule 702 does not appear to embrace *Frye,* for the rule speaks of "scientific, technical, or other specialized knowledge [that] will assist the trier of fact ...." Further doubt was cast on the continuing validity of *Frye* because the Advisory Committee Notes to Rule 702 failed to mention the *Frye* standard.

The unclear position of the Federal Rule, and its reference to assisting the trier, opened the way for renewed debate regarding the proper standard governing the admissibility of scientific evidence. Some courts and communicators feared that abandoning the *Frye* test in favor of a more liberal standard would result in admitting questionable and misleading "science" (so called "junk science"). Critics of *Frye,* including many courts, found its standard vague and hard to apply. (For example, when is a principle "generally accepted" in the relevant field?) More importantly, they pointed out that *Frye*'s demand for general acceptance requires a protracted waiting period during which a newly discovered principle or technique gains its footing. In the interim, courts are deprived of useful scientific evidence, even though the validity of the process or principle in question is accepted by leading professionals in the subspecialty in which the scientific innovation materialized. Not surprisingly, federal lower court opinions were in disarray.

The Supreme Court settled the debate, at least for the federal judiciary, in a 1993 case, Daubert v. Merrell Dow Pharmaceuticals, Inc.[8] There, two sets of parents and their minor children sued Merrill Dow for the children's birth defects, allegedly resulting from the mother's ingestion during pregnancy of Bendectin, an anti-nausea drug. The defendant presented experts who testified that on the basis of a large number of epidemiological studies and other scientific tests (such as animal studies) causation could not be established. The plaintiffs then offered their own experts to testify that based on a reanalysis of defendant's epidemiological studies, as well as several non-human studies, there was a causal link between Bendectin and the children's birth defects. The plaintiffs' evidence was rejected by the trial judge on the ground that it failed to meet

---

5.   293 F. 1013 (D.C. Cir. 1923).

6.   Id. at 1014.

7.   The Federal Rules, and thus the original text of Rule 702 became effective in 1975.

8.   509 U.S. 579 (1993). The trial judge's opinion in Daubert may be found at 727 F.Supp. 570 (S.D. Cal. 1989).

Frye's "general acceptance" test. The Ninth Circuit affirmed,[9] but the Supreme Court reversed and, after rejecting the *Frye* test, remanded the case.

Speaking through Justice Blackmun, the Court held that the *Frye* test was at odds with the "liberal thrust" of the Federal Rules of evidence and did not survive the passage of Rule 702. The Court went on to set out a new standard governing the admissibility of scientific evidence in the federal courts. Particular emphasis was placed on the language of Rule 702 which allows the introduction of "scientific . . . knowledge" that will "assist the trier" in understanding the evidence or resolving a disputed fact. The adjective "scientific" is important, said the Court, for it connotes knowledge that is the product of the methods and procedures of science, such as testing a hypothesis, careful measurement, replication of results, peer review, scientific acceptance,[10] and so forth. The focus for determining if evidence is "scientific" is on the principles embraced and the methodology employed, not on the conclusions generated. Rule 702, the Court emphasized, also makes it clear that the proffered scientific evidence must "assist the trier of fact." This requirement is closely related to the first essential (*"scientific knowledge"*),[11] but has a different focus. The focus here is on the relevancy or "fit" of the scientific knowledge (evidence presented by an expert) to the disputed issues in a particular case. It is quite possible that a reliable body of scientific knowledge would not be helpful in resolving the disputed issues before the court. To use an example suggested by the *Daubert* court:

> The study of the phases of the moon . . . may provide valid scientific "knowledge" about whether a certain night was dark. . . . However (absent credible [scientific] grounds . . .), evidence that the moon was full on a certain night will not assist the trier of fact in determining whether an individual was unusually likely to have behaved irrationally on that night.[12]

The application of Rule 702, as that rule was construed in *Daubert*, places a heavy responsibility on the trial judge. In her "gatekeeping" role she must evaluate the reliability and relevance of evidence that may pertain to a scientific field in which she has no expertise. She also needs to consider the possible application of

---

9.   951 F.2d 1128 (9th Cir. 1991).

10.   "Scientific Acceptance" is a legacy of the *Frye* test. Under *Daubert*, general acceptance by the scientific community is still a factor, but not the *only* factor, influencing admissibility.

11.   Knowledge that is not scientific would presumably be speculative or un-supported by scientific theory or methodology and hence would not "assist" the factfinder.

12.   *Daubert*, 509 U.S. at 591. This example also illustrates the close connection between the requirement that evidence be scientifically based and the requirement that it be helpful.

Rule 403, the now-familiar rule that allows her to reject relevance evidence that is "substantially outweighed" by considerations such as unfair prejudice, confusion, and time consumption. The burden of her responsibility is increased because the decision she makes will be sustained on appeal unless she "abused her discretion."[13] Often, she will need to conduct a *"Daubert* hearing," out of the jury's presence, for the purpose of considering data and arguments for and against the admissibility of scientific evidence. In cases in which expert testimony is important and each side's partisan experts reach completely different conclusions, she may wish to invoke Federal Rule 706 and select a "court appointed expert."

Recall that Federal Rule 702 speaks of "scientific, technical, or other specialized knowledge...." The issue in *Daubert* was whether the admissibility of evidence based on "scientific" knowledge was to be governed by *Frye* or some other standard. Many observers predicted that the general approach of *Daubert* would be extended to "technical or other specialized knowledge." Their prediction materialized in 1999, when it was confirmed by the Supreme Court in Kumho Tire Co., Ltd. v. Carmichael.[14] In *Kumho* the Supreme Court held that *Daubert*'s "gatekeeping" test of reliability and relevance applied not only to scientific knowledge, but to "technical or other specialized knowledge" as well. In *Kumho* a proffered "tire expert" (an engineer) claimed that through a visual and tactile inspection of the tire in question, he could determine whether the tire's failure was caused by a manufacturing or design defect, on the one hand, or consumer mistreatment (under inflation or overloading), on the other.

Applying *Daubert*'s evaluative factors, such as the testability of the expert's' hypothesis, peer review, and acceptance by other technicians, the trial judge rejected the proposed testimony. The Eleventh Circuit Court of Appeals reversed concluding that *Daubert*'s approach applied to scientific testimony, not to testimony resting on "experience" and "skill-based" observations. The Supreme Court, however, agreed with the trial judge, although it noted that factors bearing upon the reliability and relevance of non-scientific testimony might vary from factors pertinent to scientific testimony. For example, peer review,[15] quite common in the world of science, may have limited or no application to technical or specialized evidence. And in some cases involving specialized or technical testimony, the observations and experience of the expert may weigh more heavily on the admissibility decision than these

---

13. *See* General Electric Co. v. Joiner, 522 U.S. 136, 152 (1997).

14. 526 U.S. 137 (1999).

15. The Court also pointed out that there may be some instances in which

"a claim made by a scientific witness has never been the subject of peer review, for the particular application at issue may never previously have interested any scientist." Id. at 151.

factors would in assessing the proposed testimony of an expert scientist.

§ 11.4   Amended Rule 702

In the year 2000, Rule 702 was amended so as to more accurately capture the Supreme Court's approach to expert testimony as set forth in *Daubert* and *Kumho Tire*. The rule now specifies that an expert may testify to "scientific, technical, or other specialized knowledge" only if,

> (1) the testimony is based upon sufficient facts or data, (2) the testimony is the product of reliable principles and methods, and (3) the witness has applied the principles and methods reliably to the facts of the case.

The Advisor Committee's Note to Amended Rule 702 emphasizes both the trial judge's "gatekeeping" function and the variety of factors relevant to his decision to admit or exclude expert testimony. No single list of relevant concerns will suffice for all cases. A partial list includes testing by others, peer review, potential (or known) rate of error, careful standards and controls, acceptance by other persons in the field, whether the proffered scientific or technical evidence was developed especially for litigation, whether alternative explanations are adequately addressed and accounted for, and the depth of the expert's' knowledge and experience. The Advisory Committee also notes that even though the main focus for evaluating scientific evidence rests upon "principles and methodology," as opposed to conclusions, it is still important to consider whether the conclusion reached by the proffered expert departs sharply from that of his peers. If it does, there is reason to be concerned that the relevant principles and methodologies "have not been faithfully applied."[16]

§ 11.5   The Expert Witness: Sources of Knowledge and Direct Examination

The factfinder, of course, is always faced with questions of what evidence to believe and what inferences to draw. The use and evaluation of expert testimony, however, poses special difficulties. The first is determining exactly what factual assumptions underlie an expert opinion; the second is deciding which (if any) of the expert's' specialized inferences or conclusions should be accepted as true. The trier's task is made more difficult because the expert often uses technical language that describes principles and method-

---

16.   FRE 702 ACN (2000 amendment).

ologies foreign to most lay persons. To complicate matters even more, there is usually opposing expert opinion that reaches different conclusions. The starting point, however, is for the trier to identify the facts (or factual assumptions) that underlie an expert's opinion. If these facts are contested—and often they are—the basis of the expert's' opinion will be negated or weakened if the trier rejects the foundational facts in whole or in part. It thus becomes essential that there be some means by which the trier can identify the factual assumptions underlying an expert's opinion.

A simple example will make the point. A physician testifies that the plaintiff has a certain illness or injury. Three symptoms of the illness are persistent headaches, dizziness, and nausea. Earlier in the trial, the plaintiff testified that she had experienced all of these ill effects. Subsequently, however, the defendant introduces conflicting evidence, provided by estranged family members, that challenges these assertions. It is important for the trier of fact to know the extent to which the doctor's opinion rests upon the presence of these symptoms. If the trier rejects all or part of the plaintiff's testimony, it will take this into account in evaluating the accuracy of the expert physician's opinion.

There are various means by which an expert can gain knowledge of the facts that underlie his opinion: (1) he may have knowledge acquired through first-hand observation or examination; (2) he may have learned the facts prior to trial by studying the plaintiff's medical records and, perhaps, by consulting with others who have treated the patient; (3) he may learn the facts during the courtroom proceedings by observing and hearing the evidence bearing on the plaintiff's condition, and; (4) he may learn the facts when he takes the witness stand and is asked a "hypothetical" question that contains a recitation of the assumed facts. For example, counsel for the plaintiff may say, "Assuming, Doctor, that during the four weeks before the plaintiff was hospitalized, and while he was working in close proximity to the liquid chemical known as Benzene, he experienced, with increasing frequency, persistent headaches, dizziness, and nausea, do you have an opinion, within a reasonable medical certainty, as what caused these symptoms?" The hypothetical question, as you can see, not only informs the witness of the pertinent underlying "facts", but it also identifies the assumed facts on which the expert bases his opinion.

Consider further the third possibility noted above: suppose one or even several witnesses who precede the expert's testimony give all of the evidence on which the expert bases his opinion. Instead of using a hypothetical question, the direct examiner may simply ask his expert to assume, for purposes of giving his opinion, that all of the facts to which the preceding witnesses testified are true. The examiner would then, for example, continue, "Now, Doctor, do you have an opinion. . . ." This reliance on one or more prior witnesses works effectively when the prior testimony is consistent. It is not usually practical when a single witness recants or qualifies her direct testimony, or when several witnesses are inconsistent. Then, the assumed facts underlying the expert's' testimony become unclear, and a hypothetical question may be desirable. Of course, as we have noted, the expert, himself, is sometimes able to supply the underlying facts based on his personal knowledge. For example, a physician who has examined the patient may base his opinion on the "facts" he discovered during his examination. Finally, since it is common practice in every profession to rely frequently on the work of others, especially other professionals in the same or a related field, a testifying expert may rest his opinion on "facts or data . . . reasonably relied upon by experts in [this] particular field."[17] The point is that all these various means that *could* be used to provide the expert witness with a factual basis for his opinion *are allowed* by Federal Rule 703. It reads:

> **Bases of Opinion Testimony by Experts.** The facts or data . . . upon which an expert bases an opinion or inference may be those *perceived by or made known to the expert at or before the hearing.* If of a type *reasonably relied* upon by experts in the particular field . . . the facts or data need not be admissible in evidence in order for the [expert's] opinion or inference to be admitted. [Inadmissible] facts or data . . . shall not be disclosed to the jury *by the proponent* . . . unless the court determines that their probative value in assisting the jury . . . substantially outweighs their prejudicial effect.[18] [emphasis added]

Observe that the various means of informing the expert of the "facts or data" that underlie his opinion are all allowed by Rule 703. The rule's formulation is broad, for it embraces facts and data personally perceived by the witness, as well as facts and data "made known" to him. And note the timeframe: facts and data may be perceived or made known "at or before the hearing." Finally, factual materials that are not admissible may still underlie the expert's' inferences and opinions, provided these materials are "of a type reasonably relied upon" by other experts in the field. In other words, an expert's opinion may be based on his first-hand knowledge, on facts that are revealed during the trial or hearing, or on reliable "out-of-court" facts of the sort used by professionals in the expert's field.

17.   FRE 702.
18.   FRE 703.

You need to examine Rule 703 in conjunction with the other Federal rules governing expert testimony. Rule 705 is particularly important, for it specifies the testimonial form in which an expert may state his opinion or conclusion. Consider, especially, the impact of Rule 705 on the traditional means of securing expert testimony: the hypothetical question. Rule 705 states:

Disclosure of Facts or Data Underlying Expert Opinion. The expert may testify in terms of opinion or inference and give reasons therefore without first testifying to the underlying facts or data, unless the court requires otherwise. The expert may in any event be required to disclose the underlying facts or data on cross-examination.

Analyze the following hypothetical, keeping in mind both Rule 703 and Rule 705.[19]

ILLUSTRATION

Assume that in a suit against an insurance company, the issue is whether a warehouse fire had an incendiary origin (arson) or is traceable to other causes. The defendant puts Fire Marshal on the stand, qualifies him as an expert witness on the cause and origin of fires, and then asks, "Are you familiar with, and have you investigated, the warehouse fire at 914 Cargo Street, on August 23, 2005?" After receiving an affirmative answer, counsel asks, "Do you have an opinion, within a reasonable degree of probability what caused this fire?" Over objection that defense counsel must use a hypothetical question, Fire Marshal answers, "I do." When counsel then asks, "What is your opinion?", Marshal replies (over objection), "My opinion is that the source of the fire was arson." On cross, counsel for the plaintiff asks questions that elicit the factual basis for Fire Marshal's opinion. The underlying facts or data were:

(1) A personal inspection of the debris from the fire, including evidence indicating the areas of greatest

---

19. Rule 704(a) permits an expert to render an opinion even on the ultimate issue in a case. Rule 704(b) carves out a single exception to the *general rule*, embodied in Rule 704(a), that an expert *may give* his opinion as to the *ultimate issue* in a case. Under Rule 704(b), however, an expert is barred from giving his opinion as to whether the defendant in a criminal case did or did not have the mental state required as an element of the crime charged. Subsection (b) was a reaction to the "not-guilty-by-reason-of-insanity" verdict rendered in the trial of John Hinckley for the attempted assassination of President Reagan.

heat intensity, the pattern of the flames, and the condition of the warehouse electrical system.

(2) A report containing the results of a chemical analysis of the soil under warehouse where the fire probably started. [The chemist's report states that minute traces of gasoline residue were embedded in the soil near the most likely point of the fire's origin.]

(3) Conversations with three eyewitnesses (night watchman guarding other buildings) [who told Marshal that they first observed the fire and smoke on the east side of the warehouse.]

(4) A report prepared by another expert, (privately retained), as well as conversations with that expert, [whose findings, analysis, and conclusions were consistent with those of Fire Marshal.]

Counsel for the plaintiff moves to strike Fire Marshal's direct testimony on the ground that his opinion is based on hearsay that is not in evidence and, in any event, is inadmissible, and on the further ground that Marshal's opinion is based on the opinion of another expert. The trial judge again rules against the defendant on both grounds. Were the judge's rulings correct?[20]

Although asking a hypothetical question might appear to be the ideal means of eliciting an expert's opinion, experience has shown that often it is not. There are many problems in accommodating the hypothetical question to the adversary system. The lawyer asking a hypothetical often crafts it in partisan terms and includes extraneous facts—usually pointing toward (or away from) liability—that are not relevant to the expert's' opinion. Furthermore, counsel sometimes omits unfavorable relevant facts or states the relevant facts in such argumentative terms that the hypothetical partakes of closing argument. Undue length (and resulting confusion) is another problem: it is not unusual for a hypothetical question to occupy several or even a dozen pages in a trial transcript.

Traditionally, rigid requirements have attended the use of hypothetical questions. The hypothetical question is defective—and an appellate reversal could result—if a relevant fact is omitted from the question. The same is true if a relevant fact included in the hypothetical is not supported by *admitted* evidence in the record. Modern appellate courts are somewhat more forgiving in their review of "defective" hypothetical questions. Today, for example,

20. For two somewhat similar cases, see Ferrara & DiMercurio v. St. Paul Mercury Ins. Co. 240 F.3d 1 (1st Cir. 2001) and United States v. Lundy, 809 F.2d 392 (7th Cir. 1987).

appellate judges are more diligent in trying to assess the probable harm caused by the defect. They will forgive the omission of a relevant fact that is not very significant. Furthermore, they conduct their review with greater awareness of the cross-examiner's opportunity to reveal (assumed) facts omitted from the hypothetical and to ask cross-questions containing additional or fewer assumed facts.[21] Nonetheless, the common-law framework of the hypothetical remains largely intact, and the most that can be said is that sometimes the hypothetical question is more helpful to the jury than other means of eliciting expert testimony.

In any event, the use of a hypothetical question is not required by Federal Rule 705 "unless the Court requires otherwise."[22] The elimination of a general requirement that the examiner use a hypothetical question is accomplished by Rule 705's allowance of an expert's "opinion or inference" without the need to first reveal "the underlying facts or data." When a hypothetical question is used, the expert testifies that he has an opinion based on the preceding assumed facts recited by counsel, and only then does the expert render an opinion grounded on those facts. In the Illustration, counsel chose not to use a hypothetical question, the court did not rule otherwise,[23] and the expert properly gave his opinion.

The first point to be made about the judge's refusal to strike Marshal's direct testimony is that allowing an expert to give his opinion without first revealing its factual basis is not an appropriate procedure *unless* the opponent is able to use pre-trial discovery to learn what the expert's' opinion or conclusion will be *and* the data, facts, principles, and methodologies (the "foundation" or "basis") that support the expert's' opinion. Without this information, the cross-examiner is in the untenable position of asking questions designed to reveal the basis of the expert's opinion, without knowing in advance what that basis is. Suppose, for example, the cross-examiner asks the expert whether his opinion rests in part on conversations with persons who observed the outbreak of the fire. And, suppose, further, the expert answers, "I spoke with eyewitnesses, yes." Is the cross-examiner now to ask, "What did they say?" Or is the cross-examiner to move to a different inquiry and ask about another basis for the expert's opinion, thus leaving

21. "Doctor, would you change your opinion about the cause of the plaintiff's neck injury if you assumed that two days before the automobile accident in question he fell from a stepladder onto a concrete stairs, sustained a blow to the forehead, and was rendered unconscious?"

22. Judges do not often require that the direct examiner interrogate an expert witness only through the use of a hypothetical. If the examiner declines to use a hypothetical question, the cross-examiner is entitled to ask questions that will reveal the factual assumption underlying the expert's' opinion.

23. *See* cases cited supra note 20.

the jury wondering what these eyewitnesses said and whether the cross-examiner is avoiding the disclosure of helpful evidence.

Fortunately, in almost all jurisdictions, modern discovery provisions, such as those contained in the Federal Rules of Civil Procedure, allow adequate discovery of an opposing expert's opinion, as well as the basis on which it rests.[24] Armed with prior knowledge about the basis of an expert's opinion or conclusion, the cross-examiner is free to explore only those parts of the expert's foundation that he believes are weak, or to identify certain factual assumptions and ask the expert if he would change or modify his opinion if different factual assumptions were made.[25]

Note the closing sentence of Rule 703. It provides that "Facts and data otherwise inadmissible shall not be disclosed to the jury by the proponent of the opinion or inference" unless the probative value of this evidentiary material passes a special balancing test peculiar to Rule 703. That test is stringent: the facts or data are inadmissible unless "their probative value in assisting the jury to evaluate the expert's opinion substantially outweighs their prejudicial effect." Two factors are at play here. First, there is the question of how much the jury will be aided if the "inadmissible" underlying facts and data are revealed. Second, there is a concern that the jury will improperly use the underlying materials not only to evaluate the expert's opinion, but also for the truth of assertions contained in these materials (e.g., the fire started where the hearsay declarants said it did). Of course, the test applies only to the *proponent* of the expert's opinion; and, as we have seen, the test applies only to facts or data "otherwise inadmissible." Therefore (in the Illustration above) evidence resulting from Marshal's personal inspection is unaffected by the special balancing test. Knowledge gained through personal observations of the testifying witness is admissible; the proponent (or for that matter, the cross-examiner) can elicit Marshal's testimony relating to his observations. The same might be true of the chemist's report, for it could escape the hearsay rule and be received in evidence if it was a properly prepared business or public record.

Marshal's conversations with eyewitnesses and his communications with the other expert (including use of the other's expert's report)[26] appear to be "otherwise inadmissible" under Rule 703. This evidence might still come before the jury not for its truth, but

---

24. *See* Fed. R. Civ. Proc. 26(a)(2) and (b)(4)(A).

25. The different assumptions must, however, rest on a permissible foundation such as evidence in the record or facts reasonably relied on by persons in the field in question.

26. If the other expert was a public official, his report (as opposed to his informal conversations) could probably be admitted into evidence as a public report. *See* FRE 803(8)(c). This report might also qualify as a business record. *See* FRE 803(6).

rather to *reveal the basis* of the testifying expert's opinion, thus helping the jury evaluate that opinion. Let us assume that conversations with eyewitness and consultations with other experts constitute evidentiary sources that are "inadmissible" but nonetheless are "reasonably relied upon by experts" in the field of fire detection. Under this assumption (generally, an accurate one), these sources are a proper basis for an expert opinion, but the evidentiary *content* of these sources (witnesses' statements about where the fire started; the other expert's findings and conclusions) cannot be disclosed to the jury unless Rule 703's special balancing test is satisfied. Of course, the judge might, for example, conclude that the eyewitnesses' statements about the area of the building where the flames were first observed meet the special balancing test, whereas communications with the other expert do not (or vice versa).

The course and tenor of cross-examination often affects the trial judge's decision on the admissibility of "inadmissible" evidence for the purpose of assisting the jury in understanding and evaluating the expert's opinion. Suppose, for example, the cross-examiner reveals the source of some of the inadmissible evidence (facts, data, or other expert's' opinions) underlying the expert's' opinion. Without disclosing the content of this evidence, he suggests its unreliability. ("Are you telling the jury that part of your opinion that this fire was caused by arson is based on hearsay conversations with night watchmen, untrained in fire detection, and not even present at the building that burned?") Tactics like this, suggesting that the "inadmissible" basis of the expert's opinion is not credible, can "open the door" to disclosure of the underlying (and otherwise inadmissible) evidence on redirect examination.

§ 11.6   The Expert Witness: Cross–Examination and Impeachment

The technique of cross-examining an expert differs somewhat, depending largely upon which of the various modes of direct examination is used. For example, if the direct examiner does not ask a hypothetical question, the cross-examiner may want to ask questions designed to reveal the underlying basis of the expert's opinion. If the expert himself has supplied the underlying facts or data, the cross-examiner may want to ask questions designed to reveal the expert's lack of thoroughness, or defects in his observations or memory. There are several additional possibilities for weakening the force of the expert's testimony. As we have already noted, the cross-examiner may ask the expert to assume different facts than those assumed during direct examination, and to state whether these new factual assumptions would alter his opinion. The interrogator may also probe aspects of the expert's education or experience in an attempt to show that the expert's background is not well suited to developing a high degree of expertise in the particular specialty pertinent to the present case.

And like other witnesses, the expert is subject to any of the usual methods of impeachment such as bias, prior inconsistent statements, or prior "bad" acts reflecting on credibility. Bias, in particular, may be an available technique because, for example, the expert usually is paid a fee by the party who engages him. Evidence that an expert frequently testifies in trials and invariably aligns herself with one point of view or one kind of litigant (such as personal injury plaintiff) also suggests bias. Furthermore, in most jurisdictions, the examiner may confront the expert with a treatise, text, or other reliable authority and, after extracting a concession (or providing other evidence) that the proffered work is a reliable authority,[27] point to passages that contradict the expert's opinion. For example, if the expert testifies on direct that a "whiplash" injury is always manifested within several weeks after a blow is sustained, the cross-examiner may read (or have the expert read) passages from a standard text or professional periodical that indicate a longer period. Under the Federal Rules, the "learned" treatise or periodical may be used not only to challenge the expert's opinion, but also as substantive proof that the statement in the reference work is true.[28]

§ 11.7   Scientific and Technical Evidence: A Sample

There are many occasions for the application of science (including social science) and other specialized disciplines, such as statistics, in the courtroom. Some of these applications involve principles and methodologies that are rigorous and precise, yielding results that are usually highly reliable. For example, blood testing, blood typing, and the application of genetic principles, if properly conducted, produces results that are highly refined and quite dependable. So, too, does DNA testing, modern ballistics techniques, and, at a more prosaic level, speed detection by the use of radar. In contrast, handwriting analysis, the identification and meaning of various kinds of syndromes (such as battered woman and rape trauma), and the psychology of eyewitness identification involve more speculative principles, greater subjectivity, and—though often admitted—rest on less certain footing.

Assuming the *topic* on which an expert will testify is appropriate, a trial judge must make four related inquiries when deciding

---

27. It also suffices if the expert acknowledges that he relied on the proffered text, but unless he is careless, he will not have relied on a work that contradicts his views.

28. FRE 803(18) and the discussion in Ch. VII, at note 65.

whether to admit the testimony of an expert proffered to share her "scientific technical, or other specialized knowledge."[29] First, the judge must be satisfied that the witness has the necessary expertise; second, that the principles, data, scientific laws, or studies that underlie the expert's testimony are sound; third, that the methodology or application of these principles is acceptable, and fourth, that the expert's conclusions or inferences have sufficient probative value (acceptable "fit") on the issue before the court to be helpful. As to the second requirement—sound foundational principles—acceptance by the scientific or technical community may reach the point that the trial judge can take judicial notice of the reliability of the underlying principle or scientific law. For example, when police officers first began to use radar to detect the speed of automobiles, prosecutors had to provide evidence explaining the principles and reliability of radar. This evidence, of course, is no longer necessary (judicial notice is routine), but in contested cases, courts still require evidence that the radar "gun" was properly calibrated, in good working order, and that a qualified operator used appropriate procedures. Of course, the resulting "speed readout" fits perfectly with the typical issue in a prosecution for driving at an unlawful speed, which is, of course, the speed of the offending vehicle. But the speed readout would be unhelpful in answering the question whether the speeding vehicle was a car or an SUV.

DNA

Expert testimony on DNA evidence has quickly moved from the experimental into the accepted realm in both the scientific and legal communities. The basic science underlying DNA technology is now generally accepted as being reliable under the *Daubert* standard, and in fact, an increasing number of courts conclude that it should be the subject of judicial notice.[30] However, even though the basic science is widely accepted, courts still play an important role in admitting expert DNA testimony. The two questions which courts closely examine in deciding whether to admit the DNA testimony are, (1) What test was used to analyze the DNA? and, (2) What population frequency statistics were used to interpret the DNA?

DNA testing involves matching snippets of genetic code taken from specific locations along a strand of DNA. All human cells with a nucleus contain DNA and each of these cells contains the entire genetic code for a person. Every human, with the exception of identical twins, has a unique DNA "blueprint." By looking at areas along the DNA strand where it is known that individuals' genetic codes vary widely, a highly accurate determination can be made. If

29. FRE 702.

30. *See, e.g.,* United States v. Johnson, 56 F.3d 947, 952 (8th Cir. 1995).

the genetic code of the samples taken from, say, the crime scene and the suspect match, then there is a "positive DNA match."

Two methods of DNA testing have become prevalent in recent years The first test is Restriction Fragment Length Polymorphism (RFLP). RFLP involves subjecting the DNA sample to enzymes which cleave it at specific sites. In between these specific sites different people will have widely varying base pairs (adenine (A), cytosine (C), thymine (T), and guanine (G)). Thus, the segments separated out by the enzymes will significantly differ for each individual's sample DNA. RFLP is not only accurate, but the efficacy of this test has been borne out by repeated use over an extended period. However, RFLP testing does have some drawbacks; most notably, the sample must be fresh and relatively large (about the size of a dime), and it is not always possible to extract or gather such a sample.

The second method of DNA testing, Polymerase Chain Reaction (PCR), alleviates these problems. PCR amplification is a process for making many copies of selected portions of a DNA sample. Once enough copies are made, it is possible to analyze and identify the unique sections of the DNA strand.[31] This amplification procedure allows the analysis of a sample that is much smaller and more degraded than that which is permitted by RFLP testing. While both RFLP and PCR tests have routinely been accepted by courts, newer methods of DNA analysis are still scrutinized carefully. These newer tests provide some advantages over both RFLP and PCR-based tests. For instance, mitochondrial DNA testing allows the analysis of cells without a nucleus, such as from a strand of hair without a follicle. A recurring consideration in all DNA testing is the manner in which a laboratory conducts the test. Improper testing procedures could block the admissibility of DNA evidence,[32] but the trend, within limits at least, is to hold that testing irregularities affect the reliability (as opposed to the admissibility) of DNA evidence.[33]

If a crime-scene DNA sample does not match a suspect's DNA sample, then it is conclusive that the crime-scene DNA did not come from the suspect. However, the reverse of this statement is not invariably true. Currently, as noted above, the tests used to analyze DNA samples do not look at the entire strand of DNA, but examine only a fragment. Thus it may be possible for a DNA

31. PCR amplification is often paired with another test for the identification portion, Short Tandem Repeats (STR), being one of the more common pairings. *See* People v. Hill, 89 Cal.App.4th 48, 107 Cal.Rptr.2d 110, 119 (2001).

32. *See e.g.,* People v. Castro, 144 Misc.2d 956, 545 N.Y.S.2d 985, 989–996 (Sup. Ct. 1989) (court acknowledged the scientific validity of DNA typing but found that the testing laboratory failed to follow accepted scientific practices for obtaining reliable results).

33. PAUL GIANELLI & EDWARD IMWINK-ELRIED, SCIENTIFIC EVIDENCE § 18–5(B), at 35 (3d ed. 1999).

analysis to reveal that the sample DNA and suspect DNA match, when in actuality the sample is not from the suspect (a "false positive"). Since the use of sampling precludes the claim that the DNA test is 100% accurate, an expert normally testifies to the probability of accuracy. Three reasons can explain a false positive: lab error, kinship, or coincidence.

Lab error is thought to be the most common cause of false positives. The main controversy surrounding lab error is whether testimony will be received that illustrates the probability that a particular lab committed an error.[34] This probability is difficult to quantify and arriving at an estimate usually involves the use of proficiency tests. Critics of proficiency tests argue that they may not provide an accurate measure of false positives, nor, it is argued, do they provide an objective estimate of error.[35] The best way to guard against claims of lab error is to document all the steps involved in the analysis and reserve samples of the DNA that can be verified at other labs.

As to the problem of kinship, most investigations can easily be expanded to test all suspected relatives. Thus, most of the controversy over admitting a probability assessment has centered on the problem of coincidence—a false match that is the product of mere chance. Courts have responded to this controversy in different ways. Some courts have allowed expert testimony supporting the existence of a match, but have disallowed testimony relating to discrete (and general) population statistics. Most courts, however, permit testimony regarding the statistical possibility of a coincidental match and allow cross-examination to expose possibilities of inaccuracy. Some of these courts insist that the proponent of the DNA evidence adjust the figure to the most conservative possible estimate.[36]

Probability assessments of coincidental matches are made by using population bases. The controversy over allowing experts to testify about probability assessments usually centers on the size of the population database used. For subjects who are members of a small, discrete subgroup, figures based on available databases may be too broad. Additionally, it has been found that certain racial or ethnic groups are very endogamous, which further affects the possible occurrence of similar DNA patterns. For instance, for the broad subgroup "Hispanics," there may be a finding that the frequency of a mismatch of a particular DNA fragment is 1 in 10,000. For the group of Hispanics living in Houston, however, most of whom are Mexican, the frequency might be 1 in 1,000.

34. DAVID FAIGMAN ET. AL., SCIENCE IN THE LAW: FORENSIC SCIENCE ISSUES § 11-2.6.2, at 722–23 (2002).

35. Id.

36. See United States v. Chischilly, 30 F.3d 1144, 1158 (9th Cir. 1994).

Obviously, it would unfairly prejudice a defendant to use the first percentage rather than the second. Currently, however, databases do not exist for smaller population groups such as Mexican, Cuban, or West African, nor for geographic clusters of discrete members of a larger population group.

Two recent cases illustrate this problem of probability assessments based on a population database. In Government of Virgin Islands v. Penn,[37] the relevant group of possible suspects was the population of native black islanders, for whom no database was available. The government thus turned to the database for all blacks in the United States. The court admitted both the DNA evidence of a "match" and the statistical testimony addressed to coincidence, noting that while the population database used did not "produce the precise odds of finding a random match in the defendant's population, the danger of error in such application is so small as to be practically nonexistent."[38]

In United States v. Martinez,[39] the defendant was accused of raping a 14-year-old girl during a pow-wow on an Indian Reservation in South Dakota. The relevant population of suspects was thus the population of that specific Indian tribe, not a general American Indian population. The government sought to introduce evidence of the probability of a coincidental match based on the general Native American database. The court held that testimony regarding DNA profiling evidence and the conclusion of a match was admissible, but that the statistical testimony regarding the probabilities of coincidence should be excluded as substantially more prejudicial than probative.[40] Cases like these, where the defendant is a member of a discrete and insular group, and all suspects also come from this group, are problematic and the judge should be very wary of admitting statistical testimony (typically showing a very slim chance of a coincidental match) based on broad population groups.

The admissibility of statistics representing the possibility of a coincidental match has been attacked as being unfairly prejudicial when the evidence is subjected to a Rule 403 balancing test. Courts are usually concerned that jurors would either not understand the complicated statistical evidence presented by the expert or that they would misinterpret this evidence. For instance, one federal Court of Appeals expressed apprehension "that the jury will accept the DNA evidence as a statement of source probability (i.e., the likelihood that the defendant is the source of the evidentiary sample)."[41] Despite these concerns, courts will probably continue to allow at least a conservative estimate of probability evidence be-

---

37. 838 F.Supp. 1054 (D. V.I. 1993).

38. Id. at 1071.

39. 3 F.3d 1191 (8th Cir. 1993).

40. Id. at 1198.

41. *Chischilly*, 30 F.3d at 1158.

cause it is extremely helpful to the complete interpretation of DNA evidence. Evidence of a DNA match can be misleading without some broader context of interpretation.

Polygraph Tests

Polygraph evidence has traditionally been inadmissible because application of the *Frye* test for admitting scientific evidence has led to the conclusion that polygraph testing had not gained sufficient "standing and scientific recognition among physiological and psychological authorities."[42] Since the decision in *Frye*, a majority of states have followed the traditional practice and embraced the rule that polygraph evidence is per se inadmissible. However, with the passage of the Federal Rules of Evidence and, generally speaking, a modern trend favoring admissibility (acknowledged in the *Daubert* decision), courts have begun to reexamine the admissibility of polygraph evidence.

Polygraph, or "lie detector," tests are based on the premise that a lying subject's fear of detection sets in motion a series of involuntary physical responses that can be measured. Specifically, modern polygraph machines record a number of physical responses: galvanic skin responses, sweating of the palms, blood pressure, respiration, and sometimes, changes in the flow of blood to the tip of the index finger.[43] There are two main techniques used to elicit these involuntary responses: the "relevant-irrelevant" test and the more modern, control question technique. In the relevant-irrelevant test, questions of no moment (such as "Are you over 21?") are used to measure the subject's physiological state while telling the truth. The results from these questions are then compared to the subject's answers to relevant questions. If they match, the subject is telling the truth. In the control question technique, a general and vague control question is posed to the subject that usually deals with an illegal activity (such as "Have you ever stolen anything?"). Innocent subjects respond more fully and readily to these control questions than to relevant questions about the event in question; while the opposite is true for guilty subjects.

Critics of the polygraph test point out that it does not measure "fear of detection of lying" but rather it measures any form of anxiety. Thus, the subject may have feelings of anxiety unrelated to the truthfulness of a particular response. Additionally, a trained subject can be coaxed into simulating these feelings of anxiety in

42. Frye v. United States, 293 F. 1013 (D.C. Cir. 1923), which established the "general acceptance" test (*see* text at note 5) involved the admissibility of lie detector results derived from an early, less sophisticated polygraph machine.

43. Sheila K. Hyatt, *Developments in the Law of Scientific Evidence: The Admissibility of Polygraph Evidence*, 18 J. Nat'l. Ass'n. Admin. L. Judges 171, 179 (1998).

order to minimize variations or otherwise distort the results of the polygraph test.[44] Courts have also pointed to the prejudicial impact of polygraph testing, which could violate Rule 403 on the ground that the potential for prejudice substantially outweighs the probative value of test results. Other Courts have concluded that compelling a subject to undergo a polygraph test may infringe on his Fifth Amendment rights.[45]

Despite a history of opposition to polygraph testing, in recent years some courts have become more receptive to this evidence. Most notably, a recent appellate decision suggests that *Daubert* may have opened the door to polygraphic evidence in criminal cases if it is offered by the defendant.[46] In this case, the Fifth Circuit found polygraph evidence reliable because there had been significant technological advances in polygraphic techniques. Research now shows that the tests are reliable 70–90% of the time, that the technique is subject to extensive publication and research, and that polygraphy is widely used by private employers and government agencies. Additionally, the court noted that in cases where the evidence essentially amounts to one adversary's word against the other, and there is much conflicting evidence, the probative value of polygraph testimony is heightened. Finally, the court noted that polygraph evidence has an increased chance of admission in criminal trials if the government is notified prior to the testing (thus affording the prosecutor an opportunity to observe or, perhaps, participate), and the proposed evidence is offered at a pre-trial hearing.[47]

At present, jurisdictions treat polygraph evidence three different ways. The first is by applying the traditional per se exclusion rule, noted at the beginning of the section. The second response is due to the influence of *Daubert*. In some jurisdictions, polygraph evidence is not excluded automatically but instead the decision lies in the hands of the trial court. Even though courts in these jurisdictions are permitted to consider polygraph evidence, and are accorded considerable discretion, the trial judge often excludes it.[48] Finally, some jurisdictions allow polygraph evidence if both parties stipulate to its admissibility prior to the administration of the test. The differing attitudes of various jurisdictions suggest that polygraph testimony will continue to be controversial, at least for the near future.

44. See United States v. Cordoba, 991 F.Supp. 1199, 1204 (C.D.Cal 1998).

45. The most relevant Supreme Court case is Schmerber v. California, 384 U.S. 757, 764 (1966).

46. United States v. Posado, 57 F.3d 428 (5th Cir. 1995).

47. Id. at 433–36.

48. FAIGMAN ET AL., supra note 34, § 10–1.2.2, at 561–65.

Syndrome Testimony: Battered Woman Syndrome

In recent years, testimony from clinical psychologists or sociologists has begun to have a larger impact in the courtroom, especially for criminal cases. The testimony of these social scientists is used to explain personal behavior in specific situations by showing that people "typically" respond to a particular stimulus in a patterned and predictable manner. This type of evidence is usually referred to as "syndrome testimony."

Battered Woman Syndrome (BWS) was one of the first forms of syndrome testimony to gain evidentiary access in American courts. BWS describes the typical pattern of a woman's reaction to an abusive relationship. Experts commonly characterize BWS as consisting of three phases: the tension phase, the violent phase, and the quiet or loving phase.[49] The tension phase involves minor incidents of battering, eventually leading the victim to the belief that she deserves physical, sexual, or verbal abuse. The violent phase sets in as the abuser inflicts increasing, and perhaps more frequent injury. During this phase, the woman withdraws emotionally and refuses to seek help—her behavior in this phase is analogous to a disaster victim. In the final phase, the abuser becomes remorseful and makes promises not to inflict more injury. During this phase, the woman is induced to continue the relationship; however, her rapprochement is often the prelude for a cyclical repetition, characterized by more episodes and increased violence.[50]

Courts generally allow BWS evidence because it is generally reliable and its foundation rests upon considerable research.[51] The most common context for the introduction of BWS evidence is its admission to dispel commonly held notions concerning a woman's apparent failure to take protective steps. As one court put it, "[e]xpert testimony explaining why a person suffering from the battered woman syndrome would not leave her mate, would not inform police or friends, and would fear increased aggression against herself would be helpful to a jury in understanding a phenomenon not within the competence of an ordinary lay person."[52] However, courts have been wary of routinely extending the use of BWS testimony, and they continue to assess the relevance and reliability of this testimony on a case-by-case basis. For example, in one case the defense tried to use BWS to bolster a claim of duress, but the court held that the testimony was not helpful since the duress defense requires the application of an objective test, and

---

49. *See* United States v. Brown, 891 F.Supp. 1501, 1505 (D. Kan. 1995).

50. Id.

51. While BWS has generally gained scientific acceptance, it is not without criticism. For a detailed analysis on the flaws of BWS see Faigman & Wright, *Battered Woman Syndrome in the Age of Science*, 39 Ariz. L. Rev. 67 (1997).

52. State v. Allery, 101 Wash.2d 591, 682 P.2d 312, 316 (1984).

the introduction of BWS evidence would change the inquiry into a subjective one.[53]

BWS is not the only syndrome testimony that frequently appears in cases. Two other strains receiving court recognition include Child Sexual Abuse Accommodation Syndrome (CSAAS) and Rape Trauma Syndrome (RTS). Since the advent of *Daubert*, defendants have sought to introduce a variety of sociological and psychological evidence.[54] However, much of this proposed testimony does not have as firm a grounding in research and study as does CSAAS, RTS, and BWS. It seems likely, however, that as more social and psychological research becomes available, "syndrome testimony" will find increased receptivity in the courtroom.

A Note on Mathematical Evidence

Mathematical evidence can be useful in helping a trier of fact embrace or reject a factual specific proposition. Nonetheless, courts have struggled with the question of admissibility. The difficulty arises because there is often a risk that the trier will exaggerate the reliability of mathematical proof. Furthermore, the jury may fail to appreciate fully the assumptions that underlie the application of a statistical or other mathematical formula. When correctly used in the proper context, though, the problems generally associated with mathematical evidence can often be minimized.

A basic, but sometimes useful mathematical principle is the "product rule". This rule involves assessing the separate probability (expressed as a fraction) of the occurrence of each of a number of independent events (or conditions) and then, because these events allegedly concurred, multiplying these individual probabilities. The product of these two or more probabilities represents the probability of the joint occurrence of these separate events or conditions. For example, suppose that a witness reported seeing an interracial couple drive away from the crime scene in a yellow car. Assume that the probability was 1 in 10 that any given car would be yellow and 1 in 500 that an interracial couple would be in the same car. The odds that such a couple would be in a yellow car would be 1 in 5,000 ($1/10 \times 1/500$). This result suggests that the couple later apprehended—an African–American and a Caucasian occupying a yellow car—is the same couple that the witness saw earlier. The product rule indicates that there is a comparatively remote chance

---

53. United States v. Willis, 38 F.3d 170, 177 (5th Cir. 1994). *But see*, Dunn v. Roberts, 963 F.2d 308, 313–14 (10th Cir. 1992) (accused suffering BWS was entitled to expert assistance in order to develop a duress defense).

54. *See e.g.*, State v. Foret, 628 So.2d 1116, 1128 (La. 1993) (court disallowed expert testimony that said the defendant's "personality profile" was inconsistent with that of a murderer because the proposed testimony was unreliable).

that the couple apprehended is another interracial couple that, by chance, happened to be in the same area.[55]

Close examination of this example, however, will reveal some of the problems that attach to probability evidence. The first difficulty is determining the separate probability of a particular component of the composite event. How is it known that 1 in 10 cars are yellow? And what is the geographic area for this figure? Perhaps there are more yellow cars in Southern California than in Northern California (or Montana). Even more difficult is determining the probability of an interracial couple occupying the same car. It is doubtful that a reliable statistic exists that would fairly represent this probability. Again, the geographic area in which to gather data on interracial couples in the same car would have to be defined. Without a reliable probability for the happening of each of the component events, the final product will not accurately reflect the actual chance of the joint occurrence. The second difficulty is that the validity of the final product depends upon the independence of the separate events or characteristics. Suppose that the two characteristics to which a separate probability must be assigned are a male wearing a beard and a male wearing a mustache. Since many men with beards also have mustaches, these conditions are not independent of each other and, if treated as independent, would lead to faulty results.[56] While these problems are significant hurdles to the admission of simple probability evidence, they can sometimes be avoided. The probability of some independent events can be satisfactorily determined. In appropriate circumstances, courts have admitted statistical data that reveal the estimated probability of an event based on the joint occurrence of two (or more) events or conditions that comprise the principal event or condition.[57]

A more sophisticated form of mathematical evidence involves the application of Bayes' Theorem.[58] The purpose of Bayes' Theo-

---

55. *See generally*, People v. Collins, 68 Cal.2d 319, 66 Cal.Rptr. 497, 438 P.2d 33 (1968) (a leading case in the use—and misuse—of mathematical evidence).

56. While this example could lead to faulty results as it presently stands, if the incidence of men with both a beard and a mustache were known, then this could be mathematically accounted for and more accurate results could be obtained.

57. *See* Rachals v. State, 184 Ga. App. 420, 361 S.E.2d 671 (1987) (probability of large number of cardiac arrests occurring by chance during defendant-nurse's duty hours).

58. The formula can be expressed as follows:

$$O(G|E) = (P(E|G)/P(E|\text{not } G)) \times O(G)$$

This equation says that the odds that a defendant is guilty (G) taking into account newly introduced evidence (|E) equals the probability that the evidence would be presented to the jury if the defendant is found guilty, divided by the probability that the same evidence would be presented to the jury if the defendant is found not guilty, times the prior odds of the defendant's guilt. The prior odds are the odds that the defendant was guilty if the new evidence had not been introduced. RICHARD LEMPERT ET AL., A MODERN APPROACH TO EVIDENCE 229 (3d ed. 2000).

rem is to reduce to mathematical terms the final probative effect when *new* evidence is added to *pre-existing* evidence. The resulting probability, expressed as a percentage, represents the "odds" that a specified conclusion is true, after the new evidence is considered in light of the pre-existing evidence.[59] Suppose, for example, that in a criminal trial a rational factfinder believes, on the basis of the evidence already admitted, that the odds that the defendant is guilty are 50%. Subsequently, additional evidence is produced showing that the perpetrator of the crime has brown hair. Assume 50% of the population has brown hair and so does the defendant. If the defendant did commit the crime, the probability that the perpetrator's hair would be brown is 100%. The probability of brown hair if someone else committed the crime is 50%. If Bayes' Theorem is applied to these percentages, the result is 67%. This means that based on this new evidence, a *rational* factfinder should now believe that the odds that the defendant is guilty are 67%.

The application of Bayes' Theorem presents at least two problems. The first is determining the probabilities associated with the pre-existing evidence, and the second is finding an accurate and helpful way to communicate the Bayes' Theorem results, especially in a jury trial. The first problem often poses the most difficulties. In the example above we assumed that the factfinder initially believed that the odds that the defendant was guilty were 50%. This is just an assigned estimate based upon the assumed evaluation by the trier of the evidence already before it (the "pre-existing" evidence). Mathematicians customarily assign the arbitrary figure of 50% to the pre-existing evidence because it is deemed a neutral figure that does not favor either party. The problem is that it is abstractly and arbitrarily derived and has no relationship to the actual evidence in the case or, more importantly, that particular trier's belief in the reliability of that pre-existing evidence. Thus, the normal role of the factfinder, to evaluate and weigh the pre-existing evidence, is ignored. As to the second problem, it is often relatively easy to see how Bayes' Theorem can mislead a jury. Frequently, the effect of the "new evidence," when expressed mathematically, is dramatic. Furthermore, there is a supposed certainty to a mathematical result that can be misleading—the result is no better than its arithmetic input. In order to minimize false conclusions, the factfinder should be made fully aware of the limits of Bayes' Theorem. Perhaps through the repeated use of this theorem, courts will develop a protocol that makes effective use of it in selected areas of litigation. One explanatory device that some courts now use is a

---

59. Most of the decided cases consider the application of the Theorem to paternity cases in which blood test results are introduced. *See* 1 McCormick § 211, at 962–68.

display that illustrates the effect of the new evidence on various assumptions concerning the jury's assessment of the pre-existing evidence.

Yet another form of mathematical evidence that often finds favor with the courts is regression analysis. Regression analysis can help determine if a postulated relationship exists between two events or characteristics and what the strength of that relationship is.[60] Regression analysis, however, does not, by itself, explain causation; it just reveals the correlation between the events. That is, it is possible to falsely conclude that A caused B, simply on the ground that A is associated with B.

The mechanics of regression analysis can be illustrated through an example. Suppose you postulated that the more apples you ate the better your vision would be. To test this hypothesis, you asked 100 people how many apples they ate a week and the condition of their eyesight (e.g. 20/40). You could plot this information on a graph, with the number of apples eaten on the X-axis (the independent variable) and eyesight figures on the Y-axis (the dependent variable). By so doing, you could determine whether there is a correlation between the two. If more apples ingested does correlate to better eyesight, the graph would appear as an upward curving line.

This illustration, of course, is a quite simple example. Often, many more variables are included in the analysis. Regression analysis has been received in evidence by courts to illustrate a variety of relationships. In one case, for instance, regression analysis was used to show the relationship between major league baseball players' contract value, the players' game statistics, and their salary level.[61]

---

60. EXPERT EVIDENCE, 324 (Bert Black & Patrick Lee eds., 1997).

61. Selig v. United States, 565 F.Supp. 524, 537–38 (E.D.Wis. 1983).

Chapter XII

BURDENS AND PRESUMPTIONS

Table of Sections

§ 12.1 Burdens of Persuasion and Production

In an adversarial system, the burden is upon each of the opposing parties to gather his evidence, present it at trial, and to attempt to persuade the trier of fact of its efficacy. The responsibility for dispute resolution lies in the hands of neutral participants– the judge and jury. In a jury trial, the judge instructs or "charges" the jury concerning the elements of a claim or defense and directs them, first, to ascertain the historical (adjudicative) facts from the evidence, and, then, by applying the law as described in the charge, to determine whether the claim or defense is established. For example, the judge may instruct the jury that slander consists of a defamatory statement [which would be further defined], that was communicated or "published" to one other than the person allegedly defamed, (the plaintiff), and that caused the plaintiff to sustain monetary damage or harm to reputation. Depending upon what defenses are asserted, the judge also may instruct the jury, for example, that if it finds that the statement is true or that it is privileged [which would be further explained], there is no liability. Of course, in a nonjury trial, the judge alone determines the historical facts and applies the governing legal principles—that is, she alone determines the existence or nonexistence of the elements.

In both judge and jury trials, there is a need to specify the consequences of the trier's determination that all (or alternatively only some) of the elements of a claim or defense are satisfactorily proved. This specification takes the form of allocating to the plaintiff and defendant their respective obligations with regard to proving the elements of a claim or defense. Thus, in a civil trial for slander the judge should make it clear to the jurors that the plaintiff, if he is to recover, must convince them of the existence of all of the contested elements of slander: for example, the defamatory statement, its publication, and the resulting damage or harm. The assertion of certain defenses (called "affirmative" defenses) requires additional instructions that make it clear that as to these defenses the defendant has the responsibility of proof. If, for example, the defendant pleads the affirmative defense of truth, the judge will charge the jury that *if the defendant* convinces them that the defamatory statement is true, he is not liable.

This allocation of the responsibility for proof is not made on an ad hoc basis, but in accordance with precedent or statutory provisions. In most instances, especially in civil cases, a party is obligated to *plead* those elements for which he bears the responsibility of proof. A number of considerations influence the rules allocating the burden of proof, such as which party seeks to have the court alter the status quo, whether one party alleges an event that appears improbable, whether any social or public policy militates for or against recovery, and whether certain evidence is more readily available to one party than to the other.

It is no simple matter to predict which of these factors may be dominant, but it is relatively easy to ascertain from statute or precedent the allocative rules of a particular jurisdiction. The rules loosely are spoken of as governing the "burden of proof"; the preferred and more precise phrase is "burden of persuasion" (or, alternatively, "the risk of nonpersuasion"), because it connotes that the party with the responsibility for particular elements has the burden of persuading (or bears the risk of not persuading) the trier that each of these particular elements exists.[1] The burdened party must persuade the trier of the existence of these elements according to a standard or degree of certainty mandated by the type

---

1. The phrase "burden of proof" often has been used to refer to two separate and distinct responsibilities of the parties: the "burden of persuasion" and the "burden of production." These two burdens typically fall upon the party with the burden of pleading her claim or, in the case of the defendant, counterclaim or affirmative defense. It is important to stress that, as noted in the text above, the "burden of producing evidence" refers to the obligation of producing sufficient evidence for the trier of fact to find each contested element that is necessary to sustain a claim, counterclaim, or affirmative defense. The "burden of persuasion" refers to a party's obligation to persuade the trier of fact, in accordance with the applicable standard of persuasion, that the burdened party's evidentiary account of the facts is the most likely version. In a civil trial, the normal standard of proof is more likely than not ("preponderance of the evidence"); in a criminal trial, the burden of persuasion for the prosecutor is beyond a reasonable doubt.

of proceeding: in a criminal trial, the government must prove the elements of an offense beyond a reasonable doubt; in a typical civil case, a party must prove the elements of his claim by a preponderance of the evidence (sometimes expressed by the phrases "greater weight of the evidence" or "more probable than not").[2] There also are occasional intermediate standards, the most common of which is "clear and convincing" proof, that apply in particular kinds of civil cases or to particular elements within them. For example, when a party claims that his opponent engaged in fraudulent conduct, he may be required to prove the elements of fraud by clear and convincing evidence.

These standards are intended to indicate the convincing force of the evidence required to meet the burden of persuasion, not quantitatively to measure the evidence. A defendant who presents five witnesses will not always prevail over a plaintiff who presents only one. What is important is the factfinder's belief in the existence or nonexistence of the disputed factual elements. Believability is not necessarily associated with the number of witnesses nor quantity of evidence presented.

The diagrammatic framework that we will examine shortly illustrates an allocation of the burdens of persuasion to the respective parties for the various factual elements of the foregoing defamation case. To establish the framework for a particular case, one must know or assume the elements of the claims or defenses asserted. Here, assume the plaintiff must plead and prove three elements by a preponderance of the evidence: the existence of the defamatory statement [A], the communication or publication to a third party [B], and the resulting damage (or harm) [C]. Assume that the defendant, first, denies that he made the statement and second, pleads the affirmative defense that the alleged defamatory statement is true. As to this and other affirmative defenses (such as contributory negligence or assumption of risk), the defendant nor-

---

2. In criminal cases, an accused may be assigned the burden of persuading the trier of the existence of certain affirmative defenses by a preponderance of the evidence. *See* Patterson v. New York, 432 U.S. 197, 206 (1977). However, there are some limits upon the state's power to allocate a burden of persuasion to the accused. In re Winship, 397 U.S. 358, 364 (1970), held that the prosecutor was obliged to prove beyond a reasonable doubt each element or fact necessary to constitute the crime charged. *Winship,* as applied in Mullaney v. Wilbur, 421 U.S. 684, 700–01 (1975), was construed to prohibit Maine from assigning to the accused the burden of proving provocation. The case turned, however, on the fine distinction that Maine viewed provocation as simply a means of disproving "malice aforethought—an essential element of the offense charged". *See Patterson,* 432 U.S. at 215–16. Thus, it appears that a state retains considerable latitude to place upon the accused the burden of persuasion for specified defenses. However, care must be taken to define the defense (or the criminal offense itself) so that the defense assigned to the accused does not simply negate or rebut an essential element of the crime charged, but rather consists of new facts that negate or reduce criminal responsibility. This distinction has been the subject of considerable debate.

mally bears the burden of persuasion which, in the case before us, means that he must convince the factfinder that the statement is true. Thus, each party has an affirmative responsibility of proof, although the defendant will prevail if *either* the plaintiff fails to persuade the trier of the existence of elements A, B, and C *or* the defendant does persuade the trier that the alleged statement is true (element D).

Because the jury resolves only those questions that reasonably can be disputed, the plaintiff, as a first step, must offer *evidence* sufficient to allow jury consideration of the existence of each element (this is his "burden of production"). That evidence must be at least adequate to permit a reasonable jury, viewing the evidence most favorably to the plaintiff, to find that the existence of the essential elements is more probable than their nonexistence—the "preponderance" standard. In the diagram below, the evidence at a minimum must justify the jury resolution signified by Block II. If evidence pertaining to the disputed elements is insufficient to raise a jury question (that is, insufficient to move all disputed elements in the plaintiff's case to Block II), the judge, on proper motion, will direct a verdict against the plaintiff ("grant a judgment as a matter of law") on the ground that he failed to produce sufficient evidence to support his case. Put otherwise, if plaintiff's evidence has failed to create a *reasonable* dispute as to one or more disputed elements, the case is resolved by the judge (Block I).

Plaintiffs Elements	Existence of Element Reasonably Disputable	Defendant's Element
I.	II.	III.
[Judge Resolution in Favor of D]	[Jury Resolution Based on the Evidence]	[Judge Resolution in Favor of P]
A (defamatory statement)		
B (publication)		
C (damage or harm)		
		D (truth)

Thus, ultimately to meet his burden of persuasion, the plaintiff must first satisfy the essential requirement of producing evidence sufficient to move all the elements necessary to his recovery from Block I (resolution by the judge) to block II (resolution by the jury). Unless his opponent has conceded the existence of one or more elements (thereby rendering proof unnecessary),[3] the plaintiff be-

---

3. The element might be conceded, for example, in the pleadings, by stipulation, or by an admission made during discovery. Furthermore, if the facts constituting a particular element were judi-

gins this process in his case in chief by *producing* evidence to support each element. (In other words, he strives to meet his burden of production). By meeting the immediate responsibility imposed by the burden of production, the plaintiff avoids a directed verdict (often called, "judgment as a matter of law")[4] and moves the dispute at least as far as Block II. In short, he paves the way toward meeting his second and greater burden, that of persuasion.

Of course, the plaintiff, if he can, will present evidence so convincing on one or more elements that no reasonable jury could find the nonexistence of the element(s). Absent persuasive rebuttal evidence by the defendant as to those elements thus firmly established, there would be a resolution by the judge (block III) *in favor* of the plaintiff. The judge either would impose a judgment for the plaintiff (if all elements indisputably were present) or would take from jury consideration, through a peremptory instruction, those elements that were proven indisputably. If the plaintiff, during his case in chief, were able to produce evidence of such convincing force that the existence of all the necessary elements was indisputable, the state of the evidence would be reflected as follows:

Plaintiff's Elements	Existence of Element Reasonably Disputable	Defendant's Element
I.	II.	III.
[Judge Resolution]	[Jury Resolution]	[Judge Resolution]
A (defamatory statement)		➤ A
B (publication)		➤ B
C (damage or harm)		➤ C
		D (truth)

Before the judge resolves the presence of any or all elements in plaintiff's favor, however, he must give the defendant the opportunity to rebut plaintiff's evidence. The depicted state of the evidence, therefore, requires that the defendant take steps toward rebuttal or else face a judge-imposed outcome. The burden of *producing evidence now has shifted to the defendant,* although the burden of persuasion has remained fixed upon the plaintiff. Because the plaintiff must show the existence of all three elements in order to recover, the defendant can avoid a directed verdict (that is, he can

---

cially noticed, no production of evidence would be necessary. FRE 201.

4. This is the terminology of the Federal Rules of Civil Procedure. *See* Fed. R. Civ. Proc. 50.

meet the shifted burden of production) by rebutting at least one element so that he raises a jury question as to that element.[5]

Ideally, the defendant strives to present evidence of such convincing force that one or more elements would be resolved in his favor by the judge (Block I of diagram), thus entitling *him* to a directed verdict. If the defendant were thus successful, the burden of production on the element(s) he was able to move to Block I would shift to the plaintiff, who would attempt to produce sufficient rebuttal evidence to move the issue of the existence of the element(s) back into Block II. As a practical matter, however, multiple shifts in the burden of production are unusual because it is not often that the state of the evidence fluctuates back and forth between the extremes represented by Blocks I and III. Furthermore, at the close of the evidence, it is frequently the jury, as opposed to the judge, that determines whether an element (that has not been conceded) exists. Often, the conflicting evidence results in a pattern (Block II) that justifies a reasonable jury in finding for either party.

The defendant, of course, is not limited to evidence that negates the plaintiff's evidence concerning elements A, B, and C. In the case before us, he also can avoid liability by establishing the affirmative defense of truth. To do so, he must first meet *his* burden of production by providing sufficient evidence of the truth of his statement to raise a jury question (that is, to move element D into Block II). If the evidence of truth were highly convincing (for example, the plaintiff had been convicted of the alleged misconduct described in the "defamatory" statement), thus moving the affirmative defense to Block I, the defendant could shift the burden of production for this element to the plaintiff. Note, however, that the burden of *persuasion* on the element of truth would not shift to the plaintiff, but would remain fixed upon the defendant, where it was originally assigned.

Various assumptions about the state of the evidence, including the allocation of the burdens of production and persuasion, can be depicted by using the basic diagram above. Suppose, for example, that *at the conclusion* of the case, the following state of the evidence exists:

---

5. As to those elements not rebutted (i.e., not moved out of Block III by the defendant), the judge will give a peremp- tory instruction that these elements shall be taken as established.

Plaintiffs Elements	Existence of Element Reasonably Disputable	Defendant's Element
I.	II.	III.
[Judge Resolution]	[Jury Resolution]	[Judge Resolution]
A (defamatory statement)		→ A
B (publication)		→ B
C (damage or harm)	→ C	
	D ←	D (truth)

The judge would instruct the jury that it shall take as an established fact that the defendant uttered (published) a slanderous statement to a third person (elements A and B). Jury questions exist, however, as to whether the plaintiff incurred damage or harm (element C) and as to whether the defendant's statement was true (element D). Regarding these reasonably disputed elements, both plaintiff and defendant have discharged their respective *burden of production* and each must now attempt to meet his *burdens of persuasion*. Accordingly, it is necessary that the judge instruct the jury that the plaintiff has the burden of persuasion on the element of damage or harm and the defendant has the burden of persuasion on the element of truth. If the jury does not believe that damage or harm occurred, it should render a defendant's verdict. If it finds (by a preponderance of the evidence) that there was damage or harm and if it is not persuaded by the defendant that the statement was true, it will return a verdict for the plaintiff. On the other hand, if the jury is persuaded that the statement was true, it will return a defendant's verdict regardless of whether the plaintiff sustained damage or harm.

Suppose, however, that the jury is in a state of indecision or equipoise regarding the issue of damage (harm) or the issue of truth.[6] When the jury agrees that the probabilities of the existence or nonexistence of an element are equal, the *allocation of the burden of persuasion becomes decisive in determining who prevails*. Because the party to whom that burden is allocated has failed to convince the jury affirmatively of the existence of the element(s) for

6. The problem of a jury in a state of decisional balance can arise regarding the existence of any element of a claim or defense that, because of the state of the evidence, is the proper subject of jury resolution. As to any element in Block II, the jury may conclude that the probability of the existence of the element is equal to the probability of its nonexistence. Of course, if the judge is the factfinder—that is, there is no jury—the judge also resolves disputed issues of fact in accordance with the allocation of the burden of persuasion. Note again that in the illustration above, the defendant prevails if either the plaintiff fails to carry his burden of persuasion on all essential elements or the defendant carries his burden of persuasion on the element of truth.

which he is responsible, he has not discharged his burden of persuasion and the jury, in obedience to proper instructions from the court, should find against him. Thus, if the jury concludes that it is equally likely that plaintiff did or did not suffer damage (or harm) from the defamatory statement, the plaintiff loses. He has failed to meet his burden of persuading the jury that it is more likely than not (the "preponderance" standard) that he sustained a loss. Correspondingly, if the jury believes that the probabilities of the truth or falsity of the defamatory statement are equal, the defendant has failed to carry his burden of persuasion on the affirmative defense.

As noted earlier, the substantive law dictates what elements constitute a civil or criminal offense and what element(s) comprise an affirmative defense. It is usually easy to determine which party bears the ultimate responsibility of proving by the applicable standard the elements of a claim or defense. Whether a party who has met his burden of producing sufficient evidence (by moving his case in Block II) has also met his burden of persuasion depends simply upon whether the trier, at the conclusion of the case, is persuaded by the evidence favoring that party.

In a jury trial, the verdict will signify the trier's determination of whether or not a party has carried his burden. Of course, a general verdict ("We find for the defendant") may not be completely informative about which party discharged his burden of persuasion. If the defendant has denied the plaintiff's allegations supporting a recovery and also has offered an affirmative defense (e.g., truth), a verdict for the defendant can mean either that the plaintiff failed to carry his burden on his contested elements or that the defendant successfully carried his burden on the affirmative defense. In a trial to the judge, there is usually a more explicit indication in the record (often contained in an opinion, memorandum, or statement of findings and conclusions) disclosing the basis upon which a judgment is given.

The section that follows will explore the effects of a presumption upon the burden of persuasion and the burden of production. A true presumption always affects the burden of production, but in most jurisdictions, including the federal system, a presumption does not, generally speaking, reallocate the burden of persuasion. It remains where it was originally assigned.

§ 12.2 Presumptions: General Nature and Effect

A trial involves many instances in which the trier of fact makes a factual determination by a process of inference. The factfinder first finds the existence of a certain fact or set of facts and then infers the existence of a related fact or facts. Human experience yields countless situations in which one fact or group of facts, if believed to exist, can by the process of inferential reasoning lead to a related factual conclusion. For example, if there is evidence that a letter was addressed properly and thereafter stamped and posted, it may be inferred that the addressee received it. As further examples: if a vehicle is labeled with the name of a person or company, it may be inferred that the name is that of the owner; if a person cannot be found and neither family nor acquaintances have heard from him for many years, it may be inferred that he is dead. In each of these situations certain *basic* facts (proper mailing, name on vehicle, absence without word) support a finding of the *inferred* facts (receipt, ownership, death).

Although the number and variety of basic facts that can lead to inferential conclusions are countless, certain patterns, such as those in the foregoing illustrations, frequently recur. The courts and legislatures have singled out many sets of basic and inferred facts, such as mailing-receipt, absence-death, labeling-ownership, and have given to them the status of presumptions. In many of these recurring instances, there appears to be a strong likelihood of the existence of the inferred or, more accurately, *presumed* conclusion. In other instances, the probative force of the basic facts may not be very convincing, yet some policy rationale or procedural consideration (such as superior access to evidence) may make the presumed conclusion desirable. Thus, when an article is found to be damaged after having been transported by more than one carrier, a presumption is raised that the last carrier caused the damage. Here, as among several carriers, the probative value of the presumption that the damage occurred while the property was in the custody of the last carrier may appear weak. Absent any evidence that pinpoints the cause of damage, it could be argued that it is no more probable that damage occurred while the goods were on the terminal carrier than it is that the damage occurred on one of the prior carriers. On the other hand, if the goods already were damaged at the time the last carrier took custody, it perhaps is probable that the last carrier would have noted or recorded the damaged condition. More importantly, the presumption here serves as a procedural device that gives to the plaintiff (who in the setting just described is disadvantaged in ascertaining the facts) a fair chance to recover by tentatively placing the damage with the last carrier. (The last carrier is in a better position to prove that it did not damage the goods.)

Let us now distinguish a presumption from an inference. Although the language used with reference to presumptions is often indiscriminate, a genuine presumption is raised by a basic fact or facts that, when accepted as true by the trier,[7] give rise to a *mandatory* inference, properly called a *presumed fact*. That is, *once the basic fact or facts are established,* the resulting presumed fact must be accepted by the trier *unless* it is rebutted by contravening evidence. An *inference* (if that term is properly applied) never has such a compulsory effect. The trier always is at liberty either to accept or reject an inferred fact. Note further that because a presumption founded on established facts creates a compulsory finding that remains obligatory until the presumed fact is rebutted, the raising of a presumption has a mandatory procedural effect: generally, it shifts to the opposing party at least the *burden of producing evidence.* (The presumed fact resides in a "judge resolution" area: Blocks I or III.) This is not true of an inference, which results only in creating a jury question (Block II) whether the inferred fact exists.

Although the terms "presumption" and "inference" as defined above have gained general usage, terminology in this area is not uniform. For example, judges and lawyers sometimes speak of "permissive presumptions" by which term they usually mean inferences. The cases also contain the term "presumption of law," which usually means a rebuttable presumption of the kind herein denominated simply a presumption. A "conclusive presumption," often encountered in statutes, is not really a presumption at all, but rather is a rule of substantive law. This "presumption" declares that certain basic facts, once established, give rise to an *irrebuttable* conclusion. For example, it may be presumed conclusively that a child under the age of seven years (basic fact) cannot commit a felony (presumed fact). This rule, although stated in presumptive language, is merely a substantive principle that serious criminal responsibility may not be imposed upon one under the age of seven.

§ 12.3 Some Sample Presumptions

Although presumptions are found in all jurisdictions, what one jurisdiction considers a presumption, another may classify as an inference. Since there are dozens and dozens of presumptions, the illustrative list that follows is but a small sample.

Basic Fact(s)	Presumed Fact
1. Letter regularly addressed and mailed	Received by addressee
2. Vehicle lawfully stopped is struck in rear by second vehicle	Driver of second vehicle was negligent

---

7. The existence of the basic fact could be proved at the trial, or established by pleadings, during discovery, in a stipulation, or by judicial notice.

3. Violent death from external means	Death was accidental (not a suicide)
4. Absent for 7 years without explanation or any communication with family or friends; inquiries unavailing	Absentee deceased
5. Will cannot be found	Revoked by testator
6. Employee in accident while driving vehicle owned by employer	Employee was acting within scope of employment
7. Goods delivered to bailee in good condition; damaged when returned	Bailee negligent
8. Goods damaged during transit provided by more than one carrier	Last carrier caused damage

There is a measure of probative force in each of the correlative groupings above. Other considerations, however, including superior knowledge or easier access to the evidence (numbers 1, 2, 6, 7, 8) and policies favoring the settlement of estates (4, 5), the protection of survivors (3, 4), or the recovery of damages in cases of accident (2, 6), appear to be operative. The next section will examine whether the considerations behind a particular presumption support a departure from the majority rule that a presumption shifts the burden of producing evidence, but does not disturb the burden of persuasion, which remains fixed upon the party to whom it originally was assigned.

§ 12.4　Presumptions: Impact Upon Opponent and Effect of Rebuttal Evidence

It will be recalled that the effect of a presumption always may be avoided by proving the nonexistence of the basic facts that give rise to the presumed fact. However, rebuttal evidence showing the nonexistence of the basic facts often is not so compelling as to cause the judge, by instructions or otherwise, to remove from the case altogether any consideration of a presumption. If the evidence against the existence of the basic facts is not so persuasive as to cause the judge to resolve the question of their existence, he will instruct the jury that if it finds the basic fact(s) exist, the presumed fact arises. For example, where the evidence conflicts on whether a letter was properly addressed and mailed, the judge will charge the jury that no presumption of receipt will arise unless the jury first finds that the letter was properly posted.

The foregoing discussion does not consider what general effect is to be given to a presumption after the basic facts are found to exist, nor does it address the related issue of the measure of rebuttal evidence necessary to negate the presumed fact. The various jurisdictions lack uniformity in their approach to these fundamental aspects of presumptions. There are, however, two dominant views regarding the general effect of a presumption; each has substantial support. The majority view, which was first associated with Professor James Bradley Thayer,[8] a 19th Century evidence scholar, holds that when a presumption arises after the establishment of the basic facts, its only procedural effect is to shift the burden of producing evidence to the opponent. The opponent must meet the shifted burden of producing evidence, but he does not bear the ultimate burden of convincing the trier of fact of the nonexistence of the presumed fact. The second view, embraced by a significant minority of jurisdictions, holds that the procedural effect of establishing the basic facts is usually to shift the burden of persuasion. This latter position, often called the Morgan view because of its advocacy by the late Professor Edmund Morgan,[9] places great weight both on the probative link between basic and presumed facts and on the supposed utility of presumptions in advancing desirable social policy.

Professor Morgan's minority approach gives considerably greater effect to most presumptions: a shift in the burden of persuasion results in placing upon the opponent the burden of convincing the trier that the nonexistence of the presumed fact is more probable than its existence. Simply providing enough rebuttal evidence to allow a reasonable jury to find the nonexistence of the presumed fact is insufficient to negate the "Morgan" presumption because the burden of persuasion has shifted to the party against whom the presumption operates. This shift in the persuasion burden occurs if the existence of the basic facts is conceded; it also occurs if the proponent of the presumption convinces the judge that the basic facts cannot be reasonably disputed (i.e. no jury question exists). And, of course, as we have seen, the existence of the basic facts of a presumption is sometimes an issue for the jury. If so, the proponent attempts to carry his burden of convincing the trier of the truth of the basic facts so that the presumption will arise. If the presumption does arise, and the jurisdiction applies Morgan's ap-

---

8. James Thayer, Preliminary Treatise on Evidence (1898). See especially pp. 314, 336–37.

9. Edmund Morgan, Some Problems of Proof Under the Anglo-American System of Litigation, 74–81 (1956).

proach, the burden of persuasion to show the nonexistence of the presumed fact will be cast upon the opponent of the presumption.[10]

It is important to recognize, however, that few if any jurisdictions invariably adhere either to the Thayer (majority) or Morgan (minority) view of the effect of presumptions. The marked tendency is to endorse generally one view or the other, but to make occasional departures in case law or statutes for selected presumptions. Thus, a jurisdiction adopting Thayer's position may nonetheless determine that, in the case of a certain presumption, special considerations warrant the greater presumptive effect of shifting the burden of persuasion. Some departures, often contained in statutory enactments, are likely to be found in every jurisdiction.

The debate over which general approach to presumptions—Thayer or Morgan—is the more desirable one is not likely to be decisively concluded. The difficulty is that such a variety of reasons underlie presumptions that a single approach to all presumptions seems destined to fail. Thus, the majority (Thayer) approach, which does not reassign the burden of persuasion, can be criticized when it is applied to certain presumptions—for example, those that are supported both by convincing probative force and strong policy grounds. Once the basic facts are established, the cogent considerations of policy and probability that were instrumental in the initial assignment of the burden of persuasion arguably support a reallocation of this burden. The *argument for* reassigning the burden of persuasion can be advanced (and often is) when *either* probative force *or* policy considerations associated with a particular presumption appear quite strong. On the other hand, the minority (Morgan) view can be criticized when it is applied to some presumptions for its procedural effect on many routine presumptions may be greater than desirable.[11] Furthermore, the fact that a presumption is supported by the *same* considerations that underlie the initial allocation of the burden of persuasion does not *necessarily* mean that the persuasion burden should be shifted. These considerations favor *both* the initial assignment of the persuasion burden and the reallocation of that burden to the opposing party.

Thus, the continuing problem faced by legislatures and courts is whether to adopt, with some exceptions, the Thayer approach or the Morgan approach or, alternatively, to adopt an intermediate scheme that somewhat favors one view or the other but does not coincide with either. One scheme, for example, is to shift the

---

10. For a trenchant criticism of the Morgan approach, pointing out the confusion that can attend its implementation, see Ronald Lansing, *Enough is Enough: A Critique of the Morgan View* *of Rebuttable Presumptions in Civil Cases*, 62 Or. L. Rev. 485 (1983).

11. *See, e.g.,* Fed. R. Evid. 301, Comment from the Report No. 93–650 of the House Committee on the Judiciary.

burden of persuasion when there is a substantial probative relationship between the basic facts and the presumed fact. In the absence of such a nexus, a presumption shifts only the burden of production. Another approach, usually associated with the California Evidence Code, is to shift the burden of persuasion for those presumptions identified by the legislature or courts as based upon "public policy";[12] presumptions outside the public-policy category shift only the burden of producing evidence. Because many presumptions have at least some public policy underpinnings, the determination of which presumptions are within the persuasion-shifting category is not easy. Obviously, any dual approach to presumptions necessitates careful inquiry by student and practitioner as to the procedural effect assigned to a particular presumption.

     Caution must be exercised even in a jurisdiction that purports to adhere to a single view of the effect of presumptions. As previously noted, several exceptions will usually be found; that is, some presumptions will be singled out by statute or judicial opinion for special treatment. The reasons for this departure from the normal scheme will vary, but factors (singly or in combination) such as policy concerns, fairness, or probative force may justify singling out certain presumptions for special treatment. For example, the forceful policy favoring the legitimacy of children, coupled with strong probability, gives a special strength to the presumption that a child born during a couple's marriage is the legitimate offspring of the husband, and not the child of another man.

     One must be alert for yet another variance. As noted below, even among those jurisdictions that adopt the general view of Professor Thayer (and thus to shift only the burden of production), there may be differences in the measure of rebuttal evidence that is ordinarily considered sufficient to negate the presumed fact. Fortunately, most jurisdictions that adhere to Thayer's view also endorse his position concerning the measure of counterevidence necessary to rebut the presumption. That position is that a presumption *disappears after the introduction of rebuttal evidence that is sufficiently probative to allow a reasonable trier to find the nonexistence of the presumed fact.* In practical terms, this usually means that the opponent has produced evidence sufficient for the trier to find the opposite of the presumed fact—for example, to find the *nonreceipt* of a properly mailed letter. Once adequate rebuttal evidence is presented, a true Thayer presumption disappears from the case. The trier ultimately decides the issue in question—the existence or nonexistence of the fact that was the subject of the presumption— just as if no presumption was ever raised. Under this pure Thayeri-

---

12. Ann.Cal.Evid.Code   §§ 603–606 (West 1995).

an approach, the presumption is extinguished by the presentation of rebuttal evidence that the *judge* deems *sufficient* to support a finding that the presumed fact does not exist. It is of no consequence *to the disappearance of the presumption* that neither the judge nor the trier *believed* the counterevidence. The judge simply determines whether the rebuttal evidence was sufficient to support a finding contrary to that expressed in the presumed fact. Of course, even if the presumption disappears, any remaining probative value that naturally links the basic fact to the presumed fact remains intact.

A small number of variant jurisdictions, discontented with the comparative ease by which the opponent of a "Thayer" presumption can negate its effect, depart from Thayer's view in one important respect: while adhering to his view that a presumption shifts only the burden of production, they have taken steps to increase the opponent's burden of rebuttal. These jurisdictions have rules that, roughly, occupy a middle ground between the Thayer and Morgan positions. For example, a few jurisdictions allow a presumption to disappear only when the rebuttal evidence is substantial. In other of these "hybrid" jurisdictions, the presumption persists unless the rebuttal evidence makes the nonexistence of the presumed fact at least as probable as its existence.[13] Although these compromise positions appear in theory to avoid some of the shortcomings of both the majority and minority approaches, they often cause confusion and practical difficulties, especially in jury trials. For example, what constitutes substantial or equal evidence defies description and, very often, recognition as well. Further, it is not always clear whether the judge or jury makes the determination of the sufficiency of the rebuttal evidence. When the determination is left to the jury and the rebuttal evidence reasonably could be considered substantial, but is not indisputably so, the jury may be instructed concerning the existence of a presumption, but should also be told that the presumption is to be disregarded if in the jury's view the rebuttal evidence is substantial. Such an instruction is invariably difficult to follow.

As previously suggested, it is difficult to support a single approach that applies to all presumptions. Thus, a flexible scheme that treats differently various presumptions within a jurisdiction might be preferable. Yet disparate approaches introduce further complexity and confusion to an area already cluttered with ambiguity and misunderstanding. Perhaps a practical compromise, admittedly imperfect, offers the best solution. As a starting point, there is much to be said for adopting a general approach that applies to all

---

13. For a case reviewing various rebuttal formulations, their rationale, and the decisions implementing them, see Hinds v. John Hancock Mutual Life Ins. Co., 155 Me. 349, 155 A.2d 721 (1959).

presumptions except those relatively few that for compelling reasons are singled out for different treatment. This concession to uniformity avoids the difficulty of classifying a large number of presumptions into different procedural categories.

As a general approach, Thayer's position, which has been adopted by the Federal Rules of Evidence and by a slim majority of states, suffers no greater disadvantages than the competing theories. It is true, as the critics point out, that Thayer's approach does not always give a sufficient effect to presumptions. The critics are, of course, also correct in their observation that it is comparatively easy to rebut a Thayer presumption. As we have seen, an opponent need only present enough rebuttal evidence to permit a reasonable trier to find the nonexistence of the presumed fact. On the other hand, Thayer's view is easy to understand and administer. It avoids the problem of confusing juries by dividing the burden of persuasion (basic fact to proponent; presumed fact to opponent) on what is essentially a single factual issue—a division that is necessary under the Morgan view. Further, the disappearance of a Thayer presumption does not usually dissipate the force of the presumption altogether: because almost all presumptions are supported by a logical relationship between the basic and presumed fact,[14] the destruction of the presumption does not negate the residual probative force yielded by the basic facts. That is, the disappearance of a presumption only removes its compulsory effect; after a presumption vanishes, there still remains the inference that arises from the basic facts. In many jurisdictions, the judge may, in his discretion, instruct the jury concerning the existence of this residual inference. It seems especially desirable to give such an instruction in cases where either the probative relationship between the basic and presumed fact is very strong or the rebuttal evidence is barely sufficient to eliminate the presumption. Such a practice makes the Thayer view more acceptable, and may represent the best compromise in an area marked by both intense disagreement and a host of practical difficulties.

§ 12.5 Presumptions: Instructing the Jury

In civil cases, under both the predominant Thayer view of presumptions and the minority Morgan view, it is not necessary to use the term "presumption" in instructing the jury. Avoiding this term is desirable because the jury may misunderstand a presumption's function and effect. Under Thayer's approach, if there is no

---

14. Even some presumptions commonly thought to originate only in procedural convenience or fairness (e.g., goods damaged during transit: damage caused by last carrier in the series) may be regarded as based upon logical inferences. *See* In re Wood's Estate, 374 Mich. 278, 132 N.W.2d 35, 42 (1965); *See* § 12.3.

rebuttal evidence and the existence of the basic fact is undisputed, the judge either directs a verdict (if the presumed fact is dispositive) or instructs the jury that it shall consider the presumed fact as proven. In the latter instance, use of the term presumption is unnecessary. The judge simply describes the presumed fact: "You shall find that the letter in question, written by A and addressed to B, was received." If the basic fact is contested, but there is no evidence rebutting the presumed fact,[15] it still is unnecessary to mention the word "presumption": the judge simply instructs the jury that "If from the evidence you believe that the letter in question was regularly addressed and mailed, you will find that it was received." Finally, if there is sufficient rebuttal evidence directed at the presumed fact so as to entitle a reasonable jury to find the nonexistence of that fact, the presumption disappears from the case in a Thayer jurisdiction. In recognition of any residual inference, however, the judge, if permitted by local practice, should sometimes instruct the jurors that if they conclude that the letter was properly addressed and mailed, they *may* find that it was received.[16]

In jurisdictions that hold that presumptions (or at least certain presumptions) shift the burden of persuasion (Morgan's view), the jury also may receive the case without mention of the term 'presumption.' If, for example, the basic facts are admitted or indisputably established and the opponent of the presumption attacks only the presumed fact, the judge should instruct the jury [to continue the example above] that "you will find that the letter in question was received, unless from the evidence you believe its nonreceipt is more probable than its receipt." This instruction gives the maximum effect to the presumption by shifting the burden of persuasion on the issue of receipt to the party against whom the presumption operates. If the opponent attacks both the basic facts and the presumed fact, the judge should instruct "that if from the evidence you believe that the letter in question was accurately addressed and thereafter properly mailed, then you also shall find that it was received, unless you believe that its nonreceipt is more probable than its receipt."

ILLUSTRATION

Henry, aged 38, was a wealthy, but restless, husband and father. In April, 1998, he embarked on a fishing trip.

15. As a practical matter, this is unlikely to occur because the opponent will probably also offer evidence rebutting the presumed fact. But it could occur (as, for example, where the addressee is not available as a witness) that there is no evidence available to rebut the presumed fact.

16. The most appealing case for judicial comment on the residual inference is where there is a strong probative link between the basic fact(s) and the presumed fact.

The plan was, or so he told his wife and two children, to fly to Argentina, where he would meet an old friend. The two of them, with the help of a guide, would then spend two weeks fishing. But, alas, Henry did not appear at the designated meeting place—a hotel in Buenos Aires—although he was listed among the passengers on board a flight from Washington, D.C. to Buenos Aires. Nor did Henry return to his wife and family, or send them any word of his whereabouts.

Seven and a half years later (in October, 2005), his wife—or perhaps his widow—sued the Safeguard Insurance Co. to collect the face value ($2,000,000) of two insurance policies covering Henry's life. The defendant answered the wife's complaint with allegations denying that Henry was dead. At trial, the wife, who under the applicable law had the burden of establishing Henry's death, testified that neither she nor the children had heard from Henry for more than seven years. Nor had they been able to locate him. Other friends, relatives, and business associates gave similar testimony, either in person or by deposition.

(1) Assume that the defendant, Safeguard, offers no counter evidence, but simply argues that Henry's silence is insufficient proof of his death, especially since there have been no reports of his death, no circumstances suggesting an accident, and no evidence that his body has been found. Should the judge nonetheless direct a plaintiff's verdict (enter judgment for the wife as a matter of law)? If not, how should the judge instruct the jury?

(2) Assume that Safeguard offers the testimony of Barry, the old friend that Henry was supposed to meet in Buenos Aires. Barry testifies that in March, 2004, he traveled to Budapest, Hungary, on business. (Budapest also happens to have been Henry's favorite city.) There, while walking down one of the main streets, he is sure that he spotted Henry who was waiting to board a bus, about forty yards from Barry. When Barry called Henry's name, the latter turned his head toward Barry, pulled his fedora down over his forehead and quickly climbed aboard the bus, which pulled away from the curb. Should the judge direct a verdict? If not, how should she instruct the jury?

(3) Suppose there was conflicting evidence as to whether anyone had heard from Henry in the last seven years. Family members and relatives testify that they had heard nothing. However, Adam, Henry's closest friend

from college, testifies for the defense that in September, 2003, he received a card (now lost or discarded) from Henry expressing the latter's regrets that various business engagements in Europe would prevent him from attending their college reunion. On cross-examination, Adam admits the he cannot be absolutely sure the card was from Henry, but it looked like Henry's handwriting and signature, and the card arrived three weeks before their class reunion. Furthermore, as Adam recalls, the postmark was from somewhere in Eastern Europe, probably Budapest. (Assume, for purposes of this third question, that there was no testimony that Henry had been seen in Budapest or anywhere else.) Should the judge direct a verdict? If not, how should she instruct the jury?

In subpart (1) of the Illustration, Safeguard offers no rebuttal evidence. Thus, the basic fact appears to be established. If cross-examination had cast doubt on the basic fact (so that a reasonable jury could disbelieve it), then the jury would have to decide if the basic fact—that no one had heard from or seen Henry—was established. Assuming it is established beyond reasonable dispute, the judge would direct a verdict (enter judgment as a matter of law) for the wife. If the existence of the basic fact were a disputed jury question, the judge would instruct the jurors that if they found that no one had seen or heard from Henry for seven years, they should find that Henry was dead and return a verdict for the plaintiff.

In subpart (2) of the Illustration, Safeguard provides rebuttal evidence that challenges the presumed fact—that Henry is dead. The testimony of Barry is probably sufficient for the jury to find that Henry was sighted and alive in March, 2004. Barry's familiarity with Henry, coupled with "Henry's" furtive actions, and the fact that he might have chosen to live in or visit Budapest, would probably suffice to allow a reasonable trier of fact to conclude that Henry was not dead. After all, there is no evidence other than his absence and lack of communication that he is deceased. Thus, in a Thayer jurisdiction, the presumption of death—that is, the compulsion to find death—would disappear and the jurors would decide if the plaintiff and her witnesses had convinced them by a preponderance of the evidence that Henry was deceased. (Perhaps they will disbelieve Barry or conclude that he was mistaken.) However, in a Morgan jurisdiction, the burden of persuasion would shift to Safeguard to convince the jury that Henry is still alive. If the jurors believed that Henry was alive in March, 2004, when he was seen in Budapest, it is highly plausible, and probably required, that the jury conclude that he is not deceased at the time of trial—after all, the only evidence of his death is noncommunication. There is no evidence, other than Henry's continued silence, that he died between 2004 and the date of trial (2005).

In subpart (3) of the Illustration, there is conflicting evidence concerning the basic fact. Here, the judge simply instructs the jury that if it finds that no one has heard from Henry for seven years, it must find that Henry is dead. If the jury finds that the probabilities of the existence of the *basic fact* are equal to the probabilities of its nonexistence—a state of equipoise—than the jurors should return a verdict for the defendant, Safeguard. A party relying on a presumption—here the wife—bears the burden of production and persuasion as to the basic fact(s). It is only after the basic fact is established that a presumption arises. If the jury believes that no one has heard from Henry for seven years, the basic fact is established, and the jury must return a plaintiff's verdict. An unrebutted presumption, in the context of this case, yields a plaintiff's verdict in either a Morgan or a Thayer jurisdiction. However, if the jury concludes that Henry wrote to Adam in September, 2003, the basic fact is not established and the presumed fact—death—does not arise. Lacking any evidence that her husband died between 2003 and 2005, the wife cannot carry her burden of proof. The jury should be instructed that if it decides that Henry wrote to Adam in 2003, it should return a verdict for Safeguard.

Other evidentiary states can be imagined. Suppose, for example, Safeguard produced rebuttal evidence challenging both the basic fact (Adam heard from Henry) and the presumed fact (Barry saw Henry). Under Thayer's view, the presumed fact would be negated by evidence allowing a reasonable trier to find the nonexistence of the presumed fact—to find that Henry was not dead. But under Morgan's view, the judge would instruct the jurors that if it determined that no one had heard from Henry for seven years (the basic fact), they should conclude that Henry was dead, unless Safeguard convinced them by the weight (preponderance) of the evidence that Henry was still alive. Observe, again, that in instructing the jury, the judge need not use the word "presumption." And, as we have noted, it is advisable to avoid this term, for it is often misapprehended by both lay persons and lawyers.

§ 12.6 Presumptions Under the Federal Rules of Evidence

Rules 301 and 302 of the Federal Rules of Evidence deal with presumptions. No provision is made for presumptions in criminal cases, largely because at the time of the passage of the Federal Rules these presumptions were being considered in connection with a revision of the federal criminal code. This revision, however, was never enacted. In addressing civil cases, the Federal Rules neither define nor enumerate presumptions, but only state their function and probative effect. In proceedings where federal substantive law governs the claim or defense, Rule 301 adopts the Thayer view, specifying that "a presumption imposes on the party against whom it is directed the burden of going forward with the evidence to rebut or meet the presumption, but does not shift to such party the burden of proof in the sense of the risk of nonpersuasion...."[17] Although Rule 301 does not expressly adopt Thayer's view of the measure of rebuttal evidence that is required to negate the presumption (evidence "sufficient" to permit a reasonable trier to find the nonexistence of the presumed fact), most courts and commentators have concluded that Rule 301 adopts the Thayer approach in its entirety.

The Federal Rules also contain an accommodation to the varying state approaches to presumptions. Rule 302 specifies that "the effect of a presumption respecting a fact which is an element of a claim or defense as to which State law supplies the rule of decision is determined in accordance with State law."[18] Students of civil procedure will recognize that this accommodation accords with the principles and policy of Erie Railroad Co. v. Tompkins.[19] The Rule defers to state law only as to those presumed facts that constitute an element of a claim or defense; presumptions of lesser impact are governed by the Thayer approach of Federal Rule 301— even in diversity cases where state law is applicable.

As we have observed, absent a statutory override, the Thayer approach, embodied in Rule 301, governs with regard to facts underlying a federal claim or defense. This is true even if these federal elements coexist (in the same case) with state claims or defenses. Thus, in a case involving both federal and state claims, as well as in cases involving state claims with *elements* supported by a presumption and an *incidental* matter also supported by a presumption, the judge and jury may have to deal with several presumptions of differing force and effect. When this occurs, it may be difficult to instruct the jury in understandable terms as to the proper effect of the various presumptions. Sometimes a federal presumption will be raised by certain basic facts and a similar state presumption will be raised by the same basic facts. If the state rule governing the rebuttal of the presumption is different from the federal rule (Thayer), federal practice should prevail, although this issue is not definitively settled.

---

17. Fed.R.Evid. 301. The phrase "risk of nonpersuasion" is synonymous with "burden of persuasion." As previously noted in the text, the party with the burden of persuasion bears the risk that he will lose his case if he is unable to persuade the trier.

18. FRE 302.

19. 304 U.S. 64 (1938); *See* Dick v. New York Life Ins. Co., 359 U.S. 437, 446 (1959). (*Erie* doctrine embraces presumptions).

Rule 301 does not, of course, mean that all civil presumptions arising under federal law are treated in accordance with Thayer. Congress may enact a particular statutory presumption and specify its effect, for example, by stipulating that it shall persist until rebutted by clear and convincing evidence[20] or that it shall shift the burden of persuasion.[21] Sometimes courts must struggle to determine whether a statutory presumption supersedes Rule 301. For example, the courts have divided on the procedural effect of the presumption of illegal discrimination that arises under various antidiscrimination statutes. Generally, the statutes provide that a presumption of discrimination arises upon the showing of a possibly discriminatory practice, such as the rejection of a qualified minority applicant for employment. The Supreme Court has at least partially resolved the dispute. Under one major statutory scheme, Title VII, the Court has said that the defendant needs only to meet the burden of production by presenting evidence justifying his employment practices (showing a nondiscriminatory motive).[22] Finally, despite the passage of Rule 301, the federal courts have occasionally upheld the continuing validity of certain presumptions with early statutory or common law origins that, usually for compelling policy or probative reasons, have been consistently construed as shifting the burden of persuasion.[23]

§ 12.7 Conflicting Presumptions

There is usually little point in raising a presumption if the presumed fact countervails an element of a claim or defense upon which the opponent of the presumption already has the burden of persuasion. In discharging his burden, the opponent will negate the effect of a presumption under either the Thayer or the Morgan view. Of course, a presumption against the party already having the burden of persuasion would have an effect if it raised the level of persuasion required for rebuttal of the presumed fact. Thus, an opponent who already had the burden of persuasion would nonetheless be adversely affected by a presumption that could not be rebutted by the greater weight of the evidence (the usual standard

20. *See, e.g.*, 26 U.S.C.A. § 6653 (underpayment of tax treated as presumptively negligent unless taxpayer shows otherwise by clear and convincing evidence).

21. *See* Alabama By–Products Corp. v. Killingsworth, 733 F.2d 1511, 1514–15 (11th Cir.1984).

22. *See* Texas Dep't of Comm. Affairs v. Burdine, 450 U.S. 248, 254–55 (1981), *remanded to* 647 F.2d 513 (5th Cir. 1981).

23. James v. River Parishes Co., Inc., 686 F.2d 1129, 1132–33 (5th Cir. 1982) (longstanding presumption of maritime common law that a vessel found adrift was operated negligently shifts the burden of persuasion; unaffected by Rule 301); Plough, Inc. v. Mason & Dixon Lines, 630 F.2d 468, 472 (6th Cir. 1980) (Rule 301 does not affect prior statutory presumption of the 1906 Carmack Amendment imposing on common carriers the burden of persuasion in rebutting the presumption of carrier liability).

of persuasion), but rather could be rebutted only if the contrary evidence was at least clear and convincing.

It occasionally happens that evidence admitted in a case provides a foundation for establishing two sets of basic facts which then give rise to conflicting presumptions. For example, when there is evidence of a legal marriage between *H* and *W,* there often is a presumption that their marital status continues. Another presumption often arises when the basic fact of a ceremonial marriage between *H* and *W–2* is shown: any prior marriage is presumed to have been dissolved. In a case where evidence supporting both sets of basic facts is introduced, how is the court to handle the "conflicting presumptions"? It is obvious that both presumptions cannot operate with full force.

One solution, favored by Thayer and adopted by many courts, is simply to ignore both presumptions. In essence, the presumptions negate each other. Thus, it is possible in the context of conflicting presumptions to give some effect to the presumption raised against the party who normally has the burden of persuasion: the opposing presumption can at least have the effect of negating his presumption and of forcing him to produce evidence of the fact (that would have been presumed) without the added force of a presumption. Permitting such an effect, that is, allowing the opposing presumption to dispel the presumption that favors the party with the burden of proof, reaches the result favored by Thayer. Both presumptions disappear from the case. Another possible resolution, suggested by the discussion above, would be to ignore only the presumption that was *raised against* the party with the burden of persuasion. The party with the burden would still have the benefit of his presumption.

Those jurisdictions that do not routinely negate both presumptions usually inquire whether one of the two presumptions is supported by the greater weight of policy or probability, or perhaps both. If one of the presumptions is so supported to a greater extent than the other, it is given preference and the lesser presumption is ignored. Assuming the surviving presumption is in favor of the party with the burden of persuasion, the case goes forward with one operative presumption. In the example above, the presumption favoring the legality of the current marriage has strong support on both policy and probability grounds, and it would be preferred in many jurisdictions.

§ 12.8 Presumptions in Criminal Cases: Constitutional Problems

Once the basic facts are established, a true or mandatory presumption compels a finding of the presumed fact in the absence of contrary evidence. This compulsion appears to confirm that there exists a strong probative connection between the basic facts and the presumed fact. Indeed, it may be argued that in order to surmount a constitutional challenge there must be *some* probative association between the basic facts and the presumed facts. Thus, even though many presumptions rest largely upon policy grounds, it is perhaps required by the due process clause that the presumed fact rests in part upon at least modestly probative basic facts. In making this assertion, however, one must distinguish between criminal and civil cases. In the latter, where there are comparatively few constitutional restraints, probably no more is required by the Constitution than a showing of at least some rational connection between the basic facts and the presumed fact.[24] This requirement, in practice, demands only minimal probabilistic ties. It is uncertain whether a civil presumption based *entirely* upon policy (or some other nonprobative ground) would meet constitutional standards. In fact, there is reason to predict that such a presumption would be sustained,[25] but the cases offer no definitive answer.[26] In any event, the constitutionality of presumptions in civil cases is usually a distant concern.

In criminal cases, special considerations limit the scope of allowable presumptions. A directed verdict against the accused is never permitted; further, a conviction must rest upon the trier's belief beyond a reasonable doubt that each element of the charged offense exists.[27] Of course, these propositions should not necessarily forbid the use of a rebuttable presumption against the accused. The Constitution does not forbid placing upon the accused certain obligations to offer proof: it has long been an accepted practice to assign to him certain procedural burdens with respect to so-called "affirmative defenses." These defenses, such as insanity, provocation, self-defense, and entrapment, can either exonerate the accused or, in some instances, reduce the degree of his culpability. The

---

24. Usery v. Turner Elkhorn Mining Co., 428 U.S. 1, 28 (1976).

25. If by a reformulation of the substantive law the state could eliminate altogether the presumed fact from the claim or defense of which it presently is a part, then the state should have the option of providing that such fact will be presumed until sufficiently rebutted. For example, suppose a legislature enacted a presumption that if a product was shown to be defective, the manufacturer would be presumed to have been negligent. Of course, in reality this presumption has at least some probative force. But suppose it was supported only by the policy of spreading the cost of prod-

uct-related injury and of encouraging care in the design and manufacture of products. The legislative power to eliminate negligence (the presumed fact) and make the manufacturer strictly liable for its defective product suggests that the state can take the intermediate step of retaining negligence, but presuming its presence. In short, the greater power includes the lesser. *See* Ferry v. Ramsey, 277 U.S. 88, 94 (1928).

26. *Compare* Western & Atl. R.R. v. Henderson, 279 U.S. 639, 642 (1929), *with* Mobile, J. & K.C. R.R. v. Turnipseed, 219 U.S. 35, 40–41 (1910).

27. *In re Winship*, 397 U.S. 358, 364 (1970).

central feature of an affirmative defense (as that term is properly used) is that the defendant introduces additional facts that reduce or relieve his criminal responsibility. If the accused wishes to offer one of these defenses, he is usually required not only to enter an appropriate pleading or plea, but also to offer supporting evidence. Depending upon the jurisdiction and the particular affirmative defense, the accused must either carry the burden of producing evidence or discharge the greater burden of persuading the trier (usually by a preponderance of the evidence) of the existence of the defense.

The widespread recognition of affirmative defenses and the general approval of their constitutionality might suggest that presumptions, which like affirmative defenses place procedural burdens upon a criminal defendant, should be allowable even when invoked against the accused. The usual effect of a presumption is to shift to the opponent only the burden of producing evidence; the burden of persuasion is normally left undisturbed and, in the present context, would remain with the prosecution. Since even affirmative defenses that call upon the accused to carry the burden of persuasion seem to fall within constitutional bounds,[28] it would appear that presumptions having a similar or weaker procedural effect should not raise serious constitutional concerns. Whatever the logic of the foregoing suggestions, however, the United States Supreme Court has emphatically rejected them.

In the discussion that follows, you should carefully distinguish between two types of presumptions. As used by the Supreme Court a "mandatory presumption" is one which, once the basic facts are shown, *requires* the factfinder to find the presumed fact *unless* the defendant introduces at least some contrary evidence; a "permissive presumption" (also called an inference) is one which permits but *never* requires the factfinder to infer the presumed fact from the basic facts. Courts have not always been careful to state which form of presumption they are addressing, but proper classification is easy enough once one realizes that if a presumption shifts *any* evidentiary burden to the accused, it is mandatory. Obviously, a mandatory presumption has a greater impact on the accused than does a permissive presumption, since the former (but not the latter) casts a burden on the accused to respond with rebuttal evidence. We shall see, however, that even permissive presumptions have been subjected to constitutional scrutiny.

In Mullaney v. Wilbur,[29] the Court held unconstitutional Maine's mandatory presumption that shifted to the accused the burden of proving provocation. The judge had instructed the jury

---

28. *See* Patterson v. New York, 432 U.S. 197, 206 (1977).

29. 421 U.S. 684 (1975).

that if they found that the accused unlawfully and intentionally killed the victim, they should presume malice aforethought unless they were convinced by the accused that he acted from sudden provocation.[30] It was significant that under Maine law a showing of provocation was viewed as negating malice aforethought—an essential element of murder.[31] Thus, provocation can plausibly be distinguished from an affirmative defense since the latter does not negate an essential element of the prosecution's case, but rather introduces *new facts* that, if believed by the trier, relieves or reduces the defendant's criminal responsibility. In the Court's view, the effect of the presumption in *Mullaney* was to relieve the prosecution of the burden, imposed by the leading case of In Re Winship,[32] of proving malice aforethought (an element of the crime charged) beyond a reasonable doubt.

Mullaney, decided in 1975, was not the first case in which the Supreme Court invalidated a criminal presumption. However, the tenor of the Court's *Mullaney* opinion and its emphasis upon the state's inescapable duty to prove all elements of the crime charged raised the question whether a mandatory presumption could *ever* be used against an accused. As interpreted in later cases, *Mullaney* meant *at least* that a presumption may not, consistent with the requirements of due process, shift to the accused the burden of proof—even under a preponderance standard—with regard to an element of the crime.[33] Beyond that, the decision was ambiguous. It was, of course, possible to read the *Mullaney* opinion narrowly: the presumption in that case operated to shift the burden of persuasion (not simply the burden of production); furthermore, there was not an especially strong probative nexus between the basic facts (illegal and intentional killing) and the presumed fact (malice aforethought). But a broad application of *Mullaney* could render unconstitutional any presumption that shifted a procedural burden (persuasion or production) to the accused. The precise effect of *Mullaney* still remains somewhat uncertain, but the overall picture, as developed in subsequent cases, is now relatively clear.

The Supreme Court has sometimes gauged the constitutional validity of a criminal presumption by assessing the probative nexus between the basic facts and the presumed fact, while on other occasions, the Court has focused upon whether or not the presump-

---

30. Id. at 686. The defendant had to prove provocation by a preponderance of the evidence.

31. Id. at 686–87. *Patterson,* 432 U.S. at 215–16, upholding the constitutionality of an affirmative defense almost identical to the *Mullaney* presumption, distinguished *Mullaney* on this ground.

32. 397 U.S. 358 (1970).

33. *See* Sandstrom v. Montana, 442 U.S. 510, 527 (1979), (Rehnquist, J., concurring), *remanded to* 184 Mont. 391, 603 P.2d 244 (1979); Francis v. Franklin, 471 U.S. 307, 314 (1985).

tion under review operates to relieve the prosecution of its burden of proving each element of the offense charged. The Court has also been concerned with the actual effect of a presumption, as opposed to the formal or statutory effect. That is, when jury instructions might have led jurors to the belief that they were obligated to find a presumed fact, the Court has intervened.[34] The focus is on the jury instructions, not on the statutory or judicial articulation of the presumption. The leading Supreme Court cases suggest that mandatory presumptions will be subjected to a very rigorous analysis, while permissive presumptions will be evaluated under a more lenient standard that takes account of the factual context in which the presumption operates. A sample of leading cases follows.

In 1979 the Supreme Court considered the constitutionality of criminal permissive presumptions (inferences). County Court of Ulster County v. Allen[35] involved the prosecution by New York authorities of four persons (three male adults and a female minor) for various offenses, including the illegal possession of handguns. A car occupied by the defendants was stopped for speeding. The investigating officer noticed that the open handbag of the sixteen-year-old passenger was in the front seat area, and he observed within it two large-caliber handguns. At trial, the prosecutor relied upon a statutory "presumption" that *allowed an inference* of illegal possession by all persons occupying a vehicle upon a showing of the basic fact that a firearm, not on the person of any particular occupant, was within the automobile. The trial judge instructed the jury that it was permissible to infer possession by all of the defendants from their presence in the vehicle containing the handguns, but that such an inference was not mandatory; it could be ignored even if the defendants produced no rebuttal evidence. It was thus clear that, in the terminology used by the Supreme Court, the presumption was permissive, not mandatory.

The defense attacked the statute as so broad on its face that it failed to satisfy due process. By its terms, it was argued, it would sweep within the presumption (1) occupants who may not know that the vehicle in which they are riding contains a gun, and (2) persons who, even though aware of the gun, were not permitted access to it.[36] Thus, the argument continued, the statutory presumption, even if only an inference, lacks the minimal probative force essential to its constitutionality.

The Court first responded by holding that the validity of a permissive presumption (inference) was to be judged in the *context*

---

34. *See Sandstrom*, 442 U.S. at 517.

35. 442 U.S. 140 (1979).

36. The Court of Appeals found these arguments persuasive. *See* Allen v.

County Court, Ulster County, 568 F.2d 998, 1007 (2d Cir.1977), *cert. granted*, 439 U.S. 815 (1978).

of the case in which it was invoked—that is, as applied to the particular circumstances of the case in which defendant opposes it. Although the validity of a mandatory presumption must be judged on its face (abstracted from the context of the case, except for the judge's instruction), a facial assessment of a permissive presumption was deemed inappropriate. The critical difference is that the trier must abide by the mandatory presumption until it is dispelled. Absent rebuttal, the trier is not free to make an independent evaluation of the presumed facts. However, when a presumption is permissive, the trier is always free of any obligation to draw the suggested inference; furthermore, if the trier is a jury, it should be instructed to consider other evidence that tends to confirm or deny the "inferred" fact.

This predicate thus established, the Court held that as applied to the circumstances in *Allen*,[37] the inference of possession by all of the defendants was "entirely rational"[38]—that is, the inferred fact was "more likely than not to flow from the ... [basic facts]."[39] It is not appropriate, held the Court, to require that a permissive presumption meet a reasonable doubt standard: that more stringent measure of proof applies to the evidence as a whole and has no applicability to a permissive presumption that constitutes only part of the proof.[40] Finally, the Court reiterated the important distinction between permissive and mandatory presumptions.[41] Because the latter must be accepted by the jury

> even if it is the sole evidence of an element of the offense ... the prosecution [which] bears the burden of establishing guilt ... may not rest its case entirely on a presumption unless the fact proved is sufficient to support an inference of guilt beyond a reasonable doubt.[42]

Ulster County thus teaches that permissive presumptions are allowable if the basic facts, taken in the context of the other evidence in the case, make the inferred fact more likely than not. Mandatory presumptions, however, must meet a reasonable doubt

37. The opinion emphasized that the defendants were not hitchhikers or casual passengers, that the guns were in plain view, that it was improbable that a sixteen-year-old was sole custodian of two large-caliber handguns, and that circumstances suggested an inept attempt to conceal the weapons when the defendants' vehicle was stopped for speeding. *Allen*, 442 U.S. at 163–64.

38. Id. at 163.

39. Id. at 165.

40. It would be a different matter if the permissively presumed fact was the *sole* basis for a finding of guilt, since a reasonable doubt standard would necessarily apply. Id. at 167.

41. Four Justices strongly dissented in *Ulster County*, essentially on the ground that jurors are influenced by permissive presumptions and, hence, it is important to ensure that the basic facts *standing alone* make the presumed fact more likely than not. Id. at 175–77.

42. Id. at 166–67.

standard on their face, at least where the presumed fact is an element of the offense charged.[43]

One feature of the *Ulster* Court's discussion of mandatory presumptions deserves special note. The Court's dictum suggests that a mandatory presumption is permissible whenever the basic facts supply a *sufficient* basis for finding the presumed fact beyond a reasonable doubt. Whether the Supreme Court would actually permit such a judge-imposed finding is open to question. To do so would relieve the prosecution of the burden of actually convincing the jury of the presumed fact. (The jury could use the presumption to support its beyond-a-reasonable-doubt finding.) It is likely that the Court would never uphold a truly mandatory presumption, even one that shifted to the accused only the burden of production. If this suggestion is accurate, the dictum in *Ulster County* that assumes the constitutionality of mandatory presumptions will not in fact be followed. On the other hand, if a mandatory presumption is allowable—if the trier may under some circumstances *be required* to find the presumed fact—then it seems likely that the Court will hold that the due process clause requires an inevitable connection between the basic and the presumed facts.[44]

In any event, a consistent theme of the relatively recent cases is the important difference between a permissive and mandatory presumption. And the Supreme Court has been concerned with the actual, not the formal or statutory effect of a presumption. A permissive presumption, for example, is judged in the context of the surrounding evidence. Furthermore, the constitutionality of any presumption is judged by the way it is actually communicated to the jury. As we shall see below, where the jury instructions might have led jurors to believe that they were *obliged* to find the presumed fact if the basic facts were established (and no rebuttal evidence was introduced), then the presumption will be held to the standard required of mandatory presumptions. In other words, the Court looks to jury instructions rather than statutory or case law to determine the nature and probable effect of a presumption.

In Sandstrom v. Montana,[45] decided two weeks after the *Ulster County* case, the accused was charged with purposely or knowingly

---

43. Most presumptions bear upon the elements of an offense and hence come within the constitutional limitations set out in *Ulster County* and other cases. In theory, but rarely in practice, a criminal presumption could relate to a matter sufficiently distant from the elements of an offense (and hence from the guilt of the accused) so that the constitutional restrictions generally applicable to criminal cases would not apply. *See*

United States v. Nunez, 877 F.2d 1470, 1472–73 (wiretap authorization order is presumed valid.)

44. In People v. Roder, 33 Cal.3d 491, 189 Cal.Rptr. 501, 658 P.2d 1302, 1308 n. 7 (1983), the California Supreme Court noted this apparent inconsistency in the *Ulster County* opinion.

45. 442 U.S. 510 (1979), *remanded to* 184 Mont. 391, 603 P.2d 244 (1979).

causing the victim's death, an offense that Montana denominated "deliberate homicide." The accused admitted the killing, but claimed that he did not act with the requisite purpose or knowledge and, therefore, was guilty of a lesser offense. At the conclusion of the evidence, the trial judge instructed the jury that "[t]he law presumes that a person intends the ordinary consequences of his voluntary acts."[46] Under state law the intended effect of the *Sandstrom* presumption was to shift to the accused only the burden of producing some contrary evidence; the burden of persuasion remained with the prosecution.[47] However, the Supreme Court concluded that there was a significant risk that the instruction given to the jury had been misunderstood: the jurors may have thought that they were peremptorily directed to find the requisite intent or, at least, that they were directed by a mandatory presumption shifting the burden of persuasion to find intent unless the defendant proved the contrary. Under either of these possible constructions, the presumption had unconstitutional consequences. First, since the state is obliged to prove beyond a reasonable doubt *"every fact necessary to constitute the crime ... charged"*[48] and since there is no doubt that intent is an essential element of "deliberate homicide," a *conclusive* (peremptory) presumption would be unconstitutional. According to the Court, such a presumption would have the untoward effects of lifting from the prosecution its assigned burden of proving intent and of abrogating the defendant's status of innocence until proven guilty of each element of the offense charged.[49] Second, constitutional infirmities would also result from a presumption that shifted to the accused the burden of persuasion pertaining to the requisite state of mind.[50] When the state proved the basic fact of homicide—a fact that did not itself establish that the killing was knowing or purposeful—the jury might erroneously have presumed the element of intent unless persuaded otherwise by the accused.

In the 1985 case of Francis v. Franklin,[51] the Court again condemned a jury instruction that embodied a presumption. The *Francis* instruction, unlike the instruction that was invalidated in *Sandstrom,* posed no risk that the jury might have construed the presumption in question as preemptive. Nonetheless, a closely divided Court ruled that there was a reasonable possibility that the jury had interpreted the trial court's instruction as shifting the burden of persuasion on the essential element of intent, in violation

46. Id. at 513.

47. State v. Sandstrom, 176 Mont. 492, 580 P.2d 106, 109 (1978), *cert. granted,* 439 U.S. 1067 (1979).

48. In re Winship, 397 U.S. 358, 364 (1970).

49. *Sandstrom,* 442 U.S. at 521–23.

50. Id. at 524.

51. 471 U.S. 307 (1985).

of *Mullaney* and *Sandstrom*.[52] The *Francis* Court expressly refused to rule on the constitutionality of presumptions that shift only the burden of production.[53] But observe that if the production burden did shift and if a defendant failed to meet that burden, the prosecution is in fact relieved of its task of proving each element, even though technically there has been no shift in the burden of persuasion. There is an additional difficulty in cases where the defendant himself is the only person who can provide the rebuttal evidence; as a practical matter, he must testify even though he might prefer to exercise his fifth amendment right not to take the stand. It is thus highly likely that the Court's decisions, taken as a whole, invalidates *all* mandatory presumptions, except, perhaps, those mandatory presumptions addressed to a minor point or those that have such a strong probative link with the basic facts that the presumed fact *must* exist beyond any reasonable doubt. In any event, the Court is clear that there remains a significant difference between a mandatory presumption that shifts some burden to the accused and a permissive presumption that is simply an allowable inference.

A legislature can probably achieve essentially the same effect in criminal trials that the Court has seemingly condemned in its treatment of presumptions. Suppose that a statutory reform resulted in converting a fact formerly the subject of a presumption into one that constituted an affirmative defense in the sense that *additional facts* would excuse or reduce the offense. For example, suppose that the Maine legislature, confronted with the *Mullaney* ruling, redefined murder as simply unlawful and intentional killing (excising the "malice aforethought" element), and transformed lack of malice aforethought from its role as negating an essential element to an affirmative defense consisting of additional facts which, if proved, would reduce the grade of the crime to second degree murder.[54] Affirmative defenses, even those that call upon the accused to carry the burden of persuasion, are usually found constitutional. It will thus be seen that despite the Supreme Court's rather stringent requirements surrounding presumptions, a sovereign is still permitted considerable latitude in allocating elements of an offense (or defense). First, it may take an element that could be used to define the crime (e.g., lack of provocation) and denominate it an affirmative defense (provocation justifying the act charged). Furthermore, the state apparently has rather broad authority to eliminate altogether one or, perhaps, more elements of an offense.[55]

---

52. *See* supra notes 29, 45 and accompanying text.

53. *Francis*, 471 U.S. at 314 n. 3.

54. The Supreme Court upheld a murder statute essentially identical to that described in the hypothetical above

in Patterson v. New York, 432 U.S. 197 (1977).

55. For example, American legislatures have sometimes created strict liability offenses by eliminating the state's burden of establishing any *mens rea* on

For example, the state might define a crime as the illegal entry [element 1] into a dwelling [element 2] in the nighttime [element 3] with the intent to commit a felony therein [element 4] or it might state the offense more broadly, for example, by including only elements 1 and 2, or some other combination of fewer than four.

In light of the ability of the state largely to avoid the impact of the Supreme Court's decisions restricting presumptions, it is not clear why the Court has insisted upon such strict constitutional requirements. Perhaps the answer lies in the Court's view of the jury's role, especially in criminal cases. That role is not, of course, one of simply finding facts by relying upon credible evidence and drawing rational inferences. The jury's historic protective role—its interposition between the power of the state and the individual accused—carries with it the unfettered right of acquittal. Presumptions, created by the state and administered by an authoritative state official, may have undue influence and effect. Thus, while the Court generally will allow the state legislature to redefine a crime or allocate to the defendant an affirmative defense, a majority of the Justices are uneasy with any procedure that seems to slant the trial court's fact-finding process against the accused. For this reason, mandatory presumptions are particularly suspect and are unlikely to survive constitutional challenge.[56]

the part of the accused. *See* John Jeffries & Paul Stephan, *Defenses, Presumptions, and the Burden of Proof in Criminal Law,* 88 Yale L.J. 1325, 1373–76 (1979). The authors urge that legislatures should be free to employ any affirmative defenses, mandatory presumptions, or inferences, free of restrictive constructions by the courts, so long as the remaining elements of the offense are proven beyond a reasonable doubt and comprise a constitutionally adequate basis for the punishment contemplated. Id. at 1365. Thus, if a legislature could constitutionally (i.e., consistent with principles of substantive due process and proportionality) define a felony of illegal entry without including element (3) (see text above), then courts should not concern themselves with whether element (3) is cast as a presumption or an affirmative defense.

56. The difficulty of clearly instructing a lay jury about the nature and effect of a presumption may also help explain the Supreme Court's hostility toward presumptions in criminal cases.

Chapter XIII

THE BEST EVIDENCE RULE

(Proving the Content of Writings, Recordings, and Photographs)

Table of Sections

---

§ 13.1 In General: The Rule and Its Purpose

The "Best Evidence Rule" is something of an anomaly: parties are generally free to prove propositions with whatever relevant evidence they want, subject to any applicable exclusionary rules. When making choices among relevant sources of evidence to prove a proposition, self-interested parties usually balance considerations of cost and persuasiveness. In other words, there is no general requirement that parties produce the "best" or most probative evidence of a proposition—though they often find it advantageous to do so. But such a requirement does exist when proving the contents of a document or certain other recordations. Rule 1002 requires that:

> **Requirement of original**. To prove the content of a writing, recording, or photograph, the original writing, recording, or photograph is required, except as otherwise provided in these rules or by Act of Congress.

At common law, the original was preferred because its use eliminated the risk of mistranscriptions or testimonial misstatements of what the document recited. It may now be asked whether there is any longer a need for the Best Evidence Rule, given the reliability of modern means of reproduction. Because of technological accuracy, it is untenable to base one's choice between the

417

original and a copy (as opposed to a choice between the original and verbal testimony) on the ground that the copy lacks reliability because it more likely contains accidental inaccuracies or omissions. Recognizing the accuracy of most reproductions, the drafters, in Federal Rule 1003, permit the admission of a reliable "duplicate" in lieu of the original unless the authenticity of the original is in question, or unfairness would result.[1] The term "duplicate" encompasses photocopies, electronic re-recordings, chemical reproductions, and other reliable means of making accurate copies.[2]

Today, the principal impact of the Best Evidence Rule is to exclude oral testimony about the contents of a document or other recordation, not to exclude duplicates.[3] Insisting on an "original" instead of a "duplicate" seldom results in more accurate factfinding, with the exceptions, already noted, embodied in Federal Rule 1003. The same cannot be said of preferring a writing, recording, or photograph, whether original or duplicate, to oral testimony describing or reciting its contents.[4] In short, the Best Evidence Rule still serves its original purpose of enhancing accurate factfinding, but grants more flexibility to litigants and judges in light of modern technology.

§ 13.2 Application: Proving the Contents of a Writing

Before determining if the Best Evidence Rule is satisfied, you must determine if it applies at all. Recall that the rule applies only when a "writing, recording, or photograph" is offered "to prove its contents." Whether an item is a "writing" can be disputed at the margins—e.g., does a product's serial number or a car's odometer reading qualify?—but few unclear applications actually arise. In theory, any inscribed chattel can constitute a writing, but courts have exercised discretion under Rule 1001(1) in deciding if such items should be treated as writings or ordinary chattels. If application of the Best Evidence Rule to a chattel would not serve the

---

1. Unfairness might result, for example, where only part of the original is reproduced and the uncopied section modifies the copied section, or where the duplicate is otherwise misleading. Unfairness would also result in the unlikely event that there was genuine concern as to whether the duplicate faithfully reproduced the original.

2. Specifically, "[a] 'duplicate' is a counterpart produced by the same impression as the original, or from the same matrix, or by means of photography, including enlargements and miniatures, or by mechanical or electronic re-

recording, or by chemical reproduction, or by other equivalent techniques which accurately reproduces the original." FRE 1001(4).

3. Mueller & Kirkpatrick, Evidence § 10.1 at 1067, n. 11.

4. Of course, a recordation is not always more reliable evidence of a fact to which it is addressed that is oral testimony. The document is only unambiguously preferable when used solely as evidence of its own contents and not for the truth of its written assertions.

Rule's purposes, the court need not apply it.[5] Moreover, an inscribed chattel is sometimes found to be a writing, yet the inscription is far removed from the controlling issues of the case and thus is exempted from the requirements of the Best Evidence doctrine by Rule 1004(4). That subsection states that if a "writing, recording, or photograph is not closely related to a controlling issue," it is collateral and the Best Evidence Rule is inapplicable.

Subtle issues sometimes arise in determining whether a writing is being offered to prove its content—an essential element for the application of the Best Evidence Rule. This question can arise in a number of contexts. Sometimes proof of a writing's content is required by the substantive law, as when its content is the element of a charge, claim or defense. The most obvious example is an action for libel. Furthermore the substantive law sometimes prescribes that a writing subsumes, so to speak, any prior events; in other words, the law requires that the transaction in dispute be evidenced by a writing. A deed, a will, certain contracts (especially if the parol evidence is foreclosed), or a judicial judgment are transactions the law regards as essentially written, and the proponent must make his proof by the writing if it is available.[6] In these instances, the proponent does not have the option of simply proving the oral declarations that preceded the written instrument.

Note, however, that often a writing merely recites or records a perceivable event or condition such as a marriage (marriage certificate), payment of money (receipt), or the utterance of certain words (transcript). Here, the proponent wishing to prove the underlying event may proceed in either of two ways: (1) offer the testimony of an observer, or (2) offer a writing, recording, or photograph that records or recites the event. The first approach does not involve the Best Evidence Rule because the proponent is not attempting to prove the terms of the recordation,[7] but merely is presenting evidence of an event perceived by a witness with first-hand knowledge. It makes no difference that the occurrence of the event is recited in a subsequent writing, for the writing does not, so far as legal rules of proof are concerned, "erase" or supplant the preceding event. Of course, if the proponent chooses to make his proof by use of a writing, the Best Evidence Rule must be satisfied. (Sometimes the hearsay rule is also implicated and the proponent needs to invoke an exemption or exception.) The party against whom the

5. *See* United States v. Duffy, 454 F.2d 809, 812 (5th Cir. 1972) (oral testimony about laundry mark on defendant's shirt proper).

6. 2 McCormick § 233, at 66. Of course, the opponent of the evidence must make a proper objection.

7. *See e.g.,* Allstate Ins. Co. V. Swann, 27 F.3d 1539, 1543 (11th Cir. 1994).

evidence is offered has the responsibility for challenging its admissibility under Rule 1002.

The courts are in general accord with the foregoing analysis, although there has been some tendency in criminal cases to prefer a written, signed confession over the testimony of a person claiming to have heard the oral confession, later reduced to a writing.[8] Perhaps this preference can be justified as a protective measure, but analytically the proponent offering a witness to the confession does not seek to prove the terms of a writing; therefore the proponent's choice should affect only the weight of the evidence.

§ 13.3 Application: Identifying an "Original"

Once it is clear that the Best Evidence Rule applies (i.e. the evidence is a writing, recording, or photograph, and is proffered to prove the content of the recordation), an "original"—or, in many instances, a duplicate—must be identified. Often, deciding if a document is an "original" is straightforward, but where there are several writings, application of the Best Evidence Rule requires a determination of which one is (or which ones are) original. We have already noted that Rule 1003 usually permits the use of duplicates (subsequent reliable copies) in lieu of originals. It should also be noted that parties can create *multiple* originals. In determining if they have done so, the crucial question is the parties' intent. For example, if several copies of a contract, will, or other agreement are duly executed (*i.e.* signed and, if necessary, attested), the parties have manifested an intention to accord equal status to all of the identical writings, regardless of their mechanical or surface characteristics. (A properly signed and executed carbon copy, for example, is a "multiple original.")

Besides the execution of multiple copies, other circumstances sometimes suggest the creation of several originals as, for example, when one receipt is given to a customer and the other is retained by the seller (as in many sales transactions). In this retail setting, both documents are likely to be deemed originals. Beyond this kind of "intent" determination, reference to the substantive law is often necessary to ascertain what constitutes an original for purposes of the Best Evidence Rule. Suppose, for example, a defendant types an original of a libelous document; she then makes a photocopy but publishes only the latter. The copy is the operative document under the substantive law, and as such, constitutes the original with respect to the Best Evidence Rule. Similarly, if *A* writes out a contractual offer to *B*, and the offer is transmitted by telegraph, the telegram is the original—assuming the telegraph company is acting as *A*'s agent. (Similarly, the FAX received would normally be the

---

8. McCormick, supra note 6, at 69.

original.) In situations like these, the result usually turns not upon which document was created first (or even upon a party's intent), but rather the answer is found by identifying the recordation that has the operative legal effect.

In addition to the problems created by substantive legal doctrines, modern technology often blurs the line between an original and a copy. As you know, data can be entered and stored in computers and printed out on command. Every such printout of one computer file should be considered a multiple original and each should be afforded equal evidentiary status. (However, a manually retyped copy, like a handwritten copy, always constitutes secondary evidence because the risk of mistranscription is present.) Unexecuted photocopies of originals are considered duplicates, absent evidence that the parties intended to treat them as originals, which is unlikely if the copies are unsigned. Quite obviously, oral testimony purporting to give the terms of the original is quintessential secondary evidence.

§ 13.4 Application: Recordings and Photographs; Statutory Modifications

As we have seen, the Federal Rules extend application of the Best Evidence Rule beyond writings to include sound recordings and photographs. This broadening of the rule, a relatively modern development, can be traced to similar "pre-rules" extensions in several states,[9] and should not be viewed as a far-reaching or problematic change. The extension is justified because testimony about the contents of a photograph or recording is inferior in probative value to a visual or auditory examination by the factfinder. Moreover, as with documents, insisting on original photographs and recordings reduces somewhat the potential for fraud in the reproduction process.

The original of a sound recording usually is the initial recording, and the original of a photograph is the "negative or any print therefrom."[10] In most cases, the proponent would proffer these "originals" even without the force of a rule requiring it. With regard to still and motion pictures, proof of the photographic content is often unnecessary. Commonly, photographic evidence is admitted as a graphic representation of a scene or subject that a testifying witness has observed and is describing from the stand. This illustrative use of photographic evidence does not involve proving the contents of the picture; rather, it is an attempt to establish the scene itself by testimony, aided by a visual back-

---

9. People v. King, 101 Cal.App.2d 500, 225 P.2d 950, 955 (1950) (recording); Cellamare v. Third Ave. Transit Corp., 273 A.D. 260, 77 N.Y.S.2d 91, 91 (App. Div. 1948) (X-rays).

10. FRE 1001(3).

ground. But *if* the proponent *is attempting* to prove the content of a photograph (as in the case of an X-ray, or a surveillance camera photograph),[11] the Best Evidence Rule applies. The same is true of a photograph alleged to be libelous, obscene, violative of a copyright, or of an individual's privacy. In instances such as these, the photographic material is offered for its content and testimony about that content is secondary evidence.

Statutory Modifications and Excuses for Non-production

Federal or state statutory provisions sometimes modify the usual application of the Best Evidence Rule. Congress, for example, has enacted a statute allowing photographic reproduction of tax returns and certain Treasury documents. State and federal statutes permitting copies of public records are common, as are provisions applying to regularly kept business records. If no exception to the Best Evidence Rule can be discovered, care should be taken to determine what circumstances will excuse production of the original.

If the original is lost or destroyed (excepting bad faith destruction by the proponent himself) then production is excused.[12] Records are often destroyed in the ordinary course of business, and in most cases, showing that the destruction was a business practice should suffice to establish absence of bad faith by the proponent. The same result obtains when the original is in the hands of the opponent and, after due notice, he fails to produce it.[13] The proponent has afforded his opponent the opportunity to have the original admitted and the latter has declined.

ILLUSTRATION

Law enforcement authorities have information that *D* plans to rob a bank, so FBI agents plant "bait money" with known serial numbers at the target bank. *D* does, in fact, carry out the robbery. During an initial search of *D*'s house, the bait money is allegedly discovered and examined by police. When the police return a second time, however, the bills cannot be found. At trial, the prosecution offers the testimony of a police officer who will testify that the bills with the bait money serial numbers were present in the defendant's home. The defense raises a best evidence objection. What result?

11. A common example is a security (surveillance) camera that photographs customers or intruders.

12. FRE 1004(1). Production is also excused if the "original [cannot] be ob-

tained by any available judicial process or procedure...." FRE 1004(2).

13. FRE 1004(3).

The facts in the Illustration are based on United States v. Marcantoni.[14] There, the Fifth Circuit concluded that the Best Evidence Rule applied and that the testimony was secondary evidence. Production was excused, however, by Rule 1004 since the bills were either unavailable or withheld by the defendant.

§ 13.5   Role of Judge and Jury; Classes of Secondary Evidence

Typically, questions about which recordations are originals, duplicates, or secondary evidence is a preliminary question of fact decided by the trial judge pursuant to Rule 104(a). However, Rule 1008 provides:

Functions of Court and Jury

... [W]hen an issue is raised (a) whether the asserted writing ever existed, or (b) whether another writing, recording, or photograph produced at the trial is the original, or (c) whether other evidence of contents correctly reflects the contents, the issue is for the tier of fact to determine as in the case of other issues of fact.

Often, the court's resolution of these questions would go beyond mere trial administration and effectively dictate the outcome of the case. The drafters of the Federal Rules intended to protect the jury's factfinding role in these situations, subject to the court's management and the usual requirement that conditionally relevant facts be accompanied by sufficient evidence of the conditioning (underlying) facts.[15]

ILLUSTRATION

Pope, a self-employed auto mechanic, purchases a diagnostic computer from Swift Co. for use in his business; the computer subsequently malfunctions, and Pope sues Swift for breach of warranty. At trial, Pope produces a written sales contract containing ordinary UCC warranty terms. Swift then produces a written sales contract disclaiming all warranties. Each claims that his document is the original and that the other party has modified its copy. Neither writing is obviously fraudulent.

---

14. 590 F.2d 1324 (5th Cir. 1979).
15. *See* FRE 1008 ACN; FRE 104(b).

The court, pursuant to Rule 1008(b), should allow the jury to decide which document's terms control—that is, which is the original. If the judge decides which document is the original, she effectively supplants the jury's factfinding role and dictates the outcome of the case.

Finally, you should ascertain if the jurisdiction in which a best-evidence question arises prefers a particular kind of secondary evidence. A few states extend the principle of the Best Evidence Rule and thus give it an operative effect even after production of the original has been excused. That is, these states create classes of secondary evidence, preferring one class to another. The most common extension of the Best Evidence Rule to secondary evidence is to require a copy (when available) in lieu of oral testimony purporting to give the terms of the original. The Federal Rules, however, contain no provision for classes of secondary evidence. If the proponent is required to produce the original under Rules 1002 and 1003, but production is excused under Rule 1004, than any probative secondary evidence will suffice.[16] Nonetheless, the proponent's self interest will usually result in placing before the trier the most reliable secondary evidence; a copy is normally more persuasive of the contents of the original than would be oral testimony.

16. FRE 1004 ACN. *See also* United States v. Ross, 33 F.3d 1507, 1513 (11th Cir. 1994).

Appendix I

IS IT HEARSAY?

A Short Quiz

Unless otherwise noted, in the following hypotheticals, "W" refers to the witness on the stand, "DC" is the off-the-stand declarant, and "A" is the person with first-hand knowledge of what DC said or did. When the abbreviation "WA" is used, the witness and the auditor are the same person—that is, the auditor is on the stand.

1. On the issue whether Cherubino's military commission (now lost or destroyed) had an official seal, WA's testimony that the Chief of Records said it did not.

2. On the issue whether Madam Butterfly was depressed, Butterfly's statement to WA, "Where is Pinkerton? Can't he see that I am in a state of despair!"

3. On the same issue, Military Commander's statement to Butterfly in WA's presence, "I must inform you, as Pinkerton's commander, that he will never return to you."

4. On the issue whether Lt. Pinkerton and Kate were married, WA's testimony that at the wedding ceremony, attended by a few friends and presided over by Minister, Pinkerton and Kate had each said, "I take you to be my wedded [wife; husband]", and the Minister then said. "I now pronounce you husband and wife."

5. On the same issue, WA's testimony that just as the ceremony was beginning, DC (Suzuki) rushed into the chapel and said, "I object to this marriage! Pinkerton is a cheat and a bigamist! He is already married to Butterfly."

6. In a defamation suit by Pinkerton against Suzuki, WA's testimony that Suzuki called Pinkerton a "cheat and a bigamist."

7. In the same defamation suit, in which Suzuki's defense is truth, her pre-trial statement to WA, "Pinkerton can't marry Kate he is still married to Butterfly."

8. In the same defamation suit and for the same purpose as in 7, above, Suzuki, herself, testifies to her statement to WA.

425

9. In a bigamy prosecution of Pinkerton, on the issue whether Pinkerton knew before he married Kate that he was legally married to Butterfly, his statement to WA (prior to his marriage to Kate), "I was totally distressed when my commanding officer told me that my Japanese marriage to Butterfly was actually valid." [There is other evidence supporting the validity of the Japanese marriage.]

10. In the same bigamy prosecution, on the issue whether Pinkerton knew when he married Kate that he was legally married to Butterfly, his statement to WA (made a month after the marriage to Kate), "I was absolutely shocked when my commanding officer told me yesterday that my Japanese marriage to Butterfly was valid." [There is other evidence supporting the validity of the Japanese marriage.]

11. On the issue whether Scarpia, a sheriff, tortured Mario, Scarpia's statement to his deputy, in the presence of WA, "Bind him with wire and chain him to the rafters by his feet until he either talks or passes out."

12. On the issue whether Scarpia used duress to force Tosca to have sex with him, his statement to Tosca (WA); "Yield or your Mario will die, for even now he is swinging in chains from the prison rafters."

13. On the issue whether Mario was chained to the prison rafters, the statement in 12 above.

14. On the issue whether Mario disliked Scarpia, Mario's statement to WA, "That bastard, Scarpia, he arrested me on a false charge, tortured me, and raped my dearest Tosca."

15. On the issue whether Tosca was justified in stabbing Scarpia (self-defense), WA's earlier statement to Tosca, "Watch out for Scarpia, he said he would rape you before the night was over."

16. On the issue whether Don José impersonated the famous toreador, Escamillo, in order to gain entry into Carmen's skybox, the statement by José to Carmen's doorkeeper (WA), "I am Escamillo; please open the door."

17. On the issue whether Faust made a pact with Satan, testimony by WA that Satan said to Faust, "If you will agree to do my bidding after your death, I will obey all of your earthly commands."

18. On the issue whether Sarcristan violated securities laws by falsely announcing to English stockjobbers that Napoleon had won the Battle of Waterloo, testimony by Rothschild that as soon as his messenger heard the announcement, he reported it to Rothschild.

19. On the issue whether Violetta had tuberculosis, testimony by W, a nurse, that the treatment administered by Violetta's physician was the standard treatment for tuberculosis.

20. On the same issue, an authenticated page from Violetta's diary: "Again, last night I suffered chest pains and constant coughing, and when I awoke I found blood spots on my pillow."

21. On the same issue (tuberculosis), on which P has the burden of proof, D calls Violetta's physician who testifies that she was "suffering from emphysema, not tuberculosis." To discredit Physician, P calls N, a nurse, who testifies that two weeks before the trial, Physician told her that "Violetta has tuberculosis."

Answers and Comments

The tacit assumption in these problems is fundamentally important: in each instance, it is assumed that the evidence points to (helps prove or disprove) a consequential fact. Thus, for example, if Madam Butterfly's depression (question 2) were not consequential under the substantive law governing the case, evidence that tended to make her depression more (or less) likely would be irrelevant. Thus, in considering the admissibility of evidence, you should first resolve the relevance question. Only if the evidence is relevant do you need to inquire whether some other rule, such as the hearsay rule, bars admission.

1. Hearsay. This evidence, an out-of-court statement, is offered to prove there was no seal.

2. Hearsay. Madam Butterfly's statement, offered for its truth, asserts her state of mind. Note that if Butterfly were a party and her statement were offered against her by her party-opponent, that statement would be statutory (definitional) nonhearsay and thus "exempted" from the *general* definition of hearsay (Rule 801(c)) by reason of FR 801(d)(2).

3. Nonhearsay. The evidence is offered to show the probable effect of the declarant's statement on Butterfly's state of mind.

4. Nonhearsay. There are words of independent legal significance, often referred to by courts as constituting a "verbal act."

5. Nonhearsay. These statements are offered not for their truth, but rather for their probable affect on the listeners, especially Kate. The accusations decrease the likelihood that the marriage ceremony continued. Note, however, that if Suzuki's last sentence were offered to prove Pinkerton was already married, it would be hearsay.

6.   Nonhearsay. There are words of independent legal significance constituting a verbal act.

7.   Hearsay. Assuming, as the problem suggests, that this evidence is offered *by Suzuki* and not *against her* as a party admission (See FR. 801(d)(2)), the evidence is hearsay. It is offered to prove that Pinkerton was in fact a bigamist.

8.   Hearsay, as noted above in 7. The fact that Suzuki testifies as to her own prior out-of-court statement does not change its hearsay character. The statement meets the general definition of hearsay (FR 801(c)) and does not fit within FR 801(d)(1), the "definitional nonhearsay" subsection, because it was not made under oath subject to the penalty of perjury. In other words, it is not exempted from the general definition of hearsay.

9.   Nonhearsay. There are several explanations. If the prosecution offers the statement against Pinkerton, the statement comes in as a (nonhearsay) party admission. Further, if the statement were offered for the limited purpose of showing Pinkerton's awareness or knowledge that his earlier marriage was valid, the statement would not be offered for its truth.

10. Hearsay. This declaration is an out-of-court statement made by Pinkerton and presumably offered by him for its truth, namely, his good-faith ("innocent" state of mind) when he married Kate.

11. Nonhearsay (with qualifications). If Scarpia were a party, and the statement were offered against him, it would be a (non-hearsay) party admission. Further, if the substantive law made it illegal for a sheriff to order the torture of an arrestee, Scarpia's words would have independent legal significance. You can also argue that since the words constitute a command, order, or directive, they have no "truth content" (that is, as a command, they can be neither true nor false). Note, however, that the issue appears to be whether Scarpia tortured Mario which, in the context of the problem, he would have done through his agent, the deputy. The hearsay argument is along these lines: Scarpia's statement is really the equivalent of a declaration that Mario will be tortured. As such, it is offered for its truth.

12. Nonhearsay. The threats to the survival of Mario are offered to show their probable coercive effect on Tosca.

13. Hearsay. But note that if these statements are offered against Scarpia by a party-opponent, they are not hearsay. (See FR 801(d)(2) governing hearsay exemptions or "definitional" non-hearsay)

14. Nonhearsay. Recall illustration in Ch. V in which a student's derogatory remarks about Professor Sophocles are offered to show, circumstantially, that she disliked him and thus was less likely to have enrolled in his course. (Whether or not she enrolled was assumed to be the consequential proposition)

15. Nonhearsay. The warning is offered to show that Tosca was apprehensive and fearful of Scarpia and thus was justified in using a knife to defend herself. (Put otherwise: the declaration is offered not for the truth, but rather for its tendency to influence the listener's state of mind.)

16. Nonhearsay. The words have independent legal significance (verbal act). The false words constitute the impersonation.

17. Nonhearsay. Same rationale as 16, above.

18. Hearsay. The declaration concerning who won the battle is not offered for its truth (quite the contrary), but there are too many links in the chain. Observe, however, the possibility of using FR 803(1) to get into evidence the messenger's hearsay statement (that *Sarcristan* in fact *made* the announcement). If the messenger's statement was made "immediately" after he hears *Sarcristan's* statement, we overcome the hearsay (double link) problem by invoking an exception. Of course, this means only that he evidence is admissible through the use of a hearsay exception; it does not change the hearsay nature of *Sarcristan's* statement to Rothschild. Finally, consider the possibility the messenger's statement is an excited utterance.

19. Nonhearsay. the physician probably did not intend to make the assertion "Violetta has tuberculosis," but was simply treating her. If there was no intended assertion, the nonassertive nature of the evidence keeps it outside the general definition of hearsay under FR 801(a) and (c) because the doctor did not intend to make a "statement."

20. Hearsay. Although Violetta may not have been speaking to someone when she made the diary entry, she was consciously making an assertion about her physical condition. The trier of fact is asked to believe Violetta's statement and then to infer that she suffered from tuberculosis. Quite often, hearsay statements do not state directly a consequential proposition, but rather the statements are ultimately directed toward a consequential proposition. The consequential proposition is established by drawing inferences. Nonetheless, if a conscious (intended) out-of-court statement must be accepted as true in order to infer the existence of a consequential fact, the out-of-court statement meets the general definition of hearsay (FR 801(c)).

21. Nonhearsay. The nurse's testimony is not offered for its truth, but only to impeach—that if, to cast doubt on Physician's testimony A witness' prior inconsistent statement cannot be used for the truth of the matter asserted unless the statement fits either an a exemption or an exception to the hearsay rule. The statement may, however, be used for the limited (non-hearsay) purpose of impeachment.

Appendix II

FEDERAL RULES OF EVIDENCE FOR UNITED STATES COURTS

ARTICLE I. GENERAL PROVISIONS

Rule 101. Scope

These rules govern proceedings in the courts of the United States and before the United States bankruptcy judges and United States magistrate judges, to the extent and with the exceptions stated in rule 1101.

(As amended Mar. 2, 1987, eff. Oct. 1, 1987; Apr. 25, 1988, eff. Nov. 1, 1988; Apr. 22, 1993, eff. Dec. 1, 1993.)

Rule 102. Purpose and Construction

These rules shall be construed to secure fairness in administration, elimination of unjustifiable expense and delay, and promotion of growth and development of the law of evidence to the end that the truth may be ascertained and proceedings justly determined.

Rule 103. Rulings on Evidence

(a) Effect of erroneous ruling. Error may not be predicated upon a ruling which admits or excludes evidence unless a substantial right of the party is affected, and

(1) Objection. In case the ruling is one admitting evidence, a timely objection or motion to strike appears of record, stating the specific ground of objection, if the specific ground was not apparent from the context; or

(2) Offer of proof. In case the ruling is one excluding evidence, the substance of the evidence was made known to the court by offer or was apparent from the context within which questions were asked.

Once the court makes a definitive ruling on the record admitting or excluding evidence, either at or before trial, a party need not renew an objection or offer of proof to preserve a claim of error for appeal.

(b) Record of offer and ruling. The court may add any other or further statement which shows the character of the evidence, the form in which it was offered, the objection made, and the ruling thereon. It may direct the making of an offer in question and answer form.

(c) Hearing of jury. In jury cases, proceedings shall be conducted, to the extent practicable, so as to prevent inadmissible evidence from being suggested to the jury by any means, such as making statements or offers of proof or asking questions in the hearing of the jury.

(d) Plain error. Nothing in this rule precludes taking notice of plain errors affecting substantial rights although they were not brought to the attention of the court.

(As amended Apr. 17, 2000, eff. Dec. 1, 2000.)

Rule 104. Preliminary Questions

(a) Questions of admissibility generally. Preliminary questions concerning the qualification of a person to be a witness, the existence of a privilege, or the admissibility of evidence shall be determined by the court, subject to the provisions of subdivision (b). In making its determination it is not bound by the rules of evidence except those with respect to privileges.

(b) Relevancy conditioned on fact. When the relevancy of evidence depends upon the fulfillment of a condition of fact, the court shall admit it upon, or subject to, the introduction of evidence sufficient to support a finding of the fulfillment of the condition.

(c) Hearing of jury. Hearings on the admissibility of confessions shall in all cases be conducted out of the hearing of the jury. Hearings on other preliminary matters shall be so conducted when the interests of justice require, or when an accused is a witness and so requests.

(d) Testimony by accused. The accused does not, by testifying upon a preliminary matter, become subject to cross-examination as to other issues in the case.

(e) Weight and credibility. This rule does not limit the right of a party to introduce before the jury evidence relevant to weight or credibility.

(As amended Mar. 2, 1987, eff. Oct. 1, 1987.)

Rule 105. Limited Admissibility

When evidence which is admissible as to one party or for one purpose but not admissible as to another party or for another purpose is admitted, the court, upon request, shall restrict the evidence to its proper scope and instruct the jury accordingly.

Rule 106. Remainder of or Related Writings or Recorded Statements

When a writing or recorded statement or part thereof is introduced by a party, an adverse party may require the introduction at that time of any other part or any other writing or recorded statement which ought in fairness to be considered contemporaneously with it.

(As amended Mar. 2, 1987, eff. Oct. 1, 1987.)

ARTICLE II. JUDICIAL NOTICE

Rule
201. Judicial Notice of Adjudicative Facts.
    (a) Scope of Rule.
    (b) Kinds of Facts.
    (c) When Discretionary.
    (d) When Mandatory.
    (e) Opportunity to Be Heard.
    (f) Time of Taking Notice.
    (g) Instructing Jury.

Rule 201. Judicial Notice of Adjudicative Facts

(a) Scope of rule. This rule governs only judicial notice of adjudicative facts.

(b) Kinds of facts. A judicially noticed fact must be one not subject to reasonable dispute in that it is either (1) generally known within the territorial jurisdiction of the trial court or (2) capable of accurate and ready determination by resort to sources whose accuracy cannot reasonably be questioned.

(c) When discretionary. A court may take judicial notice, whether requested or not.

(d) When mandatory. A court shall take judicial notice if requested by a party and supplied with the necessary information.

(e) Opportunity to be heard. A party is entitled upon timely request to an opportunity to be heard as to the propriety of taking judicial notice and the tenor of the matter noticed. In the absence of prior notification, the request may be made after judicial notice has been taken.

(f) Time of taking notice. Judicial notice may be taken at any stage of the proceeding.

(g) Instructing jury. In a civil action or proceeding, the court shall instruct the jury to accept as conclusive any fact judicially noticed. In a criminal case, the court shall instruct the jury that it may, but is not required to, accept as conclusive any fact judicially noticed.

ARTICLE III. PRESUMPTIONS IN CIVIL ACTIONS AND PROCEEDINGS

Rule 301. Presumptions in General in Civil Actions and Proceedings

In all civil actions and proceedings not otherwise provided for by Act of Congress or by these rules, a presumption imposes on the party against whom it is directed the burden of going forward with evidence to rebut or meet the presumption, but does not shift to such party the burden of proof in the sense of the risk of nonpersuasion, which remains throughout the trial upon the party on whom it was originally cast.

Rule 302.   Applicability of State Law in Civil Actions and Proceedings

In civil actions and proceedings, the effect of a presumption respecting a fact which is an element of a claim or defense as to which State law supplies the rule of decision is determined in accordance with State law.

ARTICLE IV.   RELEVANCY AND ITS LIMITS

Rule 401.   Definition of "Relevant Evidence"

"Relevant evidence" means evidence having any tendency to make the existence of any fact that is of consequence to the determination of the action more probable or less probable than it would be without the evidence.

Rule 402. Relevant Evidence Generally Admissible; Irrelevant Evidence Inadmissible

All relevant evidence is admissible, except as otherwise provided by the Constitution of the United States, by Act of Congress, by these rules, or by other rules prescribed by the Supreme Court pursuant to statutory authority. Evidence which is not relevant is not admissible.

Rule 403. Exclusion of Relevant Evidence on Grounds of Prejudice, Confusion, or Waste of Time

Although relevant, evidence may be excluded if its probative value is substantially outweighed by the danger of unfair prejudice, confusion of the issues, or misleading the jury, or by considerations of undue delay, waste of time, or needless presentation of cumulative evidence.

Rule 404. Character Evidence Not Admissible to Prove Conduct; Exceptions; Other Crimes

(a) Character evidence generally. Evidence of a person's character or a trait of character is not admissible for the purpose of proving action in conformity therewith on a particular occasion, except:

(1) Character of accused. Evidence of a pertinent trait of character offered by an accused, or by the prosecution to rebut the same, or if evidence of a trait of character of the alleged victim of the crime is offered by an accused and admitted under Rule 404 (a) (2), evidence of the same trait of character of the accused offered by the prosecution;

(2) Character of alleged victim. Evidence of a pertinent trait of character of the alleged victim of the crime offered by an accused, or by the prosecution to rebut the same, or evidence of a character trait of peacefulness of the alleged victim offered by the prosecution in a homicide case to rebut evidence that the alleged victim was the first aggressor;

(3) Character of witness. Evidence of the character of a witness, as provided in rules 607, 608, and 609.

(b) Other crimes, wrongs, or acts. Evidence of other crimes, wrongs, or acts is not admissible to prove the character of a person in order to show action in conformity therewith. It may, however, be admissible for other purposes, such as proof of motive, opportunity, intent, preparation, plan, knowledge, identity, or absence of mistake or accident, provided that upon request by the accused, the prosecution in a criminal case shall provide reasonable notice in advance of trial, or during trial if the court excuses pretrial notice on good cause shown, of the general nature of any such evidence it intends to introduce at trial.

(As amended Mar. 2, 1987, eff. Oct. 1, 1987; Apr. 30, 1991, eff. Dec. 1, 1991; Apr. 17, 2000, eff. Dec. 1, 2000.)

Rule 405. Methods of Proving Character

(a) Reputation or opinion. In all cases in which evidence of character or a trait of character of a person is admissible, proof may be made by testimony as to reputation or by testimony in the form of an opinion. On cross-examination, inquiry is allowable into relevant specific instances of conduct.

(b) Specific instances of conduct. In cases in which character or a trait of character of a person is an essential element of a charge, claim, or defense, proof may also be made of specific instances of that person's conduct.

(As amended Mar. 2, 1987, eff. Oct. 1, 1987.)

Rule 406. Habit; Routine Practice

Evidence of the habit of a person or of the routine practice of an organization, whether corroborated or not and regardless of the presence of eyewitnesses, is relevant to prove that the conduct of the person or organization on a particular occasion was in conformity with the habit or routine practice.

Rule 407. Subsequent Remedial Measures

When, after an injury or harm allegedly caused by an event, measures are taken that, if taken previously, would have made the injury or harm less likely to occur, evidence of the subsequent measures is not admissible to prove negligence, culpable conduct, a defect in a product, a defect in a product's design, or a need for a warning or instruction. This rule does not require the exclusion of evidence of subsequent measures when offered for another purpose, such as proving ownership, control, or feasibility of precautionary measures, if controverted, or impeachment.

(As Amended Apr. 11, 1997, eff. Dec. 1, 1997.)

Rule 408. Compromise and Offers to Compromise

Evidence of (1) furnishing or offering or promising to furnish, or (2) accepting or offering or promising to accept, a valuable consideration in compromising or attempting to compromise a claim which was disputed as to either validity or amount, is not admissible to prove liability for or invalidity of the claim or its amount. Evidence of conduct or statements made in compromise negotiations is likewise not admissible. This rule does not require the exclusion of any evidence otherwise discoverable merely because it is presented in the course of compromise negotiations. This rule also does not require exclusion when the evidence is offered for another purpose, such as proving bias or prejudice of a witness, negativing a contention of undue delay, or proving an effort to obstruct a criminal investigation or prosecution.

Rule 409. Payment of Medical and Similar Expenses

Evidence of furnishing or offering or promising to pay medical, hospital, or similar expenses occasioned by an injury is not admissible to prove liability for the injury.

Rule 410. Inadmissibility of Pleas, Plea Discussions, and Related Statements

Except as otherwise provided in this rule, evidence of the following is not, in any civil or criminal proceeding, admissible against the defendant who made the plea or was a participant in the plea discussions:

(1) a plea of guilty which was later withdrawn;

(2) a plea of nolo contendere;

(3) any statement made in the course of any proceedings under Rule 11 of the Federal Rules of Criminal Procedure or comparable state procedure regarding either of the foregoing pleas; or

(4) any statement made in the course of plea discussions with an attorney for the prosecuting authority which do not result in a plea of guilty or which result in a plea of guilty later withdrawn.

However, such a statement is admissible (i) in any proceeding wherein another statement made in the course of the same plea or plea discussions has been introduced and the statement ought in fairness be considered contemporaneously with it, or (ii) in a criminal proceeding for perjury or false statement if the statement was made by the defendant under oath, on the record and in the presence of counsel.

(As amended by P.L. 94–149, § 1(9), Dec. 12, 1975, 89 Stat. 805; Apr. 30, 1979, eff. Dec. 1, 1980.)

Rule 411. Liability Insurance

Evidence that a person was or was not insured against liability is not admissible upon the issue whether the person acted negligently or otherwise wrongfully. This rule does not require the exclusion of evidence of insurance against liability when offered for another purpose, such as proof of agency, ownership, or control, or bias or prejudice of a witness.

(As amended Mar. 2, 1987, eff. Oct. 1, 1987.)

Rule 412. Sex Offense Cases; Relevance of Alleged Victim's Past Sexual Behavior or Alleged Sexual Predisposition

(a) Evidence generally inadmissible. The following evidence is not admissible in any civil or criminal proceeding involving alleged sexual misconduct except as provided in subdivisions (b) and (c):

(1) Evidence offered to prove that any alleged victim engaged in other sexual behavior.

(2) Evidence offered to prove any alleged victim's sexual predisposition.

(b) Exceptions.

(1) In a criminal case, the following evidence is admissible, if otherwise admissible under these rules:

(A) evidence of specific instances of sexual behavior by the alleged victim offered to prove that a person other than the accused was the source of semen, injury or other physical evidence;

(B) evidence of specific instances of sexual behavior by the alleged victim with respect to the person accused of the sexual misconduct offered by the accused to prove consent or by the prosecution; and

(C) evidence the exclusion of which would violate the constitutional rights of the defendant.

(2) In a civil case, evidence offered to prove the sexual behavior or sexual predisposition of any alleged victim is admissible if it is otherwise admissible under these rules and its probative value substantially outweighs the danger of harm to any victim and of unfair prejudice to any party. Evidence of an alleged victim's reputation is admissible only if it has been placed in controversy by the alleged victim.

(c) Procedure to determine admissibility.

(1) A party intending to offer evidence under subdivision (b) must:

(A) file a written motion at least 14 days before trial specifically describing the evidence and stating the purpose for which it is offered unless the court, for good cause requires a different time for filing or permits filing during trial; and

(B) serve the motion on all parties and notify the alleged victim or, when appropriate, the alleged victim's guardian or representative.

(2) Before admitting evidence under this rule the court must conduct a hearing in camera and afford the victim and parties a right to attend and be heard. The motion, related papers, and the record of the hearing must be sealed and remain under seal unless the court orders otherwise.

(Added Pub.L. 95–540, § 2(a), Oct. 28, 1978, 92 Stat. 2046, and amended Nov. 18, 1988, Pub.L. 100–690, Title VII, § 7046(a), 102 Stat. 4400; Apr. 29, 1994, eff. Dec. 1, 1994; Sept. 13, 1994, Pub.L. 103–322, Title IV, § 40141(b), 108 Stat. 1919.)

Rule 413. Evidence of Similar Crimes in Sexual Assault Cases

(a) In a criminal case in which the defendant is accused of an offense of sexual assault, evidence of the defendant's commission of another offense or offenses of sexual assault is admissible, and may be considered for its bearing on any matter to which it is relevant.

(b) In a case in which the Government intends to offer evidence under this rule, the attorney for the Government shall disclose the evidence to the defendant, including statements of witnesses or a summary of the substance of any testimony that is expected to be offered, at least fifteen days before the scheduled date of trial or at such later time as the court may allow for good cause.

(c) This rule shall not be construed to limit the admission or consideration of evidence under any other rule.

(d) For purposes of this rule and Rule 415, "offense of sexual assault" means a crime under Federal law or the law of a State (as defined in section 513 of title 18, United States Code) that involved—

(1) any conduct proscribed by chapter 109A of title 18, United States Code;

(2) contact, without consent, between any part of the defendant's body or an object and the genitals or anus of another person;

(3) contact, without consent, between the genitals or anus of the defendant and any part of another person's body;

(4) deriving sexual pleasure or gratification from the infliction of death, bodily injury, or physical pain on another person; or

(5) an attempt or conspiracy to engage in conduct described in paragraphs (1)–(4).

(Added Sept. 13, 1994, Pub.L. 103–322, Title XXXII, § 320935(a), 108 Stat. 2135, effective July 9, 1995.)

Rule 414. Evidence of Similar Crimes in Child Molestation Cases

(a) In a criminal case in which the defendant is accused of an offense of child molestation, evidence of the defendant's commission of another offense or offenses of child molestation is admissible, and may be considered for its bearing on any matter to which it is relevant.

(b) In a case in which the Government intends to offer evidence under this rule, the attorney for the Government shall disclose the evidence to the defendant, including statements of witnesses or a summary of the substance of any testimony that is expected to be offered, at least fifteen days before the scheduled date of trial or at such later time as the court may allow for good cause.

(c) This rule shall not be construed to limit the admission or consideration of evidence under any other rule.

(d) For purposes of this rule and Rule 415, "child" means a person below the age of fourteen, and "offense of child molestation" means a crime under Federal law or the law of a State (as defined in section 513 of title 18, United States Code) that involved—

(1) any conduct proscribed by chapter 109A of title 18, United States Code, that was committed in relation to a child;

(2) any conduct proscribed by chapter 110 of title 18, United States Code;

(3) contact between any part of the defendant's body or an object and the genitals or anus of a child;

(4) contact between the genitals or anus of the defendant and any part of the body of a child;

(5) deriving sexual pleasure or gratification from the infliction of death, bodily injury, or physical pain on a child; or

(6) an attempt or conspiracy to engage in conduct described in paragraphs (1)–(5).

(Added Sept. 13, 1994, Pub.L. 103–322, Title XXXII, § 320935(a), 108 Stat. 2135, effective July 9, 1995.)

Rule 415. Evidence of Similar Acts in Civil Cases Concerning Sexual Assault or Child Molestation

(a) In a civil case in which a claim for damages or other relief is predicated on a party's alleged commission of conduct constituting an offense of sexual assault or child molestation, evidence of that party's commission of another offense or offenses of sexual assault or child molestation is admissible and may be considered as provided in Rule 413 and Rule 414 of these rules.

(b) A party who intends to offer evidence under this Rule shall disclose the evidence to the party against whom it will be offered, including statements of witnesses or a summary of the substance of any testimony that is expected to be offered, at least fifteen days before the scheduled date of trial or at such later time as the court may allow for good cause.

(c) This rule shall not be construed to limit the admission or consideration of evidence under any other rule.

(Added Sept. 13, 1994, Pub.L. 103–322, Title XXXII, § 320935(a), 108 Stat. 2135, effective July 9, 1995.)

ARTICLE V.   PRIVILEGES

Rule
501. General Rule.

Rule 501.   General Rule

Except as otherwise required by the Constitution of the United States or provided by Act of Congress or in rules prescribed by the Supreme Court pursuant to statutory authority, the privilege of a witness, person, government, State, or political subdivision thereof shall be governed by the principles of the common law as they may be interpreted by the courts of the United States in the light of reason and experience. However, in civil actions and proceedings, with respect to an element of a claim or defense as to which State law supplies the rule of decision, the privilege of a witness, person, government, State, or political subdivision thereof shall be determined in accordance with State law.

ARTICLE VI. WITNESSES

Rule 601.   General Rule of Competency

Every person is competent to be a witness except as otherwise provided in these rules. However, in civil actions and proceedings, with respect to an element of a claim or defense as to which State law supplies the rule of decision, the competency of a witness shall be determined in accordance with State law.

Rule 602.   Lack of Personal Knowledge

A witness may not testify to a matter unless evidence is introduced sufficient to support a finding that the witness has personal knowledge of the matter. Evidence to prove personal knowledge may, but need not, consist of the witness' own testimony. This rule is subject to the provisions of rule 703, relating to opinion testimony by expert witnesses.

(As amended Mar. 2, 1987, eff. Oct. 1, 1987; Apr. 25, 1988, eff. Nov. 1, 1988.)

Rule 603.   Oath or Affirmation

Before testifying, every witness shall be required to declare that the witness will testify truthfully, by oath or affirmation administered in a form calculated to awaken the witness' conscience and impress the witness' mind with the duty to do so.

(As amended Mar. 2, 1987, eff. Oct. 1, 1987.)

Rule 604.   Interpreters

An interpreter is subject to the provisions of these rules relating to qualification as an expert and the administration of an oath or affirmation to make a true translation.

(As amended Mar. 2, 1987, eff. Oct. 1, 1987.)

Rule 605.   Competency of Judge as Witness

The judge presiding at the trial may not testify in that trial as a witness. No objection need be made in order to preserve the point.

Rule 606.   Competency of Juror as Witness

(a) At the trial. A member of the jury may not testify as a witness before that jury in the trial of the case in which the juror is sitting. If the juror is called so to testify, the opposing party shall be afforded an opportunity to object out of the presence of the jury.

(b) Inquiry into validity of verdict or indictment. Upon an inquiry into the validity of a verdict or indictment, a juror may not testify as to any matter or statement occurring during the course of the jury's deliberations or to the effect of anything upon that or any other juror's mind or emotions as influencing the juror to assent to or dissent from the verdict or indictment or concerning the juror's mental processes in connection therewith, except that a juror may testify on the question whether extraneous prejudicial information was improperly brought to the jury's attention or whether any outside influence was improperly brought to bear upon any juror. Nor may a juror's affidavit or evidence of any statement by the juror concerning a matter about which the juror would be precluded from testifying be received for these purposes.

(As amended P.L. 94–149, § 1(10), Dec. 12, 1975, 89 Stat. 805; Mar. 2, 1987, eff. Oct. 1, 1987.)

Rule 607. Who May Impeach

The credibility of a witness may be attacked by any party, including the party calling the witness.

(As amended Mar. 2, 1987, eff. Oct. 1, 1987.)

Rule 608. Evidence of Character and Conduct of Witness

(a) Opinion and reputation evidence of character. The credibility of a witness may be attacked or supported by evidence in the form of opinion or reputation, but subject to these limitations: (1) the evidence may refer only to character for truthfulness or untruthfulness, and (2) evidence of truthful character is admissible only after the character of the witness for truthfulness has been attacked by opinion or reputation evidence or otherwise.

(b) Specific instances of conduct. Specific instances of the conduct of a witness, for the purpose of attacking or supporting the witness' character for truthfulness, other than conviction of crime as provided in rule 609, may not be proved by extrinsic evidence. They may, however, in the discretion of the court, if probative of truthfulness or untruthfulness, be inquired into on cross-examination of the witness (1) concerning the witness' character for truthfulness or untruthfulness, or (2) concerning the character for truthfulness or untruthfulness of another witness as to which character the witness being cross-examined has testified.

The giving of testimony, whether by an accused or by any other witness, does not operate as a waiver of the accused's or the witness' privilege against self-incrimination when examined with respect to matters which relate only to character for truthfulness.

(As amended Mar. 2, 1987, eff. Oct. 1, 1987; Apr. 25, 1988, eff. Nov. 1, 1988; March 27, 2003, eff. Dec. 1, 2003.)

Rule 609. Impeachment by Evidence of Conviction of Crime

(a) General rule. For the purpose of attacking the credibility of a witness,

(1) evidence that a witness other than an accused has been convicted of a crime shall be admitted, subject to Rule 403, if the crime was punishable by death or imprisonment in excess of one year under the law under which the witness was convicted, and evidence that an accused has been convicted of such a crime shall be admitted if the court determines that the

probative value of admitting this evidence outweighs its prejudicial effect to the accused; and

(2) evidence that any witness has been convicted of a crime shall be admitted if it involved dishonesty or false statement, regardless of the punishment.

(b) Time limit. Evidence of a conviction under this rule is not admissible if a period of more than ten years has elapsed since the date of the conviction or of the release of the witness from the confinement imposed for that conviction, whichever is the later date, unless the court determines, in the interests of justice, that the probative value of the conviction supported by specific facts and circumstances substantially outweighs its prejudicial effect. However, evidence of a conviction more than 10 years old as calculated herein, is not admissible unless the proponent gives to the adverse party sufficient advance written notice of intent to use such evidence to provide the adverse party with a fair opportunity to contest the use of such evidence.

(c) Effect of pardon, annulment, or certificate of rehabilitation. Evidence of a conviction is not admissible under this rule if (1) the conviction has been the subject of a pardon, annulment, certificate of rehabilitation, or other equivalent procedure based on a finding of the rehabilitation of the person convicted, and that person has not been convicted of a subsequent crime which was punishable by death or imprisonment in excess of one year, or (2) the conviction has been the subject of a pardon, annulment, or other equivalent procedure based on a finding of innocence.

(d) Juvenile adjudications. Evidence of juvenile adjudications is generally not admissible under this rule. The court may, however, in a criminal case allow evidence of a juvenile adjudication of a witness other than the accused if conviction of the offense would be admissible to attack the credibility of an adult and the court is satisfied that admission in evidence is necessary for a fair determination of the issue of guilt or innocence.

(e) Pendency of appeal. The pendency of an appeal therefrom does not render evidence of a conviction inadmissible. Evidence of the pendency of an appeal is admissible.

(As amended Mar. 2, 1987, eff. Oct. 1, 1987; Jan. 26, 1990, eff. Dec. 1, 1990.)

Rule 610. Religious Beliefs or Opinions

Evidence of the beliefs or opinions of a witness on matters of religion is not admissible for the purpose of showing that by reason of their nature the witness' credibility is impaired or enhanced.

(As amended Mar. 2, 1987, eff. Oct. 1, 1987.)

Rule 611. Mode and Order of Interrogation and Presentation

(a) Control by court. The court shall exercise reasonable control over the mode and order of interrogating witnesses and presenting evidence so as to (1) make the interrogation and presentation effective for the ascertainment of the truth, (2) avoid needless consumption of time, and (3) protect witnesses from harassment or undue embarrassment.

(b) Scope of cross-examination. Cross-examination should be limited to the subject matter of the direct examination and matters affecting the credibility of the witness. The court may, in the exercise of discretion, permit inquiry into additional matters as if on direct examination.

(c) Leading questions. Leading questions should not be used on the direct examination of a witness except as may be necessary to develop the witness' testimony. Ordinarily leading questions should be permitted on cross-examination. When a party calls a hostile witness, an adverse party, or a witness identified with an adverse party, interrogation may be by leading questions.

(As amended Mar. 2, 1987, eff. Oct. 1, 1987.)

Rule 612. Writing Used to Refresh Memory

Except as otherwise provided in criminal proceedings by section 3500 of title 18, United States Code, if a witness uses a writing to refresh memory for the purpose of testifying, either—

(1) while testifying, or

(2) before testifying, if the court in its discretion determines it is necessary in the interests of justice,

an adverse party is entitled to have the writing produced at the hearing, to inspect it, to cross-examine the witness thereon, and to introduce in evidence those portions which relate to the testimony of the witness. If it is claimed that the writing contains matters not related to the subject matter of the testimony the court shall examine the writing in camera, excise any portions not so related, and order delivery of the remainder to the party entitled thereto. Any portion withheld over objections shall be preserved and made available to the appellate court in the event of an appeal. If a writing is not produced or delivered pursuant to order under this rule, the court shall make any order justice requires, except that in criminal cases when the prosecution elects not to comply, the order shall be one striking the testimony or, if the court in its discretion determines that the interests of justice so require, declaring a mistrial.

(As amended Mar. 2, 1987, eff. Oct. 1, 1987.)

Rule 613.   Prior Statements of Witnesses

(a) Examining witness concerning prior statement.   In examining a witness concerning a prior statement made by the witness, whether written or not, the statement need not be shown nor its contents disclosed to the witness at that time, but on request the same shall be shown or disclosed to opposing counsel.

(b) Extrinsic evidence of prior inconsistent statement of witness.   Extrinsic evidence of a prior inconsistent statement by a witness is not admissible unless the witness is afforded an opportunity to explain or deny the same and the opposite party is afforded an opportunity to interrogate the witness thereon, or the interests of justice otherwise require.   This provision does not apply to admissions of a party-opponent as defined in rule 801(d)(2).

(As amended Mar. 2, 1987, eff. Oct. 1, 1987;   Apr. 25, 1988, eff. Nov. 1, 1988.)

Rule 614.   Calling and Interrogation of Witnesses by Court

(a) Calling by court.   The court may, on its own motion or at the suggestion of a party, call witnesses, and all parties are entitled to cross-examine witnesses thus called.

(b) Interrogation by court.   The court may interrogate witnesses, whether called by itself or by a party.

(c) Objections.   Objections to the calling of witnesses by the court or to interrogation by it may be made at the time or at the next available opportunity when the jury is not present.

Rule 615.   Exclusion of Witnesses

At the request of a party the court shall order witnesses excluded so that they cannot hear the testimony of other witnesses, and it may make the order of its own motion.   This rule does not authorize exclusion of (1) a party who is a natural person, or (2) an officer or employee of a party which is not a natural person designated as its representative by its attorney, or (3) a person whose presence is shown by a party to be essential to the presentation of the party's cause, or (4) a person authorized by statute to be present.

(As amended Mar. 2, 1987, eff. Oct. 1, 1987;   Apr. 25, 1988, eff. Nov. 1, 1988;   Nov. 18, 1988, Pub.L. 100–690, Title VII, § 7075(a), 102 Stat. 4405;   Apr. 24, 1998, eff. Dec. 1, 1998.)

ARTICLE VII. OPINIONS AND EXPERT TESTIMONY

Rule 701.   Opinion Testimony by Lay Witnesses

If the witness is not testifying as an expert, the witness' testimony in the form of opinions or inferences is limited to those opinions or inferences which are (a) rationally based on the perception of the witness, and (b) helpful to a clear understanding of the witness' testimony or the determination of a fact in issue, and (c) not based on scientific, technical, or other specialized knowledge within the scope of Rule 702.

(As amended Mar. 2, 1987, eff. Oct. 1, 1987; Apr. 17, 2000, eff. Dec. 1, 2000.)

Rule 702.   Testimony by Experts

If scientific, technical, or other specialized knowledge will assist the trier of fact to understand the evidence or to determine a fact in issue, a witness qualified as an expert by knowledge, skill, experience, training, or education, may testify thereto in the form of an opinion or otherwise, if (1) the testimony is based upon sufficient facts or data, (2) the testimony is the product of reliable principles and methods, and (3) the witness has applied the principles and methods reliably to the facts of the case.

(As amended Apr. 17, 2000, eff. Dec. 1, 2000.)

Rule 703.   Bases of Opinion Testimony by Experts

The facts or data in the particular case upon which an expert bases an opinion or inference may be those perceived by or made known to the expert at or before the hearing. If of a type reasonably relied upon by experts in the particular field in forming opinions or inferences upon the subject, the facts or data need not be admissible in evidence in order for the opinion or inference to be admitted. Facts or data that are otherwise inadmissible shall not be disclosed to the jury by the proponent of the opinion or inference unless the court determines that their probative value in assisting the jury to evaluate the expert's opinion substantially outweighs their prejudicial effect.

(As amended Mar. 2, 1987, eff. Oct. 1, 1987; Apr. 17, 2000, eff. Dec. 1, 2000.)

Rule 704.   Opinion on Ultimate Issue

(a) Except as provided in subdivision (b), testimony in the form of an opinion or inference otherwise admissible is not objectionable because it embraces an ultimate issue to be decided by the trier of fact.

(b) No expert witness testifying with respect to the mental state or condition of a defendant in a criminal case may state an opinion or inference as to whether the defendant did or did not have the mental state or condition constituting an element of the crime charged or of a defense thereto. Such ultimate issues are matters for the trier of fact alone.

(As amended Pub.L. 98–473, Title II, § 406, Oct. 12, 1984, 98 Stat. 2067.)

Rule 705.   Disclosure of Facts or Data Underlying Expert Opinion

The expert may testify in terms of opinion or inference and give reasons therefor without first testifying to the underlying facts or data, unless the court requires otherwise. The expert may in any event be required to disclose the underlying facts or data on cross-examination.

(As amended Mar. 2, 1987, eff. Oct. 1, 1987; Apr. 22, 1993, eff. Dec. 1, 1993.)

Rule 706.   Court Appointed Experts

(a) Appointment. The court may on its own motion or on the motion of any party enter an order to show cause why expert witnesses should not be appointed, and may request the parties to submit nominations. The court may appoint any expert witnesses agreed upon by the parties, and may appoint expert witnesses of its own selection. An expert witness shall not be appointed by the court unless the witness consents to act. A witness so appointed shall be informed of the witness' duties by the court in writing, a copy of which shall be filed with the clerk, or at a conference in which the parties shall have opportunity to participate. A witness so appointed shall advise the parties of the witness' findings, if any; the witness' deposition may be taken by any party; and the witness may be called to testify by the court or any party. The witness shall be subject to cross-examination by each party, including a party calling the witness.

(b) Compensation. Expert witnesses so appointed are entitled to reasonable compensation in whatever sum the court may allow. The compensation thus fixed is payable from funds which may be provided by law in criminal cases and civil actions and proceedings involving just compensation under the fifth amendment. In other civil actions and proceedings the compensation shall be paid by the parties in such proportion and at such time as the court directs, and thereafter charged in like manner as other costs.

(c) Disclosure of appointment. In the exercise of its discretion, the court may authorize disclosure to the jury of the fact that the court appointed the expert witness.

(d) Parties' experts of own selection. Nothing in this rule limits the parties in calling expert witnesses of their own selection.

(As amended Mar. 2, 1987, eff. Oct. 1, 1987.)

ARTICLE VIII.   HEARSAY

Rule
801. Definitions.
    (a) Statement.
    (b) Declarant.
    (c) Hearsay.
    (d) Statements Which Are Not Hearsay.
802. Hearsay Rule.
803. Hearsay Exceptions; Availability of Declarant Immaterial.
    (1) Present Sense Impression.
    (2) Excited Utterance.
    (3) Then Existing Mental, Emotional, or Physical Condition.
    (4) Statements for Purposes of Medical Diagnosis or Treatment.
    (5) Recorded Recollection.
    (6) Records of Regularly Conducted Activity.
    (7) Absence of Entry in Records Kept in Accordance With the Provisions of Paragraph (6).
    (8) Public Records and Reports.
    (9) Records of Vital Statistics.
    (10) Absence of Public Record or Entry.
    (11) Records of Religious Organizations.
    (12) Marriage, Baptismal, and Similar Certificates.
    (13) Family Records.
    (14) Records of Documents Affecting an Interest in Property.
    (15) Statements in Documents Affecting an Interest in Property.

Rule 801. Definitions

The following definitions apply under this article:

(a) Statement. A "statement" is (1) an oral or written assertion or (2) nonverbal conduct of a person, if it is intended by the person as an assertion.

(b) Declarant. A "declarant" is a person who makes a statement.

(c) Hearsay. "Hearsay" is a statement, other than one made by the declarant while testifying at the trial or hearing, offered in evidence to prove the truth of the matter asserted.

(d) Statements which are not hearsay. A statement is not hearsay if—

(1) Prior statement by witness. The declarant testifies at the trial or hearing and is subject to cross-examination concerning the statement, and the statement is (A) inconsistent with the declarant's testimony, and was given under oath subject to the penalty of perjury at a trial, hearing, or other proceeding, or in a deposition, or (B) consistent with the declarant's testimony and is offered to rebut an express or implied charge against the declarant of recent fabrication or improper influence or motive, or (C) one of identification of a person made after perceiving the person; or

(2) Admission by party-opponent. The statement is offered against a party and is (A) the party's own statement, in either an individual or a representative capacity or (B) a statement of which the party has manifested an adoption or belief in its truth, or (C) a statement by a person authorized by the party to make a statement concerning the subject, or (D) a statement by the party's agent or servant concerning a matter within the scope of the agency or employment, made during the existence of the relationship, or (E) a statement by a coconspirator of a party during the course and in furtherance of the conspiracy. The contents of the statement shall be considered but are not alone sufficient to establish the declarant's authority under subdivision (C), the agency or employment relationship and scope thereof under subdivision (D), or the existence of the conspiracy and the participation therein of the declarant and the party against whom the statement is offered under subdivision (E).

(As amended Pub.L. 94–113, § 1, Oct. 16, 1975, 89 Stat. 576; Mar. 2, 1987, eff. Oct. 1, 1987, April 11, 1997, eff. Dec. 1, 1997.)

Rule 802.　Hearsay Rule

Hearsay is not admissible except as provided by these rules or by other rules prescribed by the Supreme Court pursuant to statutory authority or by Act of Congress.

Rule 803.　Hearsay Exceptions; Availability of Declarant Immaterial

The following are not excluded by the hearsay rule, even though the declarant is available as a witness:

(1) Present sense impression. A statement describing or explaining an event or condition made while the declarant was perceiving the event or condition, or immediately thereafter.

(2) Excited utterance. A statement relating to a startling event or condition made while the declarant was under the stress of excitement caused by the event or condition.

(3) Then existing mental, emotional, or physical condition. A statement of the declarant's then existing state of mind, emotion, sensation, or physical condition (such as intent, plan, motive, design, mental feeling, pain, and bodily health), but not including a statement of memory or belief to prove the fact remembered or believed unless it relates to the execution, revocation, identification, or terms of declarant's will.

(4) Statements for purposes of medical diagnosis or treatment. Statements made for purposes of medical diagnosis or treatment and describing medical history, or past or present symptoms, pain, or sensations, or the inception or general character of the cause or external source thereof insofar as reasonably pertinent to diagnosis or treatment.

(5) Recorded recollection. A memorandum or record concerning a matter about which a witness once had knowledge but now has insufficient recollection to enable the witness to testify fully and accurately, shown to have been made or adopted by the witness when the matter was fresh in the witness' memory and to reflect that knowledge correctly. If admitted, the memorandum or record may be read into evidence but may not itself be received as an exhibit unless offered by an adverse party.

(6) Records of regularly conducted activity. A memorandum, report, record, or data compilation, in any form, of acts, events, conditions, opinions, or diagnoses, made at or near the time by, or from information transmitted by, a person with knowledge, if kept in the course of a regularly conducted business activity, and if it was the regular practice of that business activity to make the memorandum, report, record, or data compilation, all as shown by the testimony of the custodian or other qualified witness, or by certification that complies with Rule 902(11), Rule 902(12), or a statute permitting certification, unless the source of information or the method or circumstances of preparation indicate lack of trustworthiness. The term "business" as used in this paragraph includes business, institution, association, profession, occupation, and calling of every kind, whether or not conducted for profit.

(7) Absence of entry in records kept in accordance with the provisions of paragraph (6). Evidence that a matter is not included in the memoranda, reports, records, or data compilations, in any form, kept in accordance with the provisions of paragraph (6), to prove the nonoccurrence or nonexistence of the matter, if the matter was of a kind of which a memorandum, report, record, or data compilation was regularly made and preserved, unless the sources of information or other circumstances indicate lack of trustworthiness.

(8) Public records and reports. Records, reports, statements, or data compilations, in any form, of public offices or agencies, setting forth (A) the activities of the office or agency, or (B) matters observed pursuant to duty imposed by law as to which matters there was a duty to report, excluding, however, in criminal cases matters observed by police officers and other law enforcement personnel, or (C) in civil actions and proceedings and against the Government in criminal cases, factual findings resulting from an investigation made pursuant to authority granted by law, unless the sources of information or other circumstances indicate lack of trustworthiness.

(9) Records of vital statistics. Records or data compilations, in any form, of births, fetal deaths, deaths, or marriages, if the report thereof was made to a public office pursuant to requirements of law.

(10) Absence of public record or entry. To prove the absence of a record, report, statement, or data compilation, in any form, or the nonoccurrence or nonexistence of a matter of which a record, report, statement, or data compilation, in any form, was regularly made and preserved by a public office or agency, evidence in the form of a certification in accordance with rule 902, or testimony, that diligent search failed to disclose the record, report, statement, or data compilation, or entry.

(11) Records of religious organizations. Statements of births, marriages, divorces, deaths, legitimacy, ancestry, relationship by blood or marriage, or other similar facts of personal or family history, contained in a regularly kept record of a religious organization.

(12) Marriage, baptismal, and similar certificates. Statements of fact contained in a certificate that the maker performed a marriage or other ceremony or administered a sacrament, made by a clergyman, public official, or other person authorized by the rules or practices of a religious organization or by law to perform the act certified, and purporting to have been issued at the time of the act or within a reasonable time thereafter.

(13) Family records. Statements of fact concerning personal or family history contained in family Bibles, genealogies, charts, engravings on rings, inscriptions on family portraits, engravings on urns, crypts, or tombstones, or the like.

(14) Records of documents affecting an interest in property. The record of a document purporting to establish or affect an interest in property, as proof of the content of the original recorded document and its execution and delivery by each person by whom it purports to have been executed, if the record is a record of a public office and an applicable statute authorizes the recording of documents of that kind in that office.

(15) Statements in documents affecting an interest in property. A statement contained in a document purporting to establish or affect an interest in property if the matter stated was relevant to the purpose of the document, unless dealings with the property since the document was made have been inconsistent with the truth of the statement or the purport of the document.

(16) Statements in ancient documents. Statements in a document in existence twenty years or more the authenticity of which is established.

(17) Market reports, commercial publications. Market quotations, tabulations, lists, directories, or other published compilations, generally used and relied upon by the public or by persons in particular occupations.

(18) Learned treatises. To the extent called to the attention of an expert witness upon cross-examination or relied upon by the expert witness in direct examination, statements contained in published treatises, periodicals, or pamphlets on a subject of history, medicine, or other science or art, established as a reliable authority by the testimony or admission of the witness or by other expert testimony or by judicial notice. If admitted, the statements may be read into evidence but may not be received as exhibits.

(19) Reputation concerning personal or family history. Reputation among members of a person's family by blood, adoption, or marriage, or among a person's associates, or in the community, concerning a person's birth, adoption, marriage, divorce, death, legitimacy, relationship by blood, adoption, or marriage, ancestry, or other similar fact of his personal or family history.

(20) Reputation concerning boundaries or general history. Reputation in a community, arising before the controversy, as to boundaries of or customs affecting lands in the community, and reputation as to events of general history important to the community or State or nation in which located.

(21) Reputation as to character. Reputation of a person's character among associates or in the community.

(22) Judgment of previous conviction. Evidence of a final judgment, entered after a trial or upon a plea of guilty (but not upon a plea of nolo contendere), adjudging a person guilty of a crime punishable by death or imprisonment in excess of one year, to prove any fact essential to sustain the judgment, but not including, when offered by the Government in a criminal prosecution for purposes other than impeachment, judgments against persons other than the accused. The pendency of an appeal may be shown but does not affect admissibility.

(23) Judgment as to personal, family, or general history, or boundaries. Judgments as proof of matters of personal, family or general history, or boundaries, essential to the judgment, if the same would be provable by evidence of reputation.

(24) [Transferred to Rule 807]

(As amended P.L. 94–149, § 1(11), Dec. 12, 1975, 89 Stat. 805; Mar. 2, 1987, eff. Oct. 1, 1987, April 11, 1997, eff. Dec. 1, 1997, Apr. 17, 2000, eff. Dec. 1, 2000.)

Rule 804. Hearsay Exceptions; Declarant Unavailable

(a) Definition of unavailability. "Unavailability as a witness" includes situations in which the declarant—

(1) is exempted by ruling of the court on the ground of privilege from testifying concerning the subject matter of the declarant's statement; or

(2) persists in refusing to testify concerning the subject matter of the declarant's statement despite an order of the court to do so; or

(3) testifies to a lack of memory of the subject matter of the declarant's statement; or

(4) is unable to be present or to testify at the hearing because of death or then existing physical or mental illness or infirmity; or

(5) is absent from the hearing and the proponent of statement has been unable to procure the declarant's attendance (or in the case of a hearsay exception under subdivision (b)(2), (3), or (4), the declarant's attendance or testimony) by process or other reasonable means.

A declarant is not unavailable as a witness if exemption, refusal, claim of lack of memory, inability, or absence is due to the procurement or wrongdoing of the proponent of a statement for the purpose of preventing the witness from attending or testifying.

(b) Hearsay exceptions. The following are not excluded by the hearsay rule if the declarant is unavailable as a witness:

(1) Former testimony. Testimony given as a witness at another hearing of the same or a different proceeding, or in a deposition taken in compliance with law in the course of the same or another proceeding, if the party against whom the testimony is now offered, or, in a civil action or proceeding, a predecessor in interest, had an opportunity and similar motive to develop the testimony by direct, cross, or redirect examination.

(2) Statement under belief of impending death. In a prosecution for homicide or in a civil action or proceeding, a statement made by a declarant while believing that the declarant's death was imminent, concerning the cause or circumstances of what the declarant believed to be impending death.

(3) Statement against interest. A statement which was at the time of its making so far contrary to the declarant's pecuniary or proprietary interest, or so far tended to subject the declarant to civil or criminal liability, or to render invalid a claim by the declarant against another, that a reasonable person in the declarant's position would not have made the statement unless believing it to be true. A statement tending to expose the declarant to criminal liability and offered to exculpate the accused is not admissible unless corroborating circumstances clearly indicate the trustworthiness of the statement.

(4) Statement of personal or family history. (A) A statement concerning the declarant's own birth, adoption, marriage, divorce, legitimacy, relationship by blood, adoption, or marriage, ancestry, or other similar fact of personal or family history, even though declarant had no means of acquiring personal knowledge of the matter stated; or (B) a statement concerning the foregoing matters, and death also, of another person, if the declarant was related to the other by blood, adoption, or marriage or was so intimately associated with the other's family as to be likely to have accurate information concerning the matter declared.

(5) [Transferred to Rule 807]

(6) Forfeiture by wrongdoing. A statement offered against a party that has engaged or acquiesced in wrongdoing that was intended to, and did, procure the unavailability of the declarant as a witness.

(As amended P.L. 94–149, § 1(12), (13), Dec. 12, 1975, 89 Stat. 806; Mar. 2, 1987, eff. Oct. 1, 1987; Nov. 18, 1988, P.L. 100–690, Title VII, § 7075(b), 102 Stat. 4405, Apr. 11, 1997, eff. Dec. 1, 1997.)

Rule 805. Hearsay Within Hearsay

Hearsay included within hearsay is not excluded under the hearsay rule if each part of the combined statements conforms with an exception to the hearsay rule provided in these rules.

Rule 806. Attacking and Supporting Credibility of Declarant

When a hearsay statement, or a statement defined in Rule 801(d)(2)(C), (D), or (E), has been admitted in evidence, the credibility of the declarant may be attacked, and if attacked may be supported, by any evidence which would be admissible for those purposes if declarant had testified as a witness. Evidence of a statement or conduct by the declarant at any time, inconsistent with the declarant's hearsay statement, is not subject to any requirement that the declarant may have been afforded an opportunity to deny or explain. If the party against whom a hearsay statement has been admitted calls the declarant as a witness, the party is entitled to examine the declarant on the statement as if under cross-examination.

(As amended Mar. 2, 1987, eff. Oct. 1, 1987; Apr. 11, 1997, eff. Dec. 1, 1997.)

Rule 807. Residual Exception

A statement not specifically covered by Rule 803 or 804 but having equivalent circumstantial guarantees of trustworthiness, is not excluded by the hearsay rule, if the court determines that (A) the statement is offered as evidence of a material fact; (B) the statement is more probative on the point for which it is offered than any other evidence which the proponent can procure through reasonable efforts; and (C) the general purposes of these rules and the interests of justice will best be served by admission of the statement into evidence. However, a statement may not be admitted under this exception unless the proponent of it makes known to the adverse party sufficiently in advance of the trial or hearing to provide the adverse party with a fair opportunity to prepare to meet it, the proponent's intention to offer the statement and the particulars of it, including the name and address of the declarant.

ARTICLE IX.   AUTHENTICATION AND IDENTIFICATION

Rule 901.   Requirement of Authentication or Identification

(a) **General provision.** The requirement of authentication or identification as a condition precedent to admissibility is satisfied by evidence sufficient to support a finding that the matter in question is what its proponent claims.

(b) **Illustrations.** By way of illustration only, and not by way of limitation, the following are examples of authentication or identification conforming with the requirements of this rule:

(1) **Testimony of witness with knowledge.** Testimony that a matter is what it is claimed to be.

(2) **Nonexpert opinion on handwriting.** Nonexpert opinion as to the genuineness of handwriting, based upon familiarity not acquired for purposes of the litigation.

(3) **Comparison by trier or expert witness.** Comparison by the trier of fact or by expert witnesses with specimens which have been authenticated.

(4) **Distinctive characteristics and the like.** Appearance, contents, substance, internal patterns, or other distinctive characteristics, taken in conjunction with circumstances.

(5) Voice identification. Identification of a voice, whether heard firsthand or through mechanical or electronic transmission or recording, by opinion based upon hearing the voice at any time under circumstances connecting it with the alleged speaker.

(6) Telephone conversations. Telephone conversations, by evidence that a call was made to the number assigned at the time by the telephone company to a particular person or business, if (A) in the case of a person, circumstances, including self-identification, show the person answering to be the one called, or (B) in the case of a business, the call was made to a place of business and the conversation related to business reasonably transacted over the telephone.

(7) Public records or reports. Evidence that a writing authorized by law to be recorded or filed and in fact recorded or filed in a public office, or a purported public record, report, statement, or data compilation, in any form, is from the public office where items of this nature are kept.

(8) Ancient documents or data compilation. Evidence that a document or data compilation, in any form, (A) is in such condition as to create no suspicion concerning its authenticity, (B) was in a place where it, if authentic, would likely be, and (C) has been in existence 20 years or more at the time it is offered.

(9) Process or system. Evidence describing a process or system used to produce a result and showing that the process or system produces an accurate result.

(10) Methods provided by statute or rule. Any method of authentication or identification provided by Act of Congress or by other rules prescribed by the Supreme Court pursuant to statutory authority.

Rule 902.   Self-Authentication

Extrinsic evidence of authenticity as a condition precedent to admissibility is not required with respect to the following:

(1) Domestic public documents under seal. A document bearing a seal purporting to be that of the United States, or of any State, district, Commonwealth, territory, or insular possession thereof, or the Panama Canal Zone, or the Trust Territory of the Pacific Islands, or of a political subdivision, department, officer, or agency thereof, and a signature purporting to be an attestation or execution.

(2) Domestic public documents not under seal. A document purporting to bear the signature in the official capacity of an officer or employee of any entity included in paragraph (1) hereof, having no seal, if a public officer having a seal and having official duties in the district or political subdivision of the officer or employee certifies under seal that the signer has the official capacity and that the signature is genuine.

(3) Foreign public documents. A document purporting to be executed or attested in an official capacity by a person authorized by the laws of a foreign country to make the execution or attestation, and accompanied by a final certification as to the genuineness of the signature and official position (A) of the executing or attesting person, or (B) of any foreign official whose certificate of genuineness of signature and official position relates to the execution or attestation or is in a chain of certificates of genuineness of signature and official position relating to the execution or attestation. A final certification may be made by a secretary of embassy or legation, consul general, consul, vice consul, or consular agent of the United States, or a diplomatic or consular official of the foreign country assigned or accredited to the United States. If reasonable opportunity has been given to all parties to investigate the authenticity and accuracy of official documents, the court may, for good cause shown, order that they be treated as presumptively authentic without final certification or permit them to be evidenced by an attested summary with or without final certification.

(4) Certified copies of public records. A copy of an official record or report or entry therein, or of a document authorized by law to be recorded or filed and actually recorded or filed in a public office, including data compilations in any form, certified as correct by the custodian or other person authorized to make the certification, by certificate complying with paragraph (1), (2), or (3) of this rule or complying with any Act of Congress or rule prescribed by the Supreme Court pursuant to statutory authority.

(5) Official publications. Books, pamphlets, or other publications purporting to be issued by public authority.

(6) Newspapers and periodicals. Printed materials purporting to be newspapers or periodicals.

(7) Trade inscriptions and the like. Inscriptions, signs, tags, or labels purporting to have been affixed in the course of business and indicating ownership, control, or origin.

(8) Acknowledged documents. Documents accompanied by a certificate of acknowledgment executed in the manner provided by law by a notary public or other officer authorized by law to take acknowledgments.

(9) Commercial paper and related documents. Commercial paper, signatures thereon, and documents relating thereto to the extent provided by general commercial law.

(10) Presumptions under Acts of Congress. Any signature, document, or other matter declared by Act of Congress to be presumptively or prima facie genuine or authentic.

(11) Certified domestic records of regularly conducted activity. The original or a duplicate of a domestic record of regularly conducted activity that would be admissible under Rule 803(6) if accompanied by a written declaration of its custodian or other qualified person, in a manner complying with any Act of Congress or rule prescribed by the Supreme Court pursuant to statutory authority, certifying that the record—

(A) was made at or near the time of the occurrence of the matters set forth by, or from information transmitted by, a person with knowledge of those matters;

(B) was kept in the course of the regularly conducted activity; and

(C) was made by the regularly conducted activity as a regular practice.

A party intending to offer a record into evidence under this paragraph must provide written notice of that intention to all adverse parties, and must make the record and declaration available for inspection sufficiently in advance of their offer into evidence to provide an adverse party with a fair opportunity to challenge them.

(12) Certified foreign records of regularly conducted activity. In a civil case, the original or a duplicate of a foreign record of regularly conducted activity that would be admissible under Rule 803(6) if accompanied by a written declaration by its custodian or other qualified person certifying that the record—

(A) was made at or near the time of the occurrence of the matters set forth by, or from information transmitted by, a person with knowledge of those matters;

(B) was kept in the course of the regularly conducted activity; and

(C) was made by the regularly conducted activity as a regular practice.

The declaration must be signed in a manner that, if falsely made, would subject the maker to criminal penalty under the laws of the country where the declaration is signed. A party intending to offer a record into evidence under this paragraph must provide written notice of that intention to all adverse parties, and must make the record and declaration available for inspection sufficiently in advance of their offer into evidence to provide an adverse party with a fair opportunity to challenge them.

(As amended Mar. 2, 1987, eff. Oct. 1, 1987; Apr. 25, 1988, eff. Nov. 1, 1988; Apr. 17, 2000, eff. Dec. 1, 2000.)

Rule 903.　Subscribing Witness' Testimony Unnecessary

The testimony of a subscribing witness is not necessary to authenticate a writing unless required by the laws of the jurisdiction whose laws govern the validity of the writing.

ARTICLE X.　CONTENTS OF WRITINGS, RECORDINGS, AND PHOTOGRAPHS

Rule

Rule 1001.　Definitions

For purposes of this article the following definitions are applicable:

(1) Writings and recordings. "Writings" and "recordings" consist of letters, words, or numbers, or their equivalent, set down by handwriting, typewriting, printing, photostating, photographing, magnetic impulse, mechanical or electronic recording, or other form of data compilation.

(2) Photographs. "Photographs" include still photographs, X-ray films, video tapes, and motion pictures.

(3) Original. An "original" of a writing or recording is the writing or recording itself or any counterpart intended to have the same effect by a person executing or issuing it. An "original" of a photograph includes the negative or any print therefrom. If data are stored in a computer or similar device, any printout or other output readable by sight, shown to reflect the data accurately, is an "original".

(4) Duplicate. A "duplicate" is a counterpart produced by the same impression as the original, or from the same matrix, or by means of photography, including enlargements and miniatures, or by mechanical or electronic re-recording, or by chemical reproduction, or by other equivalent technique which accurately reproduces the original.

Rule 1002. Requirement of Original

To prove the content of a writing, recording, or photograph, the original writing, recording, or photograph is required, except as otherwise provided in these rules or by Act of Congress.

Rule 1003. Admissibility of Duplicates

A duplicate is admissible to the same extent as an original unless (1) a genuine question is raised as to the authenticity of the original or (2) in the circumstances it would be unfair to admit the duplicate in lieu of the original.

Rule 1004. Admissibility of Other Evidence of Contents

The original is not required, and other evidence of the contents of a writing, recording, or photograph is admissible if—

(1) Originals lost or destroyed. All originals are lost or have been destroyed, unless the proponent lost or destroyed them in bad faith; or

(2) Original not obtainable. No original can be obtained by any available judicial process or procedure; or

(3) Original in possession of opponent. At a time when an original was under the control of the party against whom offered, that party was put on notice, by the pleadings or otherwise, that the contents would be a subject of proof at the hearing, and that party does not produce the original at the hearing; or

(4) Collateral matters. The writing, recording, or photograph is not closely related to a controlling issue.

(As amended Mar. 2, 1987, eff. Oct. 1, 1987.)

Rule 1005. Public Records

The contents of an official record, or of a document authorized to be recorded or filed and actually recorded or filed, including data compilations in any form, if otherwise admissible, may be proved by copy, certified as correct in accordance with rule 902 or testified to be correct by a witness who has compared it with the original. If a copy which complies with the foregoing cannot be obtained by the exercise of reasonable diligence, then other evidence of the contents may be given.

Rule 1006. Summaries

The contents of voluminous writings, recordings, or photographs which cannot conveniently be examined in court may be presented in the form of a chart, summary, or calculation. The originals, or duplicates, shall be made available for examination or copying, or both, by other parties at reasonable time and place. The court may order that they be produced in court.

Rule 1007. Testimony or Written Admission of Party

Contents of writings, recordings, or photographs may be proved by the testimony or deposition of the party against whom offered or by that party's written admission, without accounting for the nonproduction of the original.

(As amended Mar. 2, 1987, eff. Oct. 1, 1987.)

Rule 1008. Functions of Court and Jury

When the admissibility of other evidence of contents of writings, recordings, or photographs under these rules depends upon the fulfillment of a condition of fact, the question whether the condition has been fulfilled is ordinarily for the court to determine in accordance with the provisions of rule 104. However, when an issue is raised (a) whether the asserted writing ever existed, or (b) whether another writing, recording, or photograph produced at the trial is the original, or (c) whether other evidence of contents correctly reflects the contents, the issue is for the trier of fact to determine as in the case of other issues of fact.

ARTICLE XI. MISCELLANEOUS RULES

Rule 1101. Applicability of Rules

(a) **Courts and judges.** These rules apply to the United States district courts, the District Court of Guam, the District Court of the Virgin Islands, the District Court for the Northern

Mariana Islands, the United States courts of appeals, the United States Claims Court, and to United States bankruptcy judges and United States magistrate judges, in the actions, cases, and proceedings and to the extent hereinafter set forth. The terms "judge" and "court" in these rules include United States bankruptcy judges and United States magistrate judges.

(b) Proceedings generally. These rules apply generally to civil actions and proceedings, including admiralty and maritime cases, to criminal cases and proceedings, to contempt proceedings except those in which the court may act summarily, and to proceedings and cases under title 11, United States Code.

(c) Rule of privilege. The rule with respect to privileges applies at all stages of all actions, cases, and proceedings.

(d) Rules inapplicable. The rules (other than with respect to privileges) do not apply in the following situations:

(1) Preliminary questions of fact. The determination of questions of fact preliminary to admissibility of evidence when the issue is to be determined by the court under rule 104.

(2) Grand jury. Proceedings before grand juries.

(3) Miscellaneous proceedings. Proceedings for extradition or rendition; preliminary examinations in criminal cases; sentencing, or granting or revoking probation; issuance of warrants for arrest, criminal summonses, and search warrants; and proceedings with respect to release on bail or otherwise.

(e) Rules applicable in part. In the following proceedings these rules apply to the extent that matters of evidence are not provided for in the statutes which govern procedure therein or in other rules prescribed by the Supreme Court pursuant to statutory authority: the trial of minor and petty offenses by United States magistrates; review of agency actions when the facts are subject to trial de novo under section 706(2)(F) of title 5, United States Code; review of orders of the Secretary of Agriculture under section 2 of the Act entitled "An Act to authorize association of producers of agricultural products" approved February 18, 1922 (7 U.S.C. 292), and under sections 6 and 7(c) of the Perishable Agricultural Commodities Act, 1930 (7 U.S.C. 499f, 499g(c)); naturalization and revocation of naturalization under sections 310–318 of the Immigration and Nationality Act (8 U.S.C. 1421–1429); prize proceedings in admiralty under sections 7651–7681 of title 10, United States Code; review of orders of the Secretary of the Interior under section 2 of the Act entitled "An Act authorizing associations of producers of aquatic products" approved June 25, 1934 (15 U.S.C. 522); review of orders of petroleum control boards under section 5 of the Act entitled "An Act to regulate interstate and foreign commerce in petroleum and its products by prohibiting the shipment in such commerce of petroleum and its products produced in violation of State law, and for other purposes", approved February 22, 1935 (15 U.S.C. 715d); actions for fines, penalties, or forfeitures under part V of title IV of the Tariff Act of 1930 (19 U.S.C. 1581–1624), or under the Anti-Smuggling Act (19 U.S.C. 1701–1711); criminal libel for condemnation, exclusion of imports, or other proceedings under the Federal Food, Drug, and Cosmetic Act (21 U.S.C. 301–392); disputes between seamen under sections 4079, 4080, and 4081 of the Revised Statutes (22 U.S.C. 256–258); habeas corpus under sections 2241–2254 of title 28, United States Code; motions to vacate, set aside or correct sentence under section 2255 of title 28, United States Code; actions for penalties for refusal to transport destitute seamen under section 4578 of the Revised Statutes (46 U.S.C. 679); actions against the United States under the Act entitled "An Act authorizing suits against the United States in admiralty for damage caused by and salvage service rendered to public vessels belonging to the United States, and for other purposes", approved March 3, 1925 (46 U.S.C. 781–790), as implemented by section 7730 of title 10, United States Code.

(As amended P.L. 94–149, § 1(14), Dec. 12, 1975, 89 Stat. 806; P.L. 95–598, Title II, § 251, Nov. 6, 1978, 92 Stat. 2673; P.L. 97–164, Title I, § 142, Apr. 2, 1982, 96 Stat. 45; Mar. 2, 1987, eff. Oct. 1, 1987; Apr. 25, 1988, eff. Nov. 1, 1988; Nov. 18, 1988, Pub.L. 100–690, Title VII, § 7075(c), 102 Stat. 4405; Apr. 22, 1993, eff. Dec. 1, 1993.)

Rule 1102. Amendments

Amendments to the Federal Rules of Evidence may be made as provided in section 2072 of title 28 of the United States Code.

(As amended Apr. 30, 1991, eff. Dec. 1, 1991.)

Rule 1103. Title

These rules may be known and cited as the Federal Rules of Evidence.

*

Table of Cases

Index

References are to Pages